Horace Greeley

NINETEENTH-CENTURY CRUSADER

PREPARED AND PUBLISHED UNDER THE DIRECTION OF THE
AMERICAN HISTORICAL ASSOCIATION FROM THE INCOME
OF THE ALBERT J. BEVERIDGE MEMORIAL FUND.

FOR THEIR ZEAL AND BENEFICENCE IN CREATING THIS FUND THE ASSOCIA-
TION IS INDEBTED TO MANY CITIZENS OF INDIANA WHO DESIRED TO HONOR
IN THIS WAY THE MEMORY OF A STATESMAN AND A HISTORIAN.

Greeley at thirty, Mrs. Greeley's favorite picture.

Horace Greeley

NINETEENTH-CENTURY CRUSADER

By

GLYNDON G. VAN DEUSEN

Philadelphia

UNIVERSITY OF PENNSYLVANIA PRESS

1953

Published in Great Britain, India, and Pakistan
by Geoffrey Cumberlege: Oxford University Press
London, Bombay, and Karachi

TO THE MEMORY OF MY MOTHER AND FATHER

Acknowledgment

This book has been six years in preparation, and during that time I have received aid and encouragement from many quarters. It is with particular gratitude that I acknowledge my obligations to the Albert J. Beveridge Memorial Fund Committee, both for its criticisms of the manuscript and for permission to delay its publication a year so that I might accept a Fulbright Award as lecturer in American history in New Zealand; to Dexter Perkins, whose interest in productive scholarship has been manifested, as always, by encouragement and constructive advice; to the University of Rochester for a generous leave of absence that was all-important to the progress of the book; to Paul Wallace Gates, who read nearly half of the manuscript and whose advice and criticism did not go unheeded.

I wish to render full acknowledgment to the Boston Public Library for permission to quote the letter from Greeley to Rufus W. Griswold that is printed in chapter eleven; to Holman Hamilton for the loan of manuscript materials and even more for his friendly encouragement and support; to Roger Butterfield for encouragement and for the loan of valuable materials; to Edward C. M. Stahl for use of the letter books in the Henry A. Stahl Collection; to J. H. Cramer for letters and newspaper items concerning Greeley; to Miss Irene Neu for material on Greeley that she discovered during her own historical research; to Mrs. Edith M. Fox for aid in the use of the Greeley materials in the Collection of Regional History at Cornell University; to Edward Hubler for a Dickens item on Clay; to G. P. Putnam's Sons for permission to quote Walt Whitman's "For You O Democracy" from their COMPLETE WRITINGS OF WALT WHITMAN; to James A. Rawley for information in regard to the Morgan Papers; to Richard Lowitt for suggestions as to source materials; to Paul Adams, Herbert Bass, Don Bensch, Thomas Bonner, Chandler Bragdon, Donald Disbrow, David Leach, Cecelia Koretsky Michael, David Smith, James Stevenson, and Robert Tolf, graduate students who did research under my direction; to Robert W. Hill, Keeper of the Manuscripts in the New York Public Library, for his generous and unstinting aid; to John R. Russell, Librarian of the University of Rochester, for the greatest possible coöperation in this enterprise; to Margaret Butterfield, Archivist of Rhees Library at the University of Rochester, for efficient help, most generously given.

I wish also to acknowledge the friendly and courteous assistance of the librarians, archivists, and assistant librarians at the Library of Congress, the Albany State Library, the New York Public Library, the New York Historical Society, the Historical Society of Pennsylvania, the Huntington Library, the Buffalo Historical Society, and the Rochester Public Library. To these and to many others of the guild, I owe a debt that can never be repaid.

Finally, I wish to acknowledge my debt to my wife, Ruth Litteer Van Deusen, who read the manuscript for literary faults, and whose patience and forbearance with a struggling author are a constant marvel to me.

G. G. VAN D.

CONTENTS

ILLUSTRATIONS

Horace Greeley

NINETEENTH-CENTURY CRUSADER

Prologue

The American generation that grew up after the War of 1812 was a prey to all the seven plagues of Egypt, and more. People roasted by the thousands in steamboat explosions and railroad wrecks. Hustling, bustling cities were stricken with terror and despair by the dreadful scourge of cholera. Consumption took such a toll of the population and was so much feared that it furnished a favorite theme for the poets and poetesses of the period. The beautiful Ohio, the wide Missouri, and the Father of Waters flooded without let or hindrance, doing millions of dollars' worth of damage to what politicians even then called "Our Priceless Heritage." It was a generation that knew little or nothing about combating the fly in the wheat or the blight that stunted and rotted the potato crop, and both fly and blight abounded.

Nor were accidents and Nature alone the cause of American woes. A laissez-faire economic engine, fired by the recklessness of the frontier spirit, stoked by venturesome and often unscrupulous profit seekers, hurried time and again up blissful slopes of speculative delight, only to find a precipice at the peak and plunge headlong down into the valley of depression. In 1819, in 1837, in 1857 there was widespread and long-drawn-out panic, suffering, and despair. As if this were not enough, sectional jealousies burst out with a frequency that seemed chronic into rancorous struggles over the tariff, over internal improvements, over the disposition of the public lands, most of all over slavery. America was truly a harried land.

But curiously enough this land of troubles was also a land of great achievement. Despite scourges and disasters, its workers toiled and spun with a furious and productive energy. They expanded educational opportunities at a prodigious rate. They created a literary tradition that rivaled anything nineteenth-century Europe could offer. They forged new democratic customs and practices, both political and social. They laid the bases of an economic order at once so stable and so fruitful that, a century later, it could furnish the sinews of victory in two world wars, pour billions into European recovery after those wars, and at the same time maintain a standard of living far beyond that of any other quarter of the globe. These founders of twentieth-century America were accomplishing great things.

Such achievements would not have been possible without steadfast purpose and infinite hope, a purpose and a hope that were well-nigh universal. The practical-minded merchant, the salty-minded New England farmer, the furious abolitionist, the double-tongued politician, the quick-tempered representative of southern chivalry, the swaggering, bullying, gouging hero of the frontier, each in his own way carried the faith in his heart, each in his own way saw the American vision, dreamed the American dream. The inspiration of Thomas Jefferson and John Adams was the inspiration of Philip Hone and Joseph Peabody and Gerrit Smith and Sam Houston and Davy Crockett. It lay at the basis of Clay's American System. Calhoun yearned after it in his dry but passionate fashion, even while plans for a southern nationality formed in his busy, scheming brain. Webster saw it, blazing with a light almost like that of the Grail in "the gorgeous ensign of the republic, still full high advanced, its arms and trophies streaming in their original lustre." The glory and the dream were everywhere about.

What was this faith in America? It was partly a steady confidence in the United States as a golden land, the place of the fortunate ones, a country with a future full of richness and plenty, where the channels of trade would ever widen and lengthen, and busy industrial plants would perpetually clamor for more men of vision to control and direct them. In part it was a belief in the United States as a land of political democracy, where a people was, and always would be, the master of its rulers. Even more it was a faith in the United States as a land of fundamentally good and righteous people, where moral law, if not always triumphant, would be always powerful; where the great Declaration's assertion that all men are created equal and have unalienable rights would lie like some compelling agent of fertilization at the roots of the actions of men. And including all these faiths, and above and beyond them, was the faith in the mission of America, her mission of leadership in the progress of civilization. Old Europe, war ravaged, laboring under the weight of decadent institutions and ancient enmities, had had her day. She had played her role as guide, and now that role had fallen to the lot of a fresh and valiant younger nation. In the purposed and inexorable march of civilization toward the goal of human felicity, the United States was now and would continue to be the leader.

Such was the faith of Horace Greeley's America.

CHAPTER 1

Youth of a Yankee

HORACE GREELEY WAS BORN ON THE FAMILY FARM
near the town of Amherst, New Hampshire, February 3, 1811. He
was a blond, but no one would have guessed it at the moment of
parturition, for he arrived in the outer world so black and breathless that he could not utter even a cry of indignation—he whose life
was later to be filled with cries of indignation. At the sight of him
there was consternation in the Greeley household. Then a resource-
ful aunt took the matter in hand. Whether she swung him by the
heels, or threw cold water on his back, there is no record left to
state, but at any rate Horace gasped, breathed, lived. He had been
claimed for this world—to the vast future discomfort of liquor
dealers, slaveholders, pimps, abortionists, seducers, and Democrats.

The Greeley's young son was named Horace because his mother
had read the name in a book and liked it, and because it was also
the name of a paternal relative. But the New Englanders in the
vicinity did to him what they did to other Horaces. He became
"Hod" Greeley.

Horace was the eldest of a family of five children, two boys and
three girls. His father, Zaccheus ("Zack" to the neighborhood), was
of English ancestry. Zack's wife, Mary Woodburn Greeley, came of
Scotch-Irish stock. The ancestors on both sides, as far back as anything reliable can be found, were undistinguished, middle-class,
small-town, and country folk, mostly farmers and blacksmiths.

Zack Greeley was a rather small man, with sandy hair and whiskers, light eyes, and colorless eyebrows. He liked husking parties
and country dances, where he would sing by the hour for the
dancers, if the fiddle gave out. Zack drank a good deal of rum and
cider (he was never a day without liquor in the mowing season),
but was reputedly a very moral man. He could and usually did work
hard, and was capable of great exertion. Horace once recalled his

father's walking fifty-two miles in one day, between dawn and midnight.

Mary Woodburn Greeley was a fair-skinned, fleshy woman, stout and hearty, with immense vitality and a fund of animal spirits. She was merry, and liked to drink and dance and sing. She smoked a pipe that Horace sometimes filled and lighted for her with a coal from the fireplace. The neighbors would stop and listen to her, singing in the fields, and they admired the ease with which she handled the hay rake and the pitchfork. She was never too tired to read to the children in the evening, or to sing ballads and tell stories as she wove the family's simple clothing. For those were the good days, before the Pennsylvania frontier twisted and broke her into a silent woman, sitting and staring out into the forest. In New England there were neighbors. Life, though hard, was settled there, and Mary and Zack were young, and Horace showed more promise every day.[1]

The Greeley's eldest was a little fellow with a big head on a slender body, and a rather whiney voice. His eyes were a mild blue, and his hair was so light in color that tradition called it white. Obviously, he was a platinum blond. He was "quiet and peaceable," so Zack later remembered, but by some strange quirk that had never happened to the Greeley genes before he was afflicted by an all-consuming curiosity about books.

Horace picked up reading by the time he was three years old, partly by questioning his mother about words and letters, and partly by studying the book that lay on her knee, a toddler's method that enabled him to read very passably sidewise and upside down. He could read any book that came into his hands at four, at which ripe age he was packed off to the winter session of the district school. There spelling fascinated him and arithmetic was easy. He was a prodigy and his fame went abroad in the land. The school committee of nearby Bedford voted that no pupil from other towns should be received in their school "save Horace Greeley alone," and the Bedford minister and other friends offered to provide an education at Exeter Academy with college to follow. This offer was refused, to some extent from pride as well as from a mother's desire to keep her nine-year-old chick in the family nest.[2]

Schooling was none too regular for Horace. At the age of five he began riding horse to plough on his father's hilly, stony eighty acres. Other stints were soon forthcoming, for no preacher had a surer calling than that of a New England farm boy to labor. He had only forty-five months of district-school learning, and that was distributed in driblets over a ten-year period. But his precocity was more than a match for such a handicap. An honest teacher confessed, when Horace was thirteen, that the boy knew more than he did and might as well stay home. This ended his formal schooling. He had already read the Bible from Genesis to Revelation, the *Arabian Nights, Robinson Crusoe,* a large part of Shakespeare, and indeed every book and newspaper that he could get his hands on. His constantly widening and deepening knowledge of history, literature, and economics was picked up thereafter by the hit-and-miss method, lacking all control or direction.

Horace Greeley never remembered any of his teachers as men to whom he owed any particular debt. His mind was almost entirely self-trained. What a first-class education might have done for him no one can tell. It might have made him more tolerant of the opinions of others; it might have improved his own powers of analysis by teaching him more easily to distinguish reason from prejudice; it might have given him a deeper and surer understanding of human nature. But it could scarcely have improved his prodigious memory, his capacity for separating the significant from the unimportant, his homely, pithy, trenchant style of writing with its mastery of every shade of meaning, or the power of his appeal to the minds and hearts of his readers.

The little boy who sat an indulgent witness of the writhings and fumblings of his schoolfellows found life more pleasant than bitter on the Amherst farm. He was not at all bothered by tow shirts and linsey-woolsey pants that invariably shrank above wrists and ankles. He was used to meager house furnishings and a hard bed. Nor did he mind sitting on the floor, spoon in hand, to eat his share of bean porridge out of a five-quart pan, while he listened wide-eyed to his parents' tales of how, when they were young, New England's poor often lived through the winter on milk and potatoes. His muscular coördination was poor and he lacked interest in most games, but he loved to fish for brown and speckled trout (when they were biting), and to play checkers (when he won). He had far more than his share of admiration from his elders, and he got along well with the young folk of the neighborhood, since he seldom laughed at their mistakes and was usually willing to help with their lessons.[3] His was one of the happier New England farm existences until trouble descended upon the Greeley household.

Zack lost his farm in 1820. Openhanded hospitality, poor management, a bad note endorsement, and the panic of 1819, which spread misery and want throughout New England, all played a part in this catastrophe. Drink played a part as well, at least so Horace thought in later years. The sheriff's men appeared one day and seized most of the family goods, while Mary Greeley wept and Zack disappeared into the woods to escape debtor's prison.

Horace was deeply distressed by the seizure of the family goods. One tradition has it that he tried to hide his mother's dresses; another that he secreted a gallon of rum (a much more sensible performance, since the rum represented a much more concentrated form of wealth). But all this was of little avail.

Not long thereafter, the farm was handed over to creditors at scarcely more than a third of what it had cost. Zack was bankrupt. He fled into Vermont, making his way to the town of Westhaven, near the southern end of Lake Champlain and not far from the New York border. There he found work as a woodchopper. There, too, when he judged it safe, he hired a two-horse sleigh and returned with it to New Hampshire. On January 1, 1821, the family packed the scanty remnants of their belongings into the sleigh and started for Westhaven, where Zack had found a house for sixteen dollars a year. Three days later, after a bitterly cold journey, Horace was in his new home. He never forgot those harrowing days.[4]

Westhaven lay in a land of rocky, clayey soil and limestone ledges, where corn wilted easily in the summer heat and Canada thistles throve with vigor and abandon. But there was work to be had, and Zack and the boys fell to with a will. They spent most of two years clearing fifty acres of woodland at seven dollars an acre, and then were bilked out of part of their pay. They farmed a miserable place called Flea Knoll, with miserable results. Zack ran a sawmill on shares for little or no profit. It was all hard, unrewarding work, a pitting of man against Nature in a grim, primitive, back-breaking, hand-to-hand struggle; and a boy whose mind turned always to books and reading had no joy in it.[5]

Horace did not find much social relaxation at Westhaven to relieve the monotony of farm work. He was now a sprouting lad, tall for his age, gangling, shambling, absent-minded (what growing boy is not?), much preferring a book by a blazing pine knot to drop the handkerchief or post office. When he once took a pretty girl to a country dance it was the talk of the town. He simply did not make a hit with the adolescent Westhaven belles, for he was too serious, too apt to lecture them on their grammar, or to declaim against such follies as the wearing of corsets. This last might not have been so bad—at least it gave a girl a chance to declare coyly that she did not wear stays. But then Horace, instead of using an exploratory arm, would drop his handkerchief on the floor and ask her to stoop over and pick it up as proof of her unencumbered state.[6] After that the conversation undoubtedly languished, and for the wrong reason.

What with hard work and no social life, Horace was more and more shut up within himself. Not even the books lent him by Mr. Minot, a retired Boston banker, could wholly relieve the monotony of such an existence.

No one knows when the idea of becoming a printer entered the young boy's head, but it undoubtedly came at an early date. Life at Westhaven nurtured the seed, and in 1822 he prevailed upon his father to help him solicit a job in a printing office at nearby White-hall. The printer showed no interest in an eleven-year-old apprentice, but the idea stuck in Horace's mind. As his services became more valuable, his father became increasingly cool to the idea of losing them. But all the Greeleys were stubborn and Horace shared the persistency of the breed. In 1826 he walked by himself to East Poultney, twelve miles away, and asked Amos Bliss, editor of the *Northern Spectator,* for a job.

Bliss's first impression, somewhat akin to what he would have felt had an animated scarecrow walked into his front yard, was quickly succeeded by respect for the intelligence that peered out at him from under a ragged hat. Young Greeley was given a job. By the terms of the bargain, he was to remain five years in the *Spectator's* office. The first six months he would work for board only. Thereafter he was to have forty dollars a year as well as board. Zack agreed verbally to the indenture, thinking that it was pretty magnanimous of him to give the boy his time so long before he would become of age. It was April 18, 1826, and Horace was fifteen years old.[7]

A few months after Horace went into the printing office, Zack moved the rest of the family to Erie County, Pennsylvania, where he had bought four acres of clearing and a log hut. The apprentice spent Sunday with his family on the eve of their departure for the West. It was suggested that he go with them and find an apprenticeship somewhere on the frontier. The temptation was great, and Horace needed only his mother's urging to make him break his bargain with the *Spectator.* She remained silent, and so he said good-by and took the road back to East Poultney. Many years later he remembered that lonely walk as one of the slowest and saddest journeys of his life.

The *Spectator* was issued from a two-story, wooden house near the center of the village green. There Horace applied himself assiduously, first learning to set type and later getting some valuable training by condensing news from the city journals, with a view to conserving space and to ensnaring local interest. The other apprentices at first tried to haze him. They threw type at him and inked his hair, but he was absorbed in his work and indifferent to their jokes, so they soon let him alone.

The *Spectator* office scarcely gave a sense of economic security to the new apprentice, even after his fellows ceased troubling him. The paper was on the edge of oblivion, being in perpetually straitened circumstances. At times there would be a rapid succession of masters and occasionally two or three at once. These changes in management were confusing, but they sometimes threw responsibilities upon young Greeley. This was particularly the case when the editor was a Baptist clergyman with a charge some distance away. The cleric absented himself a good share of the time and left Horace wide discretion in preparing material for the paper. There was a thrill in such a situation. And always there was reading such as the lad had never known before, in the newspaper exchanges and in the village library.

It was a hard and simple life that the young apprentice led. Practically penniless (for most of his money was sent to the family struggling on the Erie homestead), with no talent or inclination for the country dances or the country girls, his only dissipations were checkers, participation in a local debating club, and a few awkward attempts at romantic verse to which he was moved by Byron and the efforts of Felicia Hemans. But he had developed a passion for acquiring factual information, a passion that eclipsed all other interests and left him scant time and patience for mastering the conventional niceties of existence. Even those who liked him remarked that his table manners were atrocious.[8]

The knowledge that he acquired, together with a gift for witty repartee in argument, gave him a reputation and a sense of power. He came to be regarded as an authority, especially as to past and present politics. When he spoke his mind on any subject, a propensity that he indulged more and more frequently, he was listened to with interest and respect. And he formed some friendships that were to bring him back to Vermont again and again in the years to come.

Twice during these years on the *Spectator* Greeley visited his parents in Pennsylvania. His brief summer vacations gave him just enough time to make a plodding journey to Zack's frontier farm. On one of these occasions, in the summer of 1827, the footsore youth passed through the little town of Rochester, New York, a place then humming with excitement over the abduction of William Morgan by a band of overzealous Masons.[9] There can be little doubt that Horace read in the Rochester papers about the hunt for Morgan. He may even have read the editorials in the *Rochester Telegraph,* editorials written by a young man named Thurlow Weed. But to young Greeley, Weed was not even a name in 1827. The relationship between the two men that was to prove so fateful for them both still lay in the future.

The *Spectator* closed its doors once and for all in the spring of 1830, and its nineteen-year-old apprentice, his small belongings tied up in a red handkerchief and slung across his shoulders on a stick, struck out once more for western Pennsylvania and the home folks. On his previous visits he had found the air thick with gloom. It was still the same in 1830. Mary Greeley could not reconcile herself to a log cabin, and the shadow of the great woods lay heavily upon her. The happy songs and laughter of her early days had faded into querulous complaint. Zack, forty-five and without capital, was too old to begin the rugged life of a pioneer. Hampered by his wife's despair, he found the going rough, and though he eventually acquired between two and three hundred acres of fairly good land he never could have done so without substantial help from his elder son.

Horace was not much help in 1830. He cleared and grubbed for a couple of months, but he had no mind to be a pioneer. Most of his time was spent chasing jobs in newspaper offices across the New York border and in the bustling little Pennsylvania town of Erie, where he worked five months on the *Erie Gazette* and disputed vigorously with all and sundry on political matters. The Erie employment failed in the early summer of 1831. None other appearing on the horizon, the young man's fancy turned toward the Mecca of journeymen printers. He made a last visit home, divided his Erie savings with his father, and then with twenty-five dollars in his pocket and his red-handkerchief bundle on his shoulder he started for New York.

The August days and nights were hot, the journey by foot and by boat was slow and toilsome. His feet and body ached from much walking and hard beds. He spent fifteen dollars. But just as dawn was breaking on August 17, 1831,[10] a pale, gangling, nondescript youth in scarecrow clothes might have been seen standing on the deck of a down-river Hudson steamer, peering excitedly at the wharves and stores and houses along the New York shore. New York was about to have its introduction to Horace Greeley.

When Greeley reached New York, he had been conditioned in many ways for the part he was to play. School prowess, the plaudits of admiring neighbors, the sense of power that had come from constant reading and ardent debating, had given him confidence in his mental powers, a comforting and sustaining sense of intellectual capacity. Humility, one of Lincoln's most endearing traits, was conspicuously absent in Greeley. The young man who stood on a New York dock at six in the morning with his goods slung on a stick and ten dollars in his pocket was perfectly well aware that he was not as green as he looked.

Environment had done more than breed self-confidence in young Greeley. The communities in which he had lived were simple communities, face to face with the struggle for existence, and out of their travail many lessons had come. He had learned to value the pithy, clear vernacular of a simple people, to prize the useful above the ornamental or the esthetic, and to reverence common sense. The shrewdness of the plain people had been drilled into him. "Bears were tolerably thick in the region where we were brought up," he once remarked. And he had also learned the value of patience. The young fisherman who noticed that the boys who thrashed the water with their poles and yelled, "Bite, God damn you, bite," invariably went home without a catch, had mastered a lesson that was to serve him in good stead in later years.[11]

If Horace Greeley's New England had practical experience for him, it also nourished the emotional side of his nature. It exposed him to New England piety. John Quincy Adams repeating "Now I lay me down to sleep" every night, kneeling by his bed, "saying it aloud and not mumbling it either,"[12] symbolized a New England where hymns and prayers and faith in God were fundamental parts of life. Greeley's parents, themselves not particularly devout, encouraged him to go to church and read the Bible. His religious faith developed early and, though he was "little better than a Universalist" at the age of fourteen, he was otherwise substantially orthodox.

Piety went hand in hand with moral fervor. Human slavery was wrong in the opinion of Greeley's family and neighbors. He caught the spirit of their thinking and was all on the northern side during the struggle over the Missouri Compromise, just as he was in hearty accord when East Poultney rose as one man in the late 1820's to conceal a runaway slave.[13] Drinking was a habit for which he early acquired a distaste, convinced that it was injuring his father and mother. The temperance movement of this early period was a highly moral crusade, closely allied to the religious impulse, and Greeley, one of its early converts, pledged himself on New Year's Day, 1824, never to drink distilled liquors. A little later, he helped to form a temperance society in East Poultney.

The devotion to the rights and dignity of the individual that were part and parcel of antislavery feeling and temperance reform were also an integral part of the national heritage. National pride awoke early in young Greeley, aroused by local Fourth of July celebrations with twenty to fifty Revolutionary veterans on the platform and the sentiments of the Declaration of Independence sounding very fresh and real as they were read by the orator of the day. Greeley never forgot the fiftieth anniversary of Independence as it was celebrated in Poultney, nor the feeling of religious awe that swept over the village shortly afterward when it was learned that John Adams and Thomas Jefferson had both died on that day, and that the messengers riding south and north with the sad tidings had met in Philadelphia within the shadow of Independence Hall.

If environment was influential in developing young Greeley's moral fervor and his national pride, it also had much to do with shaping his attitude toward politics and political leaders. His parents were Federalists and in his early life he was largely surrounded by Federalist, or at least by conservative, influences. The *Farmer's Cabinet* of Amherst, which he devoured every week, was Federalist in tone. So was the *Northern Spectator,* on which he served his apprenticeship. Poultney, itself, solid for New England's favorite son, gave 334 votes for Adams to four for Jackson in 1828. Political discussions which Greeley heard as a child gave the precocious boy an impression that New Hampshire Republicans were creatures full of hatred, malice, and gall. Thirty years later he asserted that these were the characteristics of the "Sham Democracy" in New Hampshire. He knew, having the same proof as the legislative orator who exclaimed, "Mr. Speaker, I ought to know something about hogs:— I was raised among 'em."

Being a Federalist in a simple New England community carried no connotation of aristocracy, no evidence that the individual voter distrusted the masses. The practically solid Poultney vote for Adams meant that the selectman and the day laborer, the man who prospered and the man who could not get ahead, the man of family background and the man of no family background voted the same ticket and held the same political beliefs. Poverty-stricken Horace Greeley, a juvenile Federalist turning logically enough into a John Quincy Adams Republican, had no suspicion that he was betraying the rights of man. Indeed, when he read how Martin Van Buren and the New York Regency had thwarted the popular will in New York State by opposing the choice of presidential electors by the people, young Greeley acquired a lasting distrust of the Red Fox of Kinderhook. And when the Antimasonic excitement flamed across the New York border into New England, Greeley became deeply suspicious of the Masonic Order as a menace to democratic institutions. He was an Adams man through and through, outraged by Jackson's shilly-shallying on the tariff and by the Jackson party's two-faced tariff stand in 1828, and he was wildly indignant about the Jacksonian campaign cries of "Bargain and Corruption," "East Room," "Billiard Table," "Sunday Riding," together with the other monstrous tales of Adams' extravagance and profligacy that accompanied the triumph of King Andrew.[14]

There was still another reason why Greeley took the conservative side of politics in those early years. Protection was a basic part of the Adams-Clay program, and young Horace found more than one lesson at hand which seemed to demonstrate the logic of the protectionist position. He saw the distress occasioned by the panic of 1819, a distress occasioned in part by the dumping of British goods on the American markets. As Zack Greeley moved down the hill toward bankruptcy, Horace saw the market for the linen, woolen, and tow cloth that his mother wove usurped by the products of Britain. He may or may not have read just then the articles that Matthew Carey began to write in 1819, but they were scarcely needed to harden his conviction that a high tariff was a necessary remedy for the poverty that surrounded him. So thought the Vermonters among whom he lived in the 1820's. They were protectionists almost to a man.

When Greeley stepped off the steamboat on to the New York dock, that August morning in 1831, he had reached not only the city where he was to spend the rest of his life, but also many of the political and moral positions that were to be his permanently. But he was only twenty. His character and his philosophy of life were far from completely formed, and they were now to be subjected to a series of influences and opportunities the like of which he had never known before.

NOTES FOR CHAPTER 1

1. Greeley Papers (N.Y.P.L.), Greeley to Moses A. Cortland, Apr. 14, 1845; Greeley Papers (Lib. of Cong.), Greeley to Mrs. Rebecca Whipple, July 21, 1853; Jas. Parton, *The Life of Horace Greeley* (N. Y., 1855), pp. 28-33; H. Greeley, *Recollections of a Busy Life* (N. Y., 1868), pp. 99-100; C. Cleveland, *The Story of a Summer* (N. Y., 1874), pp. 87, 91, 97, 199-200.
2. Greeley Papers (N.Y.P.L.), Greeley to Cortland, Apr. 14, 1845; Parton, *op. cit.*, pp. 46, 49-50; Greeley, *Recollections*, p. 47.
3. Greeley, *Recollections*, pp. 114, 117; Greeley, *What I Know of Farming* (N. Y., 1871), pp. 170-71; Parton, *op. cit.*, p. 56.
4. Greeley, *Essays Designed to Elucidate the Science of Political Economy* (Boston, 1870), pp. 64-65. Hereafter cited as *Political Economy*.
5. *New-Yorker*, Apr. 8, 1837.
6. Cleveland, *op. cit.*, pp. 95f., 149f.

7. Greeley Papers (Lib. of Cong.), The Terms of Apprenticeship; Greeley, *Recollections*, pp. 61-63.
8. Parton, *op. cit.*, pp. 94-95.
9. *New-Yorker*, July 13, 1839.
10. Parton, *op. cit.*, gives the date as August 18. I follow Greeley, *Recollections*, p. 84.
11. *New York Daily Tribune*, Oct. 29, 1853. Hereafter cited as the *Tribune*.
12. Van Wyck Brooks, *The Flowering of New England* (N. Y., 1940), p. 325.
13. *Tribune*, March 20, 1861,; Greeley, *Recollections*, p. 63.
14. *Tribune*, Aug. 3, 1841, Jan. 29, May 31, 1844; Jan. 13, 1848, Nov. 8, 1851; Greeley Papers (N.Y.P.L.), Greeley to Schuyler Colfax, Aug. 20, 27, 1854.

CHAPTER 2

The Slopes of Parnassus

THE NEW YORK TO WHICH GREELEY CAME IN 1831 was an overgrown town of some 200,000 inhabitants, its wharves, banks, stores, churches, shanties, homes, and temple-fronted mansions covering rather compactly the lower end of Manhattan Island. Gas-lighted Broadway was the finest street, stretching more than two miles up from the Battery to somewhere between Tenth and Fourteenth streets. Beyond this lay an area of farms and gardens.

New York was a growing, bustling place where business dominated life and thought. Merchants, bankers, lawyers, and brokers, in beaver hats and broadcloth, their brows furrowed with care and an acquisitive gleam in their eyes, streamed downtown in the morning and uptown in the afternoon. They were first and foremost money-makers, avid for power. The great majority of them, being good providers, were also anxious to satisfy the taste of their wives and sweethearts for crinolines, silks, and velvets. The shipping gentry among this hard-working band monopolized South Street, where a forest of masts and spars rode at anchor, merchantmen from all over the world, their bowsprits with carved figureheads projecting over a street piled with a confusion of bales, bags, and barrels and smelling of pitch and molasses, pepper and coffee. Pearl Street was the headquarters of the wholesale dry-goods merchants. The chief banks, insurance and brokerage offices were located in Wall Street, but that thoroughfare was scarcely the canyon of today. Its buildings ranged from two to six stories in height. The retail stores, where buyers haggled over prices like country customers, centered mainly on Broadway. Even in the midst of the panic of 1837, when the nation's economy stalled and failures bade fair to paralyze every sizable community, New York was preëminently a center of business life.[1]

The market and the counting place bulked large in the life of prosperous New Yorkers, but they could spend their money as well as make it. Pleasure seekers enjoyed the vaudeville and fireworks at Niblo's Garden, 576 Broadway. They could stand agape before the Siamese twins and other kindred marvels at Peale's Museum, or go to the Park Theatre, where the best plays were put on. There were summer moonlight excursions in the long, shallow, fantastically painted North River steamers, and winter sleighing parties pelted one another with snowballs as they dashed along Broadway. The *bon ton* entertained at crowded dances and at dinner parties in the splendid houses west of Broadway. Parties were also given at Delmonico's, already famous for its French cookery and rare wines, or even at the Astor House which opened in 1836 on Broadway between Barclay and Vesey streets—three hundred rooms, with black walnut furniture from top to bottom, "superior oil cloth" on the floors, and a fine cuisine.

The New York social set aped English manners, and the hajjis (who had been to Paris) looked down their noses at the common run of their associates. Dinner-table conversation turned principally upon prices, profits, and the state of the currency. Then, after commendation of the vintage, speculation would ensue as to what young beauty would next marry what middle-aged man of wealth, or as to what Grecian temple up along the Hudson would next change hands. James Fenimore Cooper, back from Europe in the early thirties, found the general lust for gold infecting even the women and the clergy. Mrs. Trollope found "dollar" an ever-recurring word in conversation, and Greeley, inclined to bridle at this, caught himself using it twice in fifteen minutes.[2] It was only a small minority that found time to reflect upon the significance of the French Revolution of 1830, or the beginning of the British Factory Acts, or even the fulminations of a Massachusetts abolitionist in a newspaper called the *Liberator*, a crazy fanatic who was shouting, "I am in earnest—I will not equivocate—I will not excuse—I will not retreat a single inch—and I *will be heard*."

There was much that was reckless, wasteful, and even sinister in the New York scene of the 1830's. The stagecoach drivers who raced one another on Broadway to the peril of pedestrian and passenger alike, the hackney coachmen who bawled and fought and mulcted their passengers, were only rougher replicas of the brighter-eyed and smoother-tongued gamblers who frequented the card rooms or gambled on the price of city lots. The city was careless of safety and health alike. The streets were rough, uneven, and often unrepaired. They were customarily dirty, and in many places there were heaps of refuse from which rose a variety of stenches. Not until 1837 were street scavengers regularly employed, and then they were too few to be effective. Each occupant swept the street in front of his place, if it was swept at all. Under such circumstances sanitation was conspicuous by its absence, especially in the rougher sections of the city. Hogs ran at large, a drove of them sure to be found clustering about such notables as Pot-Pie Palmer, whose clanging bell summoned the maids to empty the swill pails into his big cart. Water came from street pumps and rain-water cisterns. It was no wonder that thousands died in the cholera epidemics of 1832 and 1834, or that fires destroyed millions of dollars' worth of property during the decade.[3]

Recklessness and waste were accompanied by violence which seemed, indeed, to be the order of the day. Newspapers hurled outrageous insults at one another and newspaper editors fought in the streets. Four months before Greeley arrived, William Cullen Bryant, the poet-editor of the *Evening Post*, publicly cowhided William L. Stone of the *Commercial Advertiser*. If the gentry acted so, what could be expected of the rougher element? East of the Bowery, especially in the terrible Five Points section, a dense population hived and festered in small, two-story, wooden and brick buildings, or in shanties, hovels, and cellars—laborers, paupers, criminals, the desperate, the diseased, the underprivileged thrown higgledy-piggledy together. Here were recruited fight-loving gangs of Irishmen (the b'hoys) to roam the city on election day, bringing tumult and riot wherever they appeared. Here mobs emerged to beat up abolitionists and sack the churches in which they tried to meet. In January 1837, with flour at twelve to fourteen dollars a barrel and the wholesalers holding it for still higher prices, a mob burst out of the slum areas, broke into one of the big warehouses, flouted the police, pelted the Mayor with flour when he tried to make a speech, and looted and destroyed hundreds of barrels of the precious stuff. On such occasions only the city militia, or perhaps a parade of artillery, could keep or restore order.

The city had no settlement houses, and vice had few restraints. Common prostitutes flaunted their wares in the streets, and the upper galleries of the theatres were customarily reserved for them as places of assignation. There was an aristocracy of vice as well as wealth. Young bloods of means and gentlemen with gold seal rings and massive watch chains slung across paunchy stomachs frequented the high-class whore-houses such as the one at 41 Thomas Street where man-about-town Francis P. Robinson hatcheted a beauty with literary aspirations, one Dorcas Dorrance alias Helen Jewett, alias Helen Mar, alias Maria B. Benson, because she threatened to expose their relations to the heiress he was about to marry. Robinson escaped punishment because of the beauty's reputation and his own social position.[4] The trial was the sensation of the hour, but it soon gave way in the public sheets to a succession of fresher scandals.

This hustling young metropolis, pushing up the island as its population swelled—building, burning, building again bigger and better—had its drab and ugly aspects, but it was also a city of great possibilities and great charm. Its bustle and hum attracted foreigner and native alike, and its gold was not all dross. Blindly the gods of the countinghouse were forging a new civilization, and art as well as the more material aspects of life was profiting thereby. Philip Hone and other wealthy men were art patrons. William Cullen Bryant, Samuel F. B. Morse, and others were developing the Sketch Club and the National Academy of Design. There were seventeen daily papers by 1837, ranging from the ten-dollar-a-year to the penny and twopenny varieties. New York was now ahead of Philadelphia as a literary center. Bryant, Fitz-Greene Halleck, and Washington Irving (returned from Europe in 1832 after a seventeen-year absence) were literary lights of magnitude. On occasion a man named Edgar Allan Poe flaunted his black military cloak along the streets. And, although nobody that mattered was conscious of the fact, across the river in Brooklyn a big, good-natured, clumsy office boy named Walt Whitman had about reached the end of his schooling in 1831. Decidedly, New York had possibilities for a gangling Yankee with a taste for newspapers, politics, and poesy.

Ungainly and bizarre in appearance, even after he had spent nearly five dollars on a New York suit of clothes, young Greeley had some initial difficulty in finding a job. Push and pertinacity triumphed, however, and for a year and a half he lived the plain, hard life of a journeyman printer in New York, setting type, writing a paragraph for publication when the opportunity offered, living in cheap lodgings, eating cheap food, working fourteen hours a day, earning six dollars a week and living on half of that, but getting some firsthand information about the New York laboring class, and building for himself a reputation. Fellow apprentices and employers got to know Horace Greeley as an oddity who was also something of a genius, a youth careless in dress and unaware of many social conventions but efficient in his work and shrewd in argument, a talkative, witty, good-natured fellow, so generous and trusting that practical jokers and swindlers separated him from sixty dollars of his hard-earned money in a little over a year. He was finding a place for himself, and secure in that knowledge he worked on without relief through the hot and terrible cholera summer of 1832.[5]

When the New England maples flaunted their October glory, Greeley visited friends and relatives in New Hampshire and Vermont. He came back to New York in time to vote for Clay and to see six dollars in election bets buried under the Democratic landslide of 1832. Six dollars had been his limit, he wrote to a friend, "for the simple reason that I had no more to bet, for if I had had it I should have put it down." Jackson's triumph, he declared in acrid humor, would mean little else than anarchy, and the Democratic victory in New York City had been due to a thousand officeholders, backed by "the most degraded and infamous rabble that ever disgraced the bogs of Ireland." On top of all this, he found it impossible to collect twenty-five dollars in back pay and consequently faced the world without a cent in his pockets.[6] He went back to work in considerable bitterness of spirit, but new ventures were just over the horizon.

About the beginning of the new year, Greeley and a young associate, Francis V. Story, with a shoestring capital and very little credit, set up a printing establishment at 54 Liberty Street. Slowly but surely the firm prospered. Story drowned that summer, but his brother-in-law, Jonas Winchester, took his place, and the business continued. Its chief source of revenue was printing done for the New York lotteries.

Just as the firm was getting started, the country was startled by the story of a lottery addict who had lost his all and then committed suicide. Popular indignation mounted and agitation increased for outlawing this form of gambling. Such action would obviously endanger the firm of Greeley and Winchester. Under these circumstances, and as a betting man who occasionally bought a lottery ticket and put all he had on elections, Greeley did not hesitate to defend those from whom he earned his bread. He wrote an article decrying the public attitude toward lotteries and arguing that suicide proved only the weakness of the man's character, nothing whatsoever as to the advisability of licensing such forms of business. The ground of this argument was skillfully chosen and the lottery men were vastly pleased.[7] Not many years later, Greeley became convinced that all forms of gambling, including lotteries, were very wicked indeed.

Printing was one way to butter parsnips, but it did not satisfy all of Horace Greeley's aspirations. An intense interest in politics; voracious reading of contemporary newspapers and literary publications; a germination of ideas on morals, the world's progress, and the American destiny drove him constantly to put pen to paper.[8] Out of this intellectual ferment emerged a great idea and an argument. He would publish a family weekly devoted to current literature and politics, one designed to reach the masses, inform them and elevate their taste. He would at one and the same time further the progress of American civilization and make money. The firm could make the venture, for it was worth about three thousand dollars and had a steady income from the lotteries. Such arguments, together with the enthusiasm of the senior partner, convinced his associates (it was now Greeley, Winchester, and Sibbett), and on March 22, 1834, the *New-Yorker* made its bow.

The *New-Yorker* was low priced, as literary magazines went. Where others sold at from five to eight dollars a year, it cost only two dollars folio and three dollars quarto (this last an innovation in the boom year of 1836). Since it sought the improvement of the American masses, it emphasized morality in literature and understanding in politics, and urged a host of reforms such as improved typography, better spelling books, improved grammars and dictionaries (Greeley had excellent ideas on such matters, on occasion even undertaking to instruct Noah Webster in spelling and etymology). It also campaigned against murders and steamboat explosions.[9] Since it was designed for wide sale, it pretended impartiality in politics, shunned religious controversy, and served up its fare with a garnish of "sweetmeats and pepper sauce."[10] These condiments consisted of such matters as a popular song printed with music in each issue so that the readers could learn "My Bark Is On The Billow" or "Meet Me By Moonlight"; jokes that passed for side-splitting humor in the 1830's (example: fleas are subject to insanity—so many of them die cracked); and considerable detail as to horrid murders, bold robberies, and spectacular convulsions of Nature. But always its main attention was to politics and literature.

Edgar Allan Poe once declared that as a critic of belles-lettres Greeley was entitled to high respect. In some ways this was true. The *New-Yorker's* editor was a stickler for correct grammar and rhyme, giving short shrift to luckless poets who offended in those matters. His plaintive query, "How can a writer rhyme 'waving' and 'rambling' and yet desire to face the public," was only one of many such verbal spankings delivered through the columns of the *New-Yorker*. Like Dr. Johnson, Greeley despised lines in which either the thought or its expression was contemptible. Why anyone should write "The hollow winds whistle in sorrowful sounds" passed his comprehension. Once he burst out: "We assure P. M. that he *cannot* write poetry, and as the fault is Nature's and not his, he need not hope for its amendment."[11] Himself a romanticist, he was impatient with the extravagances of romanticists who flung themselves headlong into excesses of sentimental misery or wild diabolism, the Miserimus and Mephistopheles schools. No, he told one "Roswald" emphatically, the *New-Yorker* would not publish "Sulmina, a Celtic Fragment." He, Greeley, had "an utter and unconquerable aversion to the Ossianic school of prose or poetry," whichever it might be considered. "Of all the varying phases of 'Heavenly Poesie,' " he snorted on another occasion, "we least affect the superlatively tender."[12] Greeley knew good writing when he saw it. He was ahead of his time in appreciating the greatness of Wordsworth, and he was one of Melville's early admirers.

But Greeley's literary standards were not impeccable. He sadly underestimated prose, attributing lasting life to poetry alone. He was prone to extravagances of judgment where his favorites were concerned. The dilettante Nathaniel P. Willis was "the most pleasing poet of the age." Felicia Hemans, whose mellifluous, sincere, and simple verse always carried a heavy tincture of the joy of sorrow and a mighty dose of morality and religion, was "the true priestess of Nature," one who should be classed with Byron, Scott, and Bulwer as among "the miracles of the age." In 1836 he ranked Byron foremost among the poets of the nineteenth century, only to demote him below Wordsworth and Cowper two years later on the ground that to compare them as poets they must first be looked at as men. Poetry, Greeley declared, was merely the transcript of the inmost soul of the poet, and it was the soul that mattered. His admiration for such decidedly lesser lights as W. H. C. Hosmer, Lydia Sigourney, and Julia H. Scott stands out in lamentable contrast to his carping criticism of Shakespeare as too often disgustingly corrupt in language and diction, "the highest type of literary hack" whose efforts were a combination of "starry flights and paltry jokes, celestial penetration and contemptible puns."[13]

The main trouble with Greeley's literary standards, from the twentieth-century point of view, was that they were so inextricably intertwined with his Puritanical attitude in moral matters. Shakespeare's genius was less important than the low quality of Shakespeare's moral sentiments. The Bard sometimes actually showed vice triumphant and sin resulting in happiness! "Can it be seriously contended," thundered the outraged critic, "that the inculcation of moral truth is the object and drift of the author?" Instruction and elevation were what counted. It was wholly in keeping with such a point of view that he should dismiss Poe's *Israfel* with the single line, "striking but not happy," and that he should congratulate himself upon not having filled the *New-Yorker* with "the trashy though humorous absurdities of the Pickwick Papers." On the other hand, he waxed enthusiastic over a story called "The Onyx Ring," that he reprinted from *Blackwood's* in the *New-Yorker*. It was a romantic tale with Faustian colorings, highly moralistic, deeply religious, rambling, and dull.[14]

Greeley was not content to be merely editor and critic. He tried hard to be a poet. In the thirty-odd efforts that he published, the thought, if not profound, was always elevated, the rhyming was good, and the grammar was excellent. But these efforts almost invariably gave an impression of laborious straining after effect on the part of the author, and not infrequently the composition groaned aloud. Worst of all, they showed no evidence of imaginative power. A poet who could write

> We reck'd not lack of cumbrous ore
> While youth's gay dreams flew light as air

did well to speak in later years of "my youthful transgressions in the way of rhyme."[15]

Greeley also published a short story, "Adolph Bruner,"[16] the tale of "a rash, misguided union" between intellect and ignorance. It was highly romantic, emotional to the nth degree, and had a tragic ending. These were the hallmarks of the popular literature of the period, but "Adolph Bruner" was no masterpiece of its kind. Its plot was strained and its style was purplish. An author who could describe his heroine as one whose "fervent gratitude was murmured from lips of rosiest fulness and yet more eloquently spoken from eyes of brightest lustre, even while suffused with richest pearls of tenderness and sorrow" was clearly not a master in his craft.

Horace Greeley was not destined to become a rival of Edgar Allan Poe in the short story. Creative literature was not the forte of the *New-Yorker's* editor. He recognized that fact. In "The Faded Stars," a poem written about 1835, he told how those "calm ministrants to God's high glory" had filled him with romantic visions. These transports had now faded away and in their place had come a stern resolve "to war on fraud intrenched with power."[17] A few years later, he wrote regretfully to a friend that his versifying days were gone forever.[18] Already the romantic moralist in him was in the ascendant, triumphing over the romantic littérateur, and the moralist slowly and painfully learned how to express practical thoughts on concrete subjects. As the decade wore on, his ideas in regard to politics and social reform were put down in a simple, forceful prose that was in sharp contrast to the style of his literary effusions in the field of belles-lettres.

NOTES FOR CHAPTER 2

1. I. N. P. Stokes, *The Iconography of Manhattan* (6 vols.; N. Y., 1915-27), III, 517-30; Willis, *Prose Writings* (N. Y., 1885), pp. 352-54; L. Abbott, *Reminiscences* (Boston and N. Y., 1915), p. 31.

2. Willis, *op. cit.*, pp. 343, 346, 352, also *Life Here and There* (N. Y., 1850), p. 119; *New-Yorker*, Sept. 20, 1834, May 14, 1836, Sept. 23, 1837, June 16, 1838; J. F. Cooper, *Home As Found* (Boston and N. Y., n.d.), pp. 5, 28, 49, 60-61, 64, 68, 72, 78, 105, 117.

3. *Ibid.*, p. 106; *New-Yorker*, Apr. 12, 1834, Dec. 19, 1835, Apr. 23, 30, Aug. 13, Sept. 3, 1836, May 19, 1838; Stokes, *op. cit.*, III, 522-30; *Tribune*, May 30, 1857, Dec. 5, 1863.

4. *New-Yorker*, Aug. 16, 1836.

5. Henry A. Stahl Collection, Greeley to J. G. Shortall, Nov. 15, 1855; Greeley Papers (N. Y. P. L.), Greeley to Cortland, Apr. 14, 1845; Greeley, *Recollections*, pp. 83-89, 191-97. For a time, Greeley worked on the *New York Evening Post*, with which he was to cross swords so often in later years— Parton, *op. cit.*, p. 133.

6. Greeley Papers (N. Y. P. L.), Greeley to S. Mears, Nov. 8, 1832.

7. This article is not in existence. Even the indefatigable Parton failed to find it, but he had the story from one of the lottery men, Mr. Dudley S. Gregory. Greeley did not deny the story in his *Recollections*. p. 93. Cf. Parton, *op. cit.*, pp. 147-48.

8. Parton, *op. cit.*, p. 151, asserts that Greeley refused James Gordon Bennett's offer of a partnership in setting up the *New York Herald*.

9. The *New-Yorker* was meant to resemble the *Saturday Evening Post*, which was then a publication devoted primarily to the field of belles-lettres.

10. Greeley Papers (N. Y. P. L.), Greeley to O. A. Bowe, June 11, 1838.

11. *New-Yorker*, June 4, 1836.

12. *Ibid.*, May 3, 1834, Jan. 24, 1835, Mar. 26, Oct. 15, Sept. 17, 1836. In dealing with Greeley's literary standards, I am indebted to an unprinted Master's thesis by Gerald A. Smith entitled "Horace Greeley as an Editor and Critic," University of Rochester, 1947, prepared under the able supervision of Professor Margaret Denny.

13. *New-Yorker*, July 26, 1834, May 30, 1835, Apr. 23, Nov. 19, 1836, June 17, 1837; Myers, *Genius of Horace Greeley* (Columbus, O., 1929), p. 28.

14. *New-Yorker*, Nov. 19, 1836, Sept. 16, 1837, Dec. 29, 1838ff.; Greeley Papers (N. Y. P. L.), Greeley to B. F. Ransom, Jan. 23, 1839.

15. *New-Yorker*, May 10, 1834; L. A. Wilmer, *Our Press Gang* (Phila., 1859), p. 115; Ingersoll Papers, Greeley to Mrs. Ingersoll, July 30, 1860.

16. *New-Yorker*, Dec. 7, 1839.

17. Cleveland, *op. cit.*, pp. 218-19.

18. Greeley Letters (Yale Lib.), Greeley to B. F. Ransom, Mar. 15, Nov. 13, 1841.

CHAPTER 3

A Budding Politician

THE SPIRIT OF POLITICAL AND SOCIAL UNREST hovered over America during the 1830's. Antimasonry, the "blessed spirit" that preached hatred of secret societies and aristocratic power, spread out of New York State into Pennsylvania and New England. National Republicanism disintegrated and in its place a new conservative party, calling itself Whig, arose to challenge the triumphant Democracy of Jackson and Van Buren. Trade-unionism boomed, only to collapse as swiftly under the stress of hard times. There was a flurry of workingmen's parties at the beginning of the decade, and Loco Focoism spread a pattern across the East as artisans, harassed by the high cost of living, cursed banks and paper currencies and unfriendly courts of law. The mellow voice of Fanny Wright proclaimed class war and an impending revolution.

The restless and dissatisfied generally allied themselves under the banner of Jacksonian Democracy, for the doughty old hero in the White House (champion of the spoils system and foe of Nicholas Biddle's "Monster," the Bank of the United States) had come to be regarded as the standard-bearer in the war against privilege. On the other hand, the bulk of the Old Federalists and of the rapidly rising business class, aristocrats and men of property and substance, the careful and the fearful, rallied under the Whig standard, which was held aloft by black-browed Daniel Webster and a charming and arrogant Kentuckian whom Charles Dickens found "enchanting; an irresistible man,"[1] and whose name was Henry Clay. Once more, as in the days of Hamilton and Jefferson, conservatives and liberals were arrayed in opposite camps.

Much sound and fury emanated from these opposing camps. The champions of the respective sides dealt one another many a hearty blow. But it would be a grave error to conceive of this warfare as a clear-cut class struggle between capital and labor, the rich and the poor. Only in the mind of a prophetess like Fanny Wright, or an occasional union leader like Eli Moore of New York, was the issue thus clearly defined. Most Americans owned property or had a reasonable expectation of so doing. The factory system was only beginning, the relationship between masters and workmen was often close, and artisans, even if they were in economic difficulties, were more inclined to think of themselves as Americans in trouble than as the exploited serfs of the capitalist system. Jacksonian Democracy was, indeed, as often a protest of business entrepreneurs against the dead hand of vested interest as it was an uprising of discontented laborers against scrounging employers.[2]

The Jacksonians had but a dim comprehension of the problems in process of creation as the economy moved toward industrialization. They were still wedded to the old Jeffersonian dogma that that government governs best which governs least, and their program of reform was negative rather than positive. They freed the country of a Bank of the United States that was indeed a potential menace to democracy, but they had nothing to offer as a substitute for that bank's valuable services in controlling credit inflation and maintaining a stable currency. They championed hard money, but this challenge to the bankers' power over the currency was destructive rather than constructive. Even the economic theorist William Gouge, idol of the hard-money men, believed that the land was the greatest source of wealth and that the ideal social system was one in which the laws and institutions of government would be reduced to a minimum. President Jackson himself acted on one occasion as a strike breaker, sending troops to help his friend, President John H. Eaton of the Chesapeake and Ohio Canal Company, put down labor troubles along the canal.[3] The voice of Jacksonism carried overtones of working-class sympathy, especially when political expediency demanded that it should do so, but its hand was the hand of Jeffersonian laissez faire.

Greeley faced the political maelstrom of the early 1830's, a prey to conflicting emotions. The zeal of the humanitarian reformer was even then stirring within him. The *New-Yorker* showed clearly his dislike of liquor, slavery, and the exploitation of the Indians, his opposition to such social injustices as the New York State compulsory militia system and imprisonment for debt. The *New-Yorker's* editor was convinced that the nineteenth century was to be the century of the common man, the age of the education and development of the masses, "the age of 'useful knowledge' and decent mediocrity." He believed that the American and French revolutions had started a trend of immense and far-reaching significance. American democratic institutions, the July Revolution of 1830 in France, and the agitation for Irish Reform were clear and unmistakable signs of this development. He was confident that he saw shaping up in Europe a great battle between "the spirit of the age and the antiquated prejudices of despotism—between the spirit of the Twelfth and the Nineteenth Centuries—between 'Divine Right' and 'inalienable rights.' "[4] Such interests and convictions might well have inclined him, along with Bryant, to the Jacksonian side, but other considerations moved him into the camp of the Whigs.

The budding nationalism of this young Yankee lent strength to the conservative side of his nature. This nationalism was clearly apparent in the *New-Yorker,* where its editor demonstrated his intense pride in the United States and its institutions, and his anxiety to promote the national welfare. His eagerness to improve American literary taste went hand in hand with his zeal for better education, moral reforms, and a national museum of art. His literary judgments had a distinctly nationalist quality, for he was apt to exalt the virtues of American writers above their proper station.[5] Sight of the Capitol at Washington with the flag flying from the top thrilled his soul, and he had only veneration for the Father of his Country. Almost every issue of the *New-Yorker* was redolent of patriotism and morality. Such an attitude as this lent itself easily to the conviction that America was already well on the road to human felicity. Greeley believed that here at home there was no such need for sweeping reform as pressed upon king-ridden Europe, where twenty-nine sovereigns lorded it over their peoples.

So far as America was concerned, the *New-Yorker's* editor had a respect for established ways and institutions, and a dislike for radical tamperers with the status quo that was almost Burkean in character. Although he held slavery to be completely incompatible with democracy, he opposed the abolitionists, classing them with Fanny Wright as people who should be allowed free speech but who were dangerous to the country's peace and well-being. His only remedy for slavery was colonization. As for the budding woman's rights movement, he was utterly unsympathetic. If women were enfranchised, they should be made subject to military duty and recruited for the army. He opposed allowing a married woman to retain control of her property. Woman's place was in the home where, by law and by the Christian tradition, the man was the head of the household.[6]

Another aspect of Greeley's conservatism was his profound distrust of the masses. It was the blindness of the multitude, he felt, that led to flour riots, to mob action against abolitionists, and to the travesty on political democracy that resulted when the Irish rabble voted in New York. Mass ignorance, the *New-Yorker's* editor declared, was an easy prey to such troublemakers as Fanny Wright. Bulwer-Lytton's *Rienzi* was commended in the *New-Yorker* because it showed the worthlessness of freedom without knowledge, and the viciousness of demagoguery. Surveying some of the wilder apparitions of change that hovered around Jacksonism, Greeley became rather easily convinced that the Democratic party was altogether too prone to contempt for established institutions, too responsive to dangerous popular demands that stemmed from ignorance.[7] Such fears did not destroy his belief in the basic principles of political democracy. He accepted without question the value of a wide if not universal suffrage, and the wisdom of majority rule. But they did produce in him a ready response to a party in which patrician tone, leadership from above, and respect for the rights of property were emphasized.

Greeley's fear of mass ignorance was reflected in his profoundly conservative attitude toward labor, and capitalist-labor relations. In his view, capital was labor performed, labor was potential capital, and the interests and aims of both were essentially harmonious and practically identical. Those who denied this essential harmony of interest were doers of evil, for they promoted class division and weakened the national fabric by teaching the obvious untruth that the laboring class was at a fixed disadvantage in the national economy. Actually, the industrious, skillful, and honest worker was almost bound to rise in the social and economic scale. The *New-Yorker's* editor grudgingly admitted the right of labor to act as a political party, to unionize and even to strike, but he was quick to point out that gains made by striking were doubtful and illusory, and that political organization was a "yawning gulf." Far better for the worker to trust to his talents and his industry in this land of opportunity. The worker should also remember, if affluence did not come his way, that wealth brings care and sorrow, while poverty ennobles character. Greeley's comment upon Catharine Sedgwick's *The Poor Rich Man, And The Rich Poor Man*, which taught this simple lesson, was almost ecstatic.[8] Such views were perhaps natural for a man who worked fourteen hours a day and never seemed to tire.

On the economic questions most prominently connected with politics, Greeley's views were a mixture of basic conservatism and political prejudice. He said practically nothing about the tariff, for it had been taken out of politics by the Compromise of 1833, but he had already accepted the principle of protection and his sympathies were clear. An enthusiastic believer in internal improvements, he heartily supported Clay's land bill, which provided for distribution of the national income derived from the sale of public lands. He approved the sales price of one dollar and a quarter an acre for public lands, and held preëmption and graduation (Democratic steps toward a free-land policy) in abhorrence. They were akin to feudalism, monopoly, and trade-unions in their iniquitous effects, and might be counted upon to curse the West "with a population of dissipated drones and land speculators." What the poor needed, said Greeley, was equal rights and opportunities, not immunities that might be turned against them. Squatters should not be driven off the land they had occupied, but it was stupid and nonsensical to encourage them.[9]

Greeley's stand on banks and money was as Whiggish as his views on land and labor. When Biddle called in the loans of the Bank of the United States in 1834, attempting in that way to force the recharter of the Bank, Greeley's first impulse was to spring to his defense.[10] Repeatedly, the *New-Yorker's* editor laid aside his vaunted impartiality when bank politics waxed hot. He intimated that the hard money movement meant to destroy the entire credit system, and leaped easily to the conclusion that the Sub-Treasury plan would mean the destruction of all banks. His assertion that the Sub-Treasury (which merely kept government receipts in the hands of the government instead of depositing them in banks) was "a retrograde toward barbarism which cannot, in the nature of things, be real and enduring" was rather obviously overstrained political rhetoric.[11] But even though he was guilty of wildly partisan statements, even though there was at times a degree of improvisation in his economic thought,[12] there was a remarkable degree of astuteness in his attitude on certain economic questions.

Greeley saw with clarity and precision the value of the Bank of the United States as a balance wheel for the national system of currency and credit. He had an equally clear conception of the crucial, sometimes vicious, but fundamentally valuable role of the state banks in supporting the credit system by their powers of discount and their issuance of paper money. The monetary issue, as he saw it, was between a rigid, archaic, metallic currency, unresponsive to the country's needs, and a more elastic currency of gold, silver, and paper, the latter to be furnished by the banks. The paper was the important thing, not the fact that the banks furnished it. He would have preferred to have this paper currency issued by the federal government, or by one central bank, had either of these courses been within the bounds of possibility.[13] Since constitutional barriers and political wrangling made both of these courses impractical, he saw no recourse save continued reliance upon the note issues of the state banks.

Greeley could on occasion attribute a greater degree of high-mindedness to the banking fraternity than it actually possessed, but he was no idolator of laissez-faire banking. He supported the New York safety-fund system, which provided at least a partial warranty against bank failures. He approved New York's General Banking Law of 1838, an important Whig measure that opened the door of opportunity to banking entrepreneurs and undertook to safeguard the value of bank currencies. He favored recharter of the Bank of the United States with its unbridled powers restrained by legislative enactment, and urged rigid inspection and control of the bank notes and loaning power of all banks issuing paper currency.[14] Obviously, Greeley wanted the banking system cleansed and renovated.

The Whig party, Horace Greeley believed, was fundamentally sound on banks and currency. He liked its stand for a strong national government, internal improvements, and industrial development. Its dedication by Clay and Webster to the great principle of national unity satisfied his own aspiring nationalism, as did the part then being played by the business class in developing the economic potentialities of the nation. He was not puzzled, as was the *Evening Post,* by the number of genuine democrats who voted the Whig ticket, for he saw no necessary contradiction between a conservative and a democrat. The kind of conservatism that Greeley admired and practised was a determination "to hold by the present until he could see clearly how to exchange it for the better,"[15] the conservatism of Henry Clay. As the *New-Yorker's* editor defined democracy, it had three aspects: the individual to be judged by his actions, not by his station in society; an equal voice in choosing the lawmakers and officials of the nation; willingness to abide by the rule of the majority. Acceptance of these principles made one a democrat, whether one voted for Clay or Van Buren, regardless of one's position on currency and banks.[16]

From a political viewpoint democracy was indivisible, as Greeley saw it. It could not be monopolized by any one party. Could Virginia, with its championship of slavery, be called democratic? Was Calhoun a democrat? Was it democracy in Van Buren to fight to reduce the executive patronage under Adams and then fight to prevent its reduction after 1828? From 1828 to 1837, Vermont had been Whig and Rhode Island Democratic in political complexion,

but in suffrage and provision for popular education, both funda-
mentals of genuine democracy, Vermont had been even then leagues
ahead of its sister state. Greeley was fond of listing Old Federalists
who had turned Democrats and Old Jeffersonians who had become
Whigs. Grandly overlooking the fact that the great majority of Old
Federalists were now Whigs, he declared that it was as ridiculous to
identify Federalism and Whiggism as it would be to identify abolition and Freemasonry. They were simply not the same thing. Whatever the case in the past, political contests in America were not now
between aristocracy and democracy. Any such contention was sheer
humbug. Actually, party battles were based upon "conflicting interests, sectional prejudices, and diverse opinions with respect to
measures."[17] There was both logic and sophistry in these arguments.

Greeley's reasoning in regard to banks, currency, and democratic
principles was often strong and compelling, but his analysis of the
panic of 1837 was not particularly brilliant. His criticism of Jackson's Specie Circular (an attempt to check land speculation and inflation by requiring the payment of specie for public lands) was of
a pattern with his enthusiasm for land speculation in the year before the great panic. Six months before the crash, he felt that
speculation was so beneficial that it should be fostered by giving
banking powers and the right of issuing bank notes to construction
companies. Such note issues would form "the most stable currency
in the world." Even after the deluge broke over the land he was
still certain that heavy buying of foreign goods was far more important than speculation as a cause of the hard times. America
should produce more crops, shut off cotton exports, and ship specie
to Europe[18]—then the good times that he was always prophesying
were just around the corner would return.

But inadequate as were Greeley's ideas on the causes and cure of
the depression, that calamitous event had profound and lasting
effects upon his attitude toward social problems. He helped in relieving the destitute during the first winter of the panic and saw
at firsthand things that had not been dreamed of in his philosophy.
The young editor discovered that thousands of New York's inhabitants lived "in damp, narrow cellars, or rickety, wretched
tenements, unfit for cleanly brutes." He saw filth and disease, and
children wasting away from hunger, and heard the able-bodied and
ambitious pleading in vain for work.[19] He noted the marked increase in New York's petty crimes. The nation was like a human
being afflicted with some terrible sickness, and Greeley began to
look about for remedies.

Naturalization laws and the restriction of immigration came

easily to mind, but much more attractive was the idea of an exodus from city to country. Naturally, the very poor could reach only nearby rural points, especially if they had dependents, but those with some means yet available should strike for the "great West." There they should get some land, "paying a dollar and a quarter if possible; if not, 'squat,' " and in either case go to work. The more Greeley thought of this idea, the more attractive it became to him. But it was not, he recognized, a complete answer to the problems of the suffering masses. Gradually his mind turned to considering the function of government.

Down through 1836, Greeley's conception of governmental responsibility had been chiefly a negative one. Government should keep order, correct abuses, and see to it that justice was done as between citizens. The most vigorous governmental function that he envisaged was the promotion of internal improvements. During the last years of the decade he began to feel his way toward a more positive concept of the governmental function. He began urging the national government to act so as to relieve the depression. He came out for a bankruptcy law, for the distribution of $75,000,000 in Treasury notes among the states, for a $5,000,000 national expenditure in two years on internal improvements (this last was a distinct forerunner of the New Deal's PWA, since Greeley meant it to relieve the rigors of the depression). It was the obligation of government, Greeley declared, to act wherever it was necessary to conserve and guard the public welfare. Government should do good as well as prevent evil. Whatever it could do better than individuals, that it should undertake.[20] Under pressure of the public misery, a vision of far-spread governmental activity for the public good was beginning to form before his eyes. Horace Greeley, a conservative, nineteenth-century Whig, was developing a conception of the function of government surprisingly like that of the twentieth-century New Deal. This fact is at once a yardstick for Rooseveltian "radicalism" and a measure of the argument that the Whigs and Democrats of the 1830's and 1840's were antipodal in their social and economic philosophies.

NOTES FOR CHAPTER 3

1. John Forster, *The Life of Charles Dickens* (N Y., n. d.) , p. 237.

2. This point is brilliantly developed by Richard Hofstadter, *The American Political Tradition* (N. Y., 1948) , pp. 44-66. See also the foreword to J. L. Blau (ed.) , *Social Theories of Jacksonian Democracy* (N. Y., 1947) .

3. W. M. Gouge, *A Short History of Currency and Banking in the United States* (Phila., 1833) , Part I, pp. 128-40. Gouge was interested in clearing the way for the industrious man to become rich, rather than in any Jacobinical notions about establishing a terrestrial paradise that would contain neither rich nor poor. As to Jackson's strikebreaking activities, see Richard B. Morris, "Andrew Jackson, Strikebreaker," *Amer. Hist. Review*, LV (Oct. 1949) , 54-68.

4. *New-Yorker*, Dec. 27, 1834, July 15, 1837.

5. It is significant that, of all American prose writers, Cooper received the most encouragement from Greeley in the *New-Yorker*. Cooper was writing novels about America. Greeley also regarded American fugitive poetry as "greatly superior" to that of England. Hillhouse reminded him of Milton. Bryant was "the Thomson of America."—*New-Yorker*, July 5, 1834.

6. *Jeffersonian*, May 26, 1838; *New-Yorker*, Feb. 28, 1835, July 1, 1837, Jan. 25, 1840. Years later he was to refer to these ideas regarding woman as "vulgar prejudices."—*Recollections*, p. 178.

7. *New-Yorker*, Sept. 20, 1834, Jan. 20, 1836, Jan. 27, 1837, Oct. 6, 1838. ". . . a hatred of anything older than yesterday—a contempt of all authority which springs not from the rank breath of the multitude of today—is the distinctive feature of the latest political authority," he declared early in 1837.

8. *New-Yorker*, June 13, 20, 1835, Apr. 9, 23, June 25, Oct. 29, 1836.

9. *Ibid.*, Dec. 20, 1834, Sept. 10, 1836, Feb. 3, Aug. 25, 1838; *Jeffersonian*, June 23, Sept. 8, 1838.

10. *New-Yorker*, Apr. 12, 1834. Greeley presented both sides of the controversy in the issue of July 19, 1834, declaring that he sought to be impartial, but in his *Recollections*, p. 110, he was once again pro-Biddle.

11. *New-Yorker*, Mar., Apr., 1836, Jan. 4, 1840; *Jeffersonian*, Mar. 17, June 23, 1838. Anyone interested in the hard-money movement should consult the admirable analysis in A. M. Schlesinger Jr., *The Age of Jackson* (Boston, 1945) , pp. 115-31, 526-27.

12. Greeley wrote to Seward in 1842, "I have to make my own Political Economy as I go along."—Greeley Letters (U. of R.) , Greeley to W. H. Seward, July 11, 1842.

13. *New-Yorker*, Aug. 26, 1837.

14. *Ibid.*, Nov. 22, 1834, Jan. 1, 1835, Sept. 17, 24, Nov. 26, 1836, Feb. 11, Mar. 11, Aug. 26, Sept. 2, 1837; *Jeffersonian*, May 5, Sept. 29, Nov. 24, 1838. There is no record of his views on banks and banking prior to 1834.

15. Greeley, *Recollections*. p. 166.

16. *Jeffersonian*, May 26, 1838.

17. *New-Yorker,* June 24, 1837, p. 221; *Jeffersonian,* May 26, June 2, Aug. 18, Oct. 13, 20, Dec. 29, 1838; *Tribune,* Sept. 2, 1841, Aug. 3, 1842, Mar. 24, 1843, Dec. 31, 1844, Sept. 13, 1845; Greeley, *Recollections,* p. 166.
18. *New-Yorker,* Oct. 15, 1836, Apr. 1, 8, 22, 1837.
19. *Ibid.,* June 16, 1838; Greeley, *Recollections,* pp. 144-45; *Tribune,* Jan. 12, 1842.
20. *New-Yorker,* Feb. 24, Mar. 10, May 12, 1838, Jan. 12, 1839, May 30ff., 1840; *Jeffersonian,* Sept. 8, 1838.

CHAPTER 4

A Bride and an Alliance

IT HAD TAKEN A GREAT DEAL OF FAITH TO START
the *New-Yorker*. When its first number went on the streets there was
not a single subscriber.[1] Subscriptions poured in, however, at the
rate of nearly a hundred a week. Within six months 2,500 names
were on the books and by 1837 there were around 9,000, a considerably larger circulation figure than that of any other American literary magazine of the day.

This satisfying rise in circulation by no means represented affluence. Behind it lay a long story of unsatisfactory partners, rascally
circulation agents, bad bookkeeping, and delinquent subscribers
whose names Greeley began to publish in 1835. The great Ann
Street fire of August 12, 1835, gutted the publishing office, forcing
the omission of a week's issue and burning the editor's painfully
gathered collection of political statistics, poetry, books, and papers.
Living in New York became more expensive and the cost of paper
and of labor rose sharply in the middle of the decade. Still and all,
prospects seemed fairly good. Somewhat impulsively, Horace Greeley
decided to take unto himself a wife.

Her name was Mary Youngs Cheney. She was twenty-two years old
and five feet four inches in height, a vivacious, pretty little brunette
with dark curls and decided opinions. Her memory was retentive,
and her active mind (it would prove to be none too stable a mind)
had something of a philosophic bent. She also liked dancing, was
painfully neat, suffered from dyspepsia, and took no interest in
politics.[2] Save for the dyspepsia, they had little in common, and
dyspepsia is an egocentric disease. Such mutual interests as the
Dial and Transcendentalism were to prove all too frail a foundation
for a successful marriage.

Mary Cheney was a schoolteacher. She had been born in Cornwall,
Connecticut, and had come to New York to live in the early 1830's.

Greeley met her at a boardinghouse conducted on the Graham plan (no meat or stimulants of any sort and a minimum of salt, but plenty of bran bread and vegetables), where he had gone to board after discovering that coffee made his hand tremble.

These fellow converts to Sylvester Graham's system found one another congenial table companions, and something more. After the petite brunette left for a teaching position in Warrenton, North Carolina, they wrote to each other. Correspondence, together with absence, fanned the flame, although it seems likely that Greeley's determination to marry came upon him rather suddenly. Certain it is that on May 2, 1836, he was trying to find a partner in the *New-Yorker* with whom he could make a home and thus reduce his living expenses.[3] Two months later, July 5, 1836, he and Mary were married at Warrenton, in the home of Squire William Bragg.

The Squire's son, Braxton Bragg, was at West Point, preparing for the career that was to make him a general in the Confederate army. Could the Braggs have looked into the future, they would not have relished the presence of the fair-haired northern youth who shambled about the parlor before the wedding ceremony.

The bridegroom at Warrenton was twenty-five years old, and his five feet ten inches was a trifle less skinny and angular than had been the case five years before. His hands were delicate, beautifully shaped and white, save for ink stains on the first two fingers. His round, pale face, with its kindly, deep-set blue eyes and beaming smile—an alert, good-humored face with generous features—was in startling contrast to the thin, almost feminine voice with its tendency to piercing sharpness in argument. The owner of this voice was voluble, awkward in society, careless in dress, absent-minded, egotistical, obstinate, and not highly sexed.[4] He was also loyal and tenderhearted, a tremendous worker, and terribly sincere, with what George Ripley later called "a noble air of candor" in his moral earnestness. It was probably on the way to Warrenton that he attempted to persuade two slaveholders of their iniquity, only narrowly to escape being himself persuaded off a dock into thirty feet of water.[5] Mary Cheney was not marrying an easy man.

The bridal pair came back to New York and set up housekeeping. That winter they lived at 124 Green Street, close to the Battery. It was by no means the best residential section, but poverty and the groom's devotion to his work kept them within half a mile of the City Hall, usually within sixty rods of it, until some eight years later. There was a flurry of social life. They went to lectures and to an occasional dancing party. Mary had Friday at homes for literary people, as befitted the wife of the *New-Yorker's* editor.

Sparkling conversation was the order of the day when the bride poured for such celebrities as General George P. Morris, editor of the *Mirror,* Willis and Lewis Gaylord Clark of the *Knickerbocker Magazine,* Elizabeth Jessup Ames, and Anne Cora Lynch. The gathering was always brighter when the witty and whimsical Asahel Clark Kendrick of Hamilton College, whose translations of Schiller invariably had the place of honor on the *New-Yorker's* front page, was there to bend his tall form over the hand of the little hostess. Life was good. Life was even gay. Horace danced a quadrille at a Christmas Eve party. But it was not long after that that the clouds began to lower.

The panic of 1837 plunged the *New-Yorker* into a sea of difficulties. Within a year the subscription list fell to 6,000. Many subscribers began sending their payments in wildcat currency, a circumstance that made Greeley bemoan the Democratic law prohibiting New York state bank notes under five dollars. Wracked by the onslaught of the depression, the partnership of Greeley and Winchester broke up. The latter took the printing business, the only paying part of the concern, and Greeley was left with the paper and an unfit third partner, one of the seven who came and went from 1834 to 1839. Only a loan of $1,000 from lottery man Dudley S. Gregory kept the perspiring editor out of bankruptcy. By the fall of 1837 the *New-Yorker,* what with subscribers dropping away like leaves in autumn, collections impossible, and its business affairs in a chaotic mess, had become an incubus of no mean proportions. Such outside editorial writing as could be commanded paid little and the Greeleys, brought to the verge of utter destitution, served plain Graham fare to visitors without explanation or excuse.

Life seemed dark indeed, when relief suddenly appeared from an unexpected quarter. Up in Albany, the boss of the Whig party in New York State had made a decision that was to bring some profit and much pain into the life of a white-haired New York printer whose hopes and dreams were going all awry.[6]

Thurlow Weed, now the editor of the politically powerful *Albany Evening Journal,* had come a long way since his *Rochester Telegraph* days. In the space of one decade, the starveling editor in a pioneer town had become the guiding spirit of New York State Whiggery. Weed was a self-made man, and an unusual one. There was a genial, warm, affectionate Weed who enjoyed merry talk and wine and oyster suppers, and who was never too busy to do a favor for a friend. There was also Weed the politician, a political manipulator shrewd in the arts of management, a lover of rough and tumble politics, a facile bribe-giver and lobbyist whose passion was victory, without too much regard for the cost. Blest with tremendous vitality, a prodigious memory, and a capacity for inspiring the confidence of the moneyed Whigs, Weed had built up a powerful political machine. Aided by the panic, this machine had ridden to victory in the election of 1837, capturing the state legislature and a host of county offices. Its master at once began laying plans for the following year. His close friend William Henry Seward, a little, red-haired, beak-nosed lawyer with a ready tongue and much charm, was politically ambitious, and Weed was determined to make him governor of the state.[7]

One of Weed's projects for the gubernatorial campaign of 1838 was a cheap political weekly that would carry the Whig gospel into the highways and byways of the state for fifty cents a year. It was a matter of pressing importance to obtain an editor for this sheet. For some time Weed had been reading the *New-Yorker,* noting its editor's politics and his handling of political prose. Greeley was unknown to him personally, but the sagacious editor of the *Evening Journal* became convinced that he had found his man. At any rate, he had to move, for the paper's prospectus had been issued and some of the funds for it had been subscribed.

Late in November or early in December 1837, Weed went down to New York and climbed the stairs to the attic where Greeley wrote his editorials. The big, florid Albany politician and the pale, slender, white-haired New York editor, both stoop-shouldered by labor at their editorial desks, shook hands, and Weed stated his errand. Then they went together down the stairs and out into the street, still talking, and so over to Weed's room in the City Hotel where Lewis Benedict, another Albany Whig, was waiting for them.

The three men dined together that night and a bargain was struck. At Greeley's suggestion, it was agreed that the paper should be called the *Jeffersonian.* Greeley would edit it in Albany, and his salary would be $1,000 for a year's work. To the harassed editor this must have seemed like manna from heaven.

The first issue of the *Jeffersonian,* February 17, 1838, explained the reason for its title. It would mirror Jefferson's fearless and inquiring turn of mind, his trust in and sympathy for the common people. Twelve years later, Greeley was to describe the Sage of Monticello as an infidel who hated Washington and "was unscrupulous and licentious in his personal morals,"[8] but now the Whigs needed the great man's name if they were to play successfully for the common voter. Such are the exigencies of politics and the hypocrisies it breeds.

The tone of the *Jeffersonian* was moderate, even appealing. Its chief message, aside from the "right" views on currency and the Sub-Treasury, was that a man could be a good democrat and also a Whig— in fact, that a man was more apt to be a good democrat if he were a Whig. It rose to a circulation of some 15,000 copies, had a considerable influence in bringing about Seward's victory, and made Greeley a busy man indeed.

During the winter months in 1838 and 1839, when ice closed the Hudson, Greeley stayed most of the time in Albany. There he edited the *Jeffersonian* and reported the legislature's debates for the *Evening Journal,* writing some of its editorials as well. At such times the *New-Yorker* was left to the tender mercies of two new partners, W. Matlack Eldridge and Elbridge G. Paige, and to the hypercritical Park Benjamin, whom Greeley used reluctantly and intermittently as literary editor.[9] When the river was open, Greeley divided his time between New York and Albany.

It may have been for these trips on the river that he donned the first of his white overcoats, a garment bought secondhand, according to tradition, from an Irish immigrant for twenty dollars. Coat tails flying, pockets bulging with papers, he would get off the steamer at Albany on Sunday morning and shamble rapidly up State Street to the *Journal's* office, or to Weed's home at 104 Green Street where he soon had the run of the parlor and of the kitchen as well. Once the *Jeffersonian* was in press, which was usually by Tuesday morning, he would rush off to his family and his paper in New York. Eager and indefatigable, indifferent to the social niceties but warmhearted and full of ideas, he was always welcome at the home of My Lord Thurlow, to whom he looked up with great respect as a man of well-nigh infinite political sagacity.

The absorbed, absent-minded, near-sighted editor who journeyed up and down the Hudson was a man of many cares and troubles. He lost his pocketbook and spent his pay two or three months in advance before the *Jeffersonian* was a week old. A pickpocket relieved him of five dollars in silver, "the cursed Bentonian stuff," one June night on the steamboat. Eldridge and Paige were anything but satisfactory as partners. Park Benjamin left early in the spring, coming back only in October. Financial adversity forced Greeley into borrowing at usurious rates of interest, an economic course that he described ruefully as a "Cape Horn navigation." Then one Wednesday morning in August 1838 Greeley reached home to find his first child, a son, dead at birth and Mary Greeley laid low by a cruel surgical delivery. Grief and shock left her broken in health, a bedridden invalid for six months thereafter.[10]

"Howsomever," wrote Greeley to his old friend and fellow editor, O. A. Bowe, "I always crawl through some auger hole or other, though sometimes it's a dreadful crooked small one." Troubles, even domestic ones, were subordinate to politics. As campaign preliminaries warmed up in the early summer of 1838 he became "hot as ginger." "That speech," he wrote to Bowe of one Whig effort, "ought to be crammed down the throat of every Tory till he pukes up the whole humbug in a fit of awful sickness and loathing." His delight at Seward's victory in November burst forth even in the pages of the supposedly impartial *New-Yorker*.[11]

The *Jeffersonian* ceased publication in February 1839. Weed had wanted it kept on, but Mary Greeley's health was an argument against the enforced winter absences from New York. For his own part, Greeley had found the double duty extremely wearing and he was sick of the very sight of a steamboat, even though travel in such bedbug-ridden palaces had meant a $1,000 income.[12]

The next year was difficult. As usual, the *New-Yorker* paid nothing. The Greeleys lived chiefly on the twelve dollars a week earned by the head of the family through editing the *New York Whig*, a paper that he described as dying of intense stupidity. He wrote a little for other journals, but this was at best an uncertain source of income. That fall he and Molly set up housekeeping at 93 Barclay Street with one room and two bedrooms on three different floors and in different corners of the house. It was scarcely a home, but it was the best that Greeley could find downtown. In desperation he began to revolve plans for reëstablishing the *Jeffersonian*, and a project, dim as yet, for establishing a one-penny Whig daily in New York, a paper that would stress internal improvements, began to grow in his mind. But before these plans had a chance to develop he became involved in Weed's struggle to control the Whig Presidential nomination.

The Dictator of the New York Whigs was pointing for a national victory in 1840 and he was determined not to be mired again in the particular kind of mud that had engulfed him in 1832. Henry Clay had then been firmly ticketed as the Bank candidate, and the ticket had stuck. He was also unpopular with abolitionists and Antimasons, two groups that meant votes in New York State. The Kentuckian must be discarded, Weed was sure, and with Jackson's rise painfully in mind he turned his gaze upon two other military heroes. One was William Henry Harrison, far from rugged at sixty-six, but the hero of Tippecanoe. Harrison had made a respectable race for election against Van Buren in 1836. The other possibility was Winfield Scott, the six-foot-five hero of Lundy's Lane, a man in his early

fifties and very popular in New York and New England. Of the
two, Weed preferred Scott.

Clay came north to spy out the land that summer and in August
visited Saratoga Springs, where the season was at full height and
he found a host of admirers. Weed asked Greeley to go up to Saratoga and somehow, some way, persuade the Kentuckian that he
ought to wait until 1844.

Greeley had been reluctantly convinced by Weed's logic that Clay
could not win—that Scott was the man. "The Adjutant," as Weed
and Seward called the *New-Yorker's* editor, had been willing enough
to go on a political journey to Detroit that summer, talking all the
way against Clay's nomination. But facing the Old Prince at Saratoga was another matter. Besides, what was the use? Clay had an
imperious will and his heart was set on the nomination. Appearances indicated that he had it in the bag and to this Greeley's
heart, if not his judgment, said aye. "We can run Scott and lick
'em," he wrote to Bowe. "We shall probably try Clay and get licked.
Vat of it? 'Shall there be no more cakes and ale? Yes, by Saint Sims.'
I am learning philosophy, which we shall need in such case."
Greeley reached Albany. Farther than that he would not budge and
Weed himself went to the Springs. It was a bootless errand.

The "Democratic Whigs," as they styled themselves, met in national convention at Harrisburg in December, and both Greeley and
Weed were there. Both worked against Clay. Weed's was the more
important role. Greeley did his part through argument and by
means of a table of estimates that he had compiled indicating where
the vote of each state would go in case of Clay's nomination.[13] Their
efforts were instrumental in shelving the Kentuckian, but the New
York boss and his adjutant could not swing the convention to Scott.
It preferred the other hero and Harrison was nominated with John
Tyler (a states' righter who had wept at Clay's rejection) put in
second place as a gesture of appeasement to Clay's infuriated friends.
"It may not be a flush of trumps for New York," wrote Francis
Granger to Weed, "but it is a safe card for her."[14] At the time this
looked like good prophecy.

Greeley liked Harrisburg, where he found people appreciative of
his editorial talents. Various and sundry Pennsylvanians urged him
to come down and establish a Whig paper at their capital. On news
of this, promises and appeals began to come from Albany about the
reëstablishment of the *Jeffersonian*. Economic prospects seemed
more promising than they had in many a moon and his spirits rose
accordingly. "Make your politicians support you," he wrote to

Bowe. "If they don't, you know 'a man can't buy money when he ain't got none.' "[15]

Greeley's volatile spirits were rising higher. Where might not his political writing lead? Ambition was stirring. It was in 1839, and probably at this time, that he confided to paper how

> . . . even in many a waking hour
> Come dreams to madness near allied,
> The hope to scale the heights of power
> A Nation's choice, a Senate's pride.
> Full well I know such thoughts but mock
> The mind to which no more is given,
> But humblest blade and loftiest oak
> Alike may rear their heads to heaven.[16]

Stubbornly energetic, so busy with life that he could not find time for the social niceties that help make life endurable, this warm-hearted, eager, stubborn man, this character beset by dreams, was feeling his way toward a larger role than that offered by the *New-Yorker*.

But he was still tied to the *New-Yorker*—"O, that it was in the bottom of the sea!"—and the politicians were long on promises but short on actual support. The Harrisburg project fell through, and the *Jeffersonian* revival kept flitting like a will-o'-the-wisp beyond his reach. That winter, Molly had a miscarriage that left her again an invalid, news of which her husband gave to a friend in the midst of an otherwise rollicking political letter. Molly was showing distinct signs of hypochondria, but despite this distressing home situation Greeley went again to Albany, where he lived on the third floor of the Eagle Tavern and worked furiously at all the writing that came his way. He reported legislative proceedings and did some editorials for Weed's *Evening Journal* at twenty-five dollars a week; wrote for other papers (the *Harrisburg Chronicle, Boston Atlas, New York Whig,* and *Fredonia Censor*) whenever he had a chance; and chafed impotently as the *New-Yorker* ran down in his absence.[17] He and his wife had to live, and Albany was the home of the politicos who bestowed favors upon deserving journalists.

But even Albany looked like a dead-end street, for Weed and Seward would give nothing save general approval to Greeley's plan for getting out a cheap Whig daily. The poverty-stricken editor became restless. He was invited to the governor's mansion for dinner, and went. A second invitation came in February and was

declined. Once was enough for glory, he let Seward know. "For dining as an art I have due respect but am no [sic] proficient therein—
I lack education—I have no taste—no time. 'I pray thee to have me
excused.' "[18] Baffled and fuming, he was of no mind to be soothed
by paltry favors.

But while Greeley chewed the cud of bitterness, the campaign of
1840 began looming up on the horizon. The politicians moved at
last, and the word leaked out. On April 22, 1840, a jocose little item
appeared in James Gordon Bennett's *Herald*. "Greeley the Horace"
was going to establish a small weekly to be called the *Log Cabin*.
Bennett's amusement vanished when the *Cabin's* circulation jumped
in nine weeks to 56,000 copies.

The *Log Cabin,* issued simultaneously in New York and Albany
as a four-page weekly (six months for fifty cents), was Greeley's
main contribution to the Harrison campaign. The Whigs had
judged it expedient to forego adopting a platform at Harrisburg,
but the *Cabin* devoted considerable argument to what Greeley considered the issues of the day. His editorials demanded a sound and
uniform currency (euphemism for a national bank), tariff protection,
one Presidential term, restriction of Executive influence, distribution of the proceeds of the public lands and governmental economy.
There was always a Whig campaign song, with music, and every
local election was analyzed with reams of statistics. There was a hint
of the *New-Yorker,* a soupçon of the *Jeffersonian,* in this new sheet,
but that was all. The election of 1840 was too slam-bang for sober
comment to predominate in its pages.

Both parties specialized in emotion that year. The Democrats
caricatured Harrison as a superannuated old granny with an affinity
for log cabins and hard cider. They charged that he had sold white
men into slavery for debt; that he was illiterate, a defaulter, and
"the hero of forty defeats." The Whigs, taking a lesson from Democratic campaigns of previous years, produced a fanfare calculated to
convince the voters that "Whigs" and "The People" were practically
synonymous terms. The sneers at Harrison were turned to good
account and the log cabins and hard cider of the plain people became symbols of the Whig campaign. The countryside resounded
with the shouts of thousands of marchers and the Whig state convention at Utica that August had a procession five miles long.
Whigs swarmed around full-sized log cabins replete with coonskins
on the doors and latchstrings out, quaffing hard cider that the temperance brethren averred was merely sour. They rolled huge victory
balls for miles along the highways, singing the while such songs as

> It is the ball a-rolling on
> For Tippecanoe and Tyler too,

or the "Turnout Song,"

> From the White House, now Matty,
>   turn out, turn out,
> From the White House, now Matty,
>   turn out.

Little Van, "the used-up man," was stigmatized as an aristocrat, an extravagant spender of the people's money, an opponent of the War of 1812.

Henry Clay, fastidious by temperament, despised this demagoguery. Horace Greeley may have had qualms about it, for there was a defensive note in his subsequent references to the battle of 1840. But during the fight he waded in with joyous abandon.

The *Cabin* set its own pattern of misrepresentation in its first issue, when Greeley announced that the contest was between "a rough, old farmer in homespun" and "the finished gentleman who had been smiled at by Ladies and Duchesses, and whose son had been a favored guest at the table of Royalty itself." Harrison was a brave but tenderhearted hero with sound views on every issue, and his running mate, Tyler, was the noble representative of "a noble race, the frank, warm-hearted, hospitable planters of Virginia." The *Cabin* reprinted in full Congressman Charles Ogle's speech on "The Royal Splendor of the President's Palace," which portrayed Van Buren as a waster of the people's money, one who bought huge mirrors, costly carpets, and gold plate, and had the effrontery to purchase "foreign Fanny Kemble green finger cups in which to wash his pretty, tapering, soft, white, lily fingers, after dining on fricandeau de veau and omelette souffle." Even his chamber pot cost two dollars.[19] But this extravagant dandy, according to Greeley, had accepted heart and soul the extreme Loco Foco positions, and in consequence had become a promoter of class war and an enemy of the Christian religion.

So strong was Greeley's enthusiasm for campaign swashbuckling that it overmastered his budding interest in social reform. It is barely possible that he had labor's interest genuinely at heart when he appealed to artisans to vote against the Sub-Treasury, with the fantastic argument that it would reduce wages because it was calculated to overthrow banks and paper money. But when he was faced by the necessity of saying something about the President's real accomplishment in labor reform, the establishment of a ten-hour day for Federal employees, Greeley's zest for abusing Van Buren overcame his interest in the working class. The ten-hour-day order was only an electioneering trick, vicious in principle, and outside the province of government. "We do not believe such aid will ever permanently promote the interests of the working man," he declared. After the campaign was over, he showed a poorly disguised contempt for Orestes Brownson's appeal to the Democrats to resort to first principles and raise the standard of social democracy.[20] Politician Greeley was convinced that none save the Whigs could be trusted with the great task of social reform.

The embattled editor had scant reason to be proud of his role in 1840. He knew this, and in later years tried to make out that he had kept fundamental issues to the fore.[21] Nevertheless, he had learned a valuable lesson from the campaign. He had seen the *Log Cabin* rise to a circulation of 80,000 copies an issue. Wastefully produced and making small profits, it still demonstrated the potentialities of political journalism and the effectiveness of a political campaign in building up a cheap newspaper's circulation. This was something not to be forgotten, and Greeley did not forget it.

When Harrison swept to victory in November, Greeley was jubilant. It was, he believed, the knell of Loco Focoism. He went up to New Hampshire for a brief vacation, prophesying that at last the country would have what it had long needed, a government bent on economy.

When Greeley returned to New York, it was to wrestle with his ever-present problem of making a living. Independently of Weed and Seward, he decided to resume the *Log Cabin*, raising its price to a dollar and a half a year. Its circulation fell to 10,000 copies, but apparently it still made a modest profit, for Greeley told Weed that he was beginning to feel quite snug and comfortable, what with an ability to look a bank cashier in the face once more.

But the *New-Yorker* still remained a burden,[22] despite the help of a capable young Vermonter named Henry Jarvis Raymond, who had been more than glad to come down to work, as he told Greeley, "under the shadow of your wing." Even though life was easier, a comfortable living was still far from a reality. Was this the best that could be done? Greeley was not content. More and more the thought of a Whig penny daily returned to haunt the days and disturb the dreams of the young editor.

NOTES FOR CHAPTER 4

1. *New-Yorker,* Sept. 20, 1834. In the issue of March 26, 1836, he indicated his belief that there had been less than a dozen subscribers at the time of the first issue.

2. *Ibid.,* July 16, 1836; Greeley Papers (N. Y. P. L.) , Greeley to Mrs. Newhall, May 7, 1856; Greeley Papers (Lib. of Cong.) , Greeley to Mary Y. Greeley, Feb. 23 [1845?]; Cleveland, *op. cit.,* pp. 61f., 102-3; Greeley, *Recollections,* pp. 103-4.

3. Greeley Papers (N. Y. P. L.) , Greeley to B. F. Ransom, May 2, 1836.

4. Greeley Papers (Lib. of Cong.) , Greeley to C. A. Dana, Dec. 13, 1842.

5. *Tribune,* May 8, 1863.

6. *New-Yorker,* Sept. 16, 1837, Oct. 26, 1839; Greeley Papers (N. Y. P. L.) , Greeley to Castlewill, Apr. 14, 1845. Greeley to Willis Gaylord, Aug. 21, 1837, Greeley to S. Mears and B. F. Ransom, Jan. 14, 1838; Greeley, *Recollections,* pp. 103-4, 136; *Tribune,* Oct. 29, 1860.

7. G. G. Van Deusen, *Thurlow Weed: Wizard of the Lobby* (Boston, 1947) *passim.*

8. *Tribune,* Jan. 29, Feb. 5, 1850.

9. Josiah Emery, "Autobiography" (MS in Collection of Regional History, Cornell University) , pp. 41-42.

10. Greeley Papers (N. Y. P. L.) , Greeley to O. A. Bowe, June 17, 1838; Greeley Letters (U. of R.) , Greeley to Weed, Aug. 25, 1838; Greeley Papers (Lib. of Cong.) , Greeley to R. W. Griswold, Mar. 18, 1839; Merle M. Hoover, *Park Benjamin* (N. Y., 1948) , pp. 88f.

11. Greeley Papers (N. Y. P. L.) , Greeley to O. A. Bowe, June 11, 1838; *New-Yorker,* Nov. 10, 1838.

12. Greeley Papers (N. Y. P. L.) , Greeley to B. F. Ransom, Jan. 26, 1839.

13. *Tribune,* Jan. 29, 1844. Four years later *(ibid.,* Feb. 29, Mar. 4, 1848) Greeley sought to show that he had been practically without influence at Harrisburg. He was not so backward about claiming credit for Clay's nomination in 1844.

14. Weed Papers, Granger to Weed, Dec. 9, 1839; Seward Papers, Weed to Seward, Dec. 4 [1839]; Greeley Papers (N. Y. P. L.) , Greeley to O. A. Bowe, June 11, 17, 1838, Nov. 25, 1839.

15. Greeley Papers (N. Y. P. L.) , Greeley to O. A. Bowe, Dec. 14, 1839.

16. *Ibid.,* clipping "Poem by H. Greeley," N. Y., 1839.

17. *Ibid.,* Greeley to O. A. Bowe, Dec. 14, 1839.

18. *Ibid.,* Greeley to Seward, Feb. 12[1840]; Greeley Letters (U. of R.) , Greeley to Goldsmith Denniston, May 28, 1839.

19. *Log Cabin,* May 2, 16, Aug. 1, 1840.

20. *Ibid.,* May 30, Dec. 12, 1840.

21. *Tribune,* July 28, Sept. 15, 1841, Nov. 11, 1842.

22. Griswold Papers, Greeley to R. W. Griswold, Dec. 3, 5, 1840, Feb. 20, 1841.

CHAPTER 5

Microcosms

NEW YORK IN THE 1840's WAS A LITTLE WORLD OF its own, with a population that grew vigorously to the middle of the decade and then thrust forward by leaps and bounds with the mounting tide of refugees from Irish famine and German revolution. By 1850 over half a million inhabitants, a conglomerate of nationalities, thronged the lower part of Manhattan Island and was spilling over into Brooklyn and Jersey. Central Park was still a wilderness, peopled by squatters and overrun by goats. Ploughing and spading matches were still held in Harlem. But below those areas a great city was struggling into being.

It was a forward-looking city. Croton water was introduced in 1842, the beginning of an adequate water supply. Three years later New York's first telegraph pole was planted at the corner of Broadway and Wall Street. The Astor House was eclipsed by the Irving House, opening on the fashionable (west) side of Broadway opposite Stewart's Dry Goods Palace in 1848 at a cost of $500,000, with Croton water in every room and water closets and baths plentiful throughout. City aldermen were beginning to discuss the feasibility of street railways. There was a chorus of—"That bridge to Brooklyn must be built." Some daring spirits even talked of a tunnel under the East River.

New York grew too fast to keep clean. Rain customarily spread a thin black pudding over streets where the shops were wont to occupy at least half the sidewalk with their wares. Pigs, goats, and cows roamed the streets, a cow and calf even paying a lengthy visit to Wall Street during business hours one day in 1845. Vagrant dogs were so numerous that the city authorities felt impelled to authorize St. Bartholomew's days for canines, days that customarily ended with hundreds of carcasses floating in the bay.

Little attention was paid to sanitation. Thousands of quarts of milk were produced in city dairies where the cows' feed was slops from some nearby distillery. These cows were never let out of stable. Their flesh was flabby, and when they stopped giving milk and were sold as beef it often shrank in cooking to one-fourth of its original size.[1] Smells from these cow stables, from street dirt and filth, from uncared-for garbage and untended privy vaults drifted hither and yon with the prevailing winds. New York outdid Cologne's

> Nine and twenty separate stenches
> All well-defined and genuine stinks.

It was a miracle that the city was not decimated by a continual succession of plagues, or its inhabitants enervated by chronic disease.

But New Yorkers had plenty of vitality. The swearing, fighting, gambling newsboys (Gavroche in New York), the cheating, screaming, racing cabbies and omnibus drivers, the rowdy gangs that pilfered and ran, the tight-lipped men of business who bested their friends on the stock market and in trade, all these had plenty of vigor. A strong constitution was, in fact, almost a necessity. Life in the metropolis was a struggle where the fit survived: the merchant quick to press an advantage, the rowdy fireman who threw the first brick, the prize fighter who threw the first blow. Yankee Sullivan whipping William Bell in twenty-one rounds at Hart's Island in the East River; Thomas McCoy dying, pounded to a pulp, in the 120th round of his fight with Christopher Lilly up in Westchester; the "fancy" yelling "Shutters up, there's a death in the family" as a man's eyes closed under the blows of his antagonist, all symbolized the stark and often brutal struggle.

Since the struggle was hard it demanded hurry, and then diversion for tired nerves. New Yorkers became accustomed to racing. They scurried like rodents through the entrances and exits of the Wall Street business places. They raced through their meals at Sweeney's and Butter-Cake Dick's and even at Delmonico's. Stores competed for customers so strenuously that there was no time to heed the pleas of clerks for eight o'clock closings. Cabbies raced. In 1845 the new *Oregon*, meeting the new *Hendrik Hudson* just below Poughkeepsie, reversed her bows and raced her rival down river for fifteen miles before she dropped astern and resumed her upward voyage.

There was also a rush for pleasure and diversion. Crowds went on morally dubious "moonlight dancing parties" to Coney Island, or gathered to see the Mammoth Sea Serpent at the Apollo, or Tom Thumb at Barnum's Museum. People swarmed to Niblo's frog pasture in Broadway to watch a balloon ascension. They thronged the theatres to see Fanny Elssler and Placide and Christy's Minstrels. Thousands of spectators attended the yearly New York county fair, located at Castle Garden in 1846 with rowing regattas held off Broadway as an added attraction. Multitudes jammed the court rooms to watch the raucous trial of James Gordon Bennett, who had libeled the judges of the Criminal Court of Sessions, or the murder trial of John C. Colt (brother of the six-shooter's Samuel Colt), who killed printer Samuel Adams over a trifling debt and then cheated the gallows by plunging a clasp knife into his heart three hours before the time set for his execution.[2]

Then, as now, New York crowds were both sophisticated and naïve. They were not victimized by the mock auctions and confidence men that infested Broadway to the peril of rustic visitors, but any real or supposed freak of nature drew them in throngs that swelled Barnum's pocketbook. They mocked the simplicity of the denizens of "mosquito-ridden" Brooklyn, but when Dickens was publishing *Old Curiosity Shop* serially in a London magazine they would gather at the wharf and shout to an incoming ship, "Is Little Nell dead?" In many ways New Yorkers were like children, fascinated by the strange and peculiar, but indifferent to esthetic values, self-centered, artless and cruel, immature.

New York was even then a city of contrasts. The great majority of its inhabitants had no intellectual curiosity to speak of, but there was always an audience for Dr. Louis Agassiz when he lectured on the animal kingdom, or for Sir Charles Lyell's discourse on that new and fascinating subject called geology, or for Ralph Waldo Emerson's explanations of the New England character. Slums and tenements existed cheek by jowl with art exhibitions and Italian opera. Margaret Fuller, fresh from Boston and Brook Farm, found in this city where interest was so concentrated upon material gain an intellectual challenge and stimulus such as she had never known before.[3]

And always the greatest contrast that New York had to offer was that between poverty and wealth, between Mott Street and Bleecker Street, between the banker in his $1,500 carriage, and the needle-woman bending for two days over a fine shirt with ten pleats and four buttonholes for ten cents' pay. Destitution, misery, and despair stalked the Five Points as always, while the rich flourished like the green bay tree. Where the twenties had counted the wealthy by the score, the forties counted them by the hundreds. Not infrequently a lot, freestone house, and furniture cost $100,000, and as such residences multiplied so did the servants in livery. New York's wealthy were beginning to live on the same scale as Europe's noblemen.

This multiplication of wealth and comfort mirrored the rise of an industrial and financial capitalism. The American businessman, stereotyped and dull at twenty-five to Margaret Fuller, was coming into his own. Money was the open sesame to the aristocracy of America's metropolis. Money made the difference between the gay sleighing parties that laughed and shouted down Broadway and the scene across the Park where poor women, some with babies clasped in their bare arms, pale, sickly, and hungry, waited their turn to beg for bread and fuel. Money was the great desideratum, without too much nonsense about the way in which it was acquired.

Some noticed uneasily a touch of falsity here and there in all the glitter—the marble magnificence of Grace Church ending incongruously in a wooden spire, the violent contrast between the imposing marble front of Stewart's emporium and its mean brick ends. An occasional voice, like that of Henry Ward Beecher at the Cranberry Street church over in Brooklyn, was lifted to denounce current business ethics as the ruination of many a young man. If the prison inmates were to retrace their steps to their first lessons, said Beecher, many respectable businessmen would find themselves surrounded by strange visitors in their counting rooms and dwellings.[4]

People listened to Beecher on honesty as they listened to him thunder against the temptations of the flesh. That was all well enough for Sunday, but week days were another matter. Fortune beckoned, and who could say her nay? "Miss Lavinia," advertising in the *New York Sun* for a paramour, recognized the realities of the situation. "None need apply but men of capital."[5]

How would a rising young newspaper editor, blessed with ambition but cursed with a conscience, deal with such matters as these?

In the spring of 1841 Greeley faced a momentous decision. The Harrisburg offer of 1839 showed signs of renewal. The *Log Cabin* had dropped off in circulation more than he had expected. The *New-Yorker* was a headache. There were some thirty newspapers, daily and weekly, established in New York. On the other hand, Greeley knew the city and was known there. He felt, too, that it would disgrace him in his profession if he should drop both the *Cabin* and the *Yorker* and seek a fresh field. Noah Cook and James Coggeshall, two stalwart Whigs, were urging him to start a Whig daily that could be purchased by the laboring class, and the idea of mass appeal with which he had started the *New-Yorker* was still strong in his mind.[6] Moses Beach's *Sun* and Bennett's *Herald* both sold for a penny. Bennett, quarreling with all political parties, operated on a cash basis and by 1841 was boasting an annual revenue of $130,000. Why could not a cheap Whig paper do as well? Greeley was the more influenced to think it could by the fact that the politicians were urging him to the experiment and promising patronage.

It was under the influence of such reasoning that Greeley undertook his fourth full-fledged newspaper venture. He had only some $2,000, half of that in printing materials, but Coggeshall lent him $1,000, an equal amount that did not materialize was promised from another source, his old friend Dudley S. Gregory was standing by in case of need, and there was always the hope that the paper would "take" immediately.

So it was that, on April 10, 1841, a day of sleet and leaden skies with the bells of the dripping city tolling for President Harrison's funeral pageant, five thousand copies of a small folio sheet called the *New-York Tribune* hit the street. The omens of the day were not auspicious and the demand for the new paper was not exactly overwhelming. Greeley had difficulty in giving it all away.

The *Tribune,* like the city of its birth, was a microcosm. Its pages, even at the start, held up a mirror to the world, a mirror that reflected both the strange and the familiar to its readers. New Yorkers saw their city in its pride and in its shame. Statesmen and politicians could find in the *Tribune* news of governments abroad and of political parties at home. The esthete and the man of letters, the merchant and the reformer, could all find inspiration in its columns. It was a political paper and it was a family paper. It was a paper built with an eye to profit, and it was a paper dedicated to reform— "Anti-Slavery, Anti-War, Anti-Rum, Anti-Tobacco, Anti-Seduction, Anti-Grogshops, Brothels, Gambling Houses."[7] And running through it like a golden thread of continuity was the purpose that gave it its name, a dedication to the elevation of the masses. The *Tribune* stood first of all for progress and welcomed to its pages all forward-looking men and doctrines.

The *Tribune's* high-mindedness had limits. Quack nostrums for everything from colds to cancer flooded its advertising columns. These remedies might be good for something, Greeley averred when pressed on the subject. The paper could not distinguish between good and bad cures. It had to accept them all, and at the same time try to educate its readers so that the pretenses of charlatans would arouse only feelings of contempt.[8] Despite his belief that the theatre was a moral cesspool, his partners finally overrode his scruples about theatrical advertisements.[9] So profits triumphed over ethics, just as they did when he wrote editorial notices for pay, just as they did when he admitted paid articles to his news columns, just as they did when he cloaked sex appeal with virtue.

It was perfectly proper in Greeley's eyes to publish accounts of seductions, if proper horror was expressed over the deed. It was legitimate to notice lewd books, if so doing gave the editor an opportunity to denounce rival publishers for putting them out. It was even right to publish in lurid detail the double rape of eighteen-year-old Ann Murphy in the Broadway Cottage, provided sufficient horror was expressed and one could use the affair to assert that only Democrats ran bawdy houses in New York.[10] The *Tribune,* in such matters, came near making vice attractive and virtue odious, but Greeley would never admit this. There had always been much in the *Tribune* that was not Sunday school, he told a friend in later years, but this was so because progress was best served by free discussion and full exposition, rather than by suppression and concealment.[11]

It is possible that Greeley believed what he said when he defended the *Tribune's* publication of the facts of life. It is more likely that this defense was rationalization. The policy itself was probably based on the editor's acceptance of the fact that the public likes a certain amount of sex and crime news, and that publication of such items swells a newspaper's circulation. There was a large element of the realist in Greeley the romantic.

Greeley reserved for the *Tribune* full freedom of speech, but this did not mean that the paper always printed both sides of an argument, or even that it always printed what its editor held to be the truth. Again and again his own reports of events at Washington misrepresented the situation at the capital as he actually saw it.[12] When James Parton remarked that he could learn more about a current strike from the pages of the *Herald* than in any other New York newspaper, the *Tribune's* editor testily replied, "Well, I don't want to encourage those lawless proceedings." In 1841 the *Tribune* cleverly interpreted the Glentworth "pipe-laying" scandal, a first-class case of importing voters for an election, in such a way as to exculpate the Whig leaders with whom the vote-buyer had had dealings. Greeley had it that Glentworth, a consummate scoundrel it was true, had taken rascally advantage of the innocent, trusting, morally righteous Whigs.[13]

Doctrinaire, intensely partisan, obstinate as a pig, the *Tribune's* editor was not one to let devotion to the truth hinder his pursuit of moral good, party gain, or spectacular news. The man who could dramatize a visit to Niagara Falls by asserting that the wearing away of the rocks might well change the "whole topography of

Central North America" within five thousand years was very apt
to break out of the confines of a sterile state of facts, both in maintaining news interest and in conveying to the minds of his readers
the milk of the moral word that had been vouchsafed to Horace
Greeley.

Lack of patronage was a great cross to Greeley during the first
months of the *Tribune's* existence. The powerful Clay Whig merchants of the city held aloof, for they knew that he was a friend of
Weed and Seward. The Albany leaders saw this, but took no steps
to counter the absence of support.

The fact was that the Albany politicians had found Greeley too
obstreperous an adjutant to throw themselves wholeheartedly behind him. He had dared to complain about the way Weed had
managed Seward's campaign for Governor in 1838,[14] and had sput-
tered because Governor Seward had chosen a new home rather than
live in the "three-walled" Croswell house that had been Governor
Marcy's residence.[15] Worse yet were his reforming proclivities. In
1840 he had been instrumental in forcing through the state legislature a registry law for New York City voters that was most unwise
politically, a law heartily detested by Weed and Seward. This was
followed by pestiferous demands that Weed move for reforms in
the state inspection laws, a very valuable source of patronage in
the eyes of a professional politician. It was apparently beginning to
dawn upon the senior partners that in the adjutant they might have
a bear by the tail. At any rate, they took no pains to throw patronage his way. They did not even see to it that money promised by
their political friends was paid over to the harassed editor. Greeley
treasured up these things in a tenacious memory.

Would the *Tribune* be a success or a failure? For a time it was
touch and go. Just as the *New-Yorker* had done, it ran headlong
onto the shoals of bad business management. Despite a zooming
subscription list, it was losing money steadily during the first few
months of its career and Greeley was well-nigh distraught. He began
searching for someone who could bring order out of chaos in the
business department, and the search was rewarded. The perspiring
editor's attention fixed upon Thomas McElrath, a lawyer with publishing experience, recently appointed Master in Chancery by
Governor Seward. Greeley offered McElrath a partnership.

The lawyer hesitated. He had a good office and a good business,
both of which would have to be given up if he accepted Greeley's
offer. His wife and his friends opposed the step. He visited the
Tribune office, only to find disorder rampant in the business and
publication department and the paper losing $200 to $300 a week.

It looked as though he would not come in, and in desperation
Greeley wrote to Seward for aid. If the Governor would indicate
whom he would appoint as Master in Chancery in McElrath's place,
Greeley thought it would help.

Whether or not the Governor moved, McElrath at last become
convinced that the *Tribune* had real possibilities. At first he lent
Greeley $500. Then, July 31, 1841, he took an equal partnership
and put in $1,500 more. The firm of Greeley and McElrath had
started on its career.

The new partner was important for a number of reasons. He
helped to reconcile the Clay Whig merchants and, even though
slowly and reluctantly, they began to advertise in the *Tribune*.
Through his father-in-law, a man of means, McElrath brought considerable sums of money into the venture. His well-known conservatism helped to assuage fears inspired by his partner's radical
tendencies. Most important of all, he put the publication end of
the enterprise on a business basis. The manager and the editor
worked together, an effective team. "Oh! that every Greeley could
find his McElrath!" exclaimed James Parton as he surveyed the
results of the next decade, "and blessed is the McElrath that finds
his Greeley!"[16]

With McElrath's coming into the *Tribune*, the tide of fortune
began to move toward its flood. Circulation continued to zoom.
Within a year the little sheet that issued from amidst the Ann
Street filth and smells had a steady sale of over 10,000 copies, a circumstance that the happy editor celebrated by giving a dinner to
all his employees. In September and November, 1841, the *Yorker*
and the *Cabin* respectively were merged in a new venture, the
Weekly Tribune, designed to appeal to readers outside the city. Its
circulation promptly rose to over 15,000 copies a week. Advertisements increased. The *Tribune* was definitely making money by the
time it was a year old.

McElrath brought the *Tribune* from the red into the black, but
it was Greeley who made it a great newspaper. His nose for news,
his vigilance and care were basic to the reputation that the *Tribune*
quickly gained as an up-to-the-minute paper with attractive special
features. More important still, he made it a sheet that solicited and
would print ideas designed to promote the democratic way of life.
At last America had an ably edited, progressive newspaper.

And the *Tribune* was ably edited in all its departments. One of
the reasons for its success was the quality of the men that Greeley
gathered about him. George Jones, an old Poultney acquaintance,
was on the staff for a few months. Greeley offered him a partner-

ship, but he stayed on salary, and then only until a lucrative business in note-shaving drew him to Albany. Henry Jarvis Raymond, "able, ready, intelligent and indefatigable," in Greeley's estimation, was assistant in the departments of Literary Criticism, Fine Arts, and General Intelligence. Greeley differed with him on many matters, but raised his salary to $1,000. Then Webb offered more, and in 1843 Raymond moved to the more conservative and more congenial *Courier and Enquirer*. Bayard Taylor, tall, pale, twenty, and enthusiastic, was commissioned in 1844 to write letters from Europe about the German people—"but no descriptive nonsense. Of that I am damned sick." Less than four years later, Taylor had joined the ranks of the assistant editors. Meanwhile other figures of importance filled the places left vacant by Jones and Raymond.

One of the greatest sources of strength for the *Tribune's* staff lay in the intellectual circles of New England. Both of the Greeleys read and appreciated the *Dial,* and Mary Greeley sometimes summered among the New England cognoscenti. Partly on her advice, Greeley offered Margaret Fuller the position of literary critic in 1844, a place that she filled with brilliance and aplomb until she left for Europe some two years later. Charles A. Dana, another Brook Farmer, came to the *Tribune* as city editor in 1846. Three years later, the gifted George Ripley, one of the founders of the Transcendentalist movement, became literary critic. There were many stars in the *Tribune's* crown by the end of its first decade.

A galaxy of talent, a progressive spirit and a first-rate business manager were important assets, but all together they could scarcely have brought success without the catalytic touch of Greeley's personality. Pugnacious, eccentric, an exhibitionist, a demon for purity whether in copy or in the morals that he deemed important, shrill, intense, by turns scolding and beaming, Greeley dominated the office and the paper. Men complained, but obeyed. Readers cursed, but kept on reading. For here was an editor who used the columns of his paper to further great objects and achieve great ends, and to transmit his own concern for these ends and objects to the minds and hearts of the people. For countless thousands of nineteenth-century Americans, the *Tribune* was Horace Greeley, crusader for the right.

Greeley's presence was felt in the office from the moment around noon when he entered it to midnight or later when he left for home. Everyone was conscious of him, standing behind his tall painted pine desk (he liked to stand while composing) with its mass of papers so deep that he kept a strap attached to his scissors to prevent their being lost. All the staff knew that, no matter what the hour or the confusion, they would always find him at work, searching the *Tribune* for errors, reading the riot act in his high, piping voice to slipshod reporters and delinquent editors, writing editorials from notes that he kept in an old pasteboard hatbox, working on the *Whig Almanac* or the *Farmers' Library and Monthly Journal of Agriculture*,[17] dashing off a note in his crabbed script to tell Weed how to run the state or to inform Thoreau that he had found a market for one of his manuscripts. Once in a while they might find him asleep on a pile of old newspapers, waiting for the latest despatch, but this was rare. There was always so much to do.

And as he dominated the office, so he dominated the minds of his readers, hammering home into their minds and hearts his own interests and concerns, daily impressing his personality upon them. He did not mind being thought an eccentric, so that he made his personality a living thing to his reading public. Once he even described himself (half-humorously and under pretense that the description was J. Fenimore Cooper's) as a towheaded, half-bald, long-legged, slouching individual, "so rocking in gait that he walks down both sides of the street at once."[18] There was method in such half-mad gaiety, in the careless dress so habitual that it did not have to be calculated, in the light, silky hair worn long for a man and rippling down into the back of his neck, in the absurd fringe of beard that accentuated the pink-and-white benevolence of the baby face with its thick-lensed spectacles over nearsighted eyes. Like King Louis Philippe, he walked the streets carrying a fat umbrella and radiating middle-class virtue. And like Mr. Pickwick, to whose image as visualized by Cruikshank he came to bear a startling resemblance, he excited both laughter and respect.

If the *Tribune's* readers loved Greeley's virtuous eccentricity, they also admired his picturesque and effective pugnacity. When Moses Beach of the *Sun* bribed Greeley's carriers to give up routes and sent out boys to thrash the *Tribune's* boys (even applying the cowhide himself on one occasion), Greeley promptly marshaled reinforcements for his carriers the while he flayed Beach in the *Tribune*. He did his best to alienate from the *Sun* and the *Herald* those subscribers who had a sense of decency, by asserting that his two rivals had assisted a famous abortionist, Madame Restell, to make a fortune and to commit murder. "Don't cowhide Bennett, if the *Herald* slanders you," Greeley advised the *Tribune's* readers. "You cannot make him a gentleman—it has been tried a hundred times—but you may make yourself a blackguard."[19]

The *Tribune's* ideas of reform soon drew fire from other papers, and Greeley widened his range. James Watson Webb of the *Courier and Enquirer* was a fellow Whig, but Greeley did not hesitate to designate him as an "escaped State Prison bird." Bryant's *Evening Post* "would like to be an honest journal, if it could afford it." The *New York Express* was "surely the basest and paltriest of all possible journals." Even correspondents of the *Tribune* felt the lash, and its readers laughed when they read that "Alfred J. W. . . . writes four pages to prove himself a dunce, when one would have done the business effectually," or when the editor described another letter writer as an "unreasoning hog."[20]

Greeley was sometimes called to account for being abusive, but he always stoutly maintained that he was more sinned against than sinning. His opponents received only what they deserved, like the savage mastiff which had been bayoneted by the Irish soldier. "Why did you kill the dog?" asked an officer. "You should have struck him with the butt of your gun."

"And so I would, plase your Honor," replied Pat, "if the baste had run at me with his tail."[21]

Greeley exulted in the fact that the *Tribune* was *his* paper. "For whatever is distinctive in the views or doctrines of the *Tribune* there is but *one* person responsible," he wrote in 1847. In a very real sense, the paper was his life. It represented emancipation from drudgery for scant returns, from want and threadbare suits and penury in his home. It symbolized success in material things, and aspiration for an America that would be a land of happy, beautiful people. He had created it. And he loved it and watched over it as a mother over her child.

NOTES FOR CHAPTER 5

1. *Tribune,* June 25, July 7, 9, 1847.
2. *Ibid.,* Jan., Sept.-Nov., 1842.
3. *Ibid.,* Aug. 1, 1846.
4. *Ibid.,* Nov. 30, 1847. Brooklyn Items.
5. *Ibid.,* July 28, 1842. Reprint from the *Sun.*
6. Back in 1834 his firm had printed a political penny daily, the *Constitution,* to which Greeley had contributed. It had been a failure and the firm had lost money by it (Greeley, *Recollections,* pp. 139-40) . I doubt that that experience in any way influenced him to start the *Tribune.*
7. *Tribune,* Dec. 3, 1845.
8. *Ibid.,* Apr. 2, 1853, Nov. 29, 1854.
9. *Ibid.,* May 16, 1850. Greeley said at this time that probably he had not been inside a theatre more than twice in ten years.
10. *Ibid.,* Jan. 5, 6, 9, 16, Oct. 17, 1843, Nov. 2, 1846, May 27, 28, 1847.
11. Ingersoll Papers, Greeley to Mrs. Ingersoll, Aug. 16, 1860.
12. This was true in 1841 and again in 1846, to mention only two instances.

13. *Tribune,* Apr. 1of., Aug. 1, Dec. 29, 1841; Hudson, *op. cit.,* p. 548.
14. Seward Papers, Greeley to Seward, Aug. 23, 1838. He had urged Seward, against Weed's advice, to engage actively in the campaign, and had gone on to say that he thought the contest within the party over the ticket had been "most unwisely protracted." He was also very critical of the fact that there had been no Address to the Whig voters of the state, and expressed the rather sour hope that Seward would get as many votes as his running mate, Luther Bradish.
15. *Ibid.,* Weed to Seward, Dec. 2, 1838. For the story of the "three-walled house," see my *Thurlow Weed,* pp. 100-101.
16. Greeley Papers (N. Y. P. L.) McElrath to the *Tribune,* Dec. 24, 1887 (clipping) ; Greeley Papers (Lib. of Cong.) , Greeley to R. M. Griswold, July 10, 1841; *Tribune,* July 31, 1841. McElrath claimed, many years later, that the idea of the *Weekly Tribune* came from him.
17. The former was begun in 1838 and continued thereafter every year, with the exception of 1842, under various titles. The latter was begun in 1845.
18. *Tribune,* Dec. 21, 1842.
19. *Tribune,* Apr., 1841, July 21, 1841.
20. *Ibid.,* Apr. 12, 1844, Nov. 1, 1845, Feb. 18, Apr. 9, 1846, Jan. 1, 1847.
21. *Ibid.,* July 24, 1845.

CHAPTER 6

This Brave New World

T HE LAND TO WHICH THE *TRIBUNE* MADE ITS BOW was on the threshold of great events. America was beginning to spread its wings in the 1840's. At times with caution and diplomacy (as Oregon bore witness), at times with ruthless ardor (as Mexicans and Indians learned to their cost), it extended its control over the vast empire of the West. And expansion was not only in so many feet of soil. A hammering and chattering, a belching of smoke and flame rose up from forge and factory and spread slowly but steadily from East to West. A vast industrial machine was building, with its offering of jobs and goods and opportunities for making a fortune. Population swelled as hundreds of thousands of immigrants responded to the call of the land and the lure of employment as wage earners. The nation's wealth increased, it seemed, by the hour. The country so lately stricken by panic and depression now seemed impatient of all limits to its material advance.

American energy and capacity manifested themselves in other than material ways. The decade was restless spiritually. Some, horrified by the sufferings of the depression, turned to the meager certainties of the primitive past—like Thoreau, building his hut in Walden woods with bean rows close by and peace in the bee-loud glade. Most of the restless ones strove more positively for perfection. Elihu Burritt, master of forge and anvil and twenty languages, campaigned for world peace, as Elizabeth Cady Stanton did for woman's rights and Dorothea Dix for the insane. Movements for temperance and for the abolition of slavery, begun during the preceding decade, welled up into roaring tides. Phrenologists, Grahamites, land reformers, Associationists rallied their bands of devoted followers. Robert Owen explained Communism to a joint session of the United States House and Senate.

By and large, the nation's unease had a hopeful quality. Most

Americans, even those dissatisfied with the existing state of things, believed that God was benevolent, that man was good, and that society was perfectible. There was a general acceptance of the actuality of moral law and the inevitability of progress, especially progress in the United States.

For a nationalistic pride in land and people was the mode. National patriotism was invoked by labor struggling for its rights and by conservative economists like Henry Carey, whose system of internal improvements, protection, and stable currency was wrapped up in a package much admired by the Whigs. Uncle Sam and Yankee Doodle were symbols as nationalistic as Noah Webster's speller. Americans were becoming more and more conscious of themselves as a distinct people. They believed that they had a mission; that they were destined to realize the dreams of the eighteenth-century enlightenment, and to act as the trustees of liberty and happiness for Europe and mankind. America would be torchbearer for a brave new world.[1]

Greeley shared the general faith in progress. He believed that the world was on the march toward perfection as firmly as he believed in the existence of a benevolent Heavenly Father. Progress was, indeed, God's purpose, and Greeley saw the fruits of that purpose in scientific advance, in temperance and abolition movements, in English Parliamentary reform, even in the great revolutionary tides that swept across Europe in 1848. Optimistically, he proclaimed the advance toward felicity, an advance based upon the great moral law that virtue secures happiness and vice produces misery.[2]

That America was in the van of this forward movement seemed perfectly apparent to the *Tribune's* optimistic editor. He was profoundly convinced that American institutions were far superior to those of old Europe. Americans were morally purer than Europeans, though of course the moral status even of Americans was far from perfect. Noah Webster's efforts to establish an American language seemed entirely fitting and proper to Greeley, a movement as essential to our national well-being as the establishment of a truly national literature. In his nationalistic fervor he even opposed territorial expansion in the 1830's and 1840's on the ground that it would dilute American patriotism,[3] and his devotion to the tariff and internal improvements reflected a pride in America's resources and a jealous concern for her prosperity that were every whit as intense as the sentiments of his revered preceptor in economics, Henry Carey.

To Carey, the Anglophobe son of an Irish-American father, the happiness of America would best be promoted by regarding the nation as an economic unit, thus subordinating both local and foreign interests to national needs. He was an ardent protectionist and Greeley regarded his writings as little less than gospel. For years Carey's articles on the beauties of protection adorned the pages of the *Tribune,* the while his arguments were being reproduced faithfully and indefatigably on the editorial page.

If Greeley was influenced by the economic nationalism of Henry Carey, he was also swayed by the idealism of the New England Transcendentalists. He acknowledged his deep debt to their "perception and expression of moral truth." Their penchant for self-help and their insistence that virtue is the result of obedience to moral law buttressed and strengthened his own convictions, as did their firm belief in the perfectibility of man. "Not that I agree with all that is taught and received as Transcendentalism," he wrote to a friend, "but I do like its spirit and its ennobling tendencies. Its apostles are mainly among the noblest spirits living."[4]

Emerson's individualistic approach to reform did not suit Greeley's taste for legislative action, but the latter's social philosophy embraced the Sage of Concord's gospel of self-help. Greeley professed a regard for Emerson that was little short of reverence; he was also brought into close touch with Thoreau, acting for several years as the latter's literary agent; and for almost two years, at his home and in the *Tribune's* office, he met the challenge of Margaret Fuller's imperious yearnings for perfection. There can be little doubt that the individualism of these members of the Transcendentalist school had a considerable influence in the molding of Greeley's views on social problems.[5]

Amid the voices to which Greeley listened, three came from overseas. One, trumpet toned, was that of a dour Scot who lashed out at social injustice in the British Isles. A second, precise, methodical, dogmatic, was that of an English political economist. The third, chanting a weird litany of righteous indignation, logical planning, and idealistic fantasy, came from among the French utopian socialists. All had a considerable influence upon Greeley's thought.

Thomas Carlyle's *Past and Present* reached the *Tribune* office in the spring of 1843, shortly after it was written. Greeley skimmed it and was not much impressed, but a more careful reading produced a very different reaction. Within a few days he was hailing it as the greatest book the century had so far produced, and acclaiming its author as "the keenest observer and among the deepest thinkers of our time."[6]

The book that so excited Greeley's admiration did not deny the greatness of the century's material achievements; it only asserted their inadequacy, and that of the materialistic utilitarianism that accompanied them. It portrayed in stark and graphic fashion the human suffering caused by the Industrial Revolution, and assailed the rising capitalist class with embarrassing question and comment. Carlyle doubted the infallibility of supply and demand as an economic law, and poured contempt upon cash payment as the sole nexus between man and man; he satirized the simple avarice of Plugson of Undershot, "who has indomitably spun Cotton merely to gain thousands of pounds," and denounced a Mammonism that, "left to itself, has become Midas-eared."

Past and Present had some constructive ideas. It emphasized the importance of land as the source of the nation's wealth, and the value of popular migration to that land. It stressed the importance of an Industrial Aristocracy, a class of Noble Masters among Noble Workers. This aristocracy would take the lead in creating a capitalist-labor relationship based upon the idea of partnership in a common enterprise, a reciprocal sense of social responsibility, and the concept of permanent employment as opposed to short, easily terminated contracts.[7] Here was reform, indeed, but nothing very earth-shaking. Carylye's noble fury for mankind, blended with an almost superstitious reverence for great men, raged up and down behind a wall of safe conservatism. It was a combination that pleased the *Tribune's* editor.

At about the same time that Greeley was warming to Carlyle's indictment of materialism, he was also inspired by the sententious utterances of an English economist. William Atkinson's *Principles of Political Economy; or the Laws of the Formation of National Wealth, Developed by Means of the Christian Law of Government* had been first published in England in 1840. No one could accuse its author of scholarly trepidation, for he knew, or seemed to know, all the answers. One after another, he laid bare the sins of the laissez-faire economists. McCulloch and Ricardo were all wrong about the advantages of free trade. The entire train of Malthus' reasoning was fatally defective. Huskisson was a confused and confusing guide. The substitution of free trade for protection could work only injury to any national society. It lessened the nation's wealth, endangered the laborer's peculiar property right in his employment, and struck at the moral foundations of the society by tempting the people to desert their country's products for those of a foreign nation. The pursuit of national interest was not only right and proper, it was inevitable.

Atkinson's paean of praise for national self-sufficiency was published by Greeley and McElrath in 1843, with an enthusiastic introduction by Greeley in which he took up its principal arguments

PICTURES OF PROGRESS.

" COME ALONG AND HELP DIG THEM TATERS!"
" WHY, YOU MUST BE A NEW COMER IN THIS PHALANSTRY, OR YOU
WOULD KNOW THAT I BELONG TO THE EATING GROUP."

Yankee Doodle on Association, December 19, 1846. The comment of
a magazine of humor on Fourierism.

and applied them forcefully to the American scene. Here was an
arsenal of weapons for the editor's crusade against the free traders,
and he used it to good effect in the ensuing years.

Charles Fourier, unlike Carlyle and Atkinson, offered a radical
panacea for the ills of society. The French utopian and math-
ematician was determined to eliminate the evils that industrialism

had spawned by nothing less than the creation of a new social order. An incorrigible optimist (he waited at his home at noon every day for twelve years, expecting a patron to appear laden with $200,000), Fourier had no doubts as to man's natural goodness. Stifled by the excesses of industrialism, this goodness was to be set free by a reorganization of society in small units. Fourier called these units "phalanxes" and calculated that each should contain 1620 people for the best results. Laborers, capitalists, and men of talent would comprise the membership of each group. Harmony would be promoted by the exclusion from the phalanx of soldiers, policemen, lawyers, philosophers, and political economists.

Each phalanx would be a little joint-stock company, with the members investing therein their labor, capital, and talents. Out of the common product an equal subsistence portion would be given to each member and the remainder would be divided five-twelfths to labor, four-twelfths to capital, and three-twelfths to talent. The phalanx would have a common dwelling (phalanstery) with a common dining hall, seven meals a day and free love. It was to be as largely as possible a self-containing unit. The emphasis would be upon agriculture, but every member would be free to work when and where he chose.

Fourierism was Americanized by a starry-eyed epileptic named Albert Brisbane, who had absorbed its teachings from the master's own lips, twelve lessons for twelve dollars. Brisbane filtered the doctrine of its moral obliquities, called it simply Association, and poured this purified version into the receptive mind of Horace Greeley.[8]

Association, save for its denunciations of the existing order, was simply a turning back of the clock, an attempt to escape into the past. Its answer to modern life was a retreat into an idyllic, semi-pastoral community, where social problems would vanish with the removal of restraints upon the individual. The high degree of paternalistic control necessary for the operation of such a self-sufficing community was utterly inconsistent with its basic principle of individual freedom. Furthermore, the success of the plan required the coöperation of the capitalists, and they were too busy piling up fortunes to pay it any serious attention. This attempt to reverse the trends of an expanding society was headed for defeat from the start, but it had a great appeal for humanitarians. Brisbane contrived to present it as a sort of grand culmination of all the reform movements of the time, and in its heyday it outshone them all. It quite dazzled the editor of the *Tribune*.

Armed with the ideas that he absorbed from European and

American currents of thought, pricked by the suffering he saw around him, stimulated by faith in the future of America, Greeley fashioned his own concept of a brave new world.

As became a romantic idealist, the *Tribune's* editor set his sights high. His ultimate aim was a society of busy, happy people enjoying the advantages of both rural and urban life, each member of the group blessed with an equal opportunity for education and an equal chance for the honors and comforts of life. All would be socially conscious. The watchword of the nineteenth century, Greeley declared, was Brotherhood.[9]

How might such a society be achieved? Greeley's brain teemed with answers to that challenge.

One of his methods of approach was to offer solutions for specific social problems. Some of these proposals were oversimplified, and such was the case with urban congestion. Greeley's constantly reiterated advice was to go into the country and stay there, a bit of editorial wisdom to which the city masses proved stolidly unresponsive and for good and sufficient reasons. On the other hand, as in the case of education, Greeley could make some very shrewd and penetrating suggestions for reform.

Greeley saw clearly the limitations of the routinized education of his day, bound firmly as it was to the classical fetish. He demanded more and better teacher training, a free, tax-supported public school system and, at all levels, practical instruction that would stress both manual and intellectual skills, and emphasize vocational training. He would have liked, being essentially a man of peace, to see the army transformed into something like a polytechnic school for the benefit of the enlisted men. The customary classical education of the colleges moved him to scorn. "Of all horned cattle," he snorted on one occasion, "a college graduate in a newspaper office is the worst." Such pieces of advice, if not such comments, were salutary, as the subsequent course of American education was to prove.[10]

The need for educational reform was in itself indicative of an imperfect society. Greeley's watchful eye singled out other weaknesses, particularly those that were wasteful or degrading, and these drew the full fire of his attack. He was a constant and unrelenting foe of gambling, prostitution, and seduction, these being not inconsiderable parts of American life. Tobacco was in his eyes a filthy weed. Nothing excited his scorn and derision more than a "long nine—a fire at one end and a fool at the other." But liquor was a greater evil than tobacco. Resentful of the waste and degradation that it caused, Greeley began an attack upon drink that continued until the end of his life. Lucy Stone, Antoinette Blackwell, and Susan B. Anthony worked with him in these crusades.

As humanity's weaknesses aroused Greeley's reforming zeal, so did the spectacle of social injustice. He never wearied of denouncing capital punishment, and he was one of those who protested against flogging in the navy until that barbarous practice was abolished in 1850. Concentration upon social evils in the North, together with an understanding of the political difficulties involved, prevented his launching a crusade against slavery until after it began to expand, but it was always abhorrent to him. So were the feudal exactions of the Hudson River Valley patroons.[11] He urged justice for the renters in the valley, just as he urged liberating wives from what amounted to slavery to their husbands, just as he maintained that women needed a large sphere of activity and better rewards for their labor.

In all of these ways, as well as in the welcome that he habitually extended to revolutionary movements across the Atlantic, Greeley demonstrated himself a reformer. More important still were the positions that he took in regard to the sphere of government and the role of labor.

That government was a necessary evil which should be confined to the narrowest possible limits was a fundamental belief of nineteenth-century liberals. Greeley took exception to this idea. So long as government rested upon a broadly based suffrage, he felt that its expansion to meet vital social needs was a desirable thing.[12] After all, a greater degree of activity by society as such was an inevitable accompaniment of a civilization steadily progressing from the anarchic individualism of savagery toward social unity. The development of large business concerns and of organizations of labor, the growth of a thousand and one civic enterprises, even such social instruments as grist mills and hotels, were evidences of this progress toward harmonious social action. Did it not then follow, as surely as day follows night, that government of the people and by the people should also expand in response to the needs of an increasingly complex social organism?

To Greeley the answer was obvious. He was convinced that there was an inexorable tendency toward the use of government for the promotion of the general welfare. If this was Socialism he, for one, was willing to be called a Socialist. "We hold the sphere of government commensurate with its power to do good," he declared in 1849,[13] a point of view that was bound to produce conniption fits among the more conservative-minded Whigs. It was in line with this philosophy that Greeley stood not only for education legislation but also for a high tariff and internal improvements.

Greeley's zeal for internal improvements never wavered through-out the course of his life. They were the means by which he would open up the nation's wealth, which lay ready for the taking in this rich and glorious land; they were the links that he saw forming "a golden chain of benefits and blessings, admirably calculated to bind together, indissolubly, the States composing this vast re-public."[14]

Protection was simply another means of securing the nation's well-being. A protective tariff, in Greeley's estimation, was essen-tial to the prosperity of American labor. It meant national security and national independence. As manufacturing spread under its beneficent shield, prices of industrial goods would fall, work would become plentiful for everyone, and producer and consumer, labor and capital, would be united in one harmonious whole. Profoundly influenced by Clay's American System concept and by the economic nationalism of Atkinson and Carey, Greeley echoed and reëchoed their arguments about the wonders of the home market and the necessity of national self-sufficiency. What did it matter if "some hundred or two wealthy manufacturers" made fabulous profits for a time behind the shield of protection? Such exorbitant gains would soon vanish before the competition that would be stimulated, and then the tariff walls would shine in their full splendor as ramparts of the national felicity.[15]

Agriculture was another field that would be blessed by the exten-sion of state activity. During the middle 1840's Greeley aban-doned support of Clay's land policy. Falling under the influence of a utopian group which called itself the National Reformers, he began advocating free grants of public lands up to 160 acres, the exemption of homesteads from seizure for debt, and the arbitrary limiting of land inheritance to 160 or 320 acres. This was an exten-sion of governmental authority with a vengeance. In 1848 he in-troduced into Congress a Homestead Act which failed of passage. Nevertheless, the author of the homestead plank in the Republican platform of 1860 was coming into his own. He was an advocate of government-built, improved highways connecting farm regions with rural markets, and the Tribune was an early and persistent agitator for a federal department of agriculture.[16]

If government supported agriculture and nourished it, govern-ment should also provide a floor of support for labor. In 1841, Greeley took over from a Fourierism a doctrine that he maintained after his faith in Associationism waned—labor's right to work. It was the responsibility of government, he declared repeatedly, to pro-vide work sufficient to guarantee subsistence in times of unemployment. Thus he, along with other Fourierites, anticipated what was perhaps the most revolutionary principle of the New Deal, the principle of work relief.[17]

Greeley was by no means an advocate of government ownership of the means of production and distribution. He had a vigorous and articulate preference for private ownership. Now and then a querulous note would creep into his references to the increasing power of the state. Nevertheless, he saw correctly that governmental authority was bound to increase, especially that authority which emanates from Washington, and that it was the right and the duty of the national state to control men's actions where such control is clearly for the benefit of society. This was true in his earlier days, when he was plumping for tariff, internal improvements, and a stable currency. It became increasingly so in later years, as he witnessed the growth of the nation. "With a constantly expanding territory," he wrote, somewhat wryly, it is true, in 1859, "it is certain that Federal power cannot be limited. Every year will create imperative necessities for its growth and expansion."[18]

Labor's lowly status bothered Greeley immensely. The *Tribune* was constantly exposing the exploitation of man by man—the misery of domestic servants (kept on pittances in muckish quarters and subjected to all sorts of indignities), the drab drudgery and heart-rending toil of women employed in the sweated trades, the horrors of living in the "Dens of Death" pictured by the *Tribune* in an exposé of the New York slum situation. Greeley was particularly sensitive to the fortunes of printers and was widely popular with them. When New York's Typographical Union #6 was organized in 1850, he was made its first president and in that capacity and as editor of the *Tribune* he did much to improve the wages and working conditions of New York printers. In 1862, his compositors presented him with a $400 gold watch in token of their esteem.[19]

How could the lot of the worker be lightened? Greeley strove earnestly to find an answer to that fundamental problem. The *Tribune's* editor emphasized help from above the laboring class level as one means of meeting the problem. The workingman must have reading rooms, scientific lectures, lyceums, and libraries, furnished free by private philanthropy or by some public agency. His children must be guaranteed an education. Labor exchanges should be set up where those needing employees and those needing employment could meet to their common advantage. Slowly and reluctantly, he accepted the idea of limiting the hours of work by law. These proposals by no means exhausted the fertility of his imagination where labor was concerned.

Greeley had three ideas which he wanted labor to take up in unilateral fashion. One was the practice of thrift and frugality, regarding which there was a perpetual bombardment of advice in the columns of the *Tribune*. A second was Association, which he pushed vigorously in the early 1840's. The third, to which more and more emphasis was given as his interest in Association waned, was the producers' coöperative, in which workingmen would act as their own employers. These were activities in which labor could engage by itself. Perhaps more important than any of them, from a modern point of view, were his ideas concerning the regulation of the wage system.

The *Tribune's* editor professed little patience with those who, in the name of personal liberty, demanded that the law of supply and demand be allowed to regulate wages. He found it difficult to perceive the practical value, save possibly for the employer, of a freedom for labor "so extreme that those who have no shoes are perfectly at liberty to go barefoot."[20] It was necessary, he declared, to guard against slavery in the North as well as to condemn it in the South. Where tendencies toward such a status occurred in the free North they produced an increasing restlessness on the part of labor. If employers could find no way of regulating the price of labor other than the old, hit-and-miss, laissez-faire system, the time was not far off when labor would teach them a better system.[21] He had such a form of regulation ready at hand and he urged it repeatedly upon both employers and employees. It was a form of collective bargaining.

Greeley was a great believer in trade agreements jointly negotiated by the employers and the employees in any industry in a given community. Such agreements, he declared, should be regarded as morally binding, and those who refused to abide by them should be "shunned alike by journeymen and customers." In this way he hoped to remove the baneful effects of competition by the substandard producer. Again and again he used the columns of the *Tribune* to publicize agreements made in this fashion and to urge the wider adoption of this method of solving wage disputes. He used it himself in dealing with labor in the *Tribune* organization. It is not too much to say that Horace Greeley was one of the pioneers in the development of collective bargaining in the United States.[22]

The fundamental reform of the age, Greeley declared, was the lifting up of the laboring class out of ignorance, inefficiency, de-

pendence, and want to "a position of partnership and recognized
mutual helpfulness with the suppliers of the Capital which they
(the laborers) render fruitful and efficient." This was essential
to the dawn of the new day. There can be no doubt of Greeley's own
conviction that he was the friend of the workingman.[23]

Such was the new order, as visualized by the partner of Weed and
Seward. America was to become a moral paradise, where Everyman's
talents and his understanding of what was good would be developed
with painstaking care. In this Beulah land a government, responsive
to the public will but so guided by an aristocracy of brains and
achievement as to be ever watchful of the public interest, would
build tariff walls, develop internal improvements, and in general
undertake those activities best calculated to promote national
prosperity and happiness, while an uplifted and ennobled laboring
class would work in harmony with benevolent capitalists for the
good of all. There would have to be a great deal of enlightenment
all around, but progress was inevitable and the outcome would be a
genuine social and economic democracy.

NOTES FOR CHAPTER 6

1. Henry C. Carey, *The Past, the Present, and the Future* (Phila., 1848),
   passim, and *The Harmony of Interests, Agricultural, Manufacturing and
   Commercial* (N. Y., 1852), *passim*; M. Curti, *The Roots of American
   Loyalty* (N. Y., 1946), pp. 106f. and *passim*; H. Kohn, *The Idea of
   Nationalism* (N. Y., 1944), pp. 293f., 301; G. G. Van Deusen, "The
   Nationalism of Horace Greeley," in *Nationalism and Internationalism*,
   ed. E. M. Earle (N. Y., 1950), pp. 431-54.
2. Greeley, *Recollections*, pp. 68-74, 424, 429; *Hints Toward Reforms* (N. Y.,
   1853), pp. 85-111, 149-78, 225f.; *Tribune*, May 2, 1843, Apr. 1, 1848,
   Dec. 31, 1850. The main articles of Greeley's creed are summed up by
   him in his *Recollections*, pp. 68-74. His God was a personal Deity, and
   was not triune. God did not condemn anyone to eternal punishment.
3. *New-Yorker*, Oct. 8, 1836, Oct. 7, 1837, Sept. 29, 1838, Feb. 23, 1839;
   Jeffersonian, Sept. 1, 1838; *Tribune*, Feb. 2, Nov. 18, 1843, Dec. 12, 1844,
   Nov. 18, 1851; Greeley Papers (N. Y. P. L.), Greeley to O. A. Bowe,
   Mar. 30, 1842; V. Brooks, *Flowering of New England*, pp. 377-78, and *The
   World of Washington Irving*, pp. 447f.
4. Greeley Letters (Yale Lib.), Greeley to B. F. Ransom, Mar. 15, 1841.
5. Greeley, *Hints Toward Reforms*, p. 86, and the entire essay on "The
   Formation of Character"; *New-Yorker*, Apr. 3, 1841; Griswold Papers,
   Greeley to Griswold, Aug. 25, Dec. 16, 1846; Greeley Letters (Yale Lib.),
   Greeley to Thoreau, Apr. 17, 1848; R. L. Rusk, *The Life of Ralph
   Waldo Emerson* (N. Y., 1949), pp. 288, 321.
6. Greeley Letters (U. of R.), Greeley to Weed, May 14, 1843; Greeley
   Papers (N. Y. P. L.), Greeley to O. A. Bowe, May 16, 1843; *Tribune*,
   May 12, 16, 1843, Dec. 16, 1847.

7. T. Carlyle, *Past and Present* (Oxford, 1918), pp. 225-26, 242f. and *passim*.
8. For the early relations of Greeley and Brisbane, see Arthur E. Bestor, Jr., "Albert Brisbane—Propagandist for Socialism in the 1840's," *New York History*, XXVIII (Apr. 1947), 128-58, especially 150-51.
9. Greeley, *Hints Toward Reforms*, pp. 187f., 396; *Tribune*, June 9, 1845, May 8, 17, 1849, Nov. 29, 1850.
10. *New-Yorker*, Dec. 24, 1836; *Jeffersonian*, Feb. 24, Nov. 17, Dec. 1, 1838; *Tribune*, Oct. 5, 1842, Jan. 30, 1846, July 8, 1856, Aug. 15, 1865; Greeley, *An Address Before the Literary Societies of Hamilton College* (1844), *passim*, and *Hints Toward Reforms*, pp. 206ff. Also *Peoples' College* (1859), *passim*. Greeley was one of the trustees of the Peoples' College, an institution projected at Havana, New York, 1853-59, which was to give special attention to scientific agriculture and vocational training.
11. *Tribune*, Aug. 23, 1844, Feb. 1, Aug. 11, 1845; H. Christman, *Tin Horns and Calico* (N. Y., 1945), pp. 81, 182, 195, 233.
12. *Jeffersonian*, Nov. 10, 1838; Greeley, *Glances at Europe* (N. Y., 1851), p. 279.
13. Greeley, *Hints Toward Reforms*, pp. 177-78, 190ff. *Tribune*, Feb. 10, 1842, Aug. 5, 1845, Nov. 15, 1849, Sept. 18, 20, 1850, Feb. 14, 1855.
14. Greeley, "River and Harbor Improvements," *DeBow's Review*, IV (Nov. 1847), 291-96.
15. Greeley, *Hints Toward Reforms*, pp. 232-56; *Tribune*, July 26, 1847, Aug. 28, 1851.
16. *Tribune*, Apr. 18, 1842, June 26, July 29, 1845, Sept. 18, 1850, June 2, 1852, Mar. 5, 1856; E. D. Ross, "Horace Greeley and the Beginnings of the New Agriculture," *Agriculture History*, VII, No. 1 (Jan. 1933), 15-17.
17. *Tribune*, May 11, June 26, July 12, 16, 1841; Greeley, *The Crystal Palace and Its Lessons* (N. Y., 1851), pp. 30-31.
18. Greeley, *Political Economy*, pp. 128-29; *Tribune*, Jan. 20, 1859.
19. George A. Stevens, *New York Typographical Union #6* (Albany, 1912), pp. 205, 234, 286, 616-25.
20. *Tribune*, Oct. 8, 1847.
21. *Ibid.*, May 17, 1850.
22. *Ibid.*, Feb. 8, 1851, Apr. 13, Aug. 5, 1853, May 16, 1854; Stevens, *op. cit.*, pp. 235, 238, 243, 252-53; N. W. Chamberlain, *Collective Bargaining* (N. Y., 1951), pp. 23-31.
23. Pages of citations might be given for the views developed in this chapter. In addition to those already noted, the following are among the most significant:: *New-Yorker*, July 17, 24, 31, 1841; *Tribune*, May 18, Nov. 13, 30, Dec. 14, 1843, Jan. 28, May 22, Sept. 30, 1845, Aug. 11, Sept. 14, 1847; Greeley, *An Address Before the Literary Societies of Hamilton College*, *passim*; *Hints Toward Reforms*, pp. 193f., 352-57; *Recollections*, pp. 507-9.

CHAPTER 7

Not So Brave and Not So New

THE ODOR OF IDEALISM, THE REPUTATION FOR high-mindedness that Greeley acquired through his efforts for reform made him a national figure of increasing importance. Here was a successful businessman who had risen from the ranks, but who remained a champion of the masses. The combination, real or imaginary, of material success and righteousness has always been singularly attractive to the American people, and Greeley was no exception to the rule. Thousands flocked to hear him lecture, regardless of the fact that he had none of the arts or graces of the platform orator, and his listeners drank in his words almost as though they came from the gospel fount. Emerson, on the lecture circuit in the West during 1854, reported that Greeley had preceded him and had done the people's thinking for them. The *Tribune*, especially the *Weekly Tribune* (which contained all the rarest gems of the great editor's philosophy) came to be regarded as a purveyor of the pure milk of the word. Many a doughty son of the soil was convinced that Horace wrote every word of it, and was apt to come up after a lecture at Oshkosh or Kalamazoo to inquire as to when his subscription ran out. "Did you ever see Horace?" was an inevitable question at any western camp fire. Horace knew everything. He was an apostle of truth, a guide, a Daniel come to judgment—that is, he was these things for all save Democrats, ultra-conservative Whigs, practical politicians, and the wicked.

This reputation was largely undeserved, for the *Tribune's* editor was not half the reformer that he was supposed to be. There was a Greeley who yearned to build the New Jerusalem and whose sword leaped lightly to his hand, but there was also another Greeley who was calculating, conservative, and full of shifts and evasions, not to mention a third Greeley who could seek refuge from reality in Utopia. The brave new world of reformer Greeley was not half so brave or new after the other Greeleys had finished tinkering with it.

The incongruities inherent in being both a conservative and a reformer were sometimes a bit startling. It was hard, for instance, to reconcile reformer Greeley's farsighted ideas about the expanding role of government with conservative Greeley's chronic demands for retrenchment in governmental expenditures, a contradiction that was all the more striking because his demands for economy came at a time when national penny-pinching was definitely injurious to effective administration.[1] A similar incongruity appeared in his attitude toward the nativist movement.

Generally speaking, Greeley's opposition to anti-Catholic bigotry was based upon high ground. Repeatedly he would stand for the great principle of tolerance, or defend religious liberty and equality of rights as basic to the free institutions of America. He usually opposed such arguments as these to the New York nativists' attempts at fusion with the Whigs. But he also declared that one of his most important reasons for opposing nativism was its tendency to throw the Catholic church into alignment with the Democrats. That church, said Greeley, was eminently conservative in character and thought "and, though but partially Conservative ourselves, we feel the necessity, in this age of incessant Agrarian upheaval and Radical convulsion, for something which holds fast—something which opposes a steady resistance to the fierce spirit of Change and Disruption."[2] A nineteenth-century Protestant reformer who felt the necessity of sheltering himself behind the Catholic church was something of an anomaly, although perhaps the cream of the jest lay in the scathing reference to land reform by a man who went for it, lock, stock, and barrel, two years later.

Greeley's dread of upheaval and convulsion was still with him and still based upon his fear of mass ignorance, just as it had been in the previous decade. This was made evident by his reaction to Orestes A. Brownson's disillusionment with the democratic dogma after the election of 1840. Greeley praised Brownson's criticism of the prevailing tendency to regard the voice of the people as the voice of God, and accepted as right and proper the latter's fastidious shrinking from "the narrow views, crude notions, and blind instincts of the multitude." Like Brownson, Greeley felt that true democracy could exist only when the aristocrats of intellect were instructing the populace as to the best means of avoiding error. Both men were evidently convinced that the intelligence of the people was hardly a sufficient basis for good government.[3]

The "belchings" of Fanny Wright, as Greeley termed that high-spirited lady's demands for reform, aroused in him only disgust. Was she not a free thinker—one who disliked the marriage tie—

and a Democrat to boot? Greeley's soul yearned for a safely conservative hero, who would gently lead the masses out of darkness
into the radiance of the new day. The conduct of the *Tribune's*
editor as his influence grew indicated that there were at least times
when he thought of himself as admirably suited for such a role.
Small wonder that he found Carlyle's *Heroes and Hero Worship*
"a glorious volume."[4]

The Dorr Rebellion of 1842 cast a revealing light upon Greeley's
attitude toward political democracy. Here again, his fear of the
impulses of the mass dominated his reaction to the event.

This Rhode Island "War," as it was sometimes termed, derived
its name from its leader, Thomas Wilson Dorr. It was essentially a
popular movement of protest against the archaic constitution of
Rhode Island, where at least 50 per cent of the adult males could
not vote and the apportionment of members in the state legislature
was over a century behind the times. In grudging response to this
movement, the conservative government of the state summoned a
constitutional convention, chosen by those already voters. This
body, under pressure of the popular discontent, drew up an instrument that represented a substantial victory for popular rule. It was
narrowly rejected in a referendum, with the Dorrites themselves
(who had drawn up a constitution that they preferred) voting
against it.[5]

Dorr and his followers then began to flirt with the idea of using
violence as a means of gaining a complete victory. This dangerous
frame of mind was fostered by the sympathy of such respectable
New York Democrats as William Cullen Bryant and Churchill C.
Cambreleng, to say nothing of the rantings of wilder spirits such
as Alexander Ming, Jr., and Levi D. Slamm of the *New York
Plebeian.*

Dorr finally decided to take over control of the state by force, but
his attempt to seize the arsenal at Providence ended in fiasco. He
fled the state, came back for another abortive revolutionary try, and
once again fled. The existing government, which at first had trembled in its shoes, arrested and imprisoned scores of his supporters.

In 1843, after a new and liberalized constitution had been legally
adopted, Dorr ventured to return to Rhode Island, coming this
time in peaceable guise. He was promptly arrested, tried for high
treason, and sentenced to solitary confinement for life at hard labor.
After a little more than a year in prison, he was released by act of a
Democratic legislature.

Greeley had felt, even before the beginning of the excitement,
that the Rhode Island franchise should be broadened, but Dorr's

appeal to force filled him with apprehension and disgust. The *Tribune's* editor rightly pointed out that the rejected constitution of 1842 would have given the power into the hands of the reformers, and that resort to violence was a course that could only lead straight to anarchy. The more Greeley thought about the attack on the Providence arsenal, the more upset he became. A week's mulling over the subject finally produced a theory of government that, in its spirit of conservatism, might well have been derived straight from Burke's *Reflections on the French Revolution*.

Down to the Declaration of Independence, Greeley declared, governments had almost uniformly rested on prescription or force. Then the Fathers planted themselves on the principles that all men are created equal, and that government is by consent of the governed. Actually, however, the rule had been that those possessing the suffrage should extend it when, in their judgment, it was just and wise so to do. The American practice was to regard the suffrage not as a right to be acknowledged, but rather as a duty to be imposed by those who already possessed it. They imposed this duty when, in their judgment, the time had come for its extension to the hitherto unprivileged.[6]

Thus Greeley, who still professed devotion to its principles, calmly abandoned the fundamental political doctrine of the Declaration of Independence. According to his conception, the progress of political democracy rested upon the wisdom and benevolence of those already enfranchised, rather than upon the unalienable rights of man.

Greeley was quick to identify the Democratic party with ultra-radicalism because many of its leaders vigorously supported Dorr. There was some excuse for this, in view of the virulently partisan controversy that stemmed out of the affair. There was less excuse for his hearty approval of Dorr's sentence to life imprisonment and for the regret he expressed when Dorr was released from prison.[7] These manifestations of intolerance and, most of all, his carefully worked out conception of the suffrage as a duty to be imposed rather than a right to be acknowledged showed the importance of order and stability in his scheme of things. There was little of traditional American democratic idealism in such a point of view. It was more in the tradition of Federalist arrogance, such as that which had displayed itself against the Whiskey Rebellion of 1794.

Greeley's attitude toward the masses was paralleled by the position he took in regard to woman's rights. In both cases he responded readily to certain specific appeals for justice, but his attitude on fundamental principles was far closer to reaction than to radicalism.

The *Tribune's* editor recognized the justice of woman's demand for more legal protection and for a wider field of opportunity than she enjoyed, but otherwise his attitude toward feminism was obscurantist. He could never bring himself to favor woman suffrage, his attitude varying from a snort of "preposterous" to the subterfuge that he would be glad to give them the vote when the majority of women clearly expressed a desire for the privilege. He had equally narrow ideas about the marital relationship. It involved duties and obligations that were rooted in "the beneficent law of God and the unchanging nature of Man." Hence he opposed divorce on any ground save adultery. When the eccentric philosopher, Stephen Pearl Andrews, inquired whether a uterine tumor weighing thirty pounds, the result of "amative excess," was not sufficient ground for divorce, Greeley declared that such an argument was simply indecent and refused to print the question in his paper.[8]

The labor problem afforded another opportunity for developing the Greeley approach—sympathy, a desire to help, but scant interest in any fundamental reforms.

Greeley was fond of indulging in great aspirations for labor; he talked hopefully of labor exchanges and work relief; he came out, albeit slowly and reluctantly, for a ten-hour day; he even took a prominent part in arousing the consciousness of society to the misery of the urban masses. Despite all this, he scarcely deserves the title of a genuine friend of the working class.

The difference in Greeley's attitude toward workers and employers was striking, to say the least. Contemplating the world as it was, Greeley found the capitalist not such a bad fellow. To be sure, he could on occasion call the capitalist system a game of gouge and declare that the wages system must disappear; he could even denounce those avaricious employers who degraded labor by screwing down wage rates as they screwed up hours of employment.[9] But this was usually when the spirit of Fourierism was upon him. Generally, he found it much easier to excuse than denounce the shortcomings of employers. Even those who were hard on their workers, he felt, were often the victims of circumstances and should not be judged too harshly. The appalling cruelties in British factories were really due to overpopulation and a supply of labor that outran the demand. Thus British labor was victimized by circumstances over which no one had any control and, to make matters worse, the capitalists were themselves the victims of excessive competition. Labor conditions in the Lowell textile mills seemed to him practically idyllic, and he was easily convinced that the introduction of the factory system in the United States was invariably followed by great improvement in working conditions. Employers, he believed, were at least as wise, humane, and considerate as their employees, and not less likely to do right when the interests of the two appeared to conflict.[10]

Greeley's natural orientation was toward the capitalist. He was an ardent proponent of the Whig bankruptcy law of 1841 (a measure that was certainly open to criticism as too lenient to the property-owning class) and continued to defend it even after popular opinion forced its repeal. His staunch defense of limited liability for corporations was just and necessary, but repeated editorials on the subject gave no hint that he shared the concern of a man like William Cullen Bryant over the dangers to social democracy implicit in the rise of the corporate form. The idea of government ownership of any of the means of production or distribution, like the idea of government's interference in the squabbles of capital and labor, inspired only aversion in his breast. He played a substantial part in establishing the practice of selling the nation's mineral lands outright to private purchasers, a part that he recalled with pride in later years. As an advocate of Association, he argued that the rich were becoming richer and the poor poorer, but five years later, in 1851, he had become convinced that as the rich became richer the condition of the masses also improved.[11]

But the laborer, ah, the laborer! Greeley yearned for his redemption, but it was a yearning shot through and through with impatience. The workers were so slow, not to say stupid, about following the right path, even after it had been pointed out to them. Despite reiterated advice to relieve congestion and reduce their misery by going into the country, they persisted in crowding the city slums and tenements where they bred like rabbits and died like flies. They were lamentably slow about organizing producers' coöperatives, Greeley's great remedy for their ills in the existing state of society. More than this, they were extravagant and altogether too prone to think that a competence was to be acquired in some other way than by simple, honest toil.

Greeley could not help thinking that if the laborers would only practise thrift and frugality, and set up their own associations as producers, the conflict between capital and labor would be very significantly moderated, and might disappear altogether. "Labor needs not to *combat* but to *command* capital" was his cry, and he told an anxious correspondent that there was no obstacle to the laboring classes working out their own salvation, if they would only try. Perhaps the wealthy and powerful ought to help, but they could not be blamed for want of faith in the wisdom, foresight, virtue, and prudence of a laboring class the great majority of whom were spendthrifts, indifferent to their own best interest.[12]

Looking backward to the 1840's and 1850's with the advantage of historical perspective, it is easy to see that labor's best hope in that period lay in aggressive trade-unionism and the strike. Greeley was strongly opposed to both. Unionism as a basis for dignified arbitral proceedings and harmonious collective bargaining he could understand. Indeed, he had joined the printers' union in the belief that it was to be an organization of employers and journeymen who would work out their mutual problems through happy fraternal adjustments. That was good unionism. But unionization of employees for the purpose of forcing better working conditions from employers was a breeder of class conflict, and strikes caused more losses than gains. He never wearied in pointing out to strikers the stupidity of such remedies.[13]

The fact was that Greeley did not want to see a powerful labor movement develop, for he was afraid that such a development would breed discord and strife in the nation. Hence his proposals for action were generally inadequate, to say the least. In 1850, in the face of growing unrest and after recognizing that labor conditions in New York were worse than they had been twenty years before, he outlined a plan of action for the working class. The city's laborers should organize as a sort of mutual benefit society. Then they should erect a "spacious edifice" at some central point. This building would serve as a Labor Exchange and as a place for discussing labor's needs.[14] The mountain had labored and brought forth a mouse.

Like the policemen in *The Pirates of Penzance*, Greeley cried out to the workingmen, "We go, we go. Yes, forward on the foe," and like the General, labor could have replied, "Yes, but you don't go."

Labor was, indeed, very suspicious of Greeley during his rise to prominence. This suspicion moderated in later years, because of his sympathetic portrayal of working-class misery, his advocacy of the ten-hour day, his zeal for land reform, and his generally sympathetic attitude toward printers and their troubles. Yet labor might well have remained suspicious, for his acceptance of the ten-hour day was grudging, his land reform project was an illusory panacea and his unionism was of a milk and water constituency. Handicapped by his fundamental conservatism, Greeley had very little to offer labor, save his own fair attitude toward his employees and newspaper publicity for labor's wants and misery.

"This whole relation of Employer and Laborer is so full of antagonism, inequality and injustice," Greeley declared in a moment of bitter candor, "that we despair of any reform in it but a very thorough and radical one."[15] These were fine words. Actually, they signified his attempted flight from the labor problem into the Utopia of Fourierism.

There could be no question of Greeley's enthusiasm for Association. He published a short-lived Brisbane weekly, the *Future*, early in 1841. In March 1842, he opened the *Tribune* to a Brisbane column that ran for a year and a half at what Greeley called "a small compensation—not one-tenth of its actual cost to us," probably around $500 a year.[16] For years the *Tribune's* editorial and news columns spread the Fourierist gospel with considerable positive effect upon the enthusiasm of utopians and negative effect upon the paper's circulation. In the winter of 1846-47, Greeley engaged in a lengthy and often heated debate on Association with Henry J. Raymond of the *Courier and Enquirer*, a debate that ended with Greeley denouncing "Courierism" and accusing Raymond of "misrepresentation," "falsified quotations," and "a spice of roguery."

The *Tribune's* editor by no means limited his support of Association to the columns of his paper. He attended Fourierist conventions, helped to organize phalanxes from Ohio to Massachusetts, and was for several years the president of the American Union of Associationists, an organization designed to unify and give national scope to the whole movement. He also belonged to three phalanxes —the Sylvania Association of Pennsylvania, the North American Phalanx at Red Bank, New Jersey, and a converted Transcendentalist venture in Massachusetts, Brook Farm—memberships that cost him, all told, thousands of dollars.[17]

It is probable that Association attracted Greeley to some extent because of its political potentialities. At least, as he told Weed (who had scant patience with moonings over society's reorganization), advocacy of such a reform would help to convince the masses that Whiggery was on their side. Far more important in his eyes was the fact that it was both humanitarian and conservative. Here was a system that promised relief from misery and elevation for the human spirit without anything in the way of serious social disturbance. Its slow but steady development would peacefully obliterate all social ugliness, all hatred, all degradation of man by man. He never wearied of asserting that Fourierism opposed revolutionary agitation and the instigation of hostility and hatred between prop-

erty and labor; that it supporters had nothing in common with
anti-Christian and anti-property radicals.

This system requires no immediate sacrifice as a condition precedent of
ultimate benefit [he told an Association meeting in 1842]. While it may
well satisfy the most thorough Radical, it need not alarm the most timid
Conservative. While it will ensure independence and comfort to the Poor,
it increases rather than diminishes the wealth and enjoyments of the Rich.
And this is a feature of the system which has won for it my sympathies;
and enlisted in its behalf my earnest and hopeful exertions.[18]

This, then, was the key to Greeley's attitude toward Association.
As he told Raymond in 1846, Association's grand aim was to restore
the natural rights of labor without trenching on the acquired rights
or interests of capital.[19] In a word, it destroyed nothing but misery.
It was safe, for it was all things to all men. This belief was a
measure at once of his conservatism and his naïveté. Small wonder
that Seward once described him as having a trusting and confiding
nature.

Association waxed and waned in the 1840's. It was clearly
devitalized by the end of the decade, to the delight of partner
McElrath, who had never believed in it anyway and squeezed it
out of the *Tribune* columns whenever he had a chance. Greeley
stubbornly printed news of the movement until at least 1855; labor's
right to work and the glories of coöperative production continued
to color his thinking; but his ardent support of the system may be
said to have ended when he had parried the caustic thrusts of
Henry Jarvis Raymond. The conversion of the *Tribune* into a
joint-stock enterprise in 1850, with one hundred shares of $1,000
each which were owned among the "Tribune Associates," bore witness that Fourierism had been metamorphosed in Greeley's mind
into the concept of a limited liability corporation with transferable
shares. By the reversal of an ordinary process of nature, what had
been a butterfly was becoming a much less scintillating but considerably more useful organism.

Horace Greeley was a man of good will, who spoke out bravely
against the abuses of his generation. He wanted to make America
a better place in which to live. He claimed, and was generally
accorded, the title of reformer. Ultraconservatives thought him a
dangerous radical. James Watson Webb read him out of the Whig
party as such in 1847. Milder conservatives held him a trouble-
maker, as unpredictable as fire in a high wind. Weed and Seward,
conservative politicians, were forever being made uneasy by their
partner's trumpetings and questings and windmill tiltings.

But he was not so very dangerous, this man who called strikers "Jacobins," and cuffed employers one minute only to kiss them the next. The things-that-were still held him in their spell, as Thomas Ainge Devyr pointed out in an 1860 broadside which asserted that time after time politics or Greeley's timidity, or both, had prevented the *Tribune's* editor from aiding Devyr in championing the oppressed.[20] "A bound Samson," Devyr called him, and the phrase must have stung. For while his enthusiasm on behalf of goodness was forever making him formidable, his innate conservatism was always on hand to make him shrink and strip him of his strength. Moreover, he lacked vision, save in a material sense. While he had foresight that was almost uncanny about such things as the future of electricity and the mechanization of farming, he had little of that capacity for judging correctly the potentialities of movements that is the hallmark of the statesman. He lashed out at injustice, sometimes with effect. He did a great deal to keep the popular conscience awake, and his support of producers' coöperatives was definitely constructive. But it was all rather disconnected, not infrequently contradictory, and more often than not superficial. He was, as Stephen Pearl Andrews wrote in 1853, "suggestive, inspiring and disappointing." Had Andrews made his judgment a decade later, he might well have added "dangerous" to his list.

NOTES FOR CHAPTER 7

1. *Tribune*, Dec. 30, 1843, Dec. 14, 1847, Apr. 29, Nov. 23, 1848, Dec. 8, 1849, Feb. 18, 1850, Jan. 20, 1859; A. Nevins, *Ordeal of the Union* (2 vols.; N. Y., 1947), I, 160-61. Greeley's favorite targets for economy were the army and navy, but he was also avid for drastic cuts in the pay of Congress and the foreign service, and for cutting down expenses in general.
2. *Tribune*, Oct. 27, 1843, Nov. 12, 1844.
3. *Ibid.*, Aug. 1, Oct. 26, 1843; Greeley, *Address at Hamilton College* (1844), pp. 33-34.
4. Greeley, *Hints Toward Reforms*, p. 106.
5. A. M. Mowry, *The Dorr War* (Providence, R. I., 1901), pp. 120-26, 350-51, 354-55; Schlesinger, *Age of Jackson*, pp. 410-16. This so-called Freemen's Charter represented a much more substantial victory for popular government than Schlesinger indicates.
6. *Tribune*, May 24, 1842, editorial entitled "The Law of Organic Changes in Popular Government." Cf. *ibid.*, Jan. 20, 1844. In 1855, Greeley recognized the "right" to vote, but asserted that it could be held in abeyance, due either to presumed choice (women) or to public necessity. After the Civil War, he favored limited black and white suffrage in the South, based preferably on a poll tax paid some months before voting. *Ibid.*, Feb. 13, 1855, Nov. 16, 21, 27, 1866, Jan. 14, 1867.

7. *Ibid.*, June 27, 28, 1844, June 30, 1845.

8. *Ibid.*, Jan. 25, 1843, Mar. 21, 1846, Jan. 3, 1848, Mar. 22, June 15, 1850; S. P. Andrews (ed.) , *Love, Marriage and Divorce* (N. Y., 1853) , pp. 50-51.

9. *Tribune*, Sept. 9, 1843, Jan. 5, Oct. 7, Dec. 28, 1846, Aug. 11, Sept. 14, Oct. 8, 1847; Greeley, *Hints Toward Reforms*, p. 62.

10. *Ibid.*, p. 31; *Tribune*, June 24, 1841, Nov. 10, 1843, Nov. 17, 1844, Sept. 3, Oct. 8, Dec. 27, 1845, Apr. 25, Sept. 15, 1846, Oct. 22, 1851, Nov. 12, 1852.

11. *Ibid.*, July 24, 1841, Dec. 19, 1842, Feb. 27, March 7, 1843, Jan. 27, 1846, May 15, 17, 20, 1847, Oct. 22, 1851, Mar. 30, Apr. 1, 1856; Greeley, *Recollections*, pp. 251-52; Greeley and Raymond, *Association Discussed* (N. Y., 1847) , p. 9.

12. *Tribune*, July 30, Oct. 25, 1845; Aug. 20, 1849, July 24, 1850, Mar. 20, 1851; Greeley, *Hints Toward Reforms*, pp. 326-30.

13. *Tribune*, Aug. 7, 1845, Aug. 21, 1849, Aug. 6, 1850, May 1, 1852, Aug. 23, 1864; Greeley, *Hints Toward Reforms*, pp. 335-41, 364-66; Stevens, *New York Typographical Union #6*, pp. 293-94. Greeley declared in 1864 that he had joined the printers' union on the understanding that it was to include employers as well as journeymen. He deplored the fact that it had become "one-sided." This was during a strike that resulted in the *Tribune's* operating under open-shop conditions for several years.

14. *Tribune*, Feb. 9, 1850; L. D. Ingersoll, *The Life of Horace Greeley* (Phila., 1890) , pp. 628-30.

15. *Tribune*, Sept. 4-5, 1845.

16. *Ibid.*, June 30, 1846; Griswold Papers, Greeley to Griswold, Feb. 26, 1841; Bestor, *loc. cit.*, p. 153.

17. Greeley Papers (N. Y. P. L.) , Chas. Sears to Greeley, Nov. 17, 1852; *Tribune*, Feb. 1, 1844, June 30, Aug. 18, Sept. 1, 1846. For details of Greeley's Fourieristic activities, see an unpublished M. A. thesis by Cecelia Koretsky, "Horace Greeley and Fourierism in the United States," prepared at the University of Rochester under my direction.

18. *Tribune*, Apr. 20, 1842.

19. *Ibid.*, Dec. 8, 1846.

20. Greeley Papers (N. Y. P. L.) , T. A. Devyr to Greeley, Oct. 29, 1860 [broadside].

CHAPTER 8

Soundings

———

ENTHUSIASTIC AS GREELEY WAS OVER ASSOCIATION, there was one aspect of the movement that left him cold. Its leaders, generally, took no interest in political action. They were contemptuous of it. This was never the case with the *Tribune's* editor. Even in the heyday of Fourierism, he believed that a safe course to reform could be charted through the stormy seas of practical politics. With the *Tribune* firmly established, Greeley began to take soundings so that this course might be charted for the good ship *Whig*.

There were four great principles, Greeley believed, that gave, or should give, meaning to Whiggery. First was protection which, like Association, had the central aim of increasing the number of producers in the American society. A stable currency, internal improvements and the uplift of the masses were the other articles in the creed of this four-square gospel of social harmony and national welfare. It was a gospel distinctly nationalistic in its implications.

The Democratic party, to Greeley's way of thinking, did not believe in this gospel, any more than it did in democracy itself. That party's great hero, the "violent and lawless" Jackson, had done more than any other American who had ever lived to make the government over into a "centralized despotism." Its members, in the mass, believed that there was a natural antagonism between wealth and poverty, capital and labor, and many of them made it their business to foster these antagonisms for the sake of partisan advantage. Hostile to paper money, tariffs, and internal improvements, hag-ridden by a do-nothing governmental philosophy, the party of Jackson and Van Buren was essentially exclusive and undemocratic in character. Moreover it was financially untrustworthy, for since the panic of 1837 it had soiled itself by the repudiation of state debts, Mississippi being the outstanding culprit in this regard.[1] The Democratic party, in short, was the foe, as Whiggery was the proponent, of the New Day.

It was perhaps fortunate that the political aspects of reform were clearly outlined in Greeley's mind, for they made it possible for him, a Fourierite, to work hand in glove with very practical politicians. Belief in the Whig party as the proper reforming agency buttressed his wholehearted participation in the efforts of Seward and Weed to pose that organization as the foe of oppression and the friend of labor, an attempt that furnished the key to Whig political activity in New York State during the 1840's. This belief likewise lent vigor to his attacks upon the "Sham Democracy," and even enabled him to regard as virtuous the Whig distribution of the national spoils in 1841.

In principle, Greeley was opposed to the spoils system. It was as bad, he declared, for government to discharge officeholders on account of politics as it was for employers to discharge their workers on account of their political convictions. Exaggerating the proscriptions of the Jacksonian era, he urged the Whigs not to follow that evil example.

But the full flush of opportunity proved too much for Greeley's virtue when victory placed fat offices within easy reach of the party. After all, the Whigs did not get into office very often. When they did, it was necessary to turn out their enemies, lest the great reforms that were in the offing be imperiled by those representatives of a false philosophy. Greeley wrote to Washington urging the appointment of Edward Curtis (an unblushing spoilsman who was devoted to the interests of Seward and Weed) as Collector of the Port of New York. He spoke to Governor Seward in one letter on behalf of some fifty office-seekers, and the advice that the letter contained was not entirely disinterested, though it did show qualms of conscience. As befitted a good Whig, he waxed contemptuous over Park Benjamin's charge that Whig Postmaster-General Granger was removing efficient postmasters and replacing them with party hacks. And he displayed real ingenuity in virtually ignoring the Whig office seekers who had flooded into Washington during Harrison's brief term. In that connection, all of his attention was directed to the pressure exerted by the wives of Democratic appointees, who had brought their children into Harrison's very presence and with tears and supplications had so besought him that the old general had declared "he could not stand it."[2] By implication, it was these sorrowing ones and not the hordes of Whig office seekers who had caused the death of Old Tippecanoe.

A partisan stand on the spoils system was only one evidence that the *Tribune* intended to make its weight felt in politics. Arriving on the scene at the climax of New York City's mayoralty campaign in the spring of 1841, the paper vainly urged the election of Whig J. Phillips Phoenix as Mayor. Thereafter it belabored the city's Democratic administration with charges of extravagance and corruption, and Whig councilmen with demands for governmental reform and relief for the city's poor. In the city, its watchword was "retrenchment and reform."

As for the state of New York itself, where Seward had been governor since 1838 and the Whigs had been in complete control since 1839, such a slogan was obviously inappropriate. There reform was unnecessary and as for retrenchment, Governor Seward had developed a spending policy in regard to railroads and canals that was raising the state's debt by millions of dollars every year. This Greeley defended against Democratic wails of "stop and tax" with as much confidence and acerbity as he did the cause of retrenchment in the metropolis.

But if the *Tribune* devoted considerable time to state and local politics in 1841, the main attention of its editor was centered on the stirring events that were taking place in the nation's capital.

The death of William Henry Harrison had made John Tyler, a states' rights, strict constructionist Whig, President of the United States and titular head of the Whig party. But the arrogant and charming Henry Clay, still smarting over his rejection at Harrisburg, was of no mind to be relegated to a subordinate role, either in party or national affairs. Clay was in the Senate, and from that vantage point he laid down a Whig program that made bank and tariff legislation and distribution of land sales the chief objects of the special session that met on May 31, 1841. These were all pet Clay measures and Tyler's attitude toward them was by no means certain. But the Kentuckian was confidently, scornfully, so. "Tyler dares not resist. I will drive him before me," he was reported as saying. Party leadership was obviously in the balance.

It was almost inevitable, granted the impetuous drive of the one, the obstinacy of the other, and the ambition of both, that Clay and Tyler should come to blows. And so it happened. Two bank bills marshaled through Congress by the Kentuckian ran afoul of the Presidential veto—the first largely because Tyler objected to any bank with the power to discount notes and establish branches in the states, the second because the President became convinced that there was not room enough for both himself and Clay at the head of the Whig party.[3] With the second veto, all the Cabinet save Webster resigned, and party and President drifted into a hopeless wrangling that delighted their Democratic opponents.

Greeley saw this sequence of events with pain and distress, for it spelled ruin to his hopes of a constructive program. The *Tribune's* editor had his own plan for a bank, one that would be potent to maintain a stable national currency, but at the same time would be powerless to inflate the currency, influence the price structure, or exert political pressure.[4] He preferred a bank that would have branching power, but was willing to give up that attribute if necessary. Greeley's bank would have satisfied Tyler, but it was far from meeting the requirements of Henry Clay.

Throughout the bank controversy at Washington, Greeley maintained an air of anxious impartiality. Constantly he urged compromise. Constantly he sought to pour oil on troubled waters, declaring that talk of Clay's dictation and of Tyler's resistance to it was only "the wretched slang of a profligate press." It was better, he declared, to have a bank that would please the President than to have no bank at all.[5]

During early August 1841, as the bank quarrel rolled up to the crisis of the first veto, Greeley became convinced that the controversy was largely of Clay's making; that sycophants and bad advisers were setting Clay on to ruin himself and the party. But not an inkling of this was permitted to get into the *Tribune*. The news from Washington correspondents was carefully edited with a view to its "clarification." The veto elicited kind words for Tyler, together with praise for Clay and affirmation of the party's essential unity. "We are prouder than ever of the Whig party and its Statesmen in Congress," Greeley declared. Editorial honesty, upon which he was quick to insist in other papers, was evidently not of so much consequence in the *Tribune* when its editor was fighting for the maintenance of the Whig party as an effective political force.[6]

The stormy progress of events that marked the path to the second veto found Greeley still picking his course with care. On the one hand he criticized the veto power in principle, and said harsh things about the narrow-minded Virginians (Rives, Wise, and others) who stuck to the President like cockleburs. On the other hand he praised the conciliatory vein of the second veto, and warmly approved Webster's staying in the Cabinet. This was a guarantee, said Greeley, that the administration would remain Whig. Harmony was still his theme, despite the fact that like Weed he had little faith left in the President's wisdom as a party leader.

During the height of the quarrel between Clay and Tyler, Greeley was acting as correspondent for the *Madisonian*, which was the President's mouthpiece in Washington. Early that winter, high quarters at the capital (probably John C. Spencer, Secretary of

War) urged him to take charge of that paper with a view to reconciling the factions and saving the Whig party. In many ways it was a tempting offer, and Greeley went so far as to suggest that he might edit the *Madisonian* for two months without pay, meanwhile looking over the ground. A short visit to Washington convinced him that Tyler and the "Virginia animals" had become so intent on plotting for 1844 that they wanted neither him nor harmony, and he went back to New York in disgust.[7]

Greeley was outraged by this outcropping of Tyler's ambition, but even so he felt that he must struggle to mitigate the strife within the party. The *Tribune* complained querulously about the President's lack of devotion to those principles of one term, retrenchment, and a sound currency that had been firmly lodged in the breast of the noble Harrison. Nevertheless, it supported Tyler's proposal for a National Exchequer until the irate Congressional Whigs knocked it into a cocked hat. It was not until the summer of 1842 and other sins by Tyler against Greeley's economic program, that the *Tribune* finally read the President out of the Whig party.

Tyler had no love for either a high tariff or distribution. Wielding a veto power that the Whigs in Congress had not the strength to defy, he forced them to abandon the distribution of public-land-sales' proceeds as the price of establishing a tariff that returned duty levels to approximately the rates of 1832. This summary destruction of Clay's land policy was gall and wormwood to the *Tribune*.

Greeley had written a stream of editorials on the tariff, had spoken for it, had lobbied for it in Washington, and the Home League (a protectionist organization in which he was deeply interested) had been given columns of space in the *Tribune*. He was well pleased with the tariff of 1842, but the fate of distribution was another matter.

At this time, Greeley regarded distribution as not only the key to internal improvements, but the very basis of protection as well. It would furnish money for roads and canals; it would siphon off a revenue that might otherwise come to be regarded as excessive and open the way to tariff reduction.[8] He "would see the grass knee high in Broadway," he told Weed, rather than abandon distribution, and now while he applauded the tariff he denounced the administration in the same breath. Webster, till now exempt from criticism, was abused for attempting to coöperate with the President; Tyler was stigmatized as a recreant and a traitor. Pacification was at an end. The *Tribune* had gone to war.

On September 16, 1842, the *Tribune* listed two recent post-office appointments under the heading "Appointments by Judas Iscariot."

Six days before the peppery editor had contrived this lucid head-line, he had placed at the masthead the name of Henry Clay. The campaign of 1844 had begun.[9]

Whig bickering and the failure of distribution were disappoint-ments to an editor who saw the Whig party as the great agency for achieving national welfare. But even if Greeley's zeal for the national interest was thwarted by the failure of the Whig program, he could find some measure of solace in the promotion of cultural nationalism. The *Tribune's* editor helped prepare and waxed en-thusiastic over Rufus Wilmot Griswold's *Poets and Poetry* in *America,* a thoroughly nationalistic anthology that was published in 1842. The *Tribune* also gave much space to patriotic speeches and published an American history that emphasized the peculiarly glorious principles of the American people. By 1844, Greeley was demanding an international copyright law as necessary to the development of a truly national literature. Thus, when political agencies failed, Greeley summoned culture to the service of the nation.

It was paradoxical that one of the nation's leading novelists should turn upon the glorifier of national literature, but so it was. Greeley had aroused the ire of J. Fenimore Cooper, and Cooper was a litigious character, especially where Whig editors who criticized him and his novels were concerned.

Greeley himself had dealt gently with Cooper, but during 1841 Weed had written for the *Tribune* a report of his own sufferings at Cooper's hands, in the course of which he had remarked that a $400 verdict had been the judicial measure of the worth of Feni-more's character. The novelist held the *Tribune* guilty of libel for publishing such an injurious statement and sued for $3,000. The result was a $200 judgment against Greeley, plus costs of nearly $100 more.

The *Tribune's* editor, smarting under this levy, wrote an eleven-column account of these legal proceedings that poked fun at Cooper and burlesqued the trial in masterly fashion. Greeley regarded this as a masterpiece, but Cooper was not amused. The angry author threatened another suit, but Seward volunteered his services as Greeley's counsel and the case never came to trial.

If Cooper's attack on Greeley was deftly turned into comedy, it had its serious side as well. The *Tribune's* editor protested vigor-ously against the court's refusal to allow proof of statements alleged to be libelous, and it is entirely likely that these protests played a part in the New York courts' subsequent ruling that the truth could be pleaded in justification by a defendant in a suit for libel.[10]

The "Cooperage" of the *Tribune*, as Greeley whimsically termed it, may have been a welcome distraction for the pugnacious editor. It gave the *Tribune* some excellent publicity, and as comic relief it mitigated the Whigs' political gloom. But by its very nature it could afford only a brief interlude in the never-ending struggle between Whig and Democrat that was not the center of Greeley's attention.

The Whig party was momentarily staggered by the Clay-Tyler break, but most of its elements soon rallied vigorously around Kentucky's favorite son. In New York State the Whigs were roundly defeated in 1841. The following year they tried to elect the elegant Luther Bradish governor over William C. ("Farmer") Bouck. "Cheerily, cheerily, brother Whigs throughout the Union," caroled the *Tribune* on election day, "NEW YORK ADVANCES TO THE RESCUE." Late that night the paper's groaning, swearing editor conceded defeat. Bradish had been headed by over 20,000 votes. A few more such rescues and the party would be in grave danger of disintegration.

New York City was in an even more parlous condition than that which afflicted the state. Handicapped by fraudulent registrations of aliens and torn by dissension over nativism, the Whigs made miserable showings in the mayoralty elections. What with commercial Whigs voting Democratic because of the Whig protective tariff of 1842, and conservative Whigs staying home when the word reform was mentioned by the party's politicians, Greeley had his hands full of local troubles. But he was a man who always went to meet trouble more than halfway, no matter from what quarter it came.

It was more than long-standing devotion that put Clay at the *Tribune's* masthead. Thurlow Weed was convinced that it must be Clay this time, and for Weed's political acumen Greeley had as great respect as in 1839. More important still, the Kentuckian's program was wholly satisfying. Clay was committed to a protective tariff, distribution, and internal improvements, while on the slavery question he was distinctly a moderate, opposing abolition while favoring gradual emancipation and colonization. Best of all, he came out against the immediate annexation of Texas, calling the proposal a breeder of foreign war and dangerous to the integrity of the Union. Clay's program was distinctly national, and nationalist Greeley was pleased by all its positions, not the least by those on slavery and Texas.

During the early 1840's, the *Tribune's* editor was still very cautious in his treatment of slavery. He was trying so hard to be scrupulously fair to the slaveholders that he even scolded a party of Pennsylvania Negroes for rescuing a fugitive slave from his captors. In those halcyon days, the *Tribune* waxed much more violent against alcohol and Mormonism ("the greatest imposture of the age") than it did against slavery. While it was clear that Greeley regarded the South's peculiar institution as a moral evil, it was also clear that he regarded it as of secondary importance compared to national harmony.[11]

Abolitionism, on the other hand, drew Greeley's fire. It was, he declared, a sectionalizing influence, disruptive of the Whig party and through that party of "our great national interests," dangerous to the Union because of the dissensions it bred. One of his main reasons for opposing the gag rule, which stifled antislavery petitions to Congress, was that the rule inflamed abolitionism and increased its menace to national unity.[12] Here, too, Greeley's concept of the national interest transcended his moral fervor.

Slavery, said Greeley, should not be made a political question. He was particularly opposed to the suggestion that Clay be abandoned as a candidate because he was a slaveholder, and that Webster or some other northerner be named in his place for the sake of antislavery votes. The exclusion of slaveholders from office, declared Greeley, would be contrary to the spirit of the constitution. Worst of all its results would be its tendency to sectionalize the Whig party, thus divorcing that party from its national outlook. One of the best ways to guard against such a possibility was to nominate slaveholder Henry Clay.

The best interests of the cause of liberty required Clay's nomination, Greeley wrote to a friend. "I consider him less a slaveholder than many a man who never spoke to a Nigger—less at heart than any of our public men." If the abolitionists would vote for him and then ask his aid as a friend to abolish slavery, they would get farther than by any other road. "But that," added Greeley shrewdly, "would not make Gerrit Smith or Alvan Stewart great men, and it will not be done."[13] Such comments made it obvious that, to Greeley, Clay's American System was the paramount issue of the campaign.

As in the case of slavery and abolition, Greeley's attitude toward territorial expansion was based primarily upon his concern for national harmony. Oregon was a case in point. He was all for the independence of Oregon under the protection of the United States and Great Britain. But like Benton, who would have placed a statue of the Roman god Terminus upon the highest peak of the Rockies, Greeley was convinced that the area west of those mountains should not be included in the United States. It was a vastly overrated country, he declared. Nothing that frost killed could be raised there. The cost of administering such distant territories would be exorbitant, the people there would be unable to exercise a vigilant supervision over their rulers, and their interests would inevitably diverge from those of the rest of the country. National unity would be weakened, and republican freedom would be shadowed by the menace of despotism.[14] This attitude doubtless owed some of its fervor to the penchant of expansionists for linking the acquisition of Oregon with the acquisition of Texas.

Greeley's opposition to the annexation of Texas paralleled his attitude toward Oregon, save that it was made more violent by the prospect of trouble in the Union, trouble that would be bound to arise if slavery were to extend its power. When Tyler began fumbling toward the Presidency in his own right by toying with the Texas question, Greeley was at once aroused. The extension of slavery into the Mexican regions would be the diffusion of "a horrible and guilty scourge," he declared as early as 1842, grandly disregarding the fact that the Texans already had slaves. There was no reason for acquiring Texas that was not just as applicable to Cuba, Canada, and California. "A man can always perceive urgent reasons for taking the property of his neighbors if at heart he covets it," sneered Greeley bitterly. We were big enough already; Texas was burdened by war and debt; her people were too improvident and idle to make good citizens; annexation would excite the bitterest jealousy and hostility, not only in England and France but also in the rest of the civilized world. The South was reported to favor such a move, but why should the South seek "to renew the perils of the Missouri controversy? to throw the whole subject of slavery into the arena of party politics and bar-room altercation?" Once the question was raised, Greeley asserted, "We shall be afloat on a fathomless sea of troubles. Let us be wise *now*." He even quoted with approval a Richmond *Whig* editorial arguing that the North would dissolve the Union before agreeing to annex such a magnificent addition to slave territory.[15]

But John Tyler, that "Deplorable Accident . . . by the visitation of God acting President of the United States," was determined to have the Lone-Star State. Popular sentiment was swinging in that direction, swayed by tales of British interference in the affairs of the Southwest. The South was anxious to counterbalance the North's growing power in Congress, and talk of splitting Texas into several states was in the air. Webster resigned from the government

in 1843 and shortly afterward the State Department made overtures looking to annexation. In March 1844, Texas sent a representative to Washington to discuss the admission of Texas into the
Union. Under the guidance of Secretary of State John C. Calhoun,
as ardent an expansionist as ever headed the State Department, a
treaty was prepared on April 12, 1844. Tyler sent it to the Senate
ten days later, with a message urging ratification. The Senate held
it up, and by so doing threw the whole issue into the Presidential
campaign.

As annexation loomed larger and larger, Greeley warned steadily
against it. Danger, he insisted, lay in this proposal to annex a vast
territory "in which the poisonous seed of slavery has already been
thickly sown." Again he declared that it would arouse a resistance
in the free states compared to which the Missouri excitement would
be a trifle; that it would fan "the embers of Abolition into a sweeping flame." The moral repugnance of the North to the extension of
slavery was deep and, once fully aroused, would be "uncontrollable
and overpowering." This tornado of moral wrath would sweep the
Whig party toward dissolution. And what was the purpose of it all?
The originators and most zealous advocates of annexation, Greeley
declared, were bent on a dissolution of the Union and the formation
of a southern confederacy, of which Calhoun would be the master
spirit.[16]

Thus Greeley took his stand against the acquisition of Texas and
the expansion of the slave power. It was to some extent a partisan
stand, for he saw clearly the evil influence upon Clay's chances, and
upon Whiggery itself, that would be exerted by a violent slavery
controversy. But it was also a matter of high principle. Greeley believed that, if America were to achieve greatness, she must remain
a united nation; that her leaders must continually dedicate her to
upholding the dignity of the individual; that she must advance
toward a condition of society that would guarantee equality of
opportunity for all. The expansion of slavery would mean a new
lease on life (his estimate was one hundred years) for a great social
evil, one that denied both equality and the integrity of the individual, and was an ever-present threat to the national interest.
The isue was clear, and upon that issue Greeley was prepared to do
battle.

"Well, we have but one more Annual Message to read before
Henry Clay's—that's a comfort." Thus spoke Greeley the prophet
on the eve of 1844. But despite this attitude of certainty, he did not
propose to take chances about the nomination. The *Tribune* kept
its favorite continually before the public as the candidate who best

represented the country's well-being, both by reason of his views on economic subjects and by the fact that his nomination would symbolize the Whig party's refusal to be divided sectionally over slavery.[17]

That winter Greeley went to Washington, where he lobbied for Clay and lower postage until the *Tribune's* errors in printing his dispatches ("lowest post of clerks" for "locust host of clerks," "father without hope" for "future without hope," and the like) drove him back to New York in a fine frenzy of exasperation. There his weak high-pitched voice proclaimed his devotion at Clay rallies. The *Tribune* announced publication of a sheaf of Whig songs and two tracts on the tariff. A month before the convention, it announced a special *Clay Tribune* that was to run throughout the campaign, six months for fifty cents.

Greeley was one of the 40,000 Whigs who met in council at Baltimore on May 1, 1844. He did not have to exert himself for the Old Prince, who was nominated by acclamation on the first ballot, but he did work hard to land second place on the ticket for a fellow New Yorker, a handsome vote-getter from Buffalo named Millard Fillmore. This effort ended in failure, and the *Tribune* laid the blame at Webb's door. Yet Greeley must have known, even though he later denied the fact, that the blame was Thurlow Weed's. The Albany boss, determined to have Fillmore run for governor that fall, turned thumbs down on his nomination for Vice-President.

Theodore Frelinghuysen, a sober jewel shedding a New Jersey light of Protestant piety, was set in the Whig diadem beside the scintillating Clay.[18] Greeley accepted the result without a murmur, but this did not disguise the fact that once more, in his insistence upon Fillmore for second place, the "adjutant" had shown a disposition to kick over the traces.

As Greeley girded his loins for the campaign, he kept a wary eye upon the doings of the opposition. Van Buren, possibly in agreement with Clay, had also published a letter opposing the annexation of Texas. His nomination would eliminate an explosive issue and Greeley hoped that he would be the Democrats' standard-bearer. But the Texas letter was fatal to Van Buren's chances. The Democrats turned to an expansionist from Tennessee, a dark horse named James K. Polk, and proceeded to run him on a platform that was definitely pro-annexation.

Polk was "Young Hickory" to the Democrats. Greeley contemptuously labeled him a third-rate politician and termed the nomination a "Loco Foco catastrophe." But a few days after this outburst of derision, he told his readers that a hard fight lay ahead.[19]

The *Tribune* carried Clay and Frelinghuysen at its masthead under the simple designation "Whig nominations." The opposition was always dubbed "Loco" or "Loco Foco," for Greeley refused to recognize it as worthy of the name "Democrat." What kind of democracy was it, he was wont to ask, that broke up abolitionist meetings, made a mockery of the franchise in New York City, and used its party organization to squelch the right of petition and freedom of discussion? At best, it was a hollow mockery and a sham.

Whig feuds, the splinter force of nativism, and a Democratic party that called itself high tariff in the North and low tariff in the South all played a part in Clay's defeat that fall. But the crucial issue was Texas. It was clear that Polk was more of an expansionist that Clay, and as the weeks went by popular opinion in the South turned toward the Democratic candidate. This was particularly true in Kentucky, and it began to look as though Clay might be defeated in his own state. The unhappy Whig candidate explained in his Alabama letters that he had nothing personally against annexation; that he would welcome Texas as soon as it could be done with safety to the Union. These letters saved him in Kentucky and Tennessee, but they were fatal in New York, where they alienated many antislavery Whigs. There the Liberty party candidate, James G. Birney, polled almost 16,000 votes. Clay ran some 5,000 behind Polk. And with New York went the election.

Greeley worked furiously during the canvass, writing, speaking, and attending political rallies in a whirlwind of activity. The *Tribune* showered thousands of tariff tracts down upon the heads of the just and the unjust. It denied incessantly the northern Democratic allegations that Polk was fully as good a tariff man as Clay. It stood staunchly for distribution of the proceeds of the public lands, declaring that distribution was essential to the maintenance of protection. It joined Fillmore and other Whig leaders in asserting that Clay's defeat would mean the annexation of Texas, and thereby would assure throwing the balance of power in the government into the hands of the opponents of American industry. Recognizing the power of Free Soilism (the Birney party in New York State had polled over 15,000 votes in 1843), Greeley sought to vitiate its strength by showing that, if it drew off votes from the Whigs, it would help the Democrats to add slaveholding Texas to the Union. The Alabama letters were a body blow to this last tactic, but Greeley put the best possible face on the matter by dogmatically declaring that they made Clay's opposition to annexation perfectly clear.

There was always due attention to the moral side of the campaign. Clay's character was being constantly attacked by the Democrats and as constantly defended by Greeley. Clay was not a drunkard or a gambler, the *Tribune* asserted, and he swore no more than had George Washington. On the other hand, Polk's grandfather, Zeke, had been a Tory; Polk himself did not dare deny his own draft-dodging in the War of 1812; and British gold was now pouring in to support him and a low tariff.

As the danger of defeat loomed closer and closer, Greeley was tempted to the verge of unscrupulous tactics. He had received a letter supposedly written and signed by James G. Birney in which the writer confessed to being secretly a Loco Foco. This was a forgery, but Greeley found a use for it. He published it in the *Tribune,* declaring that he had his doubts about its being genuine, but also stating that a friend was willing to bet $100 on its authenticity. And much as he loathed nativism, he accepted a deal between the Whigs and the New York City natives by which the city ticket was given to the latter in return for the promise of Clay votes. The staunch opponent of bigotry voted the nativist city ticket that fall, only to watch with bitter chagrin as the nativists proved faithless to their part of the bargain.[20]

Greeley wore himself down to such an extent that he broke out with a rash of boils at the close of the campaign. When it became clear that Clay had been defeated, the *Tribune's* editor felt that the universe had gone bankrupt. Overwhelmed by grief, he sobbed like a child. He carried bitter recollection of Nativist treachery for years, and for years he charged that Birney had deliberately thrown the election to Polk by declaring that annexation would be less likely under him than under Clay.

But despite his grief and anger, Greeley's head was still unbowed, his Whiggery untamed. He had once again bade defiance to the abolitionists during the campaign, warning them of the tremendous consequences of making slavery the "Main Question," and after the smoke of battle cleared away he paid his respects to the natives and owned his devotion to the Whigs. He was still as satisfied with the Whig party as a man could reasonably expect to be, he declared. It was as American as he wanted, as republican as any that made more noise about its republicanism, and in the campaign it had gloriously upheld the national welfare. "We have not found any party," he asserted, "whose objects are more comprehensive or beneficent, whose views are more enlightened or practical, than that with which we have hitherto acted whenever it has been in the field."[21]

Thus Greeley affirmed his loyalty to his party and to the Union while, with a mind made gloomy by defeat, he turned his gaze upon the future.

NOTES FOR CHAPTER 8

1. *Tribune,* Dec. 6, 1842, Jan. 28, 1843, Aug. 29, 1846, June 10, 14, 1848, Sept. 18, 20, 1850, and *passim.* Unlike Dickens who, in the *Christmas Carol,* took a fling at Americans in general for repudiation, Greeley strove to pin the blame upon the Democrats alone.
2. *Ibid.,* Apr. 23, July 20, 1841, May 6, 1844; Seward Papers, Greeley to Seward, Aug. 11, 1841; Gratz Autograph Collection, Greeley to Seward, Jan. 14 [1840].
3. G. G. Van Deusen, *The Life of Henry Clay* (Boston, 1937), pp. 342-54; G. R. Poage, *Henry Clay and the Whig Party* (Chapel Hill, 1936), pp. 34-106.
4. *Tribune,* Apr. 17, 1841, *et seq.* Greeley wanted a bank capitalized at $20,000,000. It would purchase and sell 60-day bills of exchange, purchase notes of other banks and send them home for redemption, and itself issue notes redeemable in specie. On the other hand, it would have no power of discount or loan, no foreigner could own its stock, only the mother bank would be a bank of issue, and all profits over 7 per cent would be shared equally by the stockholders and the government.
5. *Ibid,* July 17, Aug. 4, 1841.
6. Greeley Letters (U. of R.), Greeley to Seward, Aug. 11, 1841; *Tribune,* Aug. 9-21, 1841.
7. Greeley Letters (U. of R), Greeley to Weed, Dec. 7, 15, 1841; *Tribune,* June 29, Aug. 28, 1843.
8. *Ibid.,* July 9, 1842.
9. Greeley Letters (U. of R.), Greeley to Weed, Aug. 13, 1842; *Tribune,* July 6, 11, Aug. 2, 3of., Sept. 16, 21, Oct. 3, 25, 1842.
10. E. R. Outland, *The Effingham Libels on Cooper* (Madison, 1929), pp. 183, 195-97, 200.
11. *Tribune,* June 17, Aug. 2, 5, 1841, and *passim.*
12. *Ibid.,* June 10, 14, 1841,, Mar. 5, 1842, Sept. 9, 1843, July 2, 1845. Curiously, he interpreted the Supreme Court decision in Prigg *vs.* Pa. to preclude personal liberty laws, and therefore deplored it. Actually, the decision cleared the way for such state laws.
13. Greeley Papers (N. Y. P. L.), Greeley to O. A. Bowe, Aug. 21, 1843.
14. *Tribune,* Feb. 2, July 19, Nov. 25, 1843, Jan. 22, July 26, 1845.
15. *Ibid.,* Apr. 2, Nov. 14, 1842, May 16, June 12, 1843.
16. *Ibid.,* Mar 19, 1844.
17. *Tribune,* Aug. 22, Sept. 4, Dec. 6, 1843.
18. Patterson Papers, Weed to Patterson, June 16, 1844; *Tribune,* May 8, 1844, Sept. 24, 1845, Aug. 28, 1846.
19. *Ibid.,* June 1, 5, 1844.
20. *Tribune,* July 2, 1845, Aug. 27, 1846.
21. *Ibid.,* Aug. 16, Nov. 9, 16, 1844, Feb. 2, 1852.

CHAPTER 9

The Crystallization of a "Liberal" Program

THE ELECTION OF 1844 WAS A SAD BLOW FOR THE Whig party, both in New York State and in the nation at large. It meant the predominance of Democratic policies at Washington—the annexation of Texas, permanent establishment of the Sub-Treasury and, worst of all in Greeley's eyes, the lowered (Walker) tariff of 1846. In the state, where Silas Wright had beaten Fillmore by over 10,000 votes, the Whigs were left a prey to gloom and factional fights. Bitter quarrels over nativism and abolitionism rent the air; the *Courier* and the *Express* were snarling at Greeley's radicalism; the ardent friends of Henry Clay declared that during the campaign just passed Seward and Weed had knifed the Old Prince; there was even talk of applying a liberal coat of tar and feathers to the Albany Dictator. Prospects for an advance toward felicity under Whig guidance were not exactly encouraging, and Thurlow Weed's leadership of the Whig party in New York State trembled in the balance.

Weed was thoroughly aware of the difficulties of the Whig situation and cast about for a remedy. As skillful in assaying the trends of public opinion as he was in making political adjustments, he had a clear perception of the driving force of reform. He was convinced, particularly after the 1844 defeat, that salvation for the party lay in a championship of change and improvement, a program mild enough not to alienate most conservatives, but at the same time courageous enough to rally a respectable portion of the masses into the Whig camp. Cautiously he began to orient Whig policies in the general direction of reform.

With particular reference to state politics, Weed maintained and developed his pro-Irish, antinativist attitude, professed sympathy

for the antirenters and for labor, and urged upon the state constitutional convention (which met in 1846) a program of democrati-
zation that included the election of all state officers and full suffrage
for the state's Negroes. Nationally, the Dictator took a strong stand
for protection and internal improvements and against the extension of the slave power. With this program he undertook to rebuild
the shattered Whig morale and rescue the state and nation from
the Democracy. It was a program parts of which were sure to draw
fire from the ultraconservatives, those whose interests in property
rights and the status quo transcended all other considerations. Draw
that fire it did, but Weed saw it as the only hope for victory at the
polls.[1]

The youngest partner in the Weed-Seward machine (Greeley was
ten years Seward's junior and fourteen years younger than Weed)
was an enthusiastic supporter of the general policy laid down at
Albany. Greeley's ideas on reform ranged more widely than those of
Thurlow Weed. He was interested in it for its own sake and for
the nation's good, while to Weed reform was primarily a means to
political victory. The seed of future trouble lay in this divergence
of viewpoint, but for the time being the alliance seemed a good
one to the young editor and his *Tribune* as the organ of progressive
Whiggism swung into vigorous action in the city of New York.

Beginning with its first issue and continuing throughout the
decade, the *Tribune* flung forward the banner of social and political
reform in the city at the mouth of the Hudson. Perennially, as
election time rolled round, the voters were exhorted to turn out
at the polls, eliminate thieves and rascals (i.e., Democrats) and rebuke extravagance. "Away with the Common Council tea room and
refreshments, whereby a horde of political loafers are supported!"
Greeley thundered. "Away with the carriage riding at the expense
of the city. . . . Above all, no banquets at the Alms House, or
pleasure jaunts at the expense of the city."[2]

The *Tribune* demanded that the city's prisons be renovated, that
first offenders be separated from hardened criminals, that a decent
effort at reforming criminals be made and that flogging be abolished. It urged improvement of the city's educational facilities, the
establishment of more medical and normal schools, a free evening-
school service and more educational opportunity for the children
of the city's poor. The problem of poverty was given prominence
in its columns. A series of articles begun in the *Tribune* in August
1845 exposed the miserable condition of the workers in the city's
sweated trades. Greeley urged work relief for the destitute, declaring
that the city should find remunerative labor for the unemployed,

with honest workers paid at least the means of subsistence until they found better jobs, and with shirking paupers contracted out to the lowest bidder for ten-year periods, or put in a workhouse where indigence should "be tasked and punished."[3] And a host of other demands were raised as well. Greeley wanted laws to punish seducers and to close grog shops on Sunday. He wanted better street cleaning, and an investigation of the watering of the city's milk supply. There was scarcely an aspect of the city's life upon which the *Tribune* did not bend an anxious and inquiring eye.

While the fiery editor was crusading for civic honesty and for the city's general social improvement, he also flung himself with abandon into the maelstrom of New York City politics. The New York Loco Focos were accused of waste, extravagance, and the colonizing of outside voters at election time. Loco Foco aldermen who were making themselves rich out of fat city contracts were a special object of his scorn, and many a juicy scandal in the ranks of the city Democracy was unearthed by the *Tribune's* diligent reporters. According to Greeley, nine-tenths of the breeders of the hordes of swine that roamed and polluted the city streets were Democrats, a large proportion of the Democratic aldermen were rum sellers, most of the city's gamblers were "adroit and influential Democrats," and the Democratic party drew its main support from the city's brothels and bawdy houses. Greeley declared that the news of the Democratic victory in the mayoralty campaign of 1845 brought forth a spontaneous burst of applause from the prisoners of Blackwell's Island.[4] The Whig party, on the other hand, was composed of honest, high-minded men, whose sole aim was to serve the cause of the people.

Greeley's effort to identify New York City Whigs as the true democrats of the metropolis was never more clearly or more amusingly illustrated than it was in the mayoralty campaign of 1843. In that campaign, Whiggery was, as usual, made synonymous with righteousness, while the reigning Democrats were described as gerrymanderers, spoilsmen and plunderers of the city treasury. The Whig nominee for mayor, Robert Smith, was described as a paragon of civic virtue, a man who had risen to prominence by dint of sacrifice and toil from the status of a poor but honest "Stone-Cutter." Eighteen of the thirty-four Whig candidates for the city council were also mechanics, the *Tribune* insisted.

But if the Whig candidates were thus closely identified with the interests of the masses, what of the Democrats? Only five of the Democratic candidates for the council could be called mechanics, the *Tribune* asserted, and as for the reigning Democratic mayor, Robert H. Morris, who was seeking reëlection, the less said about his democracy the better for him. Morris was the feted and pampered product of the gilded salons of the rich, a man who had been born with a gold spoon in his mouth and had never earned a day's living by manual labor in his life.

"Whigs of New York! to the Polls," thundered Greeley.

If you love to contemplate the character of an honest, industrious, generous man, working his way forward from an apprenticeship of humble poverty to a position of competence, esteem and honor, by dint of cheerful, sturdy blows with his stone hammer,—retaining in his more fortunate days that hearty sympathy with poverty and misfortune of which his youth was so thorough a school, and regarding all his brother Mechanics as brothers indeed—if you prefer such a man to a pampered child of affluence and honors—the mere instrument and puppet of party—the author of the midnight desecrations of the forms of Justice to subserve the darkest intrigues of Faction, the deliberate contemner of the Will of the People . . . then go forth this day resolved to do a noble day's work for ROBERT SMITH, the People's candidate for Mayor!

Alas and alack! In the election, the honest Whig ex-mechanic ran some 6,000 votes behind the pampered aristocrat on the Democratic ticket and, even worse, the Democrats made almost a clean sweep of the city offices. On the basis of the *Tribune's* argument, it seemed that the voters preferred rule by the classes to rule by the masses. But Greeley insisted that wholesale fraudulent voting and violence at the polls (hundreds of Whigs had been literally "Beaten from the Ground") constituted the true explanation of the Democratic victory.[5]

One of the greatest political problems that Greeley had to face in New York City politics during the 1840's was nativism or, as it called itself, the American Republican party. This movement, though in part derived from a genuine desire for civic reform, had grown mainly out of tension between native-born and foreign elements over the organization of the city's school system. In January 1840, Governor Seward, after a serious study of the situation, had proposed a plan for New York that would have put the children of immigrants in schools where they would be taught by teachers speaking their own language and of their own religious faith. From then on, the fat was in the fire, with a bitter conflict developing over this proposal between Catholics and Protestants, natives and foreign-born. The American Republican party that was the outcome derived some strength from Democratic sources, but its main source was the bosom of the Whig party.[6]

Greeley's attitude toward the American Republican party was what might have been expected from a Seward-Weed lieutenant. He stood by Seward's school plan, but put more stress on the simple principle of equal rights for all religious sects. He attacked American Republican plans for requiring a twenty-one-year residence for the suffrage and for excluding naturalized citizens from office. He warned the Whigs that American Republicanism was a Democratic device for dividing and destroying the Whig party, and told them to shun as they would the plague any coalition with the nativists. At the same time, he staunchly and repeatedly denied Democratic charges that the Whig party itself was anti-Catholic and anti-foreign. In 1844, when the American Republicans were in control of the city government, the *Tribune* was the only Whig paper that stood out against "co-operation" between local Whigs and American Republicans in the effort to make Henry Clay President. Though Greeley finally voted the nativist local ticket in accordance with the terms of the bargain, he did so with the greatest reluctance. He was a real factor in ending this brief alliance and thus in maintaining the integrity of the Whig party in New York City.[7]

Reform and anti-Nativism were unpalatable to the ultraconservative New York City Whigs, and Greeley found himself locked in almost perpetual battle with the ultraconservative Whig organs. James Watson Webb of the *New York Courier and Enquirer,* and James and Erastus Brooks of the *New York Express* were loud in their denunciation of the Whig radicals, charging them with being wild-eyed utopians and with high-handed methods in controlling the New York City Whig organization. In 1846, the *Express* declared that "some of our best Old Whigs are in the Nativist ranks, driven there and kept there by the new Whig creed we, from time to time, have had from Albany." It denounced participation in the constitutional convention of that year under Weed-Seward direction, fought Weed's proposals for the gubernatorial nomination and proposed to destroy Weed's control over the party. In this it was joined by other conservative elements among the Whigs.[8]

Greeley replied vigorously to all charges and allegations made by the conservatives. Conservatism, he declared, meant sure death to the Whig party in the city and in the state as well. The *Express* and the *Courier and Enquirer* wanted to make the party into a kind of rich men's club, a club that would set its face stolidly against all reform. Now what the party had to have was a broad base of popular support. Where would this come from if, by oppos-

ing reform, it opposed the interests and convictions of the 100,000
New York voters opposed to slavery (80,000 of whom were Whigs);
the 40,000 antirenters (about 50 per-cent Whigs); and the thousands
of repealers and social reformers? And what chances of success
would a party have that served only the interests of the wealthy?
"Who can be so silly," asked Greeley, "as not to see that if the
Rich should belong to us *because* they are rich, the Poor are at
the same time repelled from us because they are poor."9

The running fight between Greeley and the Whig conservatives
had begun to smoulder during the early 1840's. It burst fully into
the open in 1846 and remained a more or less constant factor in
the New York City and State political situation down to the time
of the Civil War and even beyond. It was an historical forerunner
of the struggle between liberals and conservatives that was to
agitate the Republican party repeatedly, both in the state and
in the nation, during the twentieth century. Modern Republican
liberals will understand what Greeley meant when he wrote to
Weed in 1846, "You will find it impossible to resist the current
within as well as around you in favor of Reforms generally. We cannot go back into the last century, and it would be alike disgraceful
and disastrous to attempt it."10

Greeley's attempt to identify the Whig party with progress and
the Democratic party with depravity and obscurantism extended
beyond New York City. In his opinion, Democratic opposition to
the full enfranchisement of New York Negroes and to the gradual
abolition of slavery in Delaware proved that the party of Jackson,
Van Buren, and Polk was only a whited sepulcher. The *Tribune*
cast a withering gaze upon the Democrats in the House of Representatives, denouncing what it termed the debauchery of some, and
poking fun at others. Its remarks about "Sausage" Sawyer, "a brute
in manners and a booby in brains," who ate his lunch of sausages
back of the Speaker's chair, were so offensive that the Democratic
majority excluded *Tribune* reporters and correspondents from the
chamber. This insult made the pages of the paper fairly quiver with
rage and indignation.

Greeley's partisanship was often vindictive. Never was this better
illustrated than by his attacks upon Jackson's character at the time
of the latter's death in 1845. Greeley recognized Old Hickory's
courage and patriotism, but then went on to call him a "jobber in
human flesh," a "slave-trader," a protagonist of lynch law, and a
man guilty of "covert, rapacious treachery to Mexico." Jackson, the
fiery editor declared, had weakened the strongest bulwarks of civil
liberty and national faith. A long array of usurpation and violence

had marked his career as President, and these had left behind them terrible legacies of disorder, crime, and calamity for the country.

The violence of Greeley's assault on the dead President was the more unbecoming because, four short years previously, he had denounced the *New York Sun* for being so indecent as to make a relatively mild criticism of Harrison's administration while Old Tip's body "lay unburied." Small wonder that the *Evening Post* called Greeley's tirade against Jackson a disgraceful "ebullition of party spleen and impotent malignity."[11]

Greeley went to extreme lengths in attacking Democrats. The Whigs, on the other hand, were depicted as arrayed in robes of celestial purity. The *Tribune's* editor asserted that many Whigs were reformers (like himself), and that the strength of the Whig party lay in "its hold on the understandings of the intelligent, the sympathies of the humane, the conscience of the religious, among our people." When the party program failed to appeal to these elements, the Whigs were weak as water. They just wouldn't come out to vote unless there were strong moral reasons for preferring Whig success.[12]

Partisanship was natural, and vigorous manifestations of party spirit were expected during the middle period. It was useful, for it built up newspapers and confirmed the faith of that great number of voters whose loyalty rested upon prejudice rather than reason. It made Greeley a valuable Whig lieutenant. And, within limits, Greeley's ability to combine idealism with intemperate assault upon his political opponents fitted in with Weed's developing plan of campaign.

The two men united in approving the revision of New York State's constitution in 1846. Greeley felt it should be used as an instrument of democratic advance, and his program for the constitutional convention centered around judicial reform, liberty of conscience, increasing the number of elective offices, redistricting, and granting full suffrage to the Negroes. These were real improvements, even if the last two would be of political advantage to the Whigs.[13]

The constitutional revision of 1846 did much toward meeting Greeley's demands and the *Tribune* supported its adoption. The best that the convention did for the Negro, however, was to provide for submission of free suffrage to the voters. There the Democrats voted it down, for the Negroes who had met the imposed property qualification had customarily voted Whig.

Greeley had peddled ballots for Negro suffrage at New York's nineteenth-ward polling place all through a chill and rainy Novem-

ber day, and it had warmed him to see that many Whigs took the
ballots, but not one Democrat. It was conclusive proof, if proof
were needed, he declared, of the hypocrisy of Democratic pretensions
to an interest in the common man.[14]

Greeley's course in connection with constitutional revision demonstrated his useful propensity for compounding democratic idealism
with Whig political advantage. This was even more apparent in his
attitude toward internal improvements and the tariff.

Internal improvements were always a central feature of Greeley's
program. They meant the opening up of undeveloped areas, the
transfer of raw materials to markets and of manufactured goods to
the vast masses of consumers in the hinterlands. They meant national
growth and prosperity for all. Steadfast advocacy of highways, railroads, and canals would therefore rally votes for the Whig party.
In these convictions Greeley never wavered, and with some slight
modification the same could be said for his devotion to high protection.

There can be no doubt that the *Tribune's* editor was honestly
convinced that a protective tariff was essential to national prosperity. Again and again he sought to demonstrate that it was good
for industry because it promoted diversification and competition;
that it was essential to agriculture because it produced and maintained a steady market for farm goods; that it was equally essential
to labor because it furnished cheap consumers' goods, and by ensuring steady employment guaranteed the worker's property—his
job. Protection was society's answer to laissez-faire heartlessness and
to the brutality and fallacy of the Malthusian doctrine. "The
Genius of the Nineteenth Century—the expanding Benevolence and
all-embracing Sympathy of the age" demanded it. Protection and
freedom were linked together, as were slavery and poverty. The
students of Hamilton College were assured in 1844 that no modern
government could possibly act on the principle of free trade for as
much as ten years, and after Britain went on a free-trade basis
Greeley attributed the misery of the British working class to that
same vicious doctrine.[15]

Conviction as to the beneficence of the tariff led to certainty as
to the effects of various tariff bills. The Whig tariff of 1842, Greeley
declared, was the sheet anchor of the country's prosperity. The
Walker tariff that the Democrats proposed to pass in 1846 was
thoroughly and completely vicious. It would stifle the spread of
textile and iron manufacturing, and some branches of industry
would be entirely ruined. Thousands would be thrown out of work,
if the Walker bill went through.

When the passage of the Walker tariff produced no such great economic collapse, Greeley was ready with an explanation. The Loco Foco journals, he said, were chagrined at the way the manufacturers were receiving the bill. The Locos had hoped for a panic, shut downs, a general discharge of laborers that would enable them to raise the cry of "the Rich against the Poor." Instead, the manufacturers had received the blow with calm manliness. Only a few establishments had closed or were likely to close. A great deal of mischief would be done, but American manufacturers were not going to allow themselves to be broken down by this or any other tariff.[16]

Greeley asserted when the Walker bill passed that its evil effects would produce a hiking of the tariff wall for years to come. He combed the news for reports of factory closings and eagerly published the few items of that sort that he found. But most of the evils that he had predicted failed to materialize. The country's industry continued to develop, textiles and all. By 1847, Greeley was confiding to a private correspondent that the tariff was becoming less and less important—within ten years the need for it would largely disappear. This opinion was not publicized, however, and even the mood that produced it seemed to vanish when political exigency required.[17]

If Greeley's protectionism was a mixture of idealism and political practicality, so was his stand in regard to the striking events that were occurring overseas. Occasionally casting an eye on the foreign-born voter, the Tribune's editor staunchly raised his voice on behalf of the oppressed in foreign lands.

In 1845, Greeley proposed for a sentiment at an Irish Repeal meeting: "The right of the Irish People and of Every People to control their own domestic legislation." In consonance with this principle, he continued to show the liveliest sympathy for the Irish, especially when thousands of Sons of the Irish Famine flocked to America. He attended dinners for Irish relief and addressed Repeal Associations. He even presided over a meeting held in Tammany Hall for the purpose of raising aid for Ireland. In 1848 he gave time, money, and pages of publicity in the Tribune to the cause of Irish freedom, all this with the understanding that the Irish patriots were going to stage a real rebellion against British authority. Greeley was sure that Britain would bow to such defiance and set the Irish "millions" free, but this did not alter the fact that the Tribune was actually inciting a popular revolt against a friendly foreign power.[18]

The Tribune's editor declared that he did no more for Ireland that he would be willing to do for Poland or Italy. He hailed the revolutions that burst across Europe in 1848 with great satisfaction. The new day was dawning, the emancipation had begun. Russia and Turkey were the only despotisms that would outlast the first half of the nineteenth century. Everywhere else the people would be in control. He was sure that Italy was united, and that the Italians could easily maintain their independence against Austria. The German Republicans were bound to be triumphant, and Kossuth and the Magyars represented justice and freedom. Hungary was a distinct nation and the Hungarians a distinct race—the Magyars' position there being similar to that of the Normans in nine-teenth-century England. The European revolutions would in all probability produce "that European Federative Republic which is the next grand step toward the Federation of the whole world.[19] Thus the American people were bombarded by a farrago of fact and fancy. Greeley was as optimistic as Giuseppe Mazzini, or some twentieth-century World Federalist.

Such optimistic enthusiasm was hard to quell, despite the rough developments that awaited it. In December 1851, after Nicholas I of Russia had gone to the aid of Austria's Franz Joseph in crushing the Magyars, and reaction was triumphant throughout Europe, Greeley called for a reorientation of American foreign policy. Congress should declare that America deemed its own freedom menaced and its cherished principles assailed when one European despot aided another to crush a people struggling for liberty.

Greeley issued this call for an extension of the Monroe Doctrine just as the exiled Kossuth came to America on a desperate quest for aid. Greeley's imagination, excited by this mission, pictured the Magyar as the leader of a great and triumphant republican up-heaval that, within a few short months would send all the European monarchs "racing toward the Russian frontier for refuge." To facilitate such a marathon, the *Tribune* played a leading role in the collection of funds for the Hungarian expatriate.[20]

All this jubilation and encouragement was in the best vein of Greeley the reformer, the liberal nationalist, the shrewd news-paper man. It warmed the hearts of the compassionate, helped to give Whiggery a reputation for being progressive, and its dramatic presentation of dramatic events was good news value. But it was scarcely realistic. That Greeley's view of the 1848 revolutions was essentially, though safely, Quixotic, and that his ardor could be quickly cooled by working-class violence, was made clear by his reaction to the first few months of the upheaval in France.

The *Tribune* greeted the abdication of Louis Philippe and the proclamation of the Second Republic with a cheer. Here was the

work of the people, the true democratic impulse. Greeley's Fourierism had a resurgence as he noted the part which the master's teachings had played in this humane and well-nigh bloodless upheaval.
The *Tribune's* readers were assured that France had far outstripped
the United States in the race for freedom, that the French revolution meant constitutional, if not republican, government for all
of Europe save Russia, and that the world was on the threshold of
a mighty social regeneration for which France was furnishing the
great example.

Then came the bloody June Days of 1848 when the workers,
desperate as they saw the fruits of the revolution slipping from
their grasp, rushed to the barricades in a movement that has been
justly called a crusade for an ideal.[21] Paris became a shambles, with
ten thousand casualties in the street fighting, as General Cavaignac
smashed the laborers' uprising and established what was virtually
a military dictatorship.

Greeley's reaction to the news of this strife was one of horror and
disgust. He suggested that the gold of reactionary Russia had
seduced the workers and promoted their violence. On the other
hand, he regarded Cavaignac as a man of "humanity, clear judgment and decision of character." It was fortunate that the General
had been there to take control of a desperate situation.

After hearing from Dana and other correspondents on the scene
of events in Paris, Greeley admitted somewhat grudgingly that
there might have been good intent back of the workers' violence,
just as there had been in the case of the Dorr convulsion. The
misery of the French workers was great and it had driven them to
these excesses. But this "criminal" revolt had accomplished nothing,
could accomplish nothing. A solution was possible, however. The
means of salvation had been discovered, and ere long they would
commend themselves to general acceptance.[22]

Once again, confronted by a capitalist-labor conflict, even a distant one, Greeley retreated into Fourierism. Thereafter the news
from France receded into the background, although he did deplore
the rise of Louis Napoleon and the Second Empire.

Greeley's attitude toward the revolutions of 1848 was primarily an
emotional response, deriving from his optimistic convictions about
the progress of the age. Such a position was sadly deficient in realism, and was substantially isolationist (despite his bluster about
dictators and his call for a Monroe Doctrine corollary, he was no
proponent of interference by the American government in these
foreign troubles). It was also fashioned in accordance with a newspaper man's sense of dramatic and political values.

Like his attitude toward reform at home and freedom abroad, Greeley's stand in regard to Texas and the war with Mexico represented an idealism that was more or less tailored to the exigencies of Whig politics. It conformed closely to the line of argument that Weed developed in the *Albany Evening Journal*. In these matters the two papers appeared to complement each other.

The foreign policy of the Polk administration was as vigorous as its domestic policy was laissez faire, and Greeley had little patience with it. He grudgingly accepted Oregon to the forty-ninth parallel, because it was popular in the North and he was powerless to prevent this acquisition of territory, but Texas and the fruits of its acquisition were a very different matter.

Tyler had declared the election of 1844 a mandate from the people as to Texas, and Congress had responded with a joint resolution of annexation four days before the Virginian gave way to James K. Polk. Texas accepted the proffered hand, and Young Hickory had been in the White House less than a year when a territory more than three times the size of Italy was added to the Union. This was only a beginning. America was on the threshold of great events, some glorious and some portentous of tragedy.

The acquisition of Texas aroused Greeley's fears and forebodings to a high pitch. He regarded it as part of a southern plot to destroy the protective tariff and frustrate northern designs for internal improvements—these fell purposes to be accomplished by increasing the political power of slavery. It meant war with Mexico, whom it despoiled. And it was morally iniquitous, because it would breed an unjust war and extend a vicious institution.

Indeed, annexation pushed the *Tribune* into an increasing emphasis upon the horrors of slavery. The story of a fatal whipping was held up to the public gaze as one of the beauties of the peculiar institution. Washington was stigmatized as the "City of the Slaves." When an irate southerner defended slavery as morally good because, as he put it, slavery was "the great southern safety-valve of white female virtue," Greeley responded bitterly: "We feel the need of some guaranty that the wife shall not be torn from her husband, the daughter from her parent, either to dig in the cane brakes of Texas or satiate the demands of the great Southern 'safety-valve' of white female virtue."[23]

When Greeley predicted that the annexation of Texas would mean war, he spoke as a true prophet. Events moved swiftly. General Taylor was posted on the Nueces River. Polk sent Slidell to Mexico City on a quest for a settlement of grievances—and California. As it became apparent that the mission was fruitless, Taylor was ordered across the no-man's land between the Nueces and the Rio Grande and posted his batteries opposite the Mexican town of Matamoras. Mexican cavalry swooped across the river. There was a sharp encounter, and Polk asked Congress for war on the ground that American blood had been shed on American soil. The war was on. Democrats defended it as just and necessary. Whigs, North and South, denounced it, and the northern Whigs openly declared it a spoilsmen's war, undertaken for the sake of slavery.

Greeley's bitterness knew no bounds. The war meant, he declared, that "so far as our government can effect it, the laws of Heaven are suspended and those of Hell established in their stead." The *Tribune's* editor quoted Shakespeare to his purpose:

> Thrice is he armed who hath his quarrel just,
> And he but naked, though locked up in steel,
> Whose conscience with injustice is corrupted.[24]

From start to finish, the *Tribune* blasted the war and those who made it.

It was as though Greeley was bent upon destroying the nation's morale. The war was not two weeks old when he informed the country that "very cool heads" in Washington had told him that the administration planned to use the struggle as an entree for a war with Great Britain. The *Tribune* abounded in tales of horror, detachments cut to pieces, a cord of American arms and legs stacked up as the price of a victory, troops fighting in the midst of yellow fever, disease, and moral degeneration. It declared that Mexico was a miserable place, even when the guns were not going off. A letter from the camp near Buena Vista was published, describing campaigning as made up principally of mud, water, and barefoot marches over prickly pear, and Greeley urged young men to read and ponder this well before enlisting. Prominence was given to a poem which depicted Mexicans as battling fiercely but vainly for God and Liberty against

> The tyrant throng
> Rushing from the land of slaves.[25]

Peace was the *Tribune's* constant cry, a cry that was made the more strident by the victories of the war. What was the sense of fighting for the benefit of the slave power? Why try to subjugate the Mexicans? That proud people would fight on forever. Our conquests could well be compared to Napoleon's conquests in Spain.

If history was philosophy, teaching by example, we should take warning from Napoleon's fate.[26]

The Mexicans had no need of an Axis Sally. Greeley did the job, and did it well, if not with great effect. For while the *Tribune* was steeping itself in gloom, the American armies were moving in triumph from one battlefield to another. Taylor drove the Mexicans before him at Resaca and Buena Vista. Scott swept into Mexico City. Mexico's power and her fighting will crumbled together.

As peace loomed, Greeley declared that he for one would accept it on any terms, even to taking a thousand miles square of desert and hostile savages, so that Polk and Company could boast of their conquests and annexations. "Sign anything, ratify anything, pay anything," he shrilled, "to end the guilt, the bloodshed, the shame, the enormous waste of this horrible contest. Even with that most unfit, unstable boundary of the Rio Grande, give us Peace; and then for the reckoning!"[27]

"There never was a good war or a bad peace," intoned the *Tribune's* editor. Nevertheless, he had the most dire suspicions that sinister plans were brewing at Washington, being sure that Polk intended to gobble up vast reaches of territory below the Rio Grande. Even that river was too far south for Greeley's comfort. He declared stubbornly that the Nueces was the true Texas boundary until a lanky Illinois Congressman named Abraham Lincoln wrote him that this was inaccurate and was embarrassing the Congressional Whigs.[28]

If Greeley was wrong about the southern boundary of Texas, he was right about the government's plans for westward expansion. A year before the war began, he had noted that administration journals were talking of California as our property and of the possible necessity of taking it by war. The administration, he sneered, wished to extend the area of freedom by preparing another empire for the establishment of slavery. Steadily he echoed Lowell's bitter accusation:

> They jest want this Californy
> So's to lug new slave states in
> To abuse ye, an' to scorn ye,
> An' to plunder ye like sin.[29]

As the war came to a close, Greeley reluctantly accepted the fact that there would be a large increase in American territory, but he declared that that territory must never be subjected to the curse of slavery. This was a position that he had taken before the war began, and he held to it with great tenacity. Months before the Wilmot Proviso attempted to prohibit slavery in all lands that might be acquired from Mexico, Greeley's stand on slavery extension had been made clear.

Greeley hailed the Proviso's passage by the House of Representatives (it was killed in the Senate) as a solemn declaration against using the flag to protect the spread of a hateful institution. "It will stand, too!" declared the embattled editor. "Let us see what candidate for Congress from a Free State will venture to avow himself in favor of receding from the position thus taken!"[30] The *Tribune* was serving notice that it was ready for the fray.

No compromise on slavery extension was Greeley's cry, and he complimented Calhoun, ironically, on taking the same position. He scouted northern fears, and Calhoun's assertion that the Proviso would lead to the dissolution of the Union. The southern masses, he declared, were loyal to the nation rather than to slavery, and the South would never break away on the ground of slavery extension (a fallacy that colored all his thinking in the years that were to come). Greeley also denied Calhoun's claim that a southerner had a right to migrate with his property into any of the territories of the Union. Laws make property, the *Tribune's* editor declared, and if the Northwest Ordinance or some similar law forbade slavery, then where that law operated, slaves were not property. This reasoning would apply to the Proviso, when it became law.[31]

Congress might have power to establish slavery in the territories ceded by Mexico, Greeley admitted, for the power of Congress over those territories was full and comprehensive. But Congress had no more *right* to legalize slavery there than it would have to legalize "Polygamy, Dueling, Counterfeiting, Cannibalism or any other iniquity condemned by and gradually receding before the moral and religious sentiment of the civilized and Christian world."[32] Moral law forbade the extension of human bondage.

Greeley's hatred of slavery as wicked and immoral, coupled with the South's dislike of his darling project for erecting a high tariff wall around the United States, were primary factors in producing his stern opposition to slavery extension. Another factor which operated to further that opposition was his new program for dealing with the nation's public lands.

"The public lands," Greeley declared in 1844, "are the great regulator of the relations of Labor and Capital, the safety-valve of our industrial and social engine."[33] Until the election of 1844, Greeley believed that this "safety-valve" could be most effectively utilized by putting into practice Clay's scheme for distributing the proceeds of land sales to both the old and new states. But after that disastrous defeat, the *Tribune's* editor shifted gradually from distribution to an agrarian program that demanded free land for settlers, limited land sales and unalienable homesteads. This program was being energetically pushed by a group (George Henry Evans, Thomas Ainge Devyr, and others) calling themselves the National Reformers. Like the Fourierites, these National Reformers were utopians and escapists, and as such they inflamed the visionary ardors of Horace Greeley. Indeed, he came to regard this free-land program as a major step in the direction of Associational bliss.[34]

It would be unjust to regard Greeley's championship of land reform as simply another evidence of his utopian propensity. Utopianism clearly played its part, but there were also a number of practical considerations that pushed the *Tribune's* editor toward the same goal. Free land, he felt, would be a means of relieving the urban misery that weighed so heavily upon his soul. As land for the landless tempted population into the West, so it would stimulate the expansion of industry into new areas, and the country would prosper as the result of a steady and symmetrical economic development. The program of the National Reformers would eliminate the evils of land monopoly and absentee landlordism that he found so strikingly exemplified by the sad plight of the English and Irish tenantry, and by the antirent troubles in the Hudson Valley.[35]

There were also political angles in Greeley's espousal of land reform. Clay's defeat, which meant the killing of the distribution policy, gave free rein to Greeley's mounting hatred of land speculation, a hatred intensified by the part speculators had played in bringing on what he called the "Texas iniquity."[36] President Polk at the head of the triumphant Democracy was urging graduation of land sales, a policy that Greeley was quick to denounce as a direct encouragement to speculation and therefore opposed to the public interest.[37] Nor was it without significance to Greeley that, by 1846, eastern workingmen in considerable numbers were being attracted to the movement for land reform.

The attraction that free land held for Greeley lay in the fact that it combined good politics with social and economic progress. It would act as a safety valve, easing the plight of the workers in the East by its offer of an escape into the broad fields of the West. Limited land allotments and guaranteed homesteads would banish the land speculator and thus promote the development of national resources. As the tariff fostered industrial production, so free land would develop the enormous agricultural potentialities of the West and all Americans would be bound closer together in the beneficence of a general prosperity.

The South and its peculiar institution did not fit easily into the pattern of the *Tribune* editor's dream. Greeley knew that southern statesmen, in general, opposed free land. He also knew that the extension of slavery into the western regions would discourage free labor from going into those areas.[38] Hence the expansion of slavery must be sternly resisted, and the free-land policy must be enacted into law over southern protests, despite the involved risk of a desperate sectional struggle.

Strong in an obstinacy that was nurtured by his ignorance of southern life and southern institutions, Greeley was convinced that the South could be brought to accept both protection and free land. He was sure that the national patriotism of the southern masses and the economic benefits of national unity would nullify such secessionist dreams as were entertained by the southern oligarchy and that, the expansion of slavery having been halted, his own program of agricultural and industrial development would prevail in all sections of the country and become the basis of a transcendent national prosperity.

Greeley's conception of a liberal Whig program was based upon certain fundamental principles. Hostility to splinter movements, such as nativism, abolitionism, and southern ultraism, was one of Greeley's tenets. He was also sternly opposed to the extension of slavery into any new territories. Positively, he stood for protection, internal improvements, and judicious championship of nationalist and democratic movements in the lands across the sea. Last but not least was the idealistic motif in domestic affairs, ranging from specific projects of moral reform and civic betterment to phalansteries and free homesteads.

There were threats aplenty to Greeley's hopes and dreams, threats in the South's opposition to protection and free land, in the hostility of eastern capitalists to a land policy that might drain the labor supply, in the expansion bound to follow a successful war with Mexico. Southern planters and eastern capitalists held no terrors for Greeley. Their opposition, he felt, could be minimized and overcome. But the Mexican War was a different matter. There he shared the gloom of Ralph Waldo Emerson, who had predicted that Mexico would be like the arsenic that a man swallows but that brings him down in turn. It made not the slightest particle of difference that the struggle ended with California and the Southwest firmly in the nation's grasp. "The War was a bad business," Greeley wrote in July of 1848; "the peace is little better; and this the country sees and feels despite the boasting of the President."[39]

NOTES FOR CHAPTER 9

1. Weed's course might well be studied by twentieth-century Republicans.
2. *Tribune,* Apr. 27, 1842, Mar. 18, 1847.
3. *Ibid.,* July 29, 1842, Dec. 26, 1845.
4. *Ibid.,* Apr. 12, 16, 1845, Aug. 20, 26, 1846.
5. *Ibid.,* Apr. 10-12, 15, 26, 1843.
6. L. D. Scisco, *Political Nativism in New York State* (N. Y., 1901), pp. 27-31; Van Deusen, *Thurlow Weed,* pp. 116-18; *Tribune,* July 21, Nov. 6, 1843.
7. *Ibid.,* Nov. 9, 15, 1843, Apr. 6, 19, May 22, June 1, 11, 17, Aug. 6, 24, Oct. 8, 17, 1844, Feb. 18, Mar. 15, 26, Apr. 1-18, Dec. 2, 1845; Scisco, *op. cit.,* pp. 49-54.
8. *Tribune,* Apr. 18, 1843, Apr. 11, 1844, May 1, 1846, July 14, 28, Sept. 20, Oct. 28, 1847; *New York Express,* 1846, *passim;* P. Hone, *The Diary of Philip Hone* (2 vols; N. Y., 1927), II, 823, 835.
9. *Tribune,* July 31, Aug. 11, 18, 26, 1846.
10. Weed Papers, Greeley to Weed, May 14, 1846.
11. *Tribune,* Apr. 26, 1841, June 17, 19-21, 1845.
12. *Ibid.,* Mar. 6, Sept. 29, Oct. 19, 1847.
13. *Ibid.,* Jan. 30, 1844, Jan. 9, May 21, June 18, 1845, Mar. 12, Oct. 12, 14, 1846.
14. *Ibid.,* Mar. 12, Oct. 12, 14, 1846; Greeley, *Letters from Texas* (N. Y., 1871), p. 55; D. R. Fox, "The Negro Vote in Old New York," *Pol. Sci. Quart.,* XXXII (June 1917), 252-75, and *Decline of Aristocracy in the Politics of New York* (N. Y., 1919), p. 269, note.
15. Atkinson, *op. cit.,* pp. vii-xvi; Greeley, *Address at Hamilton,* pp. 19f., *Protection and Free Trade* (pamphlet), *Hints Toward Reforms,* pp. 232f., 348f.; *Tribune,* Feb. 25, Apr. 24, 1852.
16. *Ibid.,* June 13, 1843, Feb. 11f., July 6f., Aug. 17, 1846.
17. *Ibid.,* Aug. 1, 8, 10, 22, 1846; Greeley Papers (Lib. of Cong.), Greeley to Brockway, Nov. 19, 1847; F. W. Taussig, *Tariff History of the United States* (8th ed., N. Y., 1931), pp. 145-47.
18. Greeley Letters (Alb. State Lib.), Greeley to Wm. Cooney, Mar. 23, 1845; *Tribune,* Aug. 26, 1845, Apr. 25, May 17-19, July 24, 27, 28, Aug. 19, Sept. 12, 1848.
19. *Ibid.,* Jan. 14, 1846. May 9, 23, 1848, May 23, 1850.
20. *Ibid.,* Dec. 11f., 1851.
21. D. C. McKay, *The National Workshops* (Cambridge, Mass., 1933), pp. 149, 155-56.
22. *Tribune,* Mar. 20f., Apr. 4f., July 13f., 1848.
23. *Ibid.,* Mar. 1, 7, July 31, Dec. 17, 1845, Jan. 8, Feb. 5, Mar. 13, Aug. 11, 18, 19, 21, 1846.
24. *Ibid.,* May 13, 1846.
25. *Ibid.,* May 23, Aug. 17, Oct. 18, 1846.
26. *Ibid.,* Mar. 18, Oct. 5, 1847.
27. *Ibid.,* Jan. 27, 1848.

28. *Ibid.*, Feb. 26, June 29, 1848.
29. *Ibid.*, June 13, 17, Dec. 17, 1845, July 1, 1846.
30. *Ibid.*, Aug. 12, 1846.
31. *Ibid.*, Feb. 22, Sept. 8, 1847, July 1, 1848.
32. *Ibid.*, July 3, 1848.
33. *Ibid.*, Jan. 25, 1844. Cf. July 10, Oct. 24, 1846.
34. *Ibid.*, May 15, Oct. 2, 1847.
35. *Ibid.*, June 21, July 30, Aug. 22, Sept. 4, 1844, Sept. 16, 1845.
36. *Ibid.*, Mar. 19, 1844, July 17, 18, 23, 1845.
37. *Ibid.*, Dec., 1845, *passim,* especially Dec. 4. See also Jan. 23, 1846.
38. *Ibid.*, Jan. 23, 1846, Jan. 28, July 24, 1848, Feb. 25, 1854.
39. *Ibid.*, July 27, 1848.

CHAPTER 10

A Strong-Minded Adjutant

THE VIOLENT PARTISANSHIP OF THE *TRIBUNE'S* editor, his stand on the tariff and slavery, the tone of moral righteousness that he gave to Whiggery, all fitted in very well with Weed's program for the Whig party in New York State. The Man in the White Coat was furnishing powerful support to the Whig cause. Within a decade, the adjutant of 1838 had developed into a powerfully ally. This was a remarkable metamorphosis. But it was not one that Weed viewed with unalloyed satisfaction.

For one thing, the Albany Dictator was disturbed by his lieutenant's penchant for rushing into all manner of reforming schemes. Himself a conservative whose reforming interest was largely for political advantage, Weed felt that Greeley went altogether too far in his search for a better world. It was all right to sponsor constitutional revision and Negro suffrage; it was expedient to oppose the extension of slavery; Greeley's opposition to capital punishment could do no harm and might win votes among the preachers. But Fourierism was, in Weed's estimation, a cockeyed dream that reflected discredit on those who were deluded by it, temperance was altogether too dangerous to be taken up as a political issue, and the Albany leader never could get up any real enthusiasm over land reform. Reformers, in Weed's opinion, were definitely a queer lot, and he looked upon Greeley's reforming activities with mounting anxiety and concern, all the more so because private remonstrances made Greeley declare morosely that Weed was taking him to task like a schoolboy.[1]

Greeley's penchant for reform might not have been so distressing to the senior partner had it not been coupled with an itch for public preferment, an affliction that broke out as the *Tribune* increased in circulation and influence. It was a disease for which the Whig boss appeared unable to find a remedy. Certainly Greeley's nomination for state printer in 1843 was no palliative, his election by a Democratic legislature being an obvious impossibility. Three years later, Greeley wanted to be a delegate to the constitutional convention but "it proved best," as he wrote somewhat cryptically to his friend Schuyler Colfax, not to run him from the counties of his choice. Indeed, there seemed to be no county from which he could run, and so he reluctantly stood aside. That same year he suggested the possibility of his having second place on the state ticket, but Weed side-stepped that also. Greeley would be the best candidate, purred the Dictator, if he didn't have so many irons in the fire. The capital Greeley had invested in reform, continued Weed, was "drawing no interest." There could be no clearer intimation that Greeley's reforming zeal was standing in the way of his political preferment.[2]

The Albany boss could easily reason that it was hard enough to get conservative Whigs to support Seward. What help would Greeley be to the ticket—a man who, in the opinion of such papers as the *Courier* and the *Express* and the *Utica Gazette* was a crazy fanatic who had just put on the cap and bells in the matter of land reform? Weed himself exchanged hard blows with the conservative Whig press, but he did so only when his authority was challenged. Greeley's insults to Brooks and Webb were not infrequently gratuitous. What, for instance, was the use of his celebrating the installation of new type for the *Tribune* with the remark: "If there be one thing that we dislike above all others, it is a flimsy, chocolate-colored, half-illegible, pitchforked-together apology for a newspaper—like the *Express* for example."[3] Stirring up the animals just to hear them bellow with rage was something that the Dictator deplored.

By 1847, Weed was thoroughly uncomfortable about the junior partner's extremism and had formed the habit of disclaiming it, sometimes openly and sometimes by indirection. Seward, who liked Greeley but considered him ultrasensitive and temperamentally unfit for political leadership, thought that these disclaimers were doing good. Then the *Tribune's* editor gave fresh cause for alarm. He laid himself open to attacks from religious conservatives by printing columns of favorable notice concerning religious revelations by a twenty-year-old zealot, and Seward wrote disgustedly to Weed that Greeley was provoking everybody and, to cap the climax had kindled the fires of religious fanaticism against himself. "If Webb had any sense or the *Express* any honesty," declared the Auburn statesman, "the *Tribune* would lose all."[4]

Greeley's divagations from the Weedian line of conservative-liberalism were only one manifestation of his unwillingness to re-

main a subordinate in the triumvirate. He became increasingly
fertile of suggestion and criticism as to Weed's management of
political campaigns, and was not backward about tendering opinions
regarding candidates. His criticisms, which were sometimes blazoned
on the editorial page, became more decided as the *Tribune's* influence expanded. At the same time, what he regarded as his constructive views were tendered with more and more emphasis and
decision. This was strikingly manifested in connection with the
Presidential campaign of 1848.

As the campaign of 1848 loomed up on the horizon, Greeley
surveyed the political situation and found it decidedly in a state
of flux. Political ambitions, Texas, and the Wilmot Proviso had
split the New York Democracy into warring factions, with the antislavery radicals (Barnburners) following Van Buren, while the
more aristocratic conservatives (Hunkers) fought under the flag of
William Learned Marcy. This split was reflected in similar squabbles
elsewhere through the Union and, by the short session of 1847, the
Democratic majorities in Congress had become fluid and unstable.

This Democratic disintegration was hailed with satisfaction by
politicians of the opposite faith, but their joy was somewhat dimmed
by the fact that Whiggery ("the Universal Kingdom of Koondom,"
as Daniel S. Dickinson termed it) was in an equally bad way. Never
an easy alliance of widely varying interests and convictions, it, too,
was suffering from the injection of slavery into politics. Conscience
and Cotton Whigs were splitting Whig radicals and conservatives
still further asunder in New York State, and similar crevices were
appearing throughout the North and West.[5]

Greeley was convinced by what he saw that both the old parties
were on the verge of breaking up, and that new ones would form
along radical and conservative lines. The best party the United
States had ever seen could be rallied in plenty of time for 1852, he
told his friend, Beman Brockway, on a platform of land reform,
labor reform, and, he hoped, abolition of the army and navy.[6] It
was evident from the tone of this letter to Brockway that Greeley
still believed it possible to avoid slavery expansion as a political
issue.

But 1852 was not 1848 and somehow, someway, the Whigs had to
elect a President.

There were heroes at hand, as ready and willing as David Copper-
field's friend Barkis. Ambition was stirring among the generals
and these "journeymen throat-cutters," as Greeley called them,
campaigned during the latter phases of the Mexican War with one
eye fixed in the direction of the White House. General Winfield

Scott, hero of the Mexico City campaign, was avid for political preferment. Zachary Taylor—"Old Zack," "Old Rough and Ready" —victor of Resaca de la Palma and Buena Vista, had the Presidential bee in his bonnet, put there by Thurlow Weed (among others) in the spring of 1846, stirred to a constant buzzing by certain Congressional "Young Indians" among whom was Abraham Lincoln, and by Blue Grass and New Orleans politicos under the aegis of Kentucky's Senator Crittenden. General William Jenkins Worth, catalogued by Greeley as "the last of our military Illuminati who has chipped the shell of his timidity and given birth to the chicken of his wisdom," became vocal on civil policies in the spring of 1848.[7] The army, as one Democrat sourly observed, had become little else than a Whig political camp. Greeley, averse on principle to things military, found this state of affairs little short of disgusting.

Greeley's ideal candidate, he told the country half-seriously, would be an abolitionist and a teetotaler, a rigid observer of the Ten Commandments, an advocate of internal improvements, protection, perpetual peace, economical government, military and naval retrenchment, and unalienable homesteads.[8] No such paragon being available, he turned to an examination of the material at hand.

The *Tribune's* editor favored Thomas Corwin (Senator from Ohio, a witty and eloquent opponent of the Mexican War) for President, with Clay for second place. But after visiting Ohio and consulting with Whig leaders there on the best means of stopping Taylor, Greeley became more and more openly pro-Clay.[9] This was particularly true after the Old Prince made a speech at his home town of Lexington in which he denounced the war and came close to climbing aboard the Wilmot Proviso. From that point on, you could even tell by looking at Greeley's boots and breeches, so Charles A. Stetson wrote to Weed, that the editor was in favor of *Clay* and no friend of *Tailor,* a comment that Mary Greeley would undoubtedly have labeled "bad joke."

But Greeley's support of Clay did not ring quite true. Seward thought in January 1848 that Greeley hoped for nothing more from Clay's candidacy than the exclusion of Taylor; that the *Tribune's* editor was secretly preparing the ground for John McLean of Ohio. This report was widely spread, so widely that Greeley thought best to deny it vigorously in the columns of the *Tribune.*[10]

Actually, Greeley was carrying water on both shoulders in his desire to prevent Taylor's nomination. Publicly, he was strong for Clay. Privately, he was doing his best to foster a McLean boom, and doing it so well that McLean's friend, J. B. Mower, was convinced

that the *Tribune's* editor was practically in the McLean camp. Deep
down in his heart, Greeley still wanted to see Corwin get the
nomination.

Greeley's flirtation with the McLeanites prompted Mower to
counsels of Machiavellian slyness. Greeley loved praise, Mower wrote
to McLean in his overpunctuated style. Indeed, he was "very particularly fond of it. Now judge, can't you write one of your very best
epistles, in answer to this, of mine, and take special care, to praise
his talents, his honesty of purpose, and his spotless integrity, so
that, I may show it to him. *You have him then.*"[11]

It is not unlikely that the ambitious old Justice wrote to Greeley,
but the *Tribune* went blithely on supporting Clay. Harry of the
West came to New York for a March week end (followed up the bay
by what his friends declared was a white eagle, but was more
probably an overgrown gull), and the *Tribune* gave great prominence to his reception. Greeley wanted the Whigs in the New York
State legislature, where Clay strength predominated, to come out for
the Kentuckian, but this Weed sternly opposed. Balked in this
project, the *Tribune's* editor vigorously sponsored a Clay-Seward
ticket, and went down to Washington where he tried hard to stir
up Clay sentiment. While there, he wrote a long letter to Clay,
posing as his fervent supporter but rather subtly pouring cold water
on his hopes by emphasizing the strength of the opposition. In this
letter, Greeley discounted Seward as a Vice-Presidential possibility,
an attitude the reverse of that which he was displaying in New York.
The machinations of the Man in the White Coat were so mul-
tifarious that they bred a certain amount of confusion in the minds
of the spectators. "Behold Horace Greeley," exclaimed the disappointed Mower. "I hope he will come out *right side up*, but I
confess that he acts very queer at times."[12]

There can be no doubt that Greeley's personal preference was
Corwin. He told Margaret Fuller that this was the case, just before
the Whig convention met, and he wrote as frankly to Margaret as
he did to anyone. But he deemed it more realistic to support Clay
with Seward for Vice-President, as the ticket best calculated to dis-
appoint the hopes of the Taylorites. McLean, whom Greeley actually
disliked, and stigmatized privately as "cautious" and "cold-hearted,"
was a poor third on the editor's list of candidates. Scott came next,
barely better than Taylor, who was not even on the list. Military
candidates, Greeley told Alvah Hunt, "will lead to wars for the
manufacture of Hero-candidates which, being a foreign manufacture, I am opposed to."[13]

"The more I see of Taylorism the more I don't like it," Greeley had written to Weed in the summer of 1847, and this attitude had deepened into vigorous hostility as the passing months had seen the Taylor movement grow. "I fear we are to have the old savage put upon us," he snarled to one of his correspondents, early in 1848. The *Tribune's* editor wanted no military hero, especially one who had never taken enough interest in politics to vote, and he had only scorn for what he called Taylor's "Rough and Ready, or rather rough and tumble way" of getting himself nominated by any group that was willing to put him up. "We cannot with any decency, support Gen. Taylor," Greeley wrote to Colfax two months before the Whig convention met. "His no-party letters, his well understood hostility to the Wilmot Proviso; his unqualified devotion to slavery; his destitution of qualifications and principles, place him at an immeasureable distance from the Presidency. . . . If we nominate Taylor, we may elect him, but we destroy the Whig party. The offset to Abolition will ruin us. I wash my hands of the business."[14] In this letter, Greeley was asserting far more than he knew about Old Zack's character and policies.

Seward, who also had little love for Taylor as a candidate, wrote to Weed in Delphic fashion that he would not care to be second to a nomination "that will emasculate the virtue of our party."[15] But in the last analysis Seward was content to leave it all to Weed, who was determined to place the accolade on Taylor's shoulder. Horace Greeley was not content and, though not so suave, he could be quite as stubborn as Weed.

The Democrats met in national conclave at Baltimore on May 27 and nominated Lewis Cass of Michigan. Cass was an opponent of the Proviso and an advocate of squatter sovereignty as the best means of settling the question of slavery in the territories. He was a patriot, earnestly trying to find the solution of a great national problem, but Greeley promptly caricatured him as a free-soil apostate, a Michigan Doughface, a reckless, dangerous demagogue and land speculator who, for his own selfish purposes, had donned the Black Cockade.

The Whigs met in the Chinese Museum Hall at Philadelphia on June 7. A week before the delegates gathered, Greeley wrote to Clay that Taylor's nomination seemed assured, but that it could be defeated if Clay's friends would unite on a third candidate.[16] Couched in the language of loyalty, this letter was a bid for Clay's withdrawal and for settlement on a compromise choice, but the Old Prince refused to budge. He was unwilling to relinquish any chance, however remote, of gaining the long-coveted scepter.

The Philadelphia convention was a politicians' convention, managed effectively from the start by Weed and his ilk. The Clay delegates, bitter but helpless, struggled vainly to stop the ears of the majority to the siren song of availability. Taylor was nominated on the fourth ballot and then, as a gesture of appeasement, the convention gave second place on the ticket to Millard Fillmore, a mildly antislavery friend of Clay, but a rival of Seward in New York State politics. There was no platform. The Whig party, discarding its old leaders and shutting its eyes to the problem of slavery expansion, was appealing to the voters simply on the record of a military hero.

Greeley was at the convention, but after Taylor's nomination he shook the dust of the city off his feet without waiting to see what happened to second place.

The *Tribune's* editor made his way back to New York, divided between disgust at the result and sorrow over Clay's disappointment. The convention had been a slaughter house of Whig principles, he told readers, and to anyone devoted to those principles Taylor's nomination seemed "though perfectly true, nevertheless impossible." Like Webster, he branded it as unfit to be made. There was, indeed, only one comfort to be derived from the result.

Thank God [said Greeley] that the day has at length come in which no man can hope to advance his own interests by defaming and slandering Henry Clay. . . . On his quiet farm at Ashland, calmly and in Christian faith and hope, he awaits his summons from the shadowy and perishable to the perfect and eternal. His has been a long, eventful day, of mingled sun and storm; but the tranquil evening has come at last, and it is serenely glorious with all the stars of Heaven.[17]

Clay was not quite so ready for the summons to the hereafter as Greeley indicated, but he must have appreciated the warmth of this tribute.

Even Greeley's acceptance of Fillmore's nomination (which was anything but pleasing to Weed and Seward) betrayed his wrath over the outcome at Philadelphia. Fillmore was all the more acceptable, sneered the junior partner with a backward glance at Weed, because he had not been part of the plan.[18]

Three years later, when Greeley could look back upon the Philadelphia doings with somewhat greater equanimity, he declared that they had cured him forever of any lingering belief in national conventions. Charles Lamb, said Greeley, had expressed his sentiments perfectly:

"All full inside?" asked a looker-on at the door of a London omnibus.

"Can't say for the rest," responded Lamb from one of the seats, "but that last piece of oyster pie did the business for me."[19]

Greeley's philippics against the Taylor nomination clearly threatened a bolt. He might support Taylor, he admitted, if that was the only way to defeat Cass, but if approaching developments should prove "that the Free States are now ripe for the uprising which *must* come sooner or later, and which this nomination had done much to precipitate, why then *we* are ready. Our present impression is that the time has not quite arrived—but we shall see."[20]

The development that was to test the readiness of the free states for an uprising was headed by the Barnburners, that Democratic splinter group which, under Van Buren's leadership, was undertaking to establish a national Free-Soil party. On June 22, the New York State Free-Soilers met at Utica and nominated Little Van. This was but the forerunner of a national convention which met at Buffalo in August, nominated Van Buren with Charles Francis Adams as his running mate, and pledged itself to "fight on, and fight ever" for "free soil, free speech, free labor and free men." The old Liberty party of the Birneyites then merged with the new Free-soilers, and apparently a new and significant party had been born.

Throughout the summer months and well on toward the close of September Greeley pursued what Weed called a course of "semi-neutrality" as between the Free-soilers and the Whigs. Privately, the *Tribune's* editor told Clay that he supposed he would have to support Taylor in the end or be broken pecuniarily and otherwise. Years later, he avowed that protection had been the rock which had barred his passage from the Whig party to the party of free soil. Undoubtedly both of these factors weighed heavily upon his mind. It is also highly probable that Van Buren's refusal to accept the homestead plank in the Buffalo platform cooled Greeley's enthusiasm for the free-soil movement. Land reform had become extremely important to him. "A whole Future of good and evil is involved in it," he told Caleb Smith.

But all that the general public could know in the summer of 1848 was that Greeley was ostentatiously refusing to commit himself, and that Taylor and Fillmore remained conspicuously absent from the *Tribune's* masthead. Its editor adjured "gentlemen of Wall Street and shrewd, sharp caculators generally" to notice that the people were determined to check the spread of slavery, and that the Whig party could not stand and ought not to stand in the free states unless it unequivocally recognized that fact. He said repeatedly that he would vote for Taylor if that were necessary to beat Cass, but he refused to come out unconditionally, alleging first that he must wait until the Buffalo convention had clarified the situation, second that political independence gave him an advantage in maintaining what he regarded as the all-important resistance to slavery extension. "We wish to be distinctly understood on this point," declared Greeley. "If Slavery could be excluded from New-Mexico and California by shivering the Whig party to atoms, we would not hesitate a moment, but insist on that sacrifice."[21] The Free-soilers were given generous and repeated praise for their sincerity and high-mindedness, and repeatedly he indicated that he might vote for Van Buren. And yet, when they urged him to join them, he declined.[22]

Thurlow Weed watched the tergiversations of the junior partner with deep concern, but treated them with superlative tact. Of course it was right, he told Greeley, to encourage the Barnburners. They would spur the Democratic party into more vigorous action against that great evil, slavery. He asked Greeley for help in drawing up an appeal to the antislavery Whigs to vote for Taylor, and the *Tribune's* editor, his vanity touched, produced a draft with the caution that his handwriting must not be seen by anyone.

During August and September, Greeley went out to Lake Superior to see some copper mines in which he had an interest. He came back almost decided to vote for Taylor, but still glorying in his position of independence and power. He could have been the Free-Soil party's oracle with any extent of circulation, had he said the word, he told Colfax. One bugle blast, if he blew it, would shake down "the whole rotten fabric" of the Whig party. But fidelity to men he loved kept him clinging "to the putrid corpse of the party butchered at Philadelphia," a party that had never loved him. He would probably lose both friends and subscribers as it was and end up "where 'he that doubteth' belongs. Well, who cares?"[23]

As the editor of the *Tribune* indulged himself in vainglorious boasts and false humility, Weed played the last card for his support. A candidate was needed to fill out an unexpired term (ninety days) in the Thirtieth Congress, and Weed asked Greeley to run as a public service. Greeley was flattered, but fearful lest the cry of bargain and sale be raised against him.

Thanking you for your kindness and aware of your great influence [he wrote to Weed], I request you not to favor my nomination farther, for reasons which must be obvious, and at the same time to absolve me from all promises to put up the (Taylor) ticket. I will do all that my judgment approves to promote Taylor's election, though I expect to be driven into opposition before he has been a year in power; but it shall not be said that I was "coaxed" or "courted" or "enticed" into anything beyond endurance of the banditti, who are about to get possession of the government. Their known enemy I must and will be.[24]

It may be that there was further discussion of detail, but certainly after this letter no further obeisance had to be made, either to modesty or to principle. And in no time at all Greeley was on the ticket.

On September 27, 1848, at a great Whig ratification meeting in Vauxhall Gardens, Greeley declared that, since no chance remained of electing any other man than Taylor or Cass, he would henceforth support the Philadelphia ticket. He still felt that Taylor's nomination had been "unwise and unjust," but loyalty to Fillmore, and to Hamilton Fish and George W. Patterson (the heads of the Whig state ticket), together with the conviction that Taylor would at least be safer than Cass on slavery extension, impelled him to work for a Whig victory. Then he sat down and a glee club, somewhat inappropriately, sang "No Use Knocking at the Door."[25] Two days later, the Whig nominations appeared for the first time at the *Tribune's* masthead, accompanied by an apology for their presence that damned Taylor with faint praise. It was, Philip Hone recorded in his diary, "abominably bad taste, as well as impolitic in the last degree."

Once embarked on the campaign, Greeley, like Cynara's lover, proved faithful after his fashion. He would do all he could for the banditti that had triumphed at Philadelphia, he wrote to Colfax, but he wouldn't shed a pint of tears at their defeat in November. "They deserve it, even if the country don't deserve (I rather guess it does) a visitation of that fat-bellied, mutton-headed, cucumber-soled Cass."[26] He refused Weed's request that he stump Ohio, but did write a couple of appeals to the Ohio Free-Soil Whigs that appeared in the *Weekly Tribune*. The laborers of Pennsylvania were also exhorted to vote Whig and thus get rid of a tariff that was rapidly ruining the country. But encomiums of Taylor were conspicuous by their absence, as were the war narratives, Mexican invasion romances and little-more-grape ditties with which the Whigs deluged the contest. Most of the songs, Greeley remarked acidly after the campaign, were "unfit to be hummed in a stable." The *Tribune* played the part of a Whig newspaper until the voters had gone to the polls, but Horace Greeley was not pleased.

The election was over, the Whigs were in, Greeley included, and New Yorkers turned to other matters. Forrest was at the Broadway. Henry Ward Beecher at Brooklyn's Plymouth Church thundered to a packed congregation, "We know what lust can do; its heavens glow like brass; its hour is like the raging of the furnace; that hour passed, and life is but the embers and the ashes of the spent furnace." Horace Greeley turned from politics to poor relief. Why could not work be provided for those who asked for it, instead of treating them scurvily but expensively as paupers? There was no answer.

It was impossible for Greeley to leave politics alone for very long. That winter he put his shoulder to the wheel, helping to elect Seward to the United States Senate over bitter conservative opposition. And early in December he went to Washington where, as a member of the House of Representatives, he was champing to do yeoman's service for the nation's good.

Greeley arrived in the nation's capital clad in the armor of righteousness. Congress abounded in wrongs to be redressed, evils to be uprooted, and who was better qualified for such work than a certain crusading editor? Furiously he plunged into the fray. "I never was better satisfied with anything than with that short winter campaign," he wrote in later years.[27] If his measure of success lay in setting the House completely by the ears, he had ample cause for satisfaction.

The mere cataloguing of Greeley's Congressional activities would be a task of considerable proportions. He stood for protection, and introduced a homestead bill that was quickly tabled. He tried to abolish flogging in the navy, and the serving of grog to sailors and marines. He offered a resolution changing the name of the nation to "Columbia," opposed a $38,000 item for army recruiting, and urged that the navy in the Pacific be put to work earning half a million dollars by transporting Argonauts from Panama to the California gold fields. His pen scribbled the preamble to a resolution abolishing the slave trade in the District of Columbia (a resolution that Congressman Abraham Lincoln found too strong), and his attitude toward slavery was such as to arouse the bitter hostility of southern members on the opposite side of the House. In addition to such matters, he undertook a special crusade against certain House practices, a crusade that threw that body into tumult and confusion.

The House had not much more than settled into session when Greeley began its reform. He had long held a rod in pickle for the practice of franking which, in his opinion, decreased the influence of newspapers and acted as a barrier to the reduction of postal rates. Nor was this all. Congressional pay and the salaries of government employees ought, he was sure, to be drastically reduced in the interest of governmental economy. He criticized his colleagues because they paid seven dollars and a half a column to Gales and Seaton for printing the House debates. House members were flayed repeatedly in the *Tribune* for wasting time, squandering the taxpayers' money, and indulging in unbecoming behavior. Greeley spread far and wide the news that the $250 extra compensation given to House employees at the end of the session was voted by members many of whom were befuddled by liquor provided in one of the side rooms by the expectant beneficiaries.

Such exposés of the waste and inefficiency of government were irritating enough, but the storm they aroused was as nothing to that produced by Greeley's crusade against the "mileage-elongators."

The mileage paid to Congressmen was computed by law on the basis of the route usually traveled by the incumbent in his journeys to and from Washington. Greeley published in the *Tribune* the mileage received by each member, together with that which he would have received if computed by the most direct route between his home and the capital. The table showed that House members received for one session an excess of $47,223.80 because of the circuitous routes they had taken or claimed to have taken, while the upper chamber was in pocket a total of $14,881.40 for the same reason. Old Bullion Benton had profited to the extent of $689.60. Abraham Lincoln's excess mileage was $676.80. The whole story was news of the first order and the *Tribune* made the most of it, to the edification of the electorate.

To say that Congress was upset by this mileage publicity would be putting it mildly. Shouts of "demagogue," as well as more uncomplimentary epithets, rent the air when Greeley would rise to speak. There was talk of a resolution of censure, and of Greeley's expulsion from the House. The fact that he had voted (unwittingly) for the books with which each Congressman furnished his library at the nation's expense was used to brand him as a hypocrite. By the close of the session Greeley was easily the most unpopular man on Capitol Hill. "I have divided the House into two parties," he wrote to a friend, "one that would like to see me extinguished and the other that wouldn't be satisfied without a hand in doing it."[28]

No sane person could have questioned the need of Congressional reform in 1849. The conduct of the public business was often grossly inefficient. Mileage was padded unmercifully by some of the members, and there were other evidences of low Congressional ethics. Greeley had ample grounds for complaint. Where he erred was in his method of attacking the abuses that he found on every hand. As Seward remarked, he tried to reform everything at once, forcing Congress to remain in session beyond the usual time for daily adjournment, and martyrizing himself five or six times a day by voting against the whole House. These tactics, like his mileage exposé in the *Tribune,* smacked of publicity-seeking and did little for the cause of reform. Greeley himself called the session a failure, from the point of view of constructive accomplishment.

In later years, as he looked back on his Congressional experience, Greeley felt that it had been worth while for bringing him "into collision with the embodied scoundrelism of the Nation." Seward and Weed drew a somewhat different lesson from the same source. The senior partners were convinced, as they assayed Congressman Greeley's worth, that "zeal, unregulated by prudence" was a serious limitation to his usefulness.[29]

NOTES FOR CHAPTER 10

1. T. W. Barnes, *Memoir of Thurlow Weed* (Boston, 1884), p. 97.
2. Greeley Papers (N. Y. H. A.), Greeley to Weed, Jan. 22, 1846, Sept. 25, Oct. 3, 1847; Greeley Papers (N. Y. P. L.), Greeley to Colfax, Apr. 22, 1846; Weed Papers, Weed to Greeley, May 15 [1846]. It is at least interesting that Greeley abandoned his strenuous advocacy of Fourierism the following year.
3. *Tribune,* July 27, 1846.
4. Weed Papers, Seward to Weed, Aug. 15, 27, 1847; *Tribune,* July 25, 1847.
5. *Ibid.,* Apr. 30, 1845, Aug. 14, 20, 1846, June 3, 1847; *Semi-Weekly Tribune,* Nov. 19, 1845.
6. B. Brockway, *Fifty Years of Journalism,* p. 116; Greeley Papers (Lib. of Cong.), Greeley to Brockway, Nov. 19, 1847.
7. *Tribune,* May 16, 1848; H. Hamilton, *Zachary Taylor* (2 vols.; Indianapolis, 1941, 1951), II, 63-75.
8. *Tribune,* July 21, 1846.
9. Greeley Letters (Yale Lib.), Greeley to Alvah Hunt, Nov. 17, 1847.
10. Weed Papers, Seward to Weed, Jan. 22, 1848; *Tribune,* Jan. 29, Feb. 1, 1848.
11. McLean Papers, J. B. Mower to McLean, Feb. 15, 1848.
12. Clay Papers, Greeley to Clay, Apr. 28, 1848; McLean Papers, Mower to McLean, June 5, 1848. In writing to Clay, Greeley was very cautious about proposing Seward for Vice-President. "Seward has no special claims on us and utterly detests the idea of being run. He is an active, energetic man and would feel in the chair of the Senate like a bear in a cage." Seward would help, Greeley declared, in New York and Pennsylvania, but if his candidacy would hurt in the South he should certainly not be nominated.
13. Fuller Correspondence, Greeley to Margaret Fuller, Apr. 4, 1848; Caleb B. Smith Papers, Greeley to Smith, Feb. 18, 1848; Greeley Letters (Yale Lib.), Greeley to Hunt, Nov. 17, 1847.
14. Caleb B. Smith Papers, Greeley to Smith, Feb. 18, 1848; Greeley Papers (N. Y. P. L.), Greeley to Colfax, Apr. 3, 1848.
15. Weed Papers, Seward to Weed, May 4, 27, 1848.
16. Clay Papers, Greeley to Clay, May 29, 1848.

17. *Tribune,* June 13, 1848.
18. *Ibid.,* June 10, 14, 1848, July 13, 1850; *Albany Evening Journal,* Apr. 22, 1850.
19. *Tribune,* Jan. 4, 1851.
20. *Ibid.,* June 10, 1848.
21. Caleb B. Smith Papers, Greeley to Smith, Feb. 18, 1848; *Tribune,* July 31, 1848, Aug. 10, 1870, Mar. 27, 1872; Clay Papers, Greeley to Clay, June 21, 1848; St. G. L. Sioussat, "Andrew Johnson and the Homestead Bill," *Miss. Valley Hist. Rev.,* V (Dec. 1918), 279.
22. *Tribune,* July 31, Aug. 12, 16, 1848, Sept. 16, 1850.
23. Greeley Papers (N. Y. P. L.), Greeley to Colfax, Sept. 15, 1848.
24. Greeley Papers (N. Y. H. A.), Greeley to Weed, Sept. 22, 1848.
25. *Tribune,* Sept. 28, 29, 1848.
26. Greeley Papers (N. Y. P. L.), Greeley to Colfax, Oct. 2, 1848.
27. Greeley Papers (Lib. of Cong.), Greeley to Brockway, Feb. 14, 1872.
28. Griswold MSS, Greeley to Griswold, Jan. 21, 1849.
29. Greeley Papers (N .Y. P. L.), Greeley to Colfax, June 5, 1854; Weed Papers, Seward to Weed, Dec. 7, 1848, July 28, 1849; Margaret Fuller Correspondence, Greeley to Margaret Fuller, Jan. 29, 1849.

CHAPTER 11

Crisis and Schism

GREELEY STAYED IN WASHINGTON FOR TAYLOR'S inauguration and what he described as "the hideously vulgar ball," then hurried back to New York and the *Tribune*. As was apt to be the case when away, he had become fretful and peevish over the inadequacies of his subordinates. "I could crucify you all," he had written to one of his henchmen when the *Tribune* had failed to publish the news of Seward's nomination for the United States Senate at earliest possible moment.[1] There were going to be no more such mistakes, if the senior editor could help it.

The *Tribune* was now an institution with some two hundred people in its employ, over half of these on full time. Before the middle of the 1850's it boasted eighteen foreign and twenty domestic correspondents, and a dozen editors. A galaxy of talent climbed the stairs (reputedly the dirtiest in the world) of the sparsely furnished Tribune Building at Spruce and Nassau streets, or posted communications to the paper from overseas. The able Dana, not quite so idealistic since his contact with Europe in revolution, was second in command. Careful, scholarly George Ripley, rescued from the shipwrecked *Harbinger* in 1849, started at five dollars a week to blaze a literary critic's trail from romanticism to realism. Bayard Taylor, globe trotter and poet, was on the staff, while the indefatigable and opinionated James S. Pike was taken on as Washington correspondent in 1850. William Henry Fry, later to be the paper's distinguished music critic, was reporting news from Paris and London.

Increasing numbers meant expansion of the *Tribune's* field of coverage as well as improvement in the quality of its offerings. More departments were added. Solon Robinson became agricultural editor in 1853, a stroke of great good fortune for the *Weekly Tribune*. Shortly thereafter, the able George M. Snow became financial editor, and Charles T. Congdon came to stand at Greeley's right hand as another member of the editorial staff. There was a distinguished list of special correspondents and contributors, both at home and abroad. Jules Le Chevalier for the 1840's and Karl Marx at the beginning of the 1850's added distinction to the paper with their interpretations of European developments. The American historian, Richard Hildreth, was a contributor, and in 1850 the *Tribune* published two poems that looked like prose, by an author who signed himself "Walter Whitman." The paper was always interesting, from Marx's analysis of the revolutions of 1848 to G. G. Foster's "City Items" and it commanded increasing attention. Even Fanny Fern's poor old huckster would not sell his copy for any money until he had read what the paper had to say.

Greeley attracted able men to the *Tribune* because his genius as an editor made work on the paper interesting and exciting. The Man in the White Coat, irascible, peevish perfectionist though he might be, had a warm heart and a wealth of ideas. One had only to compare the *Tribune* of 1841 with the paper ten years later to see that, both as to type and contents, it symbolized Greeley's faith in progress. When an editor employed the author of the Communist Manifesto as a foreign correspondent and publicized a French anarchist (Proudhon) whose motto was "Property is Theft," progressive spirits were given a sense of being abreast of the times, if not a little ahead of the main current. Conservatives like Philip Hone might find in him a tendency "to be wild, visionary and abstracted in his notions," but he had a compelling charm for active intellects that were not bound by the conventional standards of his day, and yet shrank from cutting entirely loose for a voyage upon the seas of radicalism.

The *Tribune* was in the van of progressive ideas, and its editor boasted that it was the cheapest daily in the world, but such achievements only spurred Greeley on to further efforts for improvements.[2] Always there was pressure from the senior editor's desk for accuracy, for something fresh in the way of news, for something more to aid the paper's circulation. Send by telegraph, he told Pike in Washington. Expense was no object when the material was fresh and interesting. Get hold of someone who had access to Congressional secrets and set him telegraphing. From the age of Eve, men had been anxious to learn what ought not to be known, and the *Tribune* must have some of it or be voted dull and behind the times. Bayard Taylor was posted off to California in 1849, for first-hand news of the gold rush and as a means of establishing a circulation on the Pacific coast. *Tribune* clubs, with such premiums as the Horace Greeley watch (a Waterbury, with Greeley's picture on the back) stimulated subscriptions to the *Weekly,* especially in election years. By 1850 a special edition of the *Tribune* was being sent to Europe.

If the drive in the *Tribune's* office was sometimes nerve-wracking, the *élan* of the staff was raised by recognition of their place in the enterprise. All who were connected with the *Tribune,* Greeley told Taylor, should become known to the public by some such method as initialing their articles. It would make the paper seem more like a permanent institution, besides being a sop to the self-esteem of the correspondents. There was still another and more material means of recognition.

On January 1, 1849, Greeley established the *Tribune* Association. Under its terms, the value of the *Tribune* was set at $100,000. This was divided into one hundred equal shares and a copartnership was formed. Greeley and McElrath took in six new partners, two or three of these being lesser lights in the concern such as Thomas N. Rooker, foreman of the composing room. The new partners subscribed to sixteen shares at $1,000 a share, and ten more shares were set aside for Dana, who took them up on his return from Europe. Thus the *Tribune* transmuted the basic principle of Association into that of a joint-stock corporation, much to the satisfaction of all concerned. By 1850 the number of stockholders had increased to twelve, with Greeley owning a quarter of the stock.[3]

The *Tribune* Association was conservative when it estimated the paper's value at $100,000, for at last Greeley had a sheet that was making money. True there had been a momentary setback in 1845 when a fire had gutted the establishment—an $18,000 loss that had taken everything from Greeley's boots to Webster's dictionary, with only $10,000 insurance to offset the damage. But the new building at Spruce and Nassau had been erected, and a golden tide swept in through its narrow doorway as circulation and advertising increased together. The Association divided a $25,000 profit in 1849. Two years later, men were counting themselves fortunate if they could buy the stock at $2,000 a share.[4]

The *Tribune's* editor derived more satisfaction from the paper's influence than from its income. It was his intention, he told Colfax (this aspiring young newspaperman and politician had won Greeley's lasting confidence by doing some articles for the *Tribune* on "generous" terms about Indiana crops and politics)[5] to acquire a circulation that would make the paper count in the struggles of the day. "The world is bound to move forward," he added, as happy in his certainty of progress as he was in his conviction that the theatre would soon vanish before the relentless competition of newspapers, lyceums, and public meetings. Man was perfectible, and the *Tribune's* principal reason for being was to give man a shove in the right direction.[6]

Meddling with the status quo, whether in public or private affairs, had an irresistible fascination for Greeley. If it seemed likely to do good to someone, he was apt to be drawn into action. His fingers might be burned in the process, but the urge to make things better was all-compelling.

Do you know Sarah Helen Whitman? [he wrote to Rufus Griswold in 1849]. Of course you have heard it rumored that she is to marry Poe. Well, she has seemed to me a good girl, and—you know what Poe is. Now I know a widow of doubtful age will marry almost any sort of a white man, but this seems to me a terrible conjunction. Has Mrs. Whitman no friend within your knowledge that can faithfully explain Poe to her? I never attempted this sort of thing but once, and the net product was two enemies and a precipitation of the marriage; but I do think she must be deceived. Mrs. Osgood must know her.[7]

With the urge to help others so strong in the *Tribune's* editor, it was small wonder that the paper itself should be dedicated to promoting the world's well-being. In its pages Greeley beat the drum for progress and reform with steady zeal and with a showmanship equal to that of his close friends and counselors, Henry Ward Beecher and Phineas T. Barnum. He urged coöperative production, thus making "work its own master," upon bakers and shoemakers; he demanded equal legal rights for women. Prohibition found in him an ardent and optimistic crusader, and audiences all over the country heard his shrill-voiced prediction that Demon Rum had only a few more years to live. A successful battle was launched for free, tax-supported schools in New York State, a battle that Greeley had to wage both against the Catholic church and the forces of avarice; tax-evading capitalists were roundly scourged, and the *Tribune's* editor fluttered the dovecotes with his willingness to accept that horrid, socialistic monstrosity, a tax on incomes over $1,000.[8] Such wanton tampering with the established order was gall and wormwood to conservatives.

Meanwhile the *Tribune's* virtue, like a too eager wind, buffeted the faces of practical politicians. Weed was urged to guard the state from professional office-seekers ("Next to marrying a *very* cross old maid, getting an office to live by is the poorest business I can think of"), and Greeley came out for direct election of United States Senators as a means of checking corruption and removing many

"pompous blockheads and wire-pulling knaves" from the Upper
Chamber. It would be the next best thing to abolishing the Senate
itself.[9]

The collapse of republicanism in Europe was melancholy news for
an editor so bent upon reform. This setback to the cause of progress fostered Russian expansionism and enlarged her menace to the
cause of freedom. The *Tribune* called attention to Russian designs
on the Sandwich Islands, Manchuria, and Japan, and sympathized
with the Turks when, in 1853, the legions of the Czar began moving in the direction of Constantinople. Greeley declared that it was
America's duty to rekindle the fires of liberty abroad by organizing
"a comprehensive and permanent system of Republican Propa-
gandism" for Europe. He published Walt Whitman's "Resurgemus,"
and might have taken his own motto from its lines—

> Liberty, let others despair of thee,
> But I will never despair of thee;
> Is the house shut? Is the master away?
> Nevertheless be ready, be not weary of watching,
> He will surely return; his messengers come anon.[10]

A reforming Whig was always something of an anomaly, and early
in the 1850's Greeley once again felt it necesary to explain his
political position. There had always been two great contending
principles that divided the political world, he declared. These two
principles were Liberty and Order. In a democracy, where the people rule, the tendency is for Liberty to outweigh Order. That was
why Washington, Knox, Hamilton, and a majority of the Revolutionary leaders had become Federalists, and that was why Whiggery
was such a valuable institution.

There were also other reasons for cleaving to the Whig party.
The Democrats had always been prone to an aggressive foreign
policy, while the Whigs were traditionally pacific in their attitude
toward foreign relations. The Democrats' basic laissez-faire position
was as hostile to common schools and tax-supported common roads
as it was to tariffs, corporations and internal improvements, while
the Whig party, on the other hand, was the party of progress. Whigs
supported their party for the sake of its measures; the Democrats
supported their measures for the sake of their party. The thinking
people voted Whig; the "morally rotten" tended to vote Democratic.[11]

Greeley wanted Whiggery to act as the champion of national
interests, from economic development to education, and to be always

alert to the "whispered pleadings of humanity and beneficence."[12]
It was a grand role, one that the Whigs were far from filling. But
in spite of Whig deficiencies, Greeley clung to the party until, split
wide open over slavery, its usefulness for promoting the national
good as he saw it was lost forever. Then, and only then, did he
abandon the political organization to which he had given such
loyal service.

Greeley applauded the appointment of Hugh Maxwell, a pro-
Clay and anti-Weed man, as Collector of the Port of New York in
1849, and was steadily cool to President Taylor, even though the
latter soon moved completely into the orbit of Weed and Seward.
Despite these divagations, however, the *Tribune's* editor still regarded himself as a Weed-Seward man, and joined Weed in attacking the Barnburners when they once again closed ranks with the
Hunkers in the fall of 1849. This Democratic amalgamation, Greeley declared, was proof that the Barnburner movement of 1848 had
not originated in Free-Soil principles but rather in a sordid struggle
for power between the Van Buren-Wright and Marcy-Croswell
wings of the New York Democracy. Anyone who failed to understand this was "hardly well versed in political history."[13]

The Barnburner-Hunker alignment looked none too stable, for
the former group insisted that they intended no compromise on
slavery extension. Such extension was now a burning issue, stimulated as it was by the territorial gains of the Mexican War. When
the first session of the Thirty-first Congress met in December 1849,
crisis was in the air. Disputes were raging over the Wilmot Proviso,
the existence of slavery in the District of Columbia, and the rendition of fugitive slaves. Plans for a southern convention, to meet at
Nashville the following June, symbolized the boldly expressed hopes
of southern fire-eaters. A formidable secessionist movement was
developing, and Congress was so torn by dissension that it took sixty-
three ballots to elect a Speaker of the House.

President Taylor, under Seward's influence, stood for "non-
action" by Congress, while he urged California and New Mexico
to apply as soon as possible for admission as states, the general
understanding being that they would come in without slavery. This
excited bitter opposition in the South, just as Texas' determination
to grab 125,000 square miles of New Mexico aroused fears and
hostility in the North. Circumstances pointed to the logic of compromise, and men began to watch the movements of the senior
Senator from Kentucky, "The Great Pacificator" Henry Clay.

Deeply disturbed by the threat of disunion, Clay carefully ma-
tured his plans. Then, at the end of January 1850, having gained

Webster's support in advance, he launched his proposals. California admitted as a free state, the territories organized without reference to slavery, the Texas-New Mexico boundary settled in favor of the latter but with federal compensation to Texas, prohibition of the slave trade in the District of Columbia, a more effective fugitive slave law—such were the essential features of Clay's plan.

The compromise aroused the giants of the Senate to their full oratorical powers. Webster defended it, to the disgust of northern antislavery opinion. Calhoun denounced it as altogether inadequate from the southern point of view. Seward, knowing that he spoke as the potential leader of the antislavery forces of the North, attacked it as conceding too much to the South, and invoked a "higher law" than the Constitution, a law dedicating the country to union, to justice, and to liberty.

The divergent viewpoints of the leaders, together with the outcries that came from both sides of Mason and Dixon's line, furnished the best possible proof that Clay's plan was essentially fair. More important even than its fairness was the fact that it gave nationalist sentiment a chance to formulate and express its ideas during the long months of debate on Clay's resolutions.

Congress referred Clay's proposals to a committee of thirteen, headed by the Sage of Ashland, and this committee reported out three pieces of legislation. The first, promptly dubbed the "Omnibus," linked together Clay's proposals for California, the territories, and the Texas-New Mexico boundary. Prohibition of the District of Columbia slave trade, and the Fugitive Slave Law, remained as separate pieces of legislation. Thus organized, the Compromise started on its stormy way.

Greeley had taken the stand, early in 1849, that the thwarting of Texas' land claims against New Mexico was more important than any explicit prohibition of slavery in the newly acquired territories.[14] This inclined him to look with favor on the Compromise proposals for safeguarding New Mexico's land claims and for leaving untouched the problem as to whether or not there should be slavery in New Mexico and Arizona. His violent dislike of Taylor, a deep-seated distrust of the President's plan of "non-action," and a marked aversion for the tie-up between Weed, Seward, and "Old Zack," likewise inclined him to the support of the Compromise. But on the other hand, he was convinced that the South did not want the Compromise; that the Omnibus could not pass Congress; and that it would be better to slap Texas down decisively than to pay her off for relinquishing her claim on New Mexico's territory.

These considerations tended to move him away from the Compromise.

During the first months of the debate on the Compromise, the arguments for opposing it seemed to hold sway over Greeley's mind. He attacked Webster's Seventh of March speech, taking substantially the same "higher law" position that Seward assumed two days later,[15] and published Whitman's "Blood-Money" with its sneer at Black Dan—"And still Iscariot plies his trade."[16] Seward's speech denouncing the Compromise was praised, the "higher law" pronouncement was defended, and Greeley linked himself and Seward together as moderate men who would be only too glad to surrender the Proviso in name, if such surrender were followed by no extension of slavery.

Greeley appeared to be hewing close to the Seward-Weed line, but the triumvirate was far from harmonious in its view of the situation at Washington. The two senior members were well pleased with Taylor, but Greeley wrote to Colfax that Old Zack did not "know himself from a side of sole-leather in the way of statesmanship," and had picked for his Cabinet " a horrid mixture," from the drunkard Clayton to the overbearing and selfish Ewing. Greeley was of no mind to prepare the way for Taylor's renomination. He suspected a "fix-up" in this regard, with the South bribed to admit New Mexico as a free state, right after California, thus ensuring Taylor's succeeding himself in 1852. Greeley preferred Clay to Taylor and, apparently with a view to promoting Clay's candidacy, began turning more and more to the Compromise. His old associates, the supporters of the Wilmot Proviso, were now given short shrift. Greeley addressed them injuriously as "cords of blockheads and wooden-pated friends," while Seward, who was supporting the Proviso in principle, was tartly told: "Gov. Seward, you deceive yourself with regard to the course of things in Washington."[17]

By the middle of May, Greeley was arguing in the *Tribune* with his own Washington correspondent, James S. Pike, who was for the Taylor plan, lock, stock, and barrel. He also crossed swords with the *Evening Post,* which Proviso to the hilt, was shrieking about the "apostasy" of the *Tribune's* editor. Bryant, who was much aroused by Greeley's refusal to stand by the Proviso, had charged that the latter, under Taylor's influence, had been willing while in Congress to divide the new territories with the slaveholders. The charge was false and Greeley had burst out in the *Tribune*: "You lie, villain! willfully, wickedly, basely lie!"

The violence offered by Greeley to the poet-editor of the *Evening Post* drew a chorus of condemnation, but Greeley stuck to his guns.

Twice, he declared, he had refuted the *Post's* charge in relatively mild fashion. It was only when Bryant had insisted on repeating the calumny that Greeley had told "the false witness—what he is."

Bryant never forgot the insult and it, together with endless altercations over free trade and other matters, rankled in his brain. Years later, he was invited to a breakfast that Greeley also attended. As the latter came into the room, Bryant ignored him. The host, turning to Bryant, said in a whisper, "Don't you know Mr. Greeley?" Promptly the answer came back, "No I don't; he's a blackguard—he's a blackguard."[18]

Seward was even more upset than Bryant at the course that Greeley was taking. It was positively dangerous, the Auburn statesman wrote to Weed. If Greeley made a success of the Compromise, as he could do if he tried, where would Weed and Seward be? Could not Weed get Greeley to come down to Washington and consult with the President?[19]

Three days after Seward had committed his alarm to paper, and obviously in reply to a letter from Weed, Greeley wrote to both the senior partners. He denounced Taylor because of his Cabinet, because of his foreign appointments (not one sympathetic with the European Republicans and one, Consul Walsh at Paris, a "darkest Jesuit" and monarchist), and because he was playing fast and loose with the danger of Texas swallowing a large part of New Mexico. Greeley wanted no sugar-coated promises or secret, whispered assurances from either Weed or Seward. "I think you have a great deal too high an opinion of dexterity as an attribute of statesmanship," he told Seward. "I have none at all." If New Mexican territory was stolen by Texas, Greeley continued, "I'll blister all those who ought to have prevented it and did not. . . . This Congress must not adjourn without organizing New Mexico and shutting out Texas somehow, and I shall go hard for Clay's log-roll if something better is not put ahead of it." Why the delay in the House, Greeley inquired. "I shall not say much tomorrow," he continued, "but when I take hold in earnest, I will try to make a tear somewhere. The whole business looks very dark to me."[20]

Wroth over the political intrigues that he found in Congress when he visited Washington in June, fearful that "non-action" would deliver New Mexico into the arms of Texas, anxious to turn from the slavery controversy to more constructive economic issues, Greeley became more and more of a Compromise man. He kept declaring that, once the danger to New Mexico from Texas was removed, the Compromise would vanish into thin air.[21] But the Omnibus offered a means of safeguarding New Mexican territory for freedom and of checkmating Taylor's renomination. Lacking something better, Greeley gave it his support.

Taylor's unexpected death in July 1850 removed one of the greatest barriers to the Omnibus and, indeed, to the whole Compromise. Millard Fillmore of Buffalo, the new President, was a rival of Seward and a friend of the middle way. The power of the executive branch was now thrown in support of Clay's proposals, and Weed and Seward, hitherto so powerful at the White House, were excluded from its portals. Threats of war to the knife against the new President appeared in the columns of Weed's *Albany Evening Journal.*

At first the *Tribune* appealed for Whig unity and rebuked Weed for serving notice that Fillmore must accept Taylor's approach to the problem of the territories. Greeley had no great love for Fillmore, but he continued to support the Omnibus on the ground that it was the best means of protecting New Mexico and averting what he now described as the "imminent peril" of civil war.[22] Then, quite unexpectedly, the Omnibus went down to defeat in the Senate through overshrewd tactical maneuvering, and the whole complexion of events seemed changed.

Greeley was at the Capitol when the Senate defeated the Omnibus. He watched its exultant enemies pass out of the Senate chamber. One of them, Senator A. P. Butler of South Carolina, stopped and said, "I don't wonder at *your* support of this bill, for it would give *you* all you seek." The South was confident that it had won a great victory and Greeley, also, saw or thought he saw this turn of events as paving the way for an expansion of slave territory.

After the Omnibus was lost, the *Tribune's* editor called on the northerners who had been hostile to it to assume the responsibility for getting California into the Union and for protecting New Mexico from Texan rapacity. He professed a certainty that the cause of free soil had been badly injured by the defeat of "Clay's log-roll." But a few weeks later, when the Compromise measures finally went through as separate bills under the leadership of Senator Stephen A. Douglas, Greeley's enthusiasm for their passage had distinctly waned. He greeted them coolly, even scornfully, and finally, when some New York Whigs fired a hundred guns down at the Battery in celebration of the event, he expressed himself as disgusted with their action.[23] Once more the *Tribune's* editor had taken a new tack.

Greeley's dislike of the separate compromise measures stemmed in part from the harsh features of the Fugitive Slave Law, which lacked any provision for jury trial of the fugitives and which gave the Federal Commissioner ten dollars if he found the captive a slave, five dollars if he set the Negro free. He was also outraged by the boundary bill, which gave Texas 33,333 more square miles of territory than had been provided in the Omnibus.[24] Greeley was thus forced to accept an increase in slave territory, and on that narrow but to him fundamental point he had remained rigidly obdurate throughout the struggle.

But the increase in slave territory and the obnoxious features of the Fugitive Slave Law would scarcely, in themselves, have produced the reversal in Greeley's attitude toward the Compromise. There had to be another and more compelling reason why he, who had caused Seward and Weed so much anxiety by his support of the Compromise, should now be lined up with them in attacking the compromise proposals after they had been enacted into law. There was such a reason, and it derived from New York State politics.

Political developments in New York State were taking an ominous turn in the autumn of 1850. There Fillmore and his friends, anxious to overthrow Weed and Seward, were as deaf to genuine efforts at conciliation as was the Albany Dictator. Before Fillmore had been in the White House a month, signs of a proscriptive policy began issuing from the mansion, and Greeley began warning the President not to be duped by sycophants as Tyler had been in 1841. Another struggle between liberals and conservatives within the New York State Whig party was shaping up, in part over differences on appeasing the Slave Power, in part over the Sewardites' policy of reform, in part simply a struggle between ambitious men for control of the state organization. Greeley deplored this conflict as dangerous to the Whig party's nationalist program, but if an open breach had to come he knew where he meant to stand.

While smoldering Whig discord in New York State was being fanned into flame by Fillmore's grab for power, Greeley took time to pour out his wrath on the antislavery Democrats who met in peace and harmony with the Hunkers at Syracuse and framed a unified state ticket. What single, distinctive principle laid down by the Free-soilers at the Buffalo convention of 1848, shrewdly demanded the Tribune's editor, was affirmed or even tolerated at the "keep dark—oh, hush—truck and dicker" gathering at Syracuse? Was all the antislavery of the Buffalo platform "sunk to this little measure?" This amalgamation in the name of political practicality was the same sort of proof of the opposition's sham democracy that one saw when one compared Seward with Senator A. P. Butler of South Carolina.[25] There was altogether too large an element of truth in this derisory comment to make it palatable to the Democracy.

Greeley's wrath over Democratic harmony was one way of indicating his fear of the consequences of Whig division in New York State. Some two weeks before the Whig state convention met in Syracuse, he wrote to Fillmore's Secretary of the Treasury, the same Tom Corwin whom he had wished to see nominated in 1848. Greeley urged Corwin to get the President and Seward together, have them agree on the necessity of differing amicably with one another, and then inform their followers in New York State of this decision. Whig factiousness as it was developing, said Greeley, bade fair to be more vicious, more disastrous than the factiousness of the state's Democracy. "But ten words from Washington, based on the principle of 'live and let live,'" could set all right. Obviously, Greeley believed that the first move toward conciliation should come from within the President's official family, and he looked to Corwin to make that move. He looked in vain.

When the Whig state convention met, late in September at Syracuse, the Whig conservatives and other Whig politicians, disgruntled by the Weed-Seward leadership, were determined to slap down Seward by a refusal to commend his Senate record. There ensued on the floor of the convention a struggle for control of the party, with Greeley in the thick of the fight.

The *Tribune's* editor had continued to hope against hope that this struggle could be avoided. He had been willing to have the convention commend the President and to have it go on record for giving the Compromise (Fugitive Slave Law and all) a fair trial, provided that the leadership of Seward was also commended in general terms and the right of Congress to restrict slavery was reaffirmed. But when he found the opposition obdurate in its determination not to approve Seward's course, he rolled up his sleeves and went to work. He shuffled about from one delegate to another, citing statistics on the party's strength and weakness, pleading with the delegates to support Seward and reform, snorting his contempt for the "old fogies" of conservatism and declaring that, if they left the party, their loss would be more than made up by the accession of Free-soilers that would ensue.

The final test in the convention found the pro-Seward men in the majority, and the conservatives bolted. When "Cotton," as Greeley dubbed these dissidents, followed the silvery mane of Francis Granger out of the convention hall, it may well have been to the sound of Greeley's high-pitched voice, by turns scolding them and exhorting the Sewardites. Certainly it was with his emphatic approval that the majority of the convention took a clear-cut stand in support of Seward and in opposition to slavery extension, the while it nominated Washington Hunt for Governor. The Silver Greys, as Granger's followers were promptly christened, also nominated Hunt in a separate convention, but the New York State Whig party, like the veil of the temple, had been rent from top to bottom.[26]

Greeley rightly regarded this Whig feud as much more than a quarrel over Seward's attitude toward slavery. It was, he felt, symbolic of the struggle between conservatism and liberalism within the Whig party. He was eager to press ahead for land, law, and labor reform, tariff protection for labor, cheap postage for everybody. These measures, he was certain, were much more apt to be achieved under the leadership of Weed and Seward than under that of the conservative Whig merchant class that made reverence to Cotton and looked askance at all reform. He had told Weed before the convention that, if they had some bolters of the conservative stripe and these bolters could be induced to hold a meeting with William B. Astor in the chair and denounce the Syracuse proceedings as too radical and agrarian, it might do the Whig cause much good. Greeley's conduct at the convention was a further demonstration of his conviction that to sacrifice Seward was to sacrifice progressive measures generally and lose much support from the working class.[27]

Greeley was out of New York City a good deal that fall, stumping the state for free schools and temperance, but the editorials that he wrote showed that the conservative Whigs, who were continuing to identify themselves with the Compromise, were driving him into a more extreme antislavery position than he had hitherto occupied. He had supported the Compromise during the summer and, up to the time of the Syracuse convention, had been willing to give the separate compromise bills a fair trial. After Syracuse, he became increasingly critical, not only of the Fugitive Slave Law and the New Mexico-Texas boundary adjustment, but of the very act of compromise itself.

Hunt bested Seymour for the governorship that fall by 262 votes, and after the fury of battle died down Greeley paused to take stock of the situation. He had, he averred, learned at least one thing from the controversy over the Compromise. The course of that struggle had convinced him that the way to avert disunion was not by parleying with treason, nor by shivering at the phantom of secession. No more concessions should be extorted by a minority through threats of violence and bloodshed. There should be no more giving a state $10,000,000 to prevent her raising a rebellion. Hereafter, "all talk of forcible resistance should be treated with cool contempt," and the general government should be administered with a view to extending the blessings, not of slavery but of freedom.

The Union of the compromisers, Greeley declared, was only a cloak of appeasement for the insatiable Slave Power, a lusting ogre that would inevitably reveal itself as such in some new act of agression. The genuine lovers of the Union should now concentrate on land reform, the tariff, and kindred economic measures, leaving slavery agitation alone until the South (which was the divisive and distractive force in the Union) should make new exactions, and the cotton worshippers of the North should come forth with new concessions. Then those whose mouths were not crammed with cotton would take counsel together, and meet the crisis with the quiet strength and courage of free men.[28]

NOTES FOR CHAPTER 11

1. Greeley Papers (N. Y. P. L.), Greeley to W. E. Robinson, Feb. 9, 1849, reprinted in the *New York Herald,* June 9, 1889.
2. *Tribune,* Apr. 10, 1850.
3. Greeley Papers (N. Y. P. L.), Greeley to Colfax, Mar. 17, 1850; *The Organization and By-Laws of the Tribune Association* (N. Y., 1872); *Tribune,* June 29, 1850; Parton, *op. cit.,* p. 325; Hudson, op. cit., p. 536.
4. *Tribune,* Aug. 1, 1849; Greeley Papers (N. Y. P. L.), Greeley to Colfax, Apr. 1, 1849, Jan. 10, 1849 [but obviously 1850], Dec. 26, 1850; F. E. Snow, "Unpublished Letters of Horace Greeley," *Independent,* LIX (Oct. 19, 1905), 914; Stoddard, *op. cit.,* p. 145.
5. W. H. Smith, "Schuyler Colfax," *Indiana Mag. of Hist,* XXXIV, no. 1 (Sept., 1938), 263-67.
6. Greeley Papers (N. Y. P. L.), Greeley to Colfax, Apr. 1, 1849; *Tribune,* Dec. 7, 1850.
7. Griswold MSS, Greeley to Griswold, Jan. 21, 1849.
8. *Tribune,* Sept. 1, 1849, Feb. 26, 1850.
9. Greeley Papers (N. Y. P. L.), Greeley to W. E. Robinson, May 11, 1849, *New York Herald,* June 9, 1889, Greeley to Colfax, Aug. 10, 1850; *Tribune,* Dec. 31, 1849.
10. *Ibid.,* Aug. 7, Sept. 6, 7, 1849, June 21, 1850, Dec. 1, 1853; Seward Papers, Greeley to Seward, Feb. 19, 1850.
11. Greeley, *Why I Am a Whig* (N. Y., n. d., but obviously in the early 1850's).
12. Greeley Papers (N. Y. P. L.), Greeley to "Richelieu" (W. E. Robinson) in 1850 (clipping).
13. *Tribune,* 1849-50, especially May 14, Sept. 11, Nov. 9, 1849, Jan. 11, 1850; James W. Wadsworth Papers, John Young to Wadsworth, May 25, 1849; Thomas Ewing Papers, Greeley to ———, Nov. 5, 7, 1849.
14. *Tribune,* Mar. 9, 1849; Greeley, *Recollections,* p. 231.
15. Greeley took the "higher law" position by asserting that, when the Constitution reënacted "the will of Satan" it was "nugatory among freemen." —*Tribune,* Mar. 9, 1850.
16. *Ibid.,* Mar. 22, 1850.

17. Greeley Papers (N. Y. P. L.), Greeley to Colfax, Apr. 9, 1850, Greeley to Oliver Johnson (clipping, 1850); *Tribune,* Apr. 22, 27 (p. 2), 29, May 20, July 16, 18, 23, Oct. 16, 1850; Seward Papers, Greeley to Seward, May 27, 1850.

18. *Tribune,* Mar. 6, 9, 15, Sept. 21, Oct. 18, Nov. 20, 1849, Jan. 12, 18, May 14, 1850, June 1, 1852; R. Ogden (ed.), *Life and Letters of Edwin Lawrence Godkin* (2 vols.; N. Y., 1907), I, 167-68.

19. Weed Papers, Seward to Weed, May 24, 1850.

20. Seward Papers, Greeley to Seward, May 27, 1850; Greeley Letters (N. Y. H. S.), Greeley to Weed, May 27, 1850; *Tribune,* May 28, 1850, wherein is repeated the stand heretofore outlined in regard to New Mexico. Greeley, who was now fulminating to Schuyler Colfax about the Galphin scandal, had wanted a Cabinet reorganization as early as Nov. 1849, with Caleb B. Smith in the new Cabinet. Schuyler Colfax had brought pressure on Weed for this, also. Caleb B. Smith Papers, Colfax to Smith, Nov. 8, 1849, Apr. 19, 1850.

21. Greeley Papers (N. Y. P. L.), Greeley to "Friend Robin," June 10, 1850 (clipping); *Tribune,* June 25, 29, July 3, 4, 1850.

22. *Ibid.,* July 12, 13, 27, 1850.

23. *Ibid.,* Sept. 7, 11-13, 1850, Jan. 6, 1851.

24. *Ibid.,* Nov. 28, 1850, and Nov.-Dec., 1850, *passim.*

25. *Tribune,* Sept. 16, 18, 23, 1850.

26. Greeley Papers (N. Y. P. L.), Resolutions in Greeley's handwriting, Greeley to T. L. Kane, Oct. 7, 1850; Greeley Letters (N. Y. H. S.), Greeley to Weed, Sept. 21, 1850; *Tribune,* Sept. 23, 30, Oct. 1-3, 4-14, 21, Nov. 9, 1850; Corwin Papers, Greeley to Corwin, Sept. 12, 1850.

27. Greeley Papers (N. Y. P. L.), Greeley to "Friend Robin," June 10, 1850; Greeley Letters (N. Y. H. S.), Greeley to Weed, Sept. 21, 1850; *Tribune,* Sept. 23, 1850.

28. Seward Papers, Greeley to Seward, Dec. 4, 1850; Greeley Papers (N. Y. P. L.) Greeley to Colfax, Dec. 26, 1850; *Tribune,* Nov.-Dec., especially Nov. 25, 26, Dec. 2, 6, 1850.

CHAPTER 12

The Greeleys at Home

WHILE GREELEY WAS BUILDING HIMSELF A REPU-
tation as editor, reformer, and national leader he was also, after a
fashion, trying to establish a home. At first he and Molly moved
hither and yon from one set of rooms to another, but gradually
they began settling down to longer and longer periods in one spot.
During the early 1840's they lived for some time at 35 East Nineteenth Street in one of a row of houses just alike, number 37 being
occupied by William M. Evarts and then by William Allen Butler
who was later to gain fame as the creator of Flora M'Flimsey in the
poem "Nothing to Wear." At number 37 the Greeleys kept a goat,
or goats, in the backyard, and here on one occasion, when the
absent-minded editor was trying to get into his neighbor's house
under the impression that it was his own, he plunged headlong into
the Butlers' front hall when Mrs. Butler suddenly opened the door.[1]

Late in 1844, Horace and Molly sought out a more secluded
habitation. This was an "old, desolate rookery of a house,"[2] situated
on an eight-acre plot at Turtle Bay, nearly opposite the southern
tip of Blackwell's Island. The nearest highway was the old "Boston
road" at Forty-ninth Street. This area was definitely country in
1844, being about two miles from the thickly settled parts of New
York City.

At Turtle Bay the *Tribune's* editor again took up farming, for he
had an acre patch plowed by a neighbor for the sum of five dollars.
The ploughing was poor (only five inches deep, Greeley noted with
disgust) and the estate was run down, but Margaret Fuller, who
lived there with the Greeleys, thought that as a place of abode it
was restful and charming. So it seemed to its owner, a man tor-
mented just then by half a hundred boils and worn out by his
exertions in the campaign of 1844.[3]

Early in 1850, Greeley bought for $7,000 a two and one-half story
house built of brick and painted brown, on Nineteenth Street, half-

way between Fourth Avenue and Broadway. This was because of
his wife's passion for something different. She had, as he remarked,
a "difficult taste." Apparently, neither she nor her husband was
entirely satisfied with this abode. Certainly the lure of the land was
still upon her spouse for, in 1853, they moved once more into the
country, this time to a small farm just east of the village of Chappaqua in Westchester County, some thirty-five miles from downtown
New York.

The dynamic back of this move to Chappaqua, so Greeley later
declared, was furnished by a yearning that grew upon him in "the
sober afternoon of life" for a return to rural delights.[4] This "sober
afternoon" concept was less fact (he was only forty-two in 1853)
than it was a product of nineteenth-century romanticism. A more
important motivation for the exodus to Chappaqua was Greeley's
interest in agriculture and in the *Weekly Tribune*.

The *Tribune* all through the 1840's had given considerable space
to farm news, and this space was expanded in the following decade.
The same year that the Greeleys moved to Chappaqua, a farm
department was established in the weekly edition and Solon Robinson was made its agricultural editor. James J. Mapes, who in 1847
had taken over a run-down farm not unlike the one Greeley purchased six years later and had been busily restoring it by subsoil
drainage, fertilization, and crop rotation, was a close friend of
Greeley and a steady contributor to the *Tribune*.[5] Stimulated by his
friends and associates, by the possibility of developing the *Weekly
Tribune's* already large sales in the rural areas, and by the land
lure that was in his blood, Greeley devoted more and more attention
to farming. He foresaw the development of a real science of agriculture, and he was interested in furthering that development through
the columns of his paper and by means of an experiment similar to
that conducted by Professor Mapes.

Greeley's choice of a location for his back-to-the-land movement
was in part due to the need for fairly close proximity to the *Tribune*
office, in part to the requisites laid down by his wife. Molly Greeley,
whose eye turned more to the picturesque than to the practical,
insisted that any rural location must include "1. A peerless spring
of pure, soft, living water; 2. A cascade or brawling brook; 3. Woods
largely composed of evergreens." Hence the location of the farm, as
her husband somewhat ruefully pointed out, on a rocky, wooded
hillside with a bog at the foot.[6] Obviously, farm rehabilitation
could have been carried on under more auspicious circumstances
than those furnished by the Chappaqua estate, but Greeley may

well have reconciled himself to the difficulties involved by reflecting that the results would be all the more startling.

It became the fashion for critics and fun makers to jibe at Greeley's farming efforts, and the Chappaqua wood chopper was made the butt of much merriment. The story was spread about that he had bought one dozen genuine Shanghai eggs for six dollars, put them under a hen, and hatched out snapping turtles—a bit of foolery that brought forth an indignant "There never was a more baseless fabrication" in the *Tribune*. His *What I Know about Farming* drew from Josh Billings the comment that Greeley was only a "dictionary farmer," and that "What i kno about farming is kussed little."[7]

It was true that farmer Greeley had his crotchets and limitations. He was hipped on subsoil ploughing, steam tractors and soil sewage disposal. There was something laughable about the editor of America's most powerful newspaper chirping and clucking futilely to a team of horses, or climbing thirty feet up a hemlock, ax in hand, bent on trimming off all its branches from there to the ground. Chappaqua confronted him with fruit trees and grape vines concerning which he was, as he himself declared, "ignorant as a horse." He spent thousands of dollars on buildings, drainage, liming, fertilizing, and labor, and raised crops where none had grown before and where none but goldenrod grow at the present time. Even so, Beman Brockway noted that "things had a fearfully slip shod look at Chappaqua."[8]

But the critics might laugh as they would. Horace's farming was far from being mere idle show. He followed authorities on soil chemistry like Liebig, listened to scientific associates like Mapes and George E. Waring, and his basic ideas on intensive cultivation, liming, draining, and fencing were sound and practical. Greeley had surprisingly modern views on conservation, especially of forests, and on the mechanization of agricultural production. He saw the possibilities of farm coöperatives and wrestled with the problem of distributing agricultural abundance, although he could see no answer to that problem other than a high protective tariff.[9] These views he passed on to the farmers of the nation through the columns of the *Tribune*, through books, by means of speeches at scores of agricultural fairs, and by the examples furnished to the thousands of visitors who traipsed over the grounds at Chappaqua. Greeley's influence on agriculture was definitely constructive.

Greeley was fond of his place at Chappaqua. He never tired of showing visitors his stone barn, built at a cost of over $6,000, the fields that he had reclaimed by drainage and by grubbing out rocks and stumps, the springs of crystal pure water, equipped with tin drinking cups that were periodically stolen. It was home and he loved it with a deep affection, but like the place at Turtle Bay it was a most peculiar home.

When Greeley lived at Turtle Bay, he was wont to refer half-jokingly to his house as "Castle Doleful." Twenty years later, in concluding a lugubrious account of conditions at Chappaqua, he exclaimed, "We are a forlorn household."[10] Such expressions symbolized the sadness of Greeley's home life, where tension, hypochondria, fanaticism, and neglect combined to make a hell out of that domestic heaven which every man believes is his due.

The Mary Greeley who ruled the ménage at Turtle Bay and then at Chappaqua was quite a different person from the spirited, gay little bride that Horace had taken to himself in 1836 in Squire Bragg's parlor. The woman whom Greeley habitually addressed as "Mother" was a strong-minded female, a perfectionist with decided opinions on subjects ranging from the education of children to social regeneration and the life beyond the grave. She was also a thin-lipped complainer, with an inveterate propensity for dissatisfaction with everything and everybody. Her hatred of dirt, a hatred that led her to be perpetually scrubbing out the rock basin of her favorite spring with soap, was not paralleled by any genuine taste for domesticity, and in consequence the work done about the house was characterized by a kind of furious aimlessness. This, plus her explosive temper— "Her words had a kind of crack like the report of a rifle," wrote one observer—[11] was too much for such domestics as could be lured into the trap. They came and went everlastingly, and almost the same could be said of her circle of acquaintances. "I wish it were possible for her to have one wise, devoted and helpful friend," Greeley wrote wistfully in 1859. Alice Cary, a gentle spirit indeed, was reported as saying that she never once visited the Greeleys without being insulted.[12]

Decisive and forthright in her opinions, Molly Greeley seemed to take delight in affronting those who thwarted her will or transgressed her code of the right and proper. Walking up to a passenger on a Staten Island ferry, she snatched his cigar out of his mouth and threw it overboard while Horace stood by, momentarily expecting to be knocked down by the outraged smoker. On one occasion the family became involved in a Sunday morning squabble that developed out of Molly's determination to march up Broadway to Dr. Chapin's church accompanied by the three goats that furnished milk for the children. The usually conciliatory Horace balked at this, and they went to church goatless but with Molly fuming. "It's only your cussed pride," she flung at her husband. On another occasion she remarked bitterly before one of their acquaintances that, "damn it," she was a slave in her own house and had no rights there—a completely unjust comment, to judge by the absolute way in which she ruled the rearing of the family brood, and laid down the law as to when and where she would travel.

Molly had crotchets on a wide variety of subjects. She abhorred kid gloves, apparently because of her strong aversion to the killing of animals. This dislike led to a brief but spirited exchange with Margaret Fuller. The two met on the street one day and Molly touched the angular spinster's gloved hand, then drew back with a shudder exclaiming, "Skin of a beast, skin of a beast." "What do you wear?" asked Margaret. "Silk," was the reply, whereupon Margaret, just touching Molly's outstretched hand, shuddered in turn and exclaimed, "Entrails of a worm."[13]

Greeley's attitude toward his wife seems to have been one of exemplary patience, at least in the presence of witnesses. Bearing all things, enduring all things, rarely lifting his voice in admonition or reproach, he would either attempt to stem the torrent of complaints and jibes with a mildly persuasive logic or, if this did not avail, he would pull his ax out from under the living-room sofa and go out to hack away at his evergreens. But in his letters to Margaret Fuller, Margaret Allen, and Mrs. E. W. Newhall (these latter two friends of many years standing) Greeley made clear the trials that he and his household suffered from the nervousness, the hypochondria, and the well-nigh insane manias of his helpmeet.

A letter that Greeley wrote in 1856 showed the spirit in which, with the passage of the years, he had come to view his wife's hypochondriacal tendencies. "Mother," he wrote to Mrs. Newhall, was in better health than she had been for some time.

Six weeks ago, she had fully made up her mind to die of a rather quick consumption, and came down here [from Chappaqua] to have Curtis second the motion; but he was obstinately, perversely, conceitedly, dogmatically hostile to it, and, after a determined struggle, she was obliged to give it up. I have not heard of it since, though she is complaining a good deal.[14]

Greeley's convictions as to the sanctity of the marriage contract were such as to preclude all thoughts of divorce, but a story told by Henry Jarvis Raymond may well indicate Horace's inmost convictions regarding his own marriage. While on the *Tribune,* Raymond

was tempted by the offer of a schoolteaching job in North Carolina.
Greeley said with earnestness: "Don't go to North Carolina, Raymond. I married my wife there."[15]

The Greeleys' domestic life, such as it was, centered for many
years around their efforts at raising a family. At first these efforts
seemed doomed to failure. During the first five and one-half years
of their marriage, Molly had two miscarriages and lost two children
at birth, each of these occurrences leaving her nervously distraught.[16] Perhaps the misery thus endured was in part responsible
for the habit she formed in the early 1840's of spending her summers in or near Boston, where she became acquainted with Margaret
Fuller and the other New England intellectuals. But if she went to
Boston for the relief afforded by a change of scene, the results were
of only temporary benefit.

Regardless of the woeful effects of these efforts at childbearing,
the Greeleys continued their quest for progeny and at length it was
crowned with success. In March 1844, Arthur Young Greeley was
born.

Arthur ("Pickie" to his family) had golden hair and blue eyes.
High-strung and nervous from his cradle days, he was subject to
fits of terrible temper and savage crying. His propensity for destruction was something to marvel at. Hats, letters, watches, dishes, nothing was safe in the hands of this golden boy. But he was affectionate,
and his love of fun and his bubbling joyousness were endearing
traits. Save when in his rages, he was beautiful. His father and
mother worshiped him; childless Margaret Fuller, in her own way
as imperious and as warm as he, took him to her heart. She was
his "Aunty Margaret," and he loved her with an artless and bewitch-
ing affection.[17]

Horace was Pickie's devoted slave. He was certain that Pickie was
the most beautiful child that had ever lived. None of the Italian
painters, he was convinced, "had ever seen a child so lovely."[18] He
suffered the boy's tantrums patiently, content when his watch
crystal was not smashed more than once a week, and fussed anxiously but fruitlessly over the training that was being handed out
to his son and heir.

For Molly Greeley had ideas as to how Pickie should be brought
up, and to the fulfillment of those ideas she committed all her
energies. Her purpose was so centered that she openly regretted the
birth of a daughter, Mary Inez, in November 1846. The little girl
was an unwelcome distraction until she conveniently died of dysen-
tery in 1847.[19]

Molly insisted on taking Pickie with her to spend the summers

near Boston. There she could have him all to herself. Nothing was
too costly for him. As his father said, "Pickie is a dear boy in every
sense of the word." An hour a day was spent in bathing him and
brushing his long, silken hair. Meat, candy, butter, sugar, and even
salt, if his aunt Esther is to be believed, were excluded from his
diet. The bare floor of his nursery was scrubbed daily. He was given
a real violin, and his playthings were chosen to suggest ideas to his
mind. Other children, since they might prove sources of physical or
moral contamination, were excluded from his presence. When he
was over five years old, he was still in his baby clothes—to give
him freedom of movement. Despite his father's protests, he was not
vaccinated and his long, golden hair, his mother's pride and joy,
was never cut. Molly Greeley was determined to make him a beautiful combination of intellect and nature, fully equipped with
"choice" thoughts and language.[20]

Of course Pickie was overprotected, and of course he reacted by
rebelling against his mother. She was "so particular, particular,
particular, particular," he told a highly diverted audience at the
Red Bank phalanx. She would not let him eat "dirty food," such
as other people ate. "Don't you dare to shut me up in a room!
Ain't you ashamed to strike me, you ugly creature," he would shriek.
"I don't care for Truthness; I like fun," he told his mother on
another occasion. This attitude was in marked contrast to that
which he manifested toward his father, who let him do just about
as he liked. "He has often threatened to leave his mother, but
never to leave me. He and I are very needful to each other," Horace
wrote to Margaret Fuller.[21]

Molly was so strong minded and Horace was at home so little
that the latter could exert small influence upon the boy's upbring-
ing. Still, he did his best, for he wished Pickie to develop into "an
Associationist and a Christian" and the youngster scarcely seemed
headed toward either of those goals. When Pickie was three and
one-half years old, Horace craftily prevailed upon a fellow Fourierite, Miss Emma Whiting, to take charge of the boy. She was told
that this idea had Molly's enthusiastic consent, the fact that Molly
had declared that Horace must live in some other house if Emma
Whiting came, being carefully omitted from his letter. Emma's fears
concerning her own frail health were calmed by the Delphic assur-
ance that "if you don't acquire hardihood with us, it cannot be done
anywhere." Horace raved about the "spiritual and beauteous
aspect" of the moonlit nights at Turtle Bay, and paid Emma's fare
from Chicago ($30.00) in advance.[22]

Pickie liked Miss Whiting. Molly, however, was sullen. She complained that Emma's eyes were evil, and that her "magnetism" was bad. After a few weeks of this, Emma packed herself off to the Red Bank phalanx, and Pickie reverted to his mother's tender care.

Life ran along with no more than its usual confusion at Turtle Bay until the summer of 1849, with Pickie still unvaccinated and still in his baby clothes. There were only two pieces of family news in early summer. Little Ida Greeley, born in November 1848, was "a wonder of good temper and common sense," strange contrast to her brother, and a runaway horse had strewn Horace, Molly, and Pickie along the highway, fortunately with no serious results other than the demolition of the carriage. But there was cholera in downtown New York. Suddenly, without the least warning, it struck at Castle Doleful.

On the evening of July 11, Pickie was in his usual bounding spirits, but at two o'clock in the morning the family were roused by the first symptoms of the dread disease. As the awful vomiting and purging developed, the distracted parents tried without effect the homeopathic remedies that were Molly Greeley's latest fad. A doctor was summoned and came at seven o'clock, but could stay only a short time because of the critical condition of his own wife. He left directions for treatment with the Greeleys, directions that, as Horace afterward pitifully wrote, "we did not fully understand." When the doctor came back at noon, Pickie had lost ground badly and the last desperate measures taken to stem the course of the disease were without avail. Collapse commenced at three o'clock. Two hours later Pickie was dead.[23]

The Greeleys were distracted by Pickie's death. Horace feared for Molly's reason, and he himself was deep in despair. His letter to Margaret Fuller—"Ah Margaret! the world grows dark with us. You grieve, for Rome has fallen; I mourn, for Pickie is dead!"—was overdramatic, but other letters bore convincing proof of the grievousness of his affliction.

What he was to me, even you can hardly dream [he wrote to a close friend]. You that have two sons, in whom the natural thirst of the heart was earlier satisfied, can hardly know what my one ewe-lamb was to me. That he might live, that I might grow daily better for his sake, that I might not spoil him by overweening love, were ever recurring thoughts. God be merciful to me a sinner.

The thought kept recurring that the death of this only son had a moral significance. "Pestilence is a divinely devised correction of our Physical and Moral transgressions," Greeley wrote in the *Tribune,* and he told Seward that there was consolation in the removal of the danger that he might at some time have been swerved from the path of duty by devotion to the boy's interests.[24]

Both parents in their grief turned to spiritualism, which was then in the limelight because of the recent "rappings" of the Fox sisters at Hydesville, New York. Molly, who in her wildest grief fancied that she "saw" Pickie, was an easy convert, and Horace, too, felt that there was reality behind the manifestations. The Greeleys took Katy Fox into their household for a short time, soon after Pickie's death. She held some seances at the Castle, and they "received" some banal messages from Pickie. On one of these occasions the Swedish Nightingale, Jenny Lind, was an interested participant. She accused Horace of tipping the table with his own hands, an accusation that was indignantly denied by the bereaved father. At another session with a medium, the table was tipped by a spook which proceeded to deluge the assembled company with a great wave of forecastle profanity. At length he disclosed that he had been a pirate in the flesh whereupon he was promptly sent back to the shades of eternal night. Such occurrences were not altogether convincing to the participants in these seances. Horace came to the conclusion that spiritualism was a swindle, albeit a clever one.[25]

The Greeleys had other children than Pickie and those that died in infancy. Ida Lilian, as stable as Pickie had been mercurial, survived the cholera scourge and grew to womanhood. A second son, Raphael Uhland, born in 1851, died six years later of "malignant" croup. That same year (1857) the Greeleys' last child was born, strong-willed, tempestuous Gabrielle. She, like Ida, survived her parents. But out of nine children conceived, the Greeleys lost seven. It was a heartbreaking record.

What was Greeley like as husband and father? There can be no question that he was naturally affectionate. Visitors at his home noticed this; his generosity to his family bespoke the same virtue and his correspondence contains many affectionate references to and passages for his children.

Your sore, sick father sends this to remind you how much he loves you and to entreat you not to forget him [he wrote to Pickie in 1849]. He is tired of the crowd of noisy and heartless strangers around him. . . . Most gladly would he leave them for his own crazy, old house and his boy's bright smiles. . . . How do you like the dog, my baby? I hope you and he are good friends and stand up for each other against the world. I hope to be home with you on Friday next. Kiss your mother in love to me, my dear boy, and be sure to remember your poor lorn father.[26]

There were happy times when Horace would take his family riding in the buggy or walking on the estate. There were evenings when Horace would pull out of his pocket some magazine that he had brought home, or pick up a copy of Whittier and read by the flickering light something that had struck his fancy. And there was at least one happy summer, in 1845, when he now and then went down to Rockaway with Mollie and Pickie and Margaret Fuller, and reveled in sea bathing by moonlight, and dreamed of teaching Pickie to swim.[27]

But such occasions were few and far between, for many obstacles stood between Greeley and a normal family life. The incessant demands of his newspaper work took up much time, and so did his political activities. That they so engrossed him was probably due in some measure to the lack of a genuine community of interest with his wife. Her indifference to politics, the hypochondria that grew upon her with the years, the quarrelsome querulousness with which she often overwhelmed her husband when he did come home, all served to produce an impossible family relationship and turn him to outside interests. One of these interests, more and more time-consuming as Greeley became a national figure, was lecturing to audiences both in the East and in the Middle West.

During the 1840's and 1850's in America, lecturing was in high vogue. Every state and county fair had its speakers, and there was scarcely a town of three thousand or over that did not have its village syndicate, or lyceum, an organization that provided the area with a winter lecture series. Sooner or later, these towns were visited by such giants of the lecture platform as Emerson, Beecher, Oliver Wendell Holmes, Theodore Parker, John B. Gough, and John G. Saxe. When they spoke, the people listened with avid curiosity. It was, as Carl Schurz put it, "the middle class culture in process of formation."[28] Schurz found such lecturing inspiring. Greeley found it inspiring, remunerative and, for such a busy man as he, a great drain upon both time and energy.

Greeley began giving formal lectures at least as early as 1840 on such subjects as "The Formation of Character" and "Human Life."[29] At first there was little call for his services, for his delivery was halting and his weak, high voice was scarcely suited to the lecture platform.[30] But his audiences liked his earnestness, and the "facts" that he showered down upon them in political campaigns were, to say the least, impressive. With experience, his confidence increased, and the growing prestige of the *Tribune* called him to wider and wider fields, as did his personal reputation as a figure of national importance. By 1852 he was away lecturing "a full third of the time," so he told Schuyler Colfax,[31] and thereafter the demands on his time as a speaker increased rather than diminished. There was also a corresponding increase in the remuneration involved.

At first Greeley spoke willingly without pay. As late as 1850 he was never paid in New York City, and only about half the time when he spoke away from home. But even then he sometimes received fifty dollars for a lecture, which was indeed a promise of brighter things to come. For in the latter 1850's and 1860's, Greeley came to rank in popularity as a lecturer close to such outstanding figures as Beecher and John B. Gough. In those flush times, lecturing on temperance, slavery, and kindred themes of moral import, he would take in $6,000 to $7,000 in a single winter.[32]

The monetary return from lecturing was more than acceptable to a man who was inveterately careless about money matters, and who was blessed with an expensive family. Nevertheless the incessant traveling was hard on family relationships. Sleepless nights on stage and train, six-o'clock risings so that political paragraphs for the *Tribune* might be scribbled off before the day's journey began, inadequate meals, speaking at fairs on an open-air platform and in competition with bellowing bulls, braying jacks, and squealing stallions, traveling 1090 miles and giving three lectures in three and one-half days, pushing across the prairie, rainsoaked, cramped, revolted by the endless mud or by a young Hoosier's plea of "Mother, give me some of that gin," which mother promptly produced from a pocket pistol—such experiences, coupled with the ever-present conviction that mountains of work were piling up in his office at the *Tribune,* scarcely returned a man calm and refreshed to the bosom of his family.[33]

Desire for the society of more normal people than his wife and for the pleasures of intellectual companionship also tended to disrupt the Greeley ménage by luring the paterfamilias away from the home fires. One of the first issues of the *Tribune* carried under the heading "Hints to Sick Wives" the remark of a "popular author" that "sick wives are very interesting for a short time, and very dull for a long one."[34] There can be no doubt that, as Molly's hypochondria increased, Greeley tended more and more to find an utterly chaste solace in outside companionships.

Margaret Fuller lived at Castle Doleful during her stay in New York. There was an initial period of strain between her host and herself. She was too ardent a feminist for Greeley's taste. When he openly disapproved of her tea drinking, he was rebuked for his pains. But Greeley admired her intellect and his heart warmed to her as she wrote brilliantly, if somewhat scantily, for the *Tribune*. Then, too, Margaret had a way of enlisting people's confidences and worming out their inmost secrets. The tenor of the subsequent correspondence between these two gifted and unusual people makes it practically certain that, before Margaret left for Europe, Greeley was finding an escape from the troubles and anxieties of his family life by talking them over with this New England maiden of the warm and sympathetic heart.

New York furnished Greeley with many other interesting friends. By the latter 1840's he was frequenting Miss Anne Lynch's "evenings" at her home in Waverley Place, where Bryant, Nathaniel P. Willis, Fitz-Greene Halleck, Richard Henry Stoddard, and other literary lights foregathered. Greeley was also a frequent visitor at the salon of the Cary sisters, Alice and Phoebe, after they came to New York in 1850. He knew and liked Susan B. Anthony. Antoinette Brown Blackwell sought his advice on more than one occasion. Elizabeth Cady Stanton was a friend who would straighten his tie and push his trouser leg down into his boot before she would let him appear on a public platform. Margaret Allen and her sister Alexia Graham, admirable ladies blest not so much with intellect as with warm human sympathies and charm, were his devoted friends, and Mrs. Allen was a confidante in much the same way as was Margaret Fuller.[35]

It was through the great showman, P. T. Barnum, that Greeley had first met Mrs. Allen. Barnum was something of a reformer in his own right, and as a connoisseur of the unusual had perhaps a keener appreciation of Greeley's oddities than did the latter's feminine friends. In later years, Barnum told with infinite relish of an incident that occurred before his acquaintance with the *Tribune's* editor ripened into close friendship.

On a certain Sunday morning after church, Barnum and his daughter Caroline happened to board a horsecar in which Greeley was seated. Caroline asked her father for an introduction to his friend. Barnum said, "Mr. Greeley, this is my eldest daughter, Caroline." Horace looked at her, his gaze traveling from her head to her feet and back again to her face, but made not a single sign of recognition, his thoughts doubtless concentrated on some knotty political problem. The mortified girl said afterward to her father— "Well, father, that is the most curious introduction I ever had to any person. What was the man thinking about?"[36] Had Greeley been asked the same question, he would probably have been as much at a loss for the answer as was Barnum.

Despite, or perhaps because of, such bizarre occurrences, Greeley and Barnum became very good friends, and Greeley visited frequently at Barnum's home. There the agent of Tom Thumb and Jenny Lind arranged a desk to the editor's taste. On it many an editorial signed "H. G." was written, and the library served as a private place of appointment where Greeley met politicians and office-seekers. When work was over, Barnum would try unsuccessfully to persuade his guest to put off his thick-soled cowhide boots for a pair of carpet slippers. Horace did, however, become accustomed to taking off his coat and using one of Barnum's dressing gowns.[37]

Friends, lecturing, editorial labors, campaign workdays that meant sixteen hours of labor out of twenty-four—these absorbed most of Greeley's time and attention and kept him more and more away from home. In those directions ambition and interest beckoned, and Molly's deepening queerness and irascibility had no influence other than to confirm him in his course. Thus was created a vicious circle that had been begun in the earliest years of their married life. His early absences at Albany, when his wife was at home, pregnant and alone, may well have contributed to her mental irascibility, and the Albany job was swiftly succeeded by even more absorbing and time-consuming interests. The extent to which Greeley neglected his family while they were still at Turtle Bay was inadvertently confessed by him in a letter to Margaret Fuller. From the summer of 1846 to the end of January 1848, he took dinner at home only twice, and his only week end with his family during that same period came when his daughter Mary Inez died.[38] Such a home life could scarcely be called a well-adjusted one. In fact, it could scarcely be called home life at all.

After Greeley bought his farm at Chappaqua in 1853, his wife stayed there a major part of each year that she was not traveling abroad. Greeley himself had resolved to spend most of his time there, reserving about three days a week for the *Tribune* office.[39] But, despite such good intentions, Greeley found relatively little time for his estate. When in New York, Saturdays were all he could spare for the delights of rural life, and even then his family could count with no certainty upon his being with them.

When Brockway went up to Chappaqua with Greeley in 1857 and they met Ida on the piazza, the little girl seemed completely indifferent to her father's appearance at the farm.[40] There had been all too little time for the cultivation of a normal parent-child relationship.

Greeley's family life was subnormal. The responsibility for that sad fact rested upon Horace as much as it did upon the frustrated and lonesome Molly. Her winter trips to the West Indies and her year-long jaunts to Europe in never-ending quest of the health which perpetually eluded her were probably no more due to physical maladies, real or fancied, than they were to the solitude and boredom of the life which Horace provided for her in the place they called their home.

NOTES FOR CHAPTER 12

1. Wm. A. Butler, *A Retrospect of Forty Years* (N. Y., 1911), p. 232.
2. Greeley Papers (N. Y. P. L.), Greeley to E. Whiting, Aug. 30, 1847.
3. Greeley, *Recollections,* pp. 176-77.
4. Greeley, *What the Sister Arts Teach as to Farming* (N. Y., 1853), pp. 32-33.
5. E. D. Ross, "Horace Greeley and Agriculture," *Agricultural History,* VII (Jan. 1933), 7f.
6. Greeley, *Recollections,* p. 297.
7. Seitz, *op. cit.,* p. 291.
8. Greeley, *Recollections,* p. 303; Stahl Collection, M. Allen to her sister, May 1, 1871; Greeley Letters (Onon. Hist. Soc.), Greeley to V. W. Smith, Dec. 2, 1853; Brockway, *op. cit.,* p. 71.
9. Ross, *loc. cit.,* pp. 13f.; Greeley, *What the Sister Arts Teach as to Farming,* pp. 3-33; Greeley, *What I Know of Farming,* pp. 62f., 66-68, 76, 96, 107f., 124, 134.
10. Fuller Correspondence, Greeley to M. Fuller, Jan. 29, 1849, and elsewhere; Stahl Collection, Greeley to Mrs. Alexia Graham, June 7, 1868.
11. Brockway, *op. cit.,* p. 159.
12. Greeley Letters (Lib. of Cong.), Greeley to M. Allen, July 14, 1859; Brockway, *op. cit.,* p. 167.
13. Brockway, *op. cit.,* p. 157.
14. Greeley Papers (N. Y. P. L.), Greeley to Mrs. E. W. Newhall, Sept. 12, 1856.
15. Seitz, *op. cit.,* p. 336.
16. Greeley Papers (N. Y. P. L.), Greeley to O. A. Bowe, Feb. 2, 1842; Greeley, *Recollections,* p. 426.
17. Cleveland, *op. cit.,* pp. 243f.
18. J. Benton (ed.), *Greeley on Lincoln* (N. Y., 1893), p. 193.
19. Fuller Correspondence, Greeley to M. Fuller, July 29, 1847; Griswold Papers, Greeley to Griswold, Nov. 21, 1846.
20. Cleveland, *op. cit.,* pp. 239f.; Fuller Correspondence, *passim.*
21. *Ibid.,* Greeley to M. Fuller, June 27, July 29, Nov. 19, 1848, June 23, 1849.
22. Greeley Papers (N. Y. P. L.), Greeley to E. Whiting, Aug. 30, Sept. 25, 1847; Fuller Correspondence, Greeley to M. Fuller, Sept. 14, 29, 1847.
23. Greeley Letters (U. of R.), Greeley to Colfax, Aug 2, 1849; Fuller Correspondence, Greeley to M. Fuller, July 23, 1849.
24. Greeley Papers (N. Y. P. L.), Greeley to Colfax, Aug. 2, 1849; Seward Papers, Greeley to Seward, July 18, 1849; *Tribune,* Aug 3, 1849, Apr. 21, 1889.
25. Greeley, *Recollections,* pp. 234, 237; Greeley Papers (N. Y. P. L.), Greeley to Colfax, Dec. 26, 1850; M. Hansen-Taylor and H. E. Scudder, *Life and Letters to Bayard Taylor* (2 vols.; Boston, 1885). I, 194; *Tribune,* July 11, 1858. Old Zack Greeley, out in Pennsylvania, became a thorough-paced convert to spiritualism.

26. Greeley Papers (N. Y. P. L.), *New York Herald* (clipping), June 9, 1889.
27. Barnes, *op. cit.*, pp. 131-32.
28. Schurz, *Reminiscences*, II, 157-58.
29. Greeley Papers (N. Y. P. L.), Greeley to O. A. Bowe, Nov. 20, 1840.
30. *Ibid.*, Greeley to J. W. Lake, July 2, 1840; Greeley was always deprecatory about his lecturing.
31. Greeley Papers (N. Y. P. L.), Greeley to Colfax, Jan. 20, 1852.
32. Greeley Letters (N. Y. S. Lib.), Greeley to H. F. Harrington, March 6, 1850; Anthony Collec. (N. Y. P. L.), Greeley to A. B. Wiggin, Oct. 15, 1850; Greeley Papers (N. Y. P. L.), Greeley to C. H. Plummer, Oct. 22, 1854; W. Reid, *Horace Greeley* (1879), p. 27.
33. Greeley Papers (N. Y. P. L.), Greeley to Colfax, March 17, 1850, Jan. 20, 1852, Sept. 30, 1853; Greeley, *What I Know about Farming*, pp. 225f.; *Tribune*, May 21, Dec. 7, 1849, Mar. 16, 1854; R. L. Rusk, *The Life of Ralph Waldo Emerson* (N. Y., 1949), p. 395.
34. *Tribune*, Apr. 26, 1841.
35. Greeley Papers (N. Y. P. L.), Antoinette Blackwell to Greeley, July 19, 1858; Greeley, "Alice and Phoebe Cary," *Eminent Women of the Age*, pp. 166-67; Greeley, *Recollections*, pp. 177f.; Brooks, *Times of Melville and Whitman*, pp. 22f.; Seitz, *op. cit.*, p. 337.
36. Greeley Papers (N. Y. P. L.), Reminiscence of Greeley by Barnum (clipping).
37. *Ibid.;* Benton, *op. cit.*, pp. 167-241.
38. Fuller Correspondence, Greeley to M. Fuller, Jan. 27, 1848.
39. Greeley Papers (N. Y. P. L.), Greeley to Colfax, Jan. 18, 1853.
40. Brockway, *op. cit.*, p. 158.

Interlude

———

LIFE IN NEW YORK ROARED INTO FULL TIDE WITH the 1850's. The census at the beginning of the decade put the city's population at 515,000, to which almost exactly 300,000 were added during the next ten years despite Greeley's repeated adjurations to "go forth into the fields!"[1] Indeed, the city's increase in size was much greater than the official figures indicated. Counting the New Yorkers who sprawled up and down the North and East Rivers, along the Jersey and Long Island coasts of the bay, beside the Harlem and far up into Westchester County, the total population in or near the city by 1860 had reached some 1,500,000 souls. At least, so thought the *Tribune*.

The great metropolis was filled with the hum and bustle of business activity. Banks, insurance companies, commercial warehouses, factories and stores, and nearly all the depots for the products of the interior well-nigh monopolized the lower wards. Millions of dollars' worth of business were transacted in those wards with amazing speed and dispatch. Even at the beginning of the decade, the masses of products floating into this district every hour from the Erie Canal covered acres in space, and the trains rolling in on the Erie Railroad every day could be measured by miles in length. Broadway, main artery of the city's life, was alive with activity from five in the morning to after midnight, as laborers, clerks, businessmen, shoppers, and theatre crowds milled along its sidewalks. Even in the deepest hours of the night, shadowy figures moved up and down its length as the street cleaners wielded their birch brooms in the flickering gaslight.[2]

The city's dynamic manifested itself also in a host of changes and improvements. Cab fares diminished and the huge, clumsy omnibuses were halved in number as five-cent-fare transportation came in with the horsecars on the avenues. There was an underground sewage system by 1854, even though many houses were still not serviced by it. The development of Central Park was begun in 1853, and two years later Castle Garden was established as the landing depot for the thousands of immigrants swarming into the city. Paving improved in quality and quantity, though the "Russ" pavement that covered stretches of Broadway with granite blocks wore so smooth that horses fell right and left upon its slippery surface and it had to be torn up. There was more talk than ever, though only talk, about a bridge to Brooklyn.[3]

New Yorkers had lost none of their naïveté nor of their interest in the sensational, as the years had rolled by. When Jenny Lind arrived in 1850 for a concert tour under Barnum's auspices, the black, red, and gold ensign of the short-lived German Republic was run up to greet her, there being no Swedish flag at quarantine. Apparently, one European flag did as well as another in the eyes of the port authorities. The Swedish songstress wished to visit the office of a metropolitan newspaper and so of course was taken to that of Mr. Barnum's friend, Mr. Greeley. A huge crowd blocked the entrance when she was ready to leave the *Tribune* building. She drew back, but a husky fireman roared out, "Don't be afraid, Jenny," and the Nightingale went on her way with the crowd's huzzas ringing in her ears.[4] In 1856, Niblo's Saloon judged it a good investment to have Miss Clara Darling, dressed in Indian costume and surrounded by aboriginal scenery, deliver Longfellow's "Hiawatha" to the delighted guests of the establishment. A year later, Newport resorts advertised for New York custom by spreading the news that "John Dean and his own Mary Ann" (a coachman and a wealthy New York liquor merchant's daughter, who had married despite the frenzied efforts of the latter's parents to ship her off to Europe) had summer quarters near the beach. Niagara Falls resorts countered this news with reports of a great sea serpent in "nearby" Lake Ontario. Anyone could get up a stir any time by bringing up the subject of Free Love.[5]

Barnum was always ready to capitalize upon the curiosity of New Yorkers. A brass band blared from a street balcony before each performance at his Museum. A baby show at the Museum in 1855 jammed Broadway for three days with well-dressed mothers, infants, and interested spectators, netting the master of ceremonies from $10,000 to $20,000. The great showman also advertised a free buffalo hunt, à la the Wild West, over at Hoboken, and crowds thronged across the river on specially chartered ferryboats to watch some lethargic buffaloes being driven around a ten-acre lot. But everybody was happy, the show being free, and Barnum was happiest of all. He had chartered the ferryboats.[6]

Broadway centered the comedy and tragedy of the city's life. It provided an endless number of human-interest stories, from a shirt sleeved b'hoy trudging his son home pick-a-back across the muddy street, to the sight of George (Live-Oak) Law, steamboat and railroad man, dirty as a short-boy, with little, piggy eyes and a face like a raw beefsteak, brushing people out of his way and grunting to a crony that American institutions were "self-working and self-preserving."[7] It smiled knowingly when the divorce suit that followed Forrest's public caning of Nathaniel Parker Willis (for seducing the actor's wife) resulted in a jury verdict that it was the actor, not Mrs. Forrest, who had committed adultery. It looked on with amusement, one November day in 1857, as a dashing young woman gowned in black jumped out of a swank carriage just above Bowling Green, seized a nattily dressed gentleman by the collar, beat him with a stout gutta-percha whip until he writhed and yelled, then jumped in her carriage and drove off, the cowhided one fleeing in the opposite direction.[8] That same year it saw John Morrissey, pugilist extraordinary, go on one of his famous "benders."

It was seven o'clock on the morning of May 6, 1857. The place was the barroom of the Girard House, on the corner of Chambers Street and West Broadway. Morrissey and his pal John Petrie, having made a night of it, undertook to lie on the bar and go to sleep. Barkeep Gilbert protested and Morrissey threw a pitcher at him, then reached for anything lying loose on the bar. Glassware crashed under the great mirror. Fists began to fly and the gentleman at the viands counter, one Conway, came to the barkeeper's rescue, calling out for him to use his club. A platter with a round of beef on it hurtled through the air. Conway ducked, and came up to see a pistol in Morrissey's hand. The keeper of the viands ducked again as the gun went off, the ball going through the window and neatly perforating the hat of a startled passerby. Conway drew, and the fight boiled out into Broadway where he and Morrissey exchanged pistol shots. A policeman appeared on the scene but as the arm of the law advanced Morrissey drew a knife, exclaiming, "I'll rip your damned guts out." It took a posse to subdue the future state senator and congressman, but he was soon out on $5,000 bail.[9]

When Broadway sought more formal entertainment, it ran the gamut from Shakespeare to minstrels. In so doing it accepted much that was mediocre or worse. It sighed over the vapid sentimentalities of Elizabeth Wetherell's *Queechy*. It looked in with hardened, curious eyes on meetings where shoddy evangelists ranted about hell and red heifers going straight to damnation. *Uncle Tom's Cabin*, blatantly melodramatic, played to packed houses while the Bowery b'hoys, long the sworn enemies of abolitionists, wept and cursed Simon Legree and the slaveholders. But if some of the street's tastes were open to challenge, it also took to itself much that was good. *Midsummer Night's Dream* drew crowds almost as dense as those that flocked to see the misadventures of Uncle Tom. William Makepeace Thackeray, lecturing in the winter of 1852 on the English literati of the eighteenth century, and carrying on a side flirtation that was the talk of the town with showy young brunette Miss Baxter, was very well received indeed.[10] The spritelike Maggie Mitchell, "touched by the moon," enchanted her audiences. And then one Monday evening, it was August 31, 1857, at the opening of Laura Keene's theatre, a pair of drunken legs coming through a doorway convulsed the audience with laughter before ever the face or the figure of the owner appeared. How had this "man of genius," this "comedian from his nose to his toes," managed to hide himself from the New York managers, inquired the *Tribune*. Jo Jefferson had arrived.[11]

New York furnished artistry and good fun for those who appreciated such things, but it also furnished much that was rough and brutal. The sports and the short-boys liked their entertainment in the raw. Gang fights boiled up periodically. Prize fighters mauled one another on the city docks or, to evade the law, moved over into Jersey for their encounters. On September 18, 1856, Morrissey and a crowd of the fancy saw Charley Lynch and Andy Kelly go eighty-five rounds at the Palisades in New Jersey, near Piermont. At the eighty-sixth round Kelly rose, squared off, and fell over backward on the ground, insensible. He died that day, and the *Tribune* and the other papers carried all the gory details.

The tone of the press was as low as the tastes of the fancy. James Gordon Bennett in the *Herald* set the pace, but the other daily papers were not too far behind. Even the *Tribune* shared the general contagion. It was that paper which gleefully recounted in 1853 that Bennett, "the low-mouthed, blatant, witless, brutal" proprietor of that "sewer-sheet" the *Herald,* had had nine horsewhippings, had suffered divers cuts, cuffings, and kickings, and had had "his jaws forced open and his throat spit into." When Henry Ward Beecher rebuked the newspapers for their sensational handling of Daniel Sickles' murder of his wife's lover in 1859, the *Tribune* retorted savagely that it felt virtuous rather than guilty. It had undoubtedly saved Henry Ward the odious necessity of jumping up before he had finished his breakfast and running around the corner to buy a *Herald* so as to get all the lurid details. Greeley believed in an international copyright law, but in 1857 the *Tribune* pirated Thackeray's *The Virginians* from the Harpers, who had paid $2,000 for it, and then lied brazenly in a vain attempt to cover up the steal.[12]

The contrasts furnished by New York between refinement and brutality were matched by contrasts of wealth and poverty more glaring than in any previous decade. The town boomed and business expanded, save for the sharp but short panic of 1857. Millions in gold poured in from the California diggings, and the *nouveau riche* sprang up on all sides. Marriages were made by money, as the Paul Potiphars learned from the Flora M'Flimseys.[13] Hoops and crinolines, velvet and damask silk, and the splendor of broadcloth were seated by the smug ushers of the fashionable churches before the common run were permitted to enter the sacred precincts, for why should not those who could afford to pay be given the best at the Lord's table? The wealthy and magnificent were at home in the Fifth Avenue "palaces" whose carved granite or brownstone entrances, mosaic-floored vestibules, and museum-like drawing rooms (so ornately were they furnished with chandeliers and candelabra, sofas, prie-dieu, and bric-a-brac) proclaimed the poverty of their owners' tastes.[14] This vulgar wealth and display flaunted itself in heedless fashion beside the most dire poverty and appalling crime.

New York could afford scores of Fifth Avenue palaces. It could not, seemingly, afford one model lodginghouse for the poor. Crowded together in dark, filthy tenements, in many cases eight or ten persons to a room, packed like sardines in dirty lodging cellars where the rates ran as low as nine cents a week, the poverty-stricken masses of the city festered and stank and decayed. The *Tribune* charged in 1850 that one person out of every twenty in the city ate, drank, and slept underground; that the terrible crowding of the lower classes was steadily increasing the rate of mortality; and that 10,000 children were being trained on the New York City streets for beggary, theft, and prostitution. These charges were not the products of some reporter's imagination. They were based on police investigations. It was small wonder that gangs styling themselves the Bulls Head Lights, the First Ward Buckaneers, the Bowery Boys, and the Dead Rabbits roamed over large sections of the town, raping, pillaging, and, as in the summer of 1857, engaging in riots that necessitated calling out the militia.[15]

The gangs that terrorized the city were generally hand in glove with the city politicians. New York's government, in the clutches of this gentry, was rotten and corrupt. The *Tribune* spent much time exposing the ferry and railroad "jobs" that lined the pockets and bellies of the aldermen, the official compacts with vice, the indifference to flimsy tenement construction that all too often brought disaster and death in its wake. It spent much time also denouncing the apathy of business leaders who, through blindness or indifference, were in large part responsible for the existence of such loathsome conditions.[16]

New York's social evil seemed cancerous in its nature, for like a cancer it grew and spread. In 1857, the *Tribune* estimated that 10,000 prostitutes swarmed the city streets at night, that 5,000 gamblers plied their trade on Broadway, and that 10,000 short-boys, swill-boys, killers, roughs, and rowdies made the city streets a passage perilous. "There is not in the whole world," wrote Greeley in 1858, "a beastlier animal than the New York 'rowdy.' We believe that an unprotected woman would be safer among the savage tribes of America or Africa than in the streets of New York."[17]

Such was New York City in the 1850's, a symbol and center of the nation's materialism. Here Greeley had chosen to stand and wage his fight for the good life.

For Greeley's interest in New York's vice and crime was only one aspect of his broad concern for the welfare of the national society. That concern manifested itself in both political and social activity. The winter of 1850-51 saw him blasting at liquor, usury, and land monopoly, the while he helped Weed elect Hamilton Fish to the United States Senate over the opposition of the Cotton Whigs. As Cotton faced Conscience over the question of Fish's election, the Compromise again came in for a goodly share of attention. Once again Greeley expressed dislike for it, especially for the Fugitive Slave Law, and, to emphasize his dislike, he gave both money and time to helping escaped fugitive slaves. He was left wholly skeptical by the pledge of adherence to the Compromise signed by Henry Clay and over forty members of Congress in the winter of 1851. It smacked too much of regimentation, Greeley thought. It made him feel like the apprentice threatened with a hammering if he didn't say the bean soup was good. "It's good," the lad had whimpered, "but I don't like it."[18]

No amount of palaver, declared the *Tribune's* editor, could conceal the fundamental menace of slavery to the Union and to free institutions. "We consider Slavery essentially, necessarily aggressive," he wrote in April 1851, "and inevitably a cause of agitation and disturbance so long as it shall exist."[19] Four days after publishing this forthright blast, he went on board the steamer *Baltic* for his first trip to Europe.

When Greeley packed his carpetbag for his first trip across the

Atlantic, he planned to report the World's Fair that was being held in London's Crystal Palace, and then in fairly leisurely fashion make the Grand Tour of the continent. But on arriving in London he discovered that he had been made chairman of an exposition jury that made awards for the hardware exhibited at the fair. This responsibility, together with testifying before a Parliamentary commission investigating newspaper taxation, an address before an antislavery society, and one or two other public appearances took up so much time that it was June 7 before he left England.

Greeley's tour of the continent occupied somewhat less than two months, during which time he shambled methodically and earnestly through picture galleries, visited the usual high spots of interest, and purchased various *objets d'art* that struck his fancy or were recommended to him. Returning to England, he sailed from Liverpool on August 6 for home.

Greeley's attitude toward Europe and Europeans was a compound of genuine appreciation, superficial judgment, and rather testy patriotism. He liked Notre Dame and the Madeleine. He found Roman ruins and Roman art impressive. "Earth," he declared, "has nothing else to match with St. Peters." This was intended for publication and was written at a time when he, together with Weed and Seward, was still trying to woo the Catholic vote in New York. Ten years later, writing in a Protestant religious publication, he recalled that Rome had "seemed to me the metropolis also of ecclesiastical imposture," and recounted the scorn with which he heard a guide tell the tourists that a table which they saw in a Roman cellar was the altar at which "San Pedro" and "San Paulo" had offered the sacrifice of the mass.[20]

The letters that Greeley wrote for home consumption in 1851 abounded in shallow generalizations about the immoral French, cheating Italians, and patient, long-suffering Germans, together with equally hasty judgments in other matters. He was as confident that the Second Republic in France was firmly anchored as he was that Swiss honesty was due to Swiss republicanism. Throughout the trip he held firmly to a conviction of the superiority of things American, as perhaps was only fitting in a man who labeled Webster's bombastic note to Chevalier Hulsemann "thorough and perspicuous." American energy and the glory of American institutions rose repeatedly to Greeley's mind during the tour, and it was with a glow of "unwonted rapture" that he turned his face toward home and a crossing that involved for him all the horrors of extreme seasickness. Ruins and antiquities were all right in moderate doses, he confided to Seward, but as an everyday matter he preferred a daily paper with his breakfast.[21]

Greeley took occasion on his trip abroad to offer the British some good counsel. He urged Lord Milner's Parliamentary commission to stop taxation of newspaper advertising, and tartly advised British abolitionists that the debased situation of the British laborer played into the hands of the American apologists for black slavery.[22]

But if he felt disposed to criticize some British ways, he was also frank to admit that the Crystal Palace exhibition had given added vitality to his optimism regarding the world's future. This international gathering, "the first satisfactory model of a peace Congress," he told his readers, proclaimed the ultimate certainty of universal peace. It highlighted that resistless march of invention which, with the potentialities of steam not yet half exhausted, was reaching out for and ultimately would find other and greater sources of motive power. It showed that there was no such thing as overproduction, and that there never would be until every family on the globe was fully supplied with all that was necessary to moral and intellectual growth as well as physical comfort. It demonstrated the dignity of human labor, and the need for combination and coöperation to enable the laborer to work, not *against* or *for* but *with* machinery for an assured competence. This was a vision of the future that Greeley's America has since begun to turn into reality.

Such were some of the lessons that Greeley drew from this great industrial exhibition. To be sure, he also found there evidence of the need for a protective tariff, the argument being that America must resist the tendency to centralize manufacturing and commerce in Europe. But aside from this rather obvious lugging in of his protectionism, it was clear that the exhibition had enhanced his faith in humanity.[23]

Greeley came back to troublous times within the New York State Whig party, where Sewardite Woolly Heads and Fillmore Cotton Whigs were still at bitter odds. The two groups patched up a very hollow agreement in the shape of the 1851 state ticket (for which Greeley compaigned energetically), but the election demonstrated the avidity with which Cottons and Woollies would knife each other. And most of the ticket were defeated by their Democratic rivals.

Ignoring or minimizing the way in which Woolly voters knifed Cotton candidates, the *Tribune's* editor bitterly upbraided the Cotton Whigs as recreants. Cotton must understand, he warned, that if it meant to proscribe and silence those Whigs who hated slavery and slave-catching, its task was only begun.[24]

Greeley was "cross," he told Weed, a state of mind produced by the defeat and in no degree soothed by the fact that twenty-five dollars which he had contributed for last-minute campaign expenses had gone into the wrong pockets.[25] Hence it was all the easier for the peppery editor to become involved in a vigorous controversy with New York's leading Catholic prelate, Archbishop Hughes, the close friend of Weed and Seward.

For some time Greeley had been irked by Hughes's attitude toward the 1848 revolutions, and also by the Archbishop's views regarding secular education. Comments in the *Tribune* on these matters increased after the election, and Hughes finally replied to them in an open letter. He defended the Pope for refusing religious liberty in the Papal States (to do so would only stir up discord there), clearly intimated his opinion that Kossuth was a "humbug," and opposed New York State's secularized school system because it excluded Christianity from education. This letter drew an able, three-column editorial from Greeley. His advocacy of religious toleration, his defense of European liberalism, and his argument for keeping religious teaching separate from a state-supported system of education constituted a clear demonstration of his own progressive idealism.[26]

As Greeley departed, early in December, for what was fast becoming his annual lecture tour in the Middle West, he probably reflected with some satisfaction upon the way in which he had upheld the cause of liberty in his controversy with Archbishop Hughes. It is doubtful that any such feeling of elation was present in the breast of McElrath and the other *Tribune* associates. Greeley's battle for free, secular education cost the *Tribune* some 2,000 subscribers.[27]

When Greeley returned from his jaunt into the West, he at once plunged into the activities preceding the Whig national convention of 1852. There were three outstanding contestants for the Whig nomination that year—Fillmore, Webster, and Scott. To Greeley's way of thinking, the nomination of either of the first two would give the Cotton Whigs carte blanche in proscribing the Sewardites.[28] This left Scott as Greeley's only possible choice.

Greeley's opinion of Scott was not high. "Whenever we take up that good soldier but immeasurably conceited, aristocratic ass, Gen. Scott . . . I trust the Locos will have a better man and beat us," he had written to Colfax in 1850.[29] Time had not substantially altered this opinion of Old Fuss and Feathers any more than it had altered Greeley's belief, just as strongly held, that the Whig star was

declining and that aspiring young Whig politicians would do well
to adopt a wait-and-see attitude, rather than rush headlong into
office-seeking. But the Whigs had to nominate someone, so what
was there to do but plump for the General? Before the winter was
over, despite his misgivings about the limitations of Scott's mind
and character and his nativist leanings, Greeley was thumping the
tub for Winfield Scott as the prospective Whig candidate.[30]

Openly disdainful of national conventions, just as he had been in
1848, Greeley did not even go to the Whig conclave which assembled
in Baltimore on June 16, 1852. On the news of Scott's nomination,
however, the *Tribune* praised the General as a man of "transcendent
virtue and patriotism," and asserted that it flung the Whig banner
to the breeze "with no ordinary satisfaction."[31]

But such was not Greeley's feeling about other acts of the Whig
national convention. There had been no resolution passed in favor
of free land, and Greeley, who had been vigorously but vainly pushing for a homestead bill sponsored by Andrew Johnson that spring,
had been urgent for such a resolution.[32] Worse than the absence
of an endorsement of free land was the presence of a plank committing the party to acceptance of the Compromise. This plank,
Greeley declared, was both futile and preposterous—"We defy it,
execrate it, spit upon it." Granted that nothing could be done legis-
latively about slavery where it now existed, the fact remained that
all possible social and moral pressure must be used against this
"darkest stain on our National character," and its extension must
be sternly opposed. By failing to make this clear, the platform had
become a mere "Hunker platform."[33]

The *Tribune's* editor had a platform of his own, which he submitted to the people through his paper. It included vigorous opposition to slavery extension and to slave-hunting in the free states,
the while it blasted the moral wickedness of slavery and urged the
need for its speedy termination. It was upon this platform that he
proposed to support Scott.[34]

Greeley's slashing attack upon the Whig platform enraged the
Cotton Whigs. Such an attitude, sneered Webb, could cost the party
5,000 votes in New York City alone. But Greeley flung back the
challenge. If there were 5,000 Whigs whose voting for Whig candidates depended on his agreeing not to speak against slavery, or
upon his agreeing to aid the hunting and capture of fugitive slaves,
that 5,000 might as well "take up their beds and walk; for we
mean to stay in the Whig party and not to keep silent about Slavery,
nor 'acquiesce' in fugitive slave hunting."[35]

Such bitter recriminations between Cotton and Conscience Whigs were a sad and mournful accompaniment to the passing of a great Whig patriot, who lay gasping out his life in the National Hotel at Washington. Henry Clay died on June 29, 1852, having lived to see his choice for the Presidency, Millard Fillmore, discarded for Scott as the Whig nominee.

The *Tribune* went into mourning on the day after Clay's death, and Greeley wrote an excellent editorial on the old leader who had striven all his life to preserve the Union. No one could deny Clay's arrogance, high temper, and lack of philosophical depth of mind, and Greeley recognized those limitations. But he went on to praise the warmth and frankness, the generosity and cordiality of the man whom he had loved and followed. Clay had been a rare and lofty spirit, a proponent of measures whereby a nation is strengthened through inward growth. Therein lay his greatest claim to fame.

Clay's death gave Greeley an opportunity to pay tribute to the nationalism implicit in the Kentucky leader's American System. It also gave him an opportunity to point out with scornful emphasis how the Democrats, who had consistently slandered Clay in life, heaped eulogies upon him now that he was dead. Save for those slanders, they could never have kept him from the Presidency, but now it was all

> Thou canst not say *I* did it! Never shake
> Those gory locks at *me*.[36]

There was justice in Greeley's appreciation of Clay, and there was irony, too. For in Clay's last years, Greeley had spurned his leadership on the slavery question. Some six months before Clay's death, Greeley had called upon him at the National Hotel and the old leader had listened attentively as the Man in the White Coat fulminated against the Fugitive Slave Law—an integral part of the Compromise that Clay wished to have respected as a finality. Spurred on by his fears of an as yet nonexistent slavery expansion, and by the exigencies of New York State politics, Greeley would not let sleeping dogs lie. They might never have awakened, had they not been called up by the antislavery zealots and the canny politicians of the North.

And now the campaign roared into full swing. The Democrats had blundered into the nomination of dark horse Franklin K. Pierce, a New Hampshire lawyer and politician who had emerged from the Mexican War a brigadier-general.[37] Pierce was a known friend of the Compromise, Fugitive Slave Law and all, and came out against any renewal of the slavery agitation.

The official Whig position on the Compromise was much like that of the Democracy. The Whig platform accepted it and, while Scott did so only tacitly in accepting his nomination, it was known that in 1850 he had supported it and had rejoiced at its passage. He was also strong willed, not a man to be led by Seward or anyone else.[38] Greeley must have known these facts, just as he knew that Scott had nativist leanings and was aristocratic and egregiously conceited. Yet Greeley went down the line for Scott, even before the convention. Not only did the *Tribune's* editor refuse to join the Free-Soil bolt that nominated John P. Hale at Pittsburgh in August, but he also spoke and wrote furiously on behalf of a man for whom he had at heart scarcely more respect than he had had for Zachary Taylor. This could not have been due to a regard for what he termed basic Whig principles, such as the tariff and internal improvements, for these had been the same in 1848 that they were in 1852. Wherein lay the answer?

Two factors would seem to account for Greeley's support of Scott. The first of these was the status of the slavery question in 1852, particularly as that question concerned the Whig party. That party was now clearly split between Conscience and Cotton, which meant in general that it was split not only in regard to attitudes toward slavery but also between high tariff and low tariff, broad constructionist and strict constructionist, liberal and conservative Whigs. Seward was the leader of the Conscience group, and Scott had been Seward's choice. Scott's triumph would mean the triumph of the Seward men in the struggle for the control of the party, and this would mean a correspondingly greater chance for the triumph of the type of economic nationalism that Greeley so strongly favored. This was a great stake, one for which it was well worth fighting.

A subordinate factor, but one which almost certainly played a part in Greeley's thinking on the campaign, was his growing itch for office. He wanted the nomination for governor in 1852 and, though he professed to see why his temperance views made it unwise to name him,[39] he had no wish to conceal the smothered flame. Governor Hunt was renominated and the *Tribune* put his name at its masthead. Greeley was being regular, though he paid practically no attention to Hunt or to the state ticket during the campaign. The important thing was that he had put his aspirations on record. Perhaps, in 1854. . . .

The Whig defeat in 1852 was decisive, both in the state and in the nation. Scott carried only four states and the Democratic candidate for governor in New York, Horatio Seymour, beat Hunt by 22,000 votes. Cotton Whigs had bolted the national ticket because of

Scott, and Conscience Whigs had spat upon the platform. Horace Greeley waxed disconsolate as he surveyed the ruins.

The American System, declared the *Tribune's* editor, lay cold in the grave at Ashland. All hope of a good tariff was gone and, commercially, the United States had been reannexed to Great Britain. The battle for vital American independence was lost. He would still labor, Greeley asserted, to enlighten the public on protection, free land for settlers, and the Maine law, but the Whig party had been knifed by the Cotton Whigs and "not merely discomfited but annihilated." He did not see how it could ever again be rallied. Certainly it would not be rallied by the Conscience Whigs kowtowing to the Cotton element.[40]

Greeley's pessimism after the 1852 election led him into a state of political neutrality. His politics for 1853, he asserted, would consist in standing aloof from all parties, studying "earnestly and independently" the aspects and portents of the political horizon, and concentrating upon the battle for social reform. To lie still awhile in their political grave, he told Colfax, was "the only way to a glorious resurrection." The Whig party was the one great obstacle to carrying out the government on Whig principles, and the Whig party was in a state of irremediable decay, thanks to the Cotton element.[41]

The dissatisfaction with the Whig party which the *Tribune's* editor so succinctly expressed to his Indiana friend dominated his political views throughout 1853. His spleen was undoubtedly enhanced by the fact that the Homestead bill of 1852 had been defeated, in large part by eastern Whig capitalists, and it was certainly fed by ruminations upon the way in which the Cotton Whigs had bolted the ticket. As Greeley contemplated this desertion, as he saw the developing interest of the slavocracy in Northern Mexico, Haiti, and Cuba, and as he was subjected to the attacks of the northern Cotton Whigs, he could not help feeling pessimistic about the future of the party with which he had been aligned from the moment of its birth. Strongly as he felt that no national party should be based upon slavery or antislavery,[42] a conviction was developing in his mind that at least the Whig party's attempt to bridge the gap between the South and the North had ended in failure.

True to his postelection promise, and taking for his motto a line that he mistakenly attributed to Pope—" 'T is better, sure, to sit than rise to fall"—Greeley guided the *Tribune* during 1853 into not only a state of political neutrality but also into a state of political inactivity. And slavery was accorded much the same sort of

"Hey, Mac! Which way is west?"

treatment. He could still, on occasion, become exercised over fugitive slaves; he could declare that the oligarchs of the South despised labor as they did offal;[43] he could always view reports of southern expansionist designs with grave alarm; but, by and large, the *Tribune* was as temperate in its attitude toward slavery and the slaveholders as it was Laodicean in its political comments. It concentrated on social reform.

The reforms with which Greeley occupied himself during the year 1853 were of wide variety. Campaigning for a New York State prohibition law (Maine had enacted the model in 1851) occupied much of his time, as did the fight for a free, common-school system in the state. He was deeply interested in the Peoples' College, that projected semivocational institution of higher learning into whose prospective curriculum he introduced agricultural instruction. The *Tribune* demanded reform in New York City and retrenchment in all kinds of government expenditure. It urged the granting of equal rights to women (save for the suffrage). It demanded a homestead act for labor on the soil and coöperative production for labor in the city. Its editor said to Josiah B. Grinnell, "Go West, young man, go West," and the legend began to grow that Greeley was the originator of the phrase, although an Indiana editor had first used the expression in 1851.[44]

As for tariff reform, Greeley promised not to renew that controversy if the tariff opponents would unite with him in urging a railroad to the Pacific. The best way to use the tariff, he still maintained, would be to use it in promoting new and infant industries in different parts of the country, particularly in the South and West. But the very best means of protection for national prosperity would be a Pacific railroad. Iron rails stretching to the western edge of the country would be more effective than any tariff in widening the markets of American manufacturers and making the United States instead of Great Britain the commercial center of the world.[45]

A minimum of political action, but plenty of progress and reform—such was the *Tribune's* slogan in 1853, and under it the paper prospered. It now had thirteen editors and employed directly 183 people. Greeley forced an enlargement of the paper that year, despite the croakings of advertising manager Strebeigh and the gloomy conservatism of McElrath. There was little doubt that the enlargement would pay, he wrote to Seward, who had complimented him on his move,

though the hostility of the wealth and commerce of our city work hard against us. But the People are in good sort with us; and, if our circulation goes up as I hope, cotton will advertise with us as freely as it trades with slave drivers—because it will make money by it.

Thank you for writing. I will show your letter to McElrath, to keep him from cutting down the quality of our paper, which I dread.[46]

The enlargement and other improvements meant an added expenditure of $65,000, and increased annual expenditures by more than double the amount of the net profits of any previous year. But at the end of the year the paper showed a profit of $25,000. Its shares were now worth from $2,500 to $3,000 each. For the time being, Greeley was out of debt and, despite various and sundry benefactions and other expenses, he had money to invest. Indeed, there was only one cloud on the horizon. Henry Jarvis Raymond had established the *New York Times,* and the *Times* was offering more and more strenuous competition to the *Tribune.*[47]

Raymond had started the *Times* in 1851 as a paper designedly more conservative than the *Tribune.* As such, it appealed to the Whig business interests (largely commercial) in New York City. Greeley became convinced that the *Times* was a formidable rival before it was six months old. From then on he waged relentless war upon it, declaring that it lacked backbone and character and that it made "compliances" with evil, especially with Demon Rum. Raymond, said Greeley, saw both sides of questions to such an extent that he had trouble telling the two sides apart, and Raymond's paper was "conducted with the most policy and the least principle of any paper ever started." Much of this was said privately, but plenty of it seeped into the editorial columns of the *Tribune.* Raymond was not averse to answering blow with blow, and the ill-will the two men bore each other quickly became the talk of the town.[48]

By 1853, the quarrel between the two editors had broadened and deepened into a first-class feud. Greeley was convinced, with some reason, that there was a rapprochement between Raymond and Weed and Seward, and that the *Times* was getting outlines of Seward's speeches in advance of the *Tribune.*[49] The *Times,* snarled Greeley, was a news snatcher. It employed spies and received stolen goods, and by such practices the "little viper," the "little villain" who ran it had obtained a city circulation larger than that of the *Tribune.* Raymond returned these courtesies by telling the public that Greeley had the *Tribune* puff copper companies and other interests in which he was a stockholder. Raymond also advertised in religious journals by using ministers' statements that portrayed the *Times* as more orthodox than the *Tribune.* As the struggle between the editors waxed hotter even Karl Marx was dragged into it, and his signed articles on the Eastern question poured contempt on the *Times* for supporting Russia's designs on Turkey.[50]

Old ties were loosening for the *Tribune's* editor. The very mention of Raymond's name made him choleric, and before 1853 was over the thought of Weed and Seward made him testy. He knew that they looked with favor upon the *Times*. On top of that, Weed chose to administer a public spanking to the *Tribune's* editor that fall.

Greeley's perfervid championship of the Maine Law, his policy of political inaction, and his habit of urging the support of dry candidates, regardless of party, had stirred Weed's slow wrath. In September 1853, Weed wrote an editorial for the *Albany Evening Journal* in which the *Tribune's* course of action was blandly but severely criticized. The support of prohibitionists without regard to party, remarked the Albany boss, evidently meant that Greeley no longer regarded himself as a Whig. The Dictator regretted the loss of Greeley's noble zeal in the Whig cause, but hoped that he would come back after a year or two of laboring in the cause of reform.[51] This censure was bitter to Greeley, who regarded it as virtually reading him out of the party.

Alarmed by Raymond's competition, stung by Weed's public criticism, distressed by the parlous condition of the Whig party, Greeley faced the critical year of 1854. It was to be a year of tragic significance for the nation, as well as of momentous importance to the editor of the *Tribune*.

NOTES FOR CHAPTER 13

1. D. T. Valentine, *Manual of the Corporation of the City of New York* (1917), p. 446.
2. *Tribune*, Nov. 1, 1851; W. Whitman, *New York Dissected* (N. Y., 1936), pp. 119f.
3. Whitman, *op. cit.*, pp. 119f.; Greeley, *Glances at Europe*, pp. 62f.; *Tribune*, Nov. 29, 1854, Apr. 4, May 1, Aug. 26, 1857, Apr. 26, May 3, 8, July 26, 1858; G. Myers, *The History of Tammany Hall* (N. Y., 1917), p. 169.
4. *Tribune*, Sept. 2, 24, 1850.
5. *Tribune*, Apr. 4f., 1856, June 6, 1857; Whitman, *op. cit.*, p. 227.
6. Lyman Abbott, *Reminiscences* (Boston and N. Y., 1915), pp. 25, 27; *Albany Evening Journal*, July 11, 1855. The *Journal* sneered at "Barnum the Humbug."
7. E. Duyckinck, "Diary" (MS), Dec. 25, 1852; Whitman, *op. cit.*, pp. 128-29; *Tribune*, Feb. 10, 1852, June 4, 1857, Dec. 22, 1859, May 12, 1864, Sept. 1, 1865.
8. *Ibid.*, July 24, Oct. 9f., 1850, Nov. 6, 1857.
9. *Tribune*, May 7, 8, 13, 1857; *Times*, May 7, 8, 1857.

10. Duyckinck, "Diary," Dec. 15, 1852.
11. *Tribune*, Sept. 2, 1857.
12. *Ibid.*, Dec. 15, 1853, Feb. 28, Apr. 7f., 1859; J. H. Harper, *The House of Harper* (N. Y., 1912), pp. 115-16.
13. G. W. Curtis, *The Potiphar Papers* (N. Y., 1856), p. 83 *et passim;* Whitman, *op. cit.*, pp. 19-21.
14. *Tribune*, Nov. 18, 1852, Nov. 19, 1853.
15. *Ibid.*, June 5, 13, 19, 1850, Nov. 19, 1853, July, *passim*, Oct. 26, 31, 1857; Whitman, *op. cit.*, pp. 98f.; Abbott, *op. cit.*, p. 33; Myer, *op. cit.*, pp. 182, note 5, 185f.
16. See, for example, the *Tribune* for June 1852, and the issue of Aug. 13, 1852. Cf. Myers, *op. cit.*, pp. 152-60, 167-93.
17. *Tribune*, June 3, 1857, Nov. 22, 1858.
18. *Ibid.*, Jan. 23, 1851.
19. *Ibid.*, Jan. 7-9, 23, 28, Mar. 26, April 12, 1851.
20. *Independent*, Jan. 17, 1861.
21. Greeley, *Glances*, pp. 78, 132f., 145f., 191f., 258-59, 266, 340, 348; Seward Papers, Greeley to Seward, May 16, Aug. 26, 1851; Cleveland, *op. cit.*, pp. 114f.; *Tribune*, Jan. 3, Nov. 1, 1851.
22. *Ibid.*, May 3, 1853; Greeley, *Glances*, pp. 83f.
23. Greeley, *The Crystal Palace and Its Lessons* (N. Y., 1852), pp. 19ff.
24. *Tribune*, Sept. 11-15, Oct. *passim*, Nov. 6, 8, 14f., 1851.
25. Greeley Letters (N. Y. H. S.), Greeley to Weed, Nov. 10, 1851.
26. *Tribune*, Oct. 23, Nov. 14, 20, 24, 1851.
27. *Tribune*, June 16, 1852.
28. *Ibid.*, Feb. 9, 1853.
29. Greeley Papers (N. Y. P. L.), Greeley to Colfax, Mar. 17, Dec. 26, 1850.
30. *Ibid.*, Apr. 10, 1851, Jan. 20, Apr. 22, 1852; *Tribune*, Nov. 28, 1851, Feb. 14, Apr. 9, June 14, 15, 1852.
31. *Ibid.*, June 22, 1852.
32. Greeley Papers (N. Y. P. L.), Greeley to Colfax, June 9, 1852; Seward Papers, Greeley to Seward, June 13, 1852.
33. *Tribune*, June 22, 24, 1852.
34. *Ibid.*, June 24, 1852.
35. *Ibid.*
36. *Ibid.*, June 30, July 9, 1852.
37. See the account of his nomination in Nevins, *op. cit.*, II, 18-20.
38. *Ibid.*, II, 34.
39. Barnes, *Memoir of Thurlow Weed* (Boston, 1884), p. 216.
40. *Tribune*, Nov. 5, 11, 30, 1852, Jan. 14, 1853.
41. *Ibid.*, Nov. 30, 1852, Apr. 30, May 5, July 23, Oct. 3, 1853; Greeley Papers (N. Y. P. L.), Greeley to Mrs. G. B. Kirby, Dec. 6, 1852, Greeley to Colfax, Dec. 23, 1852, Jan. 18, 1853.
42. *Tribune*, Jan. 17, 1853.
43. *Ibid.*, Nov. 18f., 1852, Aug. 13, 1853.
44. Harrison Howard Correspondence, *passim; Tribune*, Sept., *passim*, 1853; C. Morley and L. D. Everett (eds.), Bartlett's *Familiar Quotations* (Boston, 1948), p. 505. John Babson Lane Soule first used the expression in the *Terre Haute Express* in 1851.
45. *Tribune*, Apr. 20, May 19, June 16, 1853.
46. Seward Papers, Greeley to Seward, Apr. 15, 1853.

47. Barnes, *op. cit.,* p. 217; *Tribune,* Dec. 2, 1853, Apr. 10, 1854, Apr. 21, 1889; Greeley Papers (N. Y. P. L.) , Greeley to Colfax, Apr. 21, Dec. 9, 1853; Houghton Library Autograph Collection, Greeley to G. N. Sanders, Jan. 7, 1853 [4].

48. *Tribune,* Apr. 14, 1852; Brockway, *op. cit.,* p. 152; Greeley Papers (N. Y. P. L.) , Greeley to Colfax, Apr. 21, 1853.

49. Seward Papers, Greeley to Seward, Jan. 27, Apr. 15, 1853.

50. E. H. Carr, *Karl Marx* (London, 1938) , pp. 120f. These articles, signed by Marx, were actually written by Engels.

51. *Albany Evening Journal,* Sept. 6, 1853.

CHAPTER 14

A Disruption of Partnerships

ON APRIL 30, 1853, JAMES S. PIKE, WASHINGTON correspondent of the *Tribune* wrote:

We expect Mr. Pierce will give us a quiet, moderate, conservative, unexceptionable, good-for-nothing kind of an Administration, to which nobody will think of making any especial objection or opposition; and that by the close of his term there will be a pretty general fusion of all parties.

Mr. Pike was singularly mistaken in his prophecy.

It was Stephen A. Douglas of Illinois, or, rather, the historical forces of which Mr. Douglas was a tool, that upset the Pike prediction. The "Little Giant" from Illinois was the chairman of and the dominant figure in the committee on territories in the Senate. As such, he reported out of the committee in January 1854 a bill providing for the organization of the territories of Kansas and Nebraska. This bill, as finally presented to the Senate, showed the influence of the slavery question in two ways. It transferred from Congress to the people of the territories the right to decide as to whether or not they would have slavery, and it specifically repealed the Missouri Compromise of 1820, which prohibited slavery in the whole Kansas-Nebraska area.[1]

Why Douglas acted as he did in framing the Kansas-Nebraska bill is a matter of conjecture. It is probable that his interest in land speculation and in a transcontinental railroad, his desire to please the South so as to ensure the passage of the organization bill, and his Presidential aspirations, all played a part in forming his decision. But whatever his motives, the results of his action were vicious in the extreme. The bill roused the country from a state of relative harmony to one of angry altercation and blew up the fires of the slavery controversy until they were hotter than they had ever been before. More than any other measure passed or threatened during the decade, this bill was responsible for the Civil War.

The Kansas-Nebraska Bill in its final form, backed by the approval of President Pierce, appeared in the Senate on January 23, 1854. Douglas and its other supporters urged its passage as a final settlement of the agitation over slavery, and declared that the repeal of the Missouri Compromise had been clearly implied in the Compromise of 1850. They were met by a swelling chorus of denunciations and denials from a rising tide of public meetings in the North, portents of the gathering storm.

Just after this legislative bombshell was hurled upon the floor of the Senate, Greeley returned to New York from a lecture tour that had taken him as far west as Milwaukee.[2] He was shortly to be away again for a series of speeches in Ohio, but during the interim he paid his respects to Douglas's proposal.

The Nebraska bill, said Greeley, was "an infamous proposition," a repudiation.

We regard this Nebraska movement of Douglas and his backers as one of measureless treachery and infamy. Founded on a gigantic and impudent falsehood—the assumption that the Adjustment of 1850 in spirit if not in letter repealed so much of the Compromise of 1820 as was favorable to Freedom—it seeks to discomfit and humiliate the North by a surprise—a snap-judgment—an ambuscade surmounted by a flag of truce.

Douglas talked of letting the people of the territories decide for themselves as to slavery, but he carefully kept dark the crucial point—the laws that would govern the territory until the people chose to legislate slavery up or down. Thus the "lying little villain" fawned upon the South with this piece of "northern Uriah Heepism", which was in reality only a "Presidential scheme." Greeley denounced the argument that the Nebraska bill was meant to carry out the intentions of the Compromise of 1850. That pretense was "too shallow and transparent to deceive any man who has a thimbleful of brains." Benton was quoted with approval—"Whoever says that I intended the repeal of the Missouri Compromise when I voted for the Compromise of 1850 lies, Sir; he tells a lie, Sir!"[3]

Greeley returned from Ohio, where he had sounded out popular sentiment, more incensed than ever against the Nebraska bill. The terms in which he denounced the measure drew criticism, particularly from the Cotton Whig organs. He answered these in a ringing editorial, one of the best that he ever wrote.

We are charged [said Greeley] by some of the open and active promoters of as well as by the more timid and cowardly connivers at Douglas's meditated repudiation of the Missouri Compromise, with using harsh and uncharitable language in reference to that scheme and its abettors. Our

answer to the charge is, that no other language than that we use would
faithfully express our sentiments or do justice to our convictions. Were it
simply a bad measure, we might speak of it calmly and measuredly; but as
an act of deliberate bad faith, impelled by the most sordid motives and
threatening the most calamitous results, we must treat it as we do other
gigantic perfidies and crimes. The conflagration it threatens is not to be
extinguished by jets of rosewater.

"Is it a fraud?" asked Greeley, and answered, "Yes." No one—
country, Congress, or Douglas—had understood that the Compromise of 1850 would do away with the Missouri Compromise. No
northern advocate of the Compromise had so conceived it. Would
the southerners opposed to that measure have fought it so savagely,
if they had understood it as Douglas now described it?

Consider how sternly this Compromise was resisted by Calhoun, Butler,
and every Representative from South Carolina—by the two Senators and
most of Democratic [sic] Representatives from Virginia—by the delegations
from Arkansas and Mississippi (Gen. Foote only, we believe, excepted)—
by Venable and Yulee, and nearly every extreme pro-Slavery man in
Congress. What did they all mean, what *could* they mean, if the Adjustment they fought so savagely was to have the effect which Mr. Douglas now
ascribes to it?

Greeley himself had not then dreamed of such an interpretation,
and he was convinced by the conversations that he had with Clay
that the father of the measure himself had had no thought of such
a possibility. Butler had said exultantly when the Omnibus had
failed, that by it all that Greeley sought would have been given to
him. Looking at these facts, and at the way in which repeal had
been gradually slipped into the measure,

It is our earnest conviction that the bill of Douglas, in so far as it pro-
poses to disturb the Missouri Compromise, involves great perfidy, and is
bolstered up by the most audacious false pretenses and frauds. If we are
wrong in this conviction, let it be shown, and we stand condemned; but if
we are right in our view of it, who can truly say that we speak of the plot
and its contrivers more harshly than they deserve?[4]

There were many times in his career when Greeley's easily aroused
moral indignation tempted him into unnecessarily harsh judgments.
Even here, Douglas and his motives were portrayed in colors too
lurid to suit the more sober canvas of the historian. And yet, when
one considers the evil consequences of this measure and the sophis-
tries with which it was defended by its supporters, it is difficult to

criticize either the words or the arguments that Greeley used in making his attack.

Some of Greeley's contemporaries thought that there was inconsistency in his wild indignation over the application of the doctrine of popular sovereignty to Kansas and Nebraska, when he had been so willing in 1848 and 1849 to leave the question of slavery or no slavery to the people of New Mexico.[5] But this inconsistency was more apparent than real. There had been no previous statute like the Missouri Compromise to be repealed in the case of New Mexico. Furthermore, he had been convinced that slavery would not find a foothold in that province, while now he did believe, or at least professed to believe, that slavery could and would spread into Kansas. More than all this, he was convinced that the Nebraska bill represented the first step in a great plan of southern expansion, both territorially and in terms of political power, that would indefinitely prolong the South's control over the policies of the nation. It was this latter belief that inspired the animus in Greeley's opposition to the Nebraska bill. For if such a triumph of the Slave Power occurred, Greeley would have to abandon indefinitely some of his most cherished plans for promoting the nation's happiness and well-being.

Greeley's hopes and dreams for promoting national welfare centered about the West. They involved the freedom of the public lands for actual settlers, an industrial development diversified and strengthened by protection, and a Pacific railroad. Only through such projects, he asserted (citing Henry Carey's nationalistic *The Past, the Present and the Future* as proof) would America be able to obtain that prosperity and social harmony which were the twin objects of our existence as a free nation.[6]

But what was the South's attitude toward these measures? It was that section, Greeley rightly declared, which most strongly opposed free land, and an increase of southern power would block that needed reform just as surely as the Nebraska bill was now blocking a Homestead bill in the Senate.[7] The South was already strong enough to deprive the laboring masses of the benefits of protection, and the Nebraska bill would increase the slavocracy's power, thus ensuring the continued degradation of labor. Would free men lend themselves, thundered Greeley, "to the base and unholy schemes of those who would fain reduce all laborers to the weakness, ignorance and stagnation of bondage?"[8] Finally, it was this same power-seeking slavocracy that was determined to build the Pacific railroad by the southern route, through the Gadsden Purchase acquired for that purpose in 1853. This was a "moonshine route," declared the *Tribune*. It had been concocted in the interest of speculators, and would viciously sectionalize a great undertaking that should be truly national in character.[9]

The leaders of the southern slavocracy were, in Greeley's opinion, narrow-minded sectionalists, opposed to the true interests of the nation. How Henry Clay would have denounced the Nebraska bill, exclaimed the *Tribune*. If he had been alive, this calamity would not have occurred. But now all the southern Whig Senators except Bell of Tennessee joined with the Democrats in supporting the measure. "Where now is your nationality [meaning loyalty to the nation]," Greeley asked the Badgers and Claytons and Joneses of the South. One of the worst aspects of this infamous measure, he declared, was that it was arousing sectional animosities, making inevitable new political alignments and setting on foot a new contest—"one between Freedom and Slavery, waged without a truce, and with no possible compromise, for we see that compromises are merely meant to cheat us."[10]

The Kansas-Nebraska Bill was indeed creating new sectional animosities, but Greeley's course of action was producing much the same results. The *Tribune* was now featuring accounts of Negroes burned at the stake, of slave hunts, and slave tortures, and it was blasting the South as an economic handicap whose cost to the North was prodigious. Designed to counter southern boasting and prove ridiculous the southern menace of disunion, these attacks were scarcely calculated to soothe the South or to produce a temperate spirit in the North.[11]

The reopening of the slavery controversy by the passage of the Kansas-Nebraska Bill paved the way for a new political party. Everywhere men began to talk and act as though this was an inevitable event. Greeley was one of the first to share this growing conviction.[12]

Speculating on the character a new party would assume, Greeley thought it might be based on opposition to two forms of bondage, man's subjection to man and to alcohol. This he confided to a close friend, adding his belief that the opponents of liquor and the opponents of slavery were practically identical. He was certain that an anti-Nebraska and antirum platform would furnish a basis upon which a combination of Whigs, Free-soilers and right-thinking Democrats could ride to victory after victory.[13]

There was, of course, the danger that such a party as Greeley suggested would be sectional rather than national, but this was not what the *Tribune's* editor either desired or foresaw. His political speculations were, rather, predicated upon nationalist ideals. And just as he had formerly envisaged the triumph of these principles under Whig leadership, so now he began envisaging their triumph through the formation of the new party.[14]

This party, whenever it appeared and whatever it might be called (Greeley liked the title "Republican," though in 1838 he had deplored its use as a party name because "it arrogates too much—is too exclusive and Pharisaical"), would be the standard-bearer of American freedom, a party pledged to carry on the struggle that had begun with the American Revolution for the fundamental principles of American liberty. It would have a great appeal for the northern masses, and eventually the southern masses, now deluded and victimized by a slavocrat minority, would answer to its call. It would take over control of the government, and when it did so it would check forever the expansion of the Slave Power and would carry through Congress those great measures upon which, Greeley was convinced, rested the future prosperity and greatness of the American nation.[15]

The victory would not be lightly won. Greeley knew that it would be difficult to establish such a party in the South. That would be a matter of time. He also knew how binding was the force of party regularity and how strong was the economic alignment between northern merchants and southern cotton. "We are in for a long fight with slavery," he told Colfax. But he was sure that they could sweep the North that fall on the Nebraska issue. There was already clear evidence, he felt, that fusion of old-party elements in a new organization would carry Pennsylvania. The watchword now was vigilance. Years later, he recalled how, at the passage of the Kansas-Nebraska Bill, Macbeth's awful warning, "Sleep no more," had resounded throughout the land "in thundertones that would not die unheeded."[16]

The fateful measure passed the House of Representatives just before midnight on May 22, 1854. Pierce promptly signed it. With equal promptitude, Greeley began urging that northern antislavery men organize to promote the emigration of free-soil settlers to Kansas.[17] At the same time he began to consider what practical steps should be taken toward a new political orientation.

For with the passage of the Kansas-Nebraska Bill, political movements of great significance began taking place throughout the North. Fusion was the cry, and in state after state Old Democrats, Old Whigs, and Free-soilers joined together on platforms proclaiming their ineradicable opposition to slavery extension as well as to the act which was its sign and symbol. New York was the scene of one of these movements: There preparations got under way for a conven-

tion to be held at Saratoga on August 16, 1854, and in these preparations Horace Greeley was one of the moving spirits.

At first, Greeley was not disposed to press too suddenly for the
formation of a new party in New York State. His *Tribune* editorials throughout May and June of 1854 emphasized simply the
election of anti-Nebraska men to Congress, regardless of their
political affiliations. But by the middle of July he was clearly indicating his interest in an immediate new political deal. He had
long felt, he declared, that a thorough dispersion of parties at least
every twelve years would be "a public blessing." He was doubtful
if party spirit had done more good than evil (a sentiment that must
have caused acute pain to Thurlow Weed). He hoped the Saratoga
conclave would come out against liquor, against Nebraska and its
supporters, and for uniting all free states in the demand for restitu-
tion of the Missouri Compromise. Furthermore, he believed that
Saratoga should follow the lead of Michigan where (with his own
active participation) a fusion state ticket under the name "Republican" had been nominated. But, he ended somewhat lamely,
he saw no evidence that the great bulk of New York's anti-Nebraska
voters were for such a step, and he was sure that it was not contemplated by a majority of the signers of the call for the convention.[18]

The qualifications which Greeley appended to his call for a new
party were undoubtedly produced by the attitude of Thurlow Weed.
That astute leader was cold to the idea of abandoning the Whig
organization in 1854. To do so might jeopardize Seward's chances
for reëlection to the Senate. Furthermore, Weed was convinced that
Greeley wanted a ticket nominated at Saratoga with himself at the
head of it. Such a move would almost certainly put Know Nothings
and Silver Grays in control of the Whig state convention—with
disastrous results for Weed and Seward. Hence, Weed frowned on
any new party movement. He and Greeley were in close touch, and
it was evidently because of pressure from Weed that Greeley drew
back, a retrograde movement that was made unwillingly and with
various and sundry digs at professional politicians.[19]

For a month before the Saratoga convention, the *Tribune* had
little to say about that meeting or, indeed, about a new party. This
silence evoked comment, but when criticized for his inaction Greeley replied, a trifle lamely, that he had said all he thought necessary
and that the question of a new party was one for the convention to
decide.[20]

When the motley gathering of Old Whigs, Old Democrats, Abolitionists, and Free-soilers met at Saratoga, Greeley was a power in

their midst. Many wanted to nominate a state ticket, but the Whig sentiment present (Weed had exerted his influence in choosing Whig delegates) was largely averse to such a procedure. With the Whig Dictator and his cohorts opposed to a state ticket, Greeley took the position that the important thing was to unite all those opposed to the Nebraska bill on a common platform. Hence he did not push for a resolution favoring repeal of the Fugitive Slave Law, lest those who had favored the Compromise of 1850 be alienated from the new movement. And as chairman of the platform committee, he saw to it that the resolutions it produced for adoption by the convention were based on some that he had drafted in collaboration with Weed.[21]

The Saratoga platform was composed with an eye to harmony. It was an appeal to the rank and file of the Whig party. It did not mention repealing the Fugitive Slave Law, and by this omission it held out an olive branch to Cotton. It simply came out against slavery extension and against the Nebraska bill, declaring that free and slave labor could not exist on the same soil. On the question of a new party, it retreated into ambiguity, declaring that each state should act as it deemed best in maintaining or discarding the old political organizations. It expressed unqualified approval of Kansas colonization.

The convention ended with a decision to await Whig action before nominating a slate of candidates, adjourning to meet again on September 26 at Auburn. But just before adjournment, at Greeley's instigation, it altered its voting procedure so as to increase the certainty of Whig control when it should meet for the second time.[22]

Saratoga was past and Greeley had bowed, albeit unwillingly, to Weed's judgment. Moreover, he had paved the way for fusionist acceptance of the ticket the Whigs would nominate on September 20. Even though the role was hard, Greeley was playing the part of the loyal lieutenant. He was confident of victory in November, for the Democrats were split into factions ("Hard" and "Soft"), and these were nominating separate tickets. "We can elect anybody," he wrote to his confidant, Colfax, some two weeks before the Whig convention.[23] It seemed only logical that, in view of his obedient service, "anybody" should turn out to be one Horace Greeley.

Back in 1841, Greeley had declared that "an Editor who is good for much *in* his profession will rarely seek to exchange it for an office."[24] That sentiment was now forgotten. He met Weed by appointment at the Astor House, declared that he wanted to be governor, and asked if this was not the time for his nomination.

Weed told him that the convention was out of control, that the nativists (who had increased marvelously in strength and political zeal as they viewed the swelling tides of immigration after 1848) were violently opposed to him, and that the powerful temperance element favored Myron H. Clark of Canadaigua, a fervent prohibitionist of pronounced nativist sympathies. This being the situation, the Dictator did not see how he could deliver the necessary votes for his friend Greeley. He went on to explain also that Greeley's candidacy might injure Seward's chances for reëlection to the Senate. This last remark hurt badly and, though Greeley said he was satisfied not to run, he went away with decidedly ruffled feelings.[25]

A few days after the Astor House conference, Greeley went up to Albany much enthused over another idea. This time he proposed that he run for lieutenant-governor. Again Weed parried. They could not, he said, afford the Maine Law at both ends of the ticket. As Weed later recalled it, Greeley saw the force of this argument and left in good spirits.[26]

It was at one of these conferences with Weed that Greeley proffered other suggestions. He urged that a fusion ticket of Whigs and anti-Nebraska Democrats be nominated at Syracuse, and delivered a fervent warning against any dickering with the nativists, or "Know Nothings," as he had dubbed them.[27] To these counsels, delivered with emphasis in Greeley's squeaky voice, the Dictator listened benevolently but made no commitments.

The Syracuse convention was rudderless and full of conflicting currents. Maine Lawites, Know Nothings, Cotton and Conscience Whigs struggled to impose their mastery upon it. Weed had no love for Clark, and there is some evidence that he preferred even Greeley to the Canandaiguan. The Dictator tried to avoid the prohibitionists' idol and at the same time satisfy Greeley, but it was uphill work. He suggested a Harris-Greeley ticket (Ira Harris was able and reputedly "cold water," but not dry enough to suit the drys), but the prohibitionists and natives would have none of it. Then he proposed George Washington Patterson of Westfield for governor, again with Greeley in second place. This also was rejected. The cry was for Clark, and Clark was nominated, thus using up the Maine law capital.

After Clark's nomination, Weed made no further efforts for Greeley. Instead, he swung to his new favorite among the New York journalists, and Henry Jarvis Raymond, the "Little Villain" whom Greeley loathed, was given second place. The ticket was simon-pure Whig from top to bottom, save for the tincture of Know Nothingism in its head. Not one anti-Nebraska Democrat was on it. Greeley's advice had gone begging, and his bitter enemy had been made the candidate for lieutenant-governor.[28]

The *Tribune's* doughty editor was bitterly disappointed by the outcome of the Syracuse meeting. It was not so much his own rejection that angered him. He had been prepared for that. It was the fact that Raymond had been given the honor that he himself coveted, and the humiliation of having his advice about a fusion ticket completely disregarded that bit and rankled. The platform's vigorous denunciation of the Kansas-Nebraska bill scarcely provided sufficient salve for his wounded pride. But by a mighty effort he contained himself. The Whig ticket was endorsed by the adjourned Saratoga convention when it reassembled in Auburn on September 26, and no fulmination to the contrary, not so much as a squeak of protest, was heard from the office of the *Tribune*.

Four state tickets were in the field that fall, a circumstance that tended mightily to confuse the voters. The Democratic "Hards" put up Greene C. Bronson, the "Softs" renominated Governor Seymour, and the Know Nothing organization, refusing to accept Clark, ran Daniel Ullman, a Silver Grey Whig. The contest centered mainly on the liquor question, with Clark as the darling of the drys and Seymour the idol of all zealous wets. Greeley campaigned vigorously against liquor and for Clark. The latter edged out a narrow victory (some 309 votes) over Seymour, and as signs of this sorry showing developed during the campaign, Greeley's temperature mounted. Before the contest was over, his spirit was as ferocious as that of an enraged mastiff tugging at a leash.

Greeley's mental turmoil was apparent in the *Tribune*. He wrote two editorials during the campaign that indicated his belief that the Whig party was dead and that the organization of a new party, antislavery and dry, was being hampered by the selfishness and shortsighted expediency of Whig leaders in New York and Massachusetts.[29] Diplomacy restrained his language in these public pronouncements, but the stops were pulled out in private. There he vented his disgust with Weed for thwarting the progress of fusion, knuckling under to Know Nothing influence, and directing his strategy solely with a view to Seward's reëlection to the Senate. "I believe Weed has secured a Seward Assembly," Greeley snarled to Colfax, "by letting everything else go as it might. Some of those he relies on are red-mouthed Know Nothings. . . . This is just the most scoundrelly canvass that I was ever engaged in. I feel a crawling all over on account of it . . . . Yours with a sore head."[30]

Colfax was not the only recipient of Greeley's complaints. The editor went directly to the fountainhead, laying his grievances

directly before Seward. If not absolutely beaten, they would be
relatively, he told Seward a short time before the close of the campaign. And it would all be "simply for want of courage and common
sense." He knew that Weed liked him. There wasn't a dog around
Weed's house that Weed liked any better. But Weed wouldn't listen
to him, for Weed thought that he, Greeley, knew little or nothing
about politics. He would no longer try to remove this "fixed pre-
possession" on the part of the Dictator.

Here was the muttering of rebellion, and a note of it crept into
the *Tribune*. There, two days before he wrote to Seward, Greeley
had said simply, "We wear no man's livery."[31]

On election night that year, Greeley followed his usual custom of
staying at the office to make up the returns as they came in. As
usual on these occasions, he was in a state of high excitement,
groaning and swearing when the news was bad, and whooping so
that the windows rattled when fortune favored one of his pet candidates.[32]

The news that night was none too good, and the outcome of the
gubernatorial race remained in doubt for several days. During that
time, Greeley's irritation and anger reached boiling point, and on
November 9 in a *Tribune* editorial he poured out the vials of his
wrath on the Whig leadership in New York State.

It looked like Seymour, Greeley averred, although there was still
a possibility that Clark might be elected. There would obviously
be a large Whig majority in the Congressional delegation and one
in the state assembly, but "Whig" meant very little any more and
he advised nobody to put much reliance on the term. The biggest
fights in the next House of Representatives would be between
Whigs.

Why this great reverse, asked Greeley, and answered his own
question by declaring that both major parties were dead. They
had "needed to be shoveled under" after the election of 1852, and
Kansas-Nebraska had made their interment inevitable. The people
wanted a new formation of parties, and where that had taken place
the people had said, "Amen!"

But in New York, designing politicians had said, "Wait!" They
had said that it was necessary to carry the state once more, divide
the spoils, and then see what should be done. So they had made
gestures toward fusion but had nominated a straight Whig ticket
at Syracuse, a strategy that was much like asking a friend to a picnic
and then eating up all the food before he arrived. They had also put
a mediocrity at the ticket's head, and then had made the amazing

mistake of having Raymond pose as a dry, a mistake that had cost
him thousands of votes in New York City.

. . . Messrs wire workers and managers at nominating conventions! [ex-
claimed Greeley]. We entreat you to be merciful on us, your humble
journalists, hereafter. For the crockery gods you require us to fabricate,
give us tolerable clay, give us at least fair, common earth, and do not oblige
us to perform impossibilities. Remember that we do not and will not always wait to groan till after election.

The delay in forming a new party had been costly, Greeley declared. Even now, the time might have gone by when New York
could lead the Republican movement. The man who should have
led that movement lived in Auburn, and his name was William
H. Seward. But Seward had adhered to "the vacated shell of Whiggery" and had allowed "the great movement of the Free States to
go forward without a word of bold and hearty encouragement or
sympathy from its national leader."

Actually, there had been no such reverse in New York State
for the new movement as Greeley sought to picture. Fusion had
not been utterly repudiated, for Clark, at least, was a fusion candidate and twenty-nine of the thirty-one Congressmen elected were
anti-Nebraska. Raymond had run some 600 votes better than Clark,
and had a plurality of 20,000 over his nearest rival. The editor of
the *Tribune,* angry at the rejection of himself and his counsels,
painted the picture black as a means of discrediting the leadership
of Weed and Seward.

Two days after this first postelection outburst, Greeley repeated
his charge of too little and too late. He added the further assertion
that the campaign just past had lacked a great issue and had been
sordid and corrupt—"the play of Hamlet, with Hamlet not only
omitted but forgotten." The same day that this editorial appeared,
he wrote his famous letter to Seward, dissolving the partnership.[33]

Carefully and deliberately, raking up occasion after occasion when
he had felt neglected or abused, Greeley pointed out to Seward the
inadequate manner in which the senior partners had recognized his
services. Time and again nothing had been offered him, or he had
been told that it was impolitic for him to run for office, or his feelings had been lacerated by the words or actions of Weed or of
Seward. Raymond's nomination, in particular, had been "bitterly
humbling." Once again Greeley expatiated upon the errors of the
past campaign. He hoped never to be found in opposition to
Seward, and he clearly implied that he would help in the fight to

reëlect Seward to the Senate. But beginning with the morning after the first Tuesday in February, he would "take such course as seems best, without reference to the past."[34]

Why was this letter written and, being written, why was it sent? Greeley later declared that it was "probably" written because Weed had lectured him about aspiring to the nomination for governor in 1854, and that it might have been withheld, even after it was written, save that Charles A. Dana, to whom alone it was shown before it was mailed, approved it and advised sending it. On another occasion, Greeley asserted that the letter had been sent because he had felt it only fair to apprise Seward of the fact that he "had fully decided that I would no longer be devoted to Governor Seward's personal fortunes."[35] These explanations were obviously superficial. The *raison d'être* of the letter lay in both psychological and ideological factors.

A combination of circumstances had brought Greeley under very severe strain during the year 1854. Some of these circumstances were economic in character. Chappaqua was proving an expensive venture. That spring a flood had swept away a $3,000 dam that Greeley had constructed, and his farm had been gullied to pieces by torrential rains. Another worry and source of expense was the Crystal Palace Exhibition in New York, which he had helped to sponsor and which by the latter part of 1854 was deep in financial trouble. Worse still was the anxiety occasioned by the *Tribune's* situation. Denunciations of nativist intolerance and warfare with Catholic journals over prohibition and over tax-supported common schools had cost him thousands of readers in the city. The rivalry of Raymond's *Times* was a constant and increasing drain on the resources of the *Tribune*, both as to advertisers and as to subscribers. Advertising income fell as the subscription list diminished, and as the autumn came on, McElrath forced a reduction in the size of the paper. So straitened were Greeley's circumstances that he had to give up good Pennsylvania lands for which he had paid $5,000 because he could not raise the $500 necessary to save them. Once again, he was facing a piling up of debts and financial worries, an incubus all the harder to bear because of the prosperity of the preceding year.[36]

Economic difficulties did not in themselves provoke Greeley's dissolution of the partnership, but they undoubtedly made him nervous and irritable, and on top of them and around them had been piled all of his political troubles. The way in which the *Times* was replacing the *Tribune* as the political mouthpiece of Weed and Seward in the city; the rejection of his advice about the Whig platform and the elevation of the "Little Villain" to the post for which he himself had unsuccessfully applied; a series of petty but open quarrels with Weed over prohibition and other matters,[37] which had culminated with Weed's reading him the lecture on not running for governor—these had been hard to take. He had also fought almost singlehanded (or so he felt) in a vain attempt to defeat the candidacy of the none too savory Fernando Wood for Mayor of New York. To cap the climax, he had been chafing for over half a year at the New York Whigs' delay in entering the national movement for a new party, a delay that he attributed to the narrow vision and pettifogging politics of Weed and Seward.

The Greeley who was confronted in the autumn of 1854 by rebuff, defeat, and the elevation of a hated rival had been for months subjected to severe psychological strain. The election over, the floodgates of his feelings were lowered, and his accumulated grievances burst out in the *Tribune* and in his letter to Seward. The senior partners were assailed by a blast of criticism which reflected Greeley's idealism, his egotism, his stubborn intractability, and his tendency to overrate his own capacities for leadership.

Seward, who was disposed to regard Greeley's outburst as not too serious, told Weed of the letter with its "sharp, pricking thorns," and wondered if an appointment to the Board of Regents that winter would not salve the junior partner's bitterness over Raymond's nomination and election.[38] Seward also wrote to Greeley, urging him to let bygones be bygones.

In answer to Seward's letter, Greeley stated that he had no wish to reopen the past, but desired to make all clear for the future. His political life was over, and he was going to sell most of his *Tribune* stock, pay his debts, retire to his farm, and there write occasionally for the paper. He was very tired.

Thus far in this second letter, Greeley had struck a pose of noble resignation, but at this point a sense of his injuries overcame him. Bitterly he expressed the hope that his retirement would be a relief to the party that he had intended to serve. "With Myron H. Clark, the bogus Know-Nothing for governor," he sneered, and with a man like Henry J. Raymond for lieutenant-governor, it was obvious that a paper like the *Times* rather than the *Tribune* would be the proper party organ in New York City. He himself would only try to hold those in power to some kind of fidelity to temperance. Then, with a reversion to his mood of melancholy self-abnegation, he asked Seward to understand that he, himself, had never desired office (that was not in his line) but only some sort of public recognition. He could not have stood so long by Seward's side as by Weed's, for Weed, with all his faults, was still the outstanding leader in New York.[39]

Greeley's second letter to Seward seemed to mark the end of his outburst of petulance and wrath. On the surface, all seemed as before, and the triumvirate remained on friendly, even intimate terms.[40] Seward and Weed relied upon time to heal such wounds as remained in the breast of the junior partner. But this was a very great error.

NOTES FOR CHAPTER 14

1. Nevins, *op. cit.*, II, 95-96.
2. *Tribune*, Jan., *passim*, 1854; Howard Correspondence, Greeley to Howard, Jan. 30, 1854.
3. *Tribune*, Jan. 27, 30, Feb. 1, 3, 6, 1854.
4. *Ibid.*, Feb. 15, 1854.
5. See above, Chapter XI; *Tribune*, Dec. 16, 1848, p. 1, Mar. 18, June 13, 1854.
6. *Ibid.*, Aug. 28, 1851, June 21, July 19, 1854.
7. *Ibid.*, Feb. 25, 1854. Greeley rightly denounced the Graduation Act of 1854, which only aided speculators and neighboring farmers—*Ibid.*, Apr., *passim*, 1854; F. Shannon, "The Homestead Act and the Labor Surplus," *Amer. Hist. Rev.*, XLI (July 1936), 644.
8. *Tribune*, May 3, 9, July 1, 8, 24, 26, Aug. 18 (Saratoga resolutions), Dec. 6, 18, 1854.
9. *Ibid.*, Jan. 30, Apr. 4, 1854; *Albany Evening Journal*, Dec. 2, 1853; Nevins, *op. cit.*, II, 84.
10. *Tribune*, Feb. 9, 17, Mar. 3, 4, 17, 1854.
11. *Ibid.*, Feb. 6, Mar. 7, Apr. 12-25, May 18, June 9, Sept. 13, Dec. 1, 1854.
12. F. W. Seward, *op. cit.*, II, 219; J. S. Pike, *First Blows of the Civil War* (N. Y., 1879), p. 237; Weed Papers, W. Hunt to Weed, May 25, 1854.
13. Greeley Papers (N. Y. P. L.), Greeley to Colfax, Mar. 12, 1854.
14. *Tribune*, Feb. 22, Apr. 11, 15, 1854. These ideas appear repeatedly in the *Tribune* during 1854.
15. *Jeffersonian*, Aug. 4, 1838; *Tribune*, May 8f., May 20-June 20, July 1, 1854.
16. Greeley Papers (N. Y. P. L.), Greeley to Colfax, June 28, July 7, 1854; Greeley, *Recollections*, p. 294.
17. *Tribune*, May 24, 1854.
18. *Ibid.*, July 18-24, 1854; Greeley Papers (N. Y. P. L.), Greeley to Colfax, July 26, 1854.
19. Fish Papers, W. Hunt to Fish, Aug. 2, 1854; Weed Papers, Greeley to Weed, Aug. 10, 19, 1854; *Tribune*, June 17, July 24, Aug. 10, Nov. 11, 1854. On August 10, Greeley commented satirically that the Know Nothings who were afraid that Weed had sold out the Whig party to some "newfangled" antislavery organization would be relieved to read the *Evening Journal's* comment on the call for a Whig state convention. That comment called the Whig organization the best medium for working out democratic reforms.
20. *Tribune*, Aug. 15, 1854.

21. Weed Papers, Greeley to Weed, Aug. 10, 1854; *Tribune*, Aug. 18, 19, 22, Sept. 5, Nov. 9, 11, 1854.
22. Greeley, *Recollections*, p. 314; *Tribune*, Aug. 19, 1854; F. Bancroft, *The Life of William H. Seward*, (2 vols.; N. Y. and London, 1900), I, 367.
23. Greeley Papers (N. Y. P. L.), Greeley to Colfax, Sept. 7, 1854.
24. *Tribune*, June 7, 1841.
25. Barnes, *Memoir*, pp. 225-26; Greeley, *Recollections*, p. 319.
26. Barnes, *Memoir*, p. 226.
27. Greeley Papers (N. Y. P. L.), Greeley to Colfax, July 26, 1854; *Tribune*, Nov. 20, 1854. Greeley called them "Know Nothings" because they were instructed to say "I know nothing" when questioned about their society —"The Order of the Star Spangled Banner."
28. Patterson Papers, Weed to G. W. Patterson, May 29, Sept. 17, 1854, B. F. Bruce to Patterson, Sept. 21, 1854; Weed Papers, D. H. Abell to Weed, Sept. 10, 1854; *Albany Evening Journal*, July 17, 1858, June 14, 1860; Krout, "The Maine Law in New York Politics," *New York History*, XXXIV (July 1936), 266, note.
29. *Tribune*, Oct. 3, 16, 1854.
30. Greeley Papers (N. Y. P. L.), Greeley to Colfax, Nov. 6, 1854.
31. Seward Papers, Greeley to Seward, Oct. 25, 1854; *Tribune*, Oct. 23, 1854.
32. Brockway, *op. cit.*, p. 151.
33. *Tribune*, Nov. 9, 11, 1854.
34. Greeley, *Recollections*, pp. 315-20.
35. *Tribune*, May 25, 1860, Aug. 28, Sept. 13, 1865.
36. Greeley Papers (N. Y. P. L.), Greeley to O. A. Bowe, May 9, 1854, Greeley to Barnum, July 25, 1854; *Tribune*, Sept. 1, and *passim*, Oct. 24, 1854; Wilson, *Dana*, 128-29. By November 1854, the *Times* had 20,000 subscribers to the *Tribune's* 8,000 in the New York City area.—Greeley, *Recollections*, p. 320.
37. See the *Albany Evening Journal*, Apr. 27, May 9, 1854, for illustrations. Among other things, Greeley had sharply criticized making the *Journal* again the state paper.
38. F. W. Seward, *op. cit.*, II, 239. No such appointment was forthcoming.
39. Seward Papers, Greeley to Seward, Nov. 24, 1854. Clark belonged to a Canandaigua lodge that was not in good standing with the Grand Council of the Know Nothings.
40. Greeley, *Recollections*, p. 321; Weed Papers, Seward to Weed, Dec. 2, 1854, Greeley to Weed, Oct. 23, 24, 26, 1855; Derby, *Fifty Years of Journalism*, p. 135.

CHAPTER 15

A Republican Operator

K ANSAS WAS FUEL TO THE FLAME OF ANTISLAVERY
excitement, and Greeley used that fuel to the best advantage. The
Tribune's portrayal of the free-soil and proslavery forces contending
for the possession of Kansas was etched in black and white. The
slaveholding Missourians who crossed over into the territory were
"Border Ruffians," men who believed only in the law of the rifle
and the bowie knife, men who were bent upon committing mayhem
and murder. The proslavery Kansas settlers were a plundering,
shooting, burning, torturing, tobacco-chewing, whiskey-drinking set,
who would as soon shoot a Free-soiler as to look at him. They had
an irresistible penchant for violence and tumult. The Free-soilers,
on the other hand, were honest, industrious, and God-fearing. They
were interested only in their work, their homes, and freedom. Their
whole disposition was to remain quiet, avoid collisions, and pursue
their farming, resisting only as a last resort the outrages inflicted
upon them.[1]

Actually, the settlers, whether slaveholders or Free-soilers, were
fairly similar as to character and temperament, but there was little
indication of this in the pages of the *Tribune*.

Greeley beat the drum for free soil in Kansas, but he made it clear
that this was by no means his ultimate goal. For the moment, he
was fighting a defensive battle against slavery extension. This was
all that was now practicable, in view of the attitude of the great
majority of American citizens. But the final aim was the elimination
of a great social evil. With that end in view (an end that was to be
accomplished, where slavery already existed, through social pressure and education rather than by political action), he was seeking
to develop and ripen public sentiment in favor of a general emancipation. His campaign against slavery was not based so much upon
truth as upon moral considerations.

It was in keeping with this idea of a steady advance toward the elimination of slavery that Greeley announced in December 1854 that he had now gone beyond his original purpose of restoring the Missouri Compromise line. The South had destroyed that line, and now the least that the free states could regard with equanimity was the absolute prohibition of slavery in all the territories of the Union.[2]

At the end of January 1855 Greeley went to Albany, where he lent a hand in Seward's reëlection to the United States Senate. This achieved, the *Tribune's* editor blew a blast against Seward's conservative and Know Nothing opponents, and acclaimed the happy victory as one of nation-wide interest and import. In the same breath, he criticized Seward for the latter's complacency toward the Senate's peculation and extravagance, and suggested the possibility that this second term might write finis to Seward's political career. In the days that followed, the *Tribune* defended Seward against conservative attacks and applauded his denunciation of the Fugitive Slave Law, thus apparently neutralizing his words of criticism. All this blowing hot, then cold, then hot again, simply signified that Greeley was tasting the sweets of independence. A private letter to his friend George E. Baker disclosed Greeley's real attitude toward Seward. "I am no longer anybody's partisan," he wrote. "I don't care a button whether Seward stops where he is or goes higher."[3]

During the remainder of the winter of 1854, Greeley fought hard for the passage of a prohibition law that was signed on April 9 by Governor Clark. He emphasized at the same time his violent hostility to the Know Nothing party. It was divided and uncertain on questions of domestic and foreign policy, he declared with justice. Such a party "would seem as devoid of the elements of persistence as an anti-Cholera, or anti-Potato-Rot party would be." Only through fusion in a new party, he kept asserting, could the antislavery people of the North hope to challenge successfully a slavery-dominated Democracy.[4] Having thus restated his position on the most important political questions of the day, he sailed about the middle of April for another visit to the Old World.

When Greeley left New York on his second visit to Europe, it was for the express purpose of joining his family and making a tour of the continent. Molly had taken Ida and Raphael ("fair children," Horace told a friend, "but not equal to the boy you saw but did not know") with her to England the previous autumn. The three travelers had rented a lodge on Hampstead Heath for the winter. Considerable "breakage and delapidation" of the interior of the house ensued, and the harassed owners had made out a bill for damages with which they had intended to confront Molly. But sight of her in one of her states of nervous excitement had withered their determination. The bill had remained in pocket until Greeley's arrival, when it was presented to him.[5]

Carrying his carpetbag and wearing his white overcoat, Greeley descended upon London, but it was not for long. The continent beckoned, and shortly after joining his flock he shepherded them across the Channel. They were bound for Paris, where another World Exposition was being held, and in Paris they stayed for almost two months of a cold, cloudy, rainy spring.

The leisurely tempo of Greeley's life in Paris, unlike anything that he had known for years, was interrupted early in June by a spirited tilt with the French courts. Legal proceedings landed Horace Greeley in a French jail.

At about half-past five o'clock, one Saturday afternoon, as the lawyer and author, Maunsell B. Field, tells the story,[6] a fiacre containing Greeley and several French bailiffs came to a halt before the American legation in Paris. Donn Piatt, Secretary of Legation, came out to the fiacre, and the conversation that developed between him and the occupants of the fiacre became exceedingly animated. Field, who had seen this from a distance, came up into a welter of talk and gesticulation to learn that Greeley had been arrested at the behest of a Parisian sculptor, M. Leschesne, who wanted $2,500 gold for a statue that had been broken at the New York Crystal Palace Exhibition. Greeley had already been haled before a French judge, and now a contention had arisen as to what the latter had said about security for the editor's appearance in court the following week.

As the argument waxed warm, Greeley's part was contributed in high-pitched and colorful English which was completely unintelligible to the bailiffs. To state his case more forcefully, he attempted to get out of the carriage, a move which the custodians of the law interpreted as an attempt to escape into the legation. They thrust him back without ceremony and, themselves alighting, tied their tricolor scarfs about their waists with an exaggerated air of importance. At this point, the *opéra bouffe* character of the scene quite overcame Secretary Piatt. He gave way to a burst of derisive laughter, much offending the bailiffs, who heatedly inquired if it was his intention "to ridicule the colors of France." Everybody talked at once, the tumult increased, and in its midst could be heard Greeley's treble squeak of "Take me to jail! Take me to jail!" This his captors proceeded to do. Casting dark looks upon Piatt, they climbed back into the fiacre and drove their captive off to Clichy prison.

Molly was immediately notified of her husband's plight and, seizing a fine-tooth comb and his night shirt, hastened to his side. Upon seeing her spouse in durance vile, she threw up her hands in a frantic gesture, exclaiming, "Why, father!" Greeley's hands flew up in an answering gesture and he replied, "Why, mother!"

"San-tran-nuf," Greeley's phonetic reproduction of his prison name and room number, stayed in jail over Sunday. He had many visitors, for every American in Paris who possessed a scintilla of curiosity wished to see Horace in captivity. Even Martin Van Buren and Millard Fillmore are supposed to have been among those who came to express good wishes and good will. When the social pressure eased, Greeley spent his time writing a facetious account of his incarceration, with due reference to the protection the government gave him against rascally intruders, and the prison's emphasis on equality and fraternity at the expense of liberty. He was freed late Monday afternoon. Four-year-old Raffie's radiant face on seeing his father safe at home remained fixed in the latter's memory. So did the jail, for release did not mean the end of annoyance. Leschesne's suit continued, involving a tedious legal squabble before it was finally dropped.

A day or two after Greeley's release from Clichy, Andrew Dickson White found him in one of the student restaurants, together with Piatt and some other Americans. The editor was trying to order *haricots verts*. "Flawronce, donney moy—donney moy," he pleaded, unable to remember the words he wanted; then impatiently thrusting out his plate he screamed "beans" at the top of his voice. The crowd laughed and Piatt said, "Why Greeley, you don't improve a bit; you knew beans yesterday."[7]

Shortly after these contretemps, Greeley took his family (perhaps it would be more accurate to say that Molly decided to go) to Switzerland. But his appreciation of Lake Geneva and the Swiss Alps was dulled by constant apprehension of fresh arrests by disgruntled creditors of the New York exhibition. After the family had rented a cottage at Lausanne, he went back to Paris and his law suit. Toward the end of July he slipped across the Channel to England and, as quietly as possible, took boat for home. His wife and children were in poor health, his traveling plans had been spoiled and he was thoroughly disgusted with Europe.[8]

Greeley reached New York to learn that his mother had died on the day that he sailed from Liverpool. Her death meant a visit to the Pennsylvania home, but his stay there was short. Political events in which he meant to have a hand had been developing in New

York State, and so he hurried back to the city at the mouth of the Hudson.

During Greeley's absence in Europe, the road to fusion in New York had at last been cleared. A Republican state committee had been formed and on May 30, 1855, its chairman had issued a circular notifying the electorate that a convention to choose a state ticket would be called. On July 4, the committee had resolved to hold the convention at Syracuse on August 24.

News of these Republican activities galvanized Weed into activity. Convinced, as he wrote to Seward, that "the necessity for getting in line with other states is imperative," he went to New York and exerted all his arts in the cause of fusion. Through his efforts, a meeting was arranged between the Whig and Republican state committees on July 18, at the Astor House. At this meeting it was agreed that the two state conventions should meet at the same time and place, the Republicans very reluctantly agreeing to change the date of their meeting from August 24 to September 26. Thus the stage had been set for merging the Whig party into the new Republican organization.[9]

Greeley came back early in August to find the plans for fusion well laid. He at once lent his support.

Greeley's editorials during the summer and fall of 1855 had one main objective. He was determined to bring into Republicanism all those that hated the Slave Power, regardless of how they might differ on other issues. Prohibitionists were urged not to nominate a separate ticket, since the embattled editor took it for certain that all good prohibitionists would reject the candidates of "the party of Slavery and Rum." Old Whigs were urged not to fall a prey to the delusions of Washington Hunt, who was rejecting Republicanism as a sectional movement. Know Nothings and Democrats of anti-Nebraska leanings were urged to join the new movement which, in its turn, was exhorted to be tender of diverse opinions so long as men were "right" on the main question. And as always there was a rolling fire of attack on the Administration's Kansas policy.[10]

When the time came to take the final steps toward fusion, Greeley played a leading role. He was active as a member of the committee that called a Republican mass meeting in the Tabernacle on September 18 to elect New York City and County delegates to the Republican convention. He was even more active when the convention met at Syracuse, where he was chairman of the Republican platform committee and where he, a zealous dry, fought successfully against putting an endorsement of prohibition in the platform that was finally accepted as that of fusion. Denounced for thus subordinating temperance to politics, he stuck manfully to his guns. Prohibition was not working to popular satisfaction in the state and, since this was the case, Greeley had no mind to see it become a drag upon the new Republican car.

The events at Syracuse that followed hard upon platform-making were much relished by the *Tribune's* editor. The Whig delegates were accepted into the Republican convention. The Republican platform, unqualifiedly strong against Nebraska, was accepted as the fusion platform. The ticket, a combination of Old Democrats and Old Whigs, was just as he had wanted it to be. Horace Greeley was immensely pleased.[11]

Greeley's policy during the campaign of 1855 followed a line that was by now becoming thoroughly familiar to his readers. The Know Nothings were done for, he declared. All earnest opponents of slavery extension should vote Republican, for the only way to have peace between North and South was to stop the extension of slavery. Friends outside the state were urged to eschew factional strife and to keep cool until the time had arrived for the fight to make Kansas free.[12] The chief burden of his song was unity of the ranks under the Republican flag.

As a distinctly secondary theme, the *Tribune* maintained its opposition to alcohol. This was somewhat difficult, partly because of the senior editor's shying away from the temperance cause at Syracuse, and partly because the paper was steadily accepting advertising from the Liquor Dealers' Association of New York. Some readers, and especially some of the *Tribune's* newspaper rivals, professed to fear that the paper's morals had gone astray when it accepted the money of the liquor men, but Greeley explained the matter clearly. He would be glad to have the liquor dealers take their patronage elsewhere. In fact, he adjured them to do so. But he also made it clear that the *Tribune* had no choice but to take the advertisements, since their language was unexceptionable and they were paid for at the regular rates.[13]

It was perhaps to make amends for the ambiguous position of the *Tribune* regarding alcohol that, toward the close of the campaign, Greeley repeatedly attacked Stephen Pearl Andrews' club at 555 Broadway as a free-love organization. The club was an association organized by the eccentric philosopher for the purpose of providing inexpensive recreation for the common people. The idea had caught on and from two to three hundred people gathered twice a week in its comfortably furnished rooms for conversation, music, dancing, and other recreations. It was apparently just what it purported to be, and was not an agency for propagandizing Andrews' unconventional views regarding sex relations. When the police raided it, Justice Osborn discharged all the parties arrested, declaring that their arrest was utterly unwarranted. The *Tribune* admitted all this on its editorial page. But the *Tribune's* editor had the darkest of suspicions about the goings on in the club's precincts. After all, Andrews did believe in Free Love, and Greeley took a very dim view of his old friend, Albert Brisbane, who came to Andrews' support.[14]

Free love or no free love, the Know Nothings won a narrow victory in the state elections of 1855, and for the moment Greeley was depressed by the political outlook. He complained peevishly to one astounded visitor at the *Tribune's* office that American political institutions were inferior to those of Great Britain.[15] But he soon rallied. Kansas, he told his readers, was freedom's issue. Let the Know Nothings accept that fact and, for ought he cared, they might have the new Speaker or Clerk of the House.[16]

Greeley was in Washington during the winter of 1855-56. He went there primarily to help carry on the fight against slavery by taking a hand in the hot contest over the election of a Speaker of the House—a contest that deadlocked the lower chamber for two months before the Republican candidate, Nathaniel P. Banks, was elected.

As always when away from New York for any length of time, Greeley worried about the management of the *Tribune*. His letters to Dana, who ran the paper in his absence, were full of laments about the nincompoops in the *Tribune* office who passed, by some strange mischance, for being men with brains. He was constantly berating Dana for errors of judgment that would injure the *Tribune* or lessen its senior editor's influence in Washington. Dana was told again and again whom to hire, what to pay, which correspondent to keep, and what to put in or leave out of the paper. He was also warned to be chary about interpreting Washington news. "Pray allow me," snapped Greeley, "to judge with regard to what is passing under my own eyes and not under yours." Dana's attack on Bayard Clark in the *Tribune* had cost the election of Banks and the paper was being cursed all over the House. "I must give it up and go home," wailed Greeley. "I am too sick to be out of bed, too crazy to sleep, and am surrounded by horrors. . . . You keep a load on me that will kill me." But somehow, despite all these tribulations, he found time to lobby among the House members and to write dispatches calculated to influence the electorate toward his point of view on things political.[17]

After the fight for Banks was over, Greeley prided himself on having made a real contribution to the result.[18] Certain it is that he used the *Tribune* as a bludgeon over the heads of wavering Republicans, and that the news he sent to his paper, far from being an objective account of the struggle, was biased and distorted for the purpose of helping Banks and fomenting hatred of the Slave Power.[19] It is possible that these tactics helped materially in the contest. There were those, however, who believed that Greeley had been a detriment to the cause. A good many Republican journals criticized him for his imperiousness, and Weed, who had also been in Washington working for Banks, wrote to Seward that it would have been better had he and Greeley been paired from the beginning.[20]

Toward the close of the contest over the Speakership, Greeley was pummeled and caned by an irate Democratic Congressman, Albert Rust of Arkansas. Greeley had denounced a resolution introduced by Rust inviting all candidates for Speaker to withdraw from the contest, and it had been laid on the table, 100 to 99. The following day, as Greeley was on his way down from the Capitol, he was accosted by the Arkansan, a burly six-footer weighing two hundred pounds.

Rust asked Greeley if he were a "non-combatant." Greeley replied, "That is according to circumstances," and Rust (who said later that he had been infuriated by the tone of the reply) struck Greeley several times on the head, sending him reeling up against the sidewalk fence. People rushed in between them. Greeley asked, "Who is this man? I don't know him," to which Rust replied, "Damn you, you'll know me after this." They then separated, but before Greeley reached the National Hotel he found himself again in the midst of Rust and his cronies. Rust struck at Greeley's head with a heavy cane, but the latter parried the blow with his arm. Once again bystanders came between them.[21]

Greeley suffered no serious damage from Rust's attack. The *Herald's* correspondent found him in his room that night busily writing, with wet cloths bound around his head and arm. His dispatches to the *Tribune* were not interrupted. But the assault focused attention on the *Tribune's* editor, and Greeley was never one to shrink from the spotlight.

He had come to Washington, Greeley told his readers, with the understanding that he had about an even chance of going home alive. For he had come "to unmask hypocrisy, defeat treachery and rebuke meanness . . . ." He might judge harshly and make mistakes at times, but he was always ready to correct his mistakes and amend his judgments. He would carry no weapons and engage in no brawls,

but if waylaid by ruffians he would not run and would, so far as possible, defend himself. He was suffering, thanks to Border Ruffianism,
but Banks had been made Speaker of the House. That sufficed.

Greeley's account of his Washington mission was overdramatic.
He made it appear that he was suffering with all the bravery of the
martyrs of old. But privately he wrote to Dana that the latter's
course in the *Tribune* was promoting such assaults as that of Rust.
Dana was told that hereafter he should attack no man or project in
Washington without the previous approval of the senior editor.[22]

After Banks' election, Greeley stayed on in Washington to help
in the heated struggle over seating a territorial delegate from
Kansas. He supported Andrew H. Reeder, who had been chosen
by the free-state men in defiance of the "regular" election of John
W. Whitfield by the proslavery Kansans and Missourians,[23] but
Congress rejected both candidates.

Blood boiled in Congress during those weeks of the early spring.
Men exchanged insults on the floor of the House and fist fights were
narrowly averted. Not infrequently there were open threats of disunion and civil war, but these had no effect upon the vigor and
acerbity of Greeley's lobbying, or upon the dispatches that he sent
to the *Tribune*. Time and again he poured scorn upon northern
Doughfaces and southern slavocrats, and there was a great meed of
praise for Seward's speech of April 9, 1856, wherein the New York
Senator came out for the prompt admission of Kansas as a free
state.

Not all of Greeley's dispatches concerned the Kansas struggle. His
readers were told that the page boys at the Capitol were spoiled for
regular industry by their pay of sixty-two dollars a month; that
Congressional extravagance should be cut all along the line; that
subsidizing mail steamers to Europe was bad because our unbal-
anced trade with that part of the world should not be increased.
Government in business was always unfortunate, he averred, as he
denounced the project for establishing a government Bureau of
Printing and Engraving. Congress might much better pass a homestead bill giving free land to bona fide settlers, with a "perpetual
preëmption" on the quarter- or eighth-section on which the house
was built. There was even one dispatch in which he told how he
had been invited to dinner by one of the gamblers who infested
Washington, and how the invitation had been refused.[24]

Greeley's dispatches from Washington had covered a wide range
and occasionally had struck a note of triviality, but shining through
them was one central theme—the national interest. This was evident
in his steady effort to attract the Know Nothings away from a party

that he dubbed transitory and obstructive of the very reforms it favored. It was evident not only in his demands for a homestead law but also in his appeals for a Pacific railroad, "the great enterprise of our age," essential alike for the fostering of national trade and the establishment of national defense. It was evident, also, in his stern warning against territorial expansion as something that always had been and always would be dangerous to the Union, no matter where it occurred. It was implicit in his appeal for making Washington's dilapidated tomb at Mount Vernon a public property and a national shrine.[25]

Greeley's concern for the national interest was made still more evident by his attitude toward the Republican party. That party was not sectional but national, he declared. The proof of that fact lay in the party's great struggle to make freedom a truly national blessing.[26] This identification of the Republican party as a national organization was clearly in his mind when he attended a Republican organizing convention that was held in Pittsburg toward the end of February 1856.

That convention, Greeley asserted in dispatches from Pittsburg to the *Tribune,* was inaugurating "a National party, based upon the principle of Freedom." As proof of this, he pointed to the fact that every free state, eight slave states, and the most important territories had sent delegates. Such a wide representation belied the assertion that the party was sectional either in its origins or in its intent. It was his opinion that a majority of southerners favored reëstablishment of the Missouri Compromise, and the presence of slave state delegates at Pittsburg would pave the way for "a freer proclamation of the long repressed antislavery sentiment of the South."

This same conception of the Republican party as a national organism was the central theme of his address to the convention at Pittsburg, an address delivered, appropriately enough, on Washington's birthday. The party, he declared, must draw to itself all men who opposed the onward march of slavery. It must be moderate in speech and action, thereby convincing the South that it was not an enemy but a deliverer sent to free that section from the incubus of slavery. Once the people of the South understood the Republican purpose, Greeley was sure that thousands of them would enroll under its banners and it would become "a strong if not the strongest party in every Slave State."[27]

The need for moderation in Republicanism was an idea to which Greeley would revert again and again during the next four years. It fitted his own basic philosophy of cautious approach to social change, and he knew that it would be a strong drawing card with the Old Whigs and with many of the Know Nothings. He was politically right, also, in wishing to identify Republicanism as national. Not only was such a concept in harmony with his own nationalistic views, but it was also very attractive to the Old Whigs and Old Democrats who flocked to the party standards. Whiggism, particularly, had been strongly nationalist, and men like James Russell Lowell and Hamilton Fish would not have been comfortable in this new party had they not been able to think of it as national rather than sectional.

Greeley's imagination soared as he looked forward to a future of Republican ascendancy. Already, he told Dana, he could see a day coming when the *Tribune* would be able to pay less attention to politics, and could devote more of its space to the arts and science of production. To the mind of the *Tribune's* senior editor, Republicanism would stand for all that was highest and best in the life of the nation. He told Congressman E. B. Morgan that "the man who would vote against any candidate because of his religious belief cannot be a Republican . . . ."[28]

Greeley returned to New York from his Washington sojourn about the middle of April 1856. He had found it hard, he wrote to a friend, to stand the abuse of enemies and false friends of the Republican course. But he would go back to the capital when the Kansas fight became hot. Whether there or in New York, he could always be counted upon to look after Douglas's "sophistry."[29] But now, since Presidential politics was beginning to boil furiously, he judged it the part of wisdom once more to take firm command of the Tribune's editorial policy.

As Greeley turned his thoughts to the Presidential campaign of 1856, he was freed of a financial worry that had beset him during most of the winter season. Molly Greeley had been pursuing an erratic travel program in Europe, in her never-ending pursuit of health. At one time an illness had brought her close to death. Recovered, or at least partly recovered, she had plunged into a law suit that she had felt it necessary to institute "for the benefit of future travellers." Travel, sickness, and law suits in foreign parts were alike expensive, and Greeley had had to sell four shares of his *Tribune* stock in order to meet the drain on his purse.[30] But now Molly was coming home and the European expense was at an end.

Many of the reports that Greeley had received from his wandering family had been a source of anxiety for other than financial reasons. Molly's illness had been deeply disquieting, as had been one letter from her which informed him of her conviction that

Raffie was dying. Horace was afraid that such a catastrophe as Raphael's death, which would leave Molly robbed of a second son and alone in a foreign land, might have even more tragic consequences. "Mother's" sanity, he admitted to a friend, was "not of the highest order," and her mind might well become completely unhinged by such a sad event. But with the advent of spring, better news came from across the sea. The health of the wanderers had improved, and they slowly made their way toward home.

As Greeley's comment on Molly's mental stability indicated, he had now become accustomed to viewing his family with an objective, if not a critical, eye. Ida, he told Emma Newhall, was grave, prosaic, and utterly devoted to her mother. Raphael was "an inferior copy of Pickie—poetic, imaginative, good-looking, large, rather fleshy, with bland, German features and a tendency to humor."[31] Such judicious appraisals had not been evident in his comments on Pickie. Pickie had been altogether wonderful. But Pickie was gone.

Molly and the children landed in New York on June 17. It had been a long separation, and the head of the family was there to meet them. But the greeting was not prolonged. The Republican national convention was meeting in Philadelphia and the temptation to run away from his spouse and progeny was too strong to be resisted. The next day found him busily sending dispatches from the convention's smoke-filled rooms in Philadelphia.[32]

Greeley had canvassed Republican presidential possibilities for months before the convention. Seward would have been his choice, he declared with at least apparent frankness, but for the fact that conservative and Know Nothing opposition made him fatally weak in such pivotal states as Pennsylvania, New Jersey, Indiana, and Illinois.[33] The Tribune's editor found John McLean of Ohio an attractive possibility. He also had a genuine leaning toward Speaker of the House Nathaniel P. Banks. And of course there was always John Charles Frémont, "Pathmarker of the West," dashing young warrior and explorer.

Frémont was Weed's candidate. The Dictator had decided, to Seward's bitter mortification, that this was not the year for the Auburn statesman to run. But Greeley's enthusiasm for the ebullient son-in-law of Senator Benton was somewhat slower in generating than was that of the Albany boss. Greeley knew that Frémont was a romantic and appealing figure, one to whom no taint of radicalism attached. Nevertheless, he warned his readers not to listen too readily to the siren song of availability where the pathmarker was concerned. Privately, he remarked that Frémont was politically naïve, that his stamina was doubtful and that ugly rumors were

afloat about shabbiness in some of his financial dealings.[34] When he
talked with Weed about the nomination, as he did repeatedly, he
seemed to agree that Weed's arguments for Frémont were irresistible,
but outside the Dictator's room at the Astor Greeley's course was
such as to evoke from the Albany leader the despairing comment,
"I shall never comprehend Greeley, for I can never discern the
personal considerations which sway and govern him." After what
had seemed to be full agreement with Weed, Greeley had gone
fishing for delegates hostile to Frémont.[35]

Finally, however, the *Tribune's* editor mounted the bandwagon
in earnest. On June 6, 1856, in a leading editorial in the *Tribune*,
he declared that, since amalgamation of the antislavery forces with
other groups and elements in the population was essential to victory,
his choice was Frémont rather than Seward. Frémont was young,
vigorous, famous, a former Democrat, was free soil in his sympathies,
and had done nothing to render him obnoxious to either "Americans" or adopted citizens. "We have intimations," added Greeley,
"that, should he be nominated, he will be assailed by the journals
in sympathy with Border Ruffians as incompetent, unqualified, un-
deserving, &c. Candidates thus assailed have rarely failed of an
election."[36]

Greeley was at the Republican convention when Frémont was
nominated, busily engaged in helping the delegates make up their
minds. He successfully opposed formal coöperation with the Know
Nothing party organization and also, apparently, helped to write
the Republican platform. The final resolution in that document, an
appeal for the support of men of all parties in the Republican
struggle against the advance of slavery, had been urged by him upon
the Republican National Executive Committee the preceding
March, and was thoroughly Greeleyesque in character and composition. Indeed, the proceedings of the convention, where resistance to the onward march of slavery was the theme song and
the Pacific railroad was made a cardinal plank in the platform,
were thoroughly satisfying to the *Tribune's* editor.[37] He felt in his
bones that Frémont would win, and was ready to roar with the rest
of the Republican stalwarts,

> Then let the shout again
> Ring out from sea to sea,
> Free Speech, Free Press, Free Soil, Free Men,
> Fré-mont and Victory.[38]

To understand Greeley's part in the campaign of 1856, it is necessary to remember his conviction that he was face to face with a

Slave Power, always to be distinguished from the southern masses, that was resolutely bent upon a vast extension of slave territory and upon constantly increasing its control over the nation's destiny. This struggle, he believed, admitted no compromise, no striking of balances, no concessions. It was really cold war, though he did not so name it, and he meant to wage it to the limit of his strength. Hence his attitude toward the slavocrats lacked objectivity, and at times was woefully deficient in perspicuous judgment.

To Greeley, southern speeches on Kansas might be ingenious, or plausible, or clever, but they were uniformly destitute of knowledge and defiant of truth. Preston Brooks's caning of Sumner in the Senate chamber on May 22, 1856, was handled in the *Tribune* in a manner completely prejudicial to the southerner and contemptuous of fact. The *Tribune* declared that "Bully Brooks," armed with a loaded cane, had felled Sumner without warning, and all on account of a speech "which dealt not in a grain of scurrility or abuse." Greeley asserted that Brooks had intended to kill the Senator from Massachusetts.[39] The *Tribune's* editor was all for Seward's proposal to admit Kansas as a free state under the so-called Topeka constitution—an outrageous proposition that took no account of equitable or constitutional procedure in the embattled territory. He fought bitterly against Toombs's bill for a Kansas constitutional convention, a proposition that was conciliatory and in essence fair, denouncing the Georgian as a man with a "ruffian nature—utterly reckless of history and facts." Greeley also urged the House to avoid all compromise on Kansas, since he regarded any settlement of the difficulties there as politically disadvantageous to the Republicans. He was all for adjournment, lest Congress be sold out to "Toombs and Co."[40]

While Greeley was developing his efforts in this partisan fashion, two other tickets challenged Frémont in the race for the Presidency. The Democrats had nominated an old political war horse, James Buchanan of Pennsylvania, a man who, as Minister to England, had had no connection with Nebraska. "Buck," or "Old Public Functionary," as the Republicans loved to call him, took the field on a platform that supported the Kansas-Nebraska Bill and the principle of squatter sovereignty. The Know Nothings had split over slavery, dividing into a northern and a southern wing. The so-called "North Americans" rallied to Frémont. The "South Americans" joined with intransigeant Old Whigs in nominating Millard Fillmore on a platform that sought to evade the slavery issue. The fight that roared into being during the summer of 1856 was thus a three-cornered affair. Frémont and Buchanan were the principal contenders. Fillmore's supporters hoped to obtain victory by throwing the contest into the House of Representatives.

During the campaign, Greeley alternated between going out on the stump and working like mad in the *Tribune* office. He lived in what he called his "den" at 35 East Nineteenth Street, and ate at an oyster cellar on Union Square under the Everett House. Even his beloved wood-chopping was neglected, although he went out to Chappaqua on every Saturday that was free. Sometimes, even on Saturday, he would be delayed, and once he stumbled into the house in the woods at one o'clock in the morning, terrifying Molly nearly out of her wits. At such a time she would speak her mind in no uncertain fashion, and he would listen with that placidity which he put on as though it were the armor of righteousness. For the most part, Molly was out of sight and out of mind, save when she came into town in search of a doctor who could cure her ills or who would agree with her that her doom was at hand. Even then her troubles made only a momentary fluttering in his mind. He had no time for either her or the children. The campaign absorbed all his attention.[41]

Greeley's strategy for the campaign was simple. He said little of Know Nothingism, for many North Americans were working smoothly with the Republicans and he wished only to foster this new-found harmony.[42] He sped only an occasional shaft at Fillmore. Part of his time was given to a laborious defense of Frémont against the charge that he was a Catholic. Much space was given to praise of Frémont's virtues, laudation of Republicanism as a movement truly national in scope and purpose, and assaults upon Buchanan and upon the slavocracy of which "Old Buck" was a catspaw. Most of all, attention was centered upon the Kansas iniquity, the burden of his song being that Kansas should be freed from the hateful embrace of the slaveholders and speedily admitted as a free state under the Topeka constitution.[43]

Greeley did not confine his efforts to editorial writing during the campaign. He published a good life of Frémont by W. H. Bartlett, a biography that had been read and approved by the candidate and was translated into German and Welsh for the benefit of strategic political centers. Greeley himself wrote and published what purported to be a *History of the Struggle for Slavery Extension or Restriction in the United States,* but was really a piece of campaign literature. He also saw to it that speeches of Sumner, Seward, and Colfax, the report of a Congressional investigating committee regarding Kansas, and plenty of other material derogatory to Democratic policies and Democratic leadership poured off the *Tribune* presses in pamphlet form, and were circulated in Pennsylvania and other states. Such efforts, together with a considerable amount of stump speaking, made him a busy man indeed.

As the campaign ended, the *Tribune* was arguing that Buchanan's election would strengthen the hands of the southern disunionists and thus promote the dissolution of the Union. This line of argument was not followed up after Buchanan's victory, but the *Tribune's* editor was, nevertheless, obviously a prey to the gloomiest kind of despair. The result, he declared, was a blow to liberty and a triumph for the enemies of democratic government throughout the world. Slavery was enthroned and wrong had triumphed in Kansas. Descending to more sordid particulars, he pointed out that "Buck" was the darling of the thieves, gamblers, and brothelhouse keepers of the Five Points, where he had received 574 votes to 25 for all the other candidates. The President-elect had "been purchased by the slave drivers as their servant of all work. They had bought him and paid for him." Ominously, Greeley noted how the southern demand for a revival of the slave trade was now welling up in the wake of victory. The Republic was obviously on the high road to moral ruin, if it continued under such leadership.[44]

But if Greeley was downcast by defeat, he could also see that ahead the land lay bright. The Republican party, so young and untried, had yet done amazingly well. "A party of yesterday," he declared, "which has polled one million votes and chosen more than one third of the whole number of Presidential Electors . . . has a grand future before it."[45] The better to improve these future prospects, Greeley kept up his Kansas agitation and his attacks upon slavery and upon southern fire-eaters.

As the *Tribune's* editor surveyed the future, certain plans and principles seemed to him to stand out as the very essence of Republicanism. The party should remain a rock of opposition to slavery extension. It should associate itself ever more closely with internal improvements, especially with the project of a Pacific railroad. There should be protection for those industries that might well be classified as infant, such as sugar, but tariffs should be moderate and wool might well go on the free list. As to prohibition, that might be forgotten for a while. Its unsatisfactory operation in New York State had made it for the time being a political incubus. It was with such concessions and upon such grounds that he hoped to see the antislavery cohorts welded into an harmonious fighting force for the campaigns that lay ahead.[46]

Republican political prospects might be conducive to optimism, but Greeley's pockets were, as usual, empty as he prepared for his annual lecture trip in December 1856. "Like Saul of old," he wrote to Colfax, "I am debtor to Greek and Barbarian, and have spent and used up in and about the election a doleful sum, which I must now earn."

As Greeley followed his own advice and went West for the replenishment of his fortune, two comforting thoughts made light the hazards and discomforts of the journey. One was that the fight with slavery was showing signs of progress, if not of final success, because of the influence of the *Tribune* and the strength of Republicanism. The other, curiously enough, was that he had at last freed himself from the fears and perturbations of the office-seeker. He had spurned all solicitations that fall to run for governor, even though the prospects of victory had been excellent, and this putting aside of the proffered crown, even though it had not been proffered from the most authoritative quarters, gave him courage to think that he would never again be a candidate for office.

But like the alcoholic who boasts of freedom from the toils of drink when he is most securely enmeshed, Greeley knew in his heart that the itch for office might once again descend upon him. "Don't speak of this," he warned Schuyler Colfax, in reference to his being no longer an aspirant for office. "What I hate even worse than the reputation of an office-seeker, is that of a man perpetually declining office. It is enough that I shall never again wish for one."[47] For the time being, indeed, this was sufficient, but Schuyler Colfax would have had to be very naïve to believe that his New York friend had hung his harp once and for all upon the willows of renunciation.

NOTES FOR CHAPTER 15

1. Weed Papers, Greeley to Weed, Oct. 23, 1855; *Tribune,* Sept. 6, 9, Oct. 19, 25, Dec. 9, 15, 19, 25, 1854, Jan.-Feb., 1855, Apr. 8, May 13, 1856.
2. *Ibid.,* Feb. 9, 1852, July 19, 27, Dec. 16, 1854, Sept. 24, 1855.
3. *Ibid.,* Feb. 7, 9, 27, 28, 1855; Barnes, *Memoir,* p. 232.
4. *Tribune,* Feb. *passim,* March 6, 15, Apr. 4, 7, 9, 10, 1855; *Whig Almanac,* 1855, p. 10; Seward Papers, G. E. Baker to Seward, Apr. 19, 1855. Greeley held that the expansionist slavocracy's control over the Democratic party was clearly manifested by the Ostend Manifesto, with its design on Cuba.
5. Greeley Papers (N. Y. P. L.), J. F. Hardy to Greeley, Apr. 15, Aug. 1, 1855.
6. M. B. Field, *Memories of Many Years* (N. Y., 1874), pp. 117-22. See also A. D. White, *Autobiography* (2 vols.; N. Y., 1905), I, 479; Greeley, *Recollections,* pp. 332f.
7. White, *op. cit.,* I, 479.
8. Greeley Papers (N. Y. P. L.), Greeley to S. Sinclair, July 5, 1855, Greeley to O. A. Bowe, Sept. 6, 1855, Greeley to Colfax, Sept. 7, 1855; Stahl Collection, Greeley to J. G. Shortall, Nov. 15, 1855; Greeley, *Recollections,* p. 331.

9. Seward Papers, Weed to Seward, July 12 [1855], July 23, 1855; *Albany Evening Journal*, May 30, July 19, 20, 25, 27, Aug. 18, 1855; *Tribune*, July 24, 1858.

10. *Ibid.*, Aug. 24, 27, Sept. 1-19, 1855. While he stoutly defended "compulsory morality," Greeley recognized the fact that prohibition was not working well in New York State.

11. *Ibid.*, Sept. 18, 27-29, 1855, July 24, 1858, Sept. 27, 1867.

12. E. B. Washburne Papers, Greeley to Washburne, Oct. 8, 1855.

13. *Tribune*, Oct. 1-Nov. 3, 1855.

14. *Ibid.*, Aug. 25, Sept. 10, Oct. 24, 29, 1855.

15. Chas. Mason, Diary in Charles Mason Remey, "Life and Letters of Judge Charles Mason of Iowa," Vol. II, ch. 11, no pagination (typescript in Cornell Univ. Lib.).

16. Greeley Papers (N. Y. P. L.), Greeley to Colfax, Sept. 7, 1855; *Tribune*, Nov. 10, 21, 1855. The Know Nothings were often referred to as "Sam," because the question, "Have you seen Sam?" was used in identifying a member of the lodge.

17. Greeley Papers (Lib. of Cong.), Greeley to Dana, Feb. 3, 1855 [obviously 1856], Dec. 1, 1855, Jan. 28, 30, 1856; Benton, *Greeley on Lincoln*, pp. 100-110.

18. Greeley Papers (N. Y. P. L.), Greeley to O. A. Bowe, Feb. 9, 1856.

19. See, for example, his dispatches of Dec. 17-19, in the *Tribune*, Dec. 19-21, 1855, and the dispatches in the *Tribune*, Jan. 5, March 18, 19, 1856.

20. Seward Papers, Weed to Seward, Jan. 24 [1856]; *Tribune*, Feb. 6, 1856.

21. *Ibid.*, Jan. 30, 31, 1856; *New York Times*, Jan. 30, 31, 1856; Greeley, *Recollections*, pp. 345-49.

22. Benton, *Greeley on Lincoln*, p. 107; *Tribune*, Jan. 31, Feb. 6, 1856.

23. Greeley Papers (N. Y. P. L.), Greeley to J. W. Grimes, Feb. 1, 1856, Greeley to O. A. Bowe, Feb. 9, 1856.

24. *Tribune*, Feb. 9, 11, 16, March 26, Apr. 1, 11-14, 18, 1856. Greeley pushed hard, later that spring, for Galusha Grow's land bill granting a quarter section to every bona fide settler, for the cost of survey, registry and transfer. —*Tribune*, May 16, June 30, 1856.

25. *Tribune*, Sept. 8, Nov. 12, 1855, Feb. 13, 28, March 31, Apr. 2, 3, 17, 1856; Nevins, *Ordeal of the Union* (2 vols.; N. Y., 1947), II, 328.

26. *Tribune*, Dec. 20, 1855, Feb. 13, Apr. 23, 1856.

27. *Ibid.*, Feb. 23-25, March 27, 1856; G. W. Julian, *Political Recollections* (Chicago, 1884), pp. 147-48; Nevins, *Ordeal*, II, 487, 491.

28. Benton, *Greeley on Lincoln*, pp. 146f.; Greeley Papers (N. Y. P. L.), Greeley to Wm. M. Chace, etc., May 9, 1856.

29. Greeley Papers (N. Y. P. L.), Greeley to ———, N. Y., Apr. 23. 1856.

30. *Ibid.*, Greeley to "Friend R.," June 25, 1856, in *Tribune*, of Apr. 21, 1889. This sale brought him $10,000. By the end of June, the buyers had received $2,500 in dividends.

31. Greeley Letters (Yale Lib.), Greeley to Emma Newhall, March 2, 1856.

32. Greeley Letters (Albany State Lib.), Greeley to A. W. Thayer, Jan. 21, 1856; Greeley Papers (N. Y. P. L.), Greeley to Mrs. Newhall, Apr. 18, May 7, 1856, Greeley to Colfax, June 1, 1856, May 6, 1857; *Tribune*, June 18, 19, 1856.

33. Greeley Papers (N. Y. P. L.), Greeley to Brockway, Jan. 8, 1856; *Tribune*, Apr. 21, 28, 29, June 6, 1856.

34. Greeley Papers (N. Y. P. L.), Greeley to Colfax, May 17-19, 21, 1856; *Tribune,* Apr. 15, 1856, Greeley from Washington, Apr. 12, 1856.
35. Seward Papers, Weed to Seward, May 11 [1856]; *Albany Evening Journal,* July 15, 1856; G. S. Merriam, *The Life and Times of Samuel Bowles* (2 vols.; N. Y.. 1885), I, 172; Benton, *Greeley on Lincoln,* p. 133.
36. *Tribune,* June 6, 1856.
37. *Ibid.,* March 27, 1856, Greeley from Washington, March 26, June 19, 1856; Seward Papers, Trumbull Cary to Seward, May 1, 1856.
38. *Albany Evening Journal,* June 27, 1856; J. B. Ruhl, *John C. Frémont and the Republican Party* (Columbus, 1930), p. 22.
39. *Tribune,* May 23ff., June 3, 1856. The *Tribune* also characterized Senator Butler of South Carolina, Brooks's relative and a very popular member of the Senate, as an "old ruffian."
40. *Tribune,* June 26, July 1-7, 1856.
41. *Ibid.,* July 3, 4, 7, 1856; Greeley Papers (N. Y. P. L.), Greeley to Colfax, July 7, Aug. 10, 27, 1856; Nevins, *Ordeal,* II, 471-72; Ruhl, *op. cit.,* pp. 34, 35. Of course it should not be overlooked that "Toombs and Co." were also playing politics with a vengeance.
42. Parton Papers, Greeley to Parton, July 10, 1856; Greeley Papers (N. Y. P. L.), Greeley to Mrs. Newhall, Sept. 12, Oct. 9, 1856.
43. Nevins, *Ordeal,* II, 469-70; Nichols, *The Disruption of American Democracy* (N. Y., 1948), p. 18.
44. *Tribune,* Oct. 13, 1856.
45. *Ibid.,* Nov. 3, 5, 6, 8, 11, 29, 1856.
46. *Ibid.,* Nov. 6, 1856.
47. Greeley Papers (N. Y. P. L.), Greeley to Colfax, Dec. 7, 28, 1856; Fish Papers, Fish to R. A. West, Apr. 29, 1856.

CHAPTER 16

Greeley's Battle

D URING THE THREE YEARS AFTER THE ELECTION
of 1856, Greeley's life followed its usual strenuous pace, with mul-
tiple interests crowding in upon him at every hand. He continued
the struggle against weeds and water on his farm, fought hard
against the rising power of Fernando Wood in New York City
politics, lectured, traveled across the continent, and presided
jealously over the destinies of the *Tribune*. But his paramount
interest, the subject to which he devoted himself over and above
all else, was the battle that he had marked out against the Slave
Power.

It was slavery, Greeley dinned into his readers, that was the great
bar to the economic development of the West and of the South
itself. It was the Slave Power, hostile alike to free labor and free
land, opposed to protection for American industry, avid for expansion into new areas within and without the Union, that was the
real threat to the safety and prosperity of the nation. National
interest demanded that the power of the slavocracy be curbed, and
that the institution itself be set on the high road to extinction.[1]

The Slave Power, Greeley declared, had captured the party of
Pierce and Douglas and Buchanan, making it more than ever a
party of democracy in name only—a Sham Democracy. That party,
as the subservient tool of the southern oligarchs, was eager to
invade the rights of self government in countries to the south of the
United States. It stood opposed to protection, to free land, even to
land grant colleges, bound as it was hand and foot to the chariot
wheels of the great planters. Left to work its will, the Sham Democracy would transform this democratic republic into a slaveholding
oligarchy.[2]

But, fortunately for the country, a new party had come into being
at this critical juncture, a party that was committed to the true
interests of the nation. Republicanism, as Greeley understood it

(and his conception of its meaning was far broader than that of political hacks or platform resolutions) insisted upon the great truth that slavery was sectional, freedom national, and upon the equally important fact that the proper way to promote the national well-being was not by concession or retreat, but by stern resistance to the design of the Slave Power.[3] Republicanism was unalterably opposed to the extension of slavery; it was invincibly committed to the improvement of rivers and harbors, a transcontinental railroad, and protection for home industry. National in its aims and outlook, it would take root everywhere, even in the southern states. "We ought to have a formidable Republican organization and party in those states," Greeley declared in 1859. "We should have if the press was there free and the People really at liberty to speak and vote as their own judgments and consciences should dictate. And the day of such organization cannot much longer be deferred."[4]

Greeley emphasized that Republican protectionism meant national prosperity, and he was quick to declare that low tariffs were responsible for the panic of 1857. But mindful of the sensibilities of Old Democrats, he now posed, à la Jackson, as the advocate of a "judicious" tariff. In his opinion, that of 1857 was better than that of 1846. No one wanted extreme tariff boosts. The tariff was for nursing infant industries, protection against foreign dumping and the enticement of immigration. Ten years of a tariff like that of 1842, and protection would no longer be necessary for heavy industry.

A decent protective system, Greeley told the Old Democrats of his party, would be of great assistance in destroying slavery. It would do this by its diversification of southern economic effort, an achievement that would dry up the value of the ignorant and debased labor pool that formed the basis of a slave-labor economy. As protection wrought this change in the southern economic system, slavery would pass easily away. Indeed, he pointed out triumphantly, this was already beginning to happen with the expansion of American industry. Slavery was already "an impertinence and a nuisance in Baltimore and St. Louis, as it soon must be in Louisville, Richmond and even New Orleans." If further proof was needed, he would refer skeptics to the "quiet, steady growth" of manufacturing and skilled industry in Russia, a growth which was, in his opinion, making an anachronism and abomination of serfdom.[5]

Thus, with some sound reasoning and some rather facile argument, he served up protection seasoned to the palates of all, with a special sugar coating for the benefit of the Old Democrats.

The blessings of protection were not the only contributions of Republicanism that were stressed by the embattled editor. His party, he declared, earnestly desired the development of the West, an area whose vast potential fired his imagination even when he was wading in Illinois mud so deep that he lost his shoes without realizing that they were gone. Republican predominance meant free land, which (together with protection and internal improvements) was vital to the utilization of western resources. The slavocracy opposed free land and thus opposed the true interests of the West and of the nation, but Republicanism would give free land, and deal out a spate of railroads for good measure.[6] So the *Tribune* urged railroad land grants, both to the states and to private companies, as one of the major ways of developing the West and of adding to the national wealth.

Greeley knew that graft and corruption often lurked behind such land grants. His own fingers had been scorched when, in 1856, he agreed to help the Des Moines Navigation and Railroad Company in its efforts to obtain Congressional land grants, in return for its support of the passage of the Topeka constitution through the House of Representatives. The $1,000 draft that he received in Washington and handed over to one of the company's designated lobbyists came to light in a Congressional investigation and caused him no little embarrassment, for it showed how complaisant he could be toward corruption when he felt that larger ends were involved.[7] Only a person of incredible naïveté, and Greeley was not naïve, could have been unaware of what happened to $1,000 drafts in the hands of Congressional lobbyists during the 1850's. But, despite this contretemps, he continued to urge federal aid for railroad development by private interests, and to push particularly for the construction of a transcontinental railroad. A band of iron rails across the continent, he declared, would add more to the wealth and power of the nation than would a dozen Cubas.[8]

There were times when Greeley became impatient with the Congressional Republicans because they failed to see the party's proper line of attack as clearly as he did. If the Republicans in Congress, he wrote to Salmon P. Chase in 1858, were only wise enough and unselfish enough to press for reform in patronage and expenditures, and demand measures to reinvigorate prostrate industry, he would have high hopes for 1860. Abolish the army (save for the generals and their staffs), transform the navy into mail steamers, reduce expenditures to $40,000,000 a year, set the farmers and factories to work—either do this or be beaten by the Democrats in trying to do it, and the party would win the next Presidential election. "But," he added sourly, "we shall do none of this, and shall be beaten as usual."[9]

The rescue of the South from slavery and from the Democratic party was an essential part of Greeley's nationalistic dreams and visions, and his optimism in regard to the possibility of such a rescue was easily aroused. A Frémont victory in 1856 would have meant the establishment of the Republican party throughout the South, he asserted. In 1857, he characterized the victory of an antislavery municipal ticket in St. Louis, Missouri, as having an importance "impossible to exaggerate." It was, he felt certain, the beginning of the rising up of the southern masses against the dominant planter class. In 1858, he heralded an antislavery movement in Maryland. It promised speedier relief for that state, he declared, than did the movement in Missouri.[10]

Optimism as to the vulnerability of the Slave Power in its home bailiwicks led Greeley to promote an expansion of the colonization principle that he had espoused so eagerly in Kansas. There were tens of thousands of free-soil emigrants available, he told Seward, for colonizing such border states as Missouri and Virginia. He thought seriously of making a special trip to England for settlers of the right sort. If money could be found for the project, land speculators banned from it, and the political angle played down, great results might well ensue. Missouri, a Republican state by 1860, and Virginia, following suit by 1876, were to him enticing and reasonable possibilities.[11]

Such hopes were vain and more than vain. Only in St. Louis, in all the region where slavery reigned, was a notable victory for freedom gained at the polls during the latter 1850's. The border states consistently shied away from emancipation. Greeley's hopes were disappointed. With that disappointment came a keener conception of the strength of the Slave Power, and of the necessity for strongly resisting its advance.

The *Tribune's* attitude toward slavery itself varied considerably during this period. At first the paper was filled with violent assaults. Greeley was an adept at penning sly editorial notes about how the southern planter chased women with bloodhounds to compel them "to work for his pleasure and profit," but the main attack was handled by that master of irony, Charles T. Congdon.

The banner year of this onslaught was 1857. Month after month, *Tribune* editorials lashed at "the decrepitude and poverty of the southern press" and at the imbecility of the southern editor who, having no case in logic or morals for slavery, could do nothing but "work himself into a hurricane of passion, just to show that if he

Boy—Tribune, Sir   Daily Tribune, Sir? only two cents?

Southerner —No, curse your Tribune'—don't you see I'm a *white* man?

A newsboy makes a mistake. A cartoon of the 1850's.

Courtesy of the *New York Public Library*

cannot be wise he can at least be windy." There were some good things in the South, such as tourneys. The man who rode at a ring, lance in hand, at least was not making a treacherous assault with a gutta-percha cane. But even southern tourneys were indicative of the slaveholder's inferiority to the northerner, just as was the pitiful showing of the slave states in the number of patents taken out each year. The difference was due to the two systems of labor "and their influence upon intellectual activity. . . . It is not the habit of the slaveholder to create. . . . All centuries are alike to him and the nineteenth is no better than the twelfth."[12]

One of the *Tribune's* most effective satires on slavery was a series of editorials about one Benjamin Screws, Esquire, who, so it averred, was a broker in Negroes located at 159 Gravier Street, New Orleans, and an absolutely genuine article. Doubting Thomases were told to come and gaze upon his card in the *Tribune* office. Screws was the man "who has the warranted cook maids. And the blacksmiths. And the carpenters. And the pretty, wasp-waisted, bright-eyed little yellow women, for that matter, if one will but please to call for them. Everything choice, solid, muscular, fascinating, and even voluptuous, upon the premises of Benjamin Screws."[13] The mock account of the trials and tribulations of this dealer in human flesh, and of those who bought and sold through him, was calculated to make the slaveholder's blood boil.

Baited by such attacks, the Southrons could relish to the full Sam Houston's description of Greeley as the essence of sneaking villainy, a man "whose hair is white, whose skin is white, whose eyes are white, whose clothes are white, and whose liver is in my opinion of the same color."[14]

During 1858 and 1859, the *Tribune* continued to shower some dashes of its venom upon slavery. There were times when it would ring the changes on a Virginia gentleman's advertisement offering $100 for runaway Thomas Jefferson, or comment upon the way southern poets avoided the domestic affections (it had never seen a piece entitled "To My Little, Brown Sister," or "Lines to My Daughter Whom I Am Compelled to Sell").[15] But despite such sallies, the tone of the paper was very sensibly altered. This was probably due to the approaching Presidential contest and to a conviction that satirizing southern institutions was not likely to win the votes of southern Know Nothings and poor whites. Anxious to nationalize the Republican following, Greeley's tactics now consisted of asserting that Republicanism was essentially conservative, and of declaring earnestly that no legislative attempt would be made to interfere with the institution of slavery where it already existed. He even agreed that, if a state wanted to come into the Union with slavery, it had a perfect right to do so. At the same time, he sought to propagandize for freedom and Republicanism among the southern poor whites by pushing the issuance and circulation of a compendium of Helper's *Impending Crisis,* an exposé of the evil effects of slavery upon the nonslaveholding southern white.[16]

But if the *Tribune's* attitude toward the institution of slavery showed signs of alteration during the late 1850's, such was not the case with its campaign against slavery extension. Never was this more clearly illustrated than in Greeley's attitude toward the Dred Scott decision.

On March 7, 1857, Chief Justice Roger B. Taney handed down a majority decision of the Supreme Court that, though honestly made on behalf of peace, helped immeasureably to widen the gap between the sections and to provoke the Civil War.

Dred Scott, a Missouri slave, had been taken by his master into free territory, then returned to the slave state of Missouri. Acting on the assumption that Negroes as well as whites were citizens of the United States, Scott had then sued for his freedom, first in the state and then in the federal courts, his lawyer asserting that residence in a free territory had made him a free man.

The Court majority decided that he was not a citizen, and that the protection of the Constitution could be invoked only by whites. This threw the case out of the Supreme Court. But, moved by a desire to help settle the existing controversy over slavery extension, Taney and the majority added a ruling that the Missouri Compromise had always been unconstitutional because it was a deprivation of property without due process of law, and that, therefore, slaveholding in any of the territories of the Union was a constitutional right.

The Dred Scott ruling, for all its pacificatory intent, aroused a storm of bitter indignation throughout the North. Press and pulpit resounded with denunciations. Free-soilers everywhere condemned it. In New York City, George Barrell Cheever denounced it from his Church of the Puritans on Union Square. Some six months after the decision was made public, the genial and humane Dr. John W. Francis, one of the town's leading citizens, shouted to his friend Evert Duyckinck across the Sleepy Hollow railroad station (and with ladies present) that Roger B. Taney was "a son of a bitch."[17] The North was angry, and the *Tribune* blew upon the fires of its wrath.

Greeley had returned from a western lecture trip a few days before the decision was made public. Just as he appeared in New York, advance information reached the *Tribune* office as to what the court would say. Consequently he had had time for reflection and was able to commence a vigorous assault upon the opinion as soon as the news of it was released.[18]

Greeley had once declared that he would always respect and conform to every decision of the Supreme Court,[19] but at least half of that declaration was now forgotten. The day before the

court's pronouncement, he warned with passionate earnestness that
Free-soilers would not submit to any Supreme Court decision
validating the right of a slaveholder to take his slaves into any
territory in the Union. As soon as the opinion was published, and
in the days immediately following, Greeley subjected it to a drum-
fire of attack.

This decision, we need hardly say, is entitled to just so much moral
weight as would be the judgment of a majority of those congregated in
any Washington barroom. It is a dictum prescribed by the stump to the
bench—the Bowie-knife sticking in the stump ready for instant use if
needed. . . . This judgment annihilates all Compromises and brings us
face to face with the great issue in the right shape.

When Taney delivered his opinion, said Greeley, it was no wonder that his voice was almost inaudible, conscious, as he must have
been, that the decision was based on grounds altogether different
from those indicated in the opinion,

knowing that he was engaged in a pitiful attempt to impose upon the
public. However feeble his voice might have been, what he had to say was
still feebler. There is not the slightest degree of adroitness, ingenuity or
plausibility about it. Downright and bare-faced falsehood is its main staple.
Any slave-driving editor or Virginia bar-room politician could have taken
the Chief-Justice's place on the bench, and with the exception of a little
bolder speaking up, nobody would have perceived the difference.

The editor of the *Tribune,* quite wrongly, attributed to Taney
the opinion that "black men have no rights that white men are
bound to respect." But Taney's decision, said Greeley, not only
signalized the degradation of a race; it also brought measurably
nearer an invasion of the free states by slavery. "This wicked and
false judgment" has decided "that Slavery is National. . . . Let a
single case draw from the Court an official judgment that slaves
can be held and protected under National law," Greeley warned,
"and we shall see men buying slaves for the New York market,
while Mr. Toombs can call the roll of his chattels on the slope of
Bunker Hill." Greeley could visualize a New York jobber ordering
his southern agent, "Send me a Negro cook, at the lowest market
value! Buy me a waiter! Balance my account with two chamber-
maids and a truckman!"[20]

The *Tribune* was loth to let the public forget the Dred Scott
decision. For months the editorial page returned again and again
to the subject. A pamphlet on the case was printed in the *Tribune*

office and put on sale by the Fourth of July, 1857. Both the editorials and the pamphlet distorted Taney's aims and caricatured
the meaning of his words. But it was effective ammunition in the
battle against slavery and the Democratic party, for it furthered
the contention that Republicanism alone could save the nation for
freedom.

The Dred Scott decision was used by Greeley in equating Republicanism with righteousness as well as with the national welfare.
Greeley declared that the opinion was morally vicious because it
meant an extension of human degradation, and because it strengthened the power of the evil supporters of a vicious institution. He
dedicated himself to forcing a reversal of the decision, to obtaining
a readjustment of the sectional basis upon which the court was
apportioned, to creating a public sentiment that would put the
control of the government of the United States in the hands of
righteous men.

Taney was useful to Greeley in the latter's effort to rouse popular
sentiment against slavery and its supporters. Fresh aid for this
effort came from another quarter as well. Even while the *Tribune*
was fulminating against the old Chief Justice, the proslaverites in
Kansas were furnishing the fiery editor with ammunition that he
was quick to use.

The Kansas proslavery men held a constitutional convention in
1857 at Lecompton, and from this gathering emerged the so-called
Lecompton constitution, a document in which a special guarantee
of slavery was put in a special clause. It was then submitted to
the voters by means of a plebiscite. They could vote for the constitution with this clause, or for the constitution without this clause,
not against the constitution itself. And the constitution, in parts
other than the special clause, guaranteed to slaveholders the slave
property already in the state.

When the plebiscite was held, the free-soil men refused to vote,
and the rump electorate of course ratified the constitution with
slavery complete and unabridged. The proslavery men then began
demanding admission of Kansas as a state under this document.

The proceedings at Lecompton had made a travesty of popular
sovereignty. The proslavery men there had played into Greeley's
hands. As soon as the constitution was drawn up he proclaimed
it "bogus," and urged the Kansas free-soilers to boycott it. The
plebiscite was denounced as vicious and misleading, and the Free-
soilers were duly applauded when they refused to vote. Unsparing
attacks upon Lecompton and unstinting encouragement to the
obdurate Free-soilers continued throughout the year.

Greeley longed to identify Buchanan's administration with the Lecompton iniquity. It was a longing that tempted him into unscrupulous tactics. Buchanan appointed Robert J. Walker governor of the Kansas territory in 1857, and Walker did his best to prevent the renewal of civil war in Kansas, the while he tried to move the territory toward statehood in conformance with democratic practice. But no hint of his good intentions was permitted to creep into the pages of the *Tribune*. There he was viciously caricatured as a tool of the proslavery elements in the territory, the fit representative of an administration at Washington that cringed before the Slave Power.[21]

The *Tribune's* editor had use for the Kansas question in his home bailiwick. It was to be the means whereby New York State would be carried for Republicanism in 1857. Hence his attacks upon the Kansas iniquity redoubled during the state campaign of that year. He took good care to flay Governor Walker, to label President Buchanan a "Border Ruffian ex-officio," and to heap scorn upon all proposals aimed at compromising the Kansas difficulties. It must be the Topeka constitution or nothing, Greeley told his readers,[22] the Topeka constitution being a free-soil charter that prohibited slavery.

Despite these efforts to use Kansas as a means to Republican victory, the Democrats carried New York State in the fall of 1857. As always, Greeley was downcast by the defeat, but he had a ready explanation. The electorate had been befuddled by Democratic insistence that the Kansas question had been settled and was therefore no longer an issue.

Greeley's attitude toward Kansas was essentially that of Weed and Seward. He was still on friendly terms with both of his former partners and, to any casual observer, the triumvirate was still in being. But though the relationship was superficially serene, there were evidences that the *Tribune's* editor had taken a new course. The *Tribune* did not hesitate to criticize Seward when its opinions differed from those of the Senator, and Greeley kept privately asserting that he had ceased to follow Seward's lead as a politician.[23] Weed's political generalship was dealt with severely in the *Tribune*, and repeatedly Greeley attacked the Albany boss for subservience to the New York Central Railroad and for complacence in regard to the corrupt jobbing and lobbying that was becoming conspicuous in Albany.[24] Slowly but steadily, the rift in the lute was becoming more pronounced.

The reasons for this separation were various. Greeley was still smarting over what he regarded as lack of appreciation by Weed and Seward. He was without doubt increasingly concerned over the low tone of public life at Albany. But it took more than injured feelings or shady political dealings (he had endured both without revolt while the *Tribune* was growing up) to account for his mounting opposition to the leadership of his erstwhile senior partners. There was, in other words, a Senegambian lurking in the woodpile.

Greeley's main idea, politically, was to establish the power of the Republican party by wooing not only Old Whigs but also Know Nothings and Old Democrats into the Republican phalanx. Kansas was one of his means to that end, the idea being that indignation over the Kansas iniquity would act as a catalytic agent. By the action of this agent, all antislavery men would be precipitated into an harmonious political organization, and one of the most prominent leaders of that organization would be none other than the editor of the *New York Tribune,* Horace Greeley.

To Weed, the political amalgamation sought by Greeley was full of danger. A Republican party bursting at the seams with Know Nothings and Old Democrats, however useful they might be at the polls, would mean a threat to the Old Whig leadership of the party, to his own "dictatorship," and to Seward's political ambitions. Hence the Albany boss and Greeley found themselves repeatedly at odds.

This difference of opinion, and particularly the difference over the role Old Democrats should play in the Republican party manifested itself on various occasions. Greeley worked hard for Preston King's election to the United States Senate in 1857 as successor to Hamilton Fish.[25] This was a concession to the Old Democrats. Weed assented to it, but distinctly without enthusiasm. At the Republican state convention of that same year, Greeley aligned himself with such Old Democrats as David Dudley Field and John T. Hogeboom to take over control of the convention. This combination cloaked itself in moral purity, rejecting Weed's counsel because he would not come out strongly against the jobbery and corruption that was prevalent at the state capitol.[26] For the nonce, the Dictator's hold upon the party organization was shaken, and he found himself in danger of being elbowed out into the cold.

Greeley's efforts to forge his broadly based antislavery combination continued during 1858, to Weed's increasing discomfort. As enticement to the Know Nothings, Greeley urged a registry law, together with the requirement of a year's residence between naturalization and voting. He puffed John J. Crittenden in the *Tribune* and proposed that Crittenden and John Bell of Tennessee (both supporters of Know Nothingism) come up to New York for

a "great time" after Congress had adjourned. He worked hard for
a fusion of Republicans, Know Nothings and Democrats in Ulster
County, New York, where, he declared that a slave state, if it
wanted to come in as such, could not be kept out of the Union.
Indeed, the *Tribune's* conservatism became so pronounced that
Greeley, whimsically but privately, labeled it "an Old Hunker
concern." "I shall stop taking it soon," he wrote to Pike, "if it
doesn't evince a more reformatory spirit."[27] Such was the direction
of his thinking in 1858. More evidence of this passion for a popular
front against the Slave Power soon came to light.

Before the New York State convention of 1858, Greeley was
working hand in glove with a group of New York City Know
Nothing leaders and sympathizers who were intriguing to overthrow Weed's leadership, eliminate Seward as a presidential possibility and promote John J. Crittenden as a candidate for the
Republican nomination in 1860. John Bigelow rebuked this conspiracy in the *New York Evening Post,* declaring that it was being
carried on by men who were "not worthy to unloose the latchets
of Weed's shoes." Bigelow paid high tribute to Weed's leadership
of the party, but Greeley thought he knew better. He persevered
in the plan to unseat Weed, in part because he believed that so
doing would strengthen Republicanism, and in part because the
Know Nothings were willing to nominate Greeley for governor.

Before the state convention met at Syracuse in September of
1858, the *Tribune's* editor was one of the foremost in urging
fusion with the Know Nothings. When the convention met, Greeley
was in Indiana, where he had gone to deliver an agricultural
address and to be absent when he was, or was not, nominated for
governor. "The Horatian movement," Dana wrote to Pike, was
strong. But Weed was at Syracuse, determined not to be taken in a
second time. His candidate for governor, Edwin D. Morgan (an
excellent choice) was nominated, and not even a tiny portion of
the state ticket was allotted to those who had seen Sam. The
Dictator's friends had rallied around him, and Greeley's plans had
been brought to nought. But he was unrepentant, as obstinately
determined as ever upon the policy that he had identified as his
own.[28]

Greeley supported the Republican state ticket in 1858 and, as in
the previous state campaign, he tried to make Kansas a magnet
for drawing votes from all quarters. But his dissatisfaction with
what he termed the "Syracuse folly" was open and obvious. When
the contest ended with Morgan's victory, Greeley was quick to
declare that the triumph would have been much greater and of

more significance if his counsels, instead of Weed's, had been followed at Syracuse. As proof of his enduring affection for the Know Nothings, he kept on demanding a registry law and naturalization at least a year before the foreign-born voter appeared at the polls.

Greeley's policy of increasing Republican power by enlisting the Know Nothings, as well as the Old Democrats, in the party's ranks was clear and purposeful. The actual concessions that he was willing to make to the Know Nothings, other than a share in office and the probable destruction of Weed's leadership, were constructive measures that would have improved government in New York State. He was also banking on the fact that Know Nothingism was a dying movement, so that deals with its members could be safely made. If his strategy was the opposite of that which he had used during the previous decade, when he had repulsed with horror every effort of Sam to worm himself into the counsels of the Whig party,[29] the difference could be accounted for by Know Nothing weakness, the demonstrated futility of wooing the Irish vote and, last but not least, his break with Thurlow Weed.

Aside from his efforts at fusion, Greeley developed another project for aiding the spread of Republicanism. This was nothing less than a plan for fostering discord and division within the Democratic party. His catspaw in this move was to be Senator Stephen A. Douglas of Illinois.

From 1854 on, Douglas had been denounced in the *Tribune* as a "lying little villain," one of "the little northern Judas Iscariots" who had sought to earn the gratitude of the Slave Power by accepting every lie of the Border Ruffians as truth and stigmatizing every truth affirmed by the free-state men as a lie.[30]

It was this infamous creature, this man of infinite guile and infinite ambition, whose praises Greeley now began to sing.

The reason for Greeley's attitude toward Douglas lay in developments that had been occurring within the bosom of the Democratic party. President Buchanan had come out in his message to Congress in December 1857 for admission of Kansas as a state under the Lecompton constitution. Douglas held that to admit Kansas under an instrument that flouted the wishes of a majority of Kansans would be a travesty upon his doctrine of popular sovereignty. The Little Giant announced his determination to oppose the measure when it appeared in Congress. In a stormy White House interview, Buchanan threatened him with political extinction. Douglas looking the President straight in the eye, replied, "Mr. President, I wish you to remember that General Jackson is dead."[31] Thus the die was cast, and in the bitter quarrel that ensued the Democracy was cleft in twain. A majority of the northern Democrats rose to the support of Douglas, and Greeley thought he saw a glorious opportunity to make Republican capital out of a Democratic feud.

Buchanan's support of Lecompton elicited from the *Tribune* a violent series of attacks upon that measure, which was once more characterized as a betrayal of the principle of squatter sovereignty.[32] But Douglas was praised to the skies for his rejection of Lecompton.

A Democratic effort to compromise the quarrel over Lecompton appeared in Congress in the spring of 1858 in the form of the English bill. This measure provided for submitting the entire Lecompton constitution to the voters of Kansas, with the provision that, if accepted, Kansas would get the usual gift of public lands. Rejection, on the other hand, would mean delay in statehood and therefore in a land grant until the population reached the number that would entitle the Kansans to a representative in Congress. Greeley pounced upon this bill like a hawk upon a sparrow.

Anything that looked like a settlement of Kansas troubles on other grounds than those of complete victory for free soil was sure to arouse Greeley's wrath, and so it was with the English bill. He denounced it as "Lecompton Junior—the English brat," and was largely responsible for spreading the false story that it offered "enormous bribes" in public lands to the Kansans, if they would but truckle to slavery.

When Douglas came out against the English bill, his action was commended in the warmest manner. Once again, as it had done only a few weeks before, the *Tribune* sang the praises of the Senator from Illinois. Everything that the Little Giant did seemed to be looked upon with favor by his erstwhile enemy.

Greeley had met Douglas in Washington late in 1857. Whether the two men had reached an agreement of any kind is not known, but at least Greeley had become convinced that it would be wise for Illinois Republicans to support the Illinoisan's campaign for reëlection.[33] Ultimately, the Slave Power would kick the Little Giant out of the Sham Democracy, but before that happened he could do that party all sorts of damage. "I mean to write," Greeley told one of his close friends, "so as not to weaken him with his party while he strengthens himself with the general public."[34]

Greeley was not the only Republican who thought it good policy to support Douglas. Republican political leaders like United States Senator Henry Wilson of Massachusetts, Greeley's close friend Congressman Schuyler Colfax of Indiana, and Samuel Bowles of the *Springfield Republican* also favored returning Douglas unopposed to the Senate.[35] But among them all, Greeley's voice could speak with the greatest authority to the farmers of Illinois.

The *Weekly Tribune* spread throughout Illinois its praises of the author of the Kansas-Nebraska Bill. Greeley wrote editorials designed to stimulate pro-Douglas sentiment among Illinois Republicans. He counseled all good men to rally to Douglas's reëlection. His general aim was to "soften the less cantankerous Republicans" in their attitude toward Douglas and to furnish the Douglas men with material that they could use to advantage in building up support for their candidate.[36]

The great majority of Illinois Republicans did not relish Greeley's support of the Little Giant. Their attitude toward Douglas was much like that of Mr. Weller, Junior, toward veal pie: "Weal pie is wery good—ven you're sure it a'n't kittens." Douglas was emphatically kittens to this gentry in 1858. Trumbull, Herndon, and the rest of the Illinois crowd had good reason to believe that, with the Illinois Democracy badly split over Lecompton, Abraham Lincoln could be elected to the Senate. They resented the attitude of the *Tribune,* its officious meddling in their affairs. What they did was none of the *Tribune's* business. What good, either in prestige or in patronage, could come from an unholy alliance with the author of the Nebraska infamy? Such an association would disgrace the virginity of the Republican party beyond any possible redemption.[37]

Joseph Medill's *Chicago Tribune* and other Illinois Republican papers began attacking Greeley for interfering in matters that were none of his concern. Lincoln, himself, felt that Greeley was treating him badly. The *Tribune's* editor began to be appalled by the storm he had conjured up. Visions of dissipating the influence and ruining the subscription list of the *Weekly* began to dance before his eyes. He listened to Herndon, who came east for an interview and afterward continued pressure from back home, and finally Greeley gave a sulky promise that he would do what he could for Lincoln during the campaign.

Greeley had promised, but Greeley was ruffled in spirit. Now it was not Weed and Seward but Illinois Republicans who did not value his advice. True to his word, he criticized Douglas during the campaign. But he declared privately that Lincoln's speeches did not amount to much, and his positive support of the Rail Splitter was, to say the least, lukewarm. "You have got your Elephant," he sneered to Joseph Medill. "Now shoulder him! He is not so heavy after all."

When the campaign was over, Greeley lectured the Illinois

Republicans. In no uncertain terms, he explained to them what an opportunity they had missed when, rejecting his advice on strategy, they had failed to return Douglas to the Senate and two anti-Lecompton Democrats to the House with a flood of Republican votes.[38] His criticism, like the language he had employed during the campaign, was harsh. Many Republicans felt that it was undeserved. Among the Illinois politicians a hearty dislike of Greeley took root and began to flourish.

Greeley emerged from the Lincoln-Douglas campaign of 1858 in a petulant mood. He had worked out what he considered a brilliant plan of strategy, only to have it rejected by lesser men. As one consequence of this, he had developed a critical attitude toward Lincoln, and Horace Greeley's personal prejudices were seldom uprooted by subsequent events. The coolness of the *Tribune's* editor toward Lincoln was perhaps the most unfortunate result of his attempt to direct the course of the Illinois election of 1858.

Greeley had other critics than Illinois Republicans in 1858. The Cotton Republican press of New York, the Democratic newspapers of the metropolis, and particularly James Gordon Bennett's *Herald* displayed a devilish ingenuity in ridiculing his favorite ideas and in circulating stories that touched his personal honor or put him in a ridiculous role. Thus Bennett charged as often as once a week that Greeley had pillaged the fund for relief of sufferers in the Irish famine, and that he had received and disbursed $30,000 to organize the last House of Representatives. The *Herald* also declared that the *Weekly Tribune* had lost half its circulation within the year, and Bennett shed crocodile tears over "the steady decline of our unfortunate contemporary."[39] A grand to-do was also raised over testimony before a Congressional investigating committee in regard to Greeley's lobbying on behalf of a firm of New England wool manufacturers.

The evidence as to Greeley's lobbying did not amount to much. O. B. Matteson, a venal Congressman from New York State, had suggested to W. W. Stone of the firm of Lawrence, Stone and Company that $25,000 to $30,000 be put in Greeley's hands for the purpose of influencing Congressmen to vote "right" on the wool duties. Stone swore before a Congressional investigating committee that he had talked to Greeley on the subject of wool duties, but had never mentioned Matteson's proposal. Greeley swore that the question of pay for either himself or the *Tribune* was not raised or even mentioned in the conversations that he had with Stone. Matteson swore that he had meant that Greeley should be paid simply for the influence that the *Tribune* might exert on the tariff bill.[40] The incident

furnished Greeley's enemies in the New York press with an opportunity for a field day, but that was all.

Greeley was harassed by these attacks upon himself and his paper.
Reports that the *Tribune* was on the road to ruin, and canards in
regard to himself and his motives always touched him on the raw.
He knew that it was best to let slanders die a natural death, but it
was hard for him to remain silent under such assaults, and his
violent counterattacks showed his enemies that they had found a
sure way of infuriating and distracting him.

Financial storms as well as other afflictions assailed Greeley during
his battle of the late 1850's with the Slave Power. The year 1857
was a hard one for the *Tribune*. The panic of that year hit the
volume of advertising, and the subscription list showed a considerable shrinkage, though not nearly so much as indicated by the
Herald's allegations. McElrath went into bankruptcy that summer,
his financial troubles necessitating his retirement from the paper
and to some extent impairing its credit. Greeley, weighed down by
anxiety, canceled a projected trip to Europe. His *Tribune* stock
was down to fifteen shares and, as usual, he was in debt. Once again
he felt poor.

Family troubles added their weight to the burden that Greeley
had to bear. Raphael died of croup early in 1857, and Greeley was
left without a son. Warned by a telegram, just as he was finishing
a lecture tour, he had hurried home, only to be too late to see Raffie
before he died. Raffie's health had not been good and Horace had
begun anticipating his death a year before it occurred, but it was
nevertheless a sad blow in itself and no help whatever to Molly
Greeley's outlook on life. "New York is the worst place in America—
I hope in the world—for children," Greeley wrote bitterly to a
friend. They had lost five out of seven children born there, he went
on, "and their mother has sacrificed ease, happiness, constitution,
all that she could sacrifice for her children most joyfully."[41]

The birth of a bouncing baby girl named Gabrielle was hardly
compensation for the loss of Raffie. And the older daughter, Ida,
was a worry. The rigorous discipline to which she was subjected was
making her sullen, and she was beginning to stammer. But her
worried father, lacking an alternative, still left the little girl in her
mother's full charge. As though these afflictions were not enough,
there was also the never-ending drudgery of hunting up nursemaids,
cooks, and seamstresses, some of whom did not suit and the rest
of whom would not stay.[42]

But by 1859 the family situation seemed a little better, and the
Tribune had bounced back with heartening vigor from the doldrums

of 1857. Its aggregate circulation in April of 1859 was 211,750 copies. Greeley felt free to undertake a long-cherished plan. On May 9, he left New York on the Erie Railroad for an overland journey to California.

When Greeley started for the Golden Gate, his mind was teeming with a variety of projects. He meant to, and did, preach Republicanism enroute; he took occasion while in Kansas to air one of his favorite ideas—the abolition of the standing army;[43] while on the coast, he did his best to promote another long-cherished plan, the fusion of the anti-Lecompton Democrats and the Republicans. But the great reason for his trip to the Pacific was the transcontinental railroad. Greeley wanted to publicize that project and spy out the land for the best route.

Greeley went to the coast by way of Kansas, Colorado, and Utah, writing letters to the *Tribune* as he journeyed on his way. These letters bore witness, just as did those written to the *Tribune* while on his lecture tours, to those remarkably accurate powers of observation that made him a real authority on the resources, interests, and state of development of the regions that he visited. They also bore witness to the hardships of travel in the mid-nineteenth century. The hot, fetid sleeping-car air that nauseated him, the drinking water that made him ill, the trunk that he lost, the mules that annoyed him, the sleep that departed when he lay down on bags filled with Congressional documents franked through at the public expense—all were duly set down for the edification of his readers, who laughed and learned and sighed with relief when their favorite editor at last reached California.

The West loved Horace Greeley. It regarded him as simple, honest, straightforward, and devoted to its interests, an eastern Yankee shrewd enough to see the value of a western railroad. So his journey gained him laurels on the plains and in the mountains, where men magnified it into a kind of homespun odyssey. His lively account of the dangers of the trip to Placerville was soon transformed into a legend. It was a rare campfire evening that did not hear the tale of how Hank Monk, the driver, boasting that he was always on time "at any cost," had taken his reluctant passenger slithering around rocky curves and plunging down across precipitous canyon ledges. Mark Twain declared that he had heard this story no less than 481 times.[44]

Greeley made a number of speeches in California. He was a guest of Colonel Frémont at the latter's Mariposa mine and, there and elsewhere, got a bird's-eye view of California's society, its morals, and its economics. He was much impressed by the state's fertility and resources, but was sadly disappointed to find its people "in the leading strings of slavery and sham-democracy." It is likely that the anguish caused by this benighted condition of the Californians shortened his visit. Obviously, it was a people so deeply engaged in sinning that not even the hot gospeler of the *Tribune* could accomplish much in the way of their redemption.

Greeley planned to return by starting from Los Angeles and passing through Tucson and El Paso, but an outbreak of his old enemy, boils, decided him against the rigors of the overland passage. Instead, he braved another old enemy, seasickness, and came back by way of the Isthmus. Early in October, he was once more in New York, busily preparing his letters for publication in book form.

The *Overland Journey,* published the following year, closed with a moving appeal for a Pacific railroad as a "bond of union," a "new spring to our national industry, prosperity and wealth," one that would open "new vistas to national and individual aspiration." His "long, fatiguing journey," he declared, had been taken in the hope of doing something to hasten the road's completion.

Seward and Weed thought that they knew of an objective that Greeley had in mind, other than the one that he so frankly avowed. It was an objective not publicized, but more important to them than any railroad. The *Tribune's* editor, they believed, had at last come back to the political fold and was willing to make amends for previous divagations.

Greeley had remained on very good social terms with Seward, going to the latter's home more than once after 1854 for dinner and an evening of political conversation. The *Tribune* had defended Seward's "irrepressible conflict" speech, which had been made at Rochester, New York, in the fall of 1858 and which in some quarters had given Seward the reputation of being a dangerous radical. In January 1859, Greeley had written an editorial in which he had given Seward high praise, remarking that if there were six democrats in the world, one of them was the senior Senator from the state of New York. Thurlow Weed had reprinted this editorial in the *Albany Evening Journal,* fairly purring over its contents. Direct conversation strengthened the favorable impression that the editorial had made upon Weed. He told Seward that Greeley was "all right" at last politically and, what was more, was willing to be useful out in California.

The news of Greeley's return to political sanity was as pleasing to Seward as it was to Weed. Both men pictured Greeley as drumming up Seward sentiment on his way to the coast. This was as fond a delusion as was ever entertained by any knight in the clutches of La Belle Dame Sans Merci. Once more Thurlow Weed had demonstrated his inability to fathom the thoughts and purposes of the Man in the White Coat.[45]

NOTES FOR CHAPTER 16

1. *Tribune*, Aug. 3, 1857, Feb. 23, Dec. 4, 1858, Nov. 8, Dec. 9, 10, 13, 23, 1859.
2. *Ibid.*, Apr. 26, 1858, Dec. 27, 28 1859.
3. This viewpoint appears throughout the period under consideration. It is most succinctly expressed in the powerful editorials of Nov.-Dec., 1859.

   It has sometimes been asserted that Dana was responsible for the *Tribune's* nationalistic stand during these years; that Greeley was more than willing to see the slavery South leave the Union. This is an error. Greeley would have been most reluctant to see the South go. He suggested occasionally, 1857-59, that it would be an advantage to the North to be freed from the slavery incubus, but this was clearly meant to highlight the North's social and economic superiority, or to emphasize what he regarded as the bluff and bluster of the Southrons, rather than to evince a willingness to sever the Union. The reader interested in pursuing this subject further should read, in addition to the succeeding pages of this chapter the *Tribune* editorials of Dec. 10-15, 1859, and also the comment by Charles A. Dana cited in J. H. Wilson, *The Life of Charles A. Dana* (N. Y. and London, 1907), p. 151.
4. *Tribune*, Jan. 24, 1859.
5. *Ibid.*, Apr. 2, 1851, Oct. 30, 1855, Feb. 3, Mar. 4, 13, 19, Apr. 11, May 12, Aug. 28, Sept. 3, Oct. 6, 16, 26, Nov. 5, 1857, Apr. 29, June 21, July 9, Aug. 13, Oct. 4, 1858, Jan. 17, 31, Feb. 1, 7, Oct. 10, 13, Dec. 23, 1859. See also the issues of Jan. 1858 for the series of special articles by Henry C. Carey.
6. *Ibid.*, Apr. 18, 22, 1856, Feb. 3-Mar. 2, Aug. 12, 1857, Feb. 1, Mar. 9, 1858, Feb. 5, 15, 19, Mar. 2, 1859, Nov. 7, 1860.
7. Greeley Papers (N. Y. P. L.), Greeley to Colfax, July 10, Dec. 28, 1856, Jan. 3, 1856 (obviously 1857), Feb. 14, Dec. 8, 1857, Mar. 27, Apr. 1, 1858; *Tribune*, Feb. 23, Mar. 2, 14, 16, 1857, Mar. 29, 1858;*Reports of Committees of the House of Representatives*, 34th Cong., 3d. sess. (1857), III, 21-23, 133-40, 179-91. Greeley's letters to O. B. Matteson and V. W. Smith during 1857 show how concerned he was lest exposure of Matteson injure himself. Greeley claimed that he had thought the whole affair innocent of wrongdoing. Clearly, he made no personal profit by the transaction, but he must have blinded himself to the suspicious aspects of the negotiations. O. B. Matteson, who handed Greeley the draft for $1,000 was scarcely a lily of purity, and George W. Chase, the lobbyist to whom Greeley gave the draft, made a sorry showing before the investigating committee.
8. Greeley, *Recollections*, pp. 360f.; *Tribune*, May 16, Dec. 11, 29, 1856, Jan. 12, Feb. 3, July 6, 1857, Jan. 20, 29, 1859; Greeley, *Overland Journey*, pp. 368f., 384, 386; Greeley Papers (N. Y. P. L.), Greeley to Colfax, Jan. 3, 1857; Seward Papers, Greeley to Seward, Nov. 19, 1857.
9. Salmon P. Chase Papers (Hist. Soc. of Pa.), Greeley to Chase, Sept. 28, 1858; *Tribune*, Apr. 15, Aug. 3, 1857, Feb. 23, Nov. 8, 1858.

10. Seward Papers, Greeley to Seward, Apr. 29, May 7, 1857; Greeley Papers (N. Y. P. L.), Greeley to Colfax, Feb. 2, 1859. Greeley also had hopes for significant emancipation movements materializing in the border states.
11. Nevins, *Ordeal of the Union*, I, 507.
12. *Tribune*, Mar. 11, 1856, Apr. 9, June 4, 8, Aug. 10, 28, Oct. 16, 1857.
13. *Ibid.*, Nov. 26, 1857.
14. H. Watterson, *"Marse Henry," an Autobiography* (2 vols.; N. Y., 1919), I, 138. In 1836, Greeley had sneered at "the characterless adventurer and demi-savage Houston."—*New Yorker*, July 30, 1836.
15. *Tribune*, Feb. 11, Mar. 8, Apr. 6, 1859.
16. *Tribune*, Dec. 4, 1858, Jan. 1, 24, Mar. 16, Apr. 8, Dec. 6-8, 26, 1859; Morgan Papers, Morgan to Greeley, May 3, 1859.
17. *Tribune*, Apr. 19, 1857; Duyckinck, "Diary," Aug. 25, 1857.
18. *Tribune*, Feb., *passim*, Mar. 2, 5, 9, 1857. Back in December 1856 Greeley had forecast the points of Taney's decision with astonishing accuracy.—*Ibid.*, Dec. 16, 17, 1856.
19. *Ibid.*, Aug. 24, 1841.
20. *Ibid.*, Mar.-June, especially Mar. 5-16, 1857.
21. *Ibid.*, Apr. 27, May 9, Oct. 5, 29, Nov. 16-20, Dec. 19, 1857.
22. It is interesting, though not important in an analysis of Greeley's motives and objectives, that, with a free-soil majority now safe in Kansas, he was vigorously championing the exercise of popular sovereignty as a means of making Kansas free. See the *Tribune*, Nov. Dec., 1857.
23. Seward Papers, G. E. Baker to Seward, Feb. 17, 1857, Frederick Seward to Seward, 1857, Greeley to Seward, Nov. 19, 1857; Greeley Papers (N. Y. P. L.), Greeley to Colfax, Feb. 5, 1858.
24. Greeley Papers (N. Y. P. L.), Greeley to Colfax, Feb. 5, Mar. 27, 1857, Feb. 5, 1858; *Tribune*, July 25, Oct. 6, 1857. Feb. 6, 18, 20, Mar. 13, 15, 26, 31, Apr. 3, 12, 15, 21, 1858; *Albany Evening Journal*, Mar. 29, Apr. 13, 1858, Aug. 20, 1860. As to Weed's relations with the lobbyists, see my *Thurlow Weed: Wizard of the Lobby* (Boston, 1947), pp. 219-30.
25. Greeley Papers (N. Y. P. L.), Greeley to Colfax, Feb. 5, 1858.
26. Smith Papers, Greeley to V. W. Smith, Sept. 7, 1857;*Tribune*, July 25, Sept. 23-25, Oct. 6, 1857, July 19, Aug. 20, 1858; *New York Times*, Aug. 20, 1858; *Albany Evening Journal*, July 16, 1858, Nov. 8, 1862; Nevins, *Fish*, p. 66.
27. Pike, *First Blows*, p. 422.
28. *Albany Evening Journal*, May-June, July 13, 14, Aug. 14, 17, Oct. 11, 1858; *Tribune*, May 21, July 19, 24, Aug. 6, 16, 20, 28, Sept. 10-13, 1858; *New York Times*, Aug. 20, 1858; Pike, *First Blows*, p. 425; *New York Evening Post*, July 20, 1858; J. Isely, *Horace Greeley and the Republican Party, 1853-1861* (Princeton, 1947), pp. 248-54. Isely's account of Greely's aims and strategy in 1858 is excellent.
29. *Tribune*, Sept. 13, 14, Oct. 6, 14, 16, 18, 19, 29, Nov. 4, 1858, Jan. 31, Feb. 17, 26, Mar. 7, Apr. 18, 1859. See Chaps. VIII and IX.
30. *Ibid.*, Sept. 22, 1851, Feb. 6, 8, 1854, Mar. 14, 15, 19, Apr. 16, 18, 1856, June 21, Sept. 8, 1857.
31. Milton, *op cit.*, p. 273.
32. Greeley recognized that passage of the bill might be best for the Republicans since it would result, he thought, in Douglas's expulsion from the Democratic party which would be badly damaged, if not completely wrecked. This consideration was outweighed, however, by his certainty that passage

of the bill would result in renewal of the Kansas civil war.—Greeley Papers (N. Y. P. L.), Greeley to Colfax, Feb. 15, 1858; *Tribune,* Jan. 15, Mar. 11, 1858.

33. Simon Cameron was another advocate of Douglas's reëlection. But I dismiss as mere rumor the story of a deal concocted between Seward, Weed, Greeley, and Douglas, by which the old triumvirate would support Douglas for the Senate in 1858, he supporting Seward for the Presidency in 1860 as a *quid pro quo.*—J. F. Newton, *Lincoln and Herndon* (Cedar Rapids, Iowa, 1910), pp. 215-216, Herndon to Parker, Sept. 20, 1858; Nichols, *Disruption of Democracy,* p. 173. Cf. *Albany Evening Journal,* Apr. 14, 1858; *Tribune,* May 22, 1858.

34. Greeley Papers (N. Y. P. L.), Greeley to Colfax, Dec. 11, 20, 1857. Cf. *Tribune,* Nov. 12, 1858.

35. G. S. Merriam, *Life and Times of Samuel Bowles* (2 vols.; N. Y., 1885), I, 229.

36. Greeley Papers (N. Y. P. L.), Greeley to Colfax, May 6, June 14, 1858.

37. Schurz, *Reminiscences,* II, 87-88.

38. Greeley Papers (N. Y. P. L.), Herndon to Greeley, Apr. 8, July 20, 1858, Greeley to Colfax, May 12, 17, 25, June 2, 1858, Dec. 9, 12, 1859; *Tribune,* May 11, 17, Nov. 5, 12, 17, 1858, Feb. 12, 1859; Lincoln Papers, Greeley to [Joseph Medill] [copy by Lincoln], July 24, 1858; W. H. Herndon, and J. W. Weik, *Abraham Lincoln* (2 vols.; N. Y. and London, 1913), II, 59-63; Fahrney, *op. cit.,* pp. 26-29; Newton, *op. cit.,* pp. 215-24.

39. Greeley Papers (N. Y. P. L.), Greeley to Colfax, Apr. 9, 1858; *Tribune,* Apr. 12, 1858.

40. *Reports of Committees,* 35th Cong., 1st sess., IV, 967, #414, pp. 38, 76-78, 80.

41. Greeley Papers (N. Y. P. L.), Greeley to Mrs. Newhall, Aug. 3, 1858.

42. Greeley Letters (Yale Lib.), Greeley to Mrs. Newhall, March 2, 1856; Ingersoll Papers, Greeley to Mrs. Ingersoll, July 5, 1858.

43. He had helped to spread talk of the danger of the army being used by the Democratic administration against the free-soil settlers in Kansas.

44. Chase Papers (Hist. Soc. of Pa.), Greeley to Chase, May 8, 1859; Greeley, *Overland Journey,* pp. 281-82; Brooks, *Times of Melville and Whitman,* p. 288.

45. Weed Papers, D. H. Abell to Weed, June 21, 1860; *Tribune,* Jan. 17, May 3, 1859; *Albany Evening Journal,* Jan. 18, 1859; F. W. Seward, Seward at Washington, II, 360.

CHAPTER 17

A Demonstration of
Independence

NEW YORK ON THE EVE OF THE CIVIL WAR EMERGES
from the dusty pages of the *Tribune* a behemoth, protean in form,
sometimes ugly and sometimes beautiful, but always endowed with
an immense vitality. It was a monster that harbored in its bosom
infinite hope and cynical disillusion. Baseness and greatness it knew,
and its restless dynamic spewed out both shoddy values and deeply
genuine achievements. Superbly wasteful, superbly confident, alike
the scorn and wonder of Europeans, the great city stood as a sign
and symbol of American civilization.

As New York symbolized the restless striving of the nation's
spirit, so Broadway represented the very essence of New York.
Charles Dickens had found the street dull. Alexander Mackay had
found it fascinating and splendid. Like the city itself, this street, the
epitome of magnificence and monstrosity, where vendors offered
lace veils and cabbages, diamonds and human flesh, heaven and hell,
challenged the admiration and excited the contempt of mankind.
Its architecture symbolized its contradictions and incongruities.
Here and there a chaste and stately building could be found, but
these were far outbalanced by a wild and chaotic elegance of six-
story marble façades, fantastical gables and cornices, gilded arch-
ways and brownstone fronts. Ornate and glittering gambling halls
abounded. The merchandising houses of A. T. Stewart, and Lord
and Taylor, positively flaunted luxury, and luxury screamed from
the marble fronts of the great hotels. Haughwout's crockery establishment with its three hundred cast-iron Corinthian columns was
an overpowering, if depressing, sight.

This architecture represented the crass and often brutal spirit
of a materialistic civilization. But even so this civilization was not

quite surrendered to the acquisitive instinct. Ralph Waldo Emerson, lecturing at Dr. Chapin's church on Broadway near Bleecker Street, still wove his spell; George William Curtis drew great crowds when he lectured at the New-York Historical Society; the rising spires of St. Patrick Cathedral demonstrated the contribution that religion was making to the life of the spirit; and the rapid expansion of the Astor Library, in response to popular need, indicated at least a moiety of cultural vigor among the inhabitants of the metropolis. The hardships that lay just ahead were to prove how much of lofty aspiration and high idealism were to be found in the citizens of New York.

In 1860 the town was unmindful of the storm that was soon to break over the nation, and the town's mood was jovial. New Yorkers of that period relished jokes, crude or otherwise, just as they loved display. They roared with laughter when they discovered a fake bulletin planted on the *Tribune* newsboard, announcing that John Heenan, the Benicia Boy, had stopped Tom Sayers in England in the ninth round, and had thereupon been presented to the Queen. Victoria, so the record gravely read, had expressed "great astonishment at the size of his muscle," and had declared that she would put the Prince of Wales under the pugilist's guardianship during the Prince's approaching visit to America.

Royal Edward's pilgrimage that year aroused emotions altogether different from those excited by a newspaper hoax. As Lord Renfrew (and unaccompanied by Heenan), the Prince crossed over the Canadian border near Detroit, while New Yorkers followed his progress with breathless interest. They thrilled to the news of how Detroit had gone crazy, of how young and old Michiganders had lost all sense of decorum on seeing the nineteen-year-old heir to Britain's throne. The *Tribune's* own reporter extolled the Prince's virtuosity on the dance floor, and described him as "every inch a gent." At last came the great day of October 11, when "sweet-faced" Bertie moved up Broadway in a carriage that had cost $1,000, drawn by six spanking blacks. A monster regimental parade surrounded and enveloped the royal scion. On the crowded sidewalks the colors of America and Britain drooped together, the while a moving sea of small white handkerchiefs fluttered like the hearts in their owners' stiffly corseted bosoms.[1] The procession was followed by a dizzying round of festivities that was calculated to exhaust the enthusiasm of even a princely pleasure-seeker. New Yorkers, dazzled by the sight of royalty, strove to overwhelm royal grandeur by their own magnificence in display.

New York was a city of complexities and contradictions, capricious and perverse, maddening and appealing. And sitting at his *Tribune* desk was an editor who embodied those same qualities, a man whose character and motives were often as hard to decipher as were those of the city which was his home; a man behind whose young-old, whisker-fringed baby face lay stubborn opinion, much conceit, a realistic acceptance of the values in material achievement, and a benevolence that schemed and planned for the nation's good; a man who was always striving to bring into the nation's life a synthesis between capital and labor, wealth and poverty, the material and the ideal.

Tragic news flashed across the nation, just as Greeley returned from California in the autumn of 1859. On October 16, John Brown and a handful of followers raided Harpers Ferry. The little band, with its pitiful supply of weapons, was promptly captured by federal troops under the command of two United States Army officers named Jeb Stuart and Robert E. Lee. Six weeks later, Old Brown of Ossawatomie, dispenser of the Lord's justice, had earthly justice meted out to him. On a bright December day he rode out to the gallows on his own coffin, saying to his guards as he looked out at the Maryland hills, "This is a beautiful country." Then he was hanged for treason.

The country rang with the accusation that Black Republicans were to blame for Old Brown's raid; that Seward and other Republican leaders had been partners in the plot to bring about a slave insurrection. Some Republicans feared that the charge would bring a public reaction against their party. Greeley held it a blessing in disguise.

The *Tribune* vigorously denied the stories of Republican complicity in the affair at Harpers Ferry. Old Brown was mad, it declared, driven insane by the injustices he had suffered in Kansas. Plainly, it was the Kansas policy of the Sham Democracy that had been responsible for his attempt to free the slaves. But his errors had been those of a fanatic, not the crimes of a felon, and from his death good would come. He had done more than lay down his life for his friend. He had sacrificed himself and those he held dear "to deliver from bitter bondage and degradation those whom he had never seen," and surely in this there was strength and inspiration. John Brown had paid the ultimate penalty for his belief that resistance to tryants is obedience to God. But the manner of his passing would raise up new champions of freedom.

John Brown dead [said Greeley] will live in millions of hearts—will be discussed around the homely hearth of Toil and dreamed of on the couch

of Poverty and Trial. To all who have suffered for human good—who have
been persecuted for an idea—who have been hated because of their efforts
to make the daily path of the despised and unfortunate less rugged—his
memory will be fragrant through generations. . . .

Yes, John Brown dead is verily a power—like Sampson in the falling
temple of Dagon—like Ziska, dead, with his skin stretched over a drum-
head, still routing the foes he bravely fought while he lived. Time will
doubtless make plain the object and effect of this sacrifice, and show the
errors of Man overruled and made beneficent by the wisdom and loving
justice of God. So let us be reverently grateful for the privilege of living
in a world rendered noble by the daring of heroes, the suffering of martyrs—among whom let none doubt that History will accord an honored
niche to Old John Brown.

Brown's raid, declared Greeley, would drive the Slave Power to
new outrages, just as it would end Douglas's chances for the Democratic nomination in 1860. It brought ten years nearer the end of
slavery in Virginia and the Union, an end that must come, not by
bloodshed and civil war, but peacefully, through discussion and
education. Such was the judgment of the *Tribune's* editor, a judgment that was based upon much vain imagining but that, in its
appreciation of the moral significance of Brown's death, was closer
to the truth than he could know.[2]

Greeley was not at all anxious, when he thought the matter over,
to have fulfilled his prophecy that the Harpers Ferry raid would
end Douglas's chances for the Democratic nomination. Indeed, he
did what he could to help the Little Giant win the coveted prize.
To treat that event, if it occurred, as a condemnation of "Buchanan,
Lecompton and extreme Doughfaceism," he explained to Colfax,
would be sound political strategy, while at the same time the
formidable quality of the candidate would force the Republicans
to nominate their strongest man. A Democratic nomination of
Douglas would be generally regarded as "half a licking to the rotten
Lecompton, nigger-driving Democracy, which it is our business to
complete in November." There was considerable logic in this line
of argument.

But if Douglas were to be made the Democratic nominee in order
to force the Republicans to nominate their strongest man, it was
expedient to determine what kind of a program and what sort of
candidate the Republicans would select. To these problems the
Tribune's editor had devoted considerable attention, ever since the
close of the 1858 campaign.

Greeley held obstinately to the opinion that the first consideration
was fusion. The Republicans must stage such a fight, he declared, as

would draw the maximum number of Democrats, Know Nothings, and Old Whigs into their ranks. In order to do this, they must place their main emphasis upon the danger of slavery extension. Toward such extension, the party must be "frankly but inoffensively hostile." He conceded that registry laws, the tariff, the Pacific railroad, and free land were matters of great importance, but they must not be treated as predominant issues. The threat of an expanding Slave Power must overshadow all else.

The task, said the *Tribune's* editor, was to convince the more intelligent and candid of their opponents that the Republican party was not sectional, "but truly and beneficently national, and that we meditate no wrongs to the South, but rather her renovation and advancement," just as had Washington, Jefferson, and other revered southern patriots. With such a program and such an attitude, Greeley felt that the Republicans would not only triumph in the North, but would also carry Maryland, Delaware, Missouri, and possibly even Kentucky, Tennessee, and North Carolina.[3]

If this strategy were to be successful, much would depend upon the leader of the serried ranks, and Greeley emphasized the importance of choosing the right man to head the Republican ticket. This must not be done in a hurry, he declared, and from time to time in bursts of that apparent candor which so delighted his readers, he analyzed the availability of various possible recipients of the honor.

His own preference, Greeley averred, would be for some original Republican like Seward or Chase, for instance, but it was not really essential that such a one should be chosen. It was far more important that the candidate should be able to carry the four pivotal states of Pennsylvania, New Jersey, Indiana, and Illinois. That was, indeed, crucial.[4]

The emphasis placed upon these states by the *Tribune's* editor must have seemed peculiarly significant to those of his readers whose memories stretched back to the previous presidential campaign. His opposition to Seward as a candidate in 1856 had been based upon the supposition that Seward would be weak in those same four states.

Greeley never seriously considered supporting Seward for the 1860 nomination. But it gave him a kind of savage satisfaction to toy with the Auburn statesman, to defend him publicly for his "Irrepressible conflict" speech (while being privately critical of it), to hint that his own support might be won, if only he could be convinced that Seward could be elected. Greeley was glorying in his independence, and the humiliations of past years were still rankling in his breast. He knew that he could not be convinced of Seward's availability, in part because of his own bitter pride and hurt, in part because Seward's radical utterances and his long record of hostility to the Know Nothings had made him weak where any candidate would have particular need to be strong.

"Greeley came to breakfast with me this morning—he is deluded." So Richard M. Blatchford wrote to Weed in October, shortly after the editor's return from California. Not long thereafter, Greeley told Weed in a private interview that he could not support Seward. The man from Auburn would be too weak a candidate. On the day after Christmas, he said the same thing publicly in the *Tribune*, boasting at the same time that he had never looked to the Auburn statesman for counsel, nor sought to push the latter's political fortunes.[5] The old alliance had collapsed as completely as the deacon's one-hoss shay, and the *Tribune's* editor felt as free as a runaway colt. But out of this freedom much sorrow and suffering was to come.

After Lincoln's nomination, Greeley was fond of asserting that Albany corruption had played a great role in Seward's defeat. By implication, his own opposition to Seward had derived partly from that same source. He was particularly venomous in his denunciation of certain New York street-railway franchises that gridironed half a hundred of the city's best streets as the result of a deal between Weed and the promoters whereby Weed was promised large sums of money for campaign expenses, if the bills went through.[6] The *Tribune's* editor was not coy in assuming credit for having opposed these bills, early and late. This put Greeley on the side of righteousness, but it was largely bluster and an easy assumption of virtue.

It was true enough that the New York street-railway bills were not in the city's best interest. No limitations were imposed in them as to the time or mode of construction; no mention was made of compensation to the city, or of rates of fare. They were passed to the accompaniment of lavish bribery. These things were known to Greeley and at the start he opposed the measures as being unfair to the taxpayers and tainted with corruption, urging Governor Morgan to insist at least upon such amendments as would safeguard the public interest. There is evidence, however, that he viewed these bills as political dynamite rather than as moral monstrosities, and that such moral indignation as they aroused in his breast had little or no influence upon his opposition to Seward.

Greeley's editorials that spring paid no attention to Weed's bargain with the traction magnates, rumors of which had been widely current for months. This was scarcely the attitude of a man whose sensibilities were all on edge over a nefarious deal. More important still is the fact that Greeley's resistance to the bills themselves slackened as their passage became imminent. The change of tone in the *Tribune* editorials was both evident and obvious. Privately, Greeley told Morgan that he was reluctant to oppose the bills because many of the promoters were "our friends, with whom I hate to quarrel." The franchises, he thought, were only about one-tenth as valuable as was supposed, the city did need more street railways, and the disappointed cupidity of outsiders explained much of the uproar about the bills. That uproar must be stilled, to prevent disastrous consequences. Why not call in the railroad leaders and insist on some amendments in the public interest, such as the right to tax the roads?

It is evident that Greeley regarded the transit bills as really not so bad, after all. He belabored them after they were passed without amendment over the governor's veto, but his attitude during their passage was scarcely that of one who felt that the cause of civic righteousness was at stake.[7]

It is also quite clear that Greeley was not terribly bothered by Seward's connection with the political machine that rammed the traction bills through the New York legislature. It was, rather, a desire to demonstrate his political independence and, what was much more important, a sincere belief that Seward would be weak in pivotal states that now governed Greeley's attitude toward his erstwhile partner. There is no reason to doubt his later assertion that, had he thought Seward would command one more vote in the doubtful states than anyone else, he would have worked as hard for him as he did against him.

But if Greeley was opposed to Seward, he was not without a candidate as 1860 dawned. A year or so previously, Schuyler Colfax had suggested Edward Bates of Missouri as the logical Republican choice for President. Greeley had liked the idea, and had begun bringing Bates to the attention of the public.

Bates was a Missouri lawyer and politician. He had been a follower of Henry Clay. As a Whig he had voted for Fillmore in 1856, and he still belonged to a stubborn band of Old Whigs who had not yet come into the Republican camp. As to slavery, he had been an emancipationist, in principle for thirty years (he had freed his own slaves), had opposed repeal of the Missouri Compromise and had denounced Lecompton. He was also an ardent advocate of internal improvements, and Greeley retained vivid recollections of the Missourian's eloquence on that theme back in 1847 at the Chicago river and harbor improvement convention. Sixty-five years

of age, but in excellent health, modest and dignified, the silver-
haired and silver-bearded patriarch of a family that numbered no
less than seventeen children, Bates was a conservative with a twinkle.
He could even jest about his die-hard Whiggism, defining an Old
Whig as "a respectable gentleman of the old school, who takes his
liquor regularly and votes the Democratic ticket occasionally."[8]

There was much in Bates's character and personality to be commended. There was also much to support the view later expressed
by Joseph Medill of the *Chicago Tribune* when he said that Bates
was a "fossil of the Silurian era—red sandstone at least—and should
never have been quarried out of the rocks in which he was im-
bedded."[9] There is little to indicate that he had any great amount
of administrative talent, or that he was blest with imaginative insight. Basically, he was a mediocre, conservative plodder.

Greeley's interest in Missouri's favorite son was not without reservations. He knew that Bates was an old fogy, with whom he would
find it difficult, if not impossible, to maintain close and cordial
relations. He was irked by the Missourian's penchant for letter
writing, particularly when, early in 1859, an unfortunate ambiguity
on Bates's part about ignoring the Negro question required some
ingenious exegesis in a *Tribune* editorial. Then, too, the silver-
haired jurist was a firm believer, so he said, in a fugitive slave law
that would really work. This was a point of view practically
anathema to the *Tribune's* editor.[10] Nevertheless, Bates had some
good points as a candidate, and the more Greeley thought about
the subject, the more settled became his conviction that here was
the man.

Bates's conservatism, so Greeley felt, was a distinct asset. Together
with his political record, it would constitute a real attraction for the
very considerable Old Whig remnant, while the fact that he had
voted for Fillmore in 1856 would be bait for the Know Nothings.
As to the slavery question, Bates would appeal to both the North
and the South. On the one hand, he had freed his slaves and had
come out specifically against slavery extension. On the other hand,
he was a Virginian by birth, a former slaveholder, and was related to
Jefferson and to many leading South Carolina families by marriage.
Committed to a fugitive slave law and against interference with
slavery where it existed, his nomination would be calmly received
in the South, and he would certainly carry his native state of Maryland, perhaps also Missouri and Delaware. Finally, as a westerner,
he would stand out as a protagonist of internal improvements and
as one designed by Providence to act as a mediator for the other
two sections of the country—just the man, as Greeley later remarked,

"to bridge over our national transition from the side of Slavery to that of Liberty." In short, Bates would be a national man, symbol of national reconciliation and of the essentially national character of the Republican party.[11]

His mind filled with such reasonings anent the Republican nomination, Greeley went on a lecture tour in January 1860 that took him into all the states northwest of the Ohio save Minnesota. Everywhere he went he gauged political sentiment, sowed seed for Bates, and cast doubt upon Seward's ability to carry pivotal states. He was back in New York by February 18. Two days later, the *Tribune* broke ground for the Missourian as the candidate best suited to the party and to the needs of the Union. "I have done my best in an article on the Presidency in this morning's paper," Greeley wrote to Colfax. "If anybody gets mad at it, they must; and if it isn't right, I don't know how to make it so."[12]

Bates was not Greeley's exclusive preoccupation during the fateful months of the spring of 1860. He found time to protest his loyalty to the choice of the convention, whoever that might be; there was high praise for the conservative speech that Seward made in the Senate on February 29, seeking to counteract the reputation that he had acquired for radicalism; there was even time for a running debate with Robert Dale Owen on the propriety of easy divorce, a debate in which the nadir of logic was reached in Greeley's contention that marriage was for life because Webster's dictionary so defined it.[13] But even the question of divorce (that forbidden fruit which seemed to have such a fascination for Greeley) was an aside. Greeley knew whom he wanted for President. Bates was for colonization of the free blacks. Bates was a protectionist, homestead, Pacific railroad, antislavery expansionist, and a pooh-pooh-Dred-Scott-obiter-dicta Republican into the bargain. Bates was the man.[14]

Though Greeley had publicly taken his stand on the nomination, he privately affected a lofty unconcern as to the result.

I don't care what is done about the nomination [he wrote to Pike]. I know what ought to be done, and having set that forth am content. I stand in the position of the rich old fellow who, having built a church entirely out of his own means, addressed his townsmen thus:

> "I've built you a meeting-house,
>   And bought you a bell;
> Now go to meeting,
>   Or go to h———."[15]

But this was a conceit, rather than a statement of fact. Greeley meant to work and work hard to make his views on the nomination prevail.

While Greeley was making the welkin ring for Bates, Abraham Lincoln's candidacy had been attaining sizable proportions in the Northwest. What was Greeley's attitude toward Lincoln?

Greeley was definitely not a Lincoln enthusiast. The memory of 1858 was still strong, and the *Tribune's* editor still carried a chip on his shoulder. He wrote to Herndon in December 1859 mentioning the fact that he had barely seen Lincoln at Bloomington the previous winter "and understood him to say he would call on me at my hotel, but he didn't." Greeley was a Bates man, he told Herndon. He was willing to go anything that looked stronger, but did not wish "to load the team heavier than it can pull through," a comment that was probably intended to act as a restraint on the Lincoln movement.

During his lecture tour in the weeks following this letter to Herndon, Greeley found Lincoln stock strong in the old Northwest and began thinking of him in connection with second place on the ticket. Illinois Republicans were insisting that "Old Abe" get something and he was clearly the man for Vice-President, save that "we don't want two Old Whigs." As for the Presidency, if Seward and Chase couldn't be elected, neither could "Banks, or Fessenden, or Dayton, or Cameron, or Lincoln, " though Greeley held this view subject to the representations of delegates from the doubtful states. Thus the Rail Splitter's presidential aspirations were cold-shouldered in a *Tribune* editorial that bracketed him with other second string possibilities.[16]

Greeley might be lukewarm to Lincoln as a presidential candidate, but the *Tribune* urged its readers to go and hear Lincoln when he made his bow to the East at Cooper Institute on the evening of February 27, 1860, and the *Tribune's* editor played a conspicuous part on that occasion. Together with David Dudley Field, he escorted Lincoln to the platform, and after the main address made a short speech in which he told the audience that Lincoln was an illustration of what free labor and the free expression of ideas could produce.

The *Tribune's* editor could not help noting the effect that Lincoln produced on his hearers, an effect emphasized the next day in the *Tribune's* editorial comment—"No man ever before made such an impression on his first appeal to a New York audience." The *Tribune* put the speech out in pamphlet form, and Greeley wrote to an Ohio correspondent that Lincoln would make a better speech and draw a bigger crowd in Ohio than he himself would—"Think of that."[17] But none of this meant that Greeley regarded the man from Illinois as a formidable candidate for the Presidency. In Greeley's estimation, Lincoln was just a possibility, and not a very good one at that, for second place.

So far as the Republican convention was concerned, Greeley later declared that he had not expected to attend it,[18] having been denied a place on the New York delegation. This may or may not have been so, but fate provided him with an opportunity of which he was quick to take advantage. Distance and traveling conditions created a vacancy on the Oregon delegation, and he was asked to fill it. It did not take him long to accept and, when the delegates filed into the Wigwam on the corner of Chicago's Lake and Market streets, Greeley's moon face with its absurd fringe of whisker was easily discernible in the midst of the Oregonians.

The Man in the White Coat was not merely a delegate at Chicago. He was also a member of the platform committee, and took a leading part in that body's activities. His ideas were reflected in the platform's conservative obeisance to the right of each state to control its own domestic institutions, as well as in its stern opposition to slavery extension and its eager advocacy of internal improvements and a Pacific railroad. His hand was most clearly evident in the Homestead plank which, he declared afterward, he had "fixed exactly to my own liking." This protested against the sale or alienation of any of the public lands held by actual settlers, and demanded the passage of a homestead bill that had already passed the House, a broad and comprehensive measure that required no payment for lands, threw homestead privileges open to aliens and to all citizens over the age of twenty-one, and forbade alienation of any homestead for debts incurred previous to settlement. It was a plank obviously designed to facilitate the rapid development of the West.[19]

But platform making by no means occupied all of Greeley's time or attention at the Republican convention. He had started for Chicago on May 8, and had reached his destination several days before the delegates held their first formal session. During that time, and right up until the balloting began, he shuffled around from one delegation to another, telling all who would listen that Seward lacked availability; that the nomination of Bates would deflate charges of sectionalism, and would break up the middle of the road Constitutional Union party that had just nominated John Bell of Tennessee. On May 14, a column length circular, signed by Greeley, Frank P. Blair, and the members of the Missouri delegation, told all who would read that Seward should be rejected and Bates nominated. This boomeranged, hurting Bates very definitely and creating some reaction for Seward,[20] but Greeley stubbornly kept up the fight.

Victory was Greeley's theme, and his arguments all ran to the conclusion that Seward and victory were not allies. When, in the packed Tremont House lobby, one of Weed's New Yorkers loudly asserted that everybody admitted Seward to be the leader and representative man of the party, Greeley squeaked with all the energy he could muster: "No, Sir! here is one who does *not* admit it. He is one of the leading men of our party, but there are others as deserving as he is." Over and over, he declared that he would gladly work for Seward, if convinced that the latter could command one more vote in the doubtful states than anyone else; that the vote of a border slave state like Missouri was of the utmost significance; that there were several Republicans who could get larger majorities than Seward could command in New York State itself; that no less than twenty of the New York delegates were secretly opposed to the man for whom they were pledged to vote; that Seward would, in all probability, lose Pennsylvania, New Jersey, Indiana, and Illinois.

Greeley's efforts to deprive Seward of the nomination inspired both amusement and rage. Some wag pinned on Horace's back a silk Seward badge with the Senator's name and likeness conspicuously displayed. It remained there for some time, and the crowd snickered as the unconscious bearer shambled about his work. The New York delegation, however, found it hard to see the humor in such a joke. Its more sedate members, men like William M. Evarts and George W. Curtis, shook their heads in bitterness and sorrow at Greeley's obstinate blindness. The shoulder-hitters and the tough, practical ward leaders that Weed had brought along to swell his retinue filled the air with execrations of that "damned old ass" Horace Greeley.[21]

Greeley's actual influence on the convention is a matter of some doubt. He failed to swing delegates to Bates, being unable effectively to counter such arguments as that Bates could not carry his own state; that the German-Americans would not vote for him on account of his vote for Fillmore in 1856; that the Know Nothings would spurn him in their preference for John Bell. Greeley himself later and publicly discounted the weight of his opposition to Seward, pointing out that lack of availability, rather than any one man's activities, had been responsible for Seward's defeat, and that on the night of May 16 and through most of May 17 (the crucial period just before the balloting began) he had been hard at work on the platform and had had neither time nor opportunity for electioneering.

But on the other hand, it would not be wise to dismiss too lightly the part played by Greeley in disappointing the hopes of the Auburn statesman. Greeley's private opinion was that he had been in the forefront of the battle and that his share of the burden had been unreasonably heavy, considering where he lived and the bitter enmities bound to be produced by the event. The Indiana newspaperman, John D. Defrees, who was at the convention, declared that "Greeley slaughtered Seward and saved the party." Raymond assigned to his brother editor a credit in the event ten times heavier than that of all the Blairs and gubernatorial candidates put together. Weed, who was certainly in a position to know, said in a private letter to Seward that Greeley "took possession" of the Vermont delegation and that his arguments "misled many fair minded men." Certain it is that the part played by the *Tribune's* editor was sufficiently important to earn Weed's bitter resentment and thus plunge the two men into a feud that was destined to last for the rest of Greeley's life. The editor of the *Tribune* was not sufficiently influential to bring his own candidate home in triumph, but he did play a major part in clearing the way for the nomination that was all the while being diligently prepared by the bargains and promises of Lincoln's unscrupulous campaign managers.

Greeley must have felt, as the balloting neared in Chicago, that all his efforts had been doubly vain, for as the hopes of his own candidate faded those of Seward appeared to brighten. On the evening of May 16 the *Tribune's* editor telegraphed his paper that the chances of Seward's nomination were now about even, with Lincoln having "the next best look." At twenty minutes before twelve on the evening of May 17, the night before the balloting began, he sent a special message informing the *Tribune's* readers that it looked as though the opposition to Seward would be unable to concentrate on any one candidate, and that Seward would be nominated.

On the fatal day, May 18, Greeley was in the convention hall. He saw the pivotal states of Indiana and Illinois vote solidly for Lincoln on the first ballot. Then came the second ballot, when New Hampshire, Vermont, and Pennsylvania began the break to the Rail Splitter and he crept up to within three and one-half votes of Seward.

At that point a Bates supporter, Charles Gibson of St. Louis, rushed over to where Greeley was sitting amid the Oregon delegation. Gibson had just seen Weed, and he urged Greeley to hold on for Bates. If there were no nomination on the third ballot, the Dictator had promised an immediate rally of Seward men to Bates. This move was a desperate concession in the face of defeat, but even so it was too late. While Gibson was talking to Greeley the third ballot was in progress, and Seward men in droves were climbing on the Lincoln bandwagon.[22]

When Lincoln's nomination was announced, a broad smile broke over Greeley's face. Seward's defeat was his triumph, and the insults of the Sewardites were music to his ears. He met the accusation, hurled by a Seward supporter, that he had knifed the champion, with the shrill cry that it was Albany's jobbery and corruption, not he, that had killed Mr. Seward. But in his triumph, sweet as it was, there was a measure of disappointment. He still believed that, old fogy though Bates might be, he was a better choice than Lincoln.

While Greeley relished the taste of Seward's defeat, the reactions of the other members of the convention varied from jubilation to darkest gloom. Lincoln men turned Chicago upside down that night with bonfires, torchlights, fireworks, salutes and great rolling shouts for "Honest Old Abe." William M. Evarts, leader of the New York delegation, said to a fellow delegate—"Well, Curtis, at least we have saved the Declaration of Independence"—that document having been reaffirmed, after a hard struggle, in the platform. Thurlow Weed said little. One of his life's main objectives, an aim that he had pursued for over twenty years with patient, indefatigable attention, had ended in frustration. His lifetime friend and ally, the cultured leader of New York Republicanism, had gone down to defeat before a raw-boned son of the prairie. For that defeat Weed's former adjutant, the man whom he had started on the road to fame and fortune, had been in considerable measure responsible. As the Dictator chewed the cud of bitterness, he revolved these matters in his mind.

Greeley came back to New York in a very cocky mood. He had no wish to precipitate an open fight over the part he had played at Chicago, but neither did he intend to apologize for his doings or to cringe and cower if blows were rained upon his head. When two prominent Cayuga County Republicans canceled their subscriptions to the *Tribune,* stating that their sole regret in so doing was the loss of the three-cent stamp that mailed their letter, Greeley replied jauntily:

Gentlemen:
The painful regret expressed in yours of the 19th inst. excites my sympathies. I enclose a three cent stamp to replace that whose loss you deplore, and remain,

yours placidly,
Horace Greeley.

Published in Seward's home bailiwick, republished elsewhere, this reply did nothing to moderate the fires of resentment that had been lighted by the editor of the *Tribune*.

Shortly after his return to New York, Greeley undertook to explain in objective fashion the events at Chicago. Bates had lost, he declared, because Indiana and Pennsylvania had chosen Lincoln instead. Seward had lost because the delegates from Pennsylvania, New Jersey, Indiana, and Illinois had testified that he could not carry those states. The outside attendance from New York that had crowded the barrooms, denounced anti-Seward men as ingrates and traitors, and asked "If you don't nominate Seward, where will you get your money?" had also played a part in the defeat of the man from Auburn. On the other hand, the high-minded western men had preferred to split rails at fifty cents a day rather than allow money to influence their choice of a candidate (at which point in their reading of the editorial, David Davis and Leonard Swett must have been threatened with apoplexy).

As to Lincoln, Greeley continued, he had known and esteemed him ten years before, but he still thought Bates would have been the wisest choice. The latter would have attracted conservative voters, helped reconcile the slave states to a Republican victory, and would have been a valuable aid in Missouri, the one slave state that the Republicans had any chance of carrying in the summer elections. Lincoln was true, faithful, and deserving, but Bates's nomination "would have been more far-sighted, more courageous, more magnanimous."

The evening of the day on which this editorial appeared, Greeley made a speech before the Young Men's Republican Union in their hall at Stuyvesant Institute. His main theme was Democratic corruption, but he could not resist opening with a crow of triumph over Seward's defeat—"Mr. Chairman: The Past is dead: let the dead bury it, and let its mourners, if they will, go about the streets while we devote ourselves to the living Present. . . ."[23] Thus to link Seward's political ambitions with the grave was bitter insult, untimely and unwise if Greeley really wished to avoid a knock-down and drag-out fight with his former partners.

For already the guns of the Seward forces in New York were being trained on the *Tribune's* editor. Before Weed returned from the West, his *Evening Journal* branded Greeley's action at Chicago as mean-spirited revenge. Raymond took up the charge in a three-column *Times* editorial, laying the chief responsibility for Seward's defeat on Greeley's shoulders, making public disclosure of the letter Greeley had written to Seward in 1854, and charging that that letter had menaced Seward with political hostility because Seward would not help him to obtain office. Greeley, said Raymond, had maintained the role of friend since 1854, the better to play the part of betrayer. His whole plan of action had been motivated by corrosive jealousy and disappointed ambition. Webb also joined the fray, echoing in the *Courier* the charge that Greeley's motive had been revenge.[24]

Boldly, with the alacrity that always distinguished him in verbal combat, Greeley launched his answer to this challenge. He declared that his opposition to Seward in the *Tribune* had been open, rather than insinuating, an assertion that he would have been hard put to it to prove. He flatly denied Raymond's charge that lust for office had prompted him to dissolve the partnership, and kept demanding his letter until, early in June, it was returned to him through Weed and published by both sides in the controversy.

Nor did Greeley remain on the defensive in this war of words. As was his custom, he promptly carried the fight into the enemies' camp. He twitted Weed with an injurious reference to the latter's supposed ancestor, "that old changeling and hypocrite, Lord Chancellor Thurlow," and began ringing the changes on Weed's relations with the Albany lobby. He taunted Raymond with Webb's having been the first to see the now famous letter to Seward, and with being second fiddle to Webb in the Seward ranks. These skillful thrusts set Webb and Raymond to belaboring one another while the delighted *Tribune's* editor, affecting a judicial pose, remarked that probably Webb couldn't suck eggs as skillfully as Raymond, a man who had run around to two or three conventions to engineer a place for himself as lieutenant-governor and had then turned out to be a conspicuous failure in that post of public trust.[25]

As the controversy between Greeley and his detractors waxed hot, Greeley stressed more and more his dislike of the plundering methods and lack of principle of the New York school of politics, his fear that domination by Weed and Seward would have caused the Republican party to "become rotten before it was ripe." Now the gridiron bills appeared in all their horrid light, and the voters were invited to gaze upon Weed's machinations in all their nakedness.

Greeley's avowed object was to cleanse the Republican organization in New York State of all the putrid objects that tainted it. Beginning with Weed, his attack spread to the friends and allies of the Dictator. Among others, De Witt C. Littlejohn, speaker of the state assembly in 1860, was violently assailed. The time had come, Greeley told his readers, to eliminate the stench that arose from the capitol where Weed had lorded it so long. All this was in the midst of the 1860 national campaign.[26] Greeley's assaults upon Albany corruption were justified in fact but, as Weed remarked, the *Tribune's* editor had "not always been fastidious in the use of money at Elections, or in Legislation." Under ordinary circumstances, Greeley would not have washed the New York Republicans' dirty linen before the public, especially during a presidential campaign. Now he was impelled to do so by two powerful factors. One of these was his desire to meet as effectively as possible the violent denunciations of himself as an ingrate. The other was his burning ambition for public office.

Seward's term in the Senate was due to expire in 1861. Greeley wanted the post, wanted it terribly. The evidence, though circumstantial, is strong that he was seeking to destroy the chances of Seward Republicans for reëlection to the state legislature in order that he might improve the prospects of his own election to the United States Senate. His attacks upon such Seward stalwarts as Littlejohn, and Austin Myers of Syracuse, fitted altogether too well with his ambition to be merely coincidental. The Syracuse correspondent of the *New York Times* noticed this curious conjunction of facts and spread it on the pages of that paper. Greeley denied the allegation, but coupled his denial with a demand that Seward declare whether or not he meant to stand for reëlection. It was clear that Horace was suffering from a bad case of officitis.

The truth was that Greeley had high hopes of success in his bid for the Senate. A mighty company, Field, Opdyke, Bryant, Dana, even Charles Sumner of Massachusetts, were forwarding his candidacy, and the omens appeared to be auspicious. The glories of a prominent elective office seemed almost within his reach, and it was primarily on that account that he assailed the corruption of the Weed machine.[27]

The New York quarrel could not but damage Republican chances in the national campaign, a damage scarcely lessened by periods of righteously proclaimed truce during the summer and fall. As though to atone for such injury, both Weed and Greeley gave Lincoln vigorous support. Greeley was particularly outstanding in the efforts he made to swing voters out of the opposing camps and into the Republican column.

Three other tickets beside the Republican ticket were in the field in 1860. The Constitutional Unionists, their appeal based essentially on an effort to bring about a fusion of all true Unionists by grandly ignoring the slavery question, were running John Bell of Tennessee for President, with Edward Everett of Massachusetts in second place.

The Democrats had split hopelessly at Charleston, late in April, over Douglas. Now the southern wing of the party was running John Breckenridge of Kentucky on a platform demanding full protection for slavery in the territories. The northern wing of the Democracy was running Douglas on his now familiar platform of squatter sovereignty.

As soon as the convention at Chicago was over, Greeley had started building up Lincoln, an effort that continued throughout the campaign. Old Abe was exalted as a man of integrity and vision, a leader whose victorious entrance into the White House would be the nation's salvation. Lincoln was also the Rail Splitter, symbol of the ease with which, in a free society, the humblest laborer could rise to the highest office in the land.

If Lincoln was the man of the hour, slavery restriction was the theme of the day for the *Tribune*. Greeley never tired of pointing out the iniquity of the Breckenridge position, and the inadequacies of Douglas's squatter sovereignty as a curb on the appetite of the Slave Power. But at the same time, Greeley carefully emphasized that Republicanism would not interfere with slavery where it already existed, and was careful to spike such stories as that of Lincoln's being in favor of Negro suffrage—a canard that was calculated to injure him in the border slave states.

While Greeley defined and applauded the Republican position, he caricatured the Bell-Everett ticket as "The Old Gentlemen's Ticket," the "Confusion Ticket," a device of the Sham Democracy to draw off Republican votes. It was a base surrender to the Slave Power, which had said to the Constitutional Unionists, " 'Crouch, you hounds!' and the hounds crouch." To vote with the Constitutional Unionists, declared Greeley, would bring business stagnation and depression. The emphasis that Greeley put into this attack indicated the popularity of the Bell-Everett ticket with the New York businessmen.

Such were the arguments, together with guarded appeals for a "good" tariff, laudation of internal improvements, huzzas for a Pacific railroad and demands for "public lands for the landless" that constituted the essence of Greeley's campaign. They were, in his judgment, arguments of irresistible appeal. He was convinced that that appeal was felt even below Mason and Dixon's line. "A very large minority" of southerners, he believed, would vote the Republican ticket if they only dared. As late as the end of October, he predicted that Republican electors in the slave states would poll over 50,000 votes, an estimate that was nearly fifty per cent too high. He was equally confident that a Republican victory would not precipitate disunion. If South Carolina undertook "to repeat in 1861 the tantrums of 1833," she would be "treated as she was then—kindly but firmly."[28]

Aside from his editorials, Greeley labored in other ways as a campaigner. He helped to corral speakers and raise funds. The *Tribune* printed thousands of campaign documents, including a *Political Textbook for 1860* of which Greeley was co-author, and which unblushingly stated that it was meant to convey the truth "without a trace of partisan bias." By the end of July, Greeley was speaking three times a week on behalf of the Republican candidates. He even wrote a song for the campaign—a spirited ditty entitled "The March of the Free."

When Pennsylvania went Republican, early in October, Greeley's joy was unbounded. BOYS, WE'VE GOT 'EM! shrieked the *Tribune*. PENNSYLVANIA HAS DONE IT. Similar victories in Indiana and Ohio brought additional bursts of enthusiasm. But despite his exultation, his strenuous campaigning did not slacken until November brought Lincoln safely home.

With victory perched upon the proper banners, Greeley began considering how he might best obtain for his services in the campaign a suitable reward. But his consideration of this pleasing subject did not long monopolize his thoughts. For swiftly rolling up from the South, came a storm cloud that he had not foreseen— the storm cloud of disunion and civil war.[29]

NOTES FOR CHAPTER 17

1. *Tribune,* Feb. 18, Mar. 23, 31, Apr. 30, Sept. 15, 22, 26, Oct. 12-22, 1860. The Heenan-Sayers fight came a day or so later than indicated by the fake announcement, and ended in a draw. It had also been put up on the boards at the offices of the *Herald* and *Times.*
2. *Tribune,* Oct. 18-28, Nov. 2, 4, 7, 11, Dec. 3, 1859; Greeley Papers (N. Y. P. L.), Greeley to Colfax, Oct. 24, 1859.
3. *Tribune,* June 8, 1857, June 17, Dec. 10, 1858, Apr. 26, May 4, Oct. 12, Dec. 24, 31, 1859, Jan. 12, Mar. 3, May 3, 1860.
4. *Tribune,* Jan. 17, Apr. 26, Dec. 31, 1859.
5. Weed Papers, R. M. Blatchford to Weed, Oct. 14, 1859; *Tribune,* Oct. 23, 24, Dec. 20, 21, 24, 26, 28, 1859, June 2, 1860; Greeley Papers (N. Y. P. L.), Greeley to Colfax, May 7, 1860.
6. For Weed's part in this affair, see my *Thurlow Weed: Wizard of the Lobby,* pp. 245-47.
7. Morgan Papers, Greeley to Morgan, Apr. 1, 15, 1860; *Tribune,* Mar. 9, 12, 16, 23, Apr. 6, 12, 16-18, 20, 25, 1860, June 24, 1864; P. Godwin, *A Biography of William Cullen Bryant* (2 vols.; N. Y., 1883), II, 127.

8. *Tribune,* Nov. 2, 1858.

9. Hollister, *op. cit.,* p. 200.

10. *Tribune,* Apr. 16, 1859; Chase Papers (Hist. Soc. of Pa.) , Greeley to Chase, Sept. 29, 1863; Greeley Papers (N. Y. P. L.) , Greeley to Colfax, Apr. 15, 1859.

11. Greeley Papers (N. Y. P. L.), Greeley to Colfax, Feb. 14, 18, 21, Apr. 3, 1859, Feb. 3, 1860, Greeley to Herndon, Dec. 4, 1859, Greeley to Hector Orr, Feb. 11, 1860; Morgan Papers, Greeley to Morgan, Feb. 3, 1860; *Tribune,* Feb. 18, Apr. 6, 16, Oct. 12, Nov. 14, 1859, Feb. 7, 15, 1860; *New York Times,* Feb. 17, 1860, an unsigned three-column letter on Bates. A clipping of this last is in the Greeley Papers in the New York Public Library, with Greeley's name scrawled across it in his handwriting. If he did not write or inspire it, at least it represents his sentiments. See also Chase Papers (Hist. Soc. of Pa.) , Greeley to Chase, Sept. 29, 1863.

12. Greeley Papers (N. Y. P. L.) , Greeley to Colfax, Feb. 20, 1860.

13. Greeley, *Recollections,* pp. 571-618, especially p. 579.

14. *Tribune,* Feb. 24, Mar. 1, 26, 1860.

15. Pike, *First Blows,* pp. 499-500, Greeley to Pike, Feb. 26, 1860.

16. Greeley Papers (N. Y. P. L.) , Greeley to Herndon, Dec. 4, 1859, Greeley to Colfax, Feb. 3, 1860; *Tribune,* Feb. 7, 15, 20, 1860.

17. *Tribune,* Feb. 28, 1860; Lincoln Papers, Greeley to D. L. Pope, Mar. 4, 1860.

18. Chase Papers (Hist. Soc. of Pa.) , Greeley to Chase, Aug. 5, 1860.

19. *Congr. Globe,* 36th Cong. 1st. sess., pp. 1750-53; Greeley Papers (N. Y. P. L.) , Greeley to Colfax, June 20, 1860; *Tribune,* May 22, 1860; Robbins, *op. cit.,* pp. 179-80.

20. *Tribune,* May 16, 1860, special dispatch from Chicago; R. H. Luthin, *The First Lincoln Campaign* (Cambridge, 1944) , p. 138.

21. Greeley Papers (N. Y. P. L.) , Greeley to Colfax, May 26, 1860; Greeley, *Recollections,* p. 390; *Tribune,* May 22, 1860; *New York Times,* May 24, 1860; O. J. Hollister, *Life of Schuyler Colfax* (N. Y., 1886) , p. 148; Pike, *op. cit.,* p. 519.

22. Weed Papers, C. Gibson to Weed, May 31, 1860; *Tribune,* May 24, 1860; *Albany Evening Journal,* May 28, 1860.

23. *Tribune,* May 23, 1860.

24. *Ibid.,* May 23, 25, 1860; *Albany Evening Journal,* May 21, 23, 28-29, 1860; *New York Times,* May 24, 1860.

25. *Tribune,* May 28, 29, 31, June 14, 1860; *Albany Evening Journal,* May 28, 29, June 6, 12, 14, 1860.

26. *Tribune* and *Albany Evening Journal,* July-Aug., 1860.

27. Greeley Papers (Lib. of Cong.) , Greeley to Brockway, Aug. 5, Nov. 11, 1860; Weed Papers, D. C. Littlejohn to Weed, Oct. 9, 1860; *Tribune,* Oct. 6, 23, Nov. 3, Dec. 31, 1860.

28. *Tribune,* July 23, 25, Oct. 24, 26, 1860.

29. This and the preceding paragraphs are based on an examination of the *Tribune's* files from June to November, 1860. Also on the Stahl Collection, Greeley to J. G. Shortall, July 25, 1860; Greeley Papers (Lib. of Cong.), Greeley to Brockway, Nov. 11, 1860; Morgan Papers, various letters from Greeley to E. D. Morgan during the year 1860; Huntington Collection, L. A. Roberts to Greeley, Apr. 28, 1860, and reply, Greeley to T. H. Dudley, Sept. 9, 1860; H. Greeley and J. F. Cleveland, *A Political Text-book for 1860, passim.*

CHAPTER 18

A Nationalist at Bay

THE STORM OVER THE UNION BEGAN TO LOWER immediately that the election was over. At the same time, a fury of contention arose concerning the spoils of office, most of all over the Cabinet. The country was thus confronted with the spectacle of two conflicts, one of ever-increasing gravity, waged over the preservation of the nation, the other, less ominous to the peace and safety of the country but nevertheless full of bitterness and hatred, fought out among the groups and cliques of Republican office-seekers.

Anti-Seward Republicans in New York were determined to advance their own interests the while they saved the national government from the clutches of Thurlow Weed. The more they thought about it, the more virtue they saw in pushing Horace Greeley for a place in Lincoln's inner circle. Conversations ensued, rumor took wing and speculation spread.

It was reported that the *Tribune's* editor wanted to be postmaster-general, the better to launch his lightnings against governmental waste and Congressional franks. His friends waxed enthusiastic. His enemies jeered. One ex-legislator, ousted by his constituents for his part in the gridiron-bill corruption, reported it as settled that Greeley was to be Secretary of the Exterior, "his principal duties to watch the thermometer and tell how cold it is out there."[1] Reformer Joshua Leavitt of the *Independent* wrote in alarm to Salmon P. Chase that to put Greeley in the Cabinet in any position would ruin the Administration.

Greeley professed a complete lack of interest in becoming a member of Lincoln's official family. Writing to Beman Brockway he noted, only to wave grandly aside, the possibility that he might be offered a Cabinet station. Such a move, he declared, would needlessly infuriate the South and he had no interest in the honor.

What he did want was the Senate, and Seward ought to say frankly whether or not he was going to run again. It looked as though Seward wanted to be reëlected so that he could decline and then put Evarts in his place. Greeley did not believe that this would work, but at the same time he feared Weed's "very great" power.[2]

A week later, the senatorial hopes of the Man in the White Coat had appreciably dimmed. He was depressed, though he pretended indifference. His mood was illustrated by his quotation from a colored preacher: "Bressed am dey wat don't expect nothing, for *they* ain't gwine to be disappointed."[3] Nevertheless his name remained in the canvass.

For now a great battle was joining all along the line, as two groups fought for control of the Republican organization in New York State. New Yorkers who had helped to defeat Seward at Chicago—men like George Opdyke, David Dudley Field, William Cullen Bryant, Hiram Barney, and last, but not least, Horace Greeley—were merging into one coalition. Weed and Seward, backed by the machine that they had built up during their long years of power, headed the other group. Each side watched the other with respectful caution. Each strove by every means in its power to weaken its adversary and strengthen its own position (Greeley even making a fruitless effort to detach Seward from the Weed camp).[4] Each sought to control the Cabinet appointments. Almost of necessity, each faction took opposite sides on the question of compromise with the southern secessionists. The conflict between these two groups was in part a conflict of principle; it was even more a fight for control of the New York State political organization.

The Greeleyites suffered the first defeats. On December 8, 1860, Lincoln offered the State Department to Seward. This was a bitter blow to the anti-Weed men,[5] but they could not afford to falter in the fight, and promptly assayed a test of strength in the New York State legislature. On January 1, 1861, Greeley, Opdyke, and David Dudley Field went up to Albany determined to prevent the election of DeWitt C. Littlejohn, Weed's candidate for Speaker of the Assembly. The fight was brisk and brief. Littlejohn was elected. The Greeleyites had now suffered a second reverse, but a bigger battle was in the offing.

Seward's appointment as secretary of state meant a vacancy in the Senate. Who would take Seward's place? Weed's preference was William M. Evarts. Courteous and dignified, a brilliant lawyer, head of the New York delegation to Chicago in 1860, Evarts was an outstanding figure and there was much to be said for choosing him as Seward's successor. But the anti-Seward faction thought otherwise. They wanted to rally around the editor of the *Tribune*. He told Dana that he would run, and having thus given carte blanche went off on a lecture tour. And then Dana and the anti-Seward group went to work with a will.

Lincoln's support was eagerly sought by both factions in this Senate race. Indeed, the Greeleyites spread the word that their candidate had the support of the President-elect. Weed's lieutenants countered by announcing that Old Abe had placed the state's patronage in the hands of Lord Thurlow. Lincoln, amused but cautious, took "justice for all" as his motto and kept himself out of a contest that grew more and more heated as the day of election drew near.

When caucus day finally arrived, the rival factions marshaled their cohorts at the state capitol. Weed, with Moses H. Grinnell, A. Oakey Hall, and a corps of henchmen, was in the Governor's room, with Evarts by his side. Greeley did not put in an appearance, but Dana and David Dudley Field arrayed the forces of those to whom Weed contemptuously referred as the "Radicals." A succession of ballots demonstrated that the Greeley men, while not strong enough to elect their own candidate, would be strong enough to prevent the election of Evarts. But Weed had an alternate candidate in Ira Harris, who commanded some twenty votes of his own. On the ninth ballot, in response to a command that issued emphatically from the Governor's room, the Evarts men began going over to Harris, and on the following ballot Harris was elected.[6]

The strength of the Greeley men had forced Weed to turn to his second choice, but he professed great satisfaction with the result, declaring that he had thus "Paid the *first* installment on a large debt to Mr. Greeley."[7]

Greeley declared that he was not at all mortified by his defeat. Weed and Seward hadn't done anything for a year that he so thoroughly justified as he did their opposition to him.[8] But despite these brave words, the editor of the *Tribune* was a sorely disappointed man.

Weed felt that Harris was a much better risk than Greeley. Others, with or without the boss's motives, thought so, too. George William Curtis said, after the election was over, that it would have been a terrible mistake to transfer Greeley from his editorial sphere to the United States Senate. Martin Brewer Anderson, president of the fledgling University of Rochester, wrote to Weed that by his action he had saved the country from "the national calamity which Mr. Greeley's election would have entailed upon us." The stormy Polish exile, Count Gurowski, who knew Greeley well, snorted that the *Tribune's* editor was no more fit to be a Senator than he was to take command of a regiment.[9] Certainly, judging by Greeley's record in the House in 1849, and by the course of action that he was to pursue during the next four years, his absence from the Senate was no grievous loss to Lincoln's administration.

The fight over a Senate seat was only one phase of the struggle for power that was being waged by the contending factions. Even while this fight was going on, strenuous efforts were being made to control Lincoln's cabinet appointments, his selections for foreign posts, and his choice of federal officeholders within New York State itself.

Seward's appointment to the State Department had been a great disappointment to the Greeley faction's hope of dominating the Cabinet, but their efforts to control other cabinet posts were if anything stimulated by this setback. Greeley attacked Simon Cameron, who was Weed's ally, as corrupt and unfit for office— judgments which characterized the "Great Winnebago Chief" to perfection.[10] In accordance with the wishes of the Old Democrats among his allies, the *Tribune's* editor just as earnestly supported free trader Salmon P. Chase for the Treasury.[11] The faction also pushed Montgomery Blair, Gideon Welles, and Edward Bates for cabinet posts.

Late January 1861 saw Greeley heading west, bent on his usual lecture tour and eager to take advantage of the opportunity that it afforded to offer Lincoln some good advice. Carrying his valise and a red and blue blanket which, together with his white coat, made him a walking symbol of the nation, he got off the train at Springfield on the morning of February 4. He did not see the President-elect that morning and shortly departed from the city, making the air blaze with his denunciations of Cameron. The next day, however, he returned to Springfield, where he was to lecture that evening. Anxious as he was to give the President-elect guidance, he affected coyness, and it was Lincoln who called upon Greeley at the latter's hotel.[12]

The interview with Lincoln lasted several hours. Greeley urged a no-compromise policy toward the South. He also aired his views on appointments, opposing Cameron, urging that Chase and Schuyler Colfax be given cabinet posts, and pushing Colonel Frémont for the mission to France.

In addition to this interview, while Greeley was still in Springfield he wrote a letter to the President-elect on the subject of New

York State appointments. In this he warned that the very life of the Republican party depended upon justice being done to the anti-Weed Republicans. He suggested listing the offices that were to go to New York, and then, after Lincoln had made his own personal selections, allowing each faction to choose an office, turn and turn about. The Weed men might have the first choice, said Greeley magnanimously, adding craftily that the anti-Weedites must not be sacrificed because they had taken the course that had led to Lincoln's election.[13]

The Rail Splitter received this deluge of advice patiently, but still without commitment. On occasion, Mr. Lincoln could be a most irritating man.

On the evening of February 5, Greeley lectured to a large audience in Springfield. The next morning he was about to leave for another speaking engagement in St. Louis. He was to give the Missourians a literary address, which seemed innocuous enough, but leading St. Louis Republicans wired him that he would be mobbed if he came, so he turned his face toward the quieter regions of Ohio and western Pennsylvania. Meantime, Lincoln had left Springfield for Washington.

As the private train which bore Lincoln toward the nation's capital rolled to a stop in Girard, Pennsylvania, on February 16, Greeley clambered on board. He was bound for Erie, only a few miles to the east, where he was to give a lecture that evening on "America Westward of the Mississippi." His stay on the presidential special could only be of short duration, but the reporter from the *Cleveland Plain Dealer* who was on the train noticed that the man from New York seemed in no hurry to pay his respects to Lincoln. His coat collar partly turned in and partly standing up, his pockets stuffed with papers and magazines, Quaker hat perched jauntily on the back of his head, red and blue blankets over his arm, Greeley walked into the President-elect's car, sat down, and waited for Lincoln to come to him. Before he got off at Erie, he had had the pleasure of receiving Lincoln's respects and of meeting Mrs. Lincoln, a presentation that was accomplished without the broad-brimmed hat once leaving its owner's head.[14]

Rudeness to Mary Lincoln did not indicate that Horace Greeley was habitually uncivil to ladies. Had the mood struck him, he could have been altogether kind and even courtly. It is not unlikely that this display of what appeared to be bad manners was simple absent-mindedness. The attitude toward Lincoln himself was probably due to bad humor at having failed to establish a preponderant influence with the President-elect. The fight against Seward's appointment had been lost, the fight against Cameron was a losing one, and Schuyler Colfax was being edged out in the cabinet race by his fellow Hoosier, Caleb B. Smith. Moreover, Greeley could not be oblivious to the fact that a goodly number of those closest to Old Abe were still bitter because of the *Tribune's* attitude toward the Rail Splitter's candidacy for the Senate, three years before. Henry Villard informed the readers of the *Cincinnati Commercial* that, clustered around Lincoln, were many enemies of the *Tribune's* editor, men who were anxious to repay him for the tongue lashings he had given them in 1858.[15] Greeley was always a shrewd observer of the lay of the land, and his observations in Springfield and on the presidential special must have further cooled a regard for Lincoln that had never been too warm.

Greeley came back to New York late in February. Lincoln was already in Washington, the last stage of his trip having been marked by a change of route and a secret night journey. This alteration of plans, made on the advice of detective Allan Pinkerton who had uncovered what looked like an assassination plot, aroused much criticism and fortified rather than changed Greeley's opinion of the President-elect. "Lincoln is true and right, but not a Jackson or Clay, as his dodge through Maryland lamentably shows," the *Tribune's* editor wrote to a friend. "Old Abe is honest as the sun and means to be true and faithful; but he is in the web of very cunning spiders and could not break out if he would. Mrs. Abe is a Kentuckian and enjoys flattery—I mean deference. And God is above all, and all things will be well in the end. Life is not very long, and we shall rest by-and-by."[16]

Thus spoke the *Tribune's* editor in patronizing accents. He had taken Old Abe's measure and had found him honest, well meaning, and simple, the tool of men altogether too deep for him, a sort of human Old Dog Tray. Time was to tell a different story.

The never-ending struggle for political power was far from being Greeley's only concern in the winter and spring of 1860-61. That struggle was important, but only as the daily business of living is important to a man who sees himself threatened by some great misfortune, some major catastrophe. For the specter of disunion that, with Lincoln's election, thrust itself before the public gaze, became ever larger and more menacing. From November 1860 until the time, five months later, when the guns of Sumter roared out their answer to the guns of the southern Confederacy, Greeley's chief concern was how best to prevent war and establish upon a firm foundation the unity of the nation.

Could that Union be preserved and, if so, by what means? This was the question that confronted the American people, a simple question, yet stark and somber in its implications. It was paramount in the thoughts of Horace Greeley. And it was presented to his mind all the more forcefully because it constituted an ironic challenge to one of his favorite and long-standing contentions.

For over a decade, the *Tribune's* editor had been deriding the idea that the Union was in danger. One of his favorite methods of expressing scorn for such a notion had been to give the South carte blanche in the matter of separation. Just give them leave to go, he declared, and they would stay. As far back as 1849, he had told a southern prophet of separation and civil war that he would probably hear louder talk of dissolution at least fifty times in the future, and still the Union would endure. Its advantages were its best guarantee.[17]

Let Texas get out of the Union, if she wanted to, Greeley had snorted during the struggle over the Compromise of 1850. Much better so, than that she remain in it and try to bully the nation by a show of military force. This point of view was reiterated the following year. The *Tribune* then declared that if a state, backed by a decided, unquestionable majority of her people, should resolve to quit the Union, she should be allowed to go, rather than be forcibly restrained. Such would be the surest way to call her bluff. "We do not believe," Greeley had declared, "if the door of the Union were held wide open, a state could be induced to walk out in the course of the next half century." If any did, she would be glad to walk in again before she had been out two years. Self-interest would drive her back.[18] This same point of view was again expressed in 1854. It was to appear once more in 1860-61. Invariably it indicated Greeley's contempt for the possibility of disunion, rather than a willingness to see disunion take place.

During the campaign of 1860, the *Tribune* had said that threats of disunion should be discounted. Southern disunionists were a little band of theorists sheltering under the wing of the Breckenridge faction, but "without the slightest hold on public opinion at the South." Just before the nation went to the polls, Greeley declared that, if any considerable section of the Union really wanted to get out of it, he should insist that it be allowed to go. He was sure that the North felt about this just as he did. But there was no need to worry, he added comfortably, for well the South knew that such a step would mean economic disaster for the seceding states.[19]

The election figures, showing that Breckenridge had only a plurality of the southern vote, lent support to Greeley's belief that a majority of southerners were opposed to such a step. Whether or not because of these statistics, he clung to the position that he had taken just before Lincoln was elected and, on November 9, 1860, published an editorial that echoed throughout the length and breadth of the land.

Greeley declared that he would let the Cotton States "go in peace," if they felt that they could do better out of the Union than in it. "Whenever a considerable section of our Union shall deliberately resolve to go out," he said, "we shall resist all coercive measures designed to keep it in." He emphasized that such secession must be based upon popular approval in the seceding states, an approval manifested after full discussion and deliberation by a popular vote. Hasty, hot-headed movements, such as now seemed evident in the South, were to be deplored. They seemed intended to precipitate that section into rebellion. Greeley hoped that these movements would be confronted with calmness and dignity and an "unwavering trust in the inherent strength of the Union and the loyalty of the American people." A minority of southern ultras should never be allowed to engineer the destruction of the Union.[20]

Two days after this editorial appeared, Greeley in a private letter expressed the opinion that South Carolina would "simmer down" if let alone. She might take her time to do it, but there was no hurry. "We can wait."[21] Such was his conviction on Sunday, November 11. The following Friday, another significant editorial from his pen appeared in the *Tribune*.

He had not thought it worth while, said Greeley, to emphasize the unconstitutionality of secession. "The Union of these states is in its nature irrevocable, and only the earthquake of Revolution can shiver it." Still, if the fifteen slave states, finally and really wished to leave the Union, he would "insist that they be permitted to go in peace." The main thing for the country to do was to keep cool. This southern effervescence would subside, if it found no support from without. Disunion had been threatened for thirty years and probably would be for thirty years more, but it was much easier to resolve a state out of the Union than to get her out.[22]

This emphasis upon the solidity and permanence of the Union derived from Greeley's conception of the American nation as an immensely vital reality, something magnificent, unshakable, indissoluble save by the consent of its members. This idea was central in Greeley's thinking, never more so than in this time of crisis. He recurred to it again and again, even after the war had begun. The rebellious South, he declared was building its house on sand, for that house would be "founded on a denial of the vital principle of nationality" that lay at the heart of the Union—the principle embodied in free elections and acquiescence in their results. A nation, he said again, "is a reality, an entity, a vital force, and not a mere aggregation, like a Fourth of July gathering or a sleighing and supper party." A nation, said Greeley, has "a right to be," and therefore no part of the American nation could be alienated without the full consent of the American people.[23]

Greeley's thinking on the threat of secession that hovered over the land in the winter of 1860-61 was guided by the assumption that the crisis was the work of a few hotheads who must be carefully watched, but not aided by foolish northern tactics. The scheme, said the *Tribune*, was to push South Carolina into secession, produce a "point blank collision with the Federal Government," and then call upon the other slave states for help. This desperate resort was the ultras' only chance for disunion, and well they knew it.[24] Greeley hoped to foil the plot by advocating a time-consuming plan for peaceful secession. This would effectually smother the fire-eaters and allow what he felt was the preponderant Union sentiment of the southern masses to get in its work. His willingness to allow secession when a majority of southerners demanded it was exactly like his willingness to have woman suffrage when a majority of women demanded it. In both cases he felt safe, since he was convinced that there was no such demand. And in both cases he was against the proposed action.

Greeley was pinning his faith to patience and logic as the best means of averting catastrophe. On the one hand he said to the South, "Go, if your people really wish to go." On the other hand, he kept pointing out the consequences of disunion. The cost would be prohibitive. Once the South went out, the underground railroad would run overground. The West could not now, any more than in the days of Jefferson, allow the mouth of the Mississippi to fall into the hands of a foreign power. Controversy between the upper and lower South over reopening the foreign slave trade would be inevitable, the *Tribune* warned, and would probably rend apart any southern confederacy before it was well started. Meanwhile the North was cautioned that a bellicose attitude toward the South would be welcomed by the southern fire-eaters. They would be delighted with the opportunity of saying to the southern masses, "Are you going to let those northerners bluff you down?"[25]

As the clouds of southern bitterness darkened instead of scattering, as South Carolina moved steadily toward secession in December of 1860, a demand began to rise from both North and South for that traditional American remedy for crisis—compromise. Alexander H. Stephens of Georgia, ambitious and melancholic, John Letcher, the temperate and shrewd Governor of Virginia, John J. Crittenden of Kentucky, upon whose shoulders the mantle of the Great Compromiser had fallen, joined with northern Democrats such as Douglas and Vallandigham of Ohio in the search for a middle way. Republicans for the most part held aloof from these efforts, following the cautious policy of silence that Lincoln had adopted. But compromisers were to be found even within their ranks. Men like Hamilton Fish and the influential New York merchant, Moses H. Grinnell, were anxious to discover some method of effecting a peaceful reconciliation. Republican Senator Dixon of Connecticut spoke of guaranteeing to every section of the country its constitutional rights. Thurlow Weed came out in the *Albany Evening Journal* for restoration of the Missouri Compromise line and a more effective Fugitive Slave Law, and his stand was loudly applauded by New York business interests.[26] A powerful northern trend toward concession seemed to be in the making, and Greeley was filled with alarm.

The whole idea of compromise was distasteful to Greeley. He had been cured of compromises in 1850. In 1854, at the time of the Kansas-Nebraska Bill, he had declared that compromise with the South was worse than useless, since it only laid the basis for fresh exactions by the slavocracy. He took this same position in 1860-61. Northern truckling to the Slave Power would be no lasting guarantee of peace, he declared, and restoration of the Missouri Compromise line would be taken as a weakening of northern opposition to slavery extension and a virtual surrender of Mexico and Central America to the slavocrats. The madness of the South, partly real and partly simulated, would not be soothed by concessions. Using an illustration that he had employed six years before, he likened the South's condition to that of an insane person. Any pandering to that mania would only "aggravate the paroxysms and increase its dangers." The thing to do was to stand still, hoping that the insanity would gradually pass away, and that its unhappy victim would yet be seen "sitting clothed and in his right mind."[27]

If a genuine basis for settlement of the controversy were wanted, Greeley was ready to provide one. He outlined this scheme in an open letter to Unionist Leslie Combs of Kentucky. Both sides should agree that there should be no slavery in the territories. Each state should be free to decide for itself whether or not it should have slavery, and each citizen should be free to like or dislike slavery. The free states should hold every man free, if he did not want to be a slave. There should be no stirring up of rebellion in the slave states by outsiders.[28] Greeley had his tongue in his cheek as he made this proposal, with its cold comfort alike for compromisers and for southern ultras.

Where the extension of slavery was in prospect, Greeley would not budge an inch. Neither would he allow for one moment the right of a state or states to defy the laws of the Union before the federal compact had been dissolved by the consent of both North and South. The President, he declared, had a sworn duty to perform. He had to keep the mails running and collect federal revenues throughout the nation. That a state might regard itself as out of the Union was inconsequential. Violaters of the laws and disturbers of the peace must be overcome and brought to justice "without hesitation and without compromise."[29]

Such was the position taken by Greeley during the dark days of December 1860. He would make no backdown on slavery by way of compromise, which he held would foster northern servility and give a new lease of life to the Slave Power. Let the South go, *if its people really wished to go.* He suggested that the proper means for a legitimate exit would be a federal convention, similar to the one that had established the Constitution of the United States. But until the South went out in due and proper form, he thundered, it must be understood that the use of armed force against the federal government would be treason. As Henry Clay had said in 1850, open resistance to the Union, the Constitution, and the laws must be put down. When South Carolina passed her ordinance of secession, Greeley remarked that as long as she continued to pay duties on her imports into the federal treasury and kept her hands off the federal forts, she could secede as long as she pleased.[30]

Despite Greeley's insistence upon the enforcement of the federal laws, his talk about letting the South go looked to many people like craven surrender. Even Lincoln wrote to him, cautioning him to go slow. Two days after South Carolina passed her secession ordinance, Greeley replied to the President-elect in a private letter that restated his views in some detail.

It was as impossible for a state to secede at pleasure from the Union, Greeley told Lincoln, as it was for a stave to secede from a cask. Seven or eight contiguous states—" a political community large enough and strong enough to maintain a national existence"— would have a right to go, and Greeley would let them go. But if the seceding state or states went to fighting and defying the laws, the Union being as yet undissolved save by their say-so, they would have to be made to behave themselves. There would never be peace and equality in the Union until the free states said to the slave states: 'Go, if you want to.' The Cotton States, Greeley continued, were obviously going out of the Union. Nothing that could be offered would stop them. But if the Union went, it could be reconstructed. The only real danger was that there might be a backdown by the free states in "another nasty compromise wherein everything is conceded and nothing secured."[31]

Lincoln was not the only recipient of Greeley's private views on the crisis. He told Governor Edwin D. Morgan of New York that they must be conciliatory and kind in spirit, but firm in their opposition to the extension of slavery. In a letter to William H. Herndon, written a few days after he had told Lincoln of his views, Greeley used a reason for speaking softly that had not appeared in his editorials. It might be all right to talk fight, he said, if Lincoln were in the White House but, as it was, he thought it a mistake to talk roughly until they were at least in a position to "use daggers as well as speak them." This was written on the day after Christmas. Within twenty-four hours, a New Yorker who talked to the *Tribune's* editor came away with the idea that he would welcome a fight. But this impression was a mistake.[32]

Greeley wished to avoid war, if that were possible. No one dreaded it more than he. If the southern masses really wanted to separate (which he did not for a moment believe) he would let them go rather than draw saber to keep them in the Union. But he was always ready to fight if secession were engineered by a slavocrat minority in an undemocratic and therefore illegitimate manner. "I am one of the few Northern men," he told Senator Garret Davis of Kentucky in 1862, "who, to avoid it [war], would have preferred that the Cotton States should leave us in peace. But they chose to rend the Union rather than patiently, quietly dissolve it—and so left us no choice but to fight."[33]

The month of January 1861 saw the six Cotton States of the Deep South follow South Carolina out of the Union. This exodus did not alter the fundamental position of the *Tribune's* editor. He would have nothing to do with the compromise sponsored by John J. Crittenden that centered around extending the Missouri Compromise line to the Pacific. To compromise now, he told Crittenden, would encourage the South to boast that it had made the North back down. "We do not capitulate to traitors," he told the Kentucky Senator. He would not even submit such a proposal to a popular vote, for he was sure that the issue would be presented unfairly in the South. There could be no surrender of principle on the question of slavery.[34] Even to save the Union, he told his readers on January 21, he would not concede free soil to slavery. This was not placing freedom above the Union. It was simply a statement of his conviction that concessions on slavery extension could not and would not preserve a united nation.

Greeley blasted the movements that took the Cotton States out of the Union as being viciously undemocratic. The doctrine that any state could dissolve the Union, he told John L. O'Sullivan at that time, was monstrous and anarchical. The majority of the citizens of those states were loyal to the nation, but the states were in the hands of terrorists. So far as the border states were concerned, secession was simply a game of bluff. No sentiment for it existed along the border. He would not stand for states being coerced out of the Union.[35]

But northerners still shook their heads at Greeley's talk of letting the Cotton States go in peace. Weed professed complete bewilderment. Did the *Tribune* want to fight or to yield, he asked in the *Albany Evening Journal*. Raymond and Webb waxed satirical at the expense of their fellow editor. George W. Patterson wrote to Weed that Greeley was in favor of letting the South secede. He had told Patterson so, adding as his reason that it was the only part of the country where he could not travel in safety,[36] and Patterson had failed to see that Greeley's statement was merely an expression of his outraged sense of personal dignity. The position of the *Tribune's* editor was certainly not crystal clear to his contemporaries.

Actually, Greeley's attitude toward secession was quite simple and understandable. Firmly convinced of the strength of the Union, he believed that the prospect of a slow, peaceful separation would scotch the whole rebellion, and it was this kind of separation that he held out to the South. Southern spirits could only be whipped to war pitch, he asserted, by the threat of northern coercion. Two years after the critical events of the winter of 1861, he still maintained that his policy had been correct. If, he said in February of 1863, the North had proposed to the South in the winter of 1861 a free discussion of secession with a fair vote, and had said further that, if a majority of the voters declared for separation, they would agree to a national convention where the South would be let go, "I believe Secession would have been killed stone dead. But, had I been disappointed in this expectation, I should still have said, 'Let them go in peace; they will be glad enough to come back very soon.' "[37]

Greeley's diagnosis of the situation in the winter of 1861 was partially correct. The passage of time did exercise a dampening influence upon southern enthusiasm for secession, and there is some evidence that doubts as to the stability of a southern confederacy were beginning to percolate the minds of southern leaders in the last few weeks before the attack on Sumter.

But this is far from saying that Greeley's plan of action was a practicable one. His offering to let the South go was hedged about by conditions that would have caused endless trouble. It is not likely that either Buchanan's or Lincoln's government could have put this proposal in a form that the southern leaders would have been willing to accept. Even had such a proposal been formulated and accepted, had the resulting vote been in favor of secession, there is small likelihood that the succeeding course of events would have been in accordance with Greeley's ideas. Either the North would have refused to abide by the result, in which case its position would have been badly compromised by its preliminary acceptance of the principle of secession, or a southern confederacy would have emerged that would have been much more durable and much more dangerous as a neighbor than Greeley imagined. To sow the seeds of such a confederacy was to sow dragon's teeth. The *Tribune's* editor had not paid sufficient heed to the solemn warning given by Clay and Webster that there could be no such thing as peaceable secession.

Greeley's course of action was well intentioned. But the plan, as he developed it, was open to the charge of ambiguity and was confusing to the North and fruitless as a pacifying influence in the South. Based upon an exaggerated idea of the strength of Union sentiment in the South, it was the too subtle scheme of an egotistical and, in this instance, poorly informed journalist. It demonstrated in part what earlier events had suggested and later events were to prove—that Greeley was prone to mistake subtlety for wisdom, and that his views on public questions were those of a clever newspaperman, rather than those of a statesman.

It is worth noting, in passing, that Greeley's stern opposition to compromise with slavery was in no whit softened by the hatred with which he was regarded in the South. The detestation in which both he and the *Tribune* were held was enormous. Shortly before the secession crisis had arisen, an abolitionist named Dr. Holacher was seized in Georgia as he was distributing antislavery literature. The unfortunate zealot was tarred and feathered, marked "to Horace Greeley, *Tribune* office, New York city, right side up with care," and shipped off to New York.[38] Southern hatred was not calculated to lessen Greeley's abhorrence of the Slave Power.

March 4, 1861, was a lovely spring day in Washington. Greeley sat just behind Lincoln as the President read his inaugural with its moving appeal for reconciliation under the flag of the Union. "I am loathe to close. We are not enemies, but friends. . . . " The *Tribune's* editor listened moodily, only grudgingly appreciative, his ear cocked for the sound of a rifle or revolver shot. When it was over, and there had been no attempt to assassinate the Chief Executive, Greeley breathed a sigh of relief. He left the capital without waiting for the inaugural ball—a glittering but gloomy affair that the *Herald's* correspondent described as about as happy in spirit as Horace Greeley in the presence of Thurlow Weed.[39]

Greeley saw Lincoln again about a fortnight after the inauguration. The *Tribune's* editor (as he recalled the interview a few years later) was fully cognizant of the gravity of the nation's situation and warned Lincoln that he would have to fight, but the President was skeptical. Old Abe seemed a trifle absent-minded as Greeley talked about the nation's peril. Greeley came away convinced that the President's one interest lay in dealing out the spoils.[40]

The jaundiced impression that Greeley took away from this interview was partly the result of a fixed conviction as to Lincoln's mediocrity, and was in part the result of the continued struggle over appointments. Some of the coveted places were going to the Greeley faction, but many went to what Greeley considered the wrong people. He wanted to see Frémont sent to England or France, but Charles Francis Adams was given the one and William L. Dayton the other post. Isaac Henderson, candidate of the anti-Seward faction for Naval Officer (the second ranking place in the New York Customs House), was not appointed to that important place. When the news of Webb's appointment to Turkey came out, the *Tribune* made a wry face. Worse still was the distribution of lesser federal posts in New York State. The thieves hunted in gangs, Greeley declared bitterly, and three-fourths of the post offices were going into the hands of corruptionists.[41]

The rivalry between Greeley and Weed was unceasing. It cropped up everywhere. No office was too small to excite the interest and animosity of these one-time friends, now bitter foes. For one such post, that of "Superintending Architect of the Treasury Department," they unwittingly sent in the same name, a fact that afforded Lincoln considerable amusement. He wrote to Chase that the great point in favor of Christopher Adams was "that Thurlow Weed and Horace Greeley join in recommending him. I suppose the like never happened before and never will again; so that it is now or never. What say you?"[42]

As April came on and the Confederacy failed to crumble, Greeley's attitude became steadily more warlike. A government that could not enforce its own laws over its own citizens would be a sham government, he declared. Those who broke the laws would be responsible for the consequences. He had no patience with the last-minute efforts of Virginia and other border states to avert the tragedy.[43] Again and again the administration was urged to proclaim its policy and then stick to it. All his advices from the South, Greeley asserted, proved that a majority of the southern people were Unionist at heart. Rebellion dwelt only in the minds and hearts of the slavocracy. If that rebellion manifested itself in open acts of violence it must be ruthlessly crushed, once and for all.

Beauregard fired on Sumter in the early morning hours of April 12, 1861, too late for the news to be carried in the *Tribune* of that day. On April 13, Greeley announced that war was now being waged by "the Jeff. Davis rebellion." It had really begun months before, he declared, and the country was to be congratulated that all had not been lost before Lincoln came into office. "Let none," said Greeley "doubt the ultimate triumph of the Right."[44] Thus he bravely threw down the gage of battle for the readers of the *Tribune.* But in the *Independent* he wrote mournfully that "we have put back by more than fifteen degrees the hand on the dial which marks the progress of mankind toward a wholly Christian Civilization and Social Order; who shall say when it may again move forward?"[45]

Greeley continued to believe that the rebellion was the plot of a few, and that the southern masses, who had wanted to stay in the Union, had been tricked out of it. His judgment here was wrong, just as it had been in reaching the conclusion that any division of the Union could be only temporary in character. Modern scholars, such as Charles Sydnor and Clement Eaton, have shown how fixed the South was becoming in its sectionalism and in its fanatical loyalty to slavery, during the Middle Period. But at least the *Tribune's* editor had been right when he opposed compromise as an answer to the southern threat. Greeley saw truly that in the struggle between the sections a fundamental moral issue was posed by slavery. It was an issue that no compromise could charm away. All such efforts, by reason of the extension of power they afforded, would only give slavery a new lease on life and new opportunities to make further exactions in dealing with the North. Like Lincoln, like the sons of the Union who rose in answer to the President's summons, Greeley felt that the time for appeasement, if there ever had been such a time, had long since passed away.[46]

NOTES FOR CHAPTER 18

1. *Ann. Rep't. of the American Historical Association,* 1902 (2 vols.; Wash., 1903), II, 484, 487; *Tribune,* Jan. 9, 1861.
2. Greeley Papers (Lib. of Cong.), Greeley to Brockway, Nov. 11, 1860.
3. *Ibid.,* Nov. 16, 17, 1860.
4. Seward Papers, S. Wilkeson to Seward (1861); *Tribune,* Apr. 1, 1861.
5. *Ann. Rep't. of the American Historical Association,* II, 485.
6. Stanton, *op. cit.,* pp. 217-18; Brockway, *op. cit.,* pp. 242-46; Barrows, *op. cit.,* p. 98; S. D. Brummer, *Political History of New York State During the Period of the Civil War* (N. Y., 1911), pp. 134-36; *Tribune,* Sept. 4, 1865; Weed, "Recollections of Horace Greeley," in the *Galaxy,* XV (Mar., 1873), 381; Seward Papers, Weed to Seward, Feb. 3, 1861.
7. Weed Papers, Weed to A. C. Wilder, Feb. 3, 1861.
8. Brockway, *op. cit.,* p. 246.
9. *Ibid.;* Weed Papers, M. B. Anderson to Weed, Feb. 8, 1861; Gurowski, *Diary,* I, 131.
10. This title was due to the way in which Cameron had mulcted the Winnebagoes after Van Buren had appointed him Indian commissioner in Wisconsin in 1838.
11. *Tribune,* Jan. 6-14, 1861; Luthin, *Lincoln and the Patronage,* p. 34.
12. *Cincinnati Daily Commercial,* Feb. 5, 6, 1861. Dispatches from Henry Villard.
13. *Ibid.,* Feb. 6. 1861; *Tribune,* Feb. 6, 1861; Lincoln Papers, Greeley to Lincoln, Feb. 6, 1861. Greeley wanted Lincoln to appoint Rufus F. Andrews district attorney, Benjamin F. Camp surveyor of the port, and Thomas B. Carroll of Albany government printer. He also repeated his request that Frémont be made minister to France.
14. *Cleveland Plain Dealer,* Feb. 18, 1861; *Erie Weekly Gazette,* Feb. 21, 1861. I am indebted for these items, and also for those from the *Cincinnati Commercial* to Mr. J. H. Cramer of Cleveland, Ohio.
15. *Cincinnati Daily Commercial,* Jan. 10, 1861.
16. Greeley Papers (Lib. of Cong.), Greeley to Brockway, Feb. 28, 1861.
17. *Tribune,* Feb. 21, 1849.
18. *Ibid.,* Aug. 8, 1850, Oct. 17, 1851; see above Chapter XIV.
19. *Ibid.,* Sept.-Oct. (especially Oct. 30), Nov. 2, 1860.
20. *Ibid.,* Nov. 9, 1860.
21. Stahl Collection, Greeley to J. G. Shortall, Nov. 11, 1860.
22. *Ibid.,* Nov. 16, 1860. Greeley always maintained the theoretical right of a large portion of the population to leave the Union. See *The American Conflict,* I, 355-60. Also his attack on Chase's decision in the case of Shortridge & Co. *vs.* Macon (*Tribune,* June 24, 1867), and his controversy with Alexander H. Stephens over the right of secession (*ibid.,* July 6, Aug. 21, 1869). He told Stephens that he stood by the right that Jefferson had set forth in the Declaration of Independence. The trouble had been that the southern popular majority in 1861 had been bullied and terrorized into secession by a minority. That was the event which he had "for months labored earnestly though fruitlessly to avoid; for it was plain from the outset that if the question were put in this form—'Will you consent to see the South subjugated and trampled on by the North?' every Southron would answer 'No.' " Hence he had protested against any iden-

tification of the Union cause with the idea of subjugation, urging that a majority of the South were for the Union and would so show themselves after fair and full discussion. The rebellion as it took place was wrong, Greeley declared in 1869, because its impulse, cardinal purpose, and paramount object was the territorial diffusion of slavery and the augmentation of slavery's power in and over the Union.

23. *Independent,* Apr. 18, May 16, 1861. The *Independent* citations all refer to articles by Greeley, unless otherwise noted.

24. *Tribune,* Nov. 10, 19, 20, 28, 1860.

25. *Ibid.,* Nov. 13, 14, 19, 20, 24, 30, Dec. 3, 1860.

26. D. L. Dumond, *The Secession Movement, 1860-1861* (N. Y., 1931), pp. 146-54. For Weed's attitude, see my *Thurlow Weed,* pp. 266-67.

27. Greeley, *Recollections,* pp. 395-98; *Tribune,* May 2, 1854, Nov. 20, 21, 24, 27, Dec. 3, 1860, Feb. 24, 1871.

28. *Ibid.,* Dec. 28, 1860.

29. *Ibid.,* Nov. 20, 21-27, Dec. 3, 1860.

30. *Ibid.,* Dec. 3, 8, 10, 17, 21, 22, 29, 1860.

31. *Lincoln Papers,* Greeley to Lincoln, Dec. 22, 1860; Nicolay and Hay, *Abraham Lincoln,* III, 258. Here and in the *Tribune,* Dec. 10, 1860, Greeley intimated that the Cotton States possessed the elements of independent national existence. Later, he declared that this was "quite likely" a mistake.—*Ibid.,* Mar. 19, 1863.

32. Morgan Papers, Greeley to E. D. Morgan, Dec. 24, 1860; Lincoln Papers, Greeley to W. H. Herndon, Dec. 26, 1860; Weed Papers, F. P. Stanton to Weed, Dec. 27, 1860. Greeley's actual words to Herndon were—"I think we mistake in not talking smoothly at least until we are in a position to *use* daggers as well as speak them."

33. *Tribune,* Apr. 3, 1862. See also the issues of May 14, 15, Sept. 26, 1862.

34. *Ibid.,* Jan. 6, 1861. *Cf.* Jan. 8, 9, 14, 1861; *Independent,* Jan. 24, 1861. In 1864, Greeley declared that the oligarchy that had led the South out of the Union had not really wanted the Crittenden Compromise. Had they wanted it, all they had to do was to leave their representatives in Congress, when it indubitably would have been voted through.—*Tribune,* Jan. 11, 1864.

35. *Ibid.,* Feb. 6, 7, 1861; *Cincinnati Daily Commercial,* Feb. 5-8, 1861; Greeley, *Letters from Texas,* p. 44; R. R. Fahrney, *Horace Greeley and the Tribune in the Civil War* (Cedar Rapids, 1936), pp. 48-49.

36. *Albany Evening Journal,* Feb. 5, 1861; Weed Papers, Patterson to Weed, March 18, 1861.

37. *Tribune,* Feb. 2, 1863; The *Independent,* Feb. 21, 1861. Cf. Greeley's speech at Pittsburg, Sept. 19, 1872, in *True Issues,* p. 4; Ingersoll, *Greeley,* pp. 653, 656.

38. *Atlanta Confederacy,* quoted in *Tribune,* Apr. 3, 1860.

39. Benton, *Greeley on Lincoln,* p. 38; Greeley, *Recollections,* p. 404; *New York Herald,* Mar. 6, 1861; *Tribune,* Mar. 6, 1865.

40. Benton, *Greeley on Lincoln,* pp. 41-42.

41. Greeley Papers (Lib. of Cong.), Greeley to Brockway, Mar. 12, 1861.

42. Nicolay and Hay, eds., *Complete Works of Abraham Lincoln* (12 vols., Lincoln Memorial University, 1927), VI, 268-69.

43. *Tribune,* Apr. 2-9, 1861; *Independent,* Mar. 21, Apr. 4, 1861.

44. *Tribune,* Apr. 13, 1861.

45. *Independent,* Apr. 18, 1861.

46. *Tribune,* Oct. 7, 1865; C. S. Sydnor, *The Development of Southern Sectionalism* (La. State Univ. Press, 1948), pp. 240-42, 315-39, *et passim;* C. Eaton, *Freedom of Thought in the Old South* (Durham, N. C., 1940), pp. 315-30, *et passim.* Both Sydnor and Eaton show how fixed the South was becoming in its sectionalism and in its fanatical loyalty to slavery. The thesis that slavery was a dying institution and that the slavery crisis could have been solved without war is very flimsy. On this point, see the excellent article by Arthur M. Schlesinger, Jr., "The Causes of the Civil War," in the *Partisan Review,* XVI, No. 10 (Oct., 1949), 969-81. Greeley felt that slavery, confined within its existing limits, would gradually decay. Compromise of the Crittenden variety would allow it to escape from those limits, and thus rejuvenate itself.

CHAPTER 19

Windswept

To THE CASUAL OBSERVER, IT MUST HAVE SEEMED as though the flag and the bugle were dominating New York City during the Civil War. Crowds gave roaring welcome to the troops that flocked into the city from New England and the West, and gave a rousing send off to their own "darling Seventh" and "gay Seventy-first" as the heroes marched to the fray. The flags that waved from stores and homes and public buildings, the small boys skirmishing on the streets and even in hotel corridors, bore witness to the presence of a patriotic spirit. So, in a slightly different way, did Barnum, lecturing on "The Art of Money-Making" for the benefit of the army medical service; so, too, did Beecher, red, white, and blue bouquet clutched firmly in his hand, bidding a vast crowd farewell as he left for England in 1863 to lecture for the North. The Metropolitan Fair of 1864 took in over $1,000,000 for the medical work of the army. Many businessmen bought war bonds with a right good will. New Yorkers, when they were so moved, could join in the war effort as lavishly and spectacularly as they built marble palaces or welcomed visiting celebrities.[1]

Many New Yorkers were not moved to such manifestations of patriotism. At the very beginning of the struggle, there were not a few business leaders who believed, with Mayor Fernando Wood, that the city ought to declare itself independent. Many of the city's ablest men devoted themselves to watching the telegraph for news of victories or defeats that would enable them to bull or bear the stock market, and joined in the vicious gold speculation that was the bane of war financiering. Bond subscriptions not infrequently lagged in a disgraceful fashion. Jay Cooke, the financial genius of the war, found New York a disappointing market, particularly for the five-twenties. As Cooke himself described it, this city that could on occasion demonstrate a noble patriotism was also unquestionably "the center and very hotbed of Southern sentiment and scheming."[2]

War set the stage, but even so the city's life was too complex to be centered in a single play. Much of that life ambled along with apparently little concern for the men who died at Manassas, or at Gettysburg, or in the Wilderness. The papers voiced the usual complaints about the city's stinking streets; editors bemoaned the clouds of dust that choked Broadway because the city's inadequately planned water supply furnished no water for the sprinklers. The frivolous thronged to see at Barnum's "the first Esquimaux ever to visit the United States," and gaped at Commodore McNutt as Barnum's midget went down to police headquarters to apply for admission to the force so that he could arrest and take upstairs all who passed by the Museum. The more serious-minded attended such ceremonies as the laying of the cornerstone for the New York Academy of Design in 1863, or listened to Professor Agassiz as he demonstrated conclusively and definitely that the theory of evolution was false. In December 1863, so the *Tribune* declared, the sporting gentry bet and lost close to a million dollars on John Heenan, the Benicia Boy, when he fought England's pride, Sailor Tom King.

There were still other reasons for indifference to the fate of men on the battlefield. The city's cave dwellers (25,000 people, the *Tribune* estimated, lived like troglodytes in fetid, unhealthy cellar tenements) were engaged in a battle as sordid and terrible as any ever fought with musket and cannon. Such people had little opportunity for scanning the war dispatches. The *nouveau riche*, the profiteers in gold and shoddy who bought their sons out of the draft so that they might watch their wartime speculations undisturbed by parental anxiety, had little interest in the casualty lists. And even in the midst of the nation's travail new lines of industrial effort, portents of the Gilded Age to come, were beginning to challenge the attention of the leaders of industry.

One of the new industrial ventures figured in a story told by the *Tribune*. Two ladies making considerable purchases in Tiffany's saw a third enter and place a much larger order. "Shoddy, no doubt," sneered one of the first two. "No, madam," replied the newcomer. "Petroleum."[3]

Greeley saw to it that the *Tribune* portrayed the life of the city in all its various aspects, good and bad, but the editor's main interest was always the war. Once hostilities had begun, he and his paper breathed fire and slaughter against the offending southrons, particularly against the recreant leaders who were now demonstrating that they had never had any genuine loyalty to the nation that he loved. The man who, three short years before, had denounced the army as a "solecism," and had called for getting rid of the navy and closing all the navy yards save possibly one, now directed an editorial policy that called for enormous army movements against the slaveholders and for a blockade of all southern ports.

The war should be an aggressive one, declared the *Tribune*. It should be carried promptly into Virginia, and if Maryland would not coöperate so much the worse for her. Baltimore was a "pestilent city" and Maryland a "treacherous state." If the latter thwarted northern plans, the North should "plough up her rebellious soil with cannon balls, and sow it with gunpowder." Greeley was for administering "condign punishment" to those in rebellion, and he saw to it that this fact was impressed upon his readers. "If you doubt it," he shouted, "just give us a chance to serve on a jury by whom Jeff. Davis, Toombs, Benjamin, Lee, Ruffin, Rhett, etc. are tried for treason, and we will convince you!"[4]

The *Tribune's* attitude toward the border slave states was ill advised. The border areas where slaves were held or where the strongest sort of sympathy for slavery existed, but which remained in the Union, contained a white population larger than that of the Confederacy. Lincoln and Seward were trying to keep this region loyal to the government at Washington. Their policy was one of vital importance to the prosecution of the war but over it, roughshod, rode the *Tribune*. It was convinced that every slave state save Delaware was bound to secede, so what was the use of soft speech and paltering diplomacy. "We trust," it declared, "that we have at least reached the bottom of this Border State Conciliation business, so assiduously prosecuted throughout the last few months." This was undoubtedly Dana, rather than Greeley. But, coming out as a *Tribune* pronouncement, it was identified as the senior editor's own idea by countless thousands of his readers. Whoever its author, it was scarcely conducive to great joy, either at the White House or in the State Department.[5]

As fate would have it, the primary responsibility for directing *Tribune* policy was largely shifted at this juncture to the shoulders of Charles Anderson Dana. On Saturday, May 18, while Greeley was engaged in trimming some of his Chappaqua trees, his ax slipped and gashed his knee. He was some distance from the house, and before he reached it the wound had been considerably aggravated. It was slow in healing, and for well over a month the impatient editor chafed at home.

While Greeley bit his thumb in seclusion at Chappaqua, Dana in New York kept shouting for military action. On June 26 he began displaying on the editorial page the slogan, "Forward to

Richmond!" The rebel Congress, bellowed Dana, must not be allowed to meet in Richmond on July 20. By that date, the place must be in the hands of the Union Army.[6] Thus the *Tribune* began to martial public pressure against the deliberation that reigned at the capital; thus it helped, a month later, to move McDowell's half-trained army out to sore defeat at Bull Run.

Greeley, nursing his wounded knee at home while Dana sounded the tocsin, wavered in his attitude as to the wisdom of the *Tribune's* outcry. He wrote to a friend that he did not want the war hurried, a statement that appeared to indicate a distate for Dana's vociferations. He said afterward that he would have preferred not to have the slogan dinned into the ears of the public by constant repetition. On the other hand, his inclination was toward swift action. He was prone to underestimate both the enthusiasm and the equipment of the rebel soldiers, and his gorge rose at stories of how the Union Army was rotting in idleness and debauchery at the capital, its only conquests one grog shop and three or four brothels. He longed to see it march out of that sink of iniquity. He was also inclined to haste through the belief that Lincoln, his judgment swayed by "venal and wall-eyed politicians," was temporizing in the hope of avoiding a serious conflict. The war had to be won within a year, Greeley thought, or else the Union was gone. He could have moderated the *Tribune's* policy, had he chosen to do so. That he left Dana a free hand was tantamount to approval of the course taken by the junior editor. After the war was over, he declared that, while Dana was the sole author of the slogan, what Dana had urged "was exactly what should have been done." The error had been in the strategy that accompanied the march on Bull Run.[7]

Retribution was near for Dana's attempt to sway military judgment. On July 22, 1861, the *Tribune's* leading editorial chanted of victory at the battle of Bull Run, but the front-page news told of a great defeat. The panic-stricken Union Army had reeled back upon Washington, leaving artillery and baggage, dead and dying, strewn along the way. The ordeal of battle had made "Forward to Richmond!" a mockery.

At first Dana tried to bluff it out. The disaster, he declared, was due to governmental blindness, paralysis and incompetence, and he called for the immediate retirement of the Cabinet. But then the storm descended and the winds blew about the luckless *Tribune* and its editorial staff. The *Times* held its rival largely responsible for the disaster, and blistered with derision the demand for recall of the Cabinet. The *World* declared that the *Tribune's* policy had derived from Greeley's unsatiated thirst for office. The *Herald* snarled that "Massa Greeley" was linked with those "Jacobin" abolitionists who were intent on making the war a crusade against slavery. Letters of bitter condemnation poured into the *Tribune* office, some of them canceling subscriptions. The *Tribune* was already confronted by a drastic shrinkage in income, advertisements were "scarce as saints," Greeley wrote, and the senior editor thought that his beloved paper was facing nothing less than ruin.[8]

Under the triple weight of defeat, denunciation, and injury to the *Tribune,* Greeley's mind nearly gave way. He did not sleep for seven nights following the battle, and came down with a brain fever so severe that for a month he was incapable of any sustained effort. It was in this distraught condition that he sought to mollify the public and to counsel the President.

On July 25, 1861, "the repentant male Magdalen of New York journalism," as James Gordon Bennett dubbed his rival, wrote for the *Tribune* an editorial entitled "Just Once." It was Greeley, by turns bold and apologetic, scolding and coaxing, contriving to stand upright and yet bend before the storm. He declared that the ideas expressed in the *Tribune* concerning the conduct of the war were in harmony with his own convictions. He was not responsible for the "Forward to Richmond!" slogan and "would have preferred not to iterate it," but he had believed in a forward movement and did not wish to evade responsibility. He had not written the article urging Cabinet changes, but believed some changes would be advantageous. He then waxed critical of McDowell's field tactics (which he miscalled "strategy"), but ended by saying that, if necessary, he was willing to play the scapegoat for military blunders. Henceforward all criticism of army movements would be barred from the columns of the *Tribune*. There were truths that still needed to be uttered in that connection, but the paper would devote itself solely to rousing and animating the people. The thirst for office which his most savage detractor had indicated as the root of *Tribune* policy was nonexistent, and therefore could have had nothing to do with the *Tribune's* criticisms of the government. "Now let the wolves howl on!"

Thus Greeley sought to placate public opinion and at the same time defend *Tribune* policy. Critical judgment found the effort evasive and unsatisfactory. Greeley himself, recognizing that he was "all but insane" at the time he wrote the editorial, thought that it was done badly, and that the *Tribune's* influence had been broken down despite his efforts. He was sick and harassed, and a letter that he wrote to the President on July 29 showed that the course of events had thrown his mental processes into a turmoil of horrors.[9]

"You are not considered a great man," Greeley told the long-suffering Lincoln, "and I am a hopelessly broken one." After this extraordinary pronouncement, which was presumably intended to clear the ground for what followed, the "hopelessly broken one" asked the less than great man for advice and promised all sorts of support. Could the rebels be beaten, Greeley inquired. If not, there should be an armistice, a national convention, an exchange of prisoners and a disbandment of forces. Posing as a judge of public sentiment, Greeley declared that it was everywhere gathering and deepening against a continuation of the war. Particularly was this true in New York City, where "sullen, scowling, black despair" sat on every brow.

Do nothing timidly or by halves, Greeley warned the President, but do what is best, even if that means making peace with the rebels "at once and on their own terms. . . . Do the thing that is the highest right, and tell me how I am to second you."

This half-crazed epistle was thoroughly defeatist in tone. Lincoln wearily disregarded it.[10]

The battle of Bull Run did not spell finis to the Union cause, the *Tribune* absorbed its castigation and kept upright, and its distraught editor won his way back to health and vigor despite all his stewing and fretting over the conduct of affairs. Greeley bottled up a fervent desire to tell the country about the limitations of the military command. He was convinced that General Winfield Scott was a worn-out old humbug upon whom rested the responsibility for sending that "ass" McDowell to command at Bull Run; he was sure that both generals should be shot for gross mismanagement. But he kept the *Tribune* quiet about military policy, even though silence was exquisitely painful. "A man had better be a hod-carrier than a journalist," he said to a friend, the eyes in his round, pink-and-white face suffused with a melancholy that gave him the appearance of a sorrowful baby.[11]

Two weeks' convalescence at Chappaqua ended on August 16. Greeley then went gingerly down to New York, where he was assiduously nursed by the well-known abolitionist, Abigail Hopper Gibbons. He was still very weak but being in harness again, even though for only a few hours at a time, had a healing effect, and something of his former belligerency returned to him.

Greeley now felt convinced that the northern Democracy and the Catholic priesthood were leagued in an attempt to force the North into a shameful peace. History has uncovered no such conspiracy, but Greeley believed that it existed and that it must be thwarted by prodding a weak and inefficient government into one great, final

effort. If at the end of six or eight months the rebels had not been
conquered, he would be willing to call it quits and come to the
best possible terms.[12]

Despite his convictions regarding this great conspiracy, the war
did not quite monopolize Greeley's attention in the fall of 1861. It
appeared that there was also work for the *Tribune's* editor to do in
New York State politics. There his implacable enemy, Weed, was
still a power. The Dictator was busy obtaining recruits and supplies
and fostering the formation of a Union ticket of Democrats and
Republicans for the better support of the war effort. These were
activities to which objection could not well be made, but at other
points the Old Man was decidedly vulnerable. Greeley joined other
New Yorkers and Salmon P. Chase, who was using the Treasury
patronage for the same purpose, in a steady assault upon the Dictator.

The attack was merciless. The *Tribune* raked over the coals of
the gridiron street-railway scandal of 1860. It pilloried Weed as a
silent partner in wartime profiteering exploits that ran the gamut
from steamboats to shoddy. Greeley took a calculated part in an
assault upon Weed's political ally, DeWitt C. Littlejohn, an assault
that forced the latter into a libel suit against the New York editor
and thus gave Weed's opponents a legal forum in which to blast
the Dictator's reputation. The jury disagreed, but the trial created
a sensation because of the skillful way in which Greeley's lawyer,
Isaiah T. Williams, had arraigned Weed as a master of the art of
corruption. The results of all this became obvious when only one
bona fide Weed man was put on the state ticket that fall, and the
anti-Weed Republicans in New York City succeeded in electing
Greeley's friend and ally, George Opdyke, mayor. Greeley, in his
turn, had now paid two installments on his debt to Mr. Weed, and
Weed's enemies were boasting that they had the Old Man encircled
by a ring of fire that would destroy his career as the boss of New
York State.[13]

Weed went abroad that winter on a mission that rendered valuable service to the Union cause. The *Tribune* gave scant notice to
his going and heralded his return by a sour editorial which characterized the banquet given him as a dodge by which the New York
City aldermen secured for themselves a good dinner at the city's
expense.[14] Malice could scarcely go further.

Meanwhile the war was dragging slowly on. True to his word,
Greeley kept the *Tribune* from issuing arbitrary pronouncements
on military strategy and tactics during the months that followed
Bull Run. He applauded McClellan's rise to power in the army,

and was restrained in his comments on the Ball's Bluff disaster of October 1861. The *Tribune* was also tolerant of Seward's conduct of the State Department, even though Greeley declared privately that he was completely disillusioned as to Seward's sincerity and his powers of judgment.[15]

The *Tribune's* changed attitude pleased the President. During the early stages of the war, Lincoln hoped to make the paper a steadfast supporter of the administration, and a series of events late in 1861 seemed to play into his hands.

James R. Gilmore, an ardent protagonist of emancipation, had started a violently antislavery magazine called the *Continental Monthly,* the object of which was to fire the northern heart with rage against the slaveholder. One of the sponsors of this publication was Robert J. Walker, erstwhile governor of Kansas and now on intimate terms with the Lincoln administration. Greeley saw possibilities in such propaganda and in Gilmore as a propagandist. He tried to get the latter to abandon the *Monthly* and use the *Tribune* as an emancipationist vehicle. Gilmore refused to do this, countering with the proposition that Greeley write for the *Monthly.* This the *Tribune's* editor finally consented to do but suggested that, as a *quid pro quo,* Walker furnish the *Tribune* with advance information about administration policies. Walker referred the matter to Lincoln.

Lincoln was delighted with Greeley's proposal and accepted it without reservation. He wrote to Walker that he would tell the latter about government plans and policies, just as he had been doing right along, and Walker could then communicate them, *sub rosa,* to the editor of the *Tribune.* "He," said Lincoln, "will be, in effect, my mouthpiece, but I shall not be known to be the Speaker." Lincoln went on to emphasize the importance of Greeley's support. "Having him firmly behind me will be as helpful to me as an army of one hundred thousand men." He hoped, by establishing such frank and confidential relations, to prevent Greeley's kicking over the traces, and urged haste in concluding the arrangement, since it might soon be advisable "to ventilate our policy on the *Trent* affair."[16]

Greeley, also, was delighted by this entente, and for a few months all was as merry as a marriage bell. The *Tribune* stood staunchly by the administration during the crisis over the *Trent* matter, and its editor wrote Seward a four-page letter advising the release of Mason and Slidell with an accompanying lecture to Britain on her base and ungenerous conduct regarding search and seizure. The *Tribune* averred that Stanton was the right man to replace Cameron

as secretary of war, and it applauded the appointment of McClellan
to command of the army. Lincoln, on his part, succeeded in getting
his crony, Ward Lamon, to postpone filing a libel suit against
Greeley, and for this the *Tribune's* editor professed gratitude.[17]
But shortly the *Tribune's* course began once again to veer away
from support of the administration.

Greeley's reversion to a critical attitude was due to several factors.
One was his rooted conviction of Lincoln's incompetency. Now,
if ever, Greeley thought, was the time for a hero, à la Carlyle, one
who would take to himself extraordinary executive powers and,
with firmness and dispatch, see the country through its crisis. But
Lincoln, alas, was no Carlylean hero. He was rather like one of
those that he, himself, described as "augurs that won't bore"—a
procrastinator, a man of indecision with a weakness for consorting
with such "poor, worthless devils" as Ward Lamon.[18] It was little
short of tragic, thought Greeley, that the country should be cursed
with such a mediocrity at such a critical time.

The malaise produced in Greeley's mind by this fixed estimate of
Lincoln's ability was heightened by the paucity of inside news that
reached the *Tribune* office. Walker and Gilmore were fearful of
trusting Greeley with anything really important, and the Man in
the White Coat discovered that his alliance with the administration
had very litle value from the news point of view. A third factor, one
that drove Greeley nearly frantic, was the North's failure to win
decisive victories. Greeley was convinced that the superior resources
of the North should be used promptly; that crushing blows should
be struck during the winter of 1861-62. When, instead of such blows,
there was news of a reverse, he was filled with mingled fury and
despair in regard both to the military leadership and the administration at Washington.

A visitor at the *Tribune* office early in 1862 found the senior
editor in a black rage at news that had come over the wires. The
first reports of the battle of Pittsburg Landing had just arrived and
Greeley was shrieking in his high falsetto—"Battle yesterday at
Pittsburg Landing; rebels whipped us, of course. Our soldiers are
being driven into the Tennessee today. Our generals are drunk.
Buell ought to be shot, and Grant ought to be hung."[19]

Delay in winning the war was all the more tragic to Greeley because the cost of the struggle was mounting upward at what seemed
to him a prodigious rate. Inveterately penurious where government
expenses were concerned, his imagination was appalled by military
costs that he estimated at from $2,000,000 to $3,000,000 a day.
Standing still at such a rate terrified him, and standing still, at least

geographically speaking, was a part of McClellan's methodical preparation for the Peninsular campaign. Even when "Little Mac" moved, early in 1862, it was with a majestic deliberation that the bouncing editor found hard to bear. The slow advance up the Peninsula toward Richmond that spring, the delay before the "maple cannon" of Centerville, the final repulse in the Seven Days' battles were all deeply upsetting, and Greeley became increasingly critical of an administration that relied upon this "young Napoleon" with his "poor, tinsel imitation" of a war.[20]

Impatience with Lincoln, a paucity of "inside" news, and Mc-Clellan's Fabian tactics were upsetting enough, but they were by no means the only thorns in Greeley's side. As the first year of war passed away, Greeley found himself more and more concerned over the administration's attitude toward slavery. It was a point on which he found himself in close harmony with a group of radical anti-slavery Republican leaders.

Even before Sumter, it had become apparent that a number of antislavery zealots, dubbed "Jacobins" by young John Hay and by the *New York Herald,* were a powerful, driving force within the Republican party. Caustic, club-footed "Thad" Stevens of Pennsylvania, roaring "Zack" Chandler (Michigan's Xanthippe in pants), Ohio's bluff Ben Wade, and the cultured, handsome and immensely conceited Sumner of Massachusetts constituted the nucleus of the group. They were out to destroy the Slave Power and slavery as well, and they were openly scornful of Lincoln's belief that the restoration of the Union took precedence over the destruction of human bondage.[21]

Greeley had not been an extremist in his attitude toward slavery and the Negro before the outbreak of the war. He had been hostile to slavery primarily because of the Slave Power's opposition to what he regarded as all-important national objectives. Therefore, his main concern had been to check the expansion of slavery. This done, he would trust to time, moral pressure, free white colonization, and the like to bring about a gradual extinction of the peculiar institution. His attitude toward the personal rights of Negroes was illustrated by what he said and did about the Negroes in New York State. There he worked for Negro suffrage, attacked social discrimination—and scolded the Negroes shrewishly because they did not see that they must work out their own salvation. He seemed to resent the drag that they imposed upon social progress. His interest in them, he declared, was "not for their own sakes only or mainly, but for the sake of the entire community." In other words, it was primarily a national rather than a humanitarian interest.[22]

When the war began, the *Tribune* took the position that the paramount objective of the struggle was the preservation of the Union, not the destruction of the South's peculiar institution. But during the summer of 1861 the paper turned its attention to the cause rather than the objective of the conflict. That cause was slavery, the great and fundamental menace to a united nation.

This shift in the *Tribune's* attitude indicated a definite trend in Greeley's thinking, a trend that was even more clearly expressed in his private correspondence. His friends were informed as early as August 1861 of his earnest conviction that the Slave Power had stood too long athwart America's destiny. Now, once and for all, it must be destroyed by striking the shackles from the slave.[23] To one of these friends, Gerrit Smith, Greeley added the interesting observation that he felt himself to be God's humble instrument to that high purpose.[24]

The growing conviction that abolition of slavery was an essential war objective led Greeley to join the Congressional radicals in applauding every move in that direction. The *Tribune* approved the act of August 6, 1861, which confiscated slaves and other property used to promote insurrection. It applauded Frémont's Missouri order freeing the slaves of all who resisted the government, and was critical of Lincoln for rescinding the general's rash action.[25] By October of 1861, Greeley was calling openly for the emancipation of the slaves of the rebels. He professed willingness to leave the proper time for such action to the judgment of the government— "we can wait if we must"—but he made it clear that he believed such action essential as a war measure, if nothing else.[26]

Greeley became increasingly restive as the year 1861 slipped away with the rebels' slaves still in bondage. His eager mind was envisaging the happiest effects upon 4,000,000 chattels of a general order of emancipation and, though he was careful to stipulate that this meant noninterference with loyal slaveholders, it was plain that he hoped the order would mean the complete destruction of slavery. The *Tribune* was conjuring up visions of Florida as a paradise of freedom to which the whole colored population of the United States might in due time repair. The war, declared the *Tribune*, was one of Ideas. The Idea of Slavery was pitted against the Idea of Freedom. Allow the latter its full dynamic by way of an emancipation proclamation, and 4,000,000 slaves would spring to the side of the Union. Now was the time. The government could not continue to spend money at the present enormous rate for even six months longer, and the winter was a favorable season for military operations in "Jeffdom."[27]

By the beginning of 1862, Greeley's irritation with the government for its failure to share his own clear insight as to the effects of emancipation was closely linked with his mounting scorn for McClellan's slow progress toward the conquest of Richmond. From this it was only a step to ascribing political significance to McClellan's delays, and Greeley (who was now proudly identifying himself as one of the radicals) joined with the Congressional extremists in accusing the general of wanting to produce a military stalemate so that the reunited voters of the Sham Democracy could elect him President in 1864.[28]

All through the spring and summer of 1862, the *Tribune* tried to prod Lincoln toward emancipation, while the President, moving always with cautious circumspection, sought to keep the border slave states in line and at the same time avoid a quarrel with the Man in the White Coat. When the President proposed a plan for compensated emancipation in the loyal border states, when he signed the bill liberating the slaves in the District of Columbia, Greeley waxed enthusiastic. On the other hand, the *Tribune's* editor made clear his displeasure when Lincoln rescinded General Hunter's order of May 1862 setting free the slaves in Florida, South Carolina, and Georgia. Greeley also made it perfectly apparent, as division between the Jacobins and the administration began to appear over the legal status of recovered territories, that his sympathies, at least, lay with Sumner's theory of state suicide as the more effectual weapon for the extermination of the hated institution.[29]

When the Second Confiscation Act came up for discussion in the summer of 1862, Greeley raised a prodigious clamor. This bill granted freedom to the slaves of all resisting the Union, whenever such slaves came within the jurisdiction of the military, and it also authorized the arming of Negroes. The embattled editor was sure that there was transcendent virtue in this measure. It would help to destroy both war and slavery, and he pushed it with all his might. At the same time, he obviously had his doubts that the administration would enforce its provisions, and when it became law he undertook a campaign calculated to make Lincoln live up to its letter and spirit.[30]

Greeley's increasing emphasis upon emancipation coincided with the failure of the Peninsular campaign, a military setback that he found very hard to bear. When this advance on Richmond began, he had confidently predicted the speedy collapse of the rebellion. The retreat plunged him into the deep gloom. He took it as a clear indication that God was trying his people, and that He meant to save the Union only if the Unionists destroyed slavery. It seemed evident to Greeley (at least this was the impression that he conveyed to his readers) that the Most High had not been pleased by the tardy development of emancipation, and with significant emphasis he invited the public to ponder the fact that, since the veto of Hunter's proclamation, every battle had been a defeat.[31] Greeley's mind seethed with discontent, his emotions became more and more explosive, and finally the outbreak came with his famous "Prayer of Twenty Millions" editorial that appeared in the *Tribune* on August 20, 1862.

According to Greeley, twenty million northerners were praying that Lincoln would take a decided stand against the continuation of slavery, and particularly that he would enforce the confiscation act. The President was being unduly influenced, Greeley charged, by "fossil politicians hailing from the border slave states" (this was a slap at the Blairs). Whatever strengthened slavery in those states, the *Tribune's* editor told the President, fortified the rebellion. Lincoln had missed a great opportunity by not declaring in his inaugural that he would recognize no loyal person as rightfully held in bondage by a traitor. This would have made the wealthier and more cautious among the slaveholding oligarchy recoil from the secessionist movement. Lincoln had annulled Frémont's Proclamation and Hunter's Order, and now the Union generals were notoriously disregarding the Confiscation Act without rebuke from the President. But this was trying to put down the rebellion and at the same time uphold its cause, something that could not be done. Every hour of deference to slavery was an hour of added and deepened peril to a Union whose triumph was indispensable, not only to the existence of the nation but to the well-being of mankind.[32]

Lincoln, who had already decided to issue an emancipation proclamation when military circumstances were auspicious, replied publicly and mildly that his paramount objective was neither to safeguard or destroy slavery, but to save the Union. He also hinted that a new policy was in the offing. Greeley responded with a reiteration of his charge that the President had failed to execute the laws. The radicals received Lincoln's statement as proof of his lack of interest in slavery as a moral issue and, at least in public, Greeley appeared to share their opinion. Privately, he held that Old Abe's letter showed that the President was moving in the right direction.[33]

The Preliminary Emancipation Proclamation was issued immediately after the battle of Antietam in September 1862. It declared all slaves free in those states still in rebellion by January 1, 1863, and

also ordered enforcement of the Second Confiscation Act. Greeley's
first reaction was one of "heartiest approval." Upon reflection, he
qualified his enthusiasm. It was not, he declared, what he had desired and sought. He had hoped for the immediate abolition of
slavery everywhere, with compensation only "to the few thoroughly
loyal slaveholders" in Maryland, Delaware, and Missouri. The
President had adopted "a more cautious, limited, temporizing procedure." Nevertheless, with these reservations, Greeley found much
to commend in the Proclamation. It placed the government unequivocally on the side of freedom. It served to identify abolitionism
and Unionism. It entitled the government to the loyalty of the
Negroes and, by placing the North in the proper moral position,
rescued it from the danger of foreign intervention. The people, he
was certain, had been given a new intellectual and moral life
by this measure, and the nation, in a very real sense, had been
recreated. It was "the beginning of the end of the rebellion," and
he asked God's blessing upon the President.

So far as military affairs were concerned, the Proclamation gave
Greeley an access of patience. He declared that he was now willing
to stand on the defensive until January 1, if that was deemed best,
although there should be continuous preparation for one, grand,
final assault. Then, if the South did not give in, simply at the sight
of these preparations, the emancipation of its slaves would go into
effect and a few weeks, at most, of freedom and war would seal
the fate of "the slaveholders' Rebellion."[34]

The lift of Greeley's morale afforded by the Emancipation
Proclamation was fitful and uncertain. From time to time, a note
of dolorous woe would creep into his observations regarding military and political events. But his spirits were generally good until
after the November elections. This was made clearly apparent by
a series of articles that he wrote for the *Continental Monthly*,
explaining his conception of the significance of the war.

A strong sentiment of nationality, Greeley declared, had been the
master passion of Americans for generations. The very strength of
this passion had kept down hostility to slavery until the Slave
Power had sought disunion. That oligarchy had undertaken the
insane task of setting up national barriers dividing New Orleans
from the upper Mississippi and separating St. Louis from the North
and West, and war had been the result. The war was rallying the
sentiment of nationality against slavery and out of this war, with
its destruction of slavery, there was emerging a nobler idea, a truer
conception of national unity than had before been known. This
new nationalist concept was rapidly taking possession of the Ameri-

can mind. It was a true union of hearts, based on an identity of
social habits and moral convictions, and combining the many states
into one nation. "Our union will be one of bodies not merely, but
of souls." Hatred, bitterness, and alienation would vanish with the
elimination of slavery, the one great cause of the rebellion, the one
great bar to the triumph of nationalist sentiment.[35] Such was his
vision of American nationalism, resurgent, resplendent, purified by
the fires of war and rising Phoenix-like from the ashes of civil strife.
The battle was still on, but Greeley's spirit was already marching
down the road to reunion.

Gilmore's abolitionist publication was not the only vehicle of
Greeley's optimism. On December 6, 1862, an editorial entitled
"Will There Be Peace?" appeared in the *Tribune*. Three months
of the emancipation policy, six at the outside, should do the trick,
Greeley told his readers. That policy would destroy southern
resistance. "We are at all events morally certain to have peace in
Spring." A few days after this editorial appeared, he wrote to
Lincoln that his advices proved that the rebels were anxious for
peace. Emancipation, plus an offer of amnesty, the assumption of
$400,000,000 of the Confederate debt, and the payment of
$100,000,000 to the loyal slave states for freeing their bondsmen
would bring an end to slavery and "a lasting and glorious peace"
by March of 1863.[36]

Progress toward emancipation was not the only cause of Greeley's
optimistic moments in the closing months of 1862. As he looked
back over the year, he could see much that was bright and of good
omen. It was true that the war had brought an abrupt rise in prices,
especially in paper, which had gone from eight to twenty cents a
pound, and that the expenses of the *Tribune* had nearly doubled;
the *Tribune* and its editor had been near to scraping the bottom
of the barrel.[37] But the paper's new price of three cents a copy was
beginning to show a profit at last. Things were running more
smoothly, too, in the *Tribune* office. Greeley had forced the dismissal of the positive and aggressive Dana from the editorial staff
and Dana's successor as managing editor, Sidney Howard Gay,
played a valuable role on the paper without producing half so
much antagonism on the part of the senior editor.[38]

Greeley was also well satisfied with two great aspects of national
legislation. The tariff was high at last, thank God, and certain to
remain so for a generation or more.[39] In May of 1862 a homestead
bill had been passed. This was a sorry substitute for a genuinely
democratic land law, but Greeley saluted it as a panacea for economic ills. "Free homes are secure," he declared.[40]

Out of the spindrift of war were emerging the basic elements of Greeley's nationalist program, a fact that filled him with satisfaction. Nor had he been displeased by the sound drubbing he had handed out to Weed in the Union state convention of 1862, where he had personally superintended the nomination of abolitionist General James S. Wadsworth for governor and the construction of a platform which enthusiastically commended emancipation.[41] Such was the bright side of the shield in 1862.

But if the year had brought some progress toward the realization of righteousness, its close brought much that was bitter to the mouth of the *Tribune's* editor. The state gubernatorial campaign of 1862, despite Greeley's steady effort to show that the Democracy was tainted with treason and that a Democratic victory might *"add a revolution in the North to our war in the South,"*[42] ended with a decisive victory for Democrat Horatio Seymour. This was a stunning defeat, for Greeley had been responsible, more than any other one man, for Wadsworth and for a campaign centering on emancipation. The disaster brought from Republican conservatives a furious denunciation of Greeley's leadership. It also marked the end of a hope that he had cherished of riding into the United States Senate on what Weed tauntingly called "his Abolition whirlwind."[43]

Nor was the state political situation the only cause of Greeley's gloom. The Democrats had won in other states than New York, and Greeley was desperately afraid that these victories meant that the people were rejecting the emancipation policy upon which he set such store, and were turning toward peace on the Confederacy's terms.[44] Then, too, despite his enthusiasm over the Emancipation Act, his distrust of Lincoln and his administration had steadily increased. Like the Congressional Jacobins, he resented Lincoln's coolness toward Frémont, and deplored the latter's retirement from the army. Seward, also, with his control of the patronage, stood between Greeley and power in the state. During December 1862, Greeley lent a cautious hand to the Jacobins' attempt to oust Seward from the Cabinet, and shared their chagrin when the plot failed.

Worse even than Seward's triumph and Democratic victories, the failure of the Union armies to win decisive battles and the fiscal situation of the government filled Greeley with a deepening unrest. The Legal Tender Act which pumped greenbacks into the currency had inflationary implications and was difficult for him to accept, and the constant piling up of the national debt was an ever-present nightmare. By the end of the year, he was again taking up his old complaint that the power of the North was not being used. He pleaded for fighting officers. So earnest was he in this that he stood by Burnside after the bloody defeat at Fredericksburg in December 1862. Greeley complimented the unfortunate general on getting back across the Rappahannock to a strong position where he could "take measures at his leisure for his next movement." The *Tribune* even professed to see something Napoleonic in Burnside's blunderings, a fact that led the crusty old Pole, Adam Gurowski, to suspect that the paper was in its dotage, or worse.[45]

Cling though he might to the hope that emancipation would end the war, convinced though he was that the conflict was one between Light and Darkness, between democracy and aristocracy,[46] Greeley was a harassed and often discouraged man as he faced the year 1863. The thought that freeing the slaves might not have the decisive effect of which he professed to be so confident was an ugly phantom, haunting his days as well as his nights. Perhaps God, after all, had found the North unworthy and was going to destroy the Union, the better to compass the destruction of slavery.[47] A vision of peace without victory, ominous, terrifying and yet enticing, began to take form within his weary brain.

NOTES FOR CHAPTER 19

1. Wilson, *op. cit.*, III, 478-513.
2. *Ibid.*, p. 479; *Tribune*, June 1, 1863, Jan. 27, 1864; Oberholtzer, *Cooke*, I, 150, 396, 498, 576-77.
3. *Tribune*, Apr. 13, 1861, Mar. 11, Apr. 18, Aug. 4, Nov. 12, 1862, Dec. 24, 1863, Jan. 27, Feb. 16, Aug. 10, Dec., 1864, Mar. 9, 1865.
4. *Ibid.*, June 11, 1858, Apr. 24-May 4, 7, 1861; *Independent*, May 9, 1861.
5. *Tribune*, Apr. 24-26, 1861; E. C. Smith, *The Borderland in the Civil War* (N. Y., 1927), p. 3; J. G. Randall, *Lincoln and the South* (Baton Rouge, 1946), pp. 52-65.
6. Greeley Papers (Lib. of Cong.), Greeley to Mrs. Allen, June 17, 1861; Greeley Papers (N. Y. P. L.), Greeley to Mrs. Laura Bowe, May 28, 1861; Greeley Letters (N. Y. Hist. Soc.), Greeley to Thos. B. Carroll, May 23, 1861; *Tribune*, May 19-June 26, 1861. The slogan, "Forward to Richmond!" seems to have originated among the friends of Fitz Henry Warren, Washington correspondent of the *Tribune.*—Fahrney, *op. cit.*, p. 83.
7. Stahl Collection, Greeley to Mrs. Allen and Mrs. Daury, June 17, 1861; Lincoln Papers, Greeley to Lincoln, May 19, 1861; Greeley Papers (N. Y. P. L.), Greeley to Mrs. Laura Bowe, May 28, 1861, Greeley to Colfax, June 12, 1861; Greeley, *Recollections*, pp. 402-3; Greeley, *The American Conflict* (2 vols.; Hartford, 1864, 1866), I, 547-50; *Tribune*, Oct. 23, 1861, March 19, 1862, Feb. 2, 1863; *Independent*, June 27, 1861; Benton, *Greeley on Lincoln*, pp. 43-44, 77-78. Greeley's penchant for snap military judgments (see the *New-Yorker*, May 7, 1836, *Tribune*, Aug. 10, 1848, for examples of this) led him to fall in all the more easily with Dana's policy.

8. *New York Times, Herald, World, Tribune,* July 23-25, 1861; Conway, *op. cit.,* I, 336; Greeley Papers (Lib. of Cong.), Greeley to Mrs. Margaret Allen, June 17, 1861. The *Tribune* began a Sunday edition, Apr. 28, 1861, that continued throughout the war.

9. Greeley Papers (Lib. of Cong.), Greeley to Brockway, Aug. 14, 1861; Gerrit Smith Papers, Greeley to Smith, Aug. 14, 1861; *Tribune,* July 25, 1861; *New York Herald,* July 26, 1861; *New York Times,* July 26, 1861; Conway, *op. cit.,* I, 336; Reavis, *op. cit.,* pp. 182-83.

10. Lincoln Papers, Greeley to Lincoln, July 29, 1861. Also published verbatim in Nicolay and Hay, *Lincoln,* IV, 365-66; *ibid.,* IV, 367.

11. Conway, *op. cit.,* I, 331-32; *Tribune,* Apr. 21, 1889, Greeley to "Dear R.," July 27, 1861.

12. Gerrit Smith Papers, Greeley to Smith, Aug. 14, 21, Oct. 8, 1861; Conway, *op. cit.,* I, 336; Greeley Papers (N. Y. P. L.), Greeley to S. Wilkeson, Aug. 24, 1861; Stahl Collection, Greeley to Mrs. Allen, Sept. 18, 1861. Greeley's dislike of Catholicism as a force hostile to freedom was obvious in articles he wrote for the *Independent,* Jan. 10, 17, Dec. 19, 1861, and in his open letter to Archbishop Hughes in the *Tribune,* July 9, 1863, wherein he accused the Catholics of bringing on calamities the nation was suffering by (1) electing Polk in 1844, (2) supporting the Mexican War, (3) being among the foremost in degrading and abusing the Negroes. It would have required an ingenious exegesis to prove any of these points.

It was at this time that Greeley suggested to Robert Bonner that the latter make a collection of Greeley's letters of advice to young people and publish them after Greeley's death.—Greeley Papers (N. Y. P. L.), Greeley to Bonner, Oct. 1, 1861.

13. Gerrit Smith Papers, Greeley to Smith, Aug. 21, 27, Sept. 6, 25, 1861; *Tribune,* July 8, 12, Sept. 14, 16, 23, Nov.-Dec., 1861, May 27, 1879; letter of H. J. Hastings; *Albany Evening Journal,* Aug. 24, Sept. 10, 21, 1861; Van Deusen, *Weed,* pp. 295-98; *Albany Atlas and Argus,* Sept. 23, 1861.

14. *Tribune,* June 5, 1862; Van Deusen, *Weed,* pp. 275-80.

15. Greeley Papers (N. Y. P. L.), Greeley to S. Wilkeson, Aug. 24, 1861; Conway, *op. cit.,* I, 331; *Tribune,* Aug.-Dec., 1861.

16. Nicolay and Hay, *Complete Works of Abraham Lincoln,* XI, 120-22, Lincoln to Walker, Nov. 21, 1861; J. R. Gilmore, *Personal Recollections of Abraham Lincoln and the Civil War* (Boston, 1898), pp. 39-64; Fahrney, *op. cit.,* pp. 92-95.

17. Lincoln Papers, Greeley to Lincoln, Jan. 6, 1862; Greeley Papers (N. Y. P. L.), Greeley to Colfax, Apr. 11, 1862; Seward Papers, Greeley to Seward, Dec. 27, 1861; *Independent,* Nov. 28, 1861 and Jan. 2, 1862, where Greeley takes the position that he urged upon Seward, and Jan. 16, 1862, where he criticizes Seward for not adopting this line.

18. Greeley Papers (N. Y. P. L.), Greeley to Colfax, Apr. 11, 1862; *Tribune,* Aug. 23, 25, 30, Sept. 26, 1861, Feb. 17, Mar. 24, Sept. 3, 8, 11, Oct. 22, 1862; Gilmore, *Recollections,* pp. 81-94. Lincoln's expansion of executive power gave Greeley no concern, *per se.* He was perfectly willing to see *dangerous* newspapers suppressed and the right of *habeas corpus* suspended where *dangerous* public enemies were involved.

19. Brockway, *op. cit.,* p. 157.

20. *Tribune*, Nov. 26, Dec., 1861, Jan., Feb. 11, 19, July 24, Oct. 18, Dec. 17, 1862; Greeley Papers (N. Y. P. L.), Greeley to Colfax, Nov. 16, 1862.

21. An excellent analysis of the Jacobins and their role is T. H. Williams, *Lincoln and the Radicals* (Univ. of Wisconsin Press, 1941).

22. *Tribune*, Sept. 22, 1855, Mar. 18, 1856; Greeley, "Christianity and Color," in Douglass' *Monthly*, Nov., 1860, p. 366. This attitude toward the New York State Negroes was perfectly in keeping with his attitude toward labor.

23. There can be no doubt that he was influenced toward this point of view by such abolitionist friends as Gerrit Smith and Abigail Gibbons.

24. Greeley Papers (Lib. of Cong.), Greeley to Brockway, Aug. 14, 1861; Gerrit Smith Papers, Greeley to Smith, Aug. 14, 1861; Conway, *op. cit.*, I, 336; *Tribune*, May 14, July 27, 30, 31, Aug. 4, 12, 21, 30, 1861.

25. *Tribune*, July 30, Sept. 2, 16-20, 1861. Greeley was sour over Frémont's dismissal in October 1861, and applauded his reinstatement in March 1862. He wanted to think that Frémont was the great military captain designed by God to lead the nation out of the Slough of Despond. In this, as well as in other ways, he was working in harmony with the Jacobins.—*Ibid.*, Oct. 21-30, Nov. 23, 1861; *Independent*, Dec. 12, 1861, Mar. 30, 1862; Williams, *op. cit.*, pp. 34-52.

26. *Tribune*, Oct. 2, 14, 17, 23, Nov. 1, 1861.

27. *Ibid.*, Dec. 6, 10, 11, 16, 23, 1861, Jan. 14, Apr. 22, 1862; *Independent*, Oct. 24, 1861, Oct. 2, 1862.

28. *Tribune*, Feb. 22, 1862, July 6, 1863; *Independent*, Jan. 23, Feb. 27, Mar. 6, May 22, June 19, 1862; Williams, *op. cit.*, pp. 77-88.

29. *Independent*, June 12, 1862; *Tribune*, Feb. 7, 1863.

30. *Ibid.*, Mar. 29, Apr. 3, 12, 14, 17, May 19, 20, June 19, July 19, 23, 26, 1862; *Independent*, Mar. 13, Apr. 17, 24, 1862; Fahrney, *op. cit.*, pp. 125-26; Williams, *op. cit.*, pp. 158-172.

31. *Independent*, May 22, June 5, July 10, 17, Aug. 21, 1862.

32. *Tribune*, June-Aug., 1862.

33. *Independent*, Sept. 18, 1862; Greeley Papers (Lib. of Cong.), Greeley to G. M. Wright, Aug. 27, 1862; Fahrney, *op. cit.*, pp. 127-29; Williams, *op. cit.*, pp. 172-73; Benton, *Greeley on Lincoln*, pp. 61-64.

34. *Tribune*, Sept. 23, 24, 27, 1862; *Independent*, Sept. 25, Oct. 2, 1862.

35. Greeley, "National Unity," "Southern Hate of the North," "Aurora," and "Obstacles to Peace," in *Continental Monthly*, II (Sept.-Dec., 1862), 357-60, 448-51, 622-25, 714-17. In the last of these articles, Greeley asserted that nationalist sentiment was so strong that successful secession would mean the reuniting of the sections under the Confederate flag, and thus the establishment of a slave empire ruled by some master spirit of the slaveholding oligarchy.

36. *Tribune*, Dec. 6, 8, 1862; Lincoln Papers, Greeley to Lincoln, Dec. 12, 1862; *Independent*, Dec. 14, 1862. In this last, he says the war may be concluded within four weeks.

37. Gurowski Papers, Greeley to Count Adam Gurowski, Sept. 25, 1861; *Tribune*, Dec. 4, 1862; Ingersoll Papers, Greeley to Mrs. Ingersoll, Nov. 26, 1862.

38. No reason can be assigned for Dana's dismissal that appears at all satisfactory, outside of personality clashes that became more frequent with the stresses engendered by the war. Greeley denied categorically, some five years later, that Dana had suppressed any of Greeley's own articles.

This had been an alleged cause of Dana's dismissal. Greeley declared that Dana left the paper "for reasons satisfactory to himself, and with which the public has no concern." This might be taken to rule out divergence of policy as a cause of dismissal, a point of view that is also indicated by Greeley's adding that they had not differed substantially in their views on slavery—Greeley Papers (N. Y. P. L.), Greeley to Colfax, Jan. 30, 1862; Greeley, *Political Economy*, pp. 214-16; *Tribune*, Apr. 10, 1862; Gilmore, *op. cit.*, p. 81; Wilson, *Dana*, pp. 169-72; Fahrney, *op. cit.*, p. 88, note.

39. *Tribune*, June 11, 1862; Greeley Papers (N. Y. P. L.), Greeley to Colfax, Jan. 30, 1862. Greeley had applauded the Morrill tariff of 1861, regardless of the danger of its alienating England and France, a danger that Weed had seen and deplored.

40. *Tribune*, Feb. 1, May 7, 9, 21, 1862. Cf. P. Gates, "The Homestead Act in an Incongruous Land System," *American Historical Review*, XLI (1936), 656ff. Greeley was also enthusiastic about the Morrill Agricultural College Act, a much better measure.—*Tribune*, June 21, 1862.

41. Wadsworth Papers, Wadsworth to D.D. Field, Sept. 14, 1862; *Albany Evening Journal*, Oct. 25, 1862 (quoting *Albany Atlas and Argus*), and Nov. 8, 1862; Welles, *Diary*, I, 154, Sept. 27, 1862; S. D. Brummer, *Political History of New York State* (N. Y., 1911), pp. 218-26. The state committee was also reorganized with an anti-Weed majority, and a little later the party headquarters were moved from Albany to New York. These were all damaging blows to Weed's political power.

42. *Tribune*, Oct. 30, 1862.

43. Smith Papers, Greeley to Smith, Oct. 21, 1862; *Tribune*, Sept.-Nov., Dec. 12, 1862; *Albany Evening Journal*, Dec. 9, 1862. Greeley's charge that Weed knifed the ticket cannot be substantiated. See Van Deusen, *Weed*, p. 302. In 1865, Greeley declared that he had had no ambitions for office during the war (*Tribune*, Aug. 24, 1865), but see his editorial in the *Tribune*, Dec. 12, 1862, in response to an attack by Weed.

44. *Tribune*, Dec. 5, 1862.

45. Benton, *Greeley on Lincoln*, p. 64; *Tribune*, Apr. 11, Sept. 8, 11, Oct. 25, Nov. 5, 6, 10, Dec. 17, 22, 1862, Jan. 10, 1863, Aug. 6, 1870; Lincoln Papers, Greeley to Lincoln, Nov. 24, Dec. 12, 1862; Greeley Papers (N. Y. P. L.), Greeley to Colfax, Nov. 16, 20, 1862; Gurowski, Diary, II, 47; *Independent*, Oct. 30, 1862.

46. *Ibid.*, Dec. 25, 1862.

47. He had suggested this possibility in the *Independent*, July 10, 1862.

CHAPTER 20

Storm-Tossed

D URING THE EARLY MONTHS OF 1863, GREELEY remained in working harmony with the radicals. Like them, he was hostile to Seward, denounced McClellan and expressed skepticism as to Lincoln's effectiveness as a war leader. He also joined them in an unavailing search for a successor to Lincoln in 1864. Greeley's alliance with Wade, Chandler and their ilk seemed well cemented.[1]

These activities of the *Tribune's* editor were undertaken in the name of an effective prosecution of the war and the destruction of slavery. At the same time, in what looked like a complete contradiction, Greeley was exploring the possibilities of a negotiated peace that, as he freely admitted, might result in giving up the whole project of emancipation.

At the close of 1862, Greeley declared in the *Tribune* that the North had always been ready for a peace that would restore "the Union as it was," without any new concessions or guarantees to slavery. This was followed by a series of suggestions to the effect that foreign mediation was always proper. If offered, it should be met "in a conciliatory spirit." France and England were too hostile to the Union to make good mediators, but the little republic of Switzerland, a pure and disinterested state, would be completely satisfactory.[2]

While these peace soundings were being thrown out in the *Tribune,* Greeley began corresponding with the Ohio Copperhead, Clement L. Vallandigham and with another peace advocate, William Cornell (Colorado) Jewett, who had just returned from Europe on fire with the idea of mediation by Napoleon III. Vallandigham and Jewett were asked to ascertain through their contacts with the Confederacy whether or not there was any rebel disposition toward such a peace as the Union could grant, or any disposition toward arbitration or mediation by a foreign power.[3]

The peace feelers that Greeley put out through Vallandigham and Jewett had no apparent effect upon the Confederates, but Greeley's hopes of mediation were kept alive by a statement that emanated from the French ministry in Washington. M. Mercier, the French minister, declared that Napoleon III had no designs or purposes adverse to the restoration of the Union.

Greeley had entertained the deepest suspicions of the French Emperor. He had reacted violently when the French invasion of Mexico had taken place in the spring of 1862 and, only a few weeks before Mercier's statement appeared, had warned that "this country has but one substantive enemy in Europe, and that is Louis Napoleon."[4]

But Union defeats, the attitude of Jewett toward French intervention, and Mercier's assurances had changed Greeley's mind about French intentions. He approached the French minister on the subject of mediation, stipulating that any such effort should not hazard the Union (a stipulation that Mercier privately labeled "all bosh"), and the *Tribune* began championing French arbitration of the quarrel between North and South.[5]

This project for French intervention came to nothing, as had the peace soundings through Jewett and Vallandigham, but for months the possibility of bringing the war to an end through some kind of foreign mediation was dangled before the *Tribune's* readers. They were also told that it was "almost impossible to make a good War or a bad Peace" and that, if an all-out Union effort could not make a serious impression on the South in three months' time, the country should make "the best available peace." That such a settlement might well mean the retention of slavery as an American institution was clearly accepted by the *Tribune's* editor. If necessary, he declared repeatedly, the Emancipation Proclamation could be set aside and they could all go back to the Union as it was.[6] The effect of such statements upon northern morale must have been considerable.

Greeley came under heavy fire because of these peace moves. Some of his associates on the *Tribune* were highly critical. Hostile journalists like Raymond and Weed wrote him off as a defeatist. Theodore Tilton of the *Independent,* angered by his friend's willingness to back down from emancipation, wrote in quiet scorn, "It seems that the editorial opinions of the *Tribune,* like Newtown pippins, are sounder in the fall than in the spring." Seward privately heaped ridicule on the idea of intervention by a ramshackle Swiss republic whose Consul-General at Washington kept a flour and feed store near the capitol and knew no more about American history than he did about the politics of the moon. The secretary of state declared that Greeley's efforts toward mediation not only ran counter to government policy but also made him liable to legal penalties for trespassing upon State Department prerogatives. Greeley heard that his former partner was threatening him with Fort Lafayette.[7]

There can be no doubt that these peace moves by Greeley were in part the result of a war psychosis. "I never could appreciate shells unless they were oyster, with the meat still in them," he said toward the close of his life. He was particularly war-weary in the winter and spring of 1863 and his mind was full of morbid imaginings. "I believe," he wrote to Chase in January of that year, "we are on the very brink of a financial collapse and a Copperhead revolution, and that we must have crushing victories or a ruinous peace very soon."[8] The succession of Union defeats the previous year had blackened his outlook, and the Confederate victory at Chancellorsville in early May of 1863 was like Ossa upon Pelion. James R. Gilmore saw his chief come into editor Gay's private room at the *Tribune* office, carrying the latest telegram about the Chancellorsville battle, his face pallid and his step almost tottering as he exclaimed: "My God! it is horrible—horrible; and to think of it, 130,000 magnificent soldiers so cut to pieces by less than 60,000 half-starved ragamuffins!"[9] When in such an abyss of black despondency, Greeley would be willing to see the war end on almost any terms. Then the clouds would lift and he would again become hopeful of a Union victory.

This succession of moods involved Greeley in a maze of inconsistencies and contradictions. Now he would blow hot, now cold, toward Lincoln's administration; now he would remark that a good war was almost impossible, then urge the importance of an all-out military effort that should destroy the South's will to resist. He declared that he was all for propositions looking toward peace otherwise than by new concessions to slavery, and then under Raymond's prodding took it back two days later. His readers, after becoming accustomed to the *Tribune's* emphasis upon the importance of the Union, would suddenly find its senior editor declaring that disunion was far from being the worst of alternatives.[10] Once again, just as in the critical period before the outbreak of hostilities, it was difficult to tell what Greeley really wanted. Indeed, there were times when it seemed that the *Tribune's* editor himself saw through a glass darkly in his own search for his own objectives.

But Greeley's peace campaign of 1863 was more than the vagary of a troubled mind. To some extent inspired by sheer defeatism, it was also rooted in his analysis of the political situation in 1863.

As Greeley surveyed the political scene during the gloomy winter of 1863, a growing menace appeared on his horizon. The northern Democratic party, emboldened by the political successes of the preceding November and by the military stalemate, was engaged in a swelling crusade for a negotiated peace, a peace without victory.[11] The prospect of such a conclusion of the war aroused all of Greeley's old-time fears regarding Democratic policies and policy makers. The Democrats fostered dismemberment, he declared, by the encouragement their attitude gave the South. Their publications were lowering the morale of the army. They were using the Emancipation Proclamation to divide the North. If they continued to be politically victorious, they would make disgraceful and dangerous concessions to the Slave Power for the sake of peace, concessions that would bind the nation to the footstool of slavery for years to come and would blight his own vision of national felicity based upon Republican principles. Peace without victory, even a disunion peace, with the Republicans still in the ascendant at Washington was conceivable as a part of God's plan. A Democratic peace, on the other hand, had no odor of sanctity about it, and must at all costs be prevented.

It was primarily to checkmate the Peace Democracy that Greeley unleashed his peace offensive. By moves toward negotiation and foreign intervention, he tried to deprive that gentry of their attempted monopoly of peaceful intent. By manifesting a willingness to give up the Emancipation Proclamation, he sought to stop the Democratic drift that had developed in some quarters of the Union as a consequence of the freedom policy. At the same time, by insisting that the initiative in opening formal peace negotiations should come from the South, he was attempting to throw the onus for continuation of hostilities upon the Confederacy and its sympathizers.[12] It was "of vital consequence," he declared in the *Tribune*, "to convince loyal Democrats, ready to fight for the Union but not for Emancipation, that the war is waged on our side exactly and truly on their ground and for the ends they approve." If those Democrats would fight on with the Republicans, so would he, even though enormous exertions would be necessary to save the Union and kill the institution of slavery.[13] This was in fair accord with Lincoln's views.

Despite Greeley's talk of enormous exertions in Union-saving, his first reaction to Lee's invasion of the North in the summer of 1863 was of none too heroic a character. To be sure, he hoped for a Union victory over the invading forces, one that would bring with it the end of the war, but he also declared that, if the rebels beat Grant before Vicksburg and watered their horses in the Delaware, "we shall be under foot and may as well own it." Raymond rebuked this pusillanimity, declaring that the North must fight to the end. This elicited a sour *Tribune* editorial entitled "Last Ditch Heroics," which started out by flaying Raymond for being bombastic and ended with the perhaps true explanation that Greeley's real point had been the necessity of beating Lee in Pennsylvania. An article written for the *Independent* shortly after this exchange had a bolder spirit. "Let the invading host of the men-stealers come on," exclaimed Greeley. The freedom-loving North would know how to meet them.[14]

Gettysburg was like a tonic to Greeley, and the fall of Vicksburg, which came at the same time, gave an additional boost to his morale. He admitted, somewhat apologetically, that national affairs now wore a brighter aspect. From now on, he implied, the administration could count upon better support from the *Tribune*.[15] And, indeed, for the remainder of the year, heckling and black defeatism were conspicuous by their absence from the editorial columns of the North's most powerful newspaper.

As the fortunes of war were putting Greeley in a better mood, the draft riots flamed up in New York. The *Tribune's* office was one center of the mob's attention. The riots gave Greeley an opportunity to display his physical courage and to indulge his propensity for journalistic exaggeration and partisan spleen.

The conscription act of March 3, 1863, applied, with certain exemptions, to all able-bodied males between twenty and forty-five years of age. Among the exemptions was one which constituted a large loophole of escape for those who were not anxious to serve their country on the field of battle. Any draftee could obtain release from military service by providing a substitute or by paying $300 into the federal treasury.

Greeley had defended both the draft and the exemption policy as right and proper.[16] He was thus closely identified with a measure which, as the time drew near for its application, produced much discontent among New York City's working class.

The draft drawings started in New York on Saturday, July 11. Two days later, rioting began in various parts of the city and for four days mobs roamed about, looting, burning, and killing in utter disregard of appeals for order made by Mayor Opdyke and Governor Seymour. Much property was destroyed and hundreds of lives were lost before soldiers from the regular army and a suspension of the drafting quieted the rioters.[17]

Negroes and abolitionists were the principal objects of the mob's vengeance as it moved howling and yelling through the streets. The *Tribune's* editor also came in for a full share of execration. Again and again, high above the tumult, shouts of "We'll hang Horace Greeley to a sour apple tree" roared through City Hall Park and its environs. "They must have burst their throats bawling at me," Greeley wrote to a friend.[18]

Two attacks were made on the *Tribune* office. The first gained access to the counting room on the main floor, where the rioters smashed furniture and started firing papers before they were driven out by the police. The second was broken up before gaining entrance to the building. Meanwhile the inmates had been armed, preparations had been made to scald invaders with live steam and the staff was girded for a generally desperate defense.[19]

After the riots were over, reports circulated persistently that in the midst of the alarums and excursions Greeley had shown the white feather. His critics declared that he had fled in panic to Windust's restaurant in Park Row and had there hidden under a table. Some of the more unkind suggested that, looking for more effective concealment, he had crawled into a large refrigerator.

These stories of Greeley's cowardice were malicious falsehoods. He was perfectly aware of the threats that were made against his life. These threats were so notorious that, on one occasion, a hackman refused to drive him to the *Tribune* building lest they be attacked. But during the days of rioting he was in and out of the office as usual, going about the business of editing with admirable composure and turning a deaf ear to the advice of his associates that he seek safety in flight.

Greeley's fortitude on this occasion was paralleled by that of his eccentric spouse, who stood at Chappaqua prepared for all contingencies. Molly Greeley placed a keg of gunpowder in the cellar of the house in the woods, with a train leading out into a nearby glade. Her plan was to escape through a window as the rioters came in at the door, touch a match to the train and blow house and mob sky high. But the mob did not appear and this heroic preparation went for naught.[20]

Greeley's bravery in time of danger was highly creditable. Not so creditable was his analysis of the riots and of Governor Seymour's attitude toward them. The *Tribune's* editor portrayed the rioters as simply the northern wing of the rebellion. Again he defended the draft bill, calling the $300 exemption an excellent provision that would weed out poor soldiers and at the same time furbish the national treasury. Seymour was mercilessly attacked. The governor, though sometimes ultra partisan in his squabbles with the national administration, was a thoroughly loyal man, but Greeley's caricature made him practically indistinguishable from a traitor. On the flimsiest of evidence, Greeley asserted that Seymour had made a "loving speech" to the rioters, addressing them as "My Friends." Seymour had justly attacked the $300 exemption as matching "the rich man's dollar with the poor man's life," but Greeley distorted this into a Machiavellian effort to prevent army reinforcements. By this action, Greeley argued, Seymour was trying to force a conclusion of the war that would restore the Peace Democrats and their southern allies to power. Thus, as was so frequently the case, Greeley prostituted truth to the purposes of political propaganda.[21]

The riots brought only a momentary flagging of spirits to the *Tribune's* editor, so far as the war was concerned. He speedily regained his equanimity. The victories in the field had proved a lasting tonic, and the *Tribune's* improved situation was another spur to happiness and content. The paper, which had little more than made ends meet in 1861 and 1862, was now showing a reasonable profit. The political skies also had a rosier hue, and Republican victories in the state elections that fall were happy auguries for the national future. The *Tribune* declared that the people had spoken. They were demanding that the rebellion be crushed and the unity of the republic restored. The only way to achieve peace, Greeley now declared, was by energetic and successful war. The pugnacious editor even had good words for the administration at Washington. He besought the people to trust in the government and not to embarrass it by weakening demonstrations against it or its members. Fault-finding was the "cheap resource of the factious." Lincoln had really made very few mistakes. Had all his orders been carried out effectively, the war would now be over.[22]

Greeley's attitude toward the administration at Washington was viewed by the Congressional Jacobins with profound distaste. This gentry was already revolving plans for a South made Republican through Negro suffrage,[23] a project for which they were finding scant sympathy at the White House. Greeley had accounted himself one of their number, but now what looked like a rapprochement was developing between the *Tribune* and the White House. It seemed as though no one could count upon Greeley's support for any length of time. What did these butterfly gyrations mean? When, if ever, would they cease? No one, not even Greeley himself, had the answer to these conundrums.

It is possible that Greeley's seeming shift in attitude toward the national administration was to some extent due to a diversion of interest. Shortly after the July riots of 1863, he was asked by a firm of Hartford publishers to write a history of the rebellion. He hesitated, for it was a tremendous task, but it was not in his nature to refuse such a challenge. Work on *The American Conflict* began August 31, 1863. It occupied Greeley daily from ten in the morning until five in the afternoon, on into the spring of 1864. The manuscript of the 600-page first volume was finished, obviously by design, on the twenty-third birthday of the *Tribune*, April 10, 1864. But this had meant efforts that were positively herculean. Plagued by interruptions, digging up his information even as he wrote, sticking stubbornly to his editorial duties on the *Tribune* and writing for the *Independent* as well, Greeley had never spent a harder eight months than those that stretched from the fall of 1863 to the spring of 1864.[24]

That Greeley's tendency toward rapprochement with Lincoln's administration continued into the spring of 1864 was strikingly manifested by his attitude toward Seward's Mexican policy. This was a policy which combined obvious distaste for Napoleon's venture with masterly inaction. Seward felt that the government was too much occupied at home to go jousting into foreign fields. The Jacobins, however, attacking the administration at every possible point, waxed very critical of Seward's failure to take a stiff attitude toward France. Henry Winter Davis shepherded through the House of Representatives a unanimous but most undiplomatic expression of disapproval of French Mexican policy; Wade, Chandler and other Senate Radicals were all for a strong stand against Napoleon. They actually argued, Senator James Dixon of Connecticut wrote to Greeley, that war with France would strengthen the North.

Greeley would have nothing to do with this Radical attack upon the administration. A ringing editorial in the *Tribune* in May, 1864, strongly approved Seward's Mexican policy. He knew, said Greeley, that he might render Lincoln's renomination less expedient by joining in the clamor against the Secretary of State, but he would not do it. None loathed the Maximilian regime more than he, but he recognized that, for the time being, we were powerless to act against it. The paramount consideration now was "the overthrow of that deadly treason which threatens our National life." Nothing would suit the South better than for the North to become involved in war with France.[25]

It would have been a mercy to everyone concerned if Greeley's complacence with the administration and his zeal for the war could

have continued until Lee's surrender. Fate would not have it so.
In fact, his attitude toward both Lincoln and the war began to
cool while he was still deep in writing the first volume of the
Conflict. The trouble was that the war showed no sign of ending,
while the national debt continued to mount at a rate which, to the
Tribune's editor seemed positively astronomical. Once again,
Greeley began to long for peace negotiations; once more his dissatisfaction with Lincoln, never very far beneath the surface, boiled
up into view; once more he became convinced that the South would
gladly sheathe the sword, if only it were properly approached.

Immediate peace and the restoration of trade were the remedies
for the nation's ills, Greeley told United States Senator-elect Edwin
D. Morgan on January 8, 1864, in an anxious, fervid letter. His
conditions for peace were simple. There should be a complete end
of slavery, a $300,000,000 indemnification in greenbacks or five-
twenty national bonds for losses of loyal slaveholders by emancipation, and "an act of oblivion" for all political offenses to date, with
each state coming back at once into the Union. "Governor,"
exclaimed Greeley, "we could have peace on these terms (substantially) tomorrow, if we had men of real capacity at the head
of affairs. Or rather, I should conclude that we have not such men
if nothing is effected."[26]

Several years later, when the battle flags had begun to gather
dust and he could write with the advantage of hindsight, Greeley
could see "that the one providential leader, the indispensable hero
of the great drama—was Abraham Lincoln." Granted that this was
an honest judgment, rather than an obeisance before the bar of
history, it is at least deplorable that this perception was so steadily
withheld from the *Tribune's* editor during the life of the Great
Emancipator. As had been earlier the case, the winter of 1863-64
found Greeley morosely contemplating what he deemed the President's lack of capacity, and looking desperately about for a new
leader. Lincoln had made "fearful mistakes," the worst of all being
his exemption of Tennessee and parts of Louisiana and Virginia
from the Emancipation Act. This error, in Greeley's opinion, was
prolonging the rebellion in horrible fashion, especially in Tennessee. Greeley wrote off the President as one who simply failed to
comprehend that the rebellion was slavery and slavery was the
rebellion. The Gettysburg Address, that November, received only
passing notice in the *Tribune*. The cloud of prejudice that distorted Greeley's vision where the President was concerned prevented
his seeing the simple grandeur of those homely words.[27] How could
such a mediocrity as Lincoln have anything important to say on

such an occasion or, indeed, on any occasion? The only thing to do was to wait patiently until his term of office was over.

Who should replace this "less than great" man whose presence in the White House was, in Greeley's opinion, a detriment to the national welfare? Greeley did not know. All that he did know was that he wanted Lincoln discarded as the party's leader. Like the Congressional Jacobins, he wanted to find a man big enough and popular enough to push Old Abe into a back seat in the Republican car.

Greeley's first love for 1864 was General William S. Rosecrans, but Rosecrans was removed from the list of possibilities by the failure of his Tennessee campaign. As the general's star faded, Greeley's thoughts turned toward Secretary of the Treasury Salmon P. Chase, whose New York appointments had been pleasing to the *Tribune's* editor and who was "sound on the goose" in regard to the abolition of slavery.

The Salmon, as one contemporary put it, was a wary fish, often pretending indifference to the lure, only to turn and snap it up with surprising dash. Certain it is that this particular Salmon was more than willing to swallow presidential bait. As Godkin observed, other men desired the Presidency but Chase positively lusted after it. He was not a strong candidate. His passion was too patent, and he had turned his political coat too many times during the past twenty years to have a powerful appeal for the voters. But a Chase boom of sorts got under way that winter, and Greeley lent it support. Its high point came with the issuance of the Pomeroy Circular.

On February 24, 1864, Senator Pomeroy of Kansas, Chase's manager, issued a broadside which declared that it would be impossible to reelect President Lincoln, and pointed to the secretary of the treasury as the great white hope of the party. The day before this unblushing effusion appeared, Greeley had come out in the open against Lincoln's renomination.

Lincoln, explained the *Tribune's* editor, was "not one of those rare, great men who mold their age into the similitude of their own high character, massive abilities and lofty aims." To be sure, when one considered the President's antecedents, his previous experience in public affairs, and the difficulties of his position, it would have to be admitted that he had done well. It was also a fact that he was the choice of a large majority of the loyal Unionists, but these honest folk had not had time to think the matter through. Lincoln just wasn't the strongest possible candidate, and Greeley appealed to political history as proof of the necessity for subordinating personal preference to availability. It was also a fact, he added, that Presidents should not be reëlected, save under pressure of extraordinary circumstances. Such, Greeley implied, were not the circumstances of 1864.[28]

This extraordinary anti-Lincoln pronouncement suggested Chase, Frémont, Butler, and Grant, in that order, as possible alternatives to the President. It was followed by various and sundry pro-Chase hints and suggestions, but not for long. The Pomeroy Circular, an obvious attempt to undercut Lincoln by a member of his official family, boomeranged in unmistakable fashion. Greeley's interest in Chase took a sudden slump, and he advised the Ohioan to announce that he was not a candidate.[29] The Salmon had made his rush, but the bait had been snatched out of the water.

The collapse of the Chase boom did not reconcile Greeley to Lincoln. The *Tribune's* editor was avowedly looking for a candidate who would not have what he now described as Lincoln's "drifting policy" toward slavery (it was all right for Greeley to veer and twist on slavery, but not for the President to 'drift' on the same subject). The *Tribune* was strong for delaying the national convention until July or August, a move designed to discourage early commitments to a second term, and Greeley encouraged a movement for John C. Frémont, the second idol of the Jacobins.

Frémont was indeed nominated by a convention of some four hundred disaffected Republican radicals who met at Cleveland on May 31, 1864, and signalized their political naïveté by nominating another New Yorker, John Cochrane, for second place on the ticket. But by that time it was obvious that nothing could prevent the President's renomination, and the *Tribune* beat no drum for the Pathmarker of the West.[30]

On June 8, 1864, Lincoln was renominated at Baltimore, to the *Tribune's* very small joy. Greeley was gloomy, and his gloom was no whit relieved by the nomination of Andrew Johnson for Vice President. The *Tribune's* editor would have preferred a Republican, rather than a War Democrat, for second place on the ticket. Once again, and for the second time during Lincoln's term of office, he found himself in harmony with Thurlow Weed. Both men looked for a Republican defeat in November.[31]

It seemed to Greeley that there was abundant reason for despair. Grant had lost 55,000 men in the Wilderness campaign that spring, and even so had failed to take the Confederate capital. The nation's credit was declining as the premium on gold advanced, with the greenbacks becoming more and more obviously an inflationary element in the currency. Then, at the end of June 1864, came Chase's departure from the Treasury, and Greeley wrote mourn-

fully of the retirement of "one of the very few great men left in
public life."[32] If ever there was a Knight of the Dismal Countenance,
it was the *Tribune's* editor in the summer of 1864. And his gloom
was scarcely lessened by the abrupt tone of Nicolay's letters demanding correction by the *Tribune* of its false reports about Cabinet
and other proceedings at Washington.[33]

The Republican convention, Greeley told Senator Morgan, had
probably put the country a long way on the road to permanent
disunion. He characterized Raymond, who had been chairman of
the platform committee in that body, as belonging to the party
of eternal war. "Fierce, uncompromising resolves and a weak
Executive," said the desponding editor, "are two stages on the road
to ruin." But he added, "I would do nothing toward Peace save on
consultation with our strong and discreet friends." A few days later,
he wrote again to the Senator in a mood of deepening despair. The
Baltimore platform had put the North in an intolerable position,
one of repelling all proffers of conciliation and insisting on uncon-
ditional surrender. New York was "a Rebel Volcano which rumbles
ominously and does not sleep. A draft, a defeat, anything unusual,
may see us in flames and drowned in blood." Couldn't Morgan
obtain from the government, asked Greeley, some sort of proclamation to the effect that the North was anxious for peace "on any
terms consistent with the integrity and lasting security of the
Republic? I think such a Proclamation, wisely made, would help
our Finances, lighten Grant's task, and disintegrate the Rebel
forces. We cannot safely postpone it."[34]

Four days previous to writing thus dolefully to Morgan, Greeley
had declared in the *Tribune* that negotiations for peace would not
be in order until one side or the other had been "beaten into a
willingness to concede the vital matter in dispute." Then, without
any such bludgeoning having taken place, it suddenly appeared to
him that his indispensable condition for such negotiations had been
met. News which he promptly credited as reliable came that several
"distinguished Confederates," just across the Canadian border at
Niagara Falls, were telling leading Democrats who "flocked" over
the river (as Greeley put it) to confer with them that peace might
be had on the basis of reconstituting the Union.[35]

The "Distinguished Confederates" of whom Greeley had heard
were Clement C. Clay of Alabama, Professor James P. Holcombe
of Virginia and Jacob ("Jake") Thompson of Mississippi, men who
had been liberally supplied with funds and instructed by the Confederate government to encourage the machinations of the Peace
Democrats, foster a western confederacy, and sabotage the northern

war effort. Hovering near this gentry was a curious pair of free lance negotiators, George N. Sanders of Kentucky and "Colorado" Jewett, the latter being the same fantastic character with whom Greeley had corresponded a year and half before in regard to foreign mediation. It was Sanders who relayed to Greeley the gladsome tidings that peace was in the air.[36]

Greeley wrote to Jewett, requesting further information. Jewett replied that "Two ambassadors of Davis & Co." were in Canada, "with full and complete powers for a peace." Jewett quoted Sanders as urging Greeley to come to the Falls for a meeting with the Confederates, and averring that "The whole matter can be consummated by me, you, them and President Lincoln." This was speedily followed by a telegram—"Will you come here? Parties have full power."[37]

Greeley had on occasion referred to Sanders with disdain,[38] but he had also taken him seriously when it suited his purpose. Now he sent Jewett's communications on to Lincoln, together with a supporting letter that displayed his own lugubrious frame of mind.

The Confederates were anxious for peace, said Greeley, and "our bleeding, bankrupt, almost dying country also longs for peace." He urged submission of "overtures for pacification," and proposed a plan of his own that included complete amnesty and a liberal indemnity for the abolition of slavery. Greeley went on to say that he feared Lincoln did not realize how much the country wanted the war to end. A frank statement of terms might prevent a northern insurrection. At least it was desirable to learn what the South had to offer, and he urged inviting the men at Niagara Falls "to exhibit their credentials and submit their ultimatum."[39]

Lincoln replied that Greeley should go directly to the Falls. If any Confederate emissary or emissaries could be found there, empowered to offer the restoration of the Union and the abandonment of slavery in return for peace, they would be given safe conduct so that Greeley could bring such person or persons to see the President.[40]

Upon receiving Lincoln's reply, Greeley began to hedge, offering a variety of lame excuses by means of which he sought to evade the role of actual participant in the negotiations. But Lincoln held him strictly to book. On July 15, the President informed the squirming editor that he was expected to produce a negotiator or negotiators in the flesh. "I not only intend a sincere effort for peace," wrote Lincoln, "But I intend that you shall be a personal witness that it is made."[41] This last missive was delivered by Major John Hay on the morning of July 16. Greeley still hemmed and hawed but finally, on his being furnished with a safe conduct for the southern emissaries, he set out for the Falls.

Having arrived at the International Hotel on the American side of the border, Greeley sent word to the Confederates that he had a safe conduct for them if they were duly accredited and had propositions for peace. This blanket statement made no mention of the conditions for peace that Lincoln had declared must be accepted as the basis of any negotiation.

The saboteurs, somewhat astonished to find themselves thus catapulted into the character of peace negotiators, replied that they were not accredited, but could obtain credentials if given a safe conduct to Richmond. Greeley forwarded this news to President Lincoln.

Upon receiving this message from Greeley, Lincoln wrote a letter, July 18, 1864, addressed TO WHOM IT MAY CONCERN. This stated that safe conduct for the bearers and liberal terms on related points would meet any proposition that included restoration of peace, the integrity of the whole Union and the abandonment of slavery. Hay arrived at the International House with this explicit statement on July 20, and the two men crossed over to the Clifton House on the other side of the river that they might present Lincoln's conditions to the southerners.

On their arrival at the Clifton House they met Sanders at the door, and soon found themselves surrounded by a crowd of curious men and (Hay noticed appreciatively) wide-eyed, pretty women. Sanders, "A seedy-looking Rebel, with grizzled whiskers and a flavor of old clo'" according to the Major, took them up to Holcombe's room, where that "Tall, solemn, spare, false-looking man, with false teeth, false eyes, and false hair," was having tea and toast. Clay was absent, but Holcombe received the message and promised a reply. There was some desultory conversation. Then they said good-by, Greeley remarking that he hoped to see Holcombe again; that he expected to be blackguarded for what he had done, since he was not allowed to explain it; but that all he had done had been done under instructions.

Greeley's attitude at the Clifton House had been querulous, to say the least, but on his way back to the American side he recovered his spirits and Hay found him quite agreeable.[42] That same day, Greeley had an interview with Jewett, who was instructed to receive any communications that might be made by the Confederates. The Tribune's editor thereupon shook the mist of Niagara off his shoulders and made his way posthaste back to New York.

The Confederates, having been told one thing by Greeley and another by Lincoln's letter, made the most of their opportunity.

They penned a flamboyant statement which accused Lincoln of going back on his word, and blamed him for the continued infliction of misery and calamity upon the country. Jewett promptly released this to the press.[43] So ended the peace parley of 1864 at Niagara Falls, but out of it arose a notable controversy.

Greeley took a public position in regard to the negotiation that substantially bore out the charges of deceit leveled against Lincoln by the Confederates. The *Tribune's* editor was thereupon castigated by Bryant and Raymond, with Bennett taking delighted digs at "poor Greeley," that "nincompoop without genius," who was lower than "Colorado" Jewett. Stung into mad unreason by this torment, Greeley backed and filled, now declaring that Lincoln's peace terms had been "just right," two days later criticizing Lincoln for not going on with the negotiations regardless of his preliminary conditions. As to whether he, himself, regarded the abolition of slavery as prerequisite to peace, Greeley hedged, explained and tergiversated until no one could tell where he did stand.[44]

Raymond demanded that all the correspondence leading up to the Niagara Falls conference be published. This would have exposed the fact that Greeley had not informed the Confederates of Lincoln's peace terms at their first interview. But the challenge had to be met, and on August 5 Greeley, in a *Tribune* editorial, agreed to publication. Lincoln also was willing, on the condition that certain defeatist passages in Greeley's letters were deleted. He urged Greeley to come and see him. This Greeley declined to do, alleging that Lincoln was surrounded by his (Greeley's) bitterest enemies. He also refused to permit the President to delete such passages as his lament about "our bleeding, bankrupt, almost dying country," and so the correspondence went unpublished in its entirety.

While the *Tribune's* editor was taking an intransigeant position in regard to the deletion of passages from the Niagara Falls correspondence, he was bombarding the White House with criticism, complaint and lament about the lost opportunity for peace. He urged the President to invite proposals for peace and, if peace could not be made, to agree to an armistice for one year, with the rebel ports opened and a national conference summoned to settle differences and end the war.[45] This, of course, would have been tantamount to giving a new lease of life to the Confederacy.

Throughout this whole peace negotiation, Greeley's conduct had been that of a deeply dispirited and discouraged man. Apparently he felt that Lee was unconquerable, Richmond impregnable. A Democratic victory at the polls, followed by a Democratic peace, seemed inevitable to him. Such developments, he believed, would spell ruin to national progress. Far better to make the best peace possible under Republican auspices.[46] Such was the mournful reasoning that motivated his actions in the summer of 1864.

But while such motivations help to explain Greeley's actions, they do not suffice to excuse them. Irritable, suspicious, slippery, he pursued a course that was marked by confusion and evasion, if not by outright deceit. His attitude toward Lincoln, his failure to present the President's conditions for peace at the first Niagara interview, his conduct of the subsequent newspaper controversy, all placed him in an unfortunate light. This was Greeley at his worst, and at his worst he was a petty, narrow-minded, mean-spirited man.

Nothing positive for the Union resulted from Greeley's peace efforts in the summer of 1864. On the contrary, such influence as they exerted was harmful. The Confederate commissioners believed that their correspondence with him had nerved the South to new efforts, and had divided, perhaps dispirited, the North.[47] More than one Republican politician saw in this "fiasco," as Charles Francis Adams, Jr., called it, reasons for alarm over the prospects for Lincoln's reëlection. The President himself refrained from public condemnation of the *Tribune's* editor, but in private he made his opinion unmistakably plain. Greeley's usefulness to the North, said Mr. Lincoln, was at an end. He was like an old shoe, good for nothing because its stitches would not hold. "He is not truthful," said the President. "The stitches all tear out." Gideon Welles, more than once castigated in the *Tribune* for supposedly inefficient conduct of the Navy Department, zestfully recorded these remarks of the President in his diary.[48]

Just before the Niagara Falls episode, the acidulous Count Gurowski had penned a revealing comment on Greeley in his diary. Greeley, said the Count, was useful to society only in peace times. War upset his morale and confused his intellectual capacities and judgment, while lack of attention by those in power hurt his feelings and set a-bleeding "his very, very mighty amour-propre."

The critical character of this comment may have derived in part from the fact that its author had borrowed money from Greeley and had, on occasion, been dunned for the debt, but it did show discernment. Indeed, in this particular instance, the Count qualified as a nineteenth century Lord Root of the Matter.[49]

While Greeley was dabbling in peace overtures, the presidential campaign of 1864 was getting under way without much help from the *Tribune*. Greeley made it clear at the beginning of the canvass that he wanted to be counted among the regulars, but throughout the summer he showed little or no positive interest in the political situation. A prey to gloomy forebodings, he envisioned a Democratic victory, followed by a reconstruction that would surrender the whole country to the Slave Power. Under such a dispensation, he considered it likely that conspicuous opponents of slavery like himself would be driven into exile. "A long, black night settles down on our blood-stained country," he wrote melodramatically to an English friend.[50]

It was in this despairing mood that Greeley began lending support to a radical plan for deserting Lincoln and nominating a fresh candidate. Ben Butler, Henry Winter Davis, and a group of kindred spirits, angered by Lincoln's stubborn persistence in plans for a moderate reconstruction of the South and by his dismissal of Chase from the Treasury, were organizing a September bolt that was meant to eventuate in a new convention and the choice of a new candidate. Greeley joined this movement. He, Theodore Tilton of the *Independent,* and Parke Godwin of the *Evening Post,* acting as a committee for the New York branch of this conspiracy, undertook an inquiry that was specially directed to key Republican governors. They were particularly interested in the governors' opinions as to whether or not another candidate should be substituted for Lincoln. They obviously hoped that the replies would arm them with an overwhelming demand for Lincoln's withdrawal from the presidential race.

The inquiry to the governors began circulating at the wrong psychological moment for the purpose of the conspirators. As it went out into the mails, news came of McClellan's nomination at Chicago on a peace platform. This was a damper, for even the Jacobins preferred Old Abe to Little Mac. And this was not all. On September 3, the news broke that Sherman had captured Atlanta, a victory that looked like the beginning of the end for the Confederacy. The cloud of northern despair began to lift, and it was in this reinvigorated climate of opinion that the replies of the governors were penned to the Greeley-Tilton-Godwin letter. The replies were definitely cool. The force of events had broken the intrigue asunder.[51]

Greeley was susceptible to the same influences that swayed the governors. With McClellan's nomination, the *Tribune* perked up and began denouncing the hapless general as definitely inferior to Lincoln and a docile tool of the Slave Power to boot. Atlanta raised Greeley's spirits immensely, even though he tried to make Lincoln believe that it would "force a disaster," if it were not immediately followed by generous offers of peace and reunion. The *Tribune* gleefully recounted how, on the morning that the fall of the rebel citadel became known, one McClellan man had said to another on the Wall Street ferry—"Well, we will elect Little Mac *in spite of all the victories!*"[52] This imputation of Democratic disloyalty was followed by a skillful defense of Greeley's springtime zeal for postponing the Republican national convention, and by a loud hurrah for Old Abe and for the Baltimore platform. Greeley now discovered, and wrote it down unblushingly, that he had subscribed wholeheartedly to the platform when it had been adopted at the June convention. It was also now plain to the embattled editor that "utter ruin" would be the result of Lincoln's defeat. "We MUST reëlect him," exclaimed Greeley, "and, God helping us, we WILL."[53]

Privately, the *Tribune's* editor was scarcely in an amiable frame of mind. If Lincoln failed to put down the rebellion and was reëlected, Greeley told Nicolay, it would be because of "his failure to shoot three cowardly and treacherous generals and to hang six spies, during the first year of the war. . . ." But though he grumbled and muttered, he did work hard on behalf of the Republican ticket. He applauded Frémont's withdrawal from the race at the close of September, castigated the Democratic slate as "white feather," declared that Lee's army had cheered lustily when it heard of McClellan's nomination, and gave wide currency to the charge that Little Mac had been ready to surrender at Malvern Hill. At the same time, columns of space were given over to stories of rebel atrocities, and the Democrats were, rightly, denounced for their doleful stories about the national credit, and for depicting Lincoln as a vulgar and clownish buffoon, ignorant and coarse, who was persisting in a needless war in order to gratify his sordid and groveling ambition. The *Tribune's* editor also raised money, printed and spread abroad millions of campaign documents, spoke repeatedly at campaign gatherings, and in general conducted himself as befitted a fervent administration supporter.[54]

Greeley hailed Lincoln's election as an expression of the popular will. The people had decided, he said, that the nation should live and that slavery should die. In the same spirit, he applauded Lincoln's December message to Congress as a sound document, based as it was on the Union and on the extinction of slavery. Four months earlier, he had criticized Lincoln openly for insisting on those same conditions. But now Sherman was marching through Georgia.[55]

The storm-tossed editor of the *Tribune* was sighting haven as 1864 neared its close. The war's end seemed definitely in sight at last, and the November elections had returned the Republicans to power with unmistakable majorities. Even New York State politics were suffused with a healthy glow, for the running fight with Weed had been highlighted by a smashing defeat for the Dictator in the state convention, the election of a gubernatorial ticket (Fenton and Alvord) openly hostile to the Old Man, and the choice of Horace Greeley, with more votes than anyone else in the state, as a presidential elector. The people were learning at last, or so it seemed, to prefer Greeley to Weed as a leader in New York State politics, and the Dictator's furious ripostes to Greeley's charges of corruption, his counteraccusations as to Greeley's complicity in the sordid cotton speculations of one Benjamin Camp, were contemptuously denied. Complacently, Greeley watched his one-time friend and mentor stumble down the road toward political oblivion.[56]

When the state electoral college met in the senate chamber at Albany to cast its vote for Lincoln, Greeley was in one of his best moods. He was the presiding officer, and from the rostrum his whisker-fringed, pink-and-white, blue-eyed benevolence beamed down upon his fellow electors and a crowd of spectators. The appointed hour struck, but the proceedings did not get under way. A bibulous elector had quaffed too deeply of the flowing bowl, and his seat was vacant. The business of the meeting could not be transacted. Some one moved to adjourn for half a day, but the spirit of benevolence spoke from the platform. Solemnly, as befitted the dignity of the occasion, Greeley urged that they all wait in silence until "our absent brother, doubtless kept from us by some good reason," should appear in his proper station. Then, with the audience deeply moved and all the women spectators crying, he leaned down to secretary of state Chauncey Depew, and whispered, "Chauncey, how long do you think it will be before that damned, drunken fool will be able to return and take his seat?"[57]

The old Greeley, the happy crusader of peaceful times, was on his way back from the wars.

NOTES FOR CHAPTER 20

1. *Tribune,* Jan. 3, 23, 27, Feb. 19, Apr. 6, May 15, 18, June 3, 6, 15, 1863; Gilmore, *op. cit.,* pp. 100-102, 145-47; Williams, *op. cit.,* pp. 219, 231-85. Greeley also joined the Jacobins in defending Burnside and Hooker, generals who played along with the Radicals.
2. *Tribune,* Oct. 2, 14, Nov. 21, 25, 27, 29, Dec. 1, 2, 4, 18, 26, 27, 30, 31, 1862, Jan. 22, 1863.
3. *Ibid.,* May 11, June 9, 1863, Jan. 8, 1864; Reavis, *op. cit.,* pp. 156-57; J. L. Vallandingham, *A Life of Clement L. Vallandigham* (Balt., 1872) pp. 223-24; "Extracts from the Journal of Henry J. Raymond," in *Scribner's Monthly,* XIX (Mar., 1880) 705.

4. *Tribune,* Oct. 2, Dec. 2, 4, 1862.
5. *Tribune,* Jan. 9, 12, 14, 19, 30, Feb. 2, 14, 1863; *New York Times,* Jan. 29, 1863; Nicolay and Hay, *Abraham Lincoln, A History,* VI, 83-84.
6. *Tribune,* Jan. 3, 22, Feb. 11, 14, Mar. 9-16, 24, 26, 28, 30, Apr. 1, 18, May 5, 16, July 8, 1863.
7. Gerrit Smith Papers, Greeley to Smith, Feb. 1, 1863; "Extracts from the Journal of Henry J. Raymond," in *Scribner's Monthly,* XIX, 706; *New York Times,* Jan. 29, 1863; *Tribune,* Feb. 2, Mar. 11, Apr. 1, 1863; *Independent,* Feb. 5, 19, 1863.
8. Chase Papers (Hist. Soc. of Pa.), Greeley to Chase, Jan. 31, 1863; Washburne Papers, Greeley to Washburne, Oct. 9, 1871.
9. Gilmore, *op. cit.,* p. 103. Cf. the *Independent,* Jan. 1, 1863, and the reminiscence of D. P. Rhoades in the *Tribune,* Sept. 21, 1890.
10. See, for example, the *Tribune,* Mar. 23-26, 1863.
11. See, as to the Peace Democrats, E. J. Benton, "The Movement for Peace Without a Victory During the Civil War," in *Collections, The Western Reserve Historical Society,* publ. #99, Dec. 1918 (Cleveland, 1918), pp. 20-26, 35-36.
12. Stahl Collection, Greeley to Mrs. Allen, Apr. 8, 1863; Gerrit Smith Papers, Greeley to Smith, Feb. 10, 1863; *Tribune,* Feb. 21, 26, May 16, 21, 1863. In the *Independent,* Feb. 12, 1863, he declared—"The War will go on. Intervention, Mediation, Arbitration, will only be talked of; or, if seriously proffered, will prove unavailing." He then urged an all-out war.
13. *Tribune,* May 16, 1863; Nicolay Papers, Greeley to Nicolay, June 14, 1863.
14. *Tribune,* June 17, 22, 1863; *Independent,* July 2, 1863.
15. *Tribune,* July 9, 1863; *Independent,* July 9, 1863.
16. This was his public position. In private, he had defended the draft as necessary and criticized it as an anomaly—Stanton Papers, Greeley to Stanton (copy), June 12, 1863; Chase Papers (Hist. Soc. of Pa.), Greeley to Chase, Aug. 27, 30, 1863.
17. Rhodes, *History of the United States,* IV, 320-28; Randall, *Civil War and Reconstruction,* pp. 410-16; F. A. Shannon, *The Organization and Administration of the Union Army, 1861-1865* (2 vols.; Cleveland, 1928), II, 210-13; Mitchell, *Seymour,* pp. 298-336. Mitchell (p. 335) puts the dead in the New York riots at a maximum of seventy-four, but see Shannon, II, 213.
18. Greeley Papers (N. Y. P. L.), Greeley to Mrs. L. Bowe, Aug. 24, 1863.
19. *Tribune,* Feb. 23, Mar. 23, 1863.
20. Hudson, *Journalism,* pp. 557-59; *Tribune,* July 29, 1863, July 20, 1868, Feb. 22, 1870; Frohman, *op. cit.,* p. 231; G. W. Smalley, *Anglo-American Memories* (London, 1910), pp. 142-43; Cortissoz, *Reid,* I, 113; Gilmore, *op. cit.,* pp. 167-97; Cleveland, *Story of a Summer,* pp. 132-34.
21. *Tribune,* July 15, 16-21, 29, Aug. 11, 12, Nov. 2, 1863. Cf. Mitchell, *Seymour,* pp. 300-336.
22. *Tribune,* July 9, 10, 13, 15, Sept. 10, Oct. 15, 17, 22-23, Nov. 4, 5, 14, 27, Dec. 17, 1863; Greeley Papers (N. Y. P. L.), Greeley to Mrs. L. Bowe, Aug. 24, 1863; Brummer, *op. cit.,* pp. 337-40.
23. Williams, *op. cit.,* pp. 294-96.
24. Stahl Collection, Greeley to Mrs. Allen, May 16, 1864; Greeley, *Recollections,* p. 421.
25. Greeley Papers (N. Y. P. L.), Dixon to Greeley, May 27, 1864; *Tribune,* May 27, 1864; Rhodes, *Hist. of the U. S.,* IV, 471.

26. Morgan Papers, Greeley to Morgan, Jan. 8, 1864.

27. Benton, *Greeley on Lincoln*, p. 79; Lanman Correspondence, Greeley to Lanman, Oct. 2, 1863; *Tribune*, Nov. 9, 20-26, 1863. It should be said, in fairness to Greeley, that the Gettysburg address was generally received with indifference.

28. *Tribune*, Feb. 23, 1864; *Independent*, Feb. 25, 1864.

29. Ingersoll Papers, Greeley to Mrs. Ingersoll, Nov. 11, 1863; Greeley Papers (N. Y. P. L.), Chase to Greeley, Feb. 24, Mar. 2, 4, 1864; Chase Papers (Hist. Soc. of Pa.), Greeley to Chase, Mar. 2, 1864; *Tribune*, Feb. 24, 25, Mar. 11, 1864.

30. Greeley Letters (Yale Lib.), Greeley to J. P. Thompson, Apr. 6, 1864; *Tribune*, Mar. 19, Apr. 1, 13, 20, 29, June 1, 6, 1864; Ruhl, *Frémont*, p. 99; Nevins, *Frémont*, II, 655; B. J. Hendrick, *Lincoln's War Cabinet* (Boston, 1946), p. 437. It is, of course, unconstitutional to choose a party's Presidential and Vice-Presidential candidates from the same state.

31. *Independent*, June 2, 1864; *Tribune*, Jan. 3, 1868; Schurz, *Reminiscences*, III, 102.

32. *Proceedings of the National Union Convention . . . 1864* (N. Y., 1864), p. 57; *Tribune*, July 1, 7, 1864; *Independent*, July 7, 1864.

33. Nicolay Papers, Nicolay to Greeley, Apr. 25, May 26, 1864, Greeley to Nicolay, Apr. 26, May 29, 1864.

34. Morgan Papers, Greeley to Morgan, June 14, 1864. In this letter, Greeley deplores the fact that Alexander H. Stephens' attempted visit to Washington in 1863 had been repelled by the Union government. Less than a week earlier (*Tribune*, June 8, 10, 1864), he had openly defended the government for this action. To berate the government in private for what he applauded in public was not unusual for Greeley.

35. *Tribune*, June 10, July 30, 1864.

36. *The War of the Rebellion; A Compilation of the Official Records of the Union and Confederate Armies*, series I, Vol. XLIII, pt. 2, pp. 930-36; *Official Records of the Union and Confederate Navies in the War of the Rebellion*, series II, Vol. III, pp. 1105-06; E. C. Kirkland, *The Peacemakers of 1864*, (N. Y., 1927), pp. 68-74; *Independent*, July 28, 1864.

37. Severance, F. H., "The Peace Conference at Niagara Falls in 1864," in *Buff. Hist. Soc. Pub.*, XVIII (Buffalo, 1914), 83-84.

38. *Tribune*, Dec. 22, 1862.

39. *Ibid.*, Mar. 31, 1865, Greeley to Lincoln, July 7, 1864. Greeley's terms were, (1) reconstruction of the Union, (2) complete amnesty, (3) $400,000,000 indemnity for abolition of slavery, apportioned pro rata among all the slave states, loyal and secession, (4) Negroes counted for representation of slave states, (5) a national convention to ratify these changes and make any constitutional changes deemed advisable.

40. Lincoln Papers, Lincoln to Greeley, July 9, 1864. The Lincoln-Greeley correspondence is in Vols. 160-64 of the Lincoln Papers.

41. *The War of the Rebellion, etc.*, ser. III, Vol. IV, p. 496, Lincoln to Greeley, July 15, 1864; Nicolay and Hay, *Lincoln*, IX, 188-89; *Independent*, July 28, 1864; Raymond, *The Life and Public Services of Abraham Lincoln*, (N. Y., 1865), pp. 572-74.

42. W. R. Thayer, *The Life and Letters of John Hay* (2 vols.; Boston and N. Y., 1915), I, 179-81, extracts from Hay's diary.

43. Kirkland, *op. cit.*, pp. 67-85, 100-105. For Greeley's account, see *The American Conflict*, II, pp. 664-65.

44. *Tribune,* July 22-Aug. 23, 1864; *New York Herald,* July 25-29, 1864; *New York Times,* July 23-30, 1864.
45. Nicolay and Hay, *Lincoln,* IX, 196-97.
46. See Greeley's dismal picture of the situation in early August, 1864, in the *Independent,* Sept. 8, 1864. His melancholy was in nowise abated by a strike that August of *Tribune* compositors. The men blamed Greeley for not using his influence on their behalf, and the strike resulted in the *Tribune* being operated for several years under open shop conditions.— Stevens, *New York Typographical Union #6,* pp. 286-95.
47. *The War of the Rebellion,* series IV, Vol. III, pp. 584-587.
48. Welles, *Diary,* II, 111-12. Cf. Depew, *Memories,* pp. 62-63. The Lincoln Papers show Greeley still dogging the President with demands for peace overtures during the fall of 1864.—Greeley to Lincoln, Aug. 29, Sept. 16, Nov. 23, 1864.
49. Gurowski, *Diary,* III, 243-44; Gurowski Papers, Greeley to Gurowski, Sept. 25, 1861.
50. Greeley Papers (N. Y. P. L.), Greeley to Lemuel Smith, Aug. 16, 1864, Greeley to W. O. Bartlett, Aug. 30, 1864.
51. For these replies, see the Tilton Papers (N. Y. H. S.), Andrew, Buckingham, Smith and others to Greeley, Godwin and Tilton, on or about Sept. 3, 1864. See also, Williams, *op. cit.,* pp. 328-30, and Fahrney, *op. cit.,* pp. 198-200.
52. Nicolay Papers, Greeley to Nicolay, Sept. 4, 1864; *Tribune,* Sept. 5, 6, 1864.
53. *Independent,* Sept. 15, 1864. "There were among us diversities of preference as to candidates, but none with regard to principles. The only practical question was—which among those suggested for our candidates will most surely and speedily achieve success for our principles?"
54. Nicolay Papers, Greeley to Nicolay, Sept. 11, 1864; *Tribune,* Sept. 7, 16, 19-30, Oct. 7-31, 1864. The issue of Oct. 17, 1864, contains a letter from John Bright to Greeley, a letter strongly pro-Lincoln.
55. *Tribune,* Nov. 10, Dec. 7, 1864; *Independent,* Nov. 17, 1864. The Democratic appeal to the money interest and to fear, said Greeley, had given McClellan and Seymour gains only among the Roman Catholics of New York State.
56. Brummer, *op. cit.,* pp. 391-97; Van Deusen, *Weed,* pp. 312-16. Greeley was more closely connected with Camp, who had been at one time a member of the *Tribune* staff, than he was willing to admit, but there was no proof of Weed's charges.—*Tribune,* Dec. 17, 1862, June 2, 25, 28, Dec. 12, 19f., 1864; Greeley Papers (N. Y. P. L.), S. Wilkeson to Greeley, Feb. 1 [1862], B. F. Camp to Greeley, Dec. 25, 1864.
57. Depew, *Memories,* pp. 90-91.

CHAPTER 21

"For You O Democracy"

THE CONFEDERACY WAS PLAINLY DYING IN THE WIN-
ter of 1865, so plainly that Greeley began looking ahead to the
cessation of hostilities and the reconstruction of his shattered country. The vision of a new nation, rising like the Phoenix from the
ashes of civil war, roused him to a mood of passionate exaltation. As
the war had developed into a struggle for human freedom, he declared, the North had become panoplied in righteousness. Clad in
such shining armor, it would now "seek the establishment of a
Republic as perfect in construction as it is pure in theory. . . . We
shall contribute an invaluable chapter to history," he asserted. This
contribution would be "the record of a civil war undertaken by
Democracy in defense of Democracy, and of a victory consistent with
itself, and unstained by fatal excesses. This lesson the world has long
needed; and this lesson, by the grace of God, it shall now have!"[1]
Greeley was looking down Whitman's democratic vistas, and his
vision was that of the Good Gray Poet:

> Come, I will make the continent indissoluble,
> I will make the most splendid race the sun ever shone upon,
> I will make divine magnetic lands,
> > With the love of comrades,
> > With the life-long love of comrades.
>
> I will plant companionship thick as trees along all the
>   rivers of America, and along the shores of the great lakes,
>   and all over the prairies,
> I will make inseparable cities with their arms about each
>   other's necks,
> > By the love of comrades,
> > By the manly love of comrades.

For you these from me, O Democracy, to serve you ma femme!
For you, for you I am trilling these songs.

Greeley's hopes and dreams about reconstruction had begun to
develop in the spirit of Whitman's theme long before the end of the
war. The *Tribune's* editor, like the poet who wrote at times for the
Tribune, would "make the continent indissoluble," and his first
means to that end would be a just and healing peace. The initial
vindictiveness with which he looked forward to hanging the leading
traitors quickly passed away. When President Lincoln, at the close of
1863, announced his moderate plan for reconstruction under 10
per cent governments pledged to accept emancipation, Greeley regis-
tered quick approval. The President, he declared, "has hit the
Golden Mean between severity and weakness," and he heartily approved the Ashley bill, which was intended to implement Lincoln's
proposal.[2]

All this was gall and wormwood to the Congressional radicals, but
Greeley hewed straight to the line. He opposed Thad Stevens, early
in 1864, on the subject of confiscation of southern property, declaring that he had "no taste for either vengeance or spoliation," an
attitude that was all the more remarkable because he was at the
same time profoundly moved by the stories of rebel atrocities.[3] That
summer he refused to support the manifesto of Ben Wade and
Henry Winter Davis in its attack on Lincoln for his pocket veto of
their drastic reconstruction bill. Though concurring in much of the
manifesto, said Greeley, he did not want to bind himself to any one
plan of reconstruction, and was glad that the bill had been vetoed.
This was at a time when he was very much at outs with the President.[4]

It was the same story in the early months of 1865. The radicals
were then concentrating their assaults upon the reconstruction
policy of the Chief Executive, but Greeley, though his private correspondence bitterly described the President as a politician who
did not measure up to his job, issued a public note of warning to
the Congressional enemies of a moderate southern policy. He was
for a magnanimous peace, declared the *Tribune's* editor, and, in
working out the problem of how to impose the national authority
upon the rebellious states, he would trust the judgment of the
executive branch of the government. Indeed, he hoped Congress
would go home at the earliest possible moment, and not reassemble
until autumn. Greeley's sweet reasonableness toward the falling foe
even led him to criticize Lincoln's second inaugural because it did
not strike so peaceful a note as that of 1861. And it was obvious

that he had no patience at all with Stevens' rantings about "conquered provinces."[5]

Greeley's theme of peace with mercy was still the feature of the *Tribune's* editorial page as the dreary days of winter merged into the spring of 1865. His reasoning had the virtue of simplicity, and it was consistent with the logic that he had used four years earlier. The southern masses, always loyal at heart to the Union, were now at length being freed from the control of the aristocratic Slave Power. Their national loyalty would now assert itself. The whole South, "with limited and transient exceptions," would return gladly and promptly "to the ways of peace and industry," if an opportunity were given it to do so. The victors should furnish that opportunity.

The news of Lee's surrender at Appomattox reached the *Tribune* office at eleven o'clock on the evening of April 9. On the following day, the twenty-fourth anniversary of the *Tribune,* Greeley issued a call for a general amnesty. He would take the life of no man who submitted to the authority of the Union. There were southerners, murderers of black soldiers and of other captives, who richly deserved punishment, but the immediate and pressing issue was the pacification of the nation.

We plead [he said] against passions certain at this moment to be fierce and intolerant; but on our side are the Ages and the voice of History. We plead for a restoration of the Union, against a policy which would afford a momentary gratification at the cost of years of perilous hate and bitterness.

Two days later, he warned against sullying the triumph "by virtually degrading a great conflict of ideas and principles into a paltry matter of detected felony and legal retribution."[6]

Such was Greeley's attitude toward reconstruction, on the eve of the great tragedy at Ford's Theatre. It was coupled with a defense of the President against what the *Tribune* termed the sneaking Democratic calumny that, in four years' time, Honest Abe had become a millionaire. The day that this defense was printed was April 14, 1865. It was the last day of Lincoln's life, a curiously appropriate time for Greeley to come to the defense of the man he had so much berated. That evening the President went to see Laura Keene in *Our American Cousin,* and as he sat in the Presidential box John Wilkes Booth shot him down. He died the next morning.

The *Tribune* mourned with the nation. It termed the President's death a national calamity, and Greeley warned the South that it had suffered irreparable loss by the murder of this man who had been killed presumably in its interest. Now Greeley praised Lincoln's simplicity and his rare capacity for silence, pointing out how his fame had spread, and how in Europe he had become a symbol of democracy and human rights. Now the *Tribune's* editor could see how Lincoln had grown while in office, how his stature had increased as he strove to save a nation's life and to bind up its wounds. At last it had become apparent to Greeley that the martyred President had had a rare talent for stating profound truths with a superb simplicity. "The only address [at Gettysburg] which the world will remember," said Greeley, "was that of the President—" and he quoted it entire. So the tribute that came willingly because it was late fell upon the grave of the great man.[7]

Tributes to the fallen President were balm to a grief-stricken people, but they did not prevent a storm of obloquy from bursting around Greeley's head. The public leaped to the conclusion that the assassination had been plotted by men high in Confederate official-dom, and its cry for vengeance was coupled with denunciations of the man who had been asking magnanimous treatment for the rebels. Greeley was bitterly denounced by his fellow editors. Fellow members of the Union League Club cast chilly looks and caustic remarks in his direction. Hundreds, perhaps thousands, stopped their subscriptions to the *Tribune*. The policy of magnanimity had boomeranged, and its author found himself covered with a hail of abuse.

It was to Greeley's credit that he stuck to his guns. Privately, he declared that, while Booth was too vain and silly to be a great villain, Mrs. Surratt had "the materials of a Lady Macbeth in her, with just enough religion of the Roman Catholic variety to quiet the strings of conscience. If she isn't hung, nobody ever should be." But even so he was convinced that no more blood should be shed, and publicly, with a serenity which showed the scorn in which he held his detractors, he continued to call for general leniency and no martyrdoms.[8] It was a stand that demonstrated courage as well as wisdom.

The man who thus stood up for a peace of moderation and justice when the North was howling for blood and vengeance had emerged from the Civil War vigorous in both mind and body. His smooth, unwrinkled face with its fringe of whisker usually bore an expression of slightly quizzical benignity. His nearsighted peerings, sometimes sharp but on the whole kindly, added to his air of benevolence. As he had always been, Greeley was still certain of his own good will toward mankind, and equally certain that his explosive rages were always the result of dire provocation by his enemies. The feuds with

Manton Marble of the *World*, with Bryant, Bennett, Raymond, and
Weed that flared across the pages of the *Tribune* with almost
monotonous regularity were, in the estimation of its editor, invariably provoked by those graceless contemporaries. He ignored
his own petulance and irritability, qualities that were continually
tempering the generous side of his nature.

"You have leisure," Greeley shrilled one day at Samuel Wilkeson,
anent a drunken proofreader. "Oblige me by going upstairs and
choking that infernal fool for nine minutes. Now *do* oblige me."
The rage was real, even though the "drunken fool" might easily
borrow ten dollars from the boss later that day, on the strength of
a hard-luck plea.

Mark Twain, on the *Tribune's* staff in the late 1860's, saw this
combination of truculence and benevolence, and enshrined it in his
story of Greeley shaving with a dull razor. The removal of the
whiskers, said Twain, would be accompanied by a monologue in
which were commingled parts of what the editor quaintly imagined
to be "Old Hundred" and ejaculations of "Damn the damned razor,
and the damned outcast who made it."

Greeley's tendency to explosive vehemence and to profanity lent
humor to a tale that circulated in one section of the New York
press not long after his death. The story went that the editor, as he
realized that he was dying, said aloud—"Well, the devil's got you at
last, you damned old bastard." Gabrielle Greeley, so the tale continued, asked Whitelaw Reid shortly after the funeral, "Mr. Reid,
what were my father's last words?" and Reid replied, "Your father's
last words were, 'I know that my Redeemer liveth.' "[9]

There was always an element of the unpredictable in Greeley's
behavior. In one mood, he would be agreeably open in his comments
on men and events. At other times, he would be cross and silent,
or simply sink into a mood of abstraction. A cleric who went to a
dinner party, all agog to catch the flow of wisdom from the great
man's lips, came away disappointed. No pearls had been strewn.
Indeed, the only thing he could remember was Greeley's remarking
"That's damned good corn!" or words to that effect.[10] These were
displays of temperament, not unlike those of a prima donna. They
were also, to a considerable extent, exhibitionist in character.

Henry Clapp once asserted that Greeley was a "self-made man
who worshipped his creator." There was a considerable measure of
truth in the jibe, for with the passage of the years Greeley's egotism
had grown apace. He was now more than ever intolerant of opposition, impatient of criticism, and susceptible to flattery. These were
great weaknesses. They were fortunately counterbalanced by a

warmth of human feeling which manifested itself in a genuine passion for public service. It was one of the tragedies of Greeley's life that this great warmth had so few outlets, other than public service, for its expression.

For with all of his tempestuous activity, the writing of reams of editorials and of one book after another, the endless lecture tours, the perpetual running after office, the Greeley of the post-Civil War period was an increasingly lonely man. "Mother" had developed into "a queer, old-fashioned looking lady," more than ever querulous, complaining, shrill-tongued, and vehement. The servants fled when she approached. Health was equally elusive, though she pursued it with even more indefatigable ardor, whether by consultation with the best doctors of New York and Washington or by a never-ending and increasingly expensive search in the West Indies and Europe for the proper air, baths, minerals springs, and medical attention. As she spent more and more of her time abroad, Ida and Gabrielle were taken out of the Sacred Heart Convent School at Manhattanville (this school had been a Molly idea, one may be sure) to accompany her and to minister to her needs. Gabrielle, high-spirited and independent, showed little disposition to immolate herself on the altar of filial love, but patient, sweet-tempered Ida devoted herself to satisfying her mother's wants and whims. Ida's was a hard and thankless existence, as her father, who looked on in helpless anxiety, well knew, and in compensation she turned toward Rome. To her father's sorrow, she showed a marked disposition to move steadily into the Catholic fold.[11] For all of Horace's patience and Ida's sweet self-abnegation, the members of the family were drifting further and further apart from one another.

Nor was there much social life to take the place of a close family circle. A multitude of engagements and editorial cares were barriers difficult to cross, even for friends. Greeley was always welcome at Beecher's, or at Barnum's, or at the Alvin Johnson's place at 323 West Fifty-seventh Street near the Eighth Avenue entrance to the Park, where he did most of his writing, but there was less and less time for such moments of relaxation.

Once in a while, Greeley would slip out of the daily grind. He would shuffle occasionally into one of Bayard Taylor's gay salons, where Whitelaw Reid and Eastman Johnson made the evening merry with talk and laughter, and occasionally he found time to show his friends the beauties of Chappaqua. Once he took the theatrically impressive Theodore Tilton and his wife Libby, a tender and confiding little woman, with great dark eyes and soft, appealing ways, up to Chappaqua for a Saturday outing. They and two other guests were bundled into the buckboard, and Horace, his hat on the back of his head and a rein in either hand, drove them helter-skelter over the rocks and stumps of "mother's land," blissfully pointing out the field he had reclaimed by digging out rocks and by ditching, the best spring, and the stone barn that he had built at such expense. Then they jounced back to the house, and sat in the living room before a fire of red cedar. "It was a sight worth seeing to see Ida get dinner there," Greeley told them, but Ida was in Europe with her mother, so the party went to the Chappaqua hotel. Then they took the train back to New York and wound up at Barnum's house, where Horace read poetry to them all evening, beginning with Whittier's "My Psalm," but not forgetting to include "Jim Bludsoe."[12] So ended a Victorian holiday.

But such holidays were few and far between. Editorial duties, lecturing, writing, campaigning monopolized Greeley's attention. Six volumes of published works—history, autobiography, letters and essays on economic subjects—were written and published over a period of eight years (1863-71), in addition to his editorial contributions to the *Tribune,* the *Independent,* and other papers.[13] If Colbert was the work ox of Louis XIV, Greeley was the work ox of the American public.

The one source of pleasure and relaxation to which the busy editor had anything like regular recourse was the woods of Chappaqua. There he found peace, in the quiet places under the hemlocks and cedars, with only the birds and squirrels for company. There he could rest, even when he was scrambling up and down the hemlocks, ax in hand. For there was never any danger of meeting there the unspeakable Bennett, or the sanctimonious Bryant, or the venomous Thurlow Weed.

But despite the lack of a well-developed social life, Greeley did not think of himself as a man to be pitied. He knew that he had a mission, and this knowledge gave him no rest. For back of the contradictions that were the outer hallmarks of the man, back of his tempery sweetness and his swearing and beaming, back of that variableness of spirit which made him at once the crusader and the conservative, lay a deep and abiding conviction that it was his task to point the way to the rebuilding of a shattered Union.

The American nation, Greeley believed, had a geographical unity, a homogeneous national character, and a wealth of such common ties as those afforded by language and historical traditions. These bound it together and helped to make its people a nationality. Furthermore, it was a nationality in which God took a great interest and a great pride. As Greeley looked back upon that Fourth of July

Horace Greeley, America's most famous editor at the
prime of life.

1826, which witnessed the death of both John Adams and Thomas Jefferson, and as he remembered how the sad tidings of their demise were borne north and south by messengers who met in Philadelphia, almost within the shadow of Independence Hall, he was convinced that the nation had then been a witness to a miracle like those of old, an evidence of the Almighty's special regard for the United States of America.[14] What could be more obvious than that America was God's own child? This child had been cruelly hurt by bitter civil strife, but at last had arrived the time of healing provided for by the divine plan.

God's plan for America, as perceived by Horace Greeley, contained three remedies that could be utilized by mortal men in working out God's will. They were, first, the elimination of the concept of states' rights from men's thinking and, conversely, an emphasis upon the doctrine of nationalism; second, the establishment of universal amnesty and impartial suffrage as the only true basis of southern reconstruction; and, third, a broad, harmonious forward movement in the economic development of the South and of the nation as a whole. These were the great means by which national unity and national progress might be once again achieved.

The Civil War, Greeley declared, had destroyed once and for all the basis of the old theory of states' rights. If this were not so, we would have to "assimilate our national existence to a Fourth of July gathering, a mass meeting, collected by some orator's fame, some raree-show's attractions." Steadily he pushed this point of view, using in its support a highly nationalistic pamphlet written in 1864 by Professor Tayler Lewis of Union College, a pamphlet entitled State Rights. A Photograph from the Ruins of Ancient Greece.

Lewis declared in this essay that the United States must learn a lesson from Greece, whose destruction had been due to the triumph of the spirit of autonomy over the spirit of nationality. The one great state right, said Lewis, was the right of intercitizenship, which binds the states, the nation, and the Union into a harmonious and indivisible whole. Ours was a nation with traditions, martyrs, heroes. It possessed a national will and, still more important, a national soul. In its national life, the past, the present, and the future were organically one. It was a nation designed and created by God.[15]

This typical product of nineteenth-century liberal nationalism expressed Greeley's own sentiments. It was, he declared, a fit and proper statement of facts, and a million copies of the pamphlet ought to be circulated throughout the United States. For it demonstrated beyond the peradventure of a doubt that the doctrine of states' rights was a relic of the past. That doctrine had been utilized by the slavocracy in spurious argument, but even in 1861 it had had little vitality, for the great majority of southerners had always been steadfastly loyal to the Union. Now the doctrine was dead. The Civil War had decided that each citizen owed a primary and paramount allegiance to his country; that the American people did, in fact, constitute a nation.[16] Thus the doctrine of states' rights had been swallowed up by the transcendent fact of American nationality.

Scotching the doctrine of states' rights and exalting the doctrine of liberal nationalism was one means of cementing national unity. Another was summed up in Greeley's slogan, "Universal Amnesty and Impartial Suffrage." Amnesty meant forgiveness, with no strings attached. From the start of the controversy over the punishment of the South, Greeley had frowned upon treason trials, confiscation of property, and deprivation of civil rights. Such action, he believed, would only produce martyrs and bitterness, delaying the reëstablishment of national unity and hampering national progress.[17] The only proper course of action, in his opinion, was to return the southern states and the southern people to a status of equality in the Union. At the same time, and this was equally important, such amnesty must be linked with a broad and impartial suffrage.

Greeley based his demand for impartial suffrage upon high ethical and moral grounds. Negroes, he asserted, were human beings, descended from Adam and Eve, and as capable of higher development as were whites. They were a naturally loyal element of the population, and they were anxious to take advantage of the opportunities for advancement that were provided by freedom. There were over four million of them, a large proportion of the South's population. Only by establishing political and civil equality for the Negro could there be a genuine reconstruction of southern society.[18]

With genuine insight, at least from the point of view of a sound reconstruction of the southern social order, Greeley emphasized that impartial suffrage and civil equality should be given by, rather than forced from the southern whites. He wished to have the states themselves establish these reforms, though they should be sanctified by constitutional amendment lest deluded southern whites undo the good work. "We should even prefer a partial measure of justice freely accorded by the Southern Whites," he declared, "to a complete one imposed on them by the power of the triumphant Union." Reconciliation and trust between white and black in the South was the surest guarantee of solid recovery and development for that devastated section of the Union. Congress should hold reconstruction in abeyance "until it can be seen whether the manifest and rapid increase and diffusion of good will between Whites and Blacks at the South" might not result in such understanding and reconciliation.

What Congress should do about Negro suffrage depended on the attitude of the southern whites toward the southern blacks. Give the Negro the vote, Greeley told the southern whites, and the Negro would be what he had been—"just about the most docile, valuable peasantry upon earth." Let the South stand out against Negro enfranchisement and it would "find Jordan a hard row to travel."[19] Greeley was making use of the old principle of the carrot and the stick in urging the South toward impartial suffrage.

Greeley's argument for Negro suffrage paid little attention to the "natural rights" of man. Suffrage, he held, was a moral right, but the government also had a moral duty, that of protecting "the industrious, the provident, the thrifty, the well-behaved, the quiet-loving . . . against robbery and outrage at the hands of the indolent, the profligate, the wasteful, the rowdy, the dissolute."[20] Hence he could easily assent to a limited suffrage for the Negro. At one time or another, he suggested as feasible a $250 property qualification (as in New York State), a literacy test, a taxpayer test, an honest workman test, a no criminal test, and a poll tax paid some months before voting.[21] The important thing was that the limitation, whatever it might be, should be applied impartially to the whites as well as to the blacks. Only so could reconstruction be based upon principles of equity and justice.

Why was Greeley so anxious for impartial suffrage? In part it was because of his honest concern for the Negroes, his belief that it was the only effective defense against exploitation that could be placed in their hands.[22] But there were other reasons for this step that also weighed heavily with the *Tribune's* editor.

Greeley was convinced that Negro suffrage was essential to the maintenance of Republican principles. The Negroes, save for the base and wicked among them (who would naturally gravitate into the ranks of the Sham Democracy), would vote Republican. This would at least counterbalance the Democratic votes of the ignorant whites in the South. Negro suffrage would therefore be productive of a variety of blessings. It was vital to hearty southern coöperation in paying off the national debt. It would prevent southern rebellions and scotch southern demands for pensions and for payment of the Confederate war debt. It would fend off Democratic raids on the high tariff. Most important of all, it would keep the Republican party from becoming "a beaten, bankrupt party," making it rather a great national party that could hopefully contest nearly every

state in the Union.[23] Such were the practical advantages that Greeley saw accruing from impartial suffrage.

Universal amnesty and impartial suffrage constituted the second
pillar of Greeley's grand plan for achieving national health and
vigor. The third was his prosperity program, a project for achieving
a great North-South-East-West coprosperity sphere. There was, he
believed, a fundamental unity of interest between North and South,
capital and labor, agriculture and manufacturing, employer and
employed in the United States. It was a basic truth, he told Orestes
A. Brownson, that here in America the interest of each was the interest of all. This transcendent fact made possible the harmonization
of the country in all its parts and movements.[24] It was the heart-
felt desire of the *Tribune's* editor to play a major role in promoting
this national harmony by educating the American people in matters
economic.

Harmonizing the nation by means of economic measures was to a
considerable extent the function of government, in Greeley's opinion. It was imperatively necessary that government foster national
prosperity by maintaining a protective tariff. It was equally imperative that the national debt, "essentially an evil," should be paid off at
the earliest possible moment. This meant heavy taxation, though
care must be taken not to levy taxes that would discourage industry
and thus impede industrial development. It also meant paring
governmental expenditures to the bone, with government salaries
kept at minimum rates, the army drastically reduced and a large
part of the navy sold for scrap. The government's current monetary
policy must be directed toward the speedy elimination of the
greenbacks and therewith the resumption of specie payment. The
way to resume was to resume. Such drastic deflation would lower
prices and wages and favor the creditor interest, but it was the
path of honor and honesty, a path that must be followed with
unflinching courage. For after the hardships of deflation were over,
everybody would settle down and go to work with confidence in a
sound and stabilized economy. Then, with the government solvent,
the national debt largely or entirely wiped out, taxes light, prices
low and tariff high, the nation could cultivate its garden in peace,
security, and prosperity.[25]

It would be unjust to think of Greeley as simply a pawn of the
vested interests, a blind exponent of government noninterference
in economic matters, save at the behest of the businessman.
Occaasionally a note of some boldness would come twanging from
the harp of the *Tribune's* editor. "There are *no* absolute rights of
property," he warned in his *Political Economy*, which was published

in 1869. *"All* rights of property are held subordinate to the dictates of national well-being." Such remarks have a twentieth-century ring. Theodore Roosevelt said something very similar at Osawatomie in 1910, and the same concept lay at the basis of the New Deal. Greeley, like those who followed after him, saw that, as the nation's life became more complex, governmental interference in economic matters must inevitably increase. He saw, in the last years of his life, that there would have to be governmental regulation of tenements, of the atrocious conditions in the coal mines, of the rates imposed by the railroads upon a long-suffering public. He criticized the great Union Pacific robbery that centered in Crédit Mobilier, the scandalous proceedings of Fisk and Gould in their dealings in Erie, the dictatorial control exerted by the New York Central Railroad over Albany legislation.

But all too often, for one who gloried in being a reformer, Greeley's attack on economic wrongdoing had nothing more fundamental as a basis than the slogan "throw the rascals out." And all too often, his vision of expanded governmental regulation and control was a reluctant vision. For deep down in his heart, despite all his criticisms of the way in which the economic machine was being run, Greeley believed that the vital economic center of a prosperous nation was the private accumulation of wealth and free and unhampered business enterprise. The desire to become rich was "wholesome and laudable," a proper aspiration for every boy, so long as it did not make him unfaithful to social obligations or moral principles. There was no reason that it should make him forgetful of high standards. Greeley asserted that the great majority of rich men had come by their wealth honestly, just as the majority of poor men over forty years of age owed their poverty to bad habits. In the 1860's as in the 1840's it was clear to him that an odor of respectability hung about the wealthy and that an odor of things disreputable hung about the poor. Most capitalists were beneficent creatures, whose works were good and ought to be encouraged.[26]

The path marked out by the entrepreneur and beaten into shape by the feet of the businessmen who followed after was the one sure path to national prosperity, in Greeley's opinion. When the government got its feet on that path, it only cluttered up the road to a better future. Few things stirred his wrath more surely than the spectacle of government in business. He even wanted New York State to give up its canal properties to private interests, so effectively had businessmen mastered the problems of transportation. The new nation of Greeley's dreams must put its faith in free enterprise. His abhorrence of what the conservatives of a later generation were to call "creeping socialism" was clear indeed.[27]

Greeley believed that government by its very nature was not equipped to enter the field of business, but he was equally convinced that government could and should protect business from any foreign competition for the home market. The vision that had come to him in the 1820's and 1830's, that protectionist vision created for him by family hardships and by Matthew and Henry Carey and Hezekiah Niles and Henry Clay, had grown more vivid and compelling with the passage of the years. Greeley was now a more ardent protectionist than he had been when he had first broken a lance on the subject with the *Evening Post*. All the old arguments were rehashed, *ad infinitum*. The tariff would benefit the farmer by providing an urban market for his wheat and corn. It would benefit the laborer by furnishing a market for his labor. It would keep wealth at home, where it could be expended most fruitfully and profitably, for foreign goods were as dear bought as they were farfetched. It would develop the industries needed for protection against some future foreign foe. In sum, it would add constantly to the country's prosperity and safety. Had Clay been elected in 1844, Greeley declared, the United States would have had 25 per cent more wealth and 2,000,000 more people than it now had in 1869.[28]

One of the favorite theses of the *Tribune's* editor was that free trade represented anarchic individualism, while protection represented the best kind of social planning. For protection was a natural, spontaneous growth, endowed with a truly functional character. It bloomed where it was needed and withered when the need for it had departed. In other words, areas undeveloped industrially gravitated toward protection, but as they became highly industrialized they lost interest in and even became opposed to high tariff walls. This concept, based far more upon wishful thinking than upon historical fact, was illustrated in 1867 when he was calling for at least a 25 per cent increase in duties affecting American industrial interests. He declared that he expected opposition to a protective tariff from Massachusetts, but that he was astonished by the opposition to protection that came from undeveloped Missouri. Such a state, with its rich industrial potential, ought to have a better conception of its true interests.[29]

The industrialization that Greeley saw in his protectionist dream was an over-all affair. Farm and factory were to be placed cheek by jowl. Labor, industrial capital, and agriculture were to be placed in the closest possible juxtaposition. The development of industry in the farming areas of the West and South was "the keynote of American progress," an essential part of that social happiness and well-being that was the true national felicity.[30]

As Greeley surveyed the vocal opposition to protection, he found that it centered in two groups of individuals—misguided idealists and sinister creatures who were in the pay of "foreign interests." Among the former, he ranked Bryant and the *Post*. His chief bête noire among the latter was David Ames Wells, special commissioner of the revenue from 1866 to 1869.

Wells's report from the revenue office for the year 1869, indicating his conversion to tariff reform, unleashed torrents of the *Tribune's* wrath. Greeley described the commissioner as a poor, servile creature, "bought and paid for by the foreign interest." It had to be admitted that the evidences of Wells's turpitude were circumstantial, but they were sufficient for the embattled editor. Wells took exactly the positions that British industrial interests wanted him to take, and the inference to be derived from this was obvious. As the loafer had once remarked in another case of circumstantial evidence, "Where you find them sassengers plenty, you don't see no dogs." These *Tribune* attacks, coupled with similar onslaughts from other protectionist sources, stirred up so great a clamor that President Grant abolished the commissioner's office in 1870 and the able and honest Wells found himself out of a job.[31]

Another renegade protectionist upon whom Greeley poured out his wrath was the future agrarian leader, Ignatius Donnelly. This warm and expansive Minnesotan was starting in 1869 a course of political action that was to make him successively a Liberal Republican, Granger, Greenbacker, and Populist. He acted as spokesman for a sullen and angry West that was receiving low prices for its agricultural produce, the while it paid high prices for its manufactured goods. Donnelly made no bones about declaring that the Republican party must come out against high protection or lose the whole Northwest. This heresy defeated his renomination for Congress on the Republican ticket. He thereupon split the party by running on a separate ticket and a Democrat was elected to his Congressional seat.

Donnelly's action was anathema to Greeley, who promptly branded him a "soldier of fortune," a "demagogue," with a "sinuous and slimy trail," who had abandoned protection and was getting ready to turn Copperhead. Donnelly's bolt had thrown the Congressional seat away. "We think this proves him a false, selfish, unworthy man and justifies our conviction that he cares nothing for the Republican party except as it ministers to his own aggrandizement."

As to Donnelly's complaints about prices, Greeley had a simple remedy that would make unnecessary the lowering of tariff barriers. All that needed to be done was to divert 600,000 Americans from agriculture to manufacturing.[32] Thus spake the great proponent of protection and party regularity, the man who for years had been urging Americans to leave the city for the country. Three years later, the same charges of recreancy to the Republican party that he now hurled at Donnelly were to beat about his own head.[33]

Early in 1870, Jay Gould wrote to Greeley suavely complimenting him upon the valuable service he was doing to American labor by his advocacy of protection.[34] It is doubtful that Greeley was much moved by praise from such a source, but it was true enough that the *Tribune's* editor was devoting much thought to promoting the welfare of labor. The tariff was a natural means to this end. Indeed, Greeley declared that there was a natural affinity between labor and the principle of protection, since every effort of the laboring class toward organization was protective "in its scope and tendency."[35] There were also other means which could be used on behalf of labor.

It was an axiom with Greeley that labor's situation must be improved. He declared that the wage earner must be raised from drudgery and servility to a plane of self-respect, self-guidance, and genuine independence.[36] But how was this to be done? Just as before the Civil War, when confronted by this problem, Greeley made proposals that laid the burden of responsibility for improvement upon the laborers themselves.

Outside the blessings of protection, Greeley's answer to labor's needs was two-fold—coöperative production and migration from the cities of the East. He was insistent upon both as great projects of self-help through which the wage earner could obtain a healthy and important place in the American social order. "Never before on earth was it so easy for the poor to get land as it is in this country today," he declared in 1867, in bland disregard of the inadequacies of the Homestead Act. In ten years, starting with neither capital nor experience, an ambitious, hard-working man should be able to acquire an eighty-acre farm, half of it under cultivation, together with a good head of stock. At the age of twenty-five, a man ought to have at least set up for himself. And if the migrant from the East did not want to farm, let him go into manufacturing or mining in the West. Industrial emancipation for the urban workers was equally feasible, through the development of coöperatives. "We believe," he told the nation's laborers, "that ten thousand extensive, capacious and profitable manufacturing and mechanical establishments might be started during 1871 by the Working Men of this state [New York] alone."[37]

Skeptics might scoff at solving the problem of farm prices by an exodus of farm labor to manufacturing centers, the while the problem of urban congestion was solved by an exodus of city labor to the farm. And, indeed, Greeley did not continue to advocate the former remedy, after his outburst in answer to Donnelly's plaints. But his faith in coöperatives and in an urban movement to the West was vigorous and undying. For those ideas meant national development, hope for the poor, and the elimination of that ugly specter that was forever cropping up—the specter of class war.[38]

Contemplation of labor's problems always prompted Greeley to renew his search for class-strife panaceas, such as coöperatives and the westward movement. These were much more attractive to him than were specific and localized remedies for specific labor ills. Realistic attempts to meet the needs of the laboring man in a factory or in a trade usually found the *Tribune's* editor in the camp of the critics.

Labor unions were, as always, objects of suspicion, so far as Greeley was concerned. He admitted that labor had the right and duty to organize, and that such action had been productive of "signal good."[39] He continued to advocate collective bargaining. But it is difficult to discover what positive good he thought had been accomplished by unions. He believed that strikes did not pay, and that neither strikers nor anyone else should interfere with the man who was willing to work at a given job. "The law of supply and demand will rule," he declared in 1871. He asserted on one occasion that labor was a commodity, just as coal is a commodity. Strikes destroyed the labor commodity, just as coal dealers would destroy coal if they burned their coal yards.[40] Greeley opposed the eight-hour day (until shortly before his nomination for the Presidency),[41] had no objection in principle to woman and child labor, defended the right of tenement-house owners to all the rent they could get,[42] and declared that the employer had a fundamental right to employ any labor, native or foreign born, that he saw fit to hire. Capital had rights as well as labor, and this was a free land where everyone's rights must be respected. Labor must work out its own salvation, but in so doing it must not interfere with the right of the employer to hire and fire and use his money in all lawful ways.

Greeley believed that the best cure for labor's ills was the effort of abstinence (in other words, long-range saving) plus the habit of steady toil. The resolution of a labor congress that encroachments

by capital on the rights of labor must be "crushed" was all "bosh."
What needed "crushing" was the grog shop, the beer parlor, the
billiard room, the cigar store, the gambling den, and the "sink of
pollution." Keep the laboring class out of these low places, and
labor would soon be independent of capitalists through its development of coöperative industries financed by its own savings. Lacking
this program, labor congresses would not amount to much.[43]

Greeley honestly wanted to see labor prosper, but he felt that
this prosperity must be achieved within the framework of a capitalistic social order and by efforts fundamentally in harmony with
that order. Always respectful of the rights of property, always fearful of class war, he sought to protect property and prevent the
development of the class struggle. Industrial coöperatives, created
by the workers with their own savings, appealed to him as an
evolutionary development that could take place peacefully within
the capitalistic system. He wanted this to be true and so, with
characteristically hopeful imagination, he knew that it was true.
He ignored the contradictions involved in championing simultaneously coöperatives and free competition, just as he ignored the
credit and price warfare by means of which the capitalists cut the
heart out of the coöperative movement in this period,[44] just as he
ignored or at least minimized the difficulties involved in moving
urban labor out to the agrarian regions of the West and South.
Stubbornly he kept insisting that coöperatives and the back-to-the-
land movement were the answers to labor's demand for an improvement of its condition. They were safe, conservative remedies. Best
of all, acceptance of them as the proper remedies placed responsibility for the hardships of labor where, in his heart, Greeley felt it
belonged—on the shoulders of the working class.

Greeley could take this attitude toward labor and still feel that
he was labor's friend because of his unlimited faith in the American
future. America was to him a land where glorious opportunity lay
ready and waiting for all honest and industrious men. If only men
would work as hard as he had worked, and be as frugal in the hard
times as he had been, they would inevitably prosper. If they refused
to save money, if they refused to go where opportunities beckoned
in Texas or Missouri or Minnesota, they had no one but themselves
to blame for their misery.

His vision of the American future was a constant stimulus to the
Tribune's editor. So many glorious things were ready for accomplishment, if men would only put their hearts and minds to the
task! Greeley glimpsed the possibilities of an American electrical
age, one that would transform life in the city and on the farm.

He saw vast possibilities in conservation, irrigation, reforestation, flood control, tree belts in prairie states, soil analysis, the diversification of crops, social development of rural life by means of farmers' clubs. He dedicated his last book, *What I Know of Farming,* to the man who should first make a power-propelled plow that would turn over ten acres a day at a depth of two feet and at a cost of not over two dollars an acre. He dreamed of an agriculture made scientific and pleasant and exciting, of life on the farm transformed from back-breaking drudgery and poverty to dignified affluence.[45] And this was only one aspect of his dream for America.

Greeley's vision of the American future roamed far beyond a revolution in agricultural techniques. In his mind's eye he saw great tides of capital and labor flowing across and up and down the country, enriching and developing the nation. There were infinite ways in which these agencies could be utilized, and proposals that varied from the growth of hyson tea in Tennessee to the extension of industrial development in the West and South poured from his pen. America was headed straight for wealth and plenty.

Greeley was as sure that there was no excuse for the pauper in post-Civil War America, as he was that special provisions for food and shelter were necessary in order to winter live stock on the Great Plains. No amount of demonstration could convince him of the feasibility of range wintering, for he could always point triumphantly to some exceptionally hard winter when there had been considerable mortality among some of the range herds. It was so with poverty. Confronted by its existence, he could always point triumphantly to those who had escaped from it as proof of his general thesis. To his mind, attempts at excusing poverty in terms of inadequacy of opportunity only reflected discredit upon the individuals who were poverty stricken. It was so obvious that they had failed to grasp the golden opportunities which America provided.[46]

It was not only of material advance that Greeley dreamed. Moral and educational advances must vie with economic development in this happy land of the future. Through a combination of prohibitory laws and moral pressure, the curse of alcohol must be lifted from the American home. There must also be a new approach to the Indian problem. Poor Lo must be taught to be a good citizen, not first defrauded and then exterminated. Vital to the nation, also, was the problem of educating the rising generation.

Greeley was an earnest believer in the free, secular, public school system that had come so largely to prevail in the United States. He wanted that system kept intact and developed, and he fought

repeatedly with Catholics who wanted to see state money deflected
to the use of church schools. Such a move, he believed, would wreck
the public school system, particularly in the rural areas. Also
important in his eyes was the form and content of educational
training at the college level.

Greeley was still a trustee of the People's College at Havana
(now Montour Falls), New York, an institution that, because of
financial difficulties, had never got under way. In 1865, he became
interested in the movement to found Cornell University that was
inaugurated by Ezra Cornell and Andrew Dickson White. Cornell
and White were seeking to make this institution an answer to the
challenge of the times. They wanted it to be in part a liberal arts
college, but also one that would emphasize science and give professional training in agriculture and mechanics. This was altogether
in the spirit of the People's College, and Greeley became interested.
He lent a hand at the founding of the new institution, gave it editorial support in the first stormy days of its existence, and retained
a sympathetic interest in it during the rest of his life. In a minor
but very real way, Horace Greeley was one of the founders of
Cornell University.[47]

Educationally, morally, economically, the America of Greeley's
dream had to be moving ever forward. Inevitably, it had to grow
geographically as well, for the man who had opposed the annexation of Texas and the thrust beyond the Rockies had at last come
to accept the logic of Manifest Destiny. An ardent sponsor of Cuban
relief, Greeley felt that that rich island would sooner or later
gravitate into the arms of the United States. Far more important
was Canada. Some day, when Canada was ready and willing, Greeley
believed that the linkage of common interests and geographical
proximity would have its inevitable effect. When that day came,
the United States would joyfully receive the Canadians into the
American union.

For the merging of kindred peoples, with geographical propin-
quity, economic ties, common social customs and common cultural
traditions was among the signs of the times. Nationalism was on
the upsurge in Italy and Germany. It was driving the Turk out of
Europe. Even Bismarck, wrong though he was in flouting democratic principles, was championing a righteous cause in his struggle
to unify Germany. As the Franco-Prussian War came on, Greeley
did not hesitate to label Napoleon III as the aggressor, the man
who was standing in the way of needful German unification. The
news of Sedan made the editor of the *Tribune* rejoice. He felt that
the skies of international politics were brightened as a result of

the victories of the German army. Germany was at last a nation. With the accompanying Italian seizure of the Holy City, Cavour's dream had at last been realized. Serfdom had been abolished in Russia, a mighty forward step. Suffrage was broadening everywhere. Freedom was on the march, and in the forefront of her serried ranks, leader of the leaders, strode the United States. "Shall we question that these advances are irreversible?" thundered the *Tribune*. The answer, of course, was "No."[48]

Greeley did not think that the United States was a perfect nation. There were altogether too many Americans who were trying to live by stockmarket gambling instead of by honest work, too many rum swillers and bawdyhouse keepers, too many who insisted on selling liquor and tobacco in the city instead of striking out for honest employment in the rural regions. Such men were handicaps to progress, and Greeley would not rest until they were driven out of the land, along with the liquor and the vice to which they and their ilk pandered. But the great body of Americans were righteous men and women, and his mission consisted in leading a people possessed of great "national virtue" to still greater heights of social and political perfection, and to a heightened sense of their national oneness and their national greatness.

For you these from me, O Democracy. . . .

NOTES FOR CHAPTER 21

1. Early in the war, Greeley had declared himself at one with the radicals in accepting Sumner's theory of state suicide, but by the end of 1863 he was abandoning this point of view, declaring that he sought only to leave the government unembarrassed by any dogmas or theories as to the manner in which peace should be made.—*Tribune*, Mar. 15, Apr. 5, 21, 1862, Feb. 7, Nov. 12, 23, 1863; Salmon P. Chase Collection (Pierpont Morgan Lib.), Chase to Greeley, Aug. 23, 1863; Greeley Letters (Huntington Lib.), Greeley to James Graham, Sept. 4, 1863.

2. *Tribune*, Dec. 10, 11, 28, 1863.

3. *Tribune*, Jan. 1863, Feb. 5, Mar. 7, May 5, 10, 1864; Chas. H. McCarthy, *Lincoln's Plan of Reconstruction* (N. Y., 1901), pp. 247-48.

4. *Tribune*, Aug. 5, 1864.

5. *Tribune*, Jan. 2, Feb. 8, 23, Mar. 6, 27, 1865; Greeley Papers (N. Y. P. L.), F. P. Blair to Greeley, Jan. 27, 1865; Morgan Papers, Greeley to Rev. A. Brown, Feb. 26, 1865; Greeley to Mrs. L. S. Chapin (courtesy of Mr. and Mrs. Robert Fales). Greeley's letter to Brown was revealing: "Mr. A. Lincoln is a gentleman with whom I hope to be always on terms of civility, but not of cordiality. I opposed his renomination for the simple

reason that I did not deem him the man for the place. I finally supported his reelection for the country's sake, not his. I have no right to ask his favor, and I dread to give him unasked advice. I will at any time win others in saying what I think of your merits, but shall not ask A. L. to do anything for my sake." To Mrs. Chapin, Greeley wrote that Lincoln would not dare give her a post office even if he wanted to, adding contemptuously, "He wants *votes*."

6. *Tribune*, Mar. 16, Apr. 11, 13, 1865.
7. *Tribune*, Apr. 15, 17-19, 24, 1865; *Independent*, Apr. 27, 1865.
8. Stahl Collection, Greeley to Mrs. Allen, May 7, June 23, 1865; *Tribune*, Apr. 20, May 5-20, Oct. 7, 1865; Rhodes, *Hist. of the U. S.*, V, 147-49, 152.
9. Benton, *Greeley on Lincoln*, pp. 260-70; Greeley Papers (L. of C.), Greeley to B. Brockway, Dec. 8, 1870; Greeley Papers (N. Y. P. L.), Colfax to Greeley, July 15, 1868; newspaper clipping (n. d.), "The Private Habits of Horace Greeley," by Mark Twain; *N. Y. Commercial Advertiser*, June 10, 1867; Depew, *Memories*, 12; Hudson, *Journalism*, pp. 660-61; Oberholtzer, *Cooke*, I, 588-589; Reavis, *Greeley*, p. 505; Ingersoll, *Greeley*, pp. 565-68. A newspaper clipping in the possession of the author recounts the story of Greeley's "last words."
10. Zabriskie, *Greeley*, p. 356.
11. Greeley Papers (N. Y. P. L.), Ida Greeley to Greeley, Oct.-Dec., 1871; Washburne Papers, Greeley to E. B. Washburne, Oct. 9, 1871; Benton, *Greeley on Lincoln*, p. 203.
12. Benton, *Greeley on Lincoln*, pp. 194, 236-41.
13. The books were the second volume of *The American Conflict, Recollections of a Busy Life, Essays on Political Economy, Letters from Texas*, and *What I Know of Farming*.
14. *Independent*, Jan. 28, Dec. 8, 1864.
15. Tayler Lewis, *State Rights. A Photograph from the Ruins of Ancient Greece.* (Albany, 1864), pp. 21-25, 27-35, 50-55, 57; *Independent*, Aug. 18, Dec. 8, 1864. Lewis rebuked Greeley (84-87) for maintaining the right of peaceful separation, but Greeley declared that he only seemed to be at variance with Lewis on this point.
16. *Tribune*, Apr. 14, 29, Oct. 7, 1865, Mar. 28, May 7, 9, Aug. 10, 21, Sept. 22, 26, 1867, Aug. 31, 1870; Greeley, *The American Conflict*, I, 347-51.
17. *Tribune*, June 10, Sept. 12, 1865. He urged the restoration of *habeas corpus*. Let the military prisons be emptied. Actual crimes, such as murder and arson, should be punished, but political offenses should be amnestied without exception. He took issue with Thad Stevens's proposal to confiscate southern lands on the ground that it would heighten southern animosity and hatred for the North.
18. *Tribune*, May 30, 1850, Apr. 27, May 3, June 20, July 10, 31, 1865.
19. *Tribune*, June 30, 1865, Jan. 17, May 28, Nov. 19, 1866; *Independent*, Apr. 6, May 11, 1865.
20. *Tribune*, Mar. 12, 1866.
21. *Tribune*, Jan. 4, 1864, May 27, 1865, May 30, Aug. 22, Nov. 16, 21, 27, 1866.
22. *Tribune*, July 10, Oct. 7, Dec. 27, 1865.
23. Greeley Papers (N. Y. P. L.), Greeley to J. R. Lawrence, Dec. 16, 1866; *Tribune*, July 8, Aug. 1, 8, Oct. 14, 1865, July 11, 1866, Mar. 21, Apr. 22, 1867.
24. *Tribune*, Apr. 10, Nov. 19, 1866.

25. Greeley Papers (N. Y. P. L.), Greeley to Colfax, Feb. 25, 1866, McCulloch to Greeley, Mar. 5, 1866, Jay Cooke to Greeley, May 10, 1866, Greeley to Colfax, Mar. 17, 1871; Greeley, *Political Economy*, pp. 237-42; *Tribune*, Jan. 5, Feb. 8, 10, 18, 25, June 16, July 13, Sept. 11, Dec. 6, 1865, Mar. 5, 6, 1866, Jan. 9, 10, Mar. 7, 8, 16, 1867, Jan. 6, 8, Apr. 9, Aug. 1, Nov. 10-12, Dec. 3, 21, 1868, Jan. 1, 5, May 8ff., 31, June 17, Sept. 24, 25, Dec. 31, 1869, Feb. 3, Mar. 9, Aug. 6, 1870, Aug. 17, Nov. 2, 1871, Feb. 9, Apr. 12, 1872.

26. At first Greeley had been inclined to favor the Civil War income tax, but by 1869 he was bitterly opposed to it. He believed that it put a premium on perjury and was "a tax on honesty and truth." It was neither just nor wise, he felt, to tax the rich and exempt the poor, and it was unconstitutional to boot.—*Tribune*, Dec. 15, 1864, June 26, 1869, July 1, 1870.

27. Greeley, *Political Economy*, pp. 50-51; *Tribune*, Feb. 2, 1865, Apr. 5, 1866, Feb. 12, 18, 1867, Dec. 2, 1868, Feb. 13, Aug. 6, Sept. 9, 1869, Nov. 22, 1870, Jan. 16, 1871; Oberholtzer, *Cooke*, II, 165, 413-14.

28. *Tribune*, July 10, 1869.

29. Greeley, *Political Economy*, pp. 97-98.

30. *Tribune*, Jan. 11, 1870, June 28, Sept. 15, 1871.

31. *Tribune*, Jan. 6, 7, Mar. 18, 23, 31, Apr. 5, 6, June 8, Dec. 21, 1869, Feb. 3, Apr. 6, 1870, July 11, 1871; Rhodes, *Hist. of the U. S.*, VI, 217-34.

32. Anthony Collection (N. Y. P. L.), Greeley to ?, Jan. 17, 1870; *Tribune*, Nov. 19, Dec. 24, 1869.

33. In 1871 Greeley became involved in an argument over protection with John Stuart Mill that resulted in something of a Greeley triumph. The celebrated Englishman took the doubtful stand that high wages in the United States were the result of cheap and abundant land. Greeley neatly demolished this argument. Henry Demarest Lloyd then entered the fray. Admitting that Mill had been wrong, Lloyd took the position that protection was not the cause of high wages. Greeley was forced to admit that at best protection was only one cause of high wages, the main cause being productivity.—*Tribune*, Feb. 13, 22, Mar. 28, Nov. 18, 20, 1871.

34. Greeley Papers (N. Y. P. L.), Gould to Greeley, Feb. 2, 1870.

35. *Tribune*, July 1, 1871, Feb. 24, 1872.

36. Greeley, *What I Know of Farming*, pp. xi-xii.

37. *Tribune*, Apr. 29, 1867, Aug. 17, 1868, June 13, 1871. The *Tribune* is full of similar statements. On migration, for example, see the issues of Jan. 12, 1866, Mar. 13, 1867, Dec. 26, 1868, July 12, Nov. 24, 1869, Jan. 9, 14, 1871. On coöperative production, see the issues of Oct. 18, 1866, Feb. 5, 1867, Dec. 4, 1868, Feb. 2, 1869, Nov. 16, 1870, Feb. 10, 1871. On occasion Greeley would admit that it was better to buy land from the railroads in the West than to try to take up free land, but this was as far as his criticism of the Homestead Act extended.

38. *Tribune*, Apr. 19, 1864, Jan. 11, 1870.

39. Greeley, *Political Economy*, p. 344.

40. *Tribune*, Mar. 27-30, Apr. 1, June 15, 1869.

41. *Tribune*, May 28, June 8, Aug. 27, 1866.

42. *Tribune*, July 2, 1866, Mar. 23, Apr. 1, 1867.

43. *Tribune*, Aug. 27, 1866, July 19, 1870, Jan. 16, June 22, 1871.

44. P. S. Foner, *History of the Labor Movement in the United States* (N. Y., 1947), pp. 417-20.

45. Greeley, *What I Know of Farming,* pp. ix-x, 26, 185, 196-97, 234, 244, 256, 274, 284-85, 289; *Tribune,* May 14, 1870, Jan. 2, Sept. 15, Oct. 23, 1871, Apr. 13, 1872.

46. *New York Times,* May 14, 1934; C. Bengston, "Horace Greeley and the Founding of the Union Colony in Colorado," (Unpublished MS, a copy of which is in the New York Public Library); O. M. Dickerson, "Letters of Horace Greeley to Nathaniel C. Meeker," *Colorado Magazine,* XIX (Mar. 1942), 50-62, and (May 1942), 102-10; *Tribune,* Nov. 5, 1870, Jan. 21, Mar. 3, 6, 7, Apr. 12, 14, 26, 1871, Feb. 17, Mar. 4, 1872.

47. *Independent,* June 2, 1864, Aug. 3, Sept. 21, 1865; *Tribune,* Jan. 11, Feb. 19, July 6, Oct. 2, Nov. 30, Dec. 15, 1869, Jan. 29, Feb. 17, Mar. 15, Apr. 27, July 16, 1870, June 24, 1871; Greeley Papers (N. Y. P. L.), various letters, 1871; Harrison Howard Correspondence, Greeley to Howard, Aug. 8, 1871; C. L. Becker, *Cornell University: Founders and the Founding* (Ithaca, 1943), pp. 22, 63-65, 86-87, 91.

48. *Independent,* June 9, 1864; *Tribune,* Mar. 17, 1863, Dec. 24, 1864, July 6, 1865, June 8, Aug. 3, 27, 1866, Mar. 31, 1867, Jan. 1, Sept. 25, 1868, Jan. 5, 1869, July 9, Aug. 11, 25, Sept. 1-30, Nov. 10, 25, 1870, Jan. 13, Feb. 24, Mar. 4, 21, Apr. 11, 13, Aug. 28, 1871. Greeley was bitterly critical of the French Communist uprising of 1871. It was bad because it delayed the republican government that Thiers was trying to establish.

As for Greeley and Cuban relief, see Greeley Papers (N. Y. P. L.), D. Taylor to Greeley, Mar. 3, 1870.

CHAPTER 22

Pursuit of the Dream

N EW YORK CITY, MICROCOSM OF THE NATION, WAS an opulent, rollicking, roistering city at the dawn of the Gilded Age, a town filled to the brim with diamonded men, richly bejeweled women, smooth stock operators, worthy poor, toughs, bums, bawdy houses, faro dens, fortunetellers, a modicum of esthetes and moralists and an over-all reverence for silver and gold. Walt Whitman, visiting the metropolis in the fall of 1870, was given a sense of exaltation by the splendor and the color, the rich shops, the costly buildings, the scarcely ever interrupted roar of the city traffic, the "hurrying, feverish, electric crowds of men. . . ." Then, looking below the surface of all this rush and glitter, he was appalled by the lack of high standards, the flippancy and vulgarity and low cunning that he saw on every hand.[1]

New York's sprawling population (the city proper had not quite reached the million mark by 1870, but well-nigh 2,000,000 people drew their sustenance from its factories, wharves, and stores) still swarmed and struggled amid the most violent contrasts of poverty and affluence. The nation's industrial development was beginning to move with rapidity toward the great achievements of the age, and for New York this meant an era of suffering for the sweated poor, but also of booming trade, of dazzling ventures that ranged from railroads to real estate, of operas and symphonies (whether in music or in steel), of flamboyant parties where toasts were drunk in costly vintages, of Saratoga holidays, European jaunts, international marriages, a sybaritic flaunting of incomes, a megalomaniac voracity of desire. It meant that, even before 1870, there was beginning to develop an enormous concentration of wealth in the hands of a small minority of the city's inhabitants.

In 1869, the *Tribune* published in a quadruple-sheet edition the income taxes of thirty-seven columns of New Yorkers. Of these men,

sixty-seven had had incomes of over $100,000 in 1868, this without
reckoning their returns from the stocks and bonds of railroads,
banks, and other corporations that were taxed at source (a restriction that excluded from the list such men as Commodore Vanderbilt). William B. Astor's reported income was $1,079,212. The great
merchant prince, Alexander T. Stewart, reported $3,019,218.[2]

Great means lavishly expended brought into being the New York
Philharmonic Orchestra, fostered art collections, proliferated
libraries, centered the best that the American theatre could furnish
on the New York boards. It also built up the city architecturally,
occasionally with genuine beauty and splendor, but chiefly with a
profusion of tinseled and gaudy displays of bad taste. It was amazing that this enormous concentration of gold produced so few
buildings of architectural merit, so much shoddy marble, weathering
black and brown, so much chipping and crumbling brownstone, so
much iron staining itself and its surroundings an ugly rust unless
it was constantly repainted. Fisk and Gould's marble "Castle of
Erie" on the northwest corner of Twenty-third Street and Eighth
Avenue, with its profusion of gold-inlaid black walnut, plate-glass
mirrors, crimson draperies, nymphs and cupids—blatantly gaudy,
incredibly vulgar—proclaimed the triumph of a materialism that
rested not so much upon humanity and justice as it did upon
shrewdness and the acquisitive instinct.

For these were the days of a chairmaker named William Marcy
Tweed, who bossed Tammany Hall and plundered the city of millions, while prominent businessmen, in fear lest their taxes be raised,
vouched for the accuracy of his accounts. They were the days of
the sinister Peter B. Sweeny, and "Slippery Dick" Connolly, and
"Elegant Oakey" Hall, henchmen of the master vulture, and of
the corrupt justices Barnard and Cardozo, who prostituted justice
and the bench to serve the ends of the Tammany boss. They were
the days of a stock-market operator—dark, stealthy, and without
scruple—named Jay Gould; the days which saw celebrated a sanctimonious wedding of religion and rascality in the person of Daniel
Drew. Most of all, because in his glittering prodigality and impudent good humor and zest for the purchasable things of life he best
symbolized the spirit of New York, they were the days of Jim Fisk.

Jubilee Jim, with the expansive smile, the waxed and pointed
blond mustache, the hand with diamonds on its fat fingers and a
swift, unobtrusive charity in its fat palm. Impudent Jim, meeting
President Grant's carriage at Long Branch the year after the great
Gold Corner failed because the President had ordered Secretary
Boutwell to sell gold and, so the *Tribune* declared, thumbing his

nose at the chief executive of the United States. Brazen Jim, exclaiming after an Erie coup had failed: "Nothing is lost save honor!" Rake Jim, winning Josie Mansfield, losing her to Ned Stokes, sobbing, "She won't let me leave my gumshoes in the house," while his triumphant rival sneered that Josie "would as soon receive a louse." Colonel Jim, the late Colonel Jim of the Ninth Regiment of the New York National Guard, dead of Ned Stokes's bullet, lying in state in his guardsman's uniform in the Opera House while thousands mourned—with the flag on the Stock Exchange raised to half mast and then lowered lest people think that Wall Street was paying tribute to the departed—with Jay Gould remarking, "Any faults which Colonel Fisk may have committed were solely due to the exuberance of his animal spirits." Legendary Jim, immortalized in ballad as the man who always gave to the poor and who

> Did all his deeds, both the good and the bad,
> In the broad open light of the day.[3]

Jim Fisk and the New York that was his home bore a distinct resemblance to one another.

Gay, glittering, beautiful, exciting, sordid New York had a story to tell, but it was a confused and dubious story, a tale that jumbled together success and shame. New York needed a man who would preach devotion to the national interest as superior to devotion to the art of money-getting, a man with a passion for public and private morality, a man with a message. And Greeley's message, delivered with the prestige of business success behind it, had at least the virtues of clarity and simplicity.

"I long to see each honest, industrious American sitting under his own vine and fig-tree with none to molest or make him afraid."[4] So wrote Greeley in the *Independent,* a few weeks after Andrew Johnson took over control of the White House. In pursuance of this aim, his editorials in the *Tribune* and his contributions to the weekly edited by his friend Theodore Tilton exhaled an optimistic trust in man in general and the President in particular.

The *Tribune's* editor had no fear, so he declared, that any state would pass laws confronting the freedmen with the harsh alternatives of exile or serfdom. Indeed, he called upon the southern gentry to take the lead in reconstructing the South and, though he admitted that he preferred universal suffrage, he expressed a willingness to proceed slowly toward that end. Literacy or property tests for voting would be wholly acceptable to him, provided that they applied equally to white and black.

This position was definitely more moderate than that of men like Chase, Sumner, and Wendell Phillips, who were demanding the imposition of Negro suffrage on the South. Plainly, Greeley hoped to effect a meeting of minds between the President and northern and southern leaders of thought and opinion, a concurrence that would bring in its train both universal amnesty and a limited suffrage for the Negro. Harmony was his watchword. Greeley called for such a Fourth of July celebration that summer as North and South had never seen before, one that would make every American citizen realize the worth of the country and its institutions.[5]

But harmony in the Greeley mode scarcely flourished during the summer of 1865. President Johnson did nothing to foster the qualified Negro suffrage that he had professed to favor, reconstructing one state after another with no attempt at providing votes for the Negro. At the same time, reports multiplied of laws discriminating against the freedmen in Tennessee, North Carolina, Alabama, and Virginia. The South was fumbling with a great problem, but not in such a way as to endear it to the embittered North. And in the North, the doctrine of universal amnesty gained no ground. At best, sectional relations were in an aimless drift, one at least as likely to take the sections apart as it was to bring them together.

In the midst of these signs and portents, Greeley steadily pursued his policy of harmonization. Southern conservatives were told that there was a direct relationship between recognition of the Negro's rights and the re-admission of southern states by Congress. The South was also warned that a genuine reconstruction of southern society would be impossible, if 4,000,000 Negroes were left profoundly dissatisfied, apprehensive, and neither quiet nor safe.[6] The North was told that forgiveness was essential to a sound national reconstruction, that equal suffrage was vital to a maintenance of American ideals, and northern Republicans were warned that without Negro suffrage every southern state would go Democratic, an event that would set back more than fifteen degrees the shadow on the dial of human progress.[7] At the same time, northern radicals were informed that Thad Stevens' proposal to confiscate southern lands was worse than impractical—"certain to work vast and enduring mischief" upon southern opinion.[8] And while thus seeking to mold popular opinion, Greeley also urged the President to take the path of amnesty and equal suffrage.[9]

Greeley was willing, if worst came to worst, to force Negro suffrage on the South, but his spirit shrank from violence. He viewed the deepening radical hostility to Johnson's control of reconstruction with almost as much fear as he did the signs of southern recalcitrance in regard to civil rights and impartial suffrage. Just before Congress met in December 1865, he went down to Washington, "not uninvited," as he boasted later, intent on preventing a breach between Congress and the President and on bridging the gap between North and South. There he urged Johnson to call three eminent northern antislavery leaders such as Gerrit Smith and Governor Andrew of Massachusetts into council with three eminent ex-rebels such as Robert E. Lee and Alexander H. Stephens. It was Greeley's idea that Johnson should summon this group to the White House and have them live there until they had worked out a plan that would restore national harmony. He pledged the *Tribune's* support in advance to any adjustment thus agreed upon. But the President obviously had little taste for any such spectacular mode of procedure, and the plan was not adopted.[10]

Even after Congress appointed the Joint Committee on Reconstruction in December 1865 to determine whether or not the Johnson-reconstructed states were entitled to representation, Greeley continued playing the part of general conciliator.[11] He kept asserting that all was going well between the President and the national legislature, a whistling in the dark which was done simply and solely for public effect. At the same time, he kept trying to improve the situation by more direct action. Going down to Washington a second time in the role of conciliator, he urged Johnson to invite the Joint Committee on Reconstruction to the White House for friendly evening discussions of the problem involved, these discussions to continue until some basis for agreement had been found. This admonition delivered, Greeley returned to New York, where he kept preaching moderation and forebearance. He told the country that the Union party had been formed by men who agreed to differ and to tolerate differences. It could and should continue to exhibit that same spirit of wise forebearance. At the same time, he warned Johnson that his obstinate refusal to make concessions would inevitably alienate the *Tribune.*[12]

But Johnson was not one to take a lesson on obduracy from Horace Greeley. Supported by Secretary of State Seward and by Henry J. Raymond and the *Times,* backed by a strong body of opinion both within and without Washington, the President stood pat in his struggle with Congress. He would not follow Greeley's suggestions. As befitted a Democrat with strong views as to states' rights, he bent a cold and fishy eye upon Congressional attempts to

assume state prerogatives. When Congress passed a bill designed
to enlarge and strengthen the Freedmen's Bureau, a federal agency
designed to help the Negroes get a good start in the life of freedom,
Johnson vetoed it on grounds that varied from charges of unconstitutionality to the assertion that it represented undue coddling
of the colored people.

The *Tribune* reacted strongly to the Freedmen's Bureau veto.
Greeley had supported the bill as necessary, since it seemed that
the Negro was not to be allowed "to protect himself with the ballot." Now he took Johnson to task for depriving the Negroes of
much-needed aid, for virtually abandoning these "southern unionists." His editorials still called for moderation, but Greeley made
it clear that Johnson had not only abandoned the "southern unionists," but had also bade defiance to Congress by a veto that was a
virtual declaration of war.[13]

The distance between the two ends of Pennsylvania Avenue
steadily lengthened during the spring and summer of 1866, and as
it did so Greeley's attitude toward Johnson became more and more
critical. On May 16, 1866, John Russell Young of the *Tribune* staff
wrote regretfully to his friend Benjamin C. Truman, President
Johnson's secretary, that the *Tribune* "has taken a bitter stand
against Johnson, and we can't afford to see any good in him or his
policy." Greeley was at last casting Johnson to the dogs, a fact that
became increasingly apparent as the months went by. There were
a number of reasons for this action.

The *Tribune's* editor had never lost sight of the importance of
Negro votes. They were, he kept repeating, essential to the maintenance of a high protective policy, but Johnson, provokingly
enough, showed no disposition to recognize the force of this argument. Greeley was also more and more upset by reports of ill-
treatment of Negroes in the South, of blatant and flagrant denials
of civil rights to the freedmen. The Treasury Department added
to the editor's irritation. Greeley was pushing for a rapid elimination of the greenbacks from the currency, pooh-poohing the difficulties involved by asserting that, if 500,000 men were turned
out of employment by deflation, they could go to work raising corn
in the West, but Secretary of the Treasury McCulloch moved
toward contraction altogether too slowly for the editor's taste.
Finally, Greeley was becoming increasingly suspicious that the
influence of Raymond's *Times* was waxing with the administration
at Washington, just as in the previous decade it had waxed with
Weed and Seward. A complexity of influences, prejudices, and

predilections was pushing Greeley constantly toward the radical camp.[14]

The *Tribune* now began supporting all radical movements and castigating Johnson for attacking or vetoing them. This was true of the bill guaranteeing civil equality for the Negro, which Greeley supported so vigorously that its passage over the President's veto prompted Theodore Tilton to propose for a toast at the *Tribune's* twenty-fifth anniversary banquet "The Author of the Civil Rights Bill." It was also true of the Congressional report on the treatment of the Negroes in the South, and of Senator Fessenden's report from the Joint Committee on Reconstruction against the claims of the reconstructed states for immediate representation in Congress. Greeley declared that it was his intention to accept whatever plan of reconstruction was adopted by the great body of Unionists in Congress, and when the fourteenth amendment to the constitution was proposed he lined the *Tribune* up in its support. He was still for Universal Amnesty and Impartial Suffrage, he declared, but he was also for the amendment. They were not fundamentally at variance with one another. Broadly speaking, this assertion was true.[15]

Added vigor was given to Greeley's criticism of the administration by the political events of 1866, particularly by the Philadelphia convention of Johnson's supporters. This took place on August 14, and a dramatic note was added to the occasion when erstwhile enemies from North and South marched into the hall of the convention arm in arm. The affair, in the minds of men like Weed, Montgomery Blair, Dean Richmond of the old New York Democracy, and possibly Johnson himself, was the prelude to a new party to be composed of Democrats and Republican conservatives. As such, it aroused the *Tribune's* wrath.

The *Tribune* asserted that Weed had taken a "wagon-load of rich men" to Philadelphia, and there had done his best to "make the heavy fellows come down with their dust" for the new party and for Weed's incidental profit. Greeley caricatured the convention as an amalgam of Johnsonized Republicans, rebels, and Copperheads, an arm-in-arm hodgepodge that was ready and willing to surrender the colored people of the South to their exasperated and discomfited ex-masters. This was now Johnson's policy, declared Greeley. The President wouldn't give the Negro the vote, but was perfectly willing to allow southern whites to vote in the Negro's name. It was now plain that the President did not want harmony with Congress, but was seeking a further lease of power through the enlistment of Democratic support. He was playing right into the hands of the old southern Democracy, which was conspiring to resume its sway over the Union. On this issue the *Tribune* plunged headlong into the campaign of 1866.[16]

Weedites and Democrats nominated the Tammany stooge, John T. Hoffman, for governor of New York that fall. This was an amalgam of sorts, but with Tammany very much in control of the resulting situation. The *Tribune* raged at the "Siamese convention" from which this result had issued. Its readers were told that Tweedites and Weedites had joined hands in concocting a ticket for the benefit of all those who had been rebels at heart during the war, but that in so doing the Democrats had cozened Weed, knocking him flatter than if he had got into the ring with John Morrissey. All honest and patriotic men must vote for the Union Republican slate. That was the only way to keep safe from dishonor.[17]

Meanwhile the Union Republican state convention had met at Syracuse on September 5, 1866, with Greeley very much in evidence. The *Tribune's* editor piped to all who would listen that Governor Reuben E. Fenton (for whose qualities he had formerly had small respect) was just the man for renomination, and that universal amnesty and impartial suffrage was the platform on which he should be renominated.

Greeley proposed that the convention go on record that everyone who fought or paid was entitled to vote, but the convention rejected this for a resolution that simply approved the Fourteenth Amendment. The *Tribune's* editor accepted this rebuff with equanimity, on the ground that he could do more for impartial freedom by remaining regular than by continuing to carry on an unsuccessful crusade. There was also balm to be found in the easy renomination of Fenton and in seeing New York City triumph over the western part of the state in the nomination for lieutenant-governor of General Stewart L. Woodford, a rising young politician from King's County.[18]

Greeley fought the state campaign that year with relish. The *Tribune* pinned the label "Demijohnson party" on the fusionists. Its editor sneered at Raymond when the latter showed signs of bolting the "Demijohnson" ticket. "Shocking cruelty to a fugitive slave," Greeley chortled, when the Democratic papers began damning Raymond's recreancy. They ought to break their "vicious colts" in private, rather than out in the public view. At the same time, he traded insults with Weed, who was declaring that Greeley had first invited and then vindicated secession, and had later rushed around from Copperheads to rebels whining for peace upon the best available terms. There was an element of truth in this charge, but Greeley had no hesitation in branding it as utterly false. "Mr. Weed simply lies, as the old villain has long persisted in doing with regard to me."[19]

Aside from such personal feuding, Greeley spent most of the campaign of 1866 blasting the Tammany Ring, lauding Fenton and thrusting reconstruction to the fore as the chief issue. Hoffman and his "satellites" were pilloried as prorebellion and proslavery. A vote for them was a vote against equal rights and for anarchy and treason.

At the same time, Greeley took pains to point out that he was by no means in full accord with the radicals. He did not like Stevens' desire for harsh treatment of the South, any more than he did the Pennsylvanian's penchant for soft money. He abhorred Wendell Phillips's plea that the South be held under an iron-fisted military despotism. Greeley's cry was for leniency. He asked the immediate admission to Congress of the representatives of all states ratifying the Fourteenth Amendment. That amendment was all right so far as it went, but Universal Amnesty and Impartial Suffrage would be much better for the country. North-South fraternization was his watchword.[20]

Greeley's enthusiasm for the campaign of 1866 was partly the result of a direct, personal interest, for he was a candidate for Congress from a New York City district. But though he threw himself into the campaign with heart and soul, the voters showed small enthusiasm for him. Whether because of his attacks on Tammany, to which the city's voters remained conspicuously faithful that year, or because of dislike for his reconstruction views, he was snowed under by a nearly 10,000 majority for his Democratic opponent. It was not easy to take such a drubbing while his running mates, Fenton and Woodford, were riding to decisive victories in the state.[21]

Hard on the state elections of 1866 followed those in New York City, which took place on December 4. During the weeks that preceded them, Greeley took up the cudgels vigorously for an honest city administration. The chief office in dispute was that of city comptroller. Greeley urged the Republicans to nominate a Democrat as their only chance of victory and suggested a friend of Cornelius Vanderbilt, Judge George D. Barnard, a man who was later driven off the bench for corruption. This advice produced a good deal of savage criticism.

The attack upon Greeley centered in the charge that he was developing a tendency to stray off the Republican reservation. He had done so in the preceding year, when he had supported a fusionist "Citizen's Association" candidate for mayor, in place of the Republican candidate, Marshall O. Roberts. The consequence of this had been that the Tammany candidate, John T. Hoffman, had been elected mayor and thus had the road opened to the governor's chair. Now here was Greeley again proclaiming his desire to stray from the beaten path of the strict party man by nominating a "good" Democrat. The upshot of the matter was that Greeley's proposal was flatly turned down, the Republicans nominating Judge Richard Kelly of unimpeachable political antecedents for comptroller.

Tweed's unsavory ally, Richard B. ("Slippery Dick") Connolly, won the comptrollership hands down. Greeley bemoaned this as the result of Republican shortsightedness, and his wailings certainly did not endear him to his political associates. Like his campaign efforts for Kelly, they also fell on deaf ears, so far as the general electorate were concerned. For before the city campaign had begun, "Slippery Dick" had been given a good character in the editorial columns of the *Tribune,* and the electorate therefore listened with considerable indifference to Greeley's wailings over the victory of Connolly and Tammany Hall.[22]

Hard on the heels of the city election came the choice of a United States senator. Greeley coveted this post, but so did the imperious member of Congress from Utica, Roscoe Conkling. Greeley had not supported Conkling's race for the lower house of Congress that fall, pretty obviously because he feared the Utican's aspirations. Now the rivalry between the two men for the Senate came out into the open, and waxed very warm indeed.

Conkling, always careful in building his fences, had the inside track. Greeley's independence in regard to city candidates had done him no good with the Republican organization. He also injured his chances by what he fondly imagined to be a piece of political astuteness.

Not long before the election to the Senate was to take place, Greeley came out in the *Tribune* with a carefully prepared editorial reiterating his demand for universal amnesty and impartial suffrage. But the crux of this editorial statement, so far as the Senate race was concerned, lay in his assertion that universal amnesty and impartial suffrage were each desireable, in and of themselves, and that it was not necessary to couple them by any "peanut dicker." In other words, universal amnesty would be a good thing if there were no impartial suffrage, and vice versa. It was an attempt to carry water on both shoulders, to please both radicals and conservatives, and it proved a political boomerang. A great howl rose up from the radical Republican newspapers that Greeley was giving up the

Negro, and his candidacy promptly went into eclipse. He received no votes after the first ballot, and "Sandy" Conkling was swept triumphantly into the Senate seat that Greeley had so long coveted.[23]

After Conkling's victory, Greeley explained repeatedly that high principle had been the cause of his own defeat. If he had only been willing to stand flatly on the Fourteenth Amendment, said Greeley, his chances for election would have been very bright indeed. With the country's welfare in view, he had chosen instead to make a distinct avowal for impartial suffrage as a good in and of itself. By this he had hoped to encourage leading southerners to accept that idea. He had also hoped by this stand to foster a more conciliatory mood in President Johnson. But the avowal that amnesty was a good thing in itself had roused Republican fears of his being too easy on the rebels and had led to his defeat.[24]

This apologia laid its author open to the charge of protesting too much, but there was, perhaps, some truth in the explanation. Incidentally, it also gave Andrew Johnson an opportunity to write down in black and white his opinion of Horace Greeley.

The wary eye of old Frank Blair caught the reference to the President in Greeley's explanation of his course, and when Blair wrote to Johnson he suggested a wholesale revamping of the Cabinet with Greeley as postmaster-general. Johnson could not see the value of such an appointment. Greeley indeed! Greeley, who had nearly bothered the life out of Mr. Lincoln, and whose antics during the Civil War had all too often left him floundering "like a whale ashore." The trouble with Greeley, Johnson wrote, was that he ran "to goodness of heart so much as to produce infirmity of mind." He was a "sublime old child," who would be of no value whatsoever in a Cabinet position.[25] Johnson's mood was tinged with bitterness, but there was much shrewd insight in this appraisal.

Greeley made his customary lecture tour in the West that winter, returning at the end of the first week in January 1867. The trip had been a grueling one, but he plunged at once into the controversy over reconstruction, a controversy that was becoming more and more bitter. The elections of the preceding fall had resulted in a victory for the radicals and this, plus the fact that the southern states had rejected the Fourteenth Amendment, hardened the stand of the Congressional extremists. Determined now to force Negro suffrage upon the South, the legislative leaders of the Republican party were systematically overriding Presidential vetoes and Supreme Court opinion as they moved toward a system of martial law and Negro voting in the late rebel states. Congress had the bit in its teeth.

Greeley's southern policy was still by no means identical with
that of his radical confrères. To be sure, he agreed with them that
the Fourteenth Amendment was inadequate. It would mean, he
wrote to a friend, control of the fifteen slave states by the Vallandigham Democracy, and control of the nation also, unless the Democrats were blind fools. Negro suffrage was absolutely necessary to
prevent such a development. But from this point on he parted company with the men who controlled Congress. He was convinced
that the southerners whom the radicals were trying to penalize
would accept impartial suffrage, if it were presented to them as a
quid pro quo for amnesty. All that was necessary was to take a
stand for impartial suffrage as a uniform rule to be established
throughout the Union, and the South would rally to its support.
He much preferred not to force Negro suffrage on the South. He
hoped, rather, to obtain it by conciliatory means.

Such was the focal point of Greeley's thinking on reconstruction,
and toward that point he drove with typical determination. Speaker
of the House Colfax was warned that the country wanted peace, not
postponement. Senator Edwin D. Morgan was told that conservatives and radicals were on the brink of a fresh civil war that would
rage on the Hudson and Delaware as well as on the Potomac and
Mississippi, unless Congress adopted a program of compromise and
conciliation. Northern states such as Connecticut, where the *Tribune's* influence was great, were implored to adopt impartial suffrage as a means of ensuring Republican victories within their
borders and as an encouragement to southern states to go and do
likewise. Meanwhile, the *Tribune* urged universal amnesty upon
the nation, and sought to placate southern sentiment and lift
southern morale. Its attitude after the southern states rejected the
Fourteenth Amendment was distinctly conciliatory, and Greeley
demonstrated a continuing interest in southern economic development by urging the migration of northern capital to the war-torn
regions, either for investment, or in the shape of gifts to repair
the damage done by war, floods, and drouth. At the same time he
sought to foster the softening of racial lines in the South by consistently using the term "Unionist" to cover both loyal whites and
colored people, and by declaring repeatedly that reconstruction
could be successful only if it enlisted the support of both of these
elements of southern society.

But there were limits to what a newspaper editor, even the editor
of the *New York Tribune,* could accomplish. Greeley recognized his
impotence to control events. There wasn't much left for him to do,
he wrote to Senator Morgan, early in February 1867.[26] Events justi-

fied his defeatism. In March 1867, the radicals pushed their first great reconstruction acts to completion, and when Johnson vetoed these bills they were promptly passed over his veto.

Radical reconstruction bore some resemblance to seventeenth-century Lord Strafford's Irish policy of "Thorough." Ten of the rebel states (Tennessee escaped by virtue of having ratified the Fourteenth Amendment) were reorganized into five military districts, with a general in command of each district. Provision was made for the disfranchisement of rebels, particularly of rebel leaders. The people of any of these states might regain their representation in Congress when, and only when, they adopted a constitution establishing Negro suffrage and the legislature chosen under that constitution had ratified the Fourteenth Amendment. In effect, the radicals were saying to the South that it must endure military rule until it had given the vote to the Negro.

Much as Greeley deplored these drastic measures, he was in no mood to oppose them, once they were enacted into law. In fact, the *Tribune's* editor had hinted as much to Morgan and had said so openly in his paper. Regretting the passage of the March acts as a step backward into the maelstrom of national disharmony, urging futilely while the legislation was still pending that it should distinguish between reformed and unreconstructed rebels, he yet had given notice that he would accept whatever action Congress might take. Time would decide whether or not his own program would have been the wiser and safer course to pursue. "We expect, at all events," he had said, "to urge a prompt and cheerful conformity to whatever Congress shall insist upon." Only let the seceded states be reconstructed on such democratic principles as would ensure clear Republican majorities in them and he would be, perforce, content. This was Greeley's *sine qua non.* A last-minute appeal which he made for justice and generosity in dealing with the South did not obscure the fact that, for him, the predominance of long-range Republican policies, rather than immediate social justice, was the primary consideration.[27]

Such was the essence of Greeley's position. It was a stand that enabled him to deplore the harshness of the Congressional measures and at the same time to criticize Johnson for vetoing them.[28] Military rule was not an admirable thing, he was free to admit, but, after all, Congressional reconstruction was basing the reorganization of the Union upon the principle of universal, and therefore impartial, suffrage. Optimistically, he saw signs of increasing southern white acceptance of the Congressional policy, and of a successful colored-white reorganization of the late rebel territories emerging from military rule. There were some such signs, but they scarcely had the significance that Greeley attributed to them.

The best sign of all, from Greeley's point of view, was the fact that the newly enfranchised "Unionists" would know where their true interests lay. Of course those Negroes who frequented or kept thieves' grog shops, dens of infamy, and the like would customarily vote Democratic, but the rest, the great majority, would vote the right ticket. Thus he found solace for what he felt in his heart was wrong by envisaging a great Republican party, triumphant throughout the nation, invincible throughout the years, standing in monolithic fashion for universal liberty and based upon a suffrage that would be enjoyed without regard for caste, color, or race—a party that would be the trusted guardian of the nation's happiness and well-being.[29] It was a beautiful vision, and Greeley wanted to believe in it. But at the same time he kept urging wistfully that an early amnesty and prompt restoration of the southern states to representation in Congress would make all the more overpowering the Grand Old Party's predominance.

For some time now, Greeley had been cut adrift from the administration of President Johnson. Further proof of this, if proof were needed, came with the Senate's discussion of the Alaska treaty, early in April 1867. The *Tribune* poured out all the vials of its wrath upon Seward's proposal to purchase Alaska from Russia. It described the project as a "Quixotic land hunt," and a poor bargain to boot. It meant taxes, taxes, and still more taxes levied to pay for a barren territory. It was a wanton affront to Great Britain. Seward had conceived it as a cover-up for the administration's disastrous domestic policy. Such were the arguments with which the *Tribune* attacked the proposal, and the paper's scorn was in no whit mitigated by the Senate's overwhelming ratification of the treaty on April 9, 1867.[30]

Alaska was simply another club to wield over the heads of Johnson and his associates. Greeley had clearly abandoned hope of bringing together the administration and the radicals. But he had not abandoned hope of moving the country toward amnesty for the erstwhile rebels.

While the *Tribune* was belaboring the administration over Alaska, events were shaping that gave its editor an opportunity to dramatize his argument for clemency in dealing with the South. Jefferson Davis, former President of the Confederacy, the archrebel of them all, wanted to get out of Fortress Monroe where he had been languishing ever since his capture at the close of the war, and Greeley was asked to serve as his bondsman. Manfully the *Tribune's* editor stepped into the breach.

At the end of the war, Greeley had thought it might be a good idea to try Jefferson Davis for treason. The idea had appealed to him as a means of obtaining a clear adjudication on the right of secession and on the power of states to absolve their citizens from allegiance to the Union.[31] But shortly he began to alter his position, declaring that he did not believe in treason trials. They would martyr their victims, produce unnecessary bitterness, and hinder national reconciliation.[32] Amnesty should be all-inclusive.

Committed as he was to amnesty as a policy, Greeley naturally lent a sympathetic ear to the pleas of Varina Davis, who wrote pathetic letters beseeching his assistance in freeing her husband from what she described as the slow death of his imprisonment at Fortress Monroe. Greeley made inquiries which satisfied him that Davis had had nothing to do with the assassination of Lincoln, and that he had not been responsible for southern prison atrocities, and as early as June 12, 1866, began urging that the "aged and infirm" ex-President of the Confederacy be at least let out on bail. The *Tribune* declared that the farce of imprisonment should be brought to an end and that Davis should be either tried or let go. After all, it said, the Confederate leader had been and, in a sense, still was the representative of 6,000,000 people. Magnanimity toward him would be a powerful contribution "to that juster appreciation of the North at the South which is the first step toward a beneficent and perfect reconciliation."[33]

Greeley asked George Shea, a New York lawyer, to interest himself in Davis' behalf. Shea consented and, though his attempt to bring Davis to trial failed, preparations for bailing the famous prisoner were far advanced by the spring of 1867. On this matter, Shea acted in consultation with Greeley. The question of bondsmen arose, and Greeley suggested several northern men, among them Commodore Vanderbilt. Shea felt that Greeley's name would carry more weight with the country than even that of the Commodore, and Greeley consented to serve as a bondsman. He did so in the full knowledge that his action would probably injure both the *Tribune* and himself.[34]

On Monday, May 13, 1867, Horace Greeley, together with Gerrit Smith and a number of other bailsmen, met at Judge Underwood's court in Richmond. There they affixed their signatures to a bond for $100,000, under which surety Jefferson Davis was liberated from prison. Vanderbilt's signature was affixed on his behalf by his son-in-law Horace F. Clark and his friend Augustus Schell. The correspondent of the *World* noticed that, after Greeley signed, the ex-President of the Confederacy stepped up and grasped his hand, and that the spectators laughed at the expression on Horace's face, so obvious was his pleasure and satisfaction at what he had done.[35]

The day after he became bondsman for Davis, Greeley spoke to a mixed audience in the Richmond African church. The time had come, he said, for peace and national harmony. The time had also come for equality of rights for the colored people and the white people. Radical reconstruction was justified by southern acts, but he was willing to accept military rule only as long as it was necessary to keep disloyal men from seizing the reins of power in the South. Let the whites conform to the recommendations of Congress, and Greeley was sure that Congress would meet such compliance with a corresponding generosity. As for the blacks, they should set about reconstructing themselves by purchasing land in Virginia or taking up land in the West under the Homestead Act. In closing, he exhorted all "Republicans and Conservatives, whites and blacks, to bury the dead past in mutual and hearty good will, and in a general, united effort to promote the prosperity and exalt the glory of our long-distracted and bleeding, but henceforth reunited, magnificent country.[36]

Greeley meant that the signing of the Davis bond should serve as a means of healing the breach between the sections. The act was well received in the South, but the repercussions in the North were violent and bitter. What resulted can only be described as a nineteenth-century ordeal by slander. A deluge of mud descended upon the head of the unfortunate editor, mud thrown by old and valued friends as well as by his enemies. He was proclaimed a notoriety seeker who had thrust himself, unwanted, into the Davis affair. It was asserted that he had had a secret conference with Davis, had tried to influence Judge Underwood to release the famous prisoner outright, and had congratulated Davis with unseemly warmth when the latter was admitted to bail. Wendell Phillips likened Greeley's attitude toward Davis to that of a "fawning spaniel." Edwin L. Godkin in the *Nation* termed Greeley's action repulsive and inexpedient, "simply detestable," an act that made a mockery of Greeley's contention that the war had been fought on behalf of a great moral issue. The hubbub that arose in the country over this deed of magnanimity was worse, far worse, than the outcry that had arisen in 1861 over "On to Richmond."[37]

The criticism aroused by the signing of the Davis bond had a direct effect upon Greeley's personal fortunes, for his publications as well as himself were brought under the rod of the public's displeasure. The *Tribune*, particularly the *Weekly Tribune*, suffered badly for a time, though it came back nobly during the campaign of 1868.[38] Worse hit was *The American Conflict.*

The first volume of the *Conflict* had sold very well, up to the spring of 1867. Greeley was reported as saying that it had brought him some $10,000 shortly after publication, money which he had spent in paying up old debts. Inspired by his ever-present financial need and prodded by his publishers, he had rushed the second volume to completion and it had been on the stands by September 1866. By January 1, 1867, nearly 125,000 copies of volume one and nearly 50,000 copies of volume two had been sold. Hastily written, based on insufficient and often unsatisfactory data (the generals on both sides lied fearfully, the perspiring author complained to a friend), biased, oracular in its military judgments, sometimes inaccurate in detail, it was nevertheless the best thing that had been done on the war, and the public demand had been keen. But now all was changed.

For a time the sale of the *Conflict* was stopped completely by the outburst of popular indignation and, though it began again, the book never recovered anything like its former popularity. Greeley's royalties for the last six months of 1868 were only $303.75. His publishers, O. D. Case and Company, became increasingly anxious to get off their hands a book that had become a white elephant. The golden harvest was over.[39]

Greeley felt the financial loss that came as a result of the Davis affair less keenly than he did the damage to the *Tribune* and the flood of personal abuse that came from friend as well as foe. But, bludgeoned and buffeted though he was, he stuck manfully to his guns. To Mrs. H. C. Ingersoll of Bangor, Maine—"My Sometime Friend," as he sadly addressed her—he wrote simply that time would dull the edge of her resentment, for time would prove that he had been right. There were sterner words for his political enemies, and he lashed out in the *Tribune* against what he termed the howling of the Pharisees. No matter how useful and noble an act might be, he declared, there would always be found someone mean enough to conceive a base motive for it. He held such people in contempt. If given another chance to perform such a beneficent deed as that of signing Davis's bond, he would be encouraged by this experience to improve the opportunity. "My maligners of today," he told his readers, "will be protesting that they didn't mean it ere three years have passed."[40] And to the Union League Club, whose president summoned him to appear at a special meeting demanded by some thirty-six members for the purpose of inquiring into his action, he returned a blistering reply.

He would not attend the meeting to be held over his conduct, Greeley told his Union League Club critics in a letter that was published on the editorial page of the *New York Tribune.*

I do not recognize you as capable of judging, or even fully apprehending me. You evidently regard me as a weak sentimentalist, misled by maudlin philosophy. I arraign you as narrow-minded blockheads, who would like to be useful to a great and good cause, but don't know how. Your attempt to base a great, enduring party on the hate and wrath necessarily engendered by a bloody Civil War, is as though you should plant a colony on an iceberg which had somehow drifted into a tropical ocean.

. . . Understand, once for all, that I dare you and defy you. . . . So long as any man was seeking to overthrow our Government, he was my enemy; from the hour in which he laid down his arms, he was my formerly erring countryman. So long as any is at heart opposed to the National Unity, the Federal authority, or to that assertion of the Equal Rights of All Men which has become practically identified with Loyalty and Nationality, I shall do my best to deprive him of power; but whenever he ceases to be thus, I demand his restoration to all the privileges of American citizenship. I give you fair notice that I shall urge the reenfranchisement of those now proscribed for Rebellion so soon as I shall feel confident that this course is consistent with the freedom of the Blacks and the unity of the Republic, and that I shall demand a recall of all now in exile only for participating in the Rebellion, whenever the country shall have been so thoroughly pacified that its safety will not thereby be endangered. And so, gentlemen, hoping that you will henceforth comprehend me somewhat better than you have done, I remain,

Yours,   Horace Greeley.[41]

The Union League Club reconsidered its action, and the meeting for censure was not held. Instead, a resolution passed by majority vote declared that there was no cause for action, and Greeley remained a member of the organization until his death.

No act of Greeley's entire career was more deserving of praise than his bailing of Jefferson Davis. That and his subsequent conduct showed courage of a high order. Bent upon the recreation of a united nation, he had endured scorn, contumely, the loss of money and friendships with firmness and dignity. The way was to be longer and rougher than he foresaw, but by his action he had helped to start the nation down the road to reunion. The whole episode constituted a study in courage and patriotic devotion.

NOTES FOR CHAPTER 22

1. Walt Whitman, "Democratic Vistas," in *Complete Prose Works* (Boston, 1901), pp. 205-6.
2. *Tribune,* June 26, 29, July 10, 1869.
3. *Ibid.,* Aug. 13, 1870, Jan. 14, 1871, Jan. 8, 1872. Material on Fisk, aside from the files of the *Tribune,* has been derived from R. H. Fuller, *Jubilee Jim* (N. Y., 1928), and M. Minnegerode, *Certain Rich Men* (N. Y., 1927).
4. *Independent,* May 11, 1865.
5. Gerrit Smith Papers, Greeley to Smith, June 21, 27, 1865; *Independent,* May 11, June 15, 22, 1865; *Tribune,* Apr. 24, May 27, 30, June 2, 15, 20-22, 1865, Sept. 13, 1867. Cf. Rhodes, *Hist. of the U. S.,* V, 524-27.
6. *Independent,* Feb. 25, 1869; *Tribune,* July 31, 1865.
7. *Ibid.,* June 23, 26, 30, July 8, 10-14, 31, Aug. 1, 8, Sept. 12, 14, 16, 18, Oct. 7, 13, 14, 19, 23, 26, 1865; *Independent,* Oct. 26, Nov. 2, 1865.
8. *Tribune,* Sept. 12, 1865; Ingersoll, *Greeley,* pp. 642-43.
9. *Tribune,* Sept. 16, 18, Oct. 23, 26, Dec. 6, 1865; *Rhodes, Hist. of the U. S.,* V, 535.
10. *Tribune,* Sept. 11, 1866.
11. Greeley Papers (N. Y. P. L.), Greeley to Colfax, Dec. 11, 1865; *Tribune,* Dec. 6, 8, 9, 14, 15, 19-21, 23, 26, 27, 29, 1865; Ross, "Horace Greeley and the South," *South Atlantic Quarterly,* XVI, 330; Rhodes, *Hist. of the U. S.,* V, 544-54.
12. Schurz, *Reminiscences,* II, 198-212; *Tribune,* Jan. 9, Feb. 15, Sept. 11, 1866. At this time, Greeley felt free to suggest Cabinet appointments to Johnson. See the Johnson Papers, Greeley to Johnson, Jan. 28, 1866. The *Tribune's* tone at this time is in striking contrast to the violent anti-Johnsonism of Tilton's *Independent,* Feb. 29-Mar. 29, 1866.
13. *Tribune,* Feb. 20-23, 1866.
14. Greeley Papers (N. Y. P. L.), Greeley to Colfax, Feb. 25, 1866, McCulloch to Greeley, Mar. 5, 1866, July 22, 1867; Chase Papers (Hist. Soc. of Pa.), Greeley to Chase, May 4, June 3, 1866; Carey Papers, E. Peshine Smith to Carey, March 26, 1866; *Tribune,* Jan., Feb. 14, 19, March 5, 6, Nov. 17, 1866; B. C. Truman, "Anecdotes of Andrew Johson," *Century Magazine,* LXXXV (Jan. 1913), 440. Greeley broke at this time with Henry Carey over contraction of the currency, which the latter opposed.—Carey Papers, J. R. Young to Carey, June 16, 1866; Greeley to Carey, Dec. 21, 1867, Aug. 22, 1869.
15. *Tribune,* Apr. 9, 28, 30, May 14, 18, 22, 30, 31, June 5, 9, 19, Aug. 6, 7, 22, 31, Nov. 12, 1866; Greeley Papers (N. Y. P. L.), Greeley to Colfax, Feb. 25, 1866; *Independent,* Apr. 26, 1866. The *Trbiune's* increased hostility to Johnson may have been due in part to John Russell Young (see Baehr, *Tribune,* p. 54), but the drift is also apparent in editorials that are indubitably by Greeley.
16. *Tribune,* July 6, 11, 29, Aug. 13, 16, 31, 1866; *Independent,* Aug. 30, Sept. 11, 1866. Greeley's editorials were now nearly as critical of Johnson as were those of his friend Tilton in the *Independent.* Both men attacked Beecher, who had come out in support of Johnson, and Beecher quickly subsided.

17. *Tribune,* Aug. 15, 21, 24, Sept. 4, 12-15, 1866.
18. Greeley Papers (N. Y. P. L.), Greeley to Colfax, Sept. 8, 1863; C. E. Norton Autographs (Houghton Lib.), Greeley to Norton, Aug. 26, 1866; *Tribune,* Sept. 6, 7, 10, 28, 1866, Oct. 20, 1870; White, *Autobiography,* I, 160. Greeley placed Woodford in nomination. White declares that Fenton's flattery swung Greeley to his support.
19. *Tribune,* Sept. 12, 13, 19, Oct. 10, 1866.
20. *Tribune,* Sept. 12, 13, 26, 28, Oct. 12, 18, 20, 25, Nov. 1, 12, 1866.
21. *Tribune,* Nov. 7, 8, 1866, May 28, 1867. The actual majority of Greeley's opponent, Fox, was 9, 988.
22. *Tribune,* Nov. 6, 22, Dec. 6, 1865, Nov. 8-Dec. 4, 1866, Nov. 18, 1867; Stebbins, *History of New York State,* pp. 140-43.
23. Greeley Papers (Lib. of Cong.), Greeley to Capt. Strong, Aug. 30, 1866, Greeley to B. Brockway, Nov. 15, 1866; Chase Papers (Hist. Soc. of Pa.), Greeley to Chase, Nov. 22, 1866; Andrew Johnson Papers, Greeley to Fernando Wood, Nov. 12, 27, 1866; *Tribune,* Nov. 10, 13, 19, 27, 1866, Jan. 11, Feb. 4, 1868, Nov. 27, 1871; Chidsey, *The Gentleman from New York,* pp. 105-6, 111-12; White, *Autobiography,* I, 134-35.
24. *Tribune,* Feb. 4, Apr. 20, May 28, 1867.
25. B. C. Truman, "Anecdotes of Andrew Johnson," *Century Magazine,* LXXXV (Jan. 1913), 438-39; W. E. Smith, *The Francis Preston Blair Family in Politics* (2 vols.; N. Y., 1933), II, 332 and note; Johnson Papers, F. P. Blair to Johnson, Feb. 12, 14, Sept. 7, 1867.
26. Morgan Papers, Greeley to Morgan, Feb. 5, 1867.
27. *Tribune,* Feb. 16, 18, 21, 25, 1867.
28. The criticism of Johnson was especially noticeable in regard to his veto of the Reconstruction Act of March 2, and of the Tenure of Office Act.
29. *Tribune,* Mar. 21, 23, 25, 27, 29, Apr. 3-5, 10, 22, 27, 29, May 3, 18, 1867; *Independent,* May 9, 1867.
30. *Tribune,* April 1, 8-11, Sept. 23, 1867, July 16, Dec. 5, 1868.
31. *Tribune,* May 17, 1865, Nov. 27, 1866; Greeley, *Recollections,* pp. 412-14.
32. *Tribune,* June 10, 1865, Sept. 13, 1867.
33. *Greeley Papers* (N. Y. P. L.), Varina Davis to Greeley, Sept. 2, Oct. 16, Nov. 16, 1866; *Tribune,* May 15, June 4, 12, 16, Aug. 14, Nov. 9, 1866.
34. Young, *Men and Memories,* pp. 117-18.
35. *World,* May 14, 1867; *Southern Historical Association Papers,* I (Jan.-June, 1876), 319-25, letter of George Shea to the *Tribune,* Jan. 15, 1876; R. Nichols, "The United States vs. Jefferson Davis," *Amer. Hist. Rev.* XXXI (Jan. 1926), 266-84.
36. *Tribune,* May 15, 1867; Ingersoll, *Greeley,* pp. 642-43.
37. *Tribune,* May 15, 17, 20, 21, 24, 29, 1867; *Nation,* May 23, 1867; Ingersoll Papers, Greeley to Mrs. Ingersoll, May 26, 1867.
38. Greeley Papers (Lib. of Cong.), Greeley to Mrs. Whipple, Dec. 7, 1867; *Tribune,* Aug. 11, Sept. 30, Nov. 12, 1868.
39. Macpherson Papers, Greeley to Macpherson, Aug. 24, 1864; Greeley Papers (N. Y. P. L.), O. D. Case to Greeley, Oct. 13, 1865, Feb. 11, 1870, Greeley to Mrs. Bowe, Feb. 4, 1866; Stahl Collection, Greeley to Mrs. Allen, July 3, 22, Sept. 19, 1866; Greeley Papers (Lib. of Cong.), Greeley to Mrs. Allen, Sept. 14, 1866, Greeley to Mrs. Whipple, Dec. 7, 1867; Autographs (Houghton Lib.), Greeley to O. D. Case, Jan. 1, 1868, Jan. 25, Dec. 7,

1869; Howard Correspondence, Greeley to Harrison Howard, Feb. 27, 1868; *Tribune*, Oct. 12, 1866, Feb. 11, 1867; Hudson, *Journalism*, p. 527.

40. Ingersoll Papers, Greeley to Mrs. Ingersoll, May 26, 1867; *Tribune*, May 15, 20, 29, 1867.

41. Greeley, *Letter to the Union League Club* (N. Y., 1867); Greeley Papers (N. Y. P. L.), John Jay to Greeley, May 16, 1867; *Tribune*, May 23, 1867.

CHAPTER 23

Valiant Battle

THE STORM OF OBLOQUY CAUSED BY THE JEFFERSON
Davis affair continued to beat around Greeley's head, but the *Tribune's* editor went manfully on his way. As of old, he continued to
exhort his readers concerning the dangers of alcohol, the beauties
of industrial coöperation, and the need for a lenient treatment of
the South. But the path was rugged now, and in June of 1867 he
went to Niagara Falls to snatch a few days well-earned rest.

Greeley spoke at Brockport, en route to the Falls. Unfriendly
papers had it that he was howled down at the Brockport open-air
meeting, but he declared indignantly that it was only a high wind
that had made it difficult to hear him. Thousands had turned out,
and of the crowd only six at most had kept yelling "Jeff Davis" until
"silenced by the general indignation."[1]

Niagara offered the scourged editor a grand, if melancholy, solace.
It was, he informed his public, next to Yosemite, the most sublime
sight he had ever seen. It was greater than Rome seen from the
dome of St. Peters, or Italy from the southern slopes of Mount
Cenis, or the Alps from Como, or Mount Blanc and her glaciers
from "Chamouny." Yet the time would come when a child now
living would walk, dry-shod, over the American fall to Goat Island
and back, "our fall thus taking prominent position among the first
of American ruins."[2] There was a quality in these observations,
particularly in the reference to American ruins, that was not unlike
the mournfulness of Marius amidst the ruins of Carthage. The editor of the *Tribune* was passing under the rod of popular displeasure,
and his state of mind was not a happy one.

But come what might so far as his personal fortunes were concerned, Greeley was sublimely confident that he knew the answer
to the problem of reconstruction. The answer, as always, was amnesty, plus the mixed-color Republicanism that amnesty would,

in his estimation, help so much to bring. If shortsighted men crushed the South as Ireland had been crushed, he hoped that the southerners would "give us a Fenian outbreak." He was glad to call himself a radical, but he wanted it distinctly understood that he was a radical of a progressive stamp, who wanted all rights for all and no confiscation. Thad Stevens' comment on this statement of position was short and to the point. "Dishwater," snorted Old Thad.[3]

Week after week, the noise of Greeley's battle rolled in the *Tribune* and the *Independent*. Every now and then the determined warrior would cease from the main attack, while he crucified the liquor merchants, or sounded the tocsin of protection, or denounced those who, on grounds of poverty or poor health, conspired "to blast the germs of offspring in the mother's womb, and thwart the beneficent command to increase and multiply given to the progenitors of our race." But he always came back to the main line. The fight for the right was many-sided, but reconstruction held the center of the field.

Devoted though Greeley was to the reconstruction problem in national affairs, his attention was of necessity diverted from it during the summer of 1867 by matters of more immediate concern to New York State. On June 4, 1867, a duly elected convention assembled at Albany for the purpose of revising the state's constitution, and the *Tribune's* editor was one of those who answered to the first roll call. For the next few weeks, the state's constitutional problems absorbed most of his attention.

Greeley had been working hard for constitutional revision for more than a year. It was needed, he declared, to speed up justice, lessen city and state corruption, foster retrenchment, strengthen the executive power and, last but not least, establish impartial suffrage in the state.[4] Now the time had come to accomplish great things along these lines, and it was with the attitude of an embattled crusader that he took his seat on the first day of the convention.

The *Tribune's* editor drew a seat far at the rear of the convention's hall, but this in no whit diminished his ardor. On the very first day, his voice was raised for reform. The only business that day was a motion of inquiry into the costs and receipts of the canals, a motion offered by Horace Greeley. Everyone took it for what it was—a slap in the face to his fellow Republicans—for everyone knew that the Republican canal frauds were enormous. But Greeley cared little for the feelings of the Republican organization when reform was in the air. He proposed to act, he told his fellow delegates, in complete independence of party, whenever that was beneficial to the public interest. When it was necessary to hold Republicans up to public disapprobation, that should be done. But the same thing held true for the Democrats. Here and now, he wished to say that the Republicans would have to take charge of the convention, for the Democrats could be counted upon to oppose any constitution that might be framed. To this Mr. Samuel J. Tilden replied with some heat, declaring that the charge was without foundation. Thus reform was thrust into the limelight and, having successfully ruffled the feelings of both parties, Greeley cleared his decks for further action.[5]

The doughty editor's desire to tilt a lance for righteousness was soon gratified. He was made chairman of the suffrage committee, one of the hot spots of the convention. This post brought him face to face with the redoubtable Susan B. Anthony, and with the politics-ridden question of Negro suffrage as well.

With the appointment of Greeley's committee, Miss Anthony and Elizabeth Cady Stanton, both friends of the chairman, hastened to the scene. They asked permission to plead their case and Greeley introduced them to the committee. But his manner was unsympathetic. How many women would vote if they could, he asked, obviously regarding this as a "crusher." The ladies spoke of unalienable rights, but this argument also left him cold. When, he asked, did these unalienable rights begin for young men and foreigners? Such queries enveloped the hearing with a decidedly frosty air .

Miss Anthony and Mrs. Stanton were not ladies to be easily rebuffed. They continued the argument, despite the chairman's unsympathetic demeanor, but their efforts were without avail. The committee turned down woman suffrage in spite of their pleas, also in spite of a petition which they presented that bore, among many others, the name of Mary Cheyney Greeley.

On public questions, "Mother" could not boss her husband, and suffrage was indubitably a public question. Not one-tenth of the women wanted it, Horace declared. Besides, it put women in the position of men, a place for which Nature had not fitted them. Negro suffrage, however, was another matter.[6]

Under Greeley's leadership, the committee came out for abolishing all voting discriminations that were based on color. At the same time, it took the position that "the right of suffrage does not belong to men whose voting will not contribute to popular intelligence and comfort." On this peremptory ground it excluded from the franchise paupers and those who had not resided thirty days in their election districts.[7]

The convention accepted the suffrage committee's report without

any vital amendments, but over Greeley's earnest protests it voted
to submit the Negro suffrage clause to the voters in a separate article.
This action ensured the defeat of full Negro suffrage, which had to
await the ratification of the Fifteenth Amendment to the Constitution, and only came into effect in 1870. The committee, for all its
efforts, had really accomplished very little, but its sorry showing
represented by far Greeley's most constructive achievement of the
convention.

Aside from his work on the suffrage committee, Greeley dis-
guished himself by offering a variety of resolutions on behalf of
honesty and economy. He started this campaign for virtue by his
canal inquiry resolution. This was followed by a proposition that
the convention refrain from paying any newspaper to publish the
reports of its proceedings, a proposal that was voted down.[8] He then
offered a motion to deduct ten dollars a day from the pay of any
member of the state legislature who should be absent from his post
without cause, coupling this with another proposal that state senators should serve without any other compensation than a consciousness of virtue and of the gratitude of their constituents. Needless to
say, both of these motions had short shrift.

As for political corruption, Greeley urged his old remedy, a
registry law, also suggesting as helpful a considerable increase in the
number of state senators. He further proposed a vast decentralization
of the state government. This was to be done by increasing the
powers of the county board of supervisors, even giving them the
right to charter railroads. This program for action led Greeley's
fellow delegate, William J. Evarts, to remark that it was easy to get
rid of the evils of government by abolishing government. Such
decentralization, Evarts declared, would stamp the new constitution
as "heretical and visionary." This particular Greeley project then
died a-borning, but another, concerning the state canal system,
promptly took its place.

Canal corruption in New York State was a great evil. The pad-
ding of pay rolls by both parties under the spoils system, fraud in
the letting of contracts and low standards of efficiency in operation
had been prevalent for many years, and by the latter 1860's had
assumed monstrous proportions. The Canal Ring stretched its
tentacles far and wide, as loathsome as its counterpart the Tweed
Ring, if not so lucrative for its inner circle.

Greeley's remedy for canal corruption had at least the virtue of
simplicity. He would sell the canals to private business interests.
They would be better run, he declared, than they ever had been
by the state. Let the New York Central Railroad buy them if it

would, said the *Tribune's* editor. He scoffed at "that venerable bugbear, Monopoly," and dangled before the convention's gaze a selling price of $40,000,000 that could be applied to reducing the state debt and the general tax burden. He cited similar action by the state of Pennsylvania as a precedent until delegate Axtell from Clinton County put a spoke in that wheel. Axtell dryly remarked that after Pennsylvania had sold her canals the tolls had been raised, to the distinct detriment of the state's commerce. Thereafter nothing more was heard about the Pennsylvania shift to private enterprise.

The motion to sell the canals was lost, as were all of Greeley's other proposals for ending waste and corruption. Only a very restricted form of his registry law remained. The good ship *Reform* seemed fated to run into head winds when it set sail for the Promised Land with pilot Greeley at its helm.[9]

Greeley's interest in the constitutional convention waned with the summer season. By the time his committee's report on suffrage had been presented he was fairly sick of the whole business, and his malaise increased as his reform proposals were turned down with monotonous regularity by the convention. He became more and more critical of its proceedings, threatened to publish in the *Tribune* the names of the numerous absentees from the sessions of the convention, and commented satirically upon that body's passion for lengthy week-end adjournments, the slow pace of its deliberations, and the verbosity of the legal lights who predominated in its membership. It was the "talkiest" body ever assembled, he snorted, and taken altogether, its proceedings constituted a dreary waste of time. He was older than most of his fellow members, he informed them, but despite this handicap he hoped to live long enough to see their labors completed. Increasingly petulant and irascible, he tore into a colleague on one occasion with a burst of profanity that left some of the rural delegates gasping for breath. They said to one another in awe-struck tones, "Why! Mr. Greeley swears!"[10]

Toward the close of September the constitutional convention adjourned until after the state election. Greeley left the hall before the proceedings had been quite wound up, his ears affronted as he wended his way out of the place by the dreary periods of a long-winded orator. He never returned to take any part in subsequent deliberations but, being in Albany that winter, he looked in on the proceedings of the reconvened body, only to find the same man endeavoring to hold the attention of the delegates. Raising his hands in horror, the *Tribune's* editor exclaimed: "Great God! Hasn't that damned fool finished his speech yet!"[11]

Constitution-making by no means monopolized Greeley's attention during the summer of 1867. Even during the convention, he devoted much attention to his newspaper rivals and to New York City affairs. There was the customary pouring out of the vials of his wrath on Raymond and Weed, and the customary assaults upon the Tweed Ring for its waste and corruption. The city must economize, declared the *Tribune* in ringing tones. Greeley announced that the city school commissioners should work for nothing, and opposed an increase in the police force on account of the cost involved. These were peculiar notions of how to achieve good government, especially since they were not accompanied by more substantive plans for reform. Even more peculiar was his persistence in defending the very shady city judge, George G. Barnard, against the charge of corruption, a defense apparently based upon Barnard's close connection with Commodore Vanderbilt, to whom Greeley had wanted to sell the state canals, and for whom he had an intense admiration.[12] With the trumpet of New York's reform editor giving forth such uncertain sounds, the voters might well be pardoned for persisting in the error of their ways and continuing to support the Tammany Ring.

Feuding with Republican conservatives of the Raymond and Weed varieties was also carried over into state affairs, for Greeley had cast in his lot with Governor Reuben E. Fenton, the man who had ousted Weed as boss of the Republican party in the state. Being a Fentonite meant also being involved in that worthy's feud with Roscoe Conkling, whose star was rapidly rising in the state's political firmament. At the Republican state convention in the fall of 1867, Greeley opposed the followers of both the old boss, Weed, and the boss-to-be, Conkling.

Greeley was by no means all-powerful at the state convention. Some of the nominees displeased him. But he did succeed in having a resolution in favor of impartial suffrage written into the platform.

The word had gone out at Syracuse that party harmony was essential to party victory. In his heart Greeley knew that this was true, and at the beginning of the campaign he strove to play the part of the good soldier. Despite his suspicions of Conkling, his enmity toward Weed and his displeasure with some of the nominees on the state ticket, he began the contest with a soft-pedaling of party differences. The main issue before the American people, he told his readers, was Negro suffrage. As good Republicans, they must all work together for this cause. Such sentiments were all very well, but living up to them was another matter. Before the end of the campaign he was feuding merrily with Raymond, Weed, and the *Nation's* Godkin. This disappearance of party harmony boded no good for the cause. The situation was made even worse by the *Tribune's* two-fisted attacks upon Demon Rum, an onslaught that scarcely made converts for Republicanism among the ranks of the wine-bibbers.[13]

As the signs and omens had indicated, the state election of 1867 was a Democratic landslide. Greeley declared that conservative Republican apathy, plus canal frauds and bad nominations, were to blame. He, in turn, was bitterly castigated by his critics for unnecessary feuding with the conservatives and for injecting temperance into the contest. Wherever the fault lay, there can be no doubt that the severe defeat heightened the animosity that was felt toward him within the Republican party.[14]

In the New York City mayoralty campaign that immediately followed the state election, Greeley urged fusion of honest Republicans with honest Democrats. His advice went unheeded. John T. Hoffman thereupon snowed under his Republican opponent. Hoffman would probably have won, fusion or no fusion. But Greeley's declaration in the midst of the campaign that municipal matters ought to be entirely divorced from party politics, coupled with an intimation that he was supporting the regular Republican candidate because there was no reform candidate in the field, did nothing to sweeten the cup of defeat or to enhance his prestige in the Republican party.[15]

At the close of 1867 Greeley was offered the post of Minister to Austria. It was declined. Reconstruction was far more important in the editor's eyes than any such diplomatic post. The policy that determined the future course of events in the South would be of vital consequence to the nation. He proposed to be on this side of the Atlantic when that policy became a burning issue in the 1868 campaign.[16] And already he was devoting much thought to the Republican presidential nomination.

The Grant boom, which was well under way by the end of 1867, left Greeley cold. His candidate was Chase, and Chase's standard was firmly advanced. He was portrayed as the distinguished son of Ohio, now at the full maturity of his powers. A civil, not a military man, he had performed greater services than Grant during the rebellion, and his views on the great questions of the day were known while those of Grant were wrapped in the mists of obscurity. Over and beyond all this, it was obvious that Grant could never carry important border states, such as Maryland and Kentucky.

To be sure, said Greeley, with one of those characteristic wobbles that again and again impaired the strength of his position, the platform was far more important than the candidate, and he would vote for Grant, Wade, or Colfax, provided the platform was right. Issues were more important than the man. But Chase was indubitably the best man.[17]

Greeley wanted the election of 1868 fought on two main issues— Negro suffrage, which he was for, and currency inflation, which he was against. Hence the importance of an able, clear-headed, straight-thinking candidate, such as Chase. "We can elect no Republican on the spontaneous combustion principle," the *Tribune's* editor declared. "We can only triumph by the systematic and thorough enlightenment of the masses. . . ."[18]

Greeley's admonitions were not much heeded by the Republican leaders. The Grant boom flourished in a manner that was positively nauseating to the guide of the *Tribune's* policies. Disgusted, he took time off from politics, going over into New Jersey to lecture on "Self-Made Men" and other subjects on which that region regarded him as an authority. One evening, late in January 1868, he donned his white coat, clapped an old hat on his head, and shuffled in among the gay opera cloaks and dress suits at the French theatre to see military life burlesqued in Offenbach's *La Grande Duchesse de Gerolstein.* What was the use of pointing out the right political road, if the party leaders would not heed his advice. "We're a party of fools," he told Charles Sumner. It would be anything but easy to elect Grant. Hard work and lots of it would be the result of such a nomination.[19]

But if the cards fell to Grant, the *Tribune's* editor intended, with however great reluctance, to go along. As the general's nomination began to appear inevitable, Greeley began laying the groundwork for Republican success by vigorously propagating the story of a counterrevolutionary plot which, he said, was designed to subvert the very foundations of the Republic. In an open letter addressed to Democratic leader Miles O'Reilly, he declared that President Johnson had turned out to be a traitor to his erstwhile supporters. According to Greeley, Johnson was seeking to reconstruct the South on a white basis and with the rebel minority in command. Once this was done, the South would vote the Republicans out of power and give the government over "to the Rebel-sympathizing Democracy." This counterrevolution, which had its mainspring in the President's "premeditated treason to those who elected him," would be consummated with the aid of five Supreme Court judges. These men would paralyze Congressional reconstruction by a new

Dred Scott decision—a decision that would emasculate the powers of Congress laid down by Marshall and even by Taney.[20]

Greeley did not disclose the sources of his information regarding this diabolical plot, a pipe dream thoroughly in keeping with the host of malignant rumors concerning Johnson that were constantly issuing from the radical camp. But right-thinking Democrats were adjured to concentrate upon the horrendous issues at stake in the approaching contest, and not to quibble over candidates. That was what Greeley intended to do.

Early in February, Greeley went to the New York State Republican convention which selected delegates to the national nominating convention. There, albeit with a wry face, he went along with the convention's declaration for a Grant and Fenton ticket, a declaration passed without a dissenting voice. And when Grant swept the national convention in May, Greeley bowed not ungracefully to the verdict. It was clear, he asserted, that the people were for the hero of Appomattox. It was equally obvious to the *Tribune's* editor that Grant's electoral and popular majorities would exceed those of Lincoln over McClellan in 1864.[21]

Greeley's stubbornness produced throughout his life a constant repetition of patterns of thought and action. 1868 was a case in point. Just as in 1848 and in the early 1850's, the leaders of his party were rejecting his advice. Just as in 1848 and 1854, Greeley was going along, making a virtue of regularity despite his lacerated feelings. But also, as had been the case at that earlier time, the wounds that had been inflicted upon his *amour-propre* were rankling. An explosion of wrath was again in the offing, and this time the outburst would have reverberations wider and deeper than those involved in the dissolution of a partnership.

The restraint which characterized Greeley's efforts to stem the Grant boom may have been due in part to his preoccupation with another and very pressing matter of national importance. This was the impeachment of President Johnson.

When rumors of a plan to remove Johnson from office had first begun to be noised about in 1866, Greeley had been distinctly cool to the idea. Such a step, he had declared, no matter how just or even necessary, would "almost certainly plunge the country afresh into convulsion and civil war." At the very least, it would make Johnson a martyr, whether or not he were convicted. And a conviction would be decidedly doubtful. The *Tribune's* editor was clearly against impeachment as a policy. "All that Andy wants is rope enough and time enough and he will save us the trouble," he was quoted as saying.[22] Such was his position down to the end of 1867. Then his attitude toward impeachment began to change. The reasons for this change are not easily discernible. Perhaps the heat of an oncoming presidential campaign began to fire Greeley's blood, making him eager for a victim who could be sacrificed as a symbol of Democratic wickedness. Perhaps he actually believed the story of Johnson's plotting with the Supreme Court majority to fasten the grip of the "Rebel-sympathizing Democracy" upon the country. Be that as it may, the *Tribune's* attitude toward impeachment grew distinctly more favorable.

Rumor had it that President Johnson was about to remove Edwin M. Stanton from his post at the head of the War Department, thus apparently violating the Tenure of Office Act which had been passed in 1867. Greeley had approved of the Tenure of Office Act at the time of its passage, and the *Tribune* now assumed a most threatening attitude toward the President. Johnson was told that if he vetoed the act he would do so at his peril. Congress was directing reconstruction policies, and "if the President makes himself an impediment, he must be swept away."[23] Worse was to follow.

Greeley left for a western lecture tour in February 1868. During his absence from the *Tribune,* Stanton was removed from office and impeachment proceedings were instituted against the President. John Russell Young, the managing editor, thereupon began a violent campaign against Johnson, supporting impeachment to the limit. The *Tribune's* tone became more shrill, but its policy was substantially the same as that which had been outlined in its editorial columns just before Greeley left on his lecture tour.

Upon returning from the West, Greeley took up the burden of directing *Tribune* policy. The *Tribune's* hostility to the President increased, if anything, in venom. Greeley made short shrift of the *World's* Washington correspondent, who asserted upon "good authority" that, had Greeley been in New York when the impeachment proceedings were started, the tone of his paper would have been quite different. The "good authority," Greeley declared, was "either woefully mistaken or a willful liar."[24]

It is, of course, possible that Greeley's rebuke to the *World* concealed, rather than displayed, his real feelings. Chase, writing to Greeley some two months later, remarked, "I was against impeachment as a policy—so were you." John Russell Young, when he wrote his memoirs, clearly indicated that the *Tribune's* vigorous support of impeachment had been due to himself rather than to the editor-in-chief.[25] It could be that Greeley felt committed to support Young's intemperate assaults, and that the wild charges and vicious innuendoes which filled the editorial columns of the paper as the trial of the President approached its climax only represented a superior's loyalty to a subordinate who had taken a position from which it was difficult to retreat.

But loyalty to a subordinate does not suffice to explain the *Tribune's* attitude toward impeachment before Greeley left for the West or after he returned to command. Such loyalty scarcely made it necessary to declare that Johnson's presence in the White House constituted a threat of "riot, insurrection and civil war." Neither did it make it necessary for the *Tribune* to assert that Johnson's acquittal would be tantamount to giving him "a virtual charter of license to heap outrage upon outrage, evading and defying the laws, and doing his wicked worst to reestablish a vindictive Rebel domination throughout the South." The *Tribune* did not have to charge that Johnson had begun plotting to resuscitate the Democratic party even before his inauguration as President, any more than it had to state that "we are certain that neither money nor revenge will seduce any Senator into an infamous association with America's most degraded son."

Some of the worst *Tribune* editorials on impeachment bore Young's stamp rather than Greeley's, but this does not alter the fact that they were published when the latter was at the head of the paper. That they were published with Greeley's approval is indicated by a letter that he wrote to Thaddeus Stevens, asking advice as to what the *Tribune* could do further in helping to secure the President's conviction.

I am compelled to be out of town after tomorrow for three or four days [Greeley wrote to Stevens in April 1868] and am very anxious that the *Tribune* should keep up a steady fire on the impeachment question till the issue is decided. If, therefore, any fact or suggestion should occur to you meantime that seems calculated to aid us in the work, I will thank you to have it telegraphed at our expense to the *Tribune*. I do not fear the result, but I greatly desire to make the majority on the first vote as strong as possible.[26]

If the *Tribune's* editor had had any serious qualms about impeachment, he would scarcely have thus aligned himself with such a vindictive and intemperate advocate of the President's removal as Thaddeus Stevens.

The *Tribune* greeted the failure of the impeachment with a wild blast against the presiding officer at the trial, Chief Justice Chase, whom it accused of having "done more than all others, unless in a pecuniary way, to secure this result." It was a tainted verdict, the paper bellowed, for money had been used to secure the acquittal. Now Johnson could organize the military as well as the civil power in the interest of rebellion and aristocracy. But let Chase, Fessenden and company shoulder the blame. Those with true hearts would "organize for and make certain the joyful advent of Grant and Victory."

"We did our best to get him out of office last spring," Greeley wrote of Johnson the following November.[27] Truer word was never spoken.

In the interval of comparative quiet that succeeded the impeachment furor and preceded the hullabaloo of the campaign of 1868, Greeley made a bid for the Republican nomination for governor. The Fentonites rallied to his support, John Russell Young went up to Syracuse to lead the fight in his chief's behalf at the state convention, and Westchester's (and Vanderbilt's) Chauncey M. Depew put the *Tribune's* editor in nomination with a ringing speech—calling him an intellectual giant, a friend of the Negro and of labor, "the embodiment of the principles of his party." On the surface, it looked like a formidable boom.

But Depew's tub-thumping was all in vain. Roscoe Conkling's star was in the ascendant, and Conkling's choice for governor was iron manufacturer John A. Griswold of Troy. The convention applauded Greeley wildly, and then proceeded to nominate Griswold on the first ballot by an overwhelming majority. The contrast between the convention's acclaim and its votes was startling. "Everybody wondered," said Depew in later years, "how there could be so much smoke and so little fire."[28]

Some unkind spirits suggested that Greeley's humiliation at Syracuse was deliberately planned by false friends, Depew among the number, but this seems highly unlikely. At least such an explanation is unnecessary. The Conklingites had carefully organized the convention beforehand, while the attempt to organize for Greeley had been pretty much of a last-minute affair. He still commanded great affection and the *Tribune* commanded great respect as a political weapon, but by 1868 many an honest fellow had come to the conviction that, while Horace was a great man, he was scarcely fitted for the responsibilities of high office. Hence it was not surprising that the delegates should cheer one way and vote another. Godkin put it in a nutshell:

In public, few members of conventions have the courage to deny his fitness for any office in the country, and we verily believe that if he were proposed for the Chief-Justiceship of the Supreme Court or the command of the fleet, there would be clergymen and country politicians found to

maintain openly that he was equally well fitted to hear appeals in admiralty
or to be an admiral himself—such are the terrors inspired by his editorial
cowskin. But the minute the voting by ballot begins, the cowardly fellows
repudiate him under the veil of secrecy.[29]

Greeley was disappointed by the blasting of his hopes for the
governorship, but he tried hard not to show it. "I cannot understand
why I desired the nomination," he told Depew. "There is nothing
in it. No man can name the ten last governors of the state of New
York." The *Tribune* bestowed its blessing on Griswold. But it is
doubtful that Greeley's regard for Conkling was enhanced by the
course events had taken at Syracuse.[30]

Thwarted in what had well-nigh become a perennial search for
office, the *Tribune's* editor now turned to the presidential campaign. He had opposed Grant's nomination until to continue such
opposition would have been rank heresy, so it was not altogether
surprising that the *Tribune's* attitude toward the Republican candidate should be somewhat irregular. And irregular it was, a weird
combination of lyricism and sharp digs.

Grant was pictured as a good man, the country's saviour, the
nation's hero:

> And if asked what state he hails from,
> This our sole reply shall be,
> "From near Appomattox Court-House,
> With its famous apple tree!"

At the same time, the *Tribune* declared that the general was no
great leader, giving this as a conclusive reason for electing a safely
Republican Congress to which must be left the guiding of the
nation's destinies. Rising to Grant's defense against the charge
that he had no policy, the *Tribune* asserted that his plan was "not
to enforce any policy against the will of the people," a bit of praise
that was surely a masterpiece of cautious appraisement. Greeley's
real feelings were disclosed when, in a backhanded fling at the
Republicans for their stupidity in overlooking a good man, he
urged the Democrats to nominate Chase. Of course they could not
elect him, but he would poll a far better vote than anyone else
they might name.[31]

Greeley had no intention of bolting the Grant ticket, but the
Tribune's lack of enthusiasm was obvious. Grant was hurt. He
complained to his running mate, Schuyler Colfax, that Greeley had
never once called on him when in Washington. "Why don't you?"

the amiable "Smiler" wrote to Greeley, adding, as an encouragement to this act of benevolence the information that Grant read
the *Tribune* "every night." But not even this news could stoke the
fires of the *Tribune's* enthusiasm.[32]

Greeley might feel unable to hurrah for Grant, but he could
and did strike a vigorous note in dealing with the issues of the
election. Defeat of the Republican ticket, he asserted, would be
nothing short of a national disaster. The election of the Democratic
candidates, Horatio Seymour and Frank Blair, would mean that
all white Republicans would have to leave the South, while the
Negroes would be again reduced to virtual slavery. Copperhead
Seymour, first among the northern demagogues, was declared to
be the very best possible Democratic candidate because he represented the very spirit of the rebellion, and in this connection the
Tribune made much of Ku Klux Klan outrages in the South.
Seymour's victory would mean counterrevolution, a repudiation
of just debts and the triumph of that great Democratic swindle,
soft money. On the other hand, a Republican triumph would mean
impartial suffrage, equal rights and a sound currency.[33]

Greeley's campaign efforts extended beyond writing editorials on
behalf of Grant and Colfax. He interested himself in getting others
to write campaign pamphlets designed to get out the Negro vote.
He played a prominent part in raising $150,000 in New York State
for election purposes. He traveled hither and yon, making political
speeches. At the height of the contest, 240,000 copies of the *Weekly
Tribune* went out among the voters each time that sheet came
off the press. The *Tribune's* editor was also active in connection
with the state campaign, making vigorous assaults upon Tammany's
John T. Hoffman, the Democratic candidate for governor, and
repeatedly denouncing the fraudulent registrations that Tammany
judges were piling up at relentless speed in New York City. All in
all, Greeley could not be accused of sulking in his tent during the
1868 campaign.

The election turned out to be a Republican victory of considerable proportions. Grant won in the electoral college by 214
votes to 80 for Seymour. The former's popular majority, slightly
over 300,000, was one of the largest recorded up to that time,
although the splendor of its magnitude was somewhat diminished
by the fact that some 450,000 of the Republican votes were cast
by Negroes, most of whom voted as a result of the arbitrarily
imposed southern reconstruction.

But in New York State, due to unblushing frauds in New York
City, Seymour and Hoffman came in ahead of their Republican

rivals. Once more it had been demonstrated that Tammany could get out the vote, and the Tiger was left undisturbed to gorge itself at the city treasury.

Greeley mourned the Republican defeat in New York State, but he waxed ecstatic as he viewed the national outcome. Grant's popular majority, he declared exultantly, was larger and more decisive than that of almost any other presidential candidate in history (as a matter of fact, Lincoln's, in 1864, was the only one that had been larger). Only fraud and terror had prevented Grant from receiving a unanimous electoral vote. He was unmistakably the choice of every section, the South included, and from this dubious assumption Greeley augured the happiest results.

Reconstruction was now over, Greeley declared. Ku Kluxism, that masked terror of Negro rights, would now decay and die. In fact, he hoped to hear very soon of the meeting of leading Negroes and whites throughout the South and of their agreeing to live thenceforth in peace and harmony with one another. With peace in the South there would come to that area a healthful immigration of capital, labor, and business enterprise. With remarkable prescience, Greeley caught a vision of the splendid economic possibilities that lay waiting for development below Mason and Dixon's line.

The South was not the only region that would benefit from Grant's victory. That triumph of equal rights and Republican liberty would open the way to great things throughout the nation. Greeley envisaged 500,000 immigrants a year from the Old World, two-thirds of them going into the South, the rest taking their talents and proficiencies into the other quarters of the Union. Skilled as well as unskilled labor would come over the waters and, of course with the benefit of a proper tariff, diversified industry would grow by leaps and bounds throughout the nation. Ten thousand manufactories would develop in the Mississippi Valley alone. Then, as an accompaniment to prosperity, universal amnesty, and impartial suffrage, there would swiftly come a general reconciliation of the sections. Grant's election, declared the editor of the *Tribune*, "finally seals the restoration of the Union, and founds an indissoluble nationality on the basis of universal liberty and manhood suffrage.[34]

And so, it seemed, the end of the quest was in sight. The ugly scars left by the Civil War would disappear even during Grant's four years; a national Republican party, devoted to truly national ends, would rule forevermore; and one Horace Greeley would at length be free to devote himself to constructive efforts in the national interest.

Was all this simply the dream of a man who was growing old, a man whose spirits were flagging and whose sight was growing dim as he started on the downhill road? It did not have that appearance. Battles in plenty were still to be found on every hand, and Greeley showed no disposition to shrink from them. There was the great fight for prohibition, as one example. Greeley's readers were warned vigorously that wine (witness Noah!) could make people drunk just as effectively as did hard liquor. The glorious crown of temperance must be seated firmly on the American head. Agriculture was another area in which revolution could be conducted with profit to all concerned, and on December 1, 1868, Greeley read a paper on "Deep Plowing" before the American Institute Farmer's Club in New York. Then there was the never-ending conflict over protection, a matter to which he hoped, once the campaign was out of the way, to devote most if not all of his time. He was just as busy as ever, he wrote to Bayard Taylor, even "though Grant *is* elected."[35]

There was much to do. There would be still more to do if, by some strange mischance, that military Moses, the hero of Appomattox, should not lead the hosts of righteousness on toward the Promised Land.

NOTES FOR CHAPTER 23

1. Gerrit Smith Papers, Greeley to the editor of the *Syracuse Journal*, June 26, 1867; *Independent*, July 4, 11, 25, 1867.
2. *Independent*, June 27, 1867.
3. Autograph Collection (Hist. Soc. of Pa.), Greeley to J. H. Orr, July 7, 1867; Nicolay Papers, Greeley to Nicolay, July 31, 1867; Current, *Stevens*, p. 282; *Independent*, Aug. 8, 1867; *Tribune*, Oct. 5, 1867.
4. *Tribune*, Sept. 21, 1866; *Independent*, Apr. 25, 1867.
5. *Tribune*, June 4, 5, 26, 27, 1867; Alexander, *Hist. of New York State*, III, 182-83 and note.
6. *Tribune*, June 20, 26, 28, July 10-13, 17, 19, 26, 27, 31, Aug. 1, 1867; *Independent*, Aug. 1, 1867.
7. A short time subsequently, Greeley remarked, in regard to impartial suffrage, "We no more believe in Black than in White Suffrage."—*Tribune*, Dec. 28, 1867.
8. The *Albany Evening Journal* and the *Albany Argus* were paid for publishing the proceedings.
9. *Tribune*, Aug. 2, 9, 14-15, 21, 24, 29, Sept. 19, 1867, Nov. 9, 1869; Greeley, *Letter to a Politician*, p. 4; *Documents of the Convention of the State of New York* (5 vols.; Albany, 1868), III, 349. I follow the proceedings of the convention as recorded in the *Tribune*.

10. White, *Autobiography*, I, 143; *Tribune*, Aug. 6, 9, 10, 29, Sept. 7, 11, 25, 1867; Greeley Papers (Lib. of Cong), Greeley to Brockway, Feb. 14, 1872; Greeley Papers (N. Y. P. L.), Greeley to Robert Bonner, Aug. 7, 1867; Stahl Collection, Greeley to Mrs. Allen, Oct. 7, 1867.

11. Brockway, p. 153.

12. *Tribune*, Jan. 29, Feb. 8, Mar. 27, Apr. 15, 16, 22, 23, 1867; *New York Times*, and *New York Commercial Advertiser*, Apr.-May, 1867; Ogden, *Godkin*, I, 298-301; Lane, *Vanderbilt*, pp. 244-45; Myers, *Tammany Hall*, p. 243. Weed at this time was the owner of the *Commercial Advertiser.*

13. *Tribune*, Sept. 27, Oct. 2, 12, 22, 1867; *Independent*, Oct. 24, 1867; Stebbins, *Polit. Hist. of New York State*, pp. 159, 162, 164, 188, 195.

14. *Tribune*, Nov. 6, 9-12, 1867; Stebbins, *Polit. Hist. of New York State*, pp. 204, 207-11.

15. *Tribune*, Nov. 15, 18, 1867.

16. *Tribune*, Dec. 5, 1867; Greeley Papers (Lib. of Cong.), Greeley to Mrs. Whipple, Dec. 7, 1867.

17. *Tribune*, Apr. 12, 15, Nov. 7, 13, 22, Dec. 30, 1867, Jan. 11, 29, 1868; *Independent*, Jan. 16, 1868; Greeley Papers (Lib. of Cong.), Greeley to Mrs. Whipple, Dec. 7, 1867.

18. *Tribune*, Oct. 16, 18, Nov. 7, 1867; *Independent*, Sept. 5, 1867, Feb. 27, 1868.

19. M. A. DeW. Howe, *Moorfield Storey* (N. Y., 1932), pp. 59-60; *Tribune*, Jan. 22, 29, 31, 1868.

20. *Tribune*, Jan. 29, 30, Feb. 3, 1868.

21. *Tribune*, Feb. 6, May 22, 1868.

22. *Tribune*, Oct. 25, Nov. 23, 1866, Jan. 8, 21, Nov. 26, Dec. 9, 1867; Greeley Papers (N. Y. P. L.), S. P. Chase to Greeley, Jan. 17, May 25, 1868; Young, *Men and Memories*, p. 116.

23. *Tribune*, Jan. 17, 18, 20, 1868, Mar. 22, 1869.

24. *Tribune*, Mar.-May, especially Mar. 24, 1868.

25. Greeley Papers (N. Y. P. L.), Chase to Greeley, May 25, 1868; Young, *Men and Memories*, p. 116.

26. Stevens Papers, Greeley to Stevens, Apr. 20, 1868.

27. *Tribune*, Nov. 19, 1868.

28. Alexander, *Hist. of the State of New York*, III, 196, statement of Depew to Alexander.

29. *Nation*, July 16, 1868.

30. *Tribune*, July 9, 1868; Depew, *Memories*, pp. 88-89; Chidsey, *Conkling*, p. 135; Stebbins, *Polit. Hist. of New York State*, pp. 351-58.

31. *Tribune*, May 23, June 4, 9, 12, 17, 19, 1868; *True Issues*, Greeley at Cleveland, Sept. 24, 1872.

32. Greeley Papers (N. Y. P. L.), Colfax to Greeley, June 19, 1868.

33. *Tribune*, July 15, 25, 29, Aug. 6, 10, 12, Sept. 1, 22, Oct. 13, 1868; Greeley Papers (N. Y. P. L.), Greeley to O. Johnson, July 23, 1868; Gerrit Smith Papers, Greeley to Smith, July 26, 1868; *Independent*, Aug. 13, 27, Sept.-Oct., 1868.

34. *Tribune*, Nov. 5, 7, 10, 11, 24, Dec. 12, 1868; *Independent*, Nov. 12, Dec. 3, 1868.

35. *Tribune*, Apr. 29, Dec. 12, 1868; Greeley Letters (N. Y. H. S.), Greeley to Bayard Taylor, Dec. 3, 1868; *Independent*, Nov. 26, 1868.

And Still the Quest

G REELEY FACED THE SPRING OF 1869 WITH AN AIR of confidence. Grant was safely installed in the White House. The *Tribune,* rebounding from its low after the Jefferson Davis affair, had a million-dollar budget. Its receipts comfortably exceeded its expenditures, and in Whitelaw Reid, who had joined its staff in the fall of 1868, Greeley had found a second in command upon whose managerial ability and newspaper sense he could confidently rely.[1] The time had come, the *Tribune's* editor felt, for a forward movement along truly national lines.

So once more the *Tribune* resounded with denunciations of strong drink and with pleadings for prohibitory laws.[2] And even as Greeley strove to exorcise Demon Rum, he inaugurated another campaign designed to revolutionize life on the farm.

What I Know of Farming, which Greeley wrote and published during 1869 and 1870, was a compendium of plans and prophecies for a better rural life. It advocated irrigation, flood control, and tree belts for the protection of the prairie regions from the force of the winds. It urged soil analysis, the diversification of crops, the conservation of natural resources, and the establishment of farmers' clubs—this last making Greeley one of the early advocates of the Grange idea. The time would come, Greeley declared, when the farmer would "be practically an engineer," and the *Tribune's* editor looked longingly forward to the age of the machine that would furnish the farm's motive power but that, unlike horses, could be cleaned, oiled, and put away for the winter.

What our farmers need [declared Greeley] is not a steam plow as a specialty, but a locomotive that can travel with facility, not only on common wagon roads, but across even freshly-plowed fields, without embarrassment, and prove as docile to its manager's touch as an average span of horses. . . . It should be so contrived that it may be hitched in a minute to a plow, a harrow, a wagon or cart, a saw or grist-mill, a mower or reaper, a thresher or stalk-cutter, a stump or rock-puller, and made useful in pumping and draining operations, digging a cellar or laying up a wall, also in ditching or trenching. We may have to wait some years yet for a servant so dexterous and docile, yet I feel confident that our children will enjoy and appreciate his handiwork.[3]

Greeley's hopes and dreams about American agriculture centered around a farm life that should be not only scientific but also coöperative in character. "The Daniel Boone business is played out," he told his readers,[4] urging that, instead of individual pioneers, agricultural-industrial colonies should settle and develop the lands of the West and South. These colonies should consist of one hundred or more hardy, thrifty families (there would be no room in them for paupers or charity-subscription migrants) which would organize agrarian villages as centers of diversified and productive economic activity.

Union Colony, founded in 1870 in the Cache la Poudre Valley of Colorado, about half way between Cheyenne and Denver, was a materialization of Greeley's agrarian-community dream. The idea of establishing this colony seems to have originated with Nathaniel Cook Meeker, a quondam Fourierite who, in 1865, had become the agricultural editor of the Tribune. Union Colony could not well be called Fourieristic (each colonist bought and owned his own plot of ground) but it constituted a fairly close association, emphasized industrial as well as agricultural activity, and undertook a considerable variety of coöperative efforts for the benefit of the whole group. It was dear to Greeley's heart for still another reason, being run on temperance lines. Local miners and cattlemen called it "Saints' Rest."

Greeley became interested in Union Colony while it was still only an idea in the mind of Nathaniel Meeker. The presiding genius of the Tribune helped in getting the organization of the colony started, became its treasurer, invested $1,000 in its land and vigorously publicized the project in the Tribune. In 1870 he visited the colony's town center, which had been named "Greeley" in his honor, and came back to tell his readers that 10,000 similar establishments should spring into being throughout the United States.

Industrial colonies of the Union Colony type, Greeley asserted, constituted "the American idea of colonization." They were rapidly spreading out along the lines of the great Pacific railroads and he foresaw their development in the South, particularly in Virginia where there was no Ku Klux Klan to act as an impediment to their progress. It was a great opportunity for those who had gumption enough to raise the $500 to $1,000 necessary to join a colony and get out to it. There were 250,000 such people, Greeley asserted, within ten miles of Trinity steeple, hustlers such as were needed to fulfill the promise of this American dream.[5]

Colonization could scarcely succeed without adequate means of transportation, and so Greeley agitated vigorously for the continued development of American railroads. He favored land subsidies to this end (money grants could wait until the government had resumed specie payment). It was becoming apparent to him that railroad rates should be regulated by the states and by Congress, but at the same time he believed that the need for the rapid development of transportation made the continuation of land grants essential to the country's welfare.[6]

Railroad development, rural colonization projects, the fostering of scientific farming and agitation for temperance did not monopolize Greeley's enthusiasm nor exhaust his plans for promoting the welfare of the nation. Industrial development also lay close to his heart and, as became a disciple of Carey and Clay, his devotion to a protective tariff increased in vigor with the years. He urged the substantial increase of a tariff that was already high, on the ground that such a move was essential to the country's prosperity. The belaboring of free traders and "revenue reformers," those snakes in the grass like David Ames Wells who were really free traders in disguise, was almost a daily feature of the *Tribune*'s editorial columns.[7] During the spring of 1869 there also began to appear in the *Tribune* its editor's *Essays Designed to Elucidate the Science of Political Economy*. This was simply a protectionist treatise, rehashing all the old protectionist arguments. It denounced free trade as practically synonymous with anarchic individualism and was dedicated to Henry Clay.[8]

One of the principal beauties of protection was that it would do so much for the welfare of American labor. With the tariff at a sufficiently high level and the working class converted to thrift and coöperative production, Greeley honestly believed that labor trouble in the United States would become a thing of the past. Steadily he pounded away at this thesis in the columns of the *Tribune,* at the same time warning the workers against class consciousness, strikes, and labor monopolies.[9]

Greeley believed that American labor should not resist the influx of foreign labor. The immigration of labor was necessary, the *Tribune* declared, because it meant national growth and eventually an amalgam of skills and talents in a vigorously superior national character. Greeley criticized unions, such as the shoemakers' Knights of St. Crispin, for taking a dim view of the influx of foreign workers. On one occasion, he even defended the use of foreign-born labor as a means of breaking strikes.

During the summer of 1870, trouble broke out in the shoe factories in North Adams, Massachusetts. The Crispins struck and the shoe manufacturers brought in coolie laborers as strikebreakers. Greeley took the attitude that the Crispins' strike had "compelled" the manufacturers to this action. The strikers had violated the law of supply and demand, a law which applied to labor as well as to commodities like wheat and coal. Let them move out of the crowded Massachusetts towns where they glutted the labor supply, and establish their own coöperative shoe factory. Half the money spent in supporting even the briefest strike would be sufficient for this purpose. The key to the solution of the North Adams trouble was coöperation.[10]

Class consciousness among nineteenth-century American laborers was chiefly conspicuous by its absence, and even such stands as that which Greeley took in regard to the Crispins of North Adams did little to weaken his hold upon the affections of the workers. During that same year of 1870, the New York State lodge of the Crispins made the *Tribune* its state organ.[11]

Greeley's emphasis upon moral and economic issues indicated his wish to believe that reconstruction troubles were over. His hailing of the Fifteenth Amendment's guarantee of the Negro's right to vote as truly establishing impartial suffrage in the South was another indication of this same frame of mind. Nevertheless, unrest and conflict in the South kept forcing him to redefine his attitude toward the southern problem.

As it became increasingly apparent that there was a great gulf fixed between constitutional enactment and southern practice in the matter of Negro voting, Greeley began championing the Ku Klux and enforcement acts by which northern Republicans sought to guarantee the Negro's status below Mason and Dixon's line. Enforcement was now the editor's cry, but even as he uttered it he recognized its inadequacy. Once more he took up his chant for universal amnesty. Only through amnesty, he declared, could an effective approach be made to a solution of the South's difficulties.[12]

Greeley had been wrong about the automatic effectiveness of the Fifteenth Amendment. His advocacy of enforcing Negro rights was a negative and dubious approach to the southern problem. And it was scarcely clear to anyone save the *Tribune's* editor that amnesty would smooth away racial animosities. Obviously, he had no deep understanding of the problem with which he was confronted. That this was so was made even more clear by his thinking on the future of the Negro.

Back in 1865, Greeley had had a bright vision of the Negro people becoming full-fledged citizens by a kind of natural process— industry on their part, balanced by white acceptance of them as political equals. He had then denounced segregation as an even greater absurdity than colonization in some foreign land. Now, under the pressure of actual circumstance, his views began to change. He began emphasizing the existence of widespread white prejudice against the colored people, began telling the Negroes that they must not expect any great elevation of their general status. Complete political equality would be impossible of attainment, at least for a long time to come. Social equality was, of course, a mirage. Neither should the Negroes expect such special favors as outright gifts of land. Their rights under the laws and the constitution should be safeguarded like those of every other citizen, but Greeley suggested that they recognize the facts of life by segregating themselves in towns or cities or counties, and by employing one another as much as possible. He was glad to see the southern Negroes getting ahead, but they could and should have been making still more progress. He urged them to form agricultural-industrial units of the Union Colony type, and there provide vocational education for their children.[13] Some of these ideas were constructive and practical, but it was also true that the thinking of the editor of the *Tribune* was leading him straight toward acceptance of the idea of Negro ghettos.

Greeley's largely negative attitude toward the Negro was at least in part the result of his belief that the social reconstruction of the South must be left in the hands of a conservative southern white leadership. He came to believe more and more firmly as the post-Civil War years went by that, if reconstruction were to be lasting, it must be based upon soundly conservative financial policies. His horror at the wastage and corruption that characterized the black and tan legislatures of the forcibly reconstructed southern states led him to overlook, or at least to minimize the remarkably progressive social legislation of the carpetbag regimes. As the extravagance of the southern legislatures became more glaring, so Greeley became more anxious for the establishment in power of a southern white leadership that would be endowed with financial common sense.

But would such a leadership be Republican in its political sympathies? Greeley believed that the answer to this query was "Yes," if the Republican party led the way in establishing universal amnesty. Such a development, he was certain, would soften sectional antipathies, moderate partisan asperities, and make possible the creation of a powerful, conservatively led, southern Republican organization.

Such were the facts of political life, so far as the South was concerned, declared the editor of the *Tribune*. For the Republican party to ignore these facts, was to court political disaster. Look at West Virginia alone, he demanded. There Lincoln's majority of 12,714 in 1864 had sunk in 1868 to Grant's majority of 4,717 as a result of the disgust of the West Virginia voters with radicalism. "How much longer," asked Greeley, "do you think that iceberg under a July sun will be safely habitable?"[14]

The main trouble with Greeley's thinking on reconstruction was that, in his zeal for final answers, he showed a persistent tendency to oversimplify southern problems. He believed that, given universal amnesty and impartial suffrage, southern whites and southern Negroes would sit down together and iron out their difficulties. He brushed aside the intimidation of the Negroes in the South as primarily the work of unreconstructed rebels, aided and abetted by irresponsible youths and criminals. It was the Old Rebellion, seeking once more to put its foot on the necks of the Negroes, but it represented, he was sure, only a small minority of southerners.

Just as a firm but conciliatory treatment of the South in 1861 would have given the loyal southern whites an opportunity to put down the secessionists, so now a policy of law enforcement coupled with amnesty would blunt the weapons of the renegades who had instituted the reign of terror in the South, and would permit the great body of whites and blacks to rally around the standard of "All Rights for All." Regardless of southern fears of Negro rule, unmindful of the narrow-minded selfishness that was all too prominent a characteristic of the postwar southern middle class, Greeley put his trust in the southern conservatives, among whom the heirs of the old Whig tradition were the prevailing element. The conservatives, he declared, could solve the South's great problem. It was a measure of his confidence in them that he urged upon the southern conservatives the duty of educating the poor whites and the Negroes and of repressing the Ku Klux outrages that he rightly stigmatized as foreign to the spirit of American democracy.[15]

Such were the means by which Greeley sought to free the nation from the reconstruction embroglio. The urgency with which he pursued his goal was symbolized by a notice given in the *Tribune* to Confederate Colonel H. D. Capers, who was leading a movement for an industrial congress in Georgia. Greeley confessedly knew nothing of Capers' politics, though he assumed that they were conservative in character, but his heart was warmed by the colonel's interest in the development of southern industry. "We pronounce him admirably reconstructed," Greeley declared, "and fit to take a freeman's part in directing the nation's policy."[16]

Greeley's attitude toward reconstruction was publicized far and wide by his trip to Texas in the spring of 1871. This was undertaken in part, at least, at the behest of northern capitalists who felt that his presence in Texas would benefit their projects for investment there, but it was chiefly the result of his sincere desire to expedite a reconciliation of the sections. Superficially, his reason for going was to address the state fair at Houston. En route, he was besieged by invitations to talk, and amiably responded from car platforms and hotel balconies and in more formal addresses at such places as New Orleans, Galveston, and Vicksburg.

In the speeches that he made on this southern trip, Greeley denounced the Ku Kluxers, castigated the carpetbaggers and scalawags and criticized the southern landowners for lacking a constructive attitude toward the Negro. But at the same time he spoke warmly of the South's increasing loyalty to the Union, and of the improving economic and social conditions that he found on every hand. Above all, he emphasized the need for national harmony.

It was unthinkable, Greeley told the southerners, that the Mississippi should run through two separate nations. The struggle for national unity, he told a German audience, like the struggle for German unification, had been in a righteous cause. All citizens, North and South, should recognize the absolute necessity of reunion, and should work together for the common cause. The citizens of Vicksburg were told that he hoped the time would come when northerners would honor the soldierly achievements and military characters of Robert E. Lee and Stonewall Jackson, and that southerners would pay equal homage to Grant, Sherman, Thomas, and Sheridan.[17] It was a primarily emotional, but nonetheless moving appeal for the recreation of a united nation.

On his return from the South, Greeley was given a reception at the Lincoln Club rooms in Union Square. The rooms were decorated with flags and flowers. A large oil painting of the guest of honor, to say nothing of numerous photographs and lithographs of the same, looked down from the walls. Arrayed in slouchy evening dress, but with a gorgeous bouquet pinned to his coat, Greeley moved about among his admirers. Already plans for making him a presidential candidate were being bruited about. Later, writing with the advantage of hindsight, Andrew Dickson White declared that the *Tribune's* editor had given the appearance that night of a victim adorned for the sacrifice.

As the festivities within the club drew to a close, a crowd assembled in the Square outside. A raised platform had been prepared on the Broadway side of the Square. Greeley mounted this platform and delivered an address to several thousand of his fellow New Yorkers, speaking through them to all his fellow countrymen.

Half apologetically, the *Tribune's* editor defended his eager willingness to make speeches during his trip. He then took pains to deny that he had ever sought office. He had run several times, but only because he had regarded it as a duty to do so. In each case, he had run a little ahead of the average of the ticket, and for this support he was grateful. In the future, while he would never decline "any nomination that has not been offered me," he would certainly seek no office whatever. Having thus indicated the fact that he was very much available politically, he told of how in the South he had pleaded for national unity and had striven to make people understand "that we are all Americans." That had been his objective when he had expressed the wish that the North should honor Lee and the South should honor Grant. "Possibly you are not willing to go so far as that," he told his auditors. "Very well, then, there is no hurry. Take your time; I can wait. I can wait." Then he assured the crowd that the Democrats were getting ready to abandon their hostility to the rights of the colored people. He welcomed signs of this, even though it might mean Republican defeat, for he was weary of reconstruction and anxious for the time when the parties, whether in accord or in rivalry, would "endeavour to promote the prosperity, the happiness and the true glory of the American people." There was talk of a Democratic New Departure—of the Democracy's accepting the Thirteenth, Fourteenth and Fifteenth amendments. Personally, he felt that it was time for a New Departure for the whole country. "Speak to the children of Israel that they go forward."[18]

Greeley's Union Square speech demonstrated his fervent patriotism and, indeed, a certain grandeur of vision as to the nation's future. It was also indubitably political, and was thus ominous from the point of view of Grant and his followers. For the squire of Chappaqua was showing signs of an insurgency that threatened to move him far out of the regular Republican orbit.

There had been scant indication at the beginning of Grant's term of such straying from the ordered path. The *Tribune's* tone after the election of 1868 had been both fulsome and fervent in regard to the hero. "We look for his coming," it had declared, "as men who gaze through the darkest night and fervently yearn for morning."[19] Greeley had gone to Washington for the inauguration. He had even gone to the wretchedly managed inaugural ball, where tired and supperless ladies sat disconsolately on the floor, and the collapse of the checking system forced hundreds of men, including the *Tribune's* editor, to go out coatless and bareheaded into the bitter night. Despite such annoyances, his report to the *Tribune* had been almost lyrical. The new Cabinet, Greeley had declared, meant business. Singling out two of the most dubious appointments for special mention, he had asserted that A. T. Stewart, merchant extraordinary, would manage the Treasury purely as a business concern—"he cannot fail"—while Elihu B. Washburne, the new secretary of state, was described as such a fighter against prodigality and corruption that he could not be spared from a reforming cabinet.[20]

Dana's *Sun,* observing these transports of enthuiasm with ironic amusement, had speculated as to what post would be given Greeley for such ardent support, and had urged the *Times* to unite with it in urging him on the President's attention. The *Times* had declined for the moment, not knowing what office Greeley was "now after."[21] But what had Greeley cared for such ill-natured twitterings? To show his scorn, he had reprinted them in the *Tribune.* The new day was at hand. That was all that really mattered.

And, indeed, at the beginning cordial coöperation had seemed to characterize the relationship between the hero and the editor. Early in March 1869, George B. Boutwell (who had been appointed secretary of the treasury after it was discovered that Stewart was ineligible because he was actively engaged in business) had informed Greeley that the President wished to consult him about important New York offices. Two such interviews had been held and, presumably, they had been characterized by a spirit of harmony. For there had been also an offer of a place on the commission to examine and report on the condition of the Union Pacific Railroad and, during the summer of 1869, the post of Minister to England had been tendered to the *Tribune's* editor. Grant had obviously wanted to be friendly.

Greeley, however, had not received these advances with open arms. In fact, he had been definitely unreceptive. He had refused the railroad commission on plea of the priority of his editorial and literary labors. The offer of the English post was met by the suggestion that it be deferred until after the fall election of 1869. Grant had thereupon begun trying to find some other foreign mission that would be to Greeley's liking.[22] The effort was vain. Greeley did not propose to accept favors at the hands of Grant, and within a few months had begun bombarding the administration with tart comments and embarrassing criticisms.

There was a wide variety of reasons for Greeley's growing hostility to Grant. Partly it derived from a personal antipathy which Greeley privately admitted; it was in some measure due to differences of opinion as to administrative policy; last but by no means least, it arose from a feeling of injury because of the course Grant took in regard to appointments in New York State. All told, these spelled out on Greeley's part a steady increase of bad humor and a mounting disgust with Grant and all his works, an attitude which the President stubbornly but fruitlessly attempted to change by offers of appointments and invitations to dinner. The situation had its comic elements, with tragedy lurking in the background.

Grant's reconstruction policy brought more and more squeaks of rage from the *Tribune* office. The President stood by the carpetbaggers and scalawagers in their attempt to maintain control of the southern state governments, a policy that Greeley had now come to regard as nothing short of idiotic. What was the good, he asked fretfully, of persisting in a course that lost one state after another to the Democrats—"As the lean boarder told his landlady touching her bedbugs, 'I really haven't the blood to spare.' "[23]

Fully as important as reconstruction, to Greeley's way of thinking, was the government's fiscal policy, and here also he found the administration woefully lacking. As a sound-money, economy-minded financial conservative, Greeley wanted to see a drastic curtailment of the navy, the elimination of 50 per cent of the army officers, and a cut in half of the cost of government printing. In 1868 he had descended upon Congress "like a scarecrow" (the simile was Thad Stevens'), to wreck a bill giving a 20-per-cent salary increase to government employees in Washington who earned less than $2,500 a year, and he was constantly on the lookout for other signs of governmental extravagance.

Such an economical point of view found itself affronted by the administration at almost every turn. Grant had no interest in emasculating the military establishment, either on the land or on the sea. And the President, much to Greeley's disgust, actually proposed increasing the salaries of government employees.[24]

Worse still was the record of the Treasury Department, from the *Tribune* point of view. Greeley kept trumpeting for immediate resumption of specie payment and speedy retirement of the greenbacks (this last despite the fact that the existing supply of currency was inadequate for business needs), but the government refused to follow either course. The *Tribune's* editor in chief was also dreadfully worried by the two-and-one-half-billion-dollar public debt. "Banking is not the government's proper business. Paying its debts is," he scolded, and urged using 90 per cent of the gold reserve for reducing the national obligations. Boutwell did use some Treasury gold to purchase government bonds on the open market, and for this he was roundly praised, but he went nowhere near the lengths advocated by the *Tribune's* economic soothsayer. Neither did he pay any attention to another pet project of Greeley's—the issuance of an "American consol," a hundred-year bond payable in specie, bearing interest at 4 or 5 per cent and usable in refunding operations. Clearly the government was not measuring up to Greeley's standards of financial statesmanship, and the editor's choler mounted accordingly.[25]

Greeley's dissatisfaction with the government's economic policy was clearly apparent in the *Tribune's* attitude toward the attempted gold corner by Fisk and Gould in September 1869. This precious pair of robbers boosted the price of gold from 130 to over 160, and were prevented from achieving their objectives only by the Treasury's last-minute sale of the precious metal. Greeley had been one of the foremost in demanding that the Treasury sell gold to break the corner. But after the crisis was over, instead of praising Boutwell for selling gold at the critical moment, the *Tribune* assumed a supercilious air. Why had not the government sold large amounts of gold on the rising market, the paper caustically inquired. Why had it given warning to stand from under, and then taken 135 for what could have been sold as much as twenty-five points higher? Where was the government's business instinct?[26]

Greeley's state of general irritation found an outlet at the close of the gold excitement in an outburst about the misuse of the English language, a subject on which he had always had strong convictions. The gyrations of the price of gold had affected stocks in general and had resulted in the appearance of the term "panicky market." The word "panicky" aroused Greeley's wrath. It was, he declared, "a hideous neologism," a "bastard word from every point of view . . . we shall have 'physicky' and 'tonicky' and 'magicky' next— we know we shall."[27]

The Grant administration's reconstruction policy and its attitude in regard to finance went far toward sealing Greeley's conviction that the hero was too small a man for his job. An equally important factor was the steady decline of Greeley's influence in the New York State Republican party, and the role which the President played in aiding and abetting that decline.

Greeley was a supporter of Reuben E. Fenton, the junior United States Senator from New York then locked in deadly struggle with Roscoe Conkling for control of the state's Republican machine.[28] The *Tribune's* editor also waged unceasing war upon the corruption prevalent in both parties, whether in the Albany legislature or in New York's Tweed Ring. In New York, Greeley's eyes had at least been opened to the iniquities of Judge Barnard, and there Fisk and Gould and Tweed came in for almost daily poundings. Greeley kept urging a nonpartisan coalition as the only means of unseating Tweed and his cohorts, a proposal that was scarcely palatable to the regular organization men of either party.[29]

As the state election of 1869 drew near, the feud within the Republican ranks was accentuated by the *Tribune's* allegations of corruption at Albany. The party's morale vanished in the midst of a welter of charges and countercharges, and the construction of a state ticket became a difficult problem. When a slate was finally nominated, three of the candidates who had been formally selected refused to run. Thereupon the Republican state committee, hopeless of victory and perhaps moved by animus toward one who had done so much to muddy up the waters, named Greeley for the office of comptroller without so much as consulting him beforehand.[30]

Greeley's only qualification for comptroller was his indiscriminate passion for economy, but if his political enemies thought to confound him by their action they were sadly mistaken in their man. He promptly accepted the nomination and made a vigorous campaign. The issues that he selected touched but lightly upon the intricacies of state finance. He dwelt instead upon Tammany corruption, the moral turpitude of the "sleek, oily, wily, respectable Democrats," and impartial suffrage—this last because Negro suffrage in New York State came before the voters that fall in the revised state constitution.[31]

"What a comedy it would be," wrote lawyer and politician E. Peshine Smith to Henry Carey, "if Greely [sic] should blunder into the Comptrollership." It was a comedy not to be played. The Republicans were soundly drubbed in the fall elections of 1869, and in the general rout Greeley ran some 4,000 votes behind the party's candidate for secretary of state, General Franz Sigel. Several thousand voters had scratched the name of the *Tribune's* editor from their ballots. This, together with the defeat of his cherished plan for free Negro suffrage, scarcely made him out a political favorite with the New York State voters.[32]

During the winter and spring of 1870, Greeley turned momentarily from his unfruitful search for office and from national concerns to concentrate upon the new charter for New York City that Boss Tweed wanted to put through the state legislature. This instrument was designed to deliver the metropolis completely into the hands of the Ring, and was pushed through the legislature by enormous bribery. But it was cleverly constructed, and deceived many honest and upright people. The Citizens Association of New York City endorsed it. The *New York Times* called it a "vast improvement" upon the old charter. Under these circumstances, it is perhaps not to be wondered at that Greeley exerted only a dubious influence against Tweed's plot.

To be sure, the *Tribune* labeled the charter "Sweeny's shame," and Greeley trumpeted about the need for "the deliverance of our city from gigantic corruption and misrule." He also called for the destruction of that citadel of the Ring's power, the Board of Supervisors, and went to Albany as the spokesman for a taxpayers' meeting at the Union League Club which demanded no less than fifteen amendments to the charter. At Albany, so he later declared, he had earnestly but vainly urged Republican senators to defeat the unamended charter.

But, granted that Greeley tried to persuade some Republican senators to vote against the charter, such action was quite counterbalanced by good words injudiciously spoken about the charter and by his wobblings before the Albany legislature. Greeley did urge amendments upon the senate, but at the same time he praised the unamended instrument "as embodying many excellent advances to reform." He also specifically denied that he was either advocating or opposing Tweed's measure. The net result of this course, together with the mesmeric influence exerted by Tweed's gold, was that not a single one of the amendments that Greeley brought to Albany was adopted.

Another consequence of Greeley's course at Albany was a blast of charges by the *Post* to the effect that his Albany mission had been a fraud and a desertion of good government. Thus Greeley was attacked from the ranks of the reformers, of whom he was supposed to be the champion. Delightedly, the *Sun* circulated the story that, as the storm howled about his ears, Greeley sadly told a friend: "Somehow I always get sold. John Russell Young sold me; and, since then, I have been sold many times."[33]

The *Sun* alleged that Greeley had wavered at Albany because of Republican suggestions that opposing the charter would be fatal to his nomination for governor in the fall of 1870. Greeley termed this charge a "willful falsehood." But, whatever the cause, his course in regard to the charter had done little to enhance the cause of good government and had laid him open to embarrassing attacks.[34]

Rebuffed by the voters, denounced and traduced for his efforts on behalf of reform, Greeley could not but be aware of his dwindling stature in the field of politics. That awareness was made all the more keen by the realization in 1870 that Grant had definitely chosen to support Conkling rather than Fenton in New York State. Greeley would almost certainly have opposed Grant's renomination without this final blow. It is not so certain that he would have bolted the regular party organization. The probability is that the feud over the control of the Republican party in New York State was the agency which finally precipitated Greeley out of the camp of the Republican regulars and into the arms of a group of Republican liberals whom he had previously regarded with disdain.

Grant had started his administration by listening to Fenton regarding New York State patronage distribution, and this had pleased Greeley very well. But by the summer of 1870, the President was tiring of Fenton and the sun of the hero's favor was beginning to shine upon the state's senior senator, Roscoe Conkling. The war that had already been raging between Conkling and Fenton now became rancorous in the extreme. The New York State Republican party was convulsed by the strife. And Greeley, ranged on the side which was to suffer one defeat after another, became very bitter indeed.

Greeley's dislike of the national administration's attitude toward the New York political situation flared violently in the spring of 1870 over the appointment of a collector of the port of New York. With unmistakable fervor, the *Tribune* warned Grant that the new collector must come from the Fenton wing of the party. But despite threats, warnings, and advice, the President nominated Thomas Murphy, a Conklingite with a dubious record as a spoilsman, for the post. Fenton strenuously opposed the appointment and Conkling, of course, urged its acceptance, both men making speeches in the Senate that fairly crackled with bitterness and hate. The Senate confirmed Murphy, forty-eight to three, and the vast power of the port's patronage was thus put at the disposal of the Conkling forces.[35] The Fentonites retired, licking their wounds, and began to lay plans for capturing the gubernatorial nomination in the fall.

This political struggle in 1870 found Greeley in very poor health. Malaria, contracted during a visit to Nassau that spring, brought on recurrent fits of fever and ague. These, together with rheumatism and sciatica, curbed the editor's activities to some degree and also dampened his spirits. "I actually begin to feel old!" he wrote to Mrs. Allen.[36] But despite these difficulties he continued to take an active interest in politics and to manifest his customary hunger for political recognition.

As far as the Republican nomination for governor in 1870 was concerned, Greeley affected to look with some favor upon Marshall O. Roberts, a Fentonite.[37] But the Man in the White Coat also had another candidate. Sick as he was, his comments in the *Tribune* made it apparent that he was willing to have the accolade fall on his own shoulders.[38]

The Republican state convention at Saratoga in the fall of 1870 was the scene of a violent struggle between the Fenton and Conkling factions, a struggle marked by displays of wily strategy on both sides. Fentonites supported both Greeley and George W. Curtis. Grant, still trying to woo Greeley, urged his nomination. Grant's friend and Conkling's candidate for governor, General Stewart L. Woodford, at one point offered to step aside in favor of Greeley, an offer which, for some reason Greeley felt it incumbent upon himself to refuse. At one point in the balloting Conkling, with Machiavellian strategy, gave Greeley his support. But behind all these feints and jockeyings for position, Conkling held the whip hand. His man, General Woodford, was nominated on the third ballot.[39]

Greeley professed to regard the outcome at Saratoga as "all right in every way." He told Whitelaw Reid that statements concerning his own indispensability, telegraphed to the *Tribune* by its convention reporter, were all "bosh." Such comment, snapped Greeley, was "enough to physic a horse."[40] But even if he was reconciled to his own defeat, the disaster that had overtaken his wing of the party was not easy to bear.

During the campaign, the *Tribune's* editor went out to Colorado, where he visited the town named in his honor and looked after his Union Colony investments. He came back for the last three weeks of the canvass and, vigorously protesting that his trip had been the result of necessity and not of political pique, wrote editorials in support of Woodford and against Governor Hoffman, who had been renominated by the Tweed-Tammany machine.

Greeley's appeals for Republican unity in the state campaign of 1870 served to advertise the dissension within the party, but were probably responsible for his last-minute nomination for Congress from the sixth Congressional district, a nomination in which both factions of the party united. Greeley accepted this nomination "cheerfully" although, still wracked by recurrent fits of fever and ague, he was unable to campaign against his Democratic opponent, the redoubtable Samuel Sullivan ("Sunset") Cox. The editor's silence during the campaign was perhaps a handicap. A more important obstacle to his success was the fact that Bryant and the *Post* came out against him because he was the champion of tariffs and monopoly.[41]

The election of 1870 in New York State was a Republican Waterloo. Hoffman was reëlected governor and Oakey Hall, "Elegant Oakey" of the Tweed Ring, mayor of New York. Tammany's majorities in New York City were reduced to some extent, the one bright spot in the picture, but the Tiger's grip on the city remained unbroken. Greeley could note with satisfaction that he had lowered the Democratic majority in the sixth district by 60 per cent, but he still ran over 1,000 votes behind Cox.[42]

After the election, Greeley attributed the Republican defeat to feuds and apathy. It was clear from his remarks that he was a Fenton man more than ever. Clear also was his warning to Grant:

We cannot afford [said the *Tribune's* editor] to have two Republican parties in this state. If we attempt it, we shall soon have none. And, in order that we may have one, it is essential that all who habitually vote the Republican ticket shall be regarded and treated as friends by the Federal administration. If a part of them are treated as step-children, we cannot keep the field.[43]

"If Grant will only let me alone," Greeley had written to Whitelaw Reid just after the Saratoga nomination, "there is no more trouble ahead for two years at least." But Grant, it seemed, would not or could not let him alone. Dinner invitations to the White House continued to reach Greeley's desk. There was still talk of the English mission. There was also talk of Greeley's being a member of a special commission to San Domingo.

But all these offers, or hints of offers, made the cantankerous editor fume and fret. He would not go to the White House; he wouldn't, he told Reid, go to England if the mission were offered; and, vigorously, he wouldn't think of going on any commission to the Caribbean. "I never thought of going to San Domingo," he told a correspondent, "am not (I trust) wanted to go to San Domingo—and, at all events, *won't go* to San Domingo." Grant might just as well stop fussing. Greeley did not like him, and wanted no favors from his administration.[44]

But if Grant could not leave Greeley alone, neither could Greeley leave Grant alone. The New York State political embroglio forbade it. Indeed, events soon demonstrated that the state Republican feud was dragging the *Tribune's* editor more and more into open conflict with the White House.

Early in 1871, Greeley was elected chairman of the Republican General Committee of New York City and County. On taking the chair he summoned the committeemen to harmony and unity in the name of victory, but the committee was rent by faction and bitterness from the start as Fentonites and Conklingites strove with one another. Each wing accused the other, probably with some reason, of Machiavellian dealings with Tammany. The Republican state committee, a Conkling stronghold, undertook to reorganize the New York City party-control mechanism. It created a new general committee for the city. Greeley regarded this as unjust, but he professed a willingness to obey the commands from state headquarters. Not so his fellow committeemen. By a vote of ninety-one to nine they refused to obey the orders of the state committee, and remained in being, with Greeley still their chairman. There were now two New York City Republican committees. This situation lasted until the fall of the year, when the Republican state convention under the driving leadership of Conkling formally abolished Greeley's committee.

The course of events which led to the disappearance of Greeley's committee made it plain to him the utter barrenness of his political future in the state with Conkling in control. It was obvious that there was no place in Conkling's machine for the editor of the *Tribune*. War or submission were the only alternatives. Greeley's choice was war.

The fight between Greeley and Conkling was carried on in Washington, and raged in the columns of the *Tribune*. Conkling was chiefly responsible for having two *Tribune* correspondents put in jail because they reported details of a treaty that was being discussed in a secret executive session of the Senate. The *Tribune* responded with a series of bitter editorial jibes. "Conkling Supporting His Dignity" became a theme of derision. The Senator from New York, said the paper, walked in a nimbus of greatness. "If Moses's name had been Conkling when he descended from the Mount, and the Jews had asked him what he saw there, he would have promptly replied, 'Conkling.'" He was twitted with not having been in the army during the Civil War, although the *Tribune* admitted that perhaps this was not strange. Such men as he "bloom most sweetly and spread abroad most satisfactorily in times of peace, like burdocks in an unhoed garden. . . . What a plantation overseer he would have made!"[45] There was obviously little chance for further coöperation between Greeley and the head of the New York State Republican machine.

It was not merely Conkling against whom the *Tribune's* editor bore malice for the destruction of his influence in the New York State Republican party. Greeley was as bitter against Grant as he was against Utica's sandy-haired son, for he was convinced that the President was a willing assistant to the political corruptionists who manned the Conkling organization. In the spring of 1871, as the struggle over the New York committee had waxed hot, Greeley had come out against Grant's renomination. Just before leaving for Texas that summer, he had written a letter favoring a single term for Grant or any other man in the White House, and on his return to New York he had come out again in the *Tribune* on the same subject. Greeley was clearly committed against a continuation of Grant's leadership in the party. The subsequent course of events was to drive the *Tribune's* editor steadily toward rebellion from the party itself.[46]

The state campaign in the fall of 1871 centered about the Tweed Ring, for the exposé of that gang of thieves was in full swing. The *Times* was publishing incriminating documents that had been stolen from the comptroller's office by a disgruntled former member of the Ring, and Thomas Nast was pillorying Tweed and his henchmen in the famous *Harper's Weekly* cartoons. At last the Tammany Democracy was definitely on the defensive.

The *Tribune* seconded the *Times's* onslaughts against the Ring, although it oscillated between its zeal for exposure of the swindlers and its jealousy of the *Times*, averring that the assault was good despite the fact that the *Times* had obtained its evidence "in some surreptitious way."[47] Faced by the inescapable fact that even the Conkling machine would be better than the Tweed plunderers, the *Tribune* and its editor worked for the Republican ticket. But Greeley had difficulty in disguising his deep dissatisfaction with the Republican-party situation, and distrust and hatred of the Conkling leaders boiled into view in the columns of the *Tribune* on the very eve of the election.[48]

The New York State election of November 1871 toppled Tweed's house in ruin and ousted Tammany from its control over the city and the state. It was a Republican victory, but it was one that left Grant's favorite, the imperious and arrogant Conkling, bestriding the state like a colossus. Greeley knew what this meant for himself, and he was bitter in spirit as he surveyed the political scene.

The accession to power of the Republicans brought not one jot or tittle of abatement, so far as their internal feuding was concerned. The Conkling men redoubled their onslaughts on their opponents. Greeley was charged with having favored the Tweed charter, and the Greeley-Fentonites were depicted as having touched Tammany pitch and being thus defiled. Their officeholders, what were left of them, were systematically dismissed in a state-wide purge. When the legislature met, Greeley's choice for speaker of the assembly was promptly defeated by a Conklingite. Proscription was all around the veteran editor.

Manfully, Greeley struck back at his foes. The custom-house wing was hurrahing for victory and reform, he noted sardonically, but where was the reform of which they boasted? Did they suppose that the Republican rascalities so patent in the southern carpetbag and scalawag regimes would be ignored in the presidential contest of 1872? And what about paymaster Hodge in Washington, that brilliant Grant satellite who had defaulted for almost half a million dollars? Other shafts were leveled at the corruption of Conklingite leaders in the state, particularly at Thomas Murphy, the painfully vulnerable collector of the port of New York.

Collector Murphy resigned under fire toward the end of November 1871. It looked like a Greeley victory, but Grant accepted the resignation with assurances of "unqualified confidence" and promptly appointed Chester A. Arthur, another Conkling man and a cynical spoilsman, to the post. Murphy's disappearance had only served to reëmphasize the President's alignment with Greeley's foes.

Furiously, Greeley turned the *Tribune's* guns on the White House. Grant's proposals in his annual message for increasing the navy and for merging the nation's telegraph lines with the postal service in a government-owned system of communications drew scornful blasts from the *Tribune's* editor. There was also a sudden outburst of zeal for civil service reform on the part of the *Tribune,* an outburst obviously prompted by the handling of the federal patronage in New York State. Defalcations by government officials other than Hodge were prominently displayed in the news columns. Accusations of nepotism were leveled against Grant. Over and over again, Greeley stressed his long-standing devotion to the one-term principle.

The lines binding Greeley to the regular Republican organization had now largely fallen away. New York City, he announced, ought to be allowed to run its own affairs without outside interference, and he asserted his willingness to work with Tammany Democrats (brands saved from the burning) in an effort to give the city good government. Thereupon he proceeded to coöperate actively with a nonpartisan Committee of Seventy which was dedicated to establishing a wise and beneficent rule over the metropolis. At the same time he sternly warned the Republican party that it had arrived at the crossroads of destiny. Any attempt to cover up the extravagances and rascalities of Republican rule in Texas, Georgia, Arkansas, and other parts of the South would be fatal to the party's success in the campaign of 1872. The time had come to recognize that the virtual surrender by the Democratic party of its hostility to equal rights had divested current politics of half their former intensity, while at the same time it was giving an opportunity for the Republicans to clean house, just as the Democrats had done in New York.

Men and brethren! [shouted the embattled editor] there is to be a general overhauling of pretensions, a sweeping out of dark corners, a dragging to light of hidden iniquities, the coming Winter. If there be those who dread such an ordeal, they may wisely put an ocean between them and the scene of their misdoings without further delay.[49]

As Grant's renomination became a foregone conclusion, Greeley continued divesting himself of Republican party ties. He clashed in the *Tribune* with James S. Pike, who was urging party regularity. Greeley told Pike that the one-term principle, the flood of embezzlements now emanating from Washington, and the general need for elevating the standards of governmental conduct at the nation's capital were paramount considerations. Then he went on to recall how the *Tribune* had established a reputation for political independence in 1848 and 1852, in 1858 and 1860. He was glad that it was not and never would be a "reliable" party organ.[50]

On March 7, 1872, Greeley published in the *Tribune* a letter which showed better than anything that had gone before how completely he had broken with the party leadership. Addressed to William Eaton Chandler, chairman of the Republican National Committee, this letter disclosed that Greeley, a member of the committee, had purposely stayed away from its last session and had furthermore asked that his name be not attached to its call for the Republican national convention. Trustworthy assurances of reform would be one thing, Greeley told Chandler. But he was not of a mind to take part in summoning a convention that, in the last analysis, would only serve to help Grant protégés, like those that now disgraced the New York custom house, to another half-million dollars of plunder.[51]

Had Greeley signed the call to the Republican convention, he told his readers, it would have at once been argued that he was bound by the result, whatever it might be. He had no intention of being so bound. He was now standing squarely on the one-term principle, and to the *Post's* assertion that the one-term idea was "no political principle, but a political fetch," he replied: "It is an act of emancipation." Horace Greeley was well on his way across his Rubicon.

NOTES FOR CHAPTER 24

1. *Tribune*, Nov. 12, 1868; Cortissoz, *Reid*, I, 106, 139-48; Hudson, *Journalism*, pp. 560-61. John Russell Young stepped out of his post as second in command on the *Tribune* during the summer of 1869, and Reid promptly took his place. See Baehr, *Tribune*, pp. 72-74, for the circumstances connected with this change.

2. *Independent*, Dec. 9, 1869, Apr. 7, 1870. Greeley thus became one of the protagonists of the approach to prohibition that was used so successfully by the Women's Christian Temperance Union and the Anti-Saloon League.

3. Greeley, *What I Know about Farming*, p. 244. See also pp. 234, 256-85, and the *Tribune*, May 14, 1870, Jan. 2, Sept. 15, 1871, Apr. 13, 1872, and Greeley, *Letters from Texas*, pp. 1-42.

4. *Tribune*, Mar. 6, 1871, quote of "A Practical Man" by Greeley.

5. C. Bengston, "Horace Greeley and the Founding of Union Colony in Colorado" (Unpublished M.A. thesis, 1910; copy in N.Y.P.L.), pp. 20-21, 29-35, 61-63, 68-71; O. M. Dickerson, "Letters of Horace Greeley to N. C. Meeker," in *Colorado Magazine*, XIX (Mar., May, 1942), 50-62, 102-10; *Tribune*, Nov. 5, 1870, Jan. 21, Mar. 3, 6, 7, Apr. 12, 14, 26, 1871, Feb. 17, Mar. 4, 1872. In Mar. 1871, Greeley counted eleven such colonies, holding 540,000 acres of land.

    Today's Greeley Chamber of Commerce (*Facts about Greeley and Weld County*, p. 15) advertises that Greeley is unusually free from labor troubles. But the responsibility for this is not laid at the door of association.

6. *Tribune*, Aug. 27, 1866, May 4, 1868, June 15, Aug. 6, 1869, May 12, 1870, Jan. 25, June 21, Sept. 15, Nov. 22, 1871.

7. *Tribune*, Jan. 6-9, 21, Feb. 11, 12, Mar. 18, 23, 31, Apr. 5, 6, June 8, 1869.

8. Greeley, *Political Economy*, pp. 345-46; *Tribune*, May 29, 1869.

9. *Independent*, Sept. 9, 1869; *Tribune*, Mar. 27-30, June 15, 17, 21, 22, 1869, Nov. 16, 24, 1870. For a while during this period, Greeley urged the experiment of tying wages to prices. Coöperation, he declared, was definitely an improvement over the wages system, although he thought that it would probably never supersede the wages system completely.

10. *Tribune*, Nov. 13, 1869, June 15, 17, 18, 23, July 22, 1870, Aug. 8, 1871.

11. Don D. Lescohier, *The Knights of St. Crispin, 1867-1874* (Madison, Wis., 1910), p. 101.

12. *Tribune*, Feb. 18, 20, 27, June 9, July 20, 1869, Feb. 14, 19, Apr. 8, 18, 1870.

13. *Independent*, Feb. 25, 1869; *Tribune*, Jan. 30, May 25, 1865, Jan. 23, Sept. 17, 1869, Apr. 12, 1872. In "Christianity and Color," *Douglass' Monthly*, Nov. 1860, p. 366, Greeley had deplored discrimination. He urged male Negro suffrage, despite Negro incompetence to exercise it, because the whites had it.

14. *Tribune*, June 9, 11, July 20, 26, Aug. 7, 14, 16, Sept. 1, Nov. 27, 1869.

15. *Tribune*, May 5, June 16, July 19, 1871. *Tribune* correspondents in the South were reporting at this time on the ignorance of the Negro and the viciousness of the Ku Klux Klan.

16. *Tribune*, Oct. 21, 1871.

17. Greeley, *Letters from Texas*, pp. 47-53; *Tribune*, June 7, 8, 1871.

18. Greeley, *Letters from Texas,* p. 44; *Tribune,* June 13, 1871; White, *Autobiography,* I, 161.

19. *Tribune,* Dec. 24, 1868, Feb. 15, Mar. 5, 1869.

20. *Tribune,* Mar. 6, 1869.

21. *Tribune,* Mar. 8, 10, 1869. Stewart was barred from office by the law of 1789 forbidding any man engaged in business from acting as Secretary of State. Washburne's appointment was probably a courtesy one, designed to give him prestige for the post he really wanted and obtained some two weeks later, that of Minister to France.

22. Greeley Papers (N.Y.P.L.), G. S. Boutwell to Greeley, Mar. 13, 1869; Greeley to Colfax, Nov. 1, 1870; Fish Papers, Grant to Fish, Aug. 21, 1870; *Tribune,* Apr. 19, 30, 1869; W. B. Hesseltine, *Ulysses S. Grant* (N. Y., 1935) p. 216.

23. *Tribune,* Sept. 28, Oct. 7, Nov. 27, Dec. 16, 20, 1869.

24. *Tribune,* July 6, 21, Aug. 1, 1868, Dec. 10, 1869, Mar. 9, 1870.

25. Greeley Papers (N.Y.P.L.), Greeley to Colfax, Mar. 17, 1871; Greeley, *Political Economy,* pp. 237-42; *Tribune,* Dec. 3, 1868, Jan. 1, May 31, Aug. 3, Dec. 22, 1869, Aug. 17, Nov. 2, 1871, Apr. 12, 1872. Greeley hedged on currency contraction in 1870. He suggested that it might be possible to have a paper currency redeemable in sums of $100 and over. It would be in the form of bonds that would bear 4 per cent interest in coin. This was only a tentative suggestion. See the *Tribune,* Aug. 6, 1870, and Greeley, *Political Economy,* pp. 237-38.

26. *Tribune,* Sept. 24, 25, 27, Oct. 1, 1869.

27. *Tribune,* Oct. 1, 1869.

28. Greeley did not support Fenton for the United States Senate in 1869, a failure that was probably due to pique over Fenton's failure to support the *Tribune's* editor for the governorship in 1868. But after Fenton's election, Greeley again stoutly proclaimed himself a Fenton man.—*Tribune,* Jan. 9, 14, 18, 19, Apr. 1, 1869; Chidsey, *Conkling,* p. 137.

29. *Tribune,* Nov. 5, 12, 24, 1868, Mar. 13, Apr. 12, 16, July 8, 19, Sept. 11, 1869.

30. Greeley, *Letters from Texas,* p. 46; Carey Papers, E. Peshine Smith to Carey, Oct. 31, 1869; *Tribune,* Oct. 8, 1869; Alexander, *Hist. of the State of New York,* III, 225.

31. *Tribune,* Oct. 11, 16, 18, 20, 22, 28, 1869.

32. Carey Papers, Smith to Carey, Oct. 31, 1869; *Tribune,* Nov. 3, 23, Dec. 20, 1869. Greeley ran some 3,600 ahead of Sigel in New York City.

33. *Tribune,* Feb. 3, 4, 12, Mar. 30, 31, Apr. 4, 5, 6, 7, 12, 13, May 5, 1870, Feb. 10, 1872; *New York Times,* Apr. 4, 6, 7, 12, 1870; *New York Evening Post,* Apr. 1-15, 1870.

34. *Tribune,* Apr. 7, 1870.

35. *Tribune,* July 4, 12, 1870; Chidsey, *Conkling,* pp. 144-45; Alexander, *Hist. of the State of New York,* III, 232-35.

36. Fish Papers, Whitelaw Reid to Fish, July 3, 1870; Stahl Collection, Greeley to Mrs. Allen, July 22, 1870; Benton, *Greeley on Lincoln,* p. 161.

37. See R. G. Albion's sketch of Roberts in the *Dictionary of American Biography.*

38. Greeley Papers (N.Y.P.L.), Greeley to Roberts, July 24, 1870; *Tribune,* Aug. 3, 27, Sept. 1, 1870; *New York World,* Aug. 9, 1870.

39. *Tribune,* Sept. 7-9, Nov. 10, 1870; E. Cary, *George William Curtis* (Boston and New York, 1894), pp. 207-8; Alexander, *Hist. of the State of New York,* III, 236-39; Cortissoz, *Reid,* I, 200-202; Chidsey, *Conkling,* pp. 145-47.

40. Cortissoz, *Reid,* I, 201-2.

41. *Tribune*, Oct. 20-Nov. 8, 1870; Reavis, *Greeley*, p. 183.

42. *Tribune*, Nov. 7-9, 17, 1870.

43. *Tribune*, Nov. 10, 1870.

44. Greeley Papers (N.Y.P.L.), Grant to Greeley, Jan. 13; Dec. 12, 1870; Greeley to Colfax, Jan. 16, 1870; *Tribune*, June 11, 1870, Jan. 9, 12, 1871; Hollister, *Colfax*, pp. 359-60; Cortissoz, *Reid*, I, 202.

45. *Tribune*, May 19, 25, 1871.

46. *Tribune*, Jan. 6, Mar. 8, 10, Apr. 5, 7, May 6, Aug. 7, 15, 18, 22, 24, 25, 28, 30, Sept. 11, 15, 19, 20, 29, 1871, Mar. 27, 1872; Barrows, *Evarts*, p. 188; Baehr, *Tribune*, pp. 96-101; Alexander, *Hist. of the State of New York*, III, 25-264.

47. *Tribune*, July-Aug., 1871, especially, July 21, 22, 1871.

48. *Tribune*, Oct. 12, 13, 28, 30, Nov. 4, 6, 7-9, 15, 16, 1871. It is interesting that Greeley was reluctant to believe Peter B. Sweeney a thief. For a defense of Sweeney, see *Tribune*, Oct. 12, 1871. At the time of Greeley's death, Sweeney had a claim of $8,000 against Greeley's estate, a claim that he forebore to press, allegedly because the estate was so small in productive assets.—Decree of Accounting, File 144/1872, Surrogate's Office, White Plains, N. Y.) .

49. *Tribune*, Nov. 13, 18, 1871. Quote is of Nov. 13. The preceding paragraphs are based on a careful study of the files of the *Tribune* and the *Times* for the fall and winter of 1871-72.

50. *Tribune*, Feb. 28, Mar. 1, 1872.

51. *Tribune*, Mar. 7, 1872.

CHAPTER 25

The End of the Rainbow

T HERE WAS A NOTE OF FATALISM IN GREELEY'S REAC-
tion to the political situation in the winter of 1871-72. In February
1872, he wrote to a close friend that he would not support Grant if
he could help it, adding half whimsically and half seriously that he
wanted a President who could get along on less liquor and tobacco.
A month later, he wrote to another friend—"I am drifting into a
fight with Grant. I hate it . . . ." Then he added that it would
alienate many friends and probably injure the *Tribune,* "of which
so little is my own property that I dread to wreck it . . . ."
It was clear that Greeley disliked intensely the thought of the
impending struggle, and yet all the time his actions made it more
nearly inevitable. There was in this attitude a sense of his own
importance as a molder of public opinion, and perhaps some realization of an impending destiny. For rumors of his own candidacy
for the highest office in the land were constantly flying about.[1]
But if the *Tribune's* guiding spirit bolted the regular Republican
nomination, where was he to go? He could scarcely picture himself
moving into the ranks of the bourgeoning temperance party, for he
had become convinced that temperance was not a good political
issue and besides the field was too narrow for one of his catholic
interests. The eight-hour-day labor reformers were even more repug-
nant to one who regarded hard work as a virtue, and Victoria
Woodhull's weird combination of woman suffrage and free love was
of course utterly beyond the pale. So was the Democracy, that "Sham
Democracy" which he had covered with contumely and abuse these
many years. There was, in fact, only one possible refuge for Greeley,
and that was Liberal Republicanism.
During the preceding four years, slowly at first but more rapidly
as time had revealed the limitations of the hero, a movement of
revolt against Grant and all his works had been growing up within
the Republican ranks. It had rumbled like distant thunder in con-

servative-radical conflicts in the South over enfranchisement of erstwhile rebels, conflicts that had become important in such reconstructed states as Tennessee and Virginia. It had burst out, a storm of revolt, in Missouri. There, in 1870, under the leadership of reformer Carl Schurz and politician B. Gratz Brown, "liberal" Republicans had come out for universal amnesty and enfranchisement and for tariff reform, and against the national administration's painfully one-sided ideas on the subject of the distribution of the patronage.[2]

These liberals had swept Missouri in 1870, and with their victory was born the Liberal Republican movement. Fostered by the passionate idealism of the spare, lean-visaged Schurz, and by the tempestuous vigor of red-headed, red-bearded Gratz Brown, aided and abetted by the self-styled "Quadrilateral" (shades of Radetsky and the Austro-Sardinian War of 1848) of newspaper editors—Samuel Bowles of the *Springfield Republican,* Horace White of the *Chicago Tribune,* Murat Halstead of the *Cincinnati Commercial,* and Colonel Henry ("Marse") Watterson of the *Louisville Courier-Journal*—supported by an increasing number of practical politicians like New York's ousted Boss Fenton, men whose first thought was to jump on a promising bandwagon, Liberal Republicanism showed every indication of coming to a vigorous and formidable maturity.

Greeley's reaction to the first signs of this movement had been mixed, but on the whole unfavorable. He had, of course, long approved the display of magnanimity toward the southern whites, and he had greeted with approval the course taken in Virginia and Texas and Tennessee by the advocates of lenient treatment of erstwhile rebels.[3] On the other hand, he had never shown any interest in civil service reform, and his views on the tariff were not such as to make him clasp the Missouri tariff reformers or any other members of that species to his bosom.

Greeley regarded the Missouri liberals, particularly fervent advocates of tariff reduction, with an especially cold and fishy eye. Schurz and Brown, in his opinion, were not one whit better than those recreants to the public trust, David Ames Wells and William Cullen Bryant. They were free traders, masquerading as tariff reformers, and therefore they were the enemies of the nation. He had hoped for their defeat in Missouri in 1870, since their real aim was to divide and destroy the Republican party for the benefit of the Democracy and free trade. The defection of the Missouri liberals was a denial of Hamilton, Madison, Carey, Clay, Niles, DeWitt Clinton and all the rest of the protectionist school, and "of the truth and value of their doctrines, we have no more doubt than of the moral perfection of the Golden Rule." Every "revenue reformer," he told Colfax, was "a Democrat in the egg, or else just hatched with half the egg shell still sticking to him, soon to be discarded."[4]

Indifferent to Greeley's onslaughts, the Liberal Republican movement continued to grow. Steadily it sapped the strength of the Republican organization: steadily it organized in state after state, assuming a national character of its own. In January 1872 a call was issued for a national convention of liberals to meet in Cincinnati on May 1. Some of its sponsors still hoped that the movement would capture the regular Republican organization. Others, Carl Schurz among their number, were now anxious to see the formation of a new political party. Schurz was to electrify the convention when he began his opening address with the words: "This is moving day."

As the Liberal Republican movement grew strong, Greeley's attitude toward it gradually changed. Its planks, save for protection, were accepted by him as statements of just and high principle, and this acceptance became more and more emphatic during the winter of 1871-72. By that time the *Tribune* was not only demanding amnesty for the southern rebels and denouncing corruption in high places—it was also carrying such a torch for civil service reform as had never before flared from its pages. It was even beginning to suggest, gingerly but unmistakably, that the tariff was a local issue.

On January 29, 1872, after a favorable review in the *Tribune* of the history of the Missouri movement, Greeley declared that it was clear that the Cincinnati convention would never nominate Grant. Before it would thus stultify itself, it would bolt the party. Greeley then asked, would the *Tribune* also bolt? Probably not, he answered, because of the likelihood that free trade would be one of the planks in the Liberal Republican platform. The *Tribune* could not contribute to the sweeping industrial collapse and commercial bankruptcy that would follow the overthrow of protection. At the same time, he grimly warned the Republican regulars that by their higgling on amnesty and by their persecution of anti-Grant Republicans they were "madly rushing on disaster."[5]

Greeley had now made his position clear. He would come into the Liberal Republican movement for a price, and that price was the abandonment downward of tariff revision. This attitude was reëmphasized during the ensuing weeks. If a tariff plank were adopted at Cincinnati, he said, "we shall ask to be counted out." If, on the other hand, there was a clear disposition to relegate the tariff to the status of a local issue, then he and the *Tribune* would "go to Cincinnati." But it would not be as a certain German Emperor had gone to Canossa, on bended knee. It would be as at least an equal partner in the Cincinnati undertaking.

By the end of March 1872 Greeley was convinced that the liberals were yielding to his demands, and he accepted an invitation from western Liberal Republicans to participate in the convention. A couple of weeks later he spoke at a Liberal Republican meeting in Cooper Institute, where he bade defiance to Grant's New York henchmen, and promised to be present at Cincinnati in the spirit, if not in the flesh. Clearly and unmistakably, he was throwing in his lot with the liberals.[6]

It cannot be doubted that the possibility of his own nomination at Cincinnati played some part in determining Greeley's attitude toward the Liberal Republican movement. His passion for office, a passion based in part upon egotism, in part upon a desire for recognition of his contributions to the nation's welfare, and in part upon a sincere zeal for public service, had not been dimmed by repeated defeats, and when rumor began to connect his name with the nomination it found him in a receptive mood. Years later, Murat Halstead remembered how easy it had been at this time to get the *Tribune's* editor started on the problems and possibilities of the Presidency. There were other signs as well. His correspondence in 1871 with Lewis Carmichael, an Otsego County, New York, Democrat, certainly showed that Greeley was thinking of himself as at least a potential candidate.[7] Writing that same year to a Missouri Democrat who wanted him to receive the Democratic nomination, he declared that such a nomination would be inadvisable because he was "a ferocious Protectionist." But when he added, "I have no doubt that I might be nominated and elected by your help," he betrayed the not too smothered flame.

There were other manifestations, less direct but none the less real, of the direction in which Greeley's thoughts were tending. In January 1872, when talk of his candidacy was becoming widespread, he was one of the principals in the New York celebration of the 166th anniversary of Franklin's birth. One of the speakers was pleased to refer to Greeley's resemblance to America's first great printer, and the *Tribune's* editor responded with remarks in which he stressed those admirable aspects of Poor Richard which could most easily be found in his own life and character. Franklin was praised for having written an inspirational autobiography, for being frugal and abstemious, for his triumph over want and obscurity, for being a statesman who did not crucify mankind with long-winded speeches, for being an honest man and a philosopher who had deserved well of his country, in short, for having been cast in the same mould as one

Horace Greeley. The inference was as obvious as were the strenuous efforts that Greeley was making once more to explain and defend his conduct during the war. Obvious, too, was the way in which the *Tribune* now avoided belligerency on the subject of protection.

In the midst of all these signs and portents came an elaborate celebration of Greeley's sixty-first birthday. The scene was the home of his friend, Alvin J. Johnson, the map maker, at 323 West Fifty-seventh Street. It was a magnificent affair, replete with $1,500 worth of floral decorations and elaborate, but wineless, refreshments— "unique, but *comme il faut,*" as the *Sun's* reporter had it. There were several hundred guests.

Greeley had hurried back from a Maine lecture trip to be the lion of the evening. With a bouquet in his lapel and a magnificent nosegay clutched in his left hand, he stood shaking hands for four hours in the parlor on the first floor, while personal friends, newspaper moguls, and political figures—John Hay, Samuel Bowles, Murat Halstead, Edwin D. Morgan, and others—offered their congratulations.

Not all that were invited had come to this affair. This was conspicuously the case with George William Curtis of *Harper's Weekly* and Secretary of State Hamilton Fish. Their presence might have made the evening something less than harmonious, for much talk about Greeley and the next Presidency was wafted through the flower-scented air.

In the midst of all this warmth of adulation, the beaming editor could forget, for the time being, the bitter cold of the night outside. Afterward he lay awake till morning, tortured by swollen muscles, but doubtless exhilarated as well by the attention he had received. The affair had been a grand success and, who could tell, perhaps a portent of still greater successes to come.

Of course the future was veiled. Anything might happen. It was even yet possible that the Liberal Republican movement might come out for free trade. "That I cannot go," Greeley wrote to a friend, "even though it would make me President."[8]

It was under these circumstances that Whitelaw Reid went out to Cincinnati to keep the convention from going free trade, and to promote his chief's nomination.[9]

The Liberal Republican convention, a motley collection of idealists, faddists, doctrinaires, newspapermen and hard-boiled politicians, assembled in Cincinnati's great Music Hall on May 1. The platform committee hammered out a document that called for amnesty, acceptance of the Thirteenth, Fourteenth, and Fifteenth amendments and civil service reform, but sidetracked the tariff.

Reid, who was very much in evidence, insisted on this exclusion, as did William Dorsheimer of New York and other ardent Greeleyites. And on this point, Schurz and the other tariff reformers gave in. They knew that this was the price of Greeley's support, a price that they were willing to pay because they felt confident that Old White Coat had no chance of receiving the nomination.

Carl Schurz, the graceful, lean-visaged reformer, immensely earnest, intensely eloquent, was one of the leading spirits of the convention. He had fixed his presidential sights on Charles Francis Adams of Massachusetts. Adams was the most prominently mentioned possibility. At first he seemed to be the convention's choice, but a variety of circumstances worked against him and for Greeley.

The Quadrilateral, all unconsciously, helped Greeley along by ditching Judge David Davis, Lincoln's political manager in 1860 and a man strong in the Middle West. Davis was the candidate of the political realists, who were shouting "anybody to beat Grant." When it became obvious that the great newspapers would not have Davis, the "anybody to beat Grant" shouters fell back upon Greeley. Hardboiled New York politicians contributed to Old White Coat's chances by steam-rollering out of the state's delegation the handful of revenue reformers who had managed to get out to Cincinnati, thus presenting the convention with a delegation solid for the farmer of Chappaqua. Greeley was also helped by factious strife among the liberals. Schurz's support of Adams aroused the ire of B. Gratz Brown, and that red-bearded politico came to the convention in a mood to rule or ruin. He concocted a bargain with Reid and others, throwing his own strength to Greeley with the understanding that he should have second place on the ticket.

The *Tribune* editor's real strength in the West as the advocate of the Pacific railroad and free land, the popularity he had gained in the South by his policy of magnanimity, his "Go South, young man," and "Go South, northern capital" exhortations, the Jefferson Davis bail, and the Texas trip, more than offset the misgivings of the tariff reformers and the argument that his temperance views would play hob among the German elements in the population. Shrewdly and skillfully, Whitelaw Reid marshaled the strength of his friend, while the supporters of other candidates let slip precious opportunities for consolidating their forces. Greeley was nominated on the sixth ballot, and Brown easily won second place on the ticket. Once and for all, the old white hat was in the ring.[10]

The *Tribune's* editor had received the supreme honor of his career, and a flood of congratulations poured into the *Tribune's* office. Greeley clubs mushroomed throughout the country. There

was a run on white hats in St. Louis and New Orleans. Whitelaw
Reid, back in New York, exuded happiness and confidence.

But if some of the Liberal Republicans rejoiced at the news of
Greeley's nomination, others received it with anything but thanks-
giving, Bryant's *Post* closed its editorial on the event by asserting
that a candidate for the highest office in the land should be, at
least, a gentleman. Godkin's *Nation* deserted the liberal standard,
declaring bitterly that a greater degree of incredulity and disappointment had not been felt by the country since the first battle of Bull
Run. Stanley Matthews, prominent Ohio lawyer and political
leader and temporary chairman at Cincinnati, left the liberal fold.
Carl Schurz, deeply disturbed by the nomination, wrote to Greeley
with brutal frankness that it had been the result of "a successful
piece of political hucksterism," and that the whole movement had
lost its moral impulse as a result of the Cincinnati proceedings. The
stubborn and opinionated Schurz swallowed his disappointment
only with the greatest difficulty and, after finally deciding not to
bolt, campaigned against Grant rather than for Greeley. Thoughts
of a third ticket were actively entertained by some of the Liberal
Republican leaders, only to pale before the unanimity with which
the regular Republicans renominated Grant at Philadelphia in
June, and the conviction that a split of the anti-Grant vote would
ensure the President's reëlection. Gideon Welles expressed the feelings of many liberals when he remarked that it would be difficult
to find a more disagreeable and objectionable candidate for three-
fourths of the men who would have to vote for him, but that he
was better than Grant. "A crooked stick," said Welles, "may be made
available to beat a mad dog." If there was injury for Grant in such
a comment, there was only cold comfort for Greeley.[11]

It had indeed been a curious nomination, one that demonstrated
little wisdom on the part of the motley host assembled at Cincinnati. The liberals were civil service reformers, but Greeley was not
and never had been an exponent of civil service reform. Even after
his nomination, he made it clear that his great remedy for the spoils
system was the establishment of the one-term principle, thus making
merit instead of renomination the motivation of Presidential appointments. His rabid protectionism was a stench in the nostrils of
the revenue reformers. Democratic support was necessary if he were
to beat Grant, but Greeley had been insulting the Democratic
party for over thirty years in the columns of the *Tribune*. His greatest strength lay in his policy of amnesty for the South, but even
there he had his Achilles' heel, for he was a staunch exponent of
enforcement acts as protection for the Negro. Weed's jibe that it

was a nomination unfit to be made save in a lunatic asylum, and Fish's declaration that it represented a standard of qualification "near to that which elevated a Roman Emperor's horse to a Roman Consulate" were extreme statements, distinguished for their rancor rather than their objective judgment. But both comments possessed a grain of truth that did not permit their being simply laughed off by the Liberal Republicans.[12]

Greeley was fully aware of the storm of criticism that broke over his nomination. Some of it, like Schurz's letter, came directly to him. Some of it was collected from other sources and published in the *Tribune*. The Grant papers reeked with it. For a time, the *Tribune's* editor even thought that the reaction might be so strong as to make it necessary for him to decline the nomination.[13]

This barrage of complaint made for nervous irritability on the part of a man who had never bothered much about concealing his feelings, and who was at times childishly outspoken. That this was so became clear when he peremptorily adjured Schurz to stop using that juggling expression "tariff reform" when he meant "free trade." There were undoubtedly many other indications of this same state of mind.

But on the whole, Greeley exhibited remarkable patience with Schurz's cavilings about the ticket, and also took a good deal of advice from Whitelaw Reid and other counselors. Reid restrained him from plunging into violent controversy with the *World*, immediately after his nomination, and it was probably due in part to the urgent advice of Samuel Bowles that he resigned his editorship of the *Tribune*, publishing a card to that effect on May 15.[14]

The explanation of Greeley's rather surprising forebearance with counselors and critics lay in his conviction that personal considerations must be subordinated to the exigencies of a great campaign, one that was vital to the welfare of the nation. "The people have already ratified Cincinnati," he wrote to a friend less than three weeks after the nomination. He had become convinced that a wave of popular sentiment had supported and was continuing to support his selection and that, as President, he could do much to lead the country toward reunion and prosperity.[15]

Greeley's conviction that he was a candidate with a mission was clearly apparent in his acceptance of the Liberal Republican nomination. He spoke of the swelling tide of approval that had greeted his selection, and then went on to praise the platform constructed at Cincinnati in words that revealed his own vision of a new and better nation. The United States, he said, should be a land where the political rights of all would be guaranteed against either local or federal interference. It should be a land where the federal patronage would be honestly administered; where the public lands should not be handed over wholesale to rapacious railroad interests, but reserved for cultivators; where the will of the people as to the raising of revenues, by tariff or otherwise, should always prevail. And above all else, there should be a general amnesty. The people, said Greeley, were determined to have a truly national reconstruction, a "New Departure" from jealousy, strife, and hatred, a clasping of hands across the bloody chasm, a forgetfulness that they had been enemies "in the joyful consciousness that they are and must henceforth remain brethren."[16] It was a theme that became the heart and center of his speeches during the campaign.

Meantime, a cloud of trials and tribulations had swarmed like locusts upon the eager candidate. He was beset by interviewers and photographers and by hosts of politicians with ideas to sell and axes to grind. His holidays at Chappaqua disappeared in a swirl of campaign business. Insomnia laid hold upon him. The sinister malady that had plagued him when the Union Army reeled back on Washington from Bull Run once again threatened him, and early in June he wrote an ominous note to Samuel Sinclair in the *Tribune* office: "I am quite unwell of something like brain fever."

And ever the ghosts of old friendships rose up to haunt his path. "Weed is against me; Seward reported so," he told his friend John Taylor Hall. Both men had been denounced time and again in the *Tribune*, personal relations with them had ceased long ago, their political power was a thing of the past. But, somehow, they were still important. The old wounds had not healed, nor had the memories of old bonds quite disappeared.[17]

It was just at this juncture that Ossa was piled upon Pelion. Mary Greeley and the girls came back from Europe.

"Mother" had gone abroad with the faithful Ida as companion and nurse in the summer of 1870, the two being joined somewhat later by Gabrielle. The latter's presence had enabled Ida to satisfy a long-held desire to visit what Greeley called "her Mecca," and she had spent some time in Rome during the winter of 1872. "I had asked her," Greeley wrote proudly but sadly to a friend to whom he had sent Ida's letters from the Holy City, "to bear witness that the massacre of St. Bartholomew (there called death of Coligny) is glorified in the Pope's Sistine Chapel of the Vatican, and, you see, she does it quite cleverly." But Ida's Roman visit had been only a variation on the main theme of her mother's search for health. Now, after an unsuccessful two-year quest that had taken her on a weary pilgrimage all over Europe, Mary Greeley had decided to come home.[18]

Gabrielle Greeley, chaperoned by some other travelers, came on ahead of her mother and sister. She landed in New York on June 1, gravely ill of typhoid fever, and Greeley had to busy himself with provision for her care. Two week later, the other travelers sailed up the bay.

The boat that bore "Mother" and Ida docked at a Hoboken pier, where Horace stood peering anxiously through failing eyes to catch a sight of his elder daughter at the rail. When he went on board, he found his wife in her stateroom. She was as firm of will as ever, but she looked liked a little old decrepit ghost. Most of her teeth were gone, and she was hopelessly crippled with rheumatism, so crippled that she could not walk. With difficulty, Greeley got her and the rest of the family up to Chappaqua where they were settled, after a fashion, by July 1. Then, with a sigh, he took up once more the burdens of a presidential nominee.[19]

The trial of Ned Stokes for the murder of Jim Fisk held the headlines, even in the *Tribune,* during the early part of the summer, but Greeley had little time for such sensational news. There were floods of letters to be answered in longhand, and more and more visitors wended their way up to Chappaqua to see the farmer in his rural haunts, and to talk with him about the business of the campaign. Somehow, time was found to write some promised articles for a cyclopedia. More and more he was pressed to show himself in various parts of the country as an aid to his perspiring fellow candidates. Early in July, in response to urgent advice, he went reluctantly on a short trip to Boston and Newport. He told his New England auditors that he had done well as an editor, and therefore might reasonably be expected to do well in another role. It was indifferent logic, but the New Englanders were sanguine, Reid was sanguine, and "Honest Old Horace," such was his campaign sobriquet, was the most hopeful of all.[20]

The Democrats ate boiled crow at Baltimore on July 9. The alternative was certain defeat. So they took Greeley and the Cincinnati platform for good measure, but it was a bitter meal. Democrat Robert Vance of North Carolina portrayed the spirit of the occasion by telling the story of an old preacher, in whose hymn book a mischievous urchin had pasted the song, "Old Grimes is dead, that good old man, we ne'er shall see him more." The preacher opened the book the next day in church and his eye fell on this "hymn." He blinked, took off his spectacles and polished them, read and blinked again, then said: "Brethren, I have been singing out of this book for forty years; I have never recognized this as a hymn before, but it's here, and I ain't agwine to go back on my book now; so please raise the tune, and we'll sing it through if it kills us!"[21]

During July, Greeley stayed rather closely at home, in part because of his wife's grave condition, but chiefly as a calculated campaigning policy. His spirits were high, for hope was bright. He was delighted by the Democratic acceptance of the Cincinnati platform, particularly because it appeared to mean acceptance of the Thirteenth, Fourteenth, and Fifteenth amendments to the Constitution. The clouds of hatred seemed to be opening at last, and in his acceptance of the Democratic nomination he spoke of his vision of a new era in which the best elements of Democracy and Republicanism would unite in finally establishing the great principles of 1776.[22]

The August dog days found the Liberal Republican candidate ranging farther from home, but more for the purpose of being seen than of being heard on fundamental issues. He made a short trip through New England, where he extolled the scenery and glorified the history and people of the region, puffed his way up Kearsarge Mountain, reiterated his faith in America's future and denied that he had promised any office to anybody.

On his return to New York from this New England expedition, Greeley attended a picnic at the Jones Wood amusement park, where 3,000 printers from New York's Typographical Union #6 applauded enthusiastically when he told them that "the matter of wages is receiving considerable attention, and it should be gradually, calmly and coolly brought to a satisfactory close, receiving the attention which experience, study and observation alone can give." The printers applauded this Delphic utterance because they liked the man, despite his crotchets and contradictions. The National Labor Reform convention, meeting a few weeks earlier in New York, had reacted in more somber fashion to the candidate of the Cincinnati convention. The Labor Reformers had resolved that the working class had no more to hope for from Greeley than from Grant.[23]

The campaign gathered momentum as it moved into the fall of 1872. Everywhere Liberal Republican and Democratic orators denounced disfranchisement, spoilsmanship, corruption, and nepotism, criticizing the incompetence of a dull-eyed President who, endlessly puffing on his black cigars, never seemed to ask the right questions or to give the right answers. Everywhere they called loudly for amnesty, efficient government, civil service reform, and the election

DIOGENES HAS FOUND THE *HONEST MAN.*—(WHICH IS *DIOGENES,* AND WHICH IS THE *HONEST MAN?*)

Greeley and Tweed are represented as striking a bargain for the campaign of 1872.

of "Old Honesty." Everywhere they wore the "White Hat of Peace."
Everywhere Greeley's rimmed-glasses gaze beamed from campaign
literature and from thousands of fans fluttered by perspiring supporters. *Frank Leslie's Illustrated Newspaper* portrayed him as an
honest farmer, surrounded by birds and squirrels, now chopping
coon Grant out of a tree, now standing at his forge busily beating
swords into ploughshares. There was a Greeley Galop, and the
Farmer of Chappaqua Songster enabled "Old Honesty's" supporters
to split their throats in the rendition of such gems as "The Old
White Hat":

> There's a good old man who lives on a farm,
> And he's not afraid to labor;
> His heart is pure and he does no harm,
> But works for the good of his neighbor.
> He always wears an old white hat,
> And he doesn't go much on style;
> He's kind to the poor that come to his door,
> And his heart is free from guile.
>
> Then hurrah, my boys, for the old white hat
> That covers a mighty head.
> May he wear it long   .
> And be hale and strong
> When his radical foes are dead.[24]

But if the Greeleyites made the welkin ring, the regular Republicans were no less vocal. Grant was venerated as a man of
sterling honesty, the saviour of the Union, the triumphant vindica-
tor of American rights at home and overseas. Greeley, on the other
hand, was subjected to a deluge of abuse and defamation rarely
seen before or since in American politics. "Old Chappaquack" was
accused of having plotted to obtain the Democratic nomination as
early as the fall of 1871. Frederick Douglass' *The New National
Era*, the leading Negro newspaper, denounced him bitterly, declaring that he had never been a genuine opponent of slavery. He
was labeled Know Nothing, Negro trader, secessionist. It was asserted that he planned to pension Confederate soldiers, pay the
Confederate debt, and appoint to his Cabinet Confederate raiders
like Captain Raphael Semmes of the *Alabama*. His name was linked
with those of the notorious Victoria Woodhull and Tennessee
Claflin, exponents of women's rights and free love. One industrial
concern ran an advertisement that at one and the same time pro-

WHOEVER SAYS THIS ISN'T A REAL ELEPHANT IS "A LIAR!"

Greeley is linked with Tammany and the Ku Klux Klan.

claimed the merits of its product and announced that "Horace Greeley has committed suicide."

Among the most ferocious of the attacks made upon Greeley were those of cartoonist Thomas Nast. These cartoons portrayed the Liberal Republican candidate as stretching out his hand to John Wilkes Booth across Lincoln's grave, as reaching out the hand of fellowship to the South across the bloody chasm of Andersonville prison, as attempting to cover the monument of southern infamy with the old white hat and coat, as catering to Tweed and hob-nobbing with the worst elements among the Irish Catholics, as attempting to swallow and being swallowed in turn by a figure labeled "Tammany" and "KKK."[25]

One of Nast's most telling cartoons showed Greeley humped over a big bowl of steaming porridge labeled "My Own Words and Deeds." As he ladled the burning stuff into his mouth, perspiration streamed down his forehead. The caption was "Red Hot!"

Back in 1853, Greeley had written to Seward, "A man says so many things in the course of thirty years that may be quoted against him. . . . " Now, ironically enough, Nast and the Republican campaigners in general were bringing home the truth of Greeley's words. Great play was made of the harsh things that he had said about the Democrats. His description of Tammany men drinking "from the ground, like hogs" around a Hickory pole was exhumed and printed. His declarations that the Democracy was grounded in vice and ignorance, that the bawdy houses of New York were owned by Democrats, that, while not every Democrat was a horse thief, every horse thief was a Democrat, were pitilessly waved under the noses of the Democratic voters. If ever a man had to eat his own words, it was Horace Greeley in the campaign of 1872.[26]

The tactics of the Greeley opposition undoubtedly had great effect with the voters. Greeley had been hard enough for Liberals and Democrats to accept, on the bare facts of his record. The quotations from his editorials, the caricature of his remarks and attitudes by Nast, undoubtedly kept many away from the polls and drove others to vote for Grant. Mark Twain told Nast that his "simply marvellous" cartoons had been largely responsible for Grant's "prodigious victory—for civilization and progress." George F. Hoar believed that the South did not resent what Grant had done as a soldier half so much as what Greeley had said as a politician. The story of blind, old Azariah Flagg, former staunch member of the Albany Regency and a life-long Democrat, refusing to let an old friend take him to the polls because he wouldn't trust his vote to a Greeley man, symbolized the attitude of thousands of Democrats

"RED HOT!"

Greeley is eating the words and deeds with which he has assailed
the Democrats.

throughout the country. This, together with the damper that Greeley's nomination had put on the hopes of the tariff reformers, spelled disaster for his campaign.[27]

Even many of those who finally voted for the Liberal Republican candidate did so reluctantly. One man wrote to Gerrit Smith: "I have always regarded Greeley as an awkward, illbred boor, and though a sort of inspired idiot, neither a scholar, statesman or gentleman. I wouldn't give Grant's little finger for a Congressional district full of him. Yet, I want him elected."[28] It is not out of such stuff as this that political victories are fashioned.

Like Greeley, the liberals had begun the campaign with hopes of success, but defeat in North Carolina on August 1 marked the beginning of an all too apparent decline in Liberal Republican prospects. This was accented by Republican victories, early in September, in Maine and Vermont.

In an effort to turn the tide and influence the elections in the crucial "October states" of Pennsylvania, Ohio, and Indiana, Greeley went on a speaking tour that took him into New Jersey, Pennsylvania, Ohio, Kentucky, and Indiana. On this trip, with admirable spirit and candor, he again outlined his conception of the fundamental significance of the canvass.

The true issue, Greeley declared repeatedly, was the establishment of a new era in American life. Through honest and conservative administration of government finance, through fostering thrift and coöperative production among laborers, most of all through the achievement of universal amnesty and a general equality of rights, America was to experience a new birth of freedom. Party ties, however ancient, were to be dissolved in the interest of this rebirth. "I am free to confess and in no way ashamed to admit," Greeley declared, "that my party associations are not the same now that they were some years ago."[29]

The time had come for the "New Departure" in politics, Greeley asserted, and this "New Departure" would herald a "New Dawn." Again and again he dwelt on his dream of national greatness, the dream that had haunted him all his life and that had been the great objective of all his crusades. The America of the future would be a land of peace and plenty where white and colored would stand together "on a common platform of American nationality," he told his audience at Louisville.

This is the ground for which I have fought [he told citizens of Indiana], not to have a subject class; a proscribed class; an alien class; an outlaw class in this country; but to have men stand on the equal and lawful plat-

JEREMY. DIDDLER'S EXULTATION!

Grant is linked to Tammany in a pro-Greeley cartoon.

form of our common nationality, citizens, free to exercise such faculties as God has given them for their own sustenance and for the upbuilding of their own families and fortunes. That seems to me statesmanship. . . . We are henceforth to be one American people.

And again in Ohio—

Let us forget that we fought. Let us remember only that we have made peace. Let us say there shall be no degradation, no people over whom we triumph. Our triumph is their triumph. Our triumph is the uplifting of everyone to the common platform of American liberty and American nationality. Our triumph is not the triumph of a section; it is not the triumph of a race; it is not the triumph of a class. It is the triumph of the American people, making us all, in life, in heart and purpose, the people, the one people of the great American Republic. Fellow citizens, to the work of Reconciliation I dedicate myself.[30]

Old White Coat was testifying to his faith, and when he testified he did it well.

Greeley made some two hundred speeches during this western campaign trip. In Pittsburg, young Jacob Riis, then in his early twenties, went to hear Greeley address an open-air meeting, saw "his noble old head" above the throng and heard his opening appeal, only to be caught up and carried away in a marching band of uniformed Grant shouters that cut through the crowd.[31] Everywhere that he went excitement roared through the streets and the crowds seemed enthusiastic. But the early state elections had been ominous, the shadow of impending defeat hung over the tour, and Colonel Watterson found Greeley apt to break out "into a kind of lamentation, punctuated by occasional outbursts of objurgation" over his gloomy prospects. He came back to New York tired. There he faced a constant round of engagements, faced also alarming signs of a change for the worse in the condition of his wife. His burdens were increasing beyond anything that he had expected to bear, and with an increasingly feverish impatience he began longing for the end of the campaign.[32]

The political skies darkened. One after another of the "October states" went Republican. The domestic skies darkened as well.

The merry, self-willed bride whom Greeley had neglected for his work and who, as "Mother," had taken her revenge by becoming a hypochondriac, was plainly nearing the end of the road. But she had enormous vitality and down into the month of October she grimly carried on the fight against death.

A new house had been built for Molly Greeley at Chappaqua, a

THE NEXT IS ORDER—ANY THING! OH, ANY THING!

Greeley's zeal for office makes him clasp the hand of John Wilkes
Booth over the grave of the murdered Lincoln.

house with a porte-cochere and a spacious bedroom with seven windows letting in the air and the sunlight. Stubbornly she planned to take possession of this house, even to the point of having fires lighted in the place to dry the dampness from the walls. But this final flare of energy and resolution blazed and faded like the red and gold in the maple leaves outside her bedroom window. Omens of victory in the campaign might have buoyed her up, for in her queer, crabbed way she was fond of her husband and identified her fortunes with his, but as this hope dimmed no stimulus took its place, and she grew steadily weaker. Dropsy added its tortures to her burden. She had to be rubbed and moved every few minutes. She slept with difficulty and her husband, close at her bedside, scarcely slept at all.

Tortured by the strain of constant watching, bowed down under a sense of impending defeat and impending death, overwhelmed by such a flood of abuse and vituperation that, as he wrote to a friend, he scarcely knew whether he was running for the Presidency or the penitentiary, Greeley's outlook on life became constantly blacker and his mind became shot with feverish imaginings. "I disagree with you about death," he burst out in a letter to his friend, Margaret Allen, on October 25. "I wish it came faster. . . . I wish she were to be laid in her grave next week, and I to follow her the week after." There was in this letter, perhaps, remorse for the past. Certaintly there was only the gloomiest anticipation for the future.[33]

Molly Greeley died at four o'clock on the morning of October 30. Automatically, his mind a pool of melancholy darkness, Greeley went through the funeral rites, then turned to face the burial of his political hopes and dreams. The world seemed ashes now, and on the eve of the election he wrote again to Margaret Allen, as though in an attempt to find release by the expression of his despair. "I am not dead but wish I were. My house is desolate, my future dark, my heart a stone."[34] The next day brought his crushing defeat at the polls.

The country, it appeared, wished to have nothing to do with Horace's plans for a "New Departure." Business voted for Grant. The Democrats stayed away from the polls in droves. The liberals had no organization to match that of the Republicans, and the "Hero" symbol proved again a talisman of victory. Greeley carried but six states—all on the border between the sections, or in the South. He had only 43.8 per cent of the total vote. It was a Grant landslide, rushing down over the quivering remnants of Greeley and his dream.[35]

Greeley's election would probably have meant a considerable improvement in the national administration. Scandal and corruption would have had an abatement instead of an increase, as they had in Grant's second term. There was small likelihood that he would have had such a private secretary as Orville E. Babcock who, deep in collusion with the Whiskey Ring, rejoiced over the defeat of "Mr. Greeley and his beggarly crew."[36] And Greeley's passionate earnestness for national unity and national progress would have hastened, at least in some measure, the reconciliation of the sections.

But on the other hand, Greeley's election would probably have had some unfortunate consequences for himself and for the nation. Sobered though his natural ebullience and pugnacity might have been by the high dignity of his office, the chances are that he would have been a contentious President. If his record in public controversy meant anything, it meant that at the very least he would have fought furiously with Congress over printing and mileage and more fundamental economic policies. His objectives, so far as the South was concerned, would have been difficult of fulfillment, for he was pledged at once to clasping hands with the southern white conservatives and to protecting the Negro's political and civil rights. His humanitarian instincts would have been challenged and made mock of by a depression against which his economic philosophy would have afforded him no weapons. He would probably have fought with members of his own party over the question of civil service reform. His Presidency would have been a time of toil and trouble and, in all likelihood, brain fever would have claimed its victim before the end of his term.

Greeley came back to the *Tribune* after the election, exhausted and in mental torment, but putting the best possible face on his discomfiture. Jauntily, if somewhat wryly, he published a "card" on November 7, stating that he now resumed the editorship which he had relinquished "on embarking in another line of business six months ago." He declared that the *Tribune* would now function as an independent, nonpartisan journal, one that would pay much more attention than heretofore to science and industry and to the useful arts. On the surface, it looked as though the prodigal master had returned to his old position of command, but this was far from being the case.

For the campaign had done grievous things to Horace Greeley. It had stripped him, once and for all, of his reputation as a great oracle. It had left him, a battered, mud-spattered, humiliated, and nearly broken figure, emerging only with difficulty from the mire of defeat. It had sadly damaged the *Tribune,* a paper which now furnished the bread and butter of many people besides the editor in chief, and in so doing had struck at Greeley's prestige within his own business household.

The *Tribune's* chief stockholders do not seem to have been disturbed to any crucial extent by the lessening of Greeley's stature. They appear to have taken the attitude that the editor and the paper were Siamese twins that could be separated only in death. But the paper's staff, that had borne so long the squeaking and scolding and driving to which Greeley had subjected them, perhaps alarmed as well by the dimming of the *Tribune's* prospects, was roused to a mood of independence. That independence expressed itself in an editorial that Greeley took as a humiliating affront.

The same page that bore Greeley's "card" also carried a short but pungent squib entitled "Crumbs of Comfort." It came from the pen of editorial writer J. R. G. Hassard. Its author rejoiced in half-humorous and half-serious fashion that the crowds of beggars and supplicants for office who had been wont to infest the offices of the *Tribune* and implore the largess of its chief would now be seen there no more. Obviously, said Hassard, this gentry would now keep aloof "from a defeated candidate who has not influence enough at Washington or Albany to get a sweeper appointed under the Sergeant-at-Arms, or a deputy-sub-assistant temporary clerk into the paste-pot section of the folding room." At last the *Tribune's* staff would be left to do its work in peace, "for which we own ourselves profoundly grateful."

Greeley read this squib as an insult. He might much better have passed it off without notice but, melancholy, bitter, his nerves on edge, he scribbled and sent down for publication a retraction that branded Hassard's effort as "a monstrous fable."

Reid, loyal to his old chief but himself none too secure in his position, convinced, moreover, that to publish the retraction would mean a mass resignation of the editorial staff, refused to give it space in the *Tribune*. Greeley bowed to this decision, but nothing could have marked more clearly his fall from power. Furthermore, it convinced him that Whitelaw Reid, whom he had raised to eminence on the paper's staff, had betrayed him and was plotting against him.[37]

And now the dark clouds closed in from all sides. Greeley was every day more distraught, more unstable of mind. He was worried over the *Tribune's* financial status, worried lest the campaign had ruined it and his friends the coproprietors. He brooded over the malignant abuse to which he had been subjected. His financial situation, too, appeared to him in a most ominous light. Owning only six shares of *Tribune* stock, incapable of working more than a few hours at a time, his estate cumbered with over $100,000 worth of uncollectible assets, he saw want staring him and his family in the face. Wherever he turned, he saw only frustration and despair. And across his anguished sight began more and more to steal a welcome vision of the end of the road. "We are in no condition to make new contracts," he wrote to his old friend Nathaniel C. Meeker, "nor I think can we be soon. Our luck is very bad."[38] Two days later he was drawing up his last will and testament.

The will that Horace Greeley made on November 9, 1872, left all of his property to his daughter Ida, half of it for her own use and half for the education and support of Gabrielle. It was official and cast in final form, but within less than a week its anguished author was scribbling down other possible dispositions of his property. At the same time, he wrote out a desperate appeal to Commodore Vanderbilt for financial help.

The old Commodore had been an object of Greeley's admiration for years. Greeley had urged upon Congress the passage of a resolution of thanks for Vanderbilt's wartime services; he had advised Lincoln in 1864 that Vanderbilt would make an excellent secretary of the treasury. Also, most unfortunately, Greeley had fallen into the clutches of Cornelius Vanderbilt, Junior, a graceless young gambler and wastrel who had got into the editor of the *Tribune* for nearly $50,000, some of it borrowed toward the very last of the 1872 campaign.[39] Now Greeley wrote to the young man's father, wailing that he was hopelessly ruined and beseeching payment of the notes owed by Cornelius, Junior. He purposed having this half-crazed missive delivered by his daughter Ida, but that it reached its destination is highly problematical. If the Commodore did see it, he hardened his heart, for it was not until a number of years later that Chauncey Depew finally prevailed upon him to make restitution to the Greeley estate of the money borrowed by his wastrel son.[40]

Greeley's mental condition was now pitiable in the extreme. On the same day that he wrote to Vanderbilt, he put down other frenzied thoughts on paper. They were one long cry of agony and remorse.

I stand naked before my God [he wrote], the most utterly, hopelessly wretched and undone of all who ever lived. I have done more harm and wrong than any man who ever saw the light of day. And yet I take God to witness that I have never intended to injure or harm anyone. But this is no excuse.

He went on to lay his financial ruin to swindlers, to assume all blame for the failure of the Liberal Republican campaign, and to beg God to take him from a world where all he had done had turned to evil.[41]

From the middle of November onward, Greeley's mental condition grew steadily worse. Put under medical care, he was removed to the private sanitorium of Dr. George S. Choate at Pleasantville, New York. There he lingered a few days, increasingly incoherent, until his death released him from his suffering. The end came on November 29, 1872.

Greeley died because he had lost the desire to live. Worn out by the exertions and distracted by the abuse of the campaign; almost prostrated by ceaseless watching at his wife's bedside; depressed by his financial condition and by his treatment in the office of the *Tribune,* he had sunk into a mood of black despair from which there was no recovery. Over and beyond the other factors that created this depression was the ignominious defeat of his hope of becoming the leader in the march toward national unity and national grandeur. The outlook for the nation appeared dark after Grant's reëlection. It seemed as though the wounds of the Civil War would go long unhealed, and as though national selfishness and corruption had been sealed with the seal of popular approval. Greeley's dream had ended with a shattering awakening. He had reached the end of the rainbow, but no pot of gold was there. Rather, to his fevered imagining, there was only an aching void.

Early in the spring of 1872, some time before his nomination, Greeley had written to a friend: "Thank God for death, the one deliverer who never fails us!"[42] Now, in the dark November days of 1872, when death came and stood by his bedside, Greeley welcomed him with open arms. For in the depth of his bitterness and despair, the dark angel seemed to offer both release and expiation.

New York did honor to its leading editor—after he was dead. Friends came to pay their respects in the parlor of Samuel Sinclair at 69 West Forty-fifth Street, where Greeley's body lay until Tuesday, December 3. Then for a day it lay in state in the Governor's Room at the City Hall, with Thurlow Weed, William Cullen Bryant, Horatio Seymour, and A. Oakey Hall among the appointed guard of honor. Rich and poor, high and low, filed by the coffin in the Governor's Room, and it was noted that among those grieving for the departed, the poor were by far the most numerous.

On the Sunday after Greeley's death, the city's leading divines spoke of his passing from their pulpits. His friend Beecher said—

If you should write of him you should say: "A man that lived in stormy times and threw his heart and soul into what he thought the best interests of the community; who sought a yet higher honor, missed it, and died broken hearted"; for if ever a man died of a broken heart, Horace Greeley was that man.

On Wednesday, December 4, there was a funeral service in the Church of the Divine Paternity on the corner of Fifth Avenue and Forty-fifth Street, and a great funeral procession down the Avenue. Thousands lined the sidewalks. The Lincoln Club of New York marched to do honor to their deceased fellow member, as did the Typographical Society and the Union League Club. Many other societies sent marching delegations. There was a distinguished representation of the nation's press. High government dignitaries, state governors, United States senators and President Grant himself rode in the procession. There were interment ceremonies at Greenwood cemetery. Then he was gone, and the city and the nation hurried back into the glittering tumult of the Gilded Age.[43]

NOTES FOR CHAPTER XXV

1. Greeley Papers (Lib. of Cong.), Greeley to Mrs. Whipple, Feb. 13, 1872, Greeley to Brockway, Mar. 5, 1872; Benton, *Greeley on Lincoln*, p. 211; Dickerson, "Letters of Horace Greeley," *Colorado Magazine*, XIX (May 1942), 106.
2. E. D. Ross, *The Liberal Republican Movement* (N. Y., 1919), pp. 26-31.
3. *Tribune*, July 20, Aug. 7, Dec. 20, 1869, Apr. 18, Aug. 8, Nov. 21, 1870, May 5, July 19, 1871; Ross, "Horace Greeley and the South," *South Atlantic Quarterly*, XVI, 329.
4. Greeley Papers (N. Y. P. L.), Greeley to Colfax, Oct. 6, 1870; *Tribune*, Apr. 25, May 2, Aug. 10, Sept. 6, 16, 26, Nov. 19, 30, 1870, Jan. 24, 30, Feb. 6, Apr. 4, 10, 1871.
5. *Tribune*, Jan. 29, 31, 1872.
6. *Tribune*, Mar. 16, 30, Apr. 4, 10, 13, 1872; Rhodes, *Hist. of the U. S.*, VI, 412.
7. *New York Times*, July 21, 1872.
8. Greeley Papers (N. Y. P. L.), Greeley to Jas. F. Holt, Sept. 17, 1869; Greeley to L. U. Reavis, June 23, 1871, also clipping from an article by Murat Halstead; *Tribune*, Dec. 30, 1871, Jan. 18, 19, Mar. 15, Apr. 5, 12, 13, Apr. 21-May 1, 1872; Benton, *Greeley on Lincoln*, pp. 199-206; Stahl Collection, Greeley to Mrs. Allen, Mar. 14, 1872; Hudson, *Journalism*, p. 569; Reavis, *Greeley*, pp. 169-78; Murat Halstead, "Breakfasts with Horace Greeley," *Cosmopolitan*, XXXVI (Apr. 1904), 700-701.
9. Benton, *Greeley on Lincoln*, p. 215; Cortissoz, *Reid*, I, 208, 215, 223.

10. Trumbull Papers, Horace White to Trumbull, Mar. 12, 14, Apr. 25, May 4, 1872, Trumbull to White, Apr. 24, 1872; D. A. Wells Papers, C. F. Adams to Wells, Apr. 18, 1872; *Proceedings of the Liberal Republican Convention*, pp. 3-28; Julian, *Political Recollections*, p. 339; Merriam, *Bowles*, II, 184-87; Watterson, "Humor and Tragedy of the Greeley Campaign," *Century*, LXXXV (Nov. 1912), 29-33, 43, and *"Marse Henry,"* I, 242-43; Schurz, *Reminiscences*, III, 338-41; Ross, *Liberal Republican Movement*, pp. 86-105, and "Horace Greeley and the South," *South Atlantic Quarterly*, XVI (Oct. 1917), 335.

11. Greeley Papers (N. Y. P. L.), Schurz to Greeley, May 6, 1872; Schurz, *Reminiscences*, III, 341-53; Trumbull Papers, Godkin to Trumbull, May 29, 1872, Reid to Trumbull, June 2, 1872; *Nation*, May 9, 1872; Julian, *Political Recollections*, p. 340; *Tribune*, July 5, 1872; Nevins, *Post*, p. 396; Ross, *Liberal Republican Movement*, pp. 110-26.

12. C. Schurz, *Speeches, Correspondence and Political Papers of Carl Schurz* (6 vols.; N. Y., 1913), II, 382, 390-92; Fish Papers, Weed to Fish, May 22, 1872, Fish to Weed, May 27, 1872; Patterson Papers, Weed to Patterson, July 7, 1872.

13. Schurz, *Speeches, Correspondence and Political Papers*, II, 373.

14. Benton, *Greeley on Lincoln*, pp. 216-17; *Tribune*, May 15, July 5, 1872; Trumbull Papers, Greeley to Trumbull, May 21, 1872; Dickerson, "Letters of Horace Greeley," *Colorado Magazine*, XIX (May 1942), 106; Schurz, *Reminiscences*, III, 350-51; Cortissoz, *Reid*, I, 214, 220-22.

15. Greeley Papers (N. Y. P. L.), Greeley to E. F. Bullard, May 21, 1872; *Tribune*, May 22, 1872; Moulton Papers, Greeley to Mrs. Moulton, May 29, 1872.

16. *Tribune*, May 22, 1872.

17. Greeley Papers (N. Y. P. L.), Greeley to Sinclair, June 4, 5, 1872; Benton, *Greeley on Lincoln*, pp. 217, 219; Greeley Letters (N. Y. State Lib.), Greeley to Hall, May 29, 1872.

18. Cleveland, *Story of a Summer*, p. 55; Benton, *Greeley on Lincoln*, pp. 203, 208.

19. Dickerson, "Letters of Horace Greeley," *Colorado Magazine*, Vol. XIX (Mar. 1942), Greeley to Meeker, Sept. 1, 1871; Greeley Papers (Lib. of Cong.), Greeley to Mrs. Allen, June 18, 1872; Benton, *Greeley on Lincoln*, pp. 186, 214-22; Washburne Papers, Greeley to Washburne, Oct. 9, 1871; Greeley Papers (N. Y. P. L.), Ida Greeley to Greeley, Oct.-Dec., 1871.

20. Benton, *Greeley on Lincoln*, pp. 161-62; Trumbull Papers, Greeley to Trumbull, July 5, 1872; *Tribune*, July 4, 1872; Stahl Collection, Greeley to Mrs. Allen, July 2, 9, 1872.

21. *Nation*, July 4, 1872.

22. *Tribune*, July 24, 1872.

23. *Ibid.*, July 31, 1872; Ingersoll, *Greeley*, pp. 645-50; Stevens, *New York Typographical Union #6*, pp. 623-25.

24. *True Issues*, p. 30; W. M. Clark, *The Old White Hat*, sheet music furnished by Roger and Lin Butterfield. There is a considerable amount of campaign material in the Greeley Papers (N. Y. P. L.).

25. *Harper's Weekly*, July 6, 27, Aug. 3, 17, 31, Sept. 14, 21, 1872; *New York Times*, July 21, 1872; *Tribune*, July 19, 1872; *True Issues*, p. 2; newspaper clipping in Greeley Papers (N. Y. P. L.), Oct. 1, 1872; Myers, *Genius of Horace Greeley*, p. 17.

26. Seward Papers, Greeley to Seward, Apr. 12, 1853; *What Horace Greeley Knows about the Democratic Party* (campaign pamphlet), pp. 1-24; *Tribune,* Mar. 28, 1866, Oct. 6, 1871; *Times,* July 19, 1872.

27. Weed Papers, Patterson to Weed, Dec. 11, 1873; Hoar, *Autobiography,* I, 284; E. L. Masters, *Mark Twain* (N. Y., 1938), p. 93; Watterson, "Humor and Tragedy, etc.," *Century,* LXXXV (Nov. 1912), 41, 44; Depew, *Memories,* p. 92.

28. W. O. Duvall to Gerrit Smith, July 19, 1872, quoted in R. V. Harlow, *Gerrit Smith* (N. Y., 1937), p. 477.

29. *True Issues,* p. 2; Ingersoll, *Greeley,* pp. 651-52.

30. *True Issues,* pp. 7-9, 11, 13-16, 21; Ingersoll, *Greeley,* pp. 650-64.

31. *True Issues;* J. A. Riis, *The Making of an American* (N. Y., 1937), p. 69.

32. Watterson, "Humor and Tragedy, etc.,"*Century,* LXXXV (Nov. 1912), 42; *True Issues,* p. 24; Benton, *Greeley on Lincoln,* pp. 229-32; Stahl Collection, Greeley to Mrs. Allen, Oct. 4, 1872.

33. Greeley Papers (Lib. of Cong.), Greeley to Mrs. Allen, Oct. 25, 1872; Cleveland, *Story of a Summer,* p. 14.

34. Greeley Papers (Lib. of Cong.), Greeley to Mrs. Allen, Nov. 4, 1872.

35. For the figures, see A. C. McLaughlin and A. B. Hart, *Cyclopedia of American Government,* III, 32-33.

36. Misc. MSS (N. Y. H. S.), Babcock to General Badeau; Merriam, *Bowles,* p. 192.

37. *New York Sun,* Nov. 30, Dec. 19, 1872; Bigelow, *Retrospections,* V, 88-89; Cortissoz, *Reid,* 243-47; Baehr, *Tribune,* pp. 115-16; Seitz, *Greeley,* p. 397.

38. Dickerson, "Letters of Horace Greeley," *Colorado Magazine,* XIX (May 1942), 109-10.

39. Greeley Papers (N. Y. P. L.), Greeley to Colfax, Dec. 13, 1863; Morgan Papers, Greeley to E. D. Morgan, Jan. 8, 9, 1864; Lincoln Papers, Greeley to Lincoln, Nov. 23, 1864; File 144/1872, Horace Greeley Estate, Surrogate's Court, Westchester County, New York; Cornelius Vanderbilt, Jr., and his wife Ellen Vanderbilt to Greeley, 1864-72, in Greeley Papers (N. Y. P. L.), a file of letters that makes interesting though depressing reading.

40. Greeley Papers (N. Y. P. L.), Greeley to [Commodore Vanderbilt], Nov. 13, 1872; Depew, *Memories,* p. 357.

41. Greeley Papers (N. Y. P. L.), Greeley's statement, Nov. 13, 1872.

42. Benton, *Greeley on Lincoln,* p. 213.

43. Greeley Papers (N. Y. P. L.), obsequy notices; *New York World,* Dec. 2, 1872; *Tribune,* Nov. 30-Dec. 5, 1872.

Epilogue

ALL HIS LIFE, HORACE GREELEY HAD BEEN A CRU-
sader. His genuine human sympathies, his moral fervor, even the
exhibitionism that was a part of his makeup, made it inevitable
that he should crusade for a better world. He did so with apostolic
zeal. He fought against drink and against the brothel, he fought
for honest government, he fought above all for the development of
America's national prosperity and unity and power. A fervent believer in the grandeur of the American destiny, he strove to make
his country a land of happy people, a nation setting an example to
all other nations in its way of life.

Greeley's effectiveness as a crusader was limited by some of his
traits and characteristics. Culturally deficient, he was to the end
ignorant of his own limitations, and this ignorance was a great
handicap. For while he repeatedly displayed powers of discernment
and of penetrating analysis, he was also liable to be most dogmatic
on subjects that he knew least about—"by turns sagacious and
childish," as Samuel Bowles once remarked. He was also easily enraged by criticism, and this rage was apt to express itself in hasty
and vituperative comment. His sense of timing was poor, as was
shown by his course of action during the Civil War. He was sometimes wrong in his judgment of men. He was often wrong in regard
to political policies and procedures.

Partly because of his character and personality limitations, partly
because of the associates with whom he cast his political lot, partly
because of the nature of the era in which he lived, Greeley's life
contained a very large element of tragedy. He had an unhappy
home, as much the result of his own faults as of Mary Greeley's.
His partnership with Weed and Seward became less and less harmonious and finally broke up into years of feuding and bitterness.
He saw his plans for promoting the national welfare thwarted by a

bloody civil war. He saw reconstruction policies develop in ways of which he deeply disapproved and, when he sought national leadership, was covered with calumny and abuse and made to suffer the humiliation of overwhelming defeat. The city that he made his home consistently rebuffed his search for office. Playboys and scoundrels continually raided his pocketbook, holding him in contempt even while they were taking his money. The *Tribune* was a part of him, but control over it passed more and more completely out of his hands, and the final realization of that fact was probably of signal importance in plunging him into that last black fit of despair from which he never emerged.

Greeley was unquestionably an idealist, but his idealism was continually being frustrated. It was hampered by his own fear of swift or sudden change, an attitude characteristic of conservative natures. It clashed with his efforts at playing the part of a successful businessman and political leader, a part that necessitated continual compromise with the realities of existence. It was stultified by the fact that he had to make a place for himself in the midst of a people surrounded and almost overwhelmed by the rich promise of material reward that lay on every hand. There was irony in the fact that idealist Greeley founded a newspaper and carved out a career in the great city that was the center and symbol of the nation's materialism. It was significant that by far the greatest part of his paper's influence was exerted outside of New York. The great tragedy of Greeley's life was his failure to effect a satisfactory working compromise between his idealism, his conservatism, and the economic facts of life in nineteenth-century America.

But though Greeley's life was full of frustration and tragedy, it was by no means a negative life. He rose to be a national figure, and as such he commanded great prestige. Ruralites respected him for his intimate knowledge of western conditions and for his devotion to free land. City laborers admired a man who was willing to tilt a lance against injustice and who dealt fairly with his employees. His wit, his pungent sayings, his moral earnestness, last but not least his business success, gave him great personal popularity with all classes of citizens. Tens of thousands of his fellow countrymen saw him as an American symbol—hustling, sharp-witted, a man who often fretted and complained (what American does not?), but whose motto was "Excelsior," who was full of bounce and drive, and who got ahead.

And Greeley had more to his credit than the achievement of great personal popularity. It was not without effect that he spent his days combating tendencies that he loathed in an America that he loved.

The things that he loathed, the brutality, the corruption, the prodigal waste of resources, the often heartless materialism of the city and the nation, were barriers in his path. But stubbornly and with courage he fought to surmount those barriers and, with all his shortcomings and failures, he laid up to his credit some very real achievements.

The newspaper that he founded and guided to maturity was a great newspaper, its columns fed by able and often brilliant correspondents, its pages a public forum where widely variant points of view were presented in such exciting and thought-compelling fashion as has seldom if ever been seen, before or since, in the public press of America. In its pages appeared nearly every day the evidences of its editor's breadth of knowledge, of the encyclopedic ranges of information that he had at his disposal. His critics might question the depth of this knowledge, but to the average American it seemed awe inspiring. Greeley and his newspaper had a very real influence upon American thought. They brought constructive ideas and hope for improvement of conditions into the rural regions. They warred with considerable effectiveness against injustice and brutality in city life. They helped mightily in creating the tide of opinion that destroyed the institution of slavery in the United States, making to that end a contribution that ought never to be minimized.

More significant still was the service that Greeley performed as a result of his faith in his country and his countrymen, his belief in infinite American progress.

For with all his faults and shortcomings, Greeley symbolized an America that, though often shortsighted and misled, was never suffocated by the wealth pouring from its farms and furnaces. Always at heart it has been a land of aspiration, where the knee bowed to Baal has not quite touched the earth. And so it has been that the Greeley who saw visions and dreamed dreams has touched the hearts of a great host of men and women, in his own and later times. It was this Greeley who became a household word, who was venerated by the western farmers, and by not a few southern farmers and even by a laboring class that he chided far more than he helped. For through his faith in the American future, a faith expressed in his ceaseless efforts to make real the promise of America, he inspired others with hope and confidence, making them feel that their dreams also had within them the substance of reality. It is his faith, and theirs that has given him his place in American history. In that faith he still marches among us, scolding and benevolent, exhorting us to confidence and to victory in the great struggles of our own day.

Bibliography

I. *Manuscripts*

Much of Greeley's correspondence was destroyed by fire after his death, but a considerable body of material remains. The principal collections, indispensable for a study of the man and his career, are the Greeley Papers in the New York Public Library, the Greeley Papers in the Library of Congress, the Greeley Letters in the library of the New-York Historical Society, and the Henry A. Stahl Collection of Greeley letters, now in the possession of Mr. Edward C. M. Stahl at Chappaqua, New York. Of these, the letters in the New York Public Library are the most important, those of Greeley to Schuyler Colfax being particularly informative. The Library of Congress collection contains numerous letters and transcripts of letters to and from *Tribune* associates (especially Charles A. Dana), and other acquaintances and friends. The New-York Historical Society collection is smaller, but important for special periods. The Stahl Collection consists chiefly of letter books, and copies of Greeley's letters are always suspect, because of his unique handwriting. But it also contains other letters than those of Greeley, some of which are not available elsewhere, and so cannot be ignored.

Other Greeley letters are scattered throughout the country, in a wide variety of collections. The most important of these are the Rufus W. Griswold Papers in the Boston Public Library, the Margaret Fuller Correspondence in the Harvard Library, the Salmon P. Chase Papers in the Historical Society of Pennsylvania, the Edwin D. Morgan Papers in the Albany State Library, the Mrs. H. C. Ingersoll Papers in the Library of Congress, the Gerrit Smith Papers in the Syracuse University Library, the collection of Greeleyana in the Huntington Library. There are scattered but important Greeley items in such collections as the Henry Clay Papers, the Thaddeus Stevens Papers, the Elihu B. Washburne Papers in the Library of Congress. Rhees Library at the University of Rochester has a number of Greeley letters that should not be overlooked by any student of the man. The Papers of Thurlow Weed and of William Henry Seward at the University of Rochester contain much valuable Greeley material.

II. *Printed Sources*

A. *Greeley Letters and Writings*

A comprehensive bibliography of Greeley's writings is to be found in the Greeley Papers in the Library of Congress. Items particularly valuable for a study of Greeley's policies and ideas are his editorials (as cited in the text) in the *Continental Monthly*, the *Independent*, the *Jeffersonian*, the *Log Cabin*, the *New-Yorker*, the *New York Tribune*.

Particularly valuable sources for printed letters are:

J. Benton (ed.), *Greeley on Lincoln: with Mr. Greeley's Letters to Charles A. Dana and a Lady Friend...* (N. Y., 1873).

O. M. Dickerson, "Letters of Horace Greeley to Nathaniel C. Meeker," *Colorado Magazine*, XIX (March 1942), 50-62, and XIX (May 1942), 102-10.

Greeley's speeches in the West and at Portland, Maine, during the campaign of 1872 are to be found in *The True Issues of the Presidential Campaign* (n. p., n. d.).

The most significant of Greeley's published works are:

The American Conflict (2 vols.; Hartford, 1864, 1866).

Association Discussed; or, The Socialism of the Tribune Examined. Being a Controversy Between the New York Tribune and the Courier and Enquirer (N. Y., 1847).

The Crystal Palace and its Lessons (1852).

Essays Designed to Elucidate the Science of Political Economy . . . (Boston, 1870).

The Formation of Character (N. Y., n. d.).

Glances at Europe . . . (N. Y., 1851).

Hints Toward Reforms (N. Y., 1853).

Mr. Greeley's Letters from Texas . . . (N. Y., 1871).

An Overland Journey, from New York to San Francisco, in the Summer of 1859 (N. Y., 1860).

Recollections of a Busy Life (N. Y., 1868).

What I Know of Farming (N. Y., 1871).

Why I Am a Whig (N. Y., n. d.).

B. *General Background by Contemporary Writers*

Beman Brockway's *Fifty Years in Journalism* (Watertown, 1891) is a salty and valuable memoir by a shrewd observer, who recorded events as he saw them. Cecelia Cleveland's *The Story of a Summer* (N. Y., 1874) is far less reliable, being essentially a romantic reminiscence. Charles T. Congdon, *Reminiscences of a Journalist* (Boston, 1880), has to be used with care, as does Chauncey M. Depew's *My Memories of Eighty Years* (N. Y., 1922). Maunsell B. Field, *Memories of Many Men and of Some Women* (N. Y., 1874) is a spirited account that yields some good Greeley material. The same is true of James P. Gilmore, *Personal Recollections of Abraham Lincoln and the Civil War* (Boston, 1898). Adam Gurowski's *Diary* (3 vols.; Boston, N. Y., Wash., 1862, 1864, 1866) is prejudiced and opinionated, but often shows real insight. Philip Hone's *The Diary of Philip Hone, 1828-1851* (2 vols.; N. Y., 1927) has little Greeley material but is invaluable for information on New York during the 1830's and 1840's. Frederic Hudson, *Journalism in the United States* (N. Y., 1873) is a valuable account marred by inaccuracies. George W. Julian, *Political Recollections, 1840 to 1872* (Chicago, 1884), is opinionated but of considerable value. The same may be said of *The Reminiscences of Carl Schurz* (3 vols.; N. Y., 1907-8). Henry Watterson's *"Marse Henry": An Autobiography* (2 vols.; N. Y., 1919) is delightful reading, but more imaginative than factual. *The Diary of George Templeton Strong* (4 vols.; N. Y., 1952) is very critical of Greeley. It is valuable for the light it throws upon the New York scene, especially from 1850 to 1875. Thurlow Weed's *Autobiography* (Boston, 1883) is designedly benevolent and often inaccurate, but is nevertheless of considerable value. Andrew Dickson White's *Autobiography* (2 vols.; N. Y., 1905) is that of a man of strong convictions who had real literary gifts. John Russell Young's *Men and Memories* (2 vols.; N. Y., 1901) has some value, but must be used with caution.

Of the contemporary biographies of Greeley, the three most important are, in order, James Parton, *The Life of Horace Greeley* (N. Y., 1855); L. U. Reavis, *A Representative Life of Horace Greeley* (N. Y., 1872); and L. D. Ingersoll, *The Life of Horace Greeley* (Chicago, 1873).

III. *Bibliography by Chapters*

Chapter 1: *Youth of a Yankee*
Information as to Greeley's origins and early life may be found in J. Merrill, *History of Amesbury, Including the First Seventeen Years of Salisbury* . . . (Haverhill, Mass., 1880) and E. L. Parker, *The History of Londonderry* . . . (Boston, 1851), but the principal sources of information are an autobiographical sketch, Greeley to Moses A. Cortland (?), Apr. 14, 1845 (N.Y.P.L.); Horace Greeley, *Recollections of a Busy Life* (N. Y., 1868); and Parton, *op. cit.* Parton had the advantage of interviews with Greeley's early neighbors, but their recollections were bound to be romantic. Greeley's account is sober in tone and, I believe, trustworthy. Greeley reminiscences are scattered throughout the *New-Yorker* and the *Tribune*.

Chapter 2: *The Slopes of Parnassus*
The best sources for New York in the 1830's are Philip Hone, *op. cit.;* I. N. Phelps Stokes, *The Iconography of Manhattan* (6 vols.; N. Y., 1915-27); J. G. Wilson, *The Memorial History of the City of New York* (4 vols.; N. Y., 1892-93); the second volume of Martha J. Lamb, *History of the City of New York* (2 vols.; N. Y., 1877, 1880). Also useful were R. G. Albion, *The Rise of New York Port* (N. Y., 1939); J. F. Cooper, *Home as Found* (Boston and N. Y., n. d.); N. P. Willis, *Prose Writings* (N. Y., 1885) and *Life Here and There* (N. Y., 1850). The *New-Yorker* also contains many interesting items on New York life, and is, of course, the chief source of information regarding Greeley's career as a literary editor.

Chapter 3: *A Budding Politician*
This analysis of Greeley's early political ideas is based upon a study of his unpublished letters and of his editorials in the *New-Yorker*, the *Jeffersonian*, and the *Log Cabin*. To a lesser extent, it owes a debt to the excellent study of Jackson in Richard B. Hofstadter's *The American Political Tradition* (N. Y., 1948) and A. M. Schlesinger Jr.'s very able, though somewhat one-sided, *The Age of Jackson* (Boston, 1945).

Chapter 4: *A Bride and an Alliance*
Greeley's correspondence, especially that in the New York Public Library and the Library of Congress, together with the Weed and Seward Papers, the *Jeffersonian*, and the *Log Cabin*, constitute the basis of this chapter.

Chapter 5. *Microcosms*
Stokes, *op. cit.*, and Wilson, *op. cit.*, furnish material for all descriptions of New York life. The *Tribune* is a great source of information regarding the city, especially the column headed "City Items." The *Tribune* and the Greeley Papers (N.Y.P.L.) furnished most of the information regarding the founding of the paper and its general character in its early years.

Chapters 6 and 7: *This Brave New World and Not So Brave and Not So New*
Mainly based on Greeley's writings during the 1840's and 1850's. Henry C.

Carey's *The Past, the Present, and the Future* (Phila., 1848) and *The Harmony of Interests, Agricultural, Manufacturing and Commercial* (N. Y.,
1852); Thomas Carlyle's *Past and Present* (Oxford, 1918); William Atkinson's *Principles of Political Economy* (N. Y., 1843); and a study of Charles
Fourier's life and writings made in connection with my teaching at the University of Rochester were also important. Arthur E. Bestor Jr. has done an
excellent article on "Albert Brisbane . . . Propagandist for Socialism in the
1840's," in *New York History*, Vol. XXVIII (Apr. 1947). The Dorr Rebellion is adequately covered in A. M. Mowry's *The Dorr War* (Providence,
R. I., 1901). For general background, such books as Norman Ware's *The
Industrial Worker, 1840-1860* (Boston and N. Y., 1924); Alice F. Tyler, *Freedom's Ferment* (Minneapolis, 1944); J. H. Noyes, *History of American
Socialisms* (Phila., 1870); and the general histories of Edward Channing and
J. B. McMaster have been useful.

Chapter 8: *Soundings*
   The examination of Greeley's Whiggery in the 1840's is chiefly based upon
an examination of Greeley's *Tribune* editorials, although his letters in the
various collections cited in the footnotes are vital to an understanding of his
views. For general background, I have drawn upon my *The Life of Henry
Clay* (Boston, 1937) and *Thurlow Weed: Wizard of the Lobby* (Boston,
1947). G. R. Poage, *Henry Clay and the Whig Party* (Chapel Hill, 1936)
was also useful.

Chapter 9. *The Crystallization of a "Liberal" Program*
   Greeley's letters and *Tribune* editorials are again the chief sources used.
On Nativism in New York, L. D. Scisco's *Political Nativism in New York
State* (N. Y., 1901) was a reliable guide. De Alva S. Alexander's *A Political
History of the State of New York* (3 vols.; N. Y., 1906-23) was useful, though
the Whig and later Republican bias of its author necessitates caution. A. C.
Flick, *History of the State of New York* (10 vols.; N. Y., 1933-37) was help-
ful, although the pertinent chapters are of uneven merit. The second volume
of C. J. H. Hayes, *Political and Cultural History of Modern Europe* (N. Y.,
1939) was moderately useful, in dealing with the European revolutions of
1848. The same may be said of Justin H. Smith's brilliant but prejudiced
The Annexation of Texas (N. Y., 1941) and *The War with Mexico* (2 vols.;
N. Y., 1919).

Chapter 10: *A Strong-Minded Adjutant*
   The development of Greeley's relationship with Weed and Seward is best
studied in the papers of the three men, although Greeley's *Recollections* and
Weed's *Autobiography* contain some useful material. Greeley's activities in
the second session of the 30th Congress are spread on the pages of the
Congressional Globe, Vol. XX.

Chapter 11: *Crisis and Schism*
   Allan Nevins, *Ordeal of the Union* (2 vols.; N. Y., 1947), furnishes the
best background available for this chapter. Nevins' work is well written and
admirably organized. It supersedes both Rhodes and Channing. Greeley's
course during the crisis over the Compromise of 1850 and the subsequent
Whig internecine battles in New York State is best studied in his letters and
Tribune editorials. Alexander, *op. cit.*, is moderately useful. Holman Hamilton, *Zachary Taylor* (2 vols.; Indianapolis, 1941, 1951), is definitive.

Chapter 12: *The Greeleys at Home*

Greeley's writings and letters constitute the basis of this chapter. Brockway, *Fifty Years in Journalism*, is indispensable. So is Cleveland's *Story of a Summer*, although it has to be used with great care. It drips sentiment and is none too accurate. Scattered items of interest were found in such books as William A. Butler, *A Retrospect of Forty Years* (N. Y., 1911). There is a judicious appraisal of Greeley's services to the farmers in Earle D. Ross, "Horace Greeley and the Beginnings of the New Agriculture," in *Agricultural History*, VII, no. 1 (Jan. 1933), 3-17.

Chapter 13: *Interlude*

For New York in the 1850's, besides the books already cited, Walt Whitman, *New York Dissected* (N. Y., 1936), was valuable, as were also Lyman Abbott, *Reminiscences* (Boston and N. Y., 1915), and G. W. Curtis, *The Potiphar Papers* (N. Y., 1856). Especially valuable for "color" is the manuscript diary of Evert Duyckinck, now in the Manuscript Division of the New York Public Library. Information on Greeley's trip to Europe was derived from his correspondence, partly published in *Glances at Europe* (N. Y., 1851), and *The Crystal Palace and Its Lessons* (n. d., but written in New York, Nov. 1851). The *Tribune*, the *New York Times*, and Greeley's correspondence were the best sources for his political activities in 1852 and 1853. There is a good recent biography of Henry J. Raymond: Ernest F. Brown, *Raymond of the Times* (N. Y., 1951).

Chapter 14: *A Disruption of Partnerships*

G. F. Milton, *The Eve of Conflict* (Boston and N. Y., 1934); P. O. Ray, *Repeal of the Missouri Compromise* (Cleveland, 1909); and F. H. Hodder "The Railroad Background of the Kansas Nebraska Act," in the *Miss. Valley Hist. Rev.*, XII (June 1925), 3-21, are valuable for the background of the Kansas Nebraska Bill. Greeley's reaction to the bill and his part in the formation of the Republican party are best studied in his editorials and private correspondence. These same materials, plus the Weed and Seward Papers, constitute the best sources of information on the rebellion of the junior partner.

Chapters 15 and 16: *A Republican Operator* and *Greeley's Battle*

Greeley's *Recollections* are useful here, as throughout, but it has to be kept constantly in mind that he was a most persuasive pleader in his own defense, one who had no hesitation in suppressing facts that were to his disadvantage. Jeter A. Isely's *Horace Greeley and the Republican Party, 1853-1861* (Princeton, 1947) is a careful and well-written analysis of this portion of Greeley's career, particularly useful for its account of Greeley's efforts to build up Republican strength in the latter 1850's. Nevins' *Ordeal* and his *The Emergence of Lincoln* (2 vols.; N. Y., 1950) are indispensable, as is Roy F. Nichols' *The Disruption of American Democracy* (N. Y., 1948). Also useful for an understanding of the period are Avery Craven's *The Coming of the Civil War* (N. Y., 1942), A. C. Cole's *The Irrepressible Conflict* (N. Y., 1934), and G. F. Milton's *The Eve of Conflict* (Boston and N. Y., 1934). Such materials furnish background and perspective for the study of Greeley's editorials and correspondence that constitutes the heart of these chapters.

Chapter 17: *A Demonstration of Independence*

The works cited for the two preceding chapters were useful as background for this account of the role Greeley played at Chicago in 1860 and in the subsequent political events. Also valuable was R. H. Luthin's *The First Lincoln Campaign* (Cambridge, 1944). *Tribune* editorials, Greeley's correspondence, and James S. Pike's *First Blows of the Civil War* (N. Y., 1879) constitute the basic source materials.

Chapter 18: *A Nationalist at Bay*

Indispensable for a study of the struggle over the spoils during the winter of 1860-61 is H. J. Carman and R. H. Luthin, *Lincoln and the Patronage* (N. Y., 1943). The situation during the critical months from November 1860 to April 1861 is best studied in D. L. Dumond, *The Secession Movement, 1860-1861* (N. Y., 1931), and in Nevins, *Emergence of Lincoln*. D. M. Potter has an excellent article, "Horace Greeley and Peaceable Secession," in *The Journal of Southern History*, VII (May, 1941), 145-59; Greeley's course is best studied at first hand in his editorials in the *Tribune* and the *Independent*, in his *Recollections*, and in Joel Benton (ed.), *Greeley on Lincoln* (N. Y., 1893).

Chapters 19 and 20: *Windswept* and *Storm-Tossed*

Greeley's twistings and turnings during the period covered by these chapters are best followed in the *Tribune* and the *Independent*. Also significant are his contributions to the *Continental Monthly* (indicated in the footnotes to Chapter 19), his *Recollections*, and his *The American Conflict* (2 vols.; Hartford, 1864, 1866). Important as background are R. R. Fahrney, *Horace Greeley and the Tribune in the Civil War*, although I differ at some points with its analysis of Greeley's actions. T. H. Williams, *Lincoln and the Radicals* (Univ. of Wisconsin Press, 1941), is an excellent study of one of Lincoln's greatest problems. J. G. Randall, *The Civil War and Reconstruction* (Boston and N. Y., 1937), is excellent as a general study of the period; and B. J. Hendrick, *Lincoln's War Cabinet* (Boston, 1946), gives a spirited account of the men around the President. Alexander's *Political History of New York State* and A. C. Flick (ed.), *History of the State of New York* (10 vols.; N. Y., 1933-37), give the background of state politics during this period. They should be supplemented by S. D. Brummer, *Political History of New York State during the Period of the Civil War* (N. Y., 1911), a pedestrian but useful account.

Chapter 21: *For You O Democracy*

This chapter, which is chiefly an analysis of Greeley's post-Civil War political and social philosophy, is based on a study of his letters, editorials, books, and speeches during that period. Contemporary biographies, such as those by Ingersoll and Reavis, were of some use, particularly because they reproduce letters the originals of which have disappeared, but these studies are in general laudatory and uncritical.

Chapters 22, 23, and 24: *Pursuit of the Dream, Valiant Battle,* and *And Still the Quest*

Like the other chapters of the book, this is based upon the sources, but J. F. Rhodes, *History of the United States from the Compromise of 1850* (Vols. V, VI; N. Y., 1904, 1906); E. P. Oberholtzer, *A History of the United*

States since the Civil War (Vols. I-III; N. Y., 1917-26) ; Randall, *Civil War and Reconstruction;* and the biographies by Reavis and Ingersoll furnish historical background for this study of Greeley's activities during the reconstruction era. Alexander, *op. cit.,* and H. A. Stebbins, *A Political History of the State of New York, 1865-1869* (N. Y., 1913) , give the New York State political situation. A first-rate political history of the State of New York has yet to be done.

Chapter 25: *The End of the Rainbow*

E. D. Ross, *The Liberal Republican Movement* (N. Y., 1919) , is indispensable for the background of the campaign of 1872 and for the campaign itself. Of less significance, but still valuable, is T. S. Barclay, *The Liberal Republican Movement in Missouri* (Columbia, Mo., 1926) . The reminiscences of Greeley's contemporaries, previously cited, are also valuable. So, too, are John Bigelow's "Diary" for copies of the two wills left by Greeley; G. S. Merriam, *Life and Times of Samuel Bowles* (2 vols.; N. Y., 1885) ; and R. Ogden (ed.) , *Life and Letters of Edwin Lawrence Godkin* (2 vols.; N. Y., 1907) . J. S. Pike, *Horace Greeley in 1872* (N. Y., 1873) , is an astute summary and survey of Greeley's position and motivations in the campaign of 1872. Whitelaw Reid, *Horace Greeley* (N. Y., 1879) , is an appreciation by one of Greeley's closest associates, a man who was too much involved in the tragic events of 1872 to render a wholly objective judgment seven years later. Carl Schurz, *Speeches, Correspondence and Political Papers* (6 vols.; N. Y., 1913) is a mine of information regarding the campaign, and the *Proceedings of the Liberal Republican Convention* (N. Y., 1872) is an aid in understanding how Greeley came to be nominated. *True Issues* (n. p., 1872) is useful for a study of Greeley's most important campaign speeches. Greeley's Papers in the New York Public Library constitute the most valuable source of information regarding the close of his career.

INDEX

DESIGN BY GUENTHER K. WEHRHAN
COMPOSITION AND PRESSWORK BY HALLMARK-HUBNER PRESS, INC.
BINDING BY CHAS. BOHN & CO., INC., NEW YORK

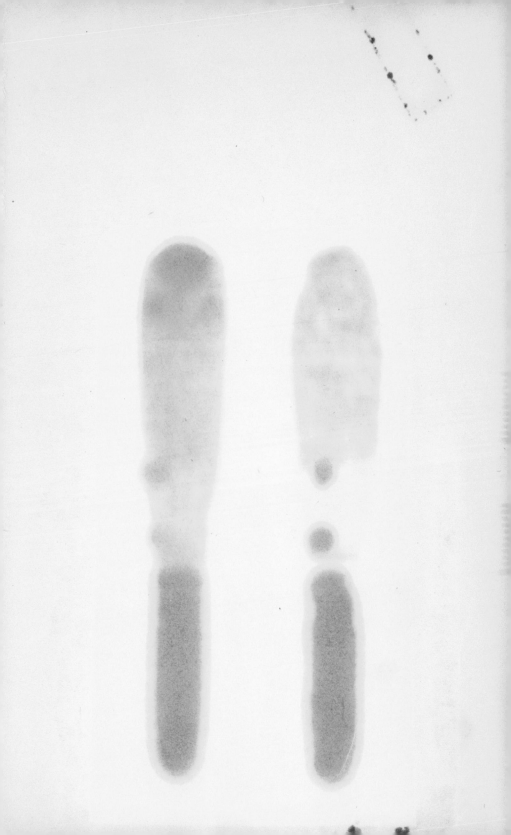